D1154896

E V E R Y M A N ' S   L I B R A R Y

EVERYMAN,
I WILL GO WITH THEE,
AND BE THY GUIDE,
IN THY MOST NEED
TO GO BY THY SIDE

HERODOTUS

The Histories

Translated by George Rawlinson

with an Introduction by
Rosalind Thomas

EVERYMAN'S LIBRARY

Alfred A. Knopf New York Toronto

234

THIS IS A BORZOI BOOK

PUBLISHED BY ALFRED A. KNOPF, INC.

First included in Everyman's Library, 1910
Introduction Copyright © 1997 by Rosalind Thomas
Bibliography, Chronology and editorial revisions Copyright © 1997
by David Campbell Publishers Ltd.
Typography by Peter B. Willberg
Third printing

All rights reserved under International and Pan-American Copyright
Conventions. Published in the United States by Alfred A. Knopf,
Inc., New York, and simultaneously in Canada by Random House
of Canada Limited, Toronto. Distributed by Random House Inc.,
New York

ISBN 0-375-40661-3

Book Design by Barbara de Wilde and Carol Devine Carson

Printed and bound in Germany
by Graphischer Grossbetrieb Pössneck GmbH

THE HISTORIES OF
HERODOTUS

———

CONTENTS

THE FIRST BOOK, ENTITLED CLIO   5
Causes of the war between Greece and Persia – 1. Mythic (ch.
1–5). 2. Historic – Aggressions of Crœsus – Previous Lydian
History (6–25). Conquests of Crœsus (26–28). Visit of Solon
to the court of Crœsus (29–33). Story of Adrastus and Atys
(34–45). Preparations of Crœsus against Cyrus – Consultation
of the oracles (46–55). Crœsus seeks a Greek alliance –
Hellenes and Pelasgi (56–58). State of Athens under Pisistratus
(59–64). Early History of Sparta (65–68). Alliance of Crœsus
with Sparta (69–70). Crœsus warned (71). Crœsus invades
Cappadocia – his war with Cyrus (72–85). Danger and deliverance of Crœsus (86, 87). His advice to Cyrus (88, 89). His
message to the Delphic oracle (90, 91). His offerings (92).
Wonders of Lydia (93). Manners and customs of the Lydians
(94). History of Cyrus – Old Assyrian Empire – Revolt of
Media (95). Early Median History (96–107). Birth and
bringing-up of Cyrus (108–122). Incitements to revolt (123,
124). He sounds the feelings of the Persians – their Ten Tribes
(125, 126). Revolt and struggle (127–130). Customs of the
Persians (131–140). Cyrus threatens the Ionian Greeks (141).
Account of the Greek settlements in Asia (142–151). Sparta
interferes to protect the Greeks (152). Sardis revolts and is
reduced (153–157). Fate of Pactyas (158–160). Reduction of
the Asiatic Greeks (161–170). The Carians, Caunians, and
Lycians attacked – their customs – they submit to the Persians
(171–176). Conquests of Cyrus in Upper Asia (177). Description
of Babylon (178–187). Cyrus marches on Babylon (188–190).
Fall of Babylon (191). Description of Babylonia (192, 193).

CONTENTS

CONTENTS

CONTENTS

CONTENTS

INTRODUCTION

Nicknamed the 'father of History' by Cicero, Herodotus is indeed the ancestor of later historians. While his methods fall short of those expected from scholars today, his search for a reliable version of the past, sifted from many sources (including eye-witness accounts) and centred on humans rather than on gods, is the beginning of all critical study of the past. The *Histories* are not easy to categorize, for they encompass geography, ethnography and biology, wrought together by a consummate story-teller; and in the centuries after Herodotus, historians inclined more towards linear political narrative in the manner of Thucydides, who became the dominant model. Yet without the example of his great predecessor, Thucydides could not have achieved what he did. When Herodotus began work, the genre of history writing as such did not exist, and for the original audience of the fifth century BC, his writing, however diffuse, must have presented a picture of their past far more coherent, more ordered and more detailed than any they could have known before.

Often regarded as an archaic writer, Herodotus was active in Athens during the middle years of the fifth century, from the generation after the Persian Wars down to the 420s, the period of Athenian supremacy and the time of Pericles. He came originally from Halicarnassus, a Greek city in Asia Minor (now Bodrum in western Turkey), on the very edge of the Persian empire, and went into exile after what was perhaps an attempt to unseat its tyrant, Lygdamis. In the *Histories*, the author refers to the numerous evils which had befallen Greece during the reigns of three Persian kings, Darius, Xerxes and Artaxerxes, who together ruled from 522 to 424 BC, which implies that he lived to witness the outbreak of the Peloponnesian War in 431.

Herodotus describes the history of the Persian invasions of Greece in 490 and 480–479 BC. Like all other Greeks, he saw these events as the story of Greek freedom triumphing over Persian slavery. But the *Histories* are not only an account of

xxi

the Persian Wars. For Herodotus traces the origins of the struggle back to the earliest signs of conflict between Greeks and non-Greeks. In the process, he ranges over the Near Eastern empires of the Medes, straddling what is now northern Iran; the Assyrians, centred in the Mesopotamian river valley of nothern Iraq; and the Lydians whose empire was centred in Sardis on the west coast of Turkey. Herodotus starts with the quarrels of the ancient period of legend and the Trojan War, and moves to the period of the Lydian empire of the late seventh and early sixth centuries, especially the reign of the wealthy Crœsus (early sixth century) who, he says, was the first ruler known to have had dealings with the Greeks which were both predatory and friendly. From there he traces the rise and fall of Crœsus' Lydian empire in the face of Persian expansion, moving further back to describe the Median empire until its own submission to Persian domination under Cyrus the Great. Thereafter, his account continues with the expansion of the Persian empire under successive Achæmenid kings to engulf Babylonia, the rest of Mesopotamia, Asia Minor (what is now modern Turkey), Phœnicia on the Levantine coast, and Egypt. On the way, he tells cautionary tales of expeditions on the edges of the known world where even the Persians could not succeed – against the Massagetæ east of the Caspian Sea, the Ethiopians, the Scythians in the area north and east of the Black Sea, culminating with the two unsuccessful attempts to gain control of that other margin of the Achæmenid-centred world, mainland Greece itself.

Herodotus does not give us a simple linear narrative, and the modern reader may at first find this disconcerting. With Persian expansion as the central thread, he also offers his audience fascinating digressions about those peoples who came into contact with the Persians, including Egyptians and Scythians, as well as those on the very cusp between myth and travellers' tales, like the Amazons, thought to inhabit an area on the edge of the world. We are given intermittent surveys of the circumstances of various Greek states, as his story seems to require them (of early Sparta and Athens, for example, at the time of Crœsus' enquiries in Book I) until the Greeks' successful resistance to the fifth-century Persian threat becomes the main focus of the narrative (Books VI–IX). Herodotus' explanation for historical action often demands a knowledge of previous events which he then describes; later misfortune may ultimately be a punishment for ancestral misdeeds, as was the case for Crœsus. And warnings for the present often involve parallels drawn from the past. Thus Corinthian envoys beg the Spartans not to allow tyrants back to Athens by invoking the long and brutal tale of their own city's period under tyranny (V 92). Such flashbacks provide some of the crucial motives and explanations for the historical processes at work. (Herodotus sometimes uses a technique at first disorienting to the modern reader, of 'ring composition' in which encircling thematic envelopes successively enclose each other until he returns to the original theme.) The whole is integrated on the moral level, as has often been pointed out, by his idea of a process of reciprocity, tit for tat, balance and counterbalance, revenge and counter-revenge. His scope is enormous, and in the course of tracing his main theme of Greek–barbarian conflict, he succeeds in drawing in much of archaic Greek history.

Everything we know about the Greeks' relationship to their history in this period suggests that while the past was important, it was important only selectively and for limited purposes. There were no professional historians, and the *Histories* were revolutionary as the first extended written work to treat the past within living memory. The earlier Greek 'genealogists' had confined themselves mainly to disentangling and rationalizing, or at least making consistent, the family relationships of mythical heroes. There was thus little written literature recording recent history.

Nor is there anything to be found in Greek literature before Herodotus anticipating the richness of the *Histories*, which seem to appear fully-fledged without any immediate parents. Their fluent style springs – astonishingly – from a tradition which so far had seen prose works only of the very driest kind. Of prose writers, the most relevant to Herodotus is undoubtedly Hecatæus of Miletus (*fl.* 500 BC), who wrote a austere text about genealogies and a more remarkable work which described the cities and areas that would be encountered while circumnavigating the Mediterranean (the *Periodos Ges*). Herodotus owes an obvious debt to this, but the fragments remaining give little hint of anything resembling the breadth and scope of his geographical and ethnographical descriptions. The same must be admitted of the other shadowy genealogists who preceded him, Akousilaos of Argos and Pherecydes of Athens. The even more obscure authors of Persian history, Charon of Lampsacus and Dionysius of Miletus, may not even be chronologically earlier than Herodotus. One suspects that their works have not survived precisely because they bore no comparison with the *Histories*.

The literature that did provide an historical narrative concentrated overwhelmingly on the very remote past, the past of heroes, of the Trojan War, and it was poetic: the Homeric *Iliad* and *Odyssey*, and the rest of the epic cycle, provided a crucial version of the Greek past, not least because they conferred status and ancestry upon later generations. Aristocratic families tended to trace themselves back to a Homeric hero if they could, and from that hero to the gods. Cities looked back to the Homeric legends for their identity and status: as was well known in antiquity, the minor significance of the Athenians in the *Iliad* was a source of chagrin and, apparently, of Athenian interpolations into the text. Such was the importance of the Homeric epics in Greek culture that even the rationalizing Thucydides, who distanced his work from frivolous and entertaining poetry and myths, looked to the *Iliad* for a substratum of historical truth, and proceeded in the early chapters of his *History* to extract usable facts (ship numbers amongst them) in order to prove that the Trojan War had been minor in scale by comparison with his own subject, the Peloponnesian War (431–404 BC).

The implications of this are vital in understanding Herodotus' achievement, and also the problems his enquiries would have faced. The first of these problems was the most taxing: how could you find out about the past at all? If the usable past, the past most evocative of a city's and family's true being, was that of the epic heroes, where did that leave what we may call more prosaically the 'recent past', the period accessible to historical enquiry, the period modern historians label the archaic period, the age of the development of the classical Greek city-state, of democracy, of Greek art and society – and the period about which Herodotus tells us much? The answer to this seems to be that it was left fragmented and in danger of oblivion. If a city's collective memory lays most emphasis on its mythical period, it follows that the time between that age and the present must wither in the collective or individual consciousness. In a world without chroniclers or any automatic system for recording past events, recollection is left to oral tradition. Occasionally, memorials, trophies and tombstones might record memories of specific events or individuals; indeed the main purpose of the memorial was to preserve the memory and fame of what otherwise would be forgotten. Poets like Alcæus who sang of their enmities might also help later historians. But effectively the past was at the mercy of memory and oral tradition, and thus of the political, familial or other rivalries and preoccupations of the teller, a fluid and endlessly changeable resource. And of course for a city to have an official collective memory of some kind, it needs to have a collective identity. Many city traditions in the classical period seem to have seen their recent past as a story of triumph against tyrants (e.g. Corinth, Athens): that image of success tended to push out other memories and other versions. This returns us to Herodotus.

One of his intentions in writing the *Histories* seems to have been to preserve the memories of past achievements before they were erased by time. In consequence, the work is full of folk-tales and oral traditions. As Herodotus states in his Pre- face: 'These are the researches of Herodotus of Halicarnassus, which he publishes in the hope of thereby preserving from decay the remembrance of what men have done, and of preventing the great and wonderful actions of the Greeks and the Barbarians from losing their due meed of glory; and withal to put on record what were their grounds of feud.' How different was this from the Homeric poet who sang of heroes to preserve or actually to confer fame on his subjects? Such an aim was especially valuable in a society primarily dependent on oral traditions – which Herodotus undoubtedly used – but it is not an aim which we would now expect of a modern historian. It is essential to appreciate Herodotus' deliberate withholding of names, for instance, and equally his listing of the ranks of the honoured. 'The Greeks who gained the greatest glory of all in the sea-fight off Salamis were the Eginetans, and after them the Athenians' (VIII 93; cf. VII 226–7 for the Thermopylæ heroes).

Such intentions, when applied to the Persian Wars, intermesh neatly with the need to recall oral tradition and collective identity, for Herodotus was putting on record an account of the wars which he thought the most plausible – and which for later generations has become the primary account. And he was doing this at a time when many conflicting versions of events were still being advanced by competing and antagonistic city-states. That would be hard enough: imagine writing a history of the Second World War, for example, from eyewitnesses, and differing national stances, with barely any documentary evidence, let alone newspapers. But the status of the Persian Wars in what we can call Greek collective identity was such that they aroused stronger passions than any other event of the recent past. There were patriotic claims from all those who had resisted the Persian invasion; awkward excuses and counter-claims from Greeks forced to fight for the Persians (like the Ionians) or those who were voluntarily pro-Persian (Thebes). Herodotus relates one malicious story, for instance, about Corinthian cowardice which he is careful to label as an Athenian tale and not accepted by other Greeks (VIII 94). What could one do about the tricky question of whether Sparta or Athens did most to defeat the Persians? Herodotus came up with an answer which had broad-reaching implications. The Persian Wars also created, or at least considerably developed, a collective Greek view of Hellenism which in the classical period increasingly set itself and its values against the barbarian world and against what were perceived as barbarian characteristics of cowardice, effeminacy and slavery. In other words, the Persian Wars served to concentrate both local and national patriotic feelings, magnifying the self-images of both the city-states and the Greek 'nation' as a whole. It will be obvious that in such circumstances Herodotus could not simply have 'written down' the facts. As with other disparate and contradictory traditions, the very act of collecting, sifting and making sense of evidence involved the creation of some kind of order, as any modern anthropologist collecting material in the field will know.

The Persian Wars provided the would-be historian, perhaps for the first time, with a subject perceived to be of as much significance as the myths and legends on which the Greek national consciousness had formerly been fed. Cities could compare their heroes' exploits with their own resistance to the enemy: Athens, for example, recollected past triumphs at the public funeral for the war dead, and set the recent expulsion of the Persians alongside the glories of the mythical past (such as expelling Amazons and Thracians from Attica). The Greek city-states found here another epic to rival the story of Troy, a set of heroes within living memory. It is perhaps no coincidence, then, that the first Greek writer who has produced anything we might recognize as history (rather than a *mélange* of legends and tales) took his central theme from these wars.

This helps us to some understanding of why the *Histories* were written as they were, indeed how they were written at all. But it would be over-simplifying to see the *Histories* primarily as a memorial to Greek achievement or to earlier Greece. There was more at stake. Let us look more closely at the period in which Herodotus was active.

He lived at a time when the Aegean and the eastern Mediterranean were dominated by Athens and the empire she had created among the surrounding Aegean islands and cities in the aftermath of the Persian Wars. Athenians justified their power – when they bothered to justify it at all – on the grounds that they had done most to defeat the Persians, but this only encouraged resentment among their former allies, now their uneasy vassals. Herodotus himself admitted with reluctance that Athens had saved Greece, and with the open acknowledgement that the claim was unpopular with non-Athenians, not least the Spartans (VII 139). In such a context, the time of the Persian Wars had special meaning as a period in which Greek fought alongside Greek against a common barbarian foe.

Some scholars believe that Herodotus was an outright

supporter of the Athenian empire and its leader Pericles, but his treatment is too balanced for that. The predominant moral and religious views of the author would also seem to preclude any easy identification with one or other city. His *Histories* are not entirely secular, the divine is a motive force, and we may recall the movement of balance and counterbalance that is so important in his narrative explanations. In particular, if there is comment, it often seems to be indirect and allusive. His emphasis on the rise and fall of states or cities commences in the very first paragraphs: 'For the cities which were formerly great, have most of them become insignificant; and such as are at present powerful, were weak in the olden time' (I 5). The continuing theme of the mutability of prosperity and happiness is expressed especially strongly in the story of the meeting of Crœsus and Solon early in Book I, and may be read as a warning to the Athenians: they too should beware that their prosperity will not last. For here Crœsus, the fabulously wealthy Lydian king, urges Solon, sage and law-giver, to admit that he, Crœsus, is the happiest of men; Solon retorts with the stories of Cleobis and Bito, and of Tellus, an obscure Athenian (I 30–32). Then Crœsus' good fortune withers and he is punished for his arrogance and an ancestral sin. About to be burnt alive, he realizes that Solon had been correct (I 86): man is indeed a creature of chance; call no man happy until he is dead – till then he is merely fortunate (I 32). This pessimistic message at the start is reinforced again in the very last paragraphs of the *Histories* (with characteristic ring composition) where the reader is left with hints of Athenian dominance, of the Persians' decline from their former excellence, and a final warning from Cyrus the Great, the man who presided over Persian expansion in the first place, not to move to 'soft countries' for fear they will cease to be men.

This raises the question of the kind of audience Herodotus was writing for. He surely intended to span the whole Greek world and not to limit himself to a particular group. He had travelled widely (and was in exile from his own native city), and had talked to a great range of informants, specialists or otherwise. His religious message and his enthusiasm for liberty were relevant to all Greeks. His fluent, entertaining narrative, at once engaging and moralizing, had general appeal. Thucydides' sour remark that his own work avoided 'the mythical element', the pleasurable and entertaining (I 21), may not have been exclusively aimed at Herodotus, but it could certainly apply to parts of the *Histories*. We may recall, for instance, the folk-tale about Polycrates and the ring (III 41–3), or the description of the wonders of Egypt, or the fantastical tales of distant places, the Ethiopians with their 'table of the Sun' and crystal coffins (III 23–4), the Arabians' methods of collecting cassia, frankincense and cinnamon (III 107–12).

Different sections of the work might appeal to different audiences, and this would have been enhanced by the way it must have been published. Ancient writers assume that Herodotus delivered lectures, and certainly we should not envisage his *Histories* as reaching only those very few who could afford to acquire a manuscript. In the fifth century as before, literature was performed to live audiences, in festivals, social gatherings and symposia, whether or not it was also intended to be read in private (silently or non-silently) from the written text. This was a period before the dominance of the written word could serve as a further barrier between educated and uneducated. In such circumstances, a text would be broken up into performance-sized sections. So we might imagine, perhaps, that any educated Greek audience could enjoy his discussion about the causes of the Nile flooding, in which Herodotus demolishes theories advanced by several Presocratic philosophers (II 19–27). Perhaps a slightly wider audience would relish the gripping accounts of the Persian invasion; the Athenians might want to hear the account of the battle of Marathon; and who knows how many would be interested in the course of the Danube? The point is that the sheer breadth and variety of the *Histories*, combined with partial publication by performance, makes it implausible to pin down his contemporary audience too precisely.

The scope and scale make it equally implausible to think that Herodotus was aiming only at immediate gratification (the other half of Thucydides' criticism) without thought for posterity. He combines with factual narrative the techniques of epic poet and oral story-teller. The audience who appreciated his narration at the end of the *Histories* (IX 115–20) of the Persian despoiling of the shrine of Protesilaus, first (Greek) casualty at Troy, at the boundary between Europe and Asia, then of the barbarous punishment meted out for this crime by the Athenians, was easily familiar with the Homeric tradition. Beside this lie interests, concerns and even language familiar in other fifth-century writers, especially the *physiologoi* or natural philosophers, who speculated on nature (*physis*), and discussed geographical phenomena and biology. Indeed, even the fantastical examples could be part of that enquiry, since exceptional phenomena are precisely those that help elucidate the peculiar workings of nature. Here he was writing in the continuing traditions of the Ionian Enlightenment, the spirit of rational enquiry prevailing among Ionian thinkers of the sixth and fifth centuries. Moreover, he writes in Ionian Greek, the language of philosophy and natural science. In his need to use oral traditions and other peoples' accounts, Herodotus could not engage in more empirical investigations (even had he wanted to), for he was dealing with something more untameable, the accumulated traditions of generations. He can tell us at one moment a folk-tale which strains the faith of the most credulous (for example, the tale of Rhampsinitus and the thief, II 121), and elsewhere assure his audience (with a twinkle in his eye?) that his policy is to repeat the tales he has heard even if he does not believe them (II 123, VII 152). He calls his work an *'historie'* in the Prologue, using the word which has become our 'history'; but at the time of the *Histories* it meant strictly 'enquiry' and was the word currently in use by early Greek philosophers and proto-scientists, enquirers into nature. Nothing could underline more forcefully the wider nature of his enterprise.

This brings us to Herodotus' interest in geography and in the nature of the many different peoples inhabiting the known world of that time. From the very opening he signals to the audience that his subject matter encompasses the achievements and wonders of barbarians as well as Greeks, and as his narrative progresses, his system is to step aside and give a geographical and ethnographic description of each area or people as it occurs. The longest description – of Egypt – is elaborated, as he says, because, 'the country ... possesses so many wonders' and 'works which defy description' (II 35); but Ionians, Spartans, Scythians, Babylonians, Libyans and many others have the anthropological spotlight turned upon them. We are also told about his own travels, personal investigations (sometimes tidied up in the telling?) and theories, for it is in these descriptions of lands and peoples that Herodotus is most present to the audience as an investigator and enquirer: he has seen only the upper chambers of the Labyrinth, he says (II 148); he is impressed by the shrine made of a single stone in Buto (II 155). We hear about Egyptian irrigation, the possible sources of the Nile, the great Scythian rivers from the Danube round the north coast of what is now the Black Sea; we hear about the land west of Egypt (North Africa), which the Greeks called Libya, and here, as for the far north, Herodotus tells us as much as he can until information of any sort literally gives out. Thus, 'As far as the Atlantes the names of the nations inhabiting the sandy ridge are known to me but beyond them my knowledge fails' (IV 185). One has a sense of his universal curiosity and quest for information of all kinds, even when it is of dubious validity. But for the fact that there are clearly subjects where he knows far more than he recounts (e.g. the 'Assyrian account'), the *Histories* stand as a compilation, brilliantly structured and ordered, of current knowledge about the world.

It is in these areas, however, that his account has been subject to the most debate, controversy and criticism. What do we do, for instance, with the statement about an area of Libya: 'Here too are the dog-faced creatures, and the creatures without heads, whom the Libyans declare to have their eyes in their breasts; and also the wild men, and wild women, and many other far less fabulous beasts' (IV 191) – creatures which recur, incidentally, in medieval maps of the world? Or 'the Atarantians, who alone of all known nations are destitute of names' (IV 184)? Or the notorious description of the hippopotamus in Book II (71) which sounds fantastical and which Herodotus allegedly took from the earlier geographer and genealogist Hecatæus? Or the mythical bird the phoenix, which at least Herodotus says he saw only in pictures (II 73)?

At times we seem perilously near to sheer fantasy, to

fabulous tales which one might be able to dignify as 'travellers' tales' much magnified in the telling, or as the confused sight-seeings of Herodotus 'the tourist'. Since antiquity, people have accused Herodotus of peddling in fictions, though whether they are supposed to be his own or those of other people is sometimes left blurred. Some modern scholars have doubted whether Herodotus always saw what he claims to have seen. It has been questioned whether he even went to Egypt, which he describes so enthusiastically and at such length; other parts are more certainly beyond his personal range, like Babylonia or Scythia. Yet further archaeological discoveries and geo-graphical exploration confirm much of what he wrote, and the most detailed examination by an Egyptologist of Herodotus' Egyptian account shows that most of it is substantiated by the evidence. The controversy will continue, with some seeking to find real confirmation of anything he says, others most struck by the impossible and inaccurate. But perhaps we should not be too fundamentalist here. Every era has differing criteria for what it regards as 'credible' or worth recounting; moreover, one should allow for the whimsical and for imaginative ideas about what lies in the unknown, and Herodotus was recalling not just what he had heard but what others too had heard. Nor should we underestimate the Greek fondness for wonders and for paradoxes (themselves often the basis for examination of nature), or the rapidity with which curiosity about other peoples could merge with pure myth (cf. the Amazons).

It is therefore insufficient simply to measure Herodotus' account against what we now know to be true, for example against absolute dimensions or geographical directions. Modern geographical consciousness is intrinsically formed by compasses and modern maps with the bird's-eye view they purport to provide. In the fifth century BC it may have been constructed around known routes, lists of towns along the coastline, and on the larger scale by ideas of grand symmetry. Thus Herodotus says the Nile and Danube mouths are 'oppo-site each other' – not entirely incorrect even by modern maps, for what it is worth – and, more surprisingly, that the rivers run parallel to each other (II 33–4). His frequent descriptions of places on the edge of the known world as 'next after' the previous place reflect the perceptions of traders and travellers in unmapped space.

Perhaps most interesting for us is the way his descriptions of remote areas and of non-Greeks are informed by and large by Greek preoccupations and perceptions. His account of the northern Scythians in Book IV, for instance, stresses the characteristics which struck a Greek as most alien and curious – their nomadism, lack of fixed settlement or buildings, their gruesome burial practices. This does not mean that his description is merely a creation of Greek imagination, as has been implied occasionally in recent work. It is more complex and diverse than that, and some of the more exotic features are in any case borne out by archaeological excavation. Yet the Scythian way of life could not help but clarify Hellenism by contrast. The exploration by one society of another is almost bound to be influenced by previous conceptions which help to make order out of new experiences, as we can see in the process by which the European discovery of America had to be accommodated by Europeans brought up on ideas of geography derived from the ancient geographers. It is fascinating to observe in Herodotus the friction between the fashionable symmetrical view of the world, which included an ocean circling the whole earth, and the messier shape that was implied by his enquiries: 'But the boundaries of Europe are quite unknown, and there is not a man who can say whether any sea girds it round either on the north or on the east, while in length it undoubtedly extends as far as both the other two [continents, Asia and Libya]' (IV 45).

He is astonishingly open-minded and curious about the barbarian customs he cites. Plutarch went so far as to accuse him of being 'a friend of the barbarians' (*philobarbaros*). Here again, on one level he is simply pointing out what is different from what was familiar to his Greek audience, these foreign habits being seen through the filter of Greek eyes, Greek perceptions about what was normal. In some cases, it is true, we may be hearing entirely Greek 'fabrications' about remote tribes, where this ethnographic lore tells us far more about the Greeks than about the people it purports to present. The tribe in North Africa who have no names, for instance, sound like the product of Greek intellectual fascination with naming. Herodotus' claim that the Egyptians do everything in quite the opposite way to other men (i.e. Greeks) may be an extrapolation from the fact that the Egyptian river behaves like no other (II 35). Yet at least there is intellectual curiosity and a desire to make sense and for these we must give the historian full credit.

He concentrates particularly on religious customs, on rituals surrounding death and marriage, and even discusses differing ideas of achieving happiness (compare the Massagetæ, I 216). This choice must reflect his own criteria for what is significant about a culture. In Book II, he presents his theory that the Greeks themselves acquired knowledge of their gods from Egypt. He is not simply mirroring Greek prejudices about 'odd' and exotic people, and it is particularly striking that his ethnography shies away from the kind of stereotypes that seem increasingly common in classical Greece, or the blanket denigration of Persians, for instance, as effeminate and luxurious, which became the standard Greek view and means of emphasizing their own superiority. His portrayal of the Persians allows them much nobility of character, brought low by progressive deterioration into slavishness and by monarchic rule. Some customs he judges. He abhors temple prostitution, for example, yet admires the Babylonian marriage market, a system involving the distribution of both wealth and beauty, in which dowries for less attractive women are provided by payments made in auction for the most beautiful, so that everyone, rich or poor, is assured of a partner (I 196). He seems well aware of the validity of mutually incompatible customs. A telling anecdote about Darius the Persian king seems to reflect Greek intellectual preoccupations more than the king's anthropological investigations. Darius questions certain Greeks and Indians about how they treat their parents' corpses: the Greeks burn the bodies, but the Indians believe they should eat them. Each group is horrified by the other. This shows, Herodotus says, that law (or custom: *nomos* covers both) is king (III 38). To the question most important of all for his audience, how the Greeks defeated the numerically superior Persian invasion, his answer seems again to rest on custom above all, the Greeks' liberty, democracy and discipline.

INTRODUCTION

Herodotus' home city, we recall, was Halicarnassus, on the southern edge of Ionia and on the western boundaries of the Persian empire. It had a remarkable mix of Greeks and non-Greek Carians, who inhabited the hinterland and were rapidly becoming Hellenized. It is tempting to think that Herodotus' open-mindedness and willingness to explore the customs and lands of non-Greeks was in part related to this background, a world in which Greeks and non-Greeks lived together, and which lay within the tentacles of the great non-Greek empires of the Near East. He remarks wryly at one point that after the initial Persian retreat, the Greeks on the mainland had no idea what lay east of Delos, that is, in Ionia along the coast of modern Turkey and islands off it, and were afraid that it would be swarming with Persian soldiers and 'full of danger' (VIII 132). The remark reads like a sly comment on the ignorance of mainland Greeks about what lay east. We may perhaps suspect a rather different relation to barbarians on the east side of the Aegean from that visible in Athenian literature and society. For Plato in the fourth century barbarians were natural enemies, for Aristotle they were natural slaves. This is far from Herodotus' view. We may also recall that it was the philosophers of the Greek cities of Asia who had initiated rational enquiry into the world. So Herodotus' intellectual background may help explain the breadth of his curiosity and the directions it took. The *Histories* came to be most appreciated in the Hellenistic period, after Alexander's conquests had spread Greek settlers over the whole of what was once the Persian empire. The edges of the known world were extending. In this new society Herodotus was both inspiration and guide.

Rosalind Thomas

A NOTE ON THE TRANSLATION

———

Rawlinson's translation is reproduced here in its original form. Alterations made have been made only in two respects, both mentioned by Rawlinson himself. Rawlinson's original caveat in the first edition of 1858 deserves reproducing (it should be noted this edition included extensive commentary and learned essays on the fresh archaeological discoveries from the Near East): 'There are, however, one or two respects in which the present translation does not lay claim to strict accuracy. Occasional passages offensive to modern delicacy have been retrenched, and others have been modified by the alteration of a few phrases. In the orthography of names, moreover, and in the rendering of the appellation of the Greek deities, the latinized forms, with which our ear is most familiar, have been adopted in preference to the closer and more literal representation of the words, which has recently obtained the sanction of some very eminent writers. In a work intended for general reading, it was thought that unfamiliar forms were to be eschewed; and that accuracy in such matters, although perhaps more scholar-like, would be dearly purchased at the expense of harshness and repulsiveness.' It was felt that in the late 1990s a translation should be more 'scholar-like'. Greek deities and those passages thought indelicate have been reinserted.

Rawlinson's original footnotes were condensed for the first publication of the *Histories* in Everyman's Library in 1910 by the Editor, E. H. Blakeney, and are reprinted in this edition, together with Blakeney's own footnotes.

R. T.

ABOUT THE TRANSLATOR

———

GEORGE RAWLINSON (1812–1902) was Camden Professor of Ancient History at Oxford between 1861 and 1889. His chief works include *The Five Great Monarchies of the Ancient Eastern World*, *The History of Ancient Egypt* and *The History of Phoenicia*.

ABOUT THE INTRODUCER

———

DR ROSALIND THOMAS is Lecturer in Ancient History at Royal Holloway, University of London, and author of *Oral Tradition and Written Record in Classical Athens* and *Literacy and Orality in Ancient Greece*. She is currently writing a book on Herodotus.

SELECT BIBLIOGRAPHY

WORK

JOHN GOULD, *Herodotus*, Weidenfeld and Nicolson, London, 1989: the best and most stimulating introduction to Herodotus.

DONALD LATEINER, *The Historical Method of Herodotus*, University of Toronto Press, Toronto, 1989: a valuable, thoughtful, dense discussion.

J. A. S. EVANS, *Herodotus, Explorer of the Past*, Princeton University Press, Princeton, 1991: concentrates on imperialism, individuals and oral tradition.

J. L. MYRES, *Herodotus, Father of History*, Clarendon Press, Oxford, 1953: readable, elegant introduction, somewhat old fashioned; concentrating particularly on geography and the Perisan Wars.

Herodotus and the Invention of History. Arethusa 20 (1987): a special edition of the journal *Arethusa* devoted to Herodotean studies. It has full bibliography, good analysis of older work and current trends in Herodotean interpretation by C. DEWALD and J. MARINCOLA, and other important essays; D. KONSTAN discusses 'Persians, Greeks and Empire'.

A. MOMIGLIANO, 'The place of Herodotus in the history of historiography', in his *Studies in Historiography*, Weidenfeld and Nicolson, London, 1966, pp. 127–42.

O. MURRAY, 'Herodotus and oral history', in H. SANCISI-WEERDENBURG and A. KUHRT, eds, *Achaemenid History II. The Greek Sources*, Instituut voor het Nabije Oosten, Leiden, 1987, pp. 93–115.

For detailed discussion of the reliability or archaeological background of any section of the *Histories*, the reader may turn to the commentaries (below), though some are not up to date with the most recent discoveries. For the Persian empire, see A. R. BURN, *Persia and the Greeks*, second edition with a Postscript by D. M. LEWIS, Duckworth, London, 1984. W. K. PRITCHETT, *The Liar School of Herodotus*, Gieben, Amsterdam, 1993 has much on the relevant archaeological evidence within a highly polemical overall argument. A stimulating discussion of Herodotus as ethnographer is by JAMES REDFIELD, 'Herodotus the Tourist', in *Classical Philology* 80 (1985), pp. 97–118.

EDITIONS AND COMMENTARIES

The standard Greek text is the Oxford Classical Text, ed. C. HUDE, *Herodoti Historiae*, 2 volumes, Clarendon Press, Oxford, 3rd edition 1927.

The commentary by W. W. HOW and J. WELLS, *A Commentary on Herodotus*, 2 volumes, Clarendon Press, Oxford, 1913 (reprinted with corrections in 1928) is still the only complete commentary in English. The most up-to-date commentary on the whole is provided by the series (in process of completion) published under the aegis of the Fondazione Lorenzo Valla, in Italian: *Erodoto. Le Storie*, Arnoldo Mondadori, Milan: the volumes on Book I and Book III by DAVID ASHERI are particularly fine (1988 and 1990 respectively). ALAN B. LLOYD, *Herodotus, Book II*, Brill, Leiden, 1975–88 provides the fullest commentary, in three volumes of which vol. I is an Introduction: a full-length discussion of and commentary on Book II on Egypt, with much of value for the rest of the *Histories*.

HISTORICAL BACKGROUND

O. MURRAY, *Early Greece*, Fontana, London, 2nd edition 1993: stimulating introduction to archaic Greece.

R. OSBORNE, *Greece in the Making 1200–479 BC*, Routledge, London, 1996: important study with concentration on recent archaeological evidence; with illustrations.

J. BOARDMAN, *The Greeks Overseas*, Thames and Hudson, London, 3rd edition 1980: lavishly illustrated account of Greek expansion around the Mediterranean.

Cambridge Ancient History, Cambridge University Press, Cambridge, 2nd edition, for detailed history and further bibliography: volume III *The Expansion of the Greek World, eighth to sixth centuries BC* (1982); volume IV *Persia, Greece and the Western Mediterranean c.525–479 BC* (1988); volume V *The Fifth Century BC* (1992).

CHRONOLOGY

DATE	GREECE/GREEK WORLD	NEAR EAST
776 BC	First Olympic Games.	
By 750	Invention of Greek alphabet.	
744–612		Assyrian Empire.
735–700	First Greek colonies founded in Sicily.	
c. 730–710	Sparta conquers Messenia.	
By 700	Homeric epics, *Iliad* and *Odyssey*.	
c. 700	Hesiod.	
c. 680		Gyges founds Lydian Empire (c. 680–645).
c. 680–640	Archilochus of Paros.	
670 on		Decline of Assyria.
664		Psammetichus I (650–625): Beginning of Saite dynasty in Egypt.
655–585	Tyranny at Corinth: Cypselus and Periander.	
650		Phraates (650–625) and rise of Median Empire.
c. 650	Tyranny of Orthagoras at Sicyon.	
632	Cylon's conspiracy at Athens.	
630	Foundation of Cyrene, North Africa, by Therans.	
621	Drakon's law code at Athens.	
620–570	Pittakos' tyranny at Mytilene. Alcaeus, Sappho, Stesichorus.	
612–609		Fall of Nineveh: Assyrian empire divided between Babylon and Persia.
late 7th century	Tyrtaeus, Alcman.	
By 600		Greek foundation of Naukratis in Egypt; greater Greek contacts with Egypt.
c. 600	Cleisthenes tyrant of Sicyon.	
597		Nebuchadrezzar (605–562) captures Babylon.
594/3	Solon archon of Athens; Solonian law code.	

DATE	GREECE/GREEK WORLD	NEAR EAST
c. 592 BC	Alcmaeon the Alcmaeonid wins victory at Olympia.	
591		Expedition of Psammetichus II of Egypt to Nubia.
c. 572	'Wooing of Agariste', daughter of Cleisthenes of Sicyon.	
569–525		Amasis king of Egypt.
c. 566	Panathenaia reorganized at Athens.	
c. 561	Peisistratus' first tyranny at Athens.	
560–546		Croesus king of Lydia.
559		Cyrus (the Great) becomes king of Persia.
559–6	Miltiades founds colony in Chersonese, Thrace.	
556	Birth of Simonides (556–468).	
550		Cyrus king of Persia conquers Media.
546		Cyrus conquers Lydia; shortly after turns to the Greeks of Asia Minor.
546–28	Peisistratus' final period of tryranny at Athens.	
539		Cyrus conquers Babylon; return of Jews from exile.
530		Death of Cyrus; succession of Cambyses.
528/7	Hippias succeeds to the tyranny at Athens.	
525		Death of Amasis of Egypt; Persians conquer Egypt.
521		Darius seizes kingship of Persia.
c. 521–491	Cleomenes king of Sparta. Expansion of Spartan power.	
514	Harmodius and Aristogeiton murder Hipparchus the Peisistratid at Athens.	
510	Peisistratid tyranny overthrown at Athens.	
508/7	Isagoras archon at Athens.	
507	Cleisthenes' reforms at Athens: Cleisthenic democracy.	

DATE	GREECE/GREEK WORLD	NEAR EAST
late 6th century BC	Xenophanes of Colophon; Pythagoras; Theognis of Megara.	
c. 500	Hecataeus of Miletus, geographer and genealogist, active.	
499–494	Ionians revolt from the Persians.	
498	Ionian rebels burn Sardis.	
494	Battle of Lade; sack of Miletus.	
492	Miltiades, the general, prosecuted for tyranny.	
490–479	Persian Wars.	
490	Xerxes' expedition against Greece; battle of Marathon.	
489	Miltiades fined for misconduct; dies.	
486		Darius dies; accession of Xerxes.
485	Gelon becomes tyrant of Syracuse.	
484	Birth of Herodotus, according to later biographers.	
480	Second Persian expedition, under Darius: battles of Artemisium, Thermopylae, Salamis.	
479	Battles of Plataea, Mycale.	
478	Origin of Athenian empire: Delian league founded under Athenian leadership.	
470s	Athenian funeral orations initiated.	
472	Aeschylus' Persae.	
468	Sophocles' first victory for tragedy.	
467–466	Greeks defeat Persians at Eurymedon (Pamphylia) under Cimon.	
465		Xerxes dies; accession of Artaxerxes (465–424).
464	Earthquake in Sparta and Messenian revolt.	

DATE	GREECE/GREEK WORLD	NEAR EAST
461 BC	Ephialtes' reforms at Athens establishing radical democracy. First Peloponnesian War between Sparta and Athens (461–446).	
459	Athenian expedition to Egypt.	
458	Aeschylus' *Oresteia*.	
456	Death of Aeschylus.	
454		Athenian disaster in Egypt.
450s–420s	Protagoras, early sophist, active.	
450s–420s	Herodotus active (dies in ?420s).	
450	Five-year truce between Athens and Sparta.	
450–449	Athenian expedition to Cyprus; death of Cimon.	
?449	'Peace of Callias' between Persians and Athens; conventional symbol of cessation of hostilities between Athens and Persia.	
447	Building of Parthenon begins at Athens.	
446	Thirty-year peace between Sparta and Athens and allies. Last dateable ode of Pindar.	
443	Ostracism of Thucydides of Melesias, leaving Pericles without a rival. Pericles' period of supremacy (and successive generalships) begins. Thurii in southern Italy founded by Athens. Herodotus is said to have joined it.	
441–439	Samos revolts from Athens.	
441	Euripides' first victory.	
?441	Sophocles' *Antigone*.	
431	Second Peloponnesian War begins (431–404). Thucydides begins writing his *History* as the war commences (dies probably in 390s).	

xliii

THE HISTORIES
OF HERODOTUS

TO THE RIGHT HONOURABLE
WILLIAM EWART GLADSTONE, M.P.,
ETC. ETC. ETC.
WHO, AMID THE CARES OF PUBLIC LIFE,
HAS CONTINUED TO FEEL AND SHOW
AN INTEREST IN CLASSICAL STUDIES,
THIS WORK IS INSCRIBED,
AS A TOKEN OF WARM REGARD,
BY THE AUTHOR.

[Original Dedication, 1858]

THE FIRST BOOK,
ENTITLED CLIO

THESE are the researches of Herodotus of Halicarnassus,[1] which he publishes, in the hope of thereby preserving from decay the remembrance of what men have done, and of preventing the great and wonderful actions of the Greeks and the Barbarians from losing their due meed of glory; and withal to put on record what were their grounds of feud.

1. According to the Persians best informed in history, the Phœnicians began the quarrel. This people, who had formerly dwelt on the shores of the Erythræan Sea,[2] having migrated to the Mediterranean and settled in the parts which they now inhabit, began at once, they say, to adventure on long voyages, freighting their vessels with the wares of Egypt and Assyria. They landed at many places on the coast, and among the rest at Argos, which was then pre-eminent above all the states included now under the common name of Hellas.[3] Here they exposed their merchandise, and traded with the natives for five or six days; at the end of which time, when almost everything was sold, there came down to the beach a number of women, and among them the daughter of the king, who was, they say, agreeing in this with the Greeks, Io, the child of Inachus. The women were standing by the stern of the ship intent upon their purchases, when the Phœnicians, with a general shout, rushed upon them. The greater part made their escape, but some were seized and carried off. Io herself was among the captives. The Phœnicians put the women

1 The mention of the author's name and country in the first sentence of his history seems to have been usual in the age in which Herodotus wrote.

2 By the Erythræan Sea Herodotus intends, not our Red Sea, which he calls the Arabian Gulf (κόλπος ᾿Αράβιος), but the Indian Ocean, or rather both the Indian Ocean and the Persian Gulf, which latter he does not consider distinct from the Ocean, being ignorant of its shape.

3 The ancient superiority of Argos is indicated by the position of Agamemnon at the time of the Trojan war (compare Thucyd. i. 9–10), and by the use of the word Argive in Homer for Greek generally. No other name of a single people is used in the same generic way.

on board their vessel, and set sail for Egypt. Thus did Io pass into Egypt, according to the Persian story,[1] which differs widely from the Phœnician: and thus commenced, according to their authors, the series of outrages.

2. At a later period, certain Greeks, with whose name they are unacquainted, but who would probably be Cretans,[2] made a landing at Tyre, on the Phœnician coast, and bore off the king's daughter, Europé. In this they only retaliated; but afterwards the Greeks, they say, were guilty of a second violence. They manned a ship of war, and sailed to Æa, a city of Colchis, on the river Phasis; from whence, after despatching the rest of the business on which they had come, they carried off Medea, the daughter of the king of the land. The monarch sent a herald into Greece to demand reparation of the wrong, and the restitution of his child; but the Greeks made answer, that having received no reparation of the wrong done them in the seizure of Io the Argive, they should give none in this instance.

3. In the next generation afterwards, according to the same authorities, Alexander the son of Priam, bearing these events in mind, resolved to procure himself a wife out of Greece by violence, fully persuaded, that as the Greeks had not given satisfaction for their outrages, so neither would he be forced to make any for his. Accordingly he made prize of Helen; upon which the Greeks decided that, before resorting to other measures, they would send envoys to reclaim the princess and require reparation of the wrong. Their demands were met by a reference to the violence which had been offered to Medea, and they were asked with what face they could now require satisfaction, when they had formerly rejected all demands for either reparation or restitution addressed to them.[3]

1 The name, thus first brought before us in its Asiatic form, may perhaps furnish an astronomical solution for the entire fable; for as the wanderings of the Greek Io have been often compared with the erratic course of the moon in the heavens, passing in succession through all the signs of the zodiac, so do we find that in the ante-Semitic period there was also an identity of name, the Egyptian title of the moon being *Yah*, and the primitive Chaldæan title being represented by a Cuneiform sign, which is phonetically *Ai*, as in modern Turkish.

2 Since no other Greeks were thought to have possessed a navy in these early times.

3 Aristophanes in the Acharnians (488–494) very wittily parodies the opening of Herodotus's history. Professing to give the causes of the Peloponnesian war, he says:—

4. Hitherto the injuries on either side had been mere acts of common violence; but in what followed the Persians consider that the Greeks were greatly to blame, since before any attack had been made on Europe, they led an army into Asia. Now as for the carrying off of women, it is the deed, they say, of a rogue; but to make a stir about such as are carried off, argues a man a fool. Men of sense care nothing for such women, since it is plain that without their own consent they would never be forced away. The Asiatics, when the Greeks ran off with their women, never troubled themselves about the matter; but the Greeks, for the sake of a single Lacedæmonian girl, collected a vast armament, invaded Asia, and destroyed the kingdom of Priam. Henceforth they ever looked upon the Greeks as their open enemies. For Asia, with all the various tribes of barbarians that inhabit it, is regarded by the Persians as their own; but Europe and the Greek race they look on as distinct and separate.[1]

5. Such is the account which the Persians give of these matters.[2] They trace to the attack upon Troy their ancient enmity towards the Greeks. The Phœnicians, however, as regards Io, vary from the Persian statements. They deny that they used any violence to remove her into Egypt; she herself, they say, having formed an intimacy with the captain, while his vessel lay at Argos,

---

————"This was nothing,
Smacking too much of our accustomed manner
To give offence. But here, sirs, was the rub:
Some sparks of ours, hot with the grape, had stol'n
A mistress of the game – Simætha named –
From the Megarians: her doughty townsmen
(For the deed moved no small extent of anger)
Reveng'd the affront upon Aspasia's train,
And bore away a brace of her fair damsels.
All Greece anon gave note of martial prelude.
And what the cause of war? marry, three women."

–MITCHELL, p. 70–2.

This is the earliest indication of a knowledge of the work of Herodotus on the part of any other Greek writer.

1 The claim made by the Persians to the natural lordship of Asia was convenient as furnishing them with pretexts for such wars as it suited their policy to engage in with non-Asiatic nations.

2 It is curious to observe the treatment which the Greek myths met with at the hands of foreigners. The Oriental mind, quite unable to appreciate poetry of such a character, stripped the legends bare of all that beautified them, and then treated them, thus vulgarised, as matters of simple history.

and perceiving herself to be with child, of her own free will accompanied the Phœnicians on their leaving the shore, to escape the shame of detection and the reproaches of her parents. Whether this latter account be true, or whether the matter happened otherwise, I shall not discuss further. I shall proceed at once to point out the person who first within my own knowledge inflicted injury on the Greeks, after which I shall go forward with my history, describing equally the greater and the lesser cities. For the cities which were formerly great, have most of them become insignificant; and such as are at present powerful, were weak in the olden time.[1] I shall therefore discourse equally of both, convinced that human happiness never continues long in one stay.

6. Crœsus, son of Alyattes, by birth a Lydian, was lord of all the nations to the west of the river Halys. This stream, which separates Syria[2] from Paphlagonia, runs with a course from south to north, and finally falls into the Euxine. So far as our knowledge goes, he was the first of the barbarians who had dealings with the Greeks, forcing some of them to become his tributaries, and entering into alliance with others. He conquered the Æolians, Ionians, and Dorians of Asia, and made a treaty with the Lacedæmonians. Up to that time all Greeks had been free. For the Cimmerian attack upon Ionia, which was earlier than Crœsus, was not a conquest of the cities, but only an inroad for plundering.

7. The sovereignty of Lydia, which had belonged to the Heraclides, passed into the family of Crœsus, who were called the Mermnadæ, in the manner which I will now relate. There was a certain king of Sardis, Candaules by name, whom the Greeks called Myrsilus. He was a descendant of Alcæus, son of Heracles. The first king of this dynasty was Agron, son of Ninus, grandson of Bel, and great-grandson of Alcæus; Candaules, son of Myrsus, was the last. The kings who reigned before Agron sprang from Lydus, son of Atys, from whom the people of the land, called

1 Thucydides remarks on the small size to which Mycênæ had dwindled compared with its former power (i. 10).

2 By Syria Herodotus here means Cappadocia, the inhabitants of which he calls Syrians (i. 72, and vii. 72), or Cappadocian Syrians (Συρίους Καππαδόκας i. 72). Herodotus regards the words Syria and Assyria, Syrians and Assyrians, as in reality the same (vii. 63); in his use of them, however, as ethnic appellatives, he always carefully distinguishes.

previously Meonians, received the name of Lydians. The Heraclides, descended from Heracles and the slave-girl of Jardanus,
having been entrusted by these princes with the management of
affairs, obtained the kingdom by an oracle. Their rule endured
for two and twenty generations of men, a space of five hundred
and five years;[1] during the whole of which period, from Agron
to Candaules, the crown descended in the direct line from father
to son.

8. Now it happened that this Candaules was in love with his
own wife; and not only so, but thought her the fairest woman
in the whole world. This fancy had strange consequences. There
was in his body-guard a man whom he specially favoured, Gyges,
the son of Dascylus. All affairs of greatest moment were entrusted by Candaules to this person, and to him he was wont to
extol the surpassing beauty of his wife. So matters went on for
a while. At length, one day, Candaules, who was fated to end ill,
thus addressed his follower: "I see thou dost not credit what I
tell thee of my lady's loveliness; but come now, since men's ears
are less credulous than their eyes, contrive some means whereby
thou mayst behold her naked." At this the other loudly exclaimed, saying, "What most unwise speech is this, master, which
thou hast uttered? Wouldst thou have me behold my mistress
when she is naked? Bethink thee that a woman, with her clothes,
puts off her bashfulness. Our fathers, in time past, distinguished
right and wrong plainly enough, and it is our wisdom to submit
to be taught by them. There is an old saying, 'Let each look on
his own.' I hold thy wife for the fairest of all womankind. Only,
I beseech thee, ask me not to do wickedly."

9. Gyges thus endeavoured to decline the king's proposal,
trembling lest some dreadful evil should befall him through it.
But the king replied to him, "Courage, friend; suspect me not of
the design to prove thee by this discourse; nor dread thy mistress, lest mischief befall thee at her hands. Be sure I will so
manage that she shall not even know that thou hast looked upon
her. I will place thee behind the open door of the chamber in
which we sleep. When I enter to go to rest she will follow me.
There stands a chair close to the entrance, on which she will lay

1 Herodotus professes to count three generations to the century (ii. 142),
thus making the generation $33\frac{1}{3}$ years. In this case the average of the generations
is but 23 years.

her clothes one by one as she takes them off. Thou wilt be able thus at thy leisure to peruse her person. Then, when she is moving from the chair toward the bed, and her back is turned on thee, be it thy care that she see thee not as thou passest through the doorway."

10. Gyges, unable to escape, could but declare his readiness. Then Candaules, when bedtime came, led Gyges into his sleeping-chamber, and a moment after the queen followed. She entered, and laid her garments on the chair, and Gyges gazed on her. After a while she moved toward the bed, and her back being then turned, he glided stealthily from the apartment. As he was passing out, however, she saw him, and instantly divining what had happened, she neither screamed as her shame impelled her, nor even appeared to have noticed aught, purposing to take vengeance upon the husband who had so affronted her. For among the Lydians, and indeed among the barbarians generally, it is reckoned a deep disgrace, even to a man, to be seen naked.[1]

11. No sound or sign of intelligence escaped her at the time. But in the morning, as soon as day broke, she hastened to choose from among her retinue, such as she knew to be most faithful to her, and preparing them for what was to ensue, summoned Gyges into her presence. Now it had often happened before that the queen had desired to confer with him, and he was accustomed to come to her at her call. He therefore obeyed the summons, not suspecting that she knew aught of what had occurred. Then she addressed these words to him: "Take thy choice, Gyges, of two courses which are open to thee. Slay Candaules, and thereby become my lord, and obtain the Lydian throne, or die this moment in his room. So wilt thou not again, obeying all behests of thy master, behold what is not lawful for thee. It must needs be, that either he perish by whose counsel this thing was done, or thou, who sawest me naked, and so didst break our usages." At these words Gyges stood awhile in mute astonishment; recovering after a time, he earnestly besought the queen that she would not compel him to so hard a choice. But finding he implored in vain, and that necessity was indeed laid on him to kill or to be killed, he made choice of life for himself,

1 The contrast between the feelings of the Greeks and the barbarians on this point is noted by Thucydides (i. 6), where we learn that the exhibition of the naked person was recent, even with the Greeks.

and replied by this inquiry: "If it must be so, and thou compellest me against my will to put my lord to death, come, let me hear how thou wilt have me set on him." "Let him be attacked," she answered, "on that spot where I was by him shown naked to you, and let the assault be made when he is asleep."

12. All was then prepared for the attack, and when night fell, Gyges, seeing that he had no retreat or escape, but must absolutely either slay Candaules, or himself be slain, followed his mistress into the sleeping-room. She placed a dagger in his hand, and hid him carefully behind the self-same door. Then Gyges, when the king was fallen asleep, entered privily into the chamber and struck him dead. Thus did the wife and kingdom of Candaules pass into the possession of Gyges, of whom Archilochus the Parian, who lived about the same time,[1] made mention in a poem written in Iambic trimeter verse.

13. Gyges was afterwards confirmed in the possession of the throne by an answer of the Delphic oracle. Enraged at the murder of their king, the people flew to arms, but after a while the partisans of Gyges came to terms with them, and it was agreed that if the Delphic oracle declared him king of the Lydians, he should reign; if otherwise, he should yield the throne to the Heraclides. As the oracle was given in his favour he became king. The Pythoness, however, added that, in the fifth generation from Gyges, vengeance should come for the Heraclides; a prophecy of which neither the Lydians nor their princes took any account till it was fulfilled. Such was the way in which the Mermnadæ deposed the Heraclides, and themselves obtained the sovereignty.

14. When Gyges was established on the throne, he sent no small presents to Delphi, as his many silver offerings at the Delphic shrine testify. Besides this silver he gave a vast number of vessels of gold, among which the most worthy of mention are the goblets, six in number, and weighing altogether thirty talents, which stand in the Corinthian treasury, dedicated by him. I call it the Corinthian treasury, though in strictness of speech it

---

1 There are strong grounds for believing that Archilochus was later than Callinus, who is proved by Grote to have written after the great Cimmerian invasion in the reign of Ardys. But there is nothing to show at what time in the reign of Ardys this invasion happened. Archilochus may have been contemporary both with Gyges and Ardys. The Cimmerian invasion may have been early in the reign of the latter prince, say B.C. 675.

is the treasury not of the whole Corinthian people, but of Cypselus, son of Eetion. Excepting Midas, son of Gordias,[1] king of Phrygia, Gyges was the first of the barbarians whom we know to have sent offerings to Delphi. Midas dedicated the royal throne whereon he was accustomed to sit and administer justice, an object well worth looking at. It lies in the same place as the goblets presented by Gyges. The Delphians call the whole of the silver and the gold which Gyges dedicated, after the name of the donor, Gygian.

As soon as Gyges was king he made an inroad on Miletus and Smyrna, and took the city of Colophon. Afterwards, however, though he reigned eight and thirty years, he did not perform a single noble exploit. I shall therefore make no further mention of him, but pass on to his son and successor in the kingdom, Ardys.

15. Ardys took Priêné and made war upon Miletus. In his reign the Cimmerians, driven from their homes by the nomads of Scythia, entered Asia and captured Sardis, all but the citadel. He reigned forty-nine years, and was succeeded by his son, Sadyattes, who reigned twelve years. At his death his son Alyattes mounted the throne.

16. This prince waged war with the Medes under Cyaxares, the grandson of Deïoces,[2] drove the Cimmerians out of Asia, conquered Smyrna, the Colophonian colony,[3] and invaded Clazomenæ. From this last contest he did not come off as he could have wished, but met with a sore defeat; still, however, in the course of his reign, he performed other actions very worthy of note, of which I will now proceed to give an account.

17. Inheriting from his father a war with the Milesians, he pressed the siege against the city by attacking it in the following manner. When the harvest was ripe on the ground he marched his army into Milesia to the sound of pipes and harps, and flutes masculine and feminine.[4] The buildings that were scattered over

1 Every Phrygian king mentioned in ancient history is either Midas, son of Gordias, or Gordias, son of Midas.

2 Vide infra, chaps. 73–4.

3 Vide infra, ch. 150.

4 Aulus Gellius understood the "male and female flutes," as flutes played by men, and flutes played by women. But it is more probable that flutes of different tones or pitches are intended. The flute, the pitch of which was lower, would be called *male*; the more treble or shrill-sounding one would be the *female*.

the country he neither pulled down nor burnt, nor did he even tear away the doors, but left them standing as they were. He cut down, however, and utterly destroyed all the trees and all the corn throughout the land, and then returned to his own dominions. It was idle for his army to sit down before the place, as the Milesians were masters of the sea. The reason that he did not demolish their buildings was, that the inhabitants might be tempted to use them as homesteads from which to go forth to sow and till their lands; and so each time that he invaded the country he might find something to plunder.

18. In this way he carried on the war with the Milesians for eleven years, in the course of which he inflicted on them two terrible blows; one in their own country in the district of Limeneium, the other in the plain of the Mæander. During six of these eleven years, Sadyattes, the son of Ardys, who first lighted the flames of this war, was king of Lydia, and made the incursions. Only the five following years belong to the reign of Alyattes, son of Sadyattes, who (as I said before) inheriting the war from his father, applied himself to it unremittingly. The Milesians throughout the contest received no help at all from any of the Ionians, excepting those of Chios, who lent them troops in requital of a like service rendered them in former times, the Milesians having fought on the side of the Chians during the whole of the war between them and the people of Erythræ.

19. It was in the twelfth year of the war that the following mischance occurred from the firing of the harvest-fields. Scarcely had the corn been set alight by the soldiers when a violent wind carried the flames against the temple of Athena Assesia, which caught fire and was burnt to the ground. At the time no one made any account of the circumstance; but afterwards, on the return of the army to Sardis, Alyattes fell sick. His illness continued, whereupon, either advised thereto by some friend, or perchance himself conceiving the idea, he sent messengers to Delphi to inquire of the god concerning his malady. On their arrival the Pythoness declared that no answer should be given them until they had rebuilt the temple of Athena, burnt by the Lydians at Assêsus in Milesia.

20. Thus much I know from information given me by the Delphians; the remainder of the story the Milesians add.

The answer made by the oracle came to the ears of Periander, son of Cypselus, who was a very close friend to Thrasybulus,

tyrant of Miletus at that period. He instantly despatched a messenger to report the oracle to him, in order that Thrasybulus,
forewarned of its tenor, might the better adapt his measures to
the posture of affairs.

21. Alyattes, the moment that the words of the oracle were
reported to him, sent a herald to Miletus in hopes of concluding
a truce with Thrasybulus and the Milesians for such a time as
was needed to rebuild the temple. The herald went upon his way;
but meantime Thrasybulus had been apprised of everything; and
conjecturing what Alyattes would do, he contrived this artifice.
He had all the corn that was in the city, whether belonging to
himself or to private persons, brought into the market-place, and
issued an order that the Milesians should hold themselves in
readiness, and, when he gave the signal, should, one and all, fall
to drinking and revelry.

22. The purpose for which he gave these orders was the
following. He hoped that the Sardian herald, seeing so great store
of corn upon the ground, and all the city given up to festivity, would
inform Alyattes of it, which fell out as he anticipated. The herald
observed the whole, and when he had delivered his message, went
back to Sardis. This circumstance alone, as I gather, brought about
the peace which ensued. Alyattes, who had hoped that there was
now a great scarcity of corn in Miletus, and that the people were
worn down to the last pitch of suffering, when he heard from the
herald on his return from Miletus tidings so contrary to those he
had expected, made a treaty with the enemy by which the two
nations became close friends and allies. He then built at Assêsus
two temples to Athena instead of one,[1] and shortly after recovered
from his malady. Such were the chief circumstances of the war
which Alyattes waged with Thrasybulus and the Milesians.

23. This Periander, who apprised Thrasybulus of the oracle,
was son of Cypselus, and tyrant of Corinth.[2] In his time a very
wonderful thing is said to have happened. The Corinthians and
the Lesbians agree in their account of the matter. They relate

1 The feeling that restitution should be twofold, when made to the gods,
was a feature of the religion of Rome. It was not recognised in Greece.

2 Bähr says (Not. ad loc.), Periander was tyrant in the *ancient* sense of the
word, in which it is simply equivalent to the Latin "rex" and the Greek ἄναξ,
or βασιλεύς, because he inherited the crown from his father Cypselus. But it
would rather seem that the word bears here its usual sense of a king who rules
with a usurped and unconstitutional authority.

that Arion of Methymna, who as a player on the harp, was second to no man living at that time, and who was, so far as we know, the first to invent the dithyrambic measure,[1] to give it its name, and to recite in it at Corinth, was carried to Tænarum on the back of a dolphin.

24. He had lived for many years at the court of Periander, when a longing came upon him to sail across to Italy and Sicily. Having made rich profits in those parts, he wanted to recross the seas to Corinth. He therefore hired a vessel, the crew of which were Corinthians, thinking that there was no people in whom he could more safely confide; and, going on board, he set sail from Tarentum. The sailors, however, when they reached the open sea, formed a plot to throw him overboard and seize upon his riches. Discovering their design, he fell on his knees, beseeching them to spare his life, and making them welcome to his money. But they refused; and required him either to kill himself outright, if he wished for a grave on the dry land, or without loss of time to leap overboard into the sea. In this strait Arion begged them, since such was their pleasure, to allow him to mount upon the quarter-deck, dressed in his full costume, and there to play and sing, and promising that, as soon as his song was ended, he would destroy himself. Delighted at the prospect of hearing the very best harper in the world, they consented, and withdrew from the stern to the middle of the vessel: while Arion dressed himself in the full costume of his calling, took his harp, and standing on the quarter-deck, chanted the Orthian.[2] His strain ended, he flung himself, fully attired as he was, headlong into the sea. The Corinthians then sailed on to Corinth. As for Arion, a dolphin, they say, took him upon his back and carried him to Tænarum, where he went ashore, and thence proceeded to Corinth in his musician's dress, and told all that had happened

1 The invention of the Dithyramb, or Cyclic chorus, was ascribed to Arion, not only by Herodotus, but also by Aristotle, by Hellanicus, by Dicæarchus, and, implicitly, by Pindar, who said it was invented at Corinth. Perhaps it is best to conclude with a recent writer that Arion did not invent, but only improved the dithyramb. The dithyramb was originally a mere hymn in honour of Dionysus, with the circumstances of whose birth the word is somewhat fancifully connected (Eurip. Bacch. 526). It was sung by a κῶμος, or band of revellers, directed by a leader.

2 According to the scholiast on Aristophanes, the Orphian was pitched in a high key, as the name would imply, and was a lively spirited air.

to him. Periander, however, disbelieved the story, and put Arion in ward, to prevent his leaving Corinth, while he watched anxiously for the return of the mariners. On their arrival he summoned them before him and asked them if they could give him any tidings of Arion. They returned for answer that he was alive and in good health in Italy, and that they had left him at Tarentum,[1] where he was doing well. Thereupon Arion appeared before them, just as he was when he jumped from the vessel: the men, astonished and detected in falsehood, could no longer deny their guilt. Such is the account which the Corinthians and Lesbians give; and there is to this day at Tænarum, an offering of Arion's at the shrine, which is a small figure in bronze, representing a man seated upon a dolphin.[2]

25. Having brought the war with the Milesians to a close, and reigned over the land of Lydia for fifty-seven years, Alyattes died. He was the second prince of his house who made offerings at Delphi. His gifts, which he sent on recovering from his sickness, were a great bowl of pure silver, with a salver in steel curiously inlaid, a work among all the offerings at Delphi the best worth looking at. Glaucus, the Chain, made it, the man who first invented the art of inlaying steel.[3]

26. On the death of Alyattes, Crœsus, his son, who was thirty-five years old, succeeded to the throne. Of the Greek cities, Ephesus was the first that he attacked. The Ephesians, when he laid siege to the place, made an offering of their city to Artemis, by stretching a rope from the town wall to the temple of the goddess,[4] which was distant from the ancient city, then

---

1 In memory of this legend, the Tarentines were fond of exhibiting Arion, astride upon his dolphin, on their coins.

2 Various attempts have been made to rationalise the legend of Arion. The truth seems to be, that the legend grew out of the figure at Tænarum, which was known by its inscription to be an offering of Arion's. The figure itself remained at Tænarum more than seven hundred years. It was seen by Ælian in the third century after Christ.

3 It is questionable whether by κόλλησις is to be understood the inlaying, or merely the welding of iron together. The only two descriptions which eye-witnesses have left us of the salver, lead in opposite directions.

4 An analogous case is mentioned by Plutarch (Solon. c. 12). The fugitives implicated in the insurrection of Cylon at Athens connected themselves with the altar by a cord. Through the breaking of the cord they lost their sacred character. So, too, when Polycrates dedicated the island of Rheneia to the Delian Apollo, he connected it with Delos by a chain (Thucyd. iii. 104).

besieged by Crœsus, a space of seven furlongs.[1] They were, as I said, the first Greeks whom he attacked. Afterwards, on some pretext or other, he made war in turn upon every Ionian and Æolian state, bringing forward, where he could, a substantial ground of complaint; where such failed him, advancing some poor excuse.

27. In this way he made himself master of all the Greek cities in Asia, and forced them to become his tributaries; after which he began to think of building ships, and attacking the islanders. Everything had been got ready for this purpose, when Bias of Priênê (or, as some say, Pittacus the Mytilenean) put a stop to the project. The king had made inquiry of this person, who was lately arrived at Sardis, if there were any news from Greece; to which he answered, "Yes, sire, the islanders are gathering ten thousand horse, designing an expedition against thee and against thy capital." Crœsus, thinking he spake seriously, broke out, "Ah, might the gods put such a thought into their minds as to attack the sons of the Lydians with cavalry!" "It seems, oh! king," rejoined the other, "that thou desirest earnestly to catch the islanders on horseback upon the mainland, – thou knowest well what would come of it. But what thinkest thou the islanders desire better, now that they hear thou art about to build ships and sail against them, than to catch the Lydians at sea, and there revenge on them the wrongs of their brothers upon the mainland, whom thou holdest in slavery?" Crœsus was charmed with the turn of the speech; and thinking there was reason in what was said, gave up his ship-building and concluded a league of amity with the Ionians of the isles.

28. Crœsus afterwards, in the course of many years, brought under his sway almost all the nations to the west of the Halys. The Lycians and Cilicians alone continued free; all the other tribes he reduced and held in subjection. They were the following: the Lydians, Phrygians, Mysians, Mariandynians, Chalybians, Paphlagonians, Thynian and Bithynian Thracians, Carians, Ionians, Dorians, Æolians and Pamphylians.[2]

---

1 We learn by this that the site of Ephesus had changed between the time of Crœsus and that of Herodotus. The building seen by Herodotus was that burnt, B.C. 356.

2 It is not quite correct to speak of the Cilicians as dwelling *within* (*i.e.*, west of) the Halys, for the Halys in its upper course ran *through* Cilicia (διὰ Κιλίκων, ch. 72), and that country lay chiefly *south* of the river. Lycia and Cilicia

29. When all these conquests had been added to the Lydian empire, and the prosperity of Sardis was now at its height, there came thither, one after another, all the sages of Greece living at the time, and among them Solon, the Athenian.[1] He was on his travels, having left Athens to be absent ten years, under the pretence of wishing to see the world, but really to avoid being forced to repeal any of the laws which, at the request of the Athenians, he had made for them. Without his sanction the Athenians could not repeal them, as they had bound themselves under a heavy curse to be governed for ten years by the laws which should be imposed on them by Solon.[2]

30. On this account, as well as to see the world, Solon set out upon his travels, in the course of which he went to Egypt to the court of Amasis,[3] and also came on a visit to Crœsus at Sardis. Crœsus received him as his guest, and lodged him in the royal palace. On the third or fourth day after, he bade his servants conduct Solon over his treasuries,[4] and show him all their greatness and magnificence. When he had seen them all, and, so far as time allowed, inspected them, Crœsus addressed this question to him. "Stranger of Athens, we have heard much of thy wisdom and of thy travels through many lands, from love of knowledge and a wish to see the world. I am curious therefore to inquire of thee, whom, of all the men that thou hast seen, thou deemest the most happy?" This he asked because he thought himself the happiest of mortals: but Solon answered him without flattery, according to his true sentiments, "Tellus of Athens, sire." Full of astonishment at what he heard, Crœsus demanded

---

would be likely to maintain their independence, being both countries of great natural strength. They lie upon the high mountain-range of Taurus, which runs from east to west along the south of Asia Minor, within about a degree of the shore, and sends down from the main chain a series of lateral branches or spurs, which extend to the sea along the whole line of coast from the Gulf of Makri, opposite Rhodes, to the plain of Tarsus. The mountains of the interior are in many parts covered with snow during the whole or the greater part of the year.

1 Solon's visit to Crœsus was rejected as fabulous before the time of Plutarch (Solon. c. 27), on account of chronological difficulties. Crœsus most probably reigned from B.C. 568 to B.C. 554. Solon certainly outlived the first usurpation of the government at Athens by Pisistratus, which was B.C. 560.

2 The travels of Solon are attested by Plato (Tim. p. 21) and others.

3 Amasis began to reign B.C. 569. Solon might sail from Athens to Egypt, thence to Cyprus (Herod. v. 113), and from Cyprus to Lydia.

4 Vide infra, vi. 125.

sharply, "And wherefore dost thou deem Tellus happiest?" To which the other replied, "First, because his country was flourishing in his days, and he himself had sons both beautiful and good, and he lived to see children born to each of them, and these children all grew up; and further because, after a life spent in what our people look upon as comfort, his end was surpassingly glorious. In a battle between the Athenians and their neighbours near Eleusis, he came to the assistance of his countrymen, routed the foe, and died upon the field most gallantly. The Athenians gave him a public funeral on the spot where he fell, and paid him the highest honours."

31. Thus did Solon admonish Crœsus by the example of Tellus, enumerating the manifold particulars of his happiness. When he had ended, Crœsus inquired a second time, who after Tellus seemed to him the happiest, expecting that at any rate, he would be given the second place. "Cleobis and Bito," Solon answered; "they were of Argive race; their fortune was enough for their wants, and they were besides endowed with so much bodily strength that they had both gained prizes at the Games. Also this tale is told of them:– There was a great festival in honour of the goddess Hera at Argos, to which their mother must needs be taken in a car.[1] Now the oxen did not come home from the field in time: so the youths, fearful of being too late, put the yoke on their own necks, and themselves drew the car in which their mother rode. Five and forty furlongs did they draw her, and stopped before the temple. This deed of theirs was witnessed by the whole assembly of worshippers, and then their life closed in the best possible way. Herein, too, God showed forth most evidently, how much better a thing for man death is than life. For the Argive men, who stood around the car, extolled the vast strength of the youths; and the Argive women extolled the mother who was blessed with such a pair of sons; and the mother herself, overjoyed at the deed and at the praises it had won, standing straight before the image, besought the goddess to bestow on Cleobis and Bito, the sons who had so mightily honoured her, the highest blessing to which mortals can attain. Her prayer

1 Cicero and others relate that the ground of the necessity was the circumstances that the youths' mother was priestess of Hera at the time. Servius says a pestilence had destroyed the oxen, which contradicts Herodotus. Otherwise the tale is told with fewer varieties than most ancient stories.

ended, they offered sacrifice and partook of the holy banquet, after which the two youths fell asleep in the temple. They never woke more, but so passed from the earth. The Argives, looking on them as among the best of men, caused statues of them to be made, which they gave to the shrine at Delphi."

32. When Solon had thus assigned these youths the second place, Crœsus broke in angrily, "What, stranger of Athens, is my happiness, then, so utterly set at nought by thee, that thou dost not even put me on a level with private men?"

"Oh! Crœsus," replied the other, "thou askedst a question concerning the condition of man, of one who knows that the power above us is full of jealousy,[1] and fond of troubling our lot. A long life gives one to witness much, and experience much oneself, that one would not choose. Seventy years I regard as the limit of the life of man.[2] In these seventy years are contained, without reckoning intercalary months, twenty-five thousand and two hundred days. Add an intercalary month to every other year, that the seasons may come round at the right time, and there will be, besides the seventy years, thirty-five such months, making an addition of one thousand and fifty days. The whole number of the days contained in the seventy years will thus be twenty-six thousand two hundred and fifty,[3] whereof not one but will produce events unlike the rest. Hence man is wholly accident. For thyself, oh! Crœsus, I see that thou art wonderfully

---

1 The φθόνος ("jealousy") of God is a leading feature in Herodotus's conception of the Deity, and no doubt is one of the chief moral conclusions which he drew from his own survey of human events, and intended to impress on us by his history. (Vide infra, iii. 40, vii. 46, and especially vii. 10, § 5–6.) Herodotus's φθονερὸς θεὸς is not simply the "*Deus ultor*" of religious Romans, much less the "*jealous* God" of Scripture. The idea of an avenging God is *included* in the Herodotean conception, but is far from being the whole of it. Prosperity, not pride, eminence, not arrogance, provokes him. He does not like any one to be great or happy but himself (vii. 46, end). What is most remarkable is, that with such a conception of the Divine Nature, Herodotus could maintain such a placid, cheerful, childlike temper. Possibly he was serene because he felt secure in his mediocrity.

2 "The days of our years are threescore years and ten" (Ps. xc. 10).

3 No commentator on Herodotus has succeeded in explaining the curious mistake whereby the solar year is made to average 375 days. That Herodotus knew the true solar year was not 375, but more nearly 365 days, is clear from book ii. ch. 4. Two inaccuracies produce the error in Herodotus. In the first place he makes Solon count his months at 30 days each, whereas it is notorious that the Greek months, after the system of intercalation was introduced, were

rich, and art the lord of many nations; but with respect to that whereon thou questionest me, I have no answer to give, until I hear that thou hast closed thy life happily. For assuredly he who possesses great store of riches is no nearer happiness than he who has what suffices for his daily needs, unless it so hap that luck attend upon him, and so he continue in the enjoyment of all his good things to the end of life. For many of the wealthiest men have been unfavoured of fortune, and many whose means were moderate have had excellent luck. Men of the former class excel those of the latter but in two respects; these last excel the former in many. The wealthy man is better able to content his desires, and to bear up against a sudden buffet of calamity. The other has less ability to withstand these evils (from which, however, his good luck keeps him clear), but he enjoys all these following blessings: he is whole of limb, a stranger to disease, free from misfortune, happy in his children, and comely to look upon. If, in addition to all this, he end his life well, he is of a truth the man of whom thou art in search, the man who may rightly be termed happy. Call him, however, until he die, not happy but fortunate. Scarcely, indeed, can any man unite all these advantages: as there is no country which contains within it all that it needs, but each, while it possesses some things, lacks others, and the best country is that which contains the most; so no single human being is complete in every respect – something is always lacking. He who unites the greatest number of advantages, and retaining them to the day of his death, then dies peaceably, that man alone, sire, is, in my judgment, entitled to bear the name of 'happy.' But in every matter it behoves us to mark well the end: for oftentimes God gives men a gleam of happiness, and then plunges them into ruin."

33. Such was the speech which Solon addressed to Crœsus, a speech which brought him neither largess nor honour. The king saw him depart with much indifference, since he thought that a man must be an arrant fool who made no account of present good, but bade men always wait and mark the end.

34. After Solon had gone away a dreadful vengeance, sent of God, came upon Crœsus, to punish him, it is likely, for deeming

---

alternately of 29 and 30 days. By this error his first number is raised from 24,780 to 25,200; and also his second number from 1033 to 1050. Secondly, he omits to mention that from time to time (every 4th τριετηρὶς probably) the intercalary month was omitted altogether.

himself the happiest of men. First he had a dream in the night, which foreshowed him truly the evils that were about to befall him in the person of his son. For Crœsus had two sons, one blasted by a natural defect, being deaf and dumb; the other, distinguished far above all his co-mates in every pursuit. The name of the last was Atys. It was this son concerning whom he dreamt a dream, that he would die by the blow of an iron weapon. When he woke, he considered earnestly with himself, and, greatly alarmed at the dream, instantly made his son take a wife, and whereas in former years the youth had been wont to command the Lydian forces in the field, he now would not suffer him to accompany them. All the spears and javelins, and weapons used in the wars, he removed out of the male apartments, and laid them in heaps in the chambers of the women, fearing lest perhaps one of the weapons that hung against the wall might fall and strike him.

35. Now it chanced that while he was making arrangements for the wedding, there came to Sardis a man under a misfortune, who had upon him the stain of blood. He was by race a Phrygian, and belonged to the family of the king. Presenting himself at the palace of Crœsus, he prayed to be admitted to purification according to the customs of the country. Now the Lydian method of purifying is very nearly the same as the Greek. Crœsus granted the request, and went through all the customary rites, after which he asked the suppliant of his birth and country, addressing him as follows:– "Who art thou, stranger, and from what part of Phrygia fleddest thou to take refuge at my hearth? And whom, moreover, what man or what woman, hast thou slain?" "Oh! king," replied the Phrygian, "I am the son of Gordias, son of Midas. I am named Adrastus.[1] The man I unintentionally slew was my own brother. For this my father drove me from the land, and I lost all. Then fled I here to thee." "Thou art the offspring," Crœsus rejoined, "of a house friendly to mine, and thou art come to friends. Thou shalt want for nothing so long as thou abidest in my dominions. Bear thy misfortune as easily as thou mayest, so will it go best with thee." Thenceforth Adrastus lived in the palace of the king.

36. It chanced that at this very same time there was in the Mysian Olympus a huge monster of a boar, which went forth

---

1 Adrastus is "the doomed" – "the man unable to escape." Atys is "the youth under the influence of Até" – "the man judicially blind."

often from this mountain-country, and wasted the corn-fields of the Mysians. Many a time had the Mysians collected to hunt the beast, but instead of doing him any hurt, they came off always with some loss to themselves. At length they sent ambassadors to Crœsus, who delivered their message to him in these words: "Oh! king, a mighty monster of a boar has appeared in our parts, and destroys the labour of our hands. We do our best to take him, but in vain. Now therefore we beseech thee to let thy son accompany us back, with some chosen youths and hounds, that we may rid our country of the animal." Such was the tenor of their prayer.

But Crœsus bethought him of his dream, and answered, "Say no more of my son going with you; that may not be in any wise. He is but just joined in wedlock, and is busy enough with that. I will grant you a picked band of Lydians, and all my huntsmen and hounds; and I will charge those whom I send to use all zeal in aiding you to rid your country of the brute."

37. With this reply the Mysians were content; but the king's son, hearing what the prayer of the Mysians was, came suddenly in, and on the refusal of Crœsus to let him go with them, thus addressed his father: "Formerly, my father, it was deemed the noblest and most suitable thing for me to frequent the wars and hunting-parties, and win myself glory in them; but now thou keepest me away from both, although thou hast never beheld in me either cowardice or lack of spirit. What face meanwhile must I wear as I walk to the forum or return from it? What must the citizens, what must my young bride think of me? What sort of man will she suppose her husband to be? Either, therefore, let me go to the chase of this boar, or give me a reason why it is best for me to do according to thy wishes."

38. Then Crœsus answered, "My son, it is not because I have seen in thee either cowardice or aught else which has displeased me that I keep thee back; but because a vision which came before me in a dream as I slept, warned me that thou wert doomed to die young, pierced by an iron weapon. It was this which first led me to hasten on thy wedding, and now it hinders me from sending thee upon this enterprise. Fain would I keep watch over thee, if by any means I may cheat fate of thee during my own lifetime. For thou art the one and only son that I possess; the other, whose hearing is destroyed, I regard as if he were not."

39. "Ah! father," returned the youth, "I blame thee not for keeping watch over me after a dream so terrible; but if thou mistakest, if thou dost not apprehend the dream aright, 'tis no blame for me to show thee wherein thou errest. Now the dream, thou saidst thyself, foretold that I should die stricken by an iron weapon. But what hands has a boar to strike with? What iron weapon does he wield? Yet this is what thou fearest for me. Had the dream said that I should die pierced by a tusk, then thou hadst done well to keep me away; but it said a weapon. Now here we do not combat men, but a wild animal. I pray thee, therefore, let me go with them."

40. "There thou hast me, my son," said Crœsus, "thy interpretation is better than mine. I yield to it, and change my mind, and consent to let thee go."

41. Then the king sent for Adrastus, the Phrygian, and said to him, "Adrastus, when thou wert smitten with the rod of affliction – no reproach, my friend – I purified thee, and have taken thee to live with me in my palace, and have been at every charge. Now, therefore, it behoves thee to requite the good offices which thou hast received at my hands by consenting to go with my son on this hunting party, and to watch over him, if perchance you should be attacked upon the road by some band of daring robbers. Even apart from this, it were right for thee to go where thou mayest make thyself famous by noble deeds. They are the heritage of thy family, and thou too art so stalwart and strong."

42. Adrastus answered, "Except for thy request, Oh! king, I would rather have kept away from this hunt; for methinks it ill beseems a man under a misfortune such as mine to consort with his happier compeers; and besides, I have no heart to it. On many grounds I had stayed behind; but, as thou urgest it, and I am bound to pleasure thee (for truly it does behove me to requite thy good offices), I am content to do as thou wishest. For thy son, whom thou givest into my charge, be sure thou shalt receive him back safe and sound, so far as depends upon a guardian's carefulness."

43. Thus assured, Crœsus let them depart, accompanied by a band of picked youths, and well provided with dogs of chase. When they reached Olympus, they scattered in quest of the animal; he was soon found, and the hunters, drawing round him in a circle, hurled their weapons at him. Then the stranger, the man

who had been purified of blood, whose name was Adrastus, he also hurled his spear at the boar, but missed his aim, and struck Atys. Thus was the son of Crœsus slain by the point of an iron weapon, and the warning of the vision was fulfilled. Then one ran to Sardis to bear the tidings to the king, and he came and informed him of the combat and of the fate that had befallen his son.

44. If it was a heavy blow to the father to learn that his child was dead, it yet more strongly affected him to think that the very man whom he himself once purified had done the deed. In the violence of his grief he called aloud on Zeus Catharsius,[1] to be a witness of what he had suffered at the stranger's hands. Afterwards he invoked the same god as Zeus Ephistius and Hetæreus – using the one term because he had unwittingly harboured in his house the man who had now slain his son; and the other, because the stranger, who had been sent as his child's guardian, had turned out his most cruel enemy.

45. Presently the Lydians arrived, bearing the body of the youth, and behind them followed the homicide. He took his stand in front of the corse, and, stretching forth his hands to Crœsus, delivered himself into his power with earnest entreaties that he would sacrifice him upon the body of his son – "his former misfortune was burthen enough; now that he had added to it a second, and had brought ruin on the man who purified him, he could not bear to live." Then Crœsus, when he heard these words, was moved with pity towards Adrastus, notwithstanding the bitterness of his own calamity; and so he answered, "Enough, my friend; I have all the revenge that I require, since thou givest sentence of death against thyself. But in sooth it is not thou who hast injured me, except so far as thou hast unwittingly dealt the blow. Some god is the author of my misfortune, and I was forewarned of it a long time ago." Crœsus after this buried the body of his son, with such honours as befitted the occasion. Adrastus, son of Gordias, son of Midas, the destroyer of his brother in time past, the destroyer now of his purifier, regarding himself as the most unfortunate wretch whom he had

1 Zeus was Catharsius, "the god of purifications," not on account of the resemblance of the rites of purification with those of Zeus Μειλίχιος, but simply in the same way that he was Ephistius and Hetærêüs, god of hearths, and of companionship, because he presided over all occasions of obligation between man and man, and the purified person contracted an obligation towards his purifier.

ever known, so soon as all was quiet about the place, slew himself upon the tomb. Crœsus, bereft of his son, gave himself up to mourning for two full years.

46. At the end of this time the grief of Crœsus was interrupted by intelligence from abroad. He learnt that Cyrus, the son of Cambyses, had destroyed the empire of Astyages, the son of Cyaxares; and that the Persians were becoming daily more powerful. This led him to consider with himself whether it were possible to check the growing power of that people before it came to a head. With this design he resolved to make instant trial of the several oracles in Greece, and of the one in Libya.[1] So he sent his messengers in different directions, some to Delphi, some to Abæ in Phocis, and some to Dodôna; others to the oracle of Amphiaraüs; others to that of Trophonius; others, again, to Branchidæ in Milesia.[2] These were the Greek oracles which he consulted. To Libya he sent another embassy, to consult the oracle of Ammon. These messengers were sent to test the knowledge of the oracles, that, if they were found really to return true answers, he might send a second time, and inquire if he ought to attack the Persians.

47. The messengers who were despatched to make trial of the oracles were given the following instructions: they were to keep count of the days from the time of their leaving Sardis, and, reckoning from that date, on the hundredth day they were to consult the oracles, and to inquire of them what Crœsus the son of Alyattes, king of Lydia, was doing at that moment. The answers given them were to be taken down in writing, and brought back to him. None of the replies remain on record except that of the oracle at Delphi. There, the moment that the Lydians entered the sanctuary,[3] and before they put their questions, the Pythoness thus answered them in hexameter verse:—

I can count the sands, and I can measure the ocean;
I have ears for the silent, and know what the dumb man
    meaneth;

1 "*The one* in Libya" (Africa) – that of Ammon, because Egypt was regarded by Herodotus as in Asia, not in Africa.

2 The oracle at Abæ seems to have ranked next to that at Delphi. The Orientals do not appear to have possessed any indigenous oracles.

3 The μέγαρον was the "inner shrine," the sacred chamber where the oracles were given.

Lo! on my sense there striketh the smell of a shell-covered
   tortoise,
Boiling now on a fire, with the flesh of a lamb, in a cauldron, –
Brass is the vessel below, and brass the cover above it.

48. These words the Lydians wrote down at the mouth of
the Pythoness as she prophesied, and then set off on their return
to Sardis. When all the messengers had come back with the
answers which they had received, Crœsus undid the rolls, and
read what was written in each. Only one approved itself to him,
that of the Delphic oracle. This he had no sooner heard than he
instantly made an act of adoration, and accepted it as true, declaring that the Delphic was the only really oracular shrine, the
only one that had discovered in what way he was in fact employed. For on the departure of his messengers he had set himself to think what was most impossible for any one to conceive
of his doing,[1] and then, waiting till the day agreed on came, he
acted as he had determined. He took a tortoise and a lamb, and
cutting them in pieces with his own hands, boiled them both
together in a brazen cauldron, covered over with a lid which was
also of brass.

49. Such then was the answer returned to Crœsus from Delphi. What the answer was which the Lydians who went to the
shrine of Amphiaraüs and performed the customary rites, obtained of the oracle there, I have it not in my power to mention,
for there is no record of it. All that is known is, that Crœsus
believed himself to have found there also an oracle which spoke
the truth.

50. After this Crœsus, having resolved to propitiate the Delphic god with a magnificent sacrifice, offered up three thousand
of every kind of sacrificial beast, and besides made a huge pile,
and placed upon it couches coated with silver and with gold, and

1 It is impossible to discuss such a question as the nature of the ancient
oracles, which has had volumes written upon it, within the limits of a note. I
will only observe that in forming our judgment on the subject, two points
should be kept steadily in view: (1) the fact that the Pythoness whom St. Paul
met with on his first entrance into European Greece, was *really possessed* by an
evil spirit, which St. Paul cast out, thereby depriving her masters of all their
hopes of gain (Acts xvi. 16–19): and (2) the phenomena of Mesmerism. In one
or other of these, or in both of them combined, will be found the simplest,
and probably the truest explanation, of all that is really marvellous in the
responses of the oracles.

golden goblets, and robes and vests of purple; all which he burnt in the hope of thereby making himself more secure of the favour of the god. Further he issued his orders to all the people of the land to offer a sacrifice according to their means. When the sacrifice was ended, the king melted down a vast quantity of gold, and ran it into ingots, making them six palms long, three palms broad, and one palm in thickness. The number of ingots was a hundred and seventeen, four being of refined gold, in weight two talents and a half; the others of pale gold, and in weight two talents. He also caused a statue of a lion to be made in refined gold, the weight of which was ten talents. At the time when the temple of Delphi was burnt to the ground,[1] this lion fell from the ingots on which it was placed; it now stands in the Corinthian treasury, and weighs only six talents and a half, having lost three talents and a half by the fire.

51. On the completion of these works Crœsus sent them away to Delphi, and with them two bowls of an enormous size, one of gold, the other of silver, which used to stand, the latter upon the right, the former upon the left, as one entered the temple. They too were moved at the time of the fire; and now the golden one is in the Clazomenian treasury, and weighs eight talents and forty-two minæ; the silver one stands in the corner of the ante-chapel, and holds six hundred amphoræ. This is known, because the Delphians fill it at the time of the Theophania.[2] It is said by the Delphians to be a work of Theodore the Samian,[3] and I think that they say true, for assuredly it is the work of no common artist. Crœsus sent also four silver casks, which are in the Corinthian treasury, and two lustral vases, a golden and a silver one. On the former is inscribed the name of the Lacedæmonians, and they claim it as a gift of theirs, but wrongly, since it was really given by Crœsus. The inscription upon it was cut by a Delphian, who wished to pleasure the Lacedæmonians. His name is known to me, but I forbear to mention it. The boy, through whose hand the water runs, is (I confess) a Lacedæmonian gift, but they did not give either of the

1 Vide infra, ii. 180, v. 62. It was burnt accidentally.

2 Both in Julius Pollux and in Philostratus there is mention of the Theophania, as a festival celebrated by the Greeks. No particulars are known of it.

3 Pausanias ascribed to Theodore of Samos the invention of casting in bronze, and spoke of him also as an architect (III. xii. § 8; VIII. xiv. § 5). Pliny agreed with both statements (Nat. Hist. xxxv. 12).

lustral vases. Besides these various offerings, Crœsus sent to Delphi many others of less account, among the rest a number of round silver basins. Also he dedicated a female figure in gold, three cubits high, which is said by the Delphians to be the statue of his baking-woman; and further, he presented the necklace and the girdles of his wife.

52. These were the offerings sent by Crœsus to Delphi. To the shrine of Amphiaraus, with whose valour and misfortune he was acquainted,[1] he sent a shield entirely of gold, and a spear, also of solid gold, both head and shaft. They were still existing in my day at Thebes, laid up in the temple of Ismenian Apollo.

53. The messengers who had the charge of conveying these treasures to the shrines, received instructions to ask the oracles whether Crœsus should go to war with the Persians, and if so, whether he should strengthen himself by the forces of an ally. Accordingly, when they had reached their destinations and presented the gifts, they proceeded to consult the oracles in the following terms:– "Crœsus, king of Lydia and other countries, believing that these are the only real oracles in all the world, has sent you such presents as your discoveries deserved, and now inquires of you whether he shall go to war with the Persians, and if so, whether he shall strengthen himself by the forces of a confederate." Both the oracles agreed in the tenor of their reply, which was in each case a prophecy that if Crœsus attacked the Persians, he would destroy a mighty empire, and a recommendation to him to look and see who were the most powerful of the Greeks, and to make alliance with them.

54. At the receipt of these oracular replies Crœsus was overjoyed, and feeling sure now that he would destroy the empire of the Persians, he sent once more to Pytho, and presented to the Delphians, the number of whom he had ascertained, two gold staters apiece.[2] In return for this the Delphians granted to Crœsus and the Lydians the privilege of precedency in consulting the oracle, exemption from all charges, the most honourable seat at the festivals, and the perpetual right of becoming at pleasure citizens of their town.

---

1 For the story of Amphiaraus, cf. Pausan. i. 34, ii. 13, § 6. Æschylus Sept. contr. Th. 564 et seqq. The "misfortune" is his being engulfed near Orôpus, or (as some said) at Harma in Bœotia.

2 For the value of the stater, see note on Book vii. ch. 28.

55. After sending these presents to the Delphians, Crœsus a third time consulted the oracle, for having once proved its truthfulness, he wished to make constant use of it. The question whereto he now desired an answer was — "Whether his kingdom would be of long duration?" The following was the reply of the Pythoness:—

> Wait till the time shall come when a mule is monarch of Media;
> Then, thou delicate Lydian, away to the pebbles of Hermus;
> Haste, oh! haste thee away, nor blush to behave like a coward.

56. Of all the answers that had reached him, this pleased him far the best, for it seemed incredible that a mule should ever come to be king of the Medes, and so he concluded that the sovereignty would never depart from himself or his seed after him. Afterwards he turned his thoughts to the alliance which he had been recommended to contract, and sought to ascertain by inquiry which was the most powerful of the Grecian states. His inquiries pointed out to him two states as pre-eminent above the rest. These were the Lacedæmonians and the Athenians, the former of Doric the latter of Ionic blood. And indeed these two nations had held from very early times the most distinguished place in Greece, the one being a Pelasgic the other a Hellenic people, and the one having never quitted its original seats, while the other had been excessively migratory; for during the reign of Deucalion, Phthiôtis was the country in which the Hellenes dwelt, but under Dorus, the son of Hellen, they moved to the tract at the base of Ossa and Olympus, which is called Histiæôtis; forced to retire from that region by the Cadmeians,[1] they settled, under the name of Macedni, in the chain of Pindus. Hence they once more removed and came to Dryopis; and from Dryopis having entered the Peloponnese in this way, they became known as Dorians.

57. What the language of the Pelasgi was I cannot say with any certainty. If, however, we may form a conjecture from the tongue spoken by the Pelasgi of the present day, — those, for instance, who live at Creston above the Tyrrhenians, who

---

1 The Cadmeians were the Græco-Phœnician race (their name merely signifying "the Easterns"), who in the ante-Trojan times, occupied the country which was afterwards called Bœotia. Hence the Greek tragedians, in plays of which ancient Thebes is the scene, invariably speak of the Thebans as Καδμεῖοι, Καδμεῖος λεώς.

formerly dwelt in the district named Thessaliôtis, and were neighbours of the people now called the Dorians, – or those again who founded Placia and Scylacé upon the Hellespont, who had previously dwelt for some time with the Athenians,[1] – or those, in short, of any other of the cities which have dropped the name but are in fact Pelasgian; if, I say, we are to form a conjecture from any of these, we must pronounce that the Pelasgi spoke a barbarous language. If this were really so, and the entire Pelasgic race spoke the same tongue, the Athenians, who were certainly Pelasgi, must have changed their language at the same time that they passed into the Hellenic body; for it is a certain fact that the people of Creston speak a language unlike any of their neighbours, and the same is true of the Placianians, while the language spoken by these two people is the same; which shows that they both retain the idiom which they brought with them into the countries where they are now settled.

58. The Hellenic race has never, since its first origin, changed its speech. This at least seems evident to me. It was a branch of the Pelasgic, which separated from the main body, and at first was scanty in numbers and of little power; but it gradually spread and increased to a multitude of nations, chiefly by the voluntary entrance into its ranks of numerous tribes of barbarians. The Pelasgi, on the other hand, were, as I think, a barbarian race which never greatly multiplied.

59. On inquiring into the condition of these two nations, Crœsus found that one, the Athenian, was in a state of grievous oppression and distraction under Pisistratus, the son of Hippocrates, who was at that time tyrant of Athens. Hippocrates, when he was a private citizen, is said to have gone once upon a time to Olympia to see the games, when a wonderful prodigy happened to him. As he was employed in sacrificing, the cauldrons which stood near, full of water and of the flesh of the victims, began to boil without the help of fire, so that the water overflowed the pots. Chilon the Lacedæmonian, who happened to be there and to witness the prodigy, advised Hippocrates, if he were unmarried, never to take into his house a wife who could bear him a child; if he already had one, to send her back to her friends; if he had a son, to disown him. Chilon's advice did not at all please Hippocrates, who disregarded it, and some time after

1 Vide infra, vi. 137.

became the father of Pisistratus. This Pisistratus, at a time when there was civil contention in Attica between the party of the Sea-coast headed by Megacles the son of Alcmæon, and that of the Plain headed by Lycurgus, one of the Aristolaïds, formed the project of making himself tyrant, and with this view created a third party.[1] Gathering together a band of partisans, and giving himself out for the protector of the Highlanders, he contrived the following stratagem. He wounded himself and his mules, and then drove his chariot into the market-place, professing to have just escaped an attack of his enemies, who had attempted his life as he was on his way into the country. He besought the people to assign him a guard to protect his person, reminding them of the glory which he had gained when he led the attack upon the Megarians, and took the town of Nisæa,[2] at the same time performing many other exploits. The Athenians, deceived by his story, appointed him a band of citizens to serve as a guard, who were to carry clubs instead of spears, and to accompany him wherever he went. Thus strengthened, Pisistratus broke into revolt and seized the citadel. In this way he acquired the sovereignty of Athens, which he continued to hold without disturbing the previously existing offices or altering any of the laws. He administered the state according to the established usages, and his arrangements were wise and salutary.

60. However, after a little time, the partisans of Megacles and those of Lycurgus agreed to forget their differences, and united to drive him out. So Pisistratus, having by the means described first made himself master of Athens, lost his power again before it had time to take root. No sooner, however, was he departed than the factions which had driven him out quarrelled anew, and at last Megacles, wearied with the struggle, sent a herald to Pisistratus, with an offer to re-establish him on the throne if he would marry his daughter. Pisistratus consented, and on these terms an agreement was concluded between the two, after which they proceeded to devise the mode of his restoration. And here the device on which they hit was the silliest that I find on record, more especially considering that the Greeks have been from very

1 There can be no doubt that these local factions must also have been political parties.

2 Plutarch mentions a war between Athens and Megara, under the conduct of Solon, in which Pisistratus was said to have distinguished himself (Solon. c. 8), as having occurred before Solon's legislation, i.e. before B.C. 594.

ancient times distinguished from the barbarians by superior sagacity and freedom from foolish simpleness, and remembering that the persons on whom this trick was played were not only Greeks but Athenians, who have the credit of surpassing all other Greeks in cleverness. There was in the Pæanian district a woman named Phya,[1] whose height only fell short of four cubits by three fingers' breadth, and who was altogether comely to look upon. This woman they clothed in complete armour, and, instructing her as to the carriage which she was to maintain in order to beseem her part, they placed her in a chariot and drove to the city. Heralds had been sent forward to precede her, and to make proclamation to this effect: "Citizens of Athens, receive again Pisistratus with friendly minds. Athena, who of all men honours him the most, herself conducts him back to her own citadel." This they proclaimed in all directions, and immediately the rumour spread throughout the country districts that Athena was bringing back her favourite. They of the city also, fully persuaded that the woman was the veritable goddess, prostrated themselves before her, and received Pisistratus back.

61. Pisistratus, having thus recovered the sovereignty, married, according to agreement, the daughter of Megacles. As, however, he had already a family of grown up sons, and the Alcmæonidæ were supposed to be under a curse,[2] he determined that there should be no issue of the marriage and he lay with her in an unnatural manner. His wife at first kept this matter to herself, but after a time, either her mother questioned her, or it may be that she told it of her own accord. At any rate, she informed her mother, and so it reached her father's ears. Megacles, indignant at receiving an affront from such a quarter, in his anger instantly made up his differences with the opposite

1 Grote has some just remarks upon the observations with which Herodotus accompanies the story of Phya. It seems clear that the Greeks of the age of Pisistratus fully believed in the occasional presence upon earth of the Gods. Grote refers to the well-known appearance of the God Pan to Phidippides a little before the battle of Marathon, which Herodotus himself states to have been received as true by the Athenians (vi. 105). [The woman's height would be about 6 English feet.]

2 Vide infra, v. 70–1; Thucyd. i. 126; Plut. Solon. c. 12. The curse rested on them upon account of their treatment of the partisans of Cylon. The archon of the time, Megacles, not only broke faith with them after he had, by a pledge to spare their lives, induced them to leave the sacred precinct of Athena in the Acropolis, but also slew a number at the altar of the Eumenides.

faction, on which Pisistratus, aware of what was planning against him, took himself out of the country. Arrived at Eretria, he held a council with his children to decide what was to be done. The opinion of Hippias prevailed, and it was agreed to aim at regaining the sovereignty. The first step was to obtain advances of money from such states as were under obligations to them. By these means they collected large sums from several countries, especially from the Thebans, who gave them far more than any of the rest. To be brief, time passed, and all was at length got ready for their return. A band of Argive mercenaries arrived from the Peloponnese, and a certain Naxian named Lygdamis, who volunteered his services, was particularly zealous in the cause, supplying both men and money.

62. In the eleventh year of their exile the family of Pisistratus set sail from Eretria on their return home. They made the coast of Attica, near Marathon, where they encamped, and were joined by their partisans from the capital and by numbers from the country districts, who loved tyranny better than freedom. At Athens, while Pisistratus was obtaining funds, and even after he landed at Marathon, no one paid any attention to his proceedings. When, however, it became known that he had left Marathon, and was marching upon the city, preparations were made for resistance, the whole force of the state was levied, and led against the returning exiles. Meantime the army of Pisistratus, which had broken up from Marathon, meeting their adversaries near the temple of the Pallenian Athena,[1] pitched their camp opposite them. Here a certain soothsayer, Amphilytus by name, an Acarnanian, moved by a divine impulse, came into the presence of Pisistratus, and approaching him uttered this prophecy in the hexameter measure:—

Now has the cast been made, the net is out-spread in the water,
Through the moonshiny night the tunnies will enter the meshes.

63. Such was the prophecy uttered under a divine inspiration. Pisistratus, apprehending its meaning, declared that he accepted the oracle, and instantly led on his army. The Athenians from the city had just finished their midday meal, after which they

1 Pallênê was a village of Attica, near Gargettus, which is the modern *Garitô*. It was famous for its temple of Athena [Minerva], which was of such magnificence as to be made the subject of a special treatise by Themison, whose book, entitled *Pallenis*, is mentioned by Athenæus (vi. 6, p. 235).

had betaken themselves, some to dice, others to sleep, when Pisistratus with his troops fell upon them and put them to the rout. As soon as the flight began, Pisistratus bethought himself of a most wise contrivance, whereby the Athenians might be induced to disperse and not unite in a body any more. He mounted his sons on horseback and sent them on in front to overtake the fugitives, and exhort them to be of good cheer, and return each man to his home. The Athenians took the advice, and Pisistratus became for the third time master of Athens.

64. Upon this he set himself to root his power more firmly, by the aid of a numerous body of mercenaries, and by keeping up a full exchequer, partly supplied from native sources, partly from the countries about the river Strymon.[1] He also demanded hostages from many of the Athenians who had remained at home, and not left Athens at his approach; and these he sent to Naxos, which he had conquered by force of arms, and given over into the charge of Lygdamis. Farther, he purified the island of Delos, according to the injunctions of an oracle, after the following fashion. All the dead bodies which had been interred within sight of the temple he dug up, and removed to another part of the isle.[2] Thus was the tyranny of Pisistratus established at Athens, many of the Athenians having fallen in the battle, and many others having fled the country together with the son of Alcmæon.

65. Such was the condition of the Athenians when Crœsus made inquiry concerning them.[3] Proceeding to seek information concerning the Lacedæmonians, he learnt that, after passing through a period of great depression, they had lately been victorious in a war with the people of Tegea; for, during the joint reign of Leo and Agasicles, kings of Sparta, the Lacedæmonians, successful in all their other wars, suffered continual defeat at the

1 The revenues of Pisistratus were derived in part from the income-tax of five per cent. which he levied from his subjects (Thucyd. vi. 54. Αθηναίους εἰκοστὴν πρασσόμενοι τῶν γιγνομένων), in part probably from the silver-mines at Laurium, which a little later were so remarkably productive (Herod. vii. 144). He had also a third source of revenue, of which Herodotus here speaks, consisting apparently either of lands or mines lying near the Strymon, and belonging to him probably in his private capacity. That part of Thrace was famous for its gold and silver mines.

2 Compare Thucyd. iii. 104.

3 The embassy of Crœsus cannot possibly have been subsequent to the final establishment of Pisistratus at Athens, which was in B.C. 542 at the earliest. It probably occurred during his first term of power.

hands of the Tegeans. At a still earlier period they had been the very worst governed people in Greece, as well in matters of internal management as in their relations towards foreigners, from whom they kept entirely aloof. The circumstances which led to their being well governed were the following:— Lycurgus, a man of distinction among the Spartans, had gone to Delphi, to visit the oracle. Scarcely had he entered into the inner fane, when the Pythoness exclaimed aloud,

> Oh! thou great Lycurgus, that com'st to my beautiful dwelling,
> Dear to Jove, and to all who sit in the halls of Olympus,
> Whether to hail thee a god I know not, or only a mortal,
> But my hope is strong that a god thou wilt prove, Lycurgus.

Some report besides, that the Pythoness delivered to him the entire system of laws which are still observed by the Spartans. The Lacedæmonians, however, themselves assert that Lycurgus, when he was guardian of his nephew, Labotas, king of Sparta, and regent in his room, introduced them from Crete; for as soon as he became regent, he altered the whole of the existing customs, substituting new ones, which he took care should be observed by all. After this he arranged whatever appertained to war, establishing the Enomotiæ, Triacades, and Syssitia,[1] besides which he instituted the senate,[2] and the ephoralty. Such was the way in which the Lacedæmonians became a well-governed people.

66. On the death of Lycurgus they built him a temple, and ever since they have worshipped him with the utmost reverence. Their soil being good and the population numerous, they sprang up rapidly to power, and became a flourishing people. In consequence they soon ceased to be satisfied to stay quiet; and, regarding the Arcadians as very much their inferiors, they sent to consult the oracle about conquering the whole of Arcadia. The Pythoness thus answered them:

---

1 The ἐνωμοτίαι were divisions of the Spartan cohort (λόχος). Of the τριηκάδες nothing seems to be known. They may have been also divisions of the army — but divisions confined to the camp, not existing in the field. The word συσσίτια would seem in this place not to have its ordinary signification, "common meals" or "messes," but to be applied to the "set of persons who were appointed to mess together."

2 It is quite inconceivable that Lycurgus should in any sense have instituted the senate. Lycurgus appears to have made scarcely any changes in the *constitution*. What he did was to alter the customs and habits of the people.

Cravest thou Arcady? Bold is thy craving. I shall not content it.
Many the men that in Arcady dwell, whose food is the acorn –
They will never allow thee. It is not I that am niggard.
I will give thee to dance in Tegea, with noisy foot-fall,
And with the measuring line mete out the glorious champaign.

When the Lacedæmonians received this reply, leaving the rest of
Arcadia untouched, they marched against the Tegeans, carrying
with them fetters, so confident had this oracle (which was, in
truth, but of base metal) made them that they would enslave the
Tegeans. The battle, however, went against them, and many fell
into the enemy's hands. Then these persons, wearing the fetters
which they had themselves brought, and fastened together in a
string, measured the Tegean plain as they executed their labours.
The fetters in which they worked were still, in my day, preserved
at Tegea where they hung round the walls of the temple of
Athena Alea.[1]

67. Throughout the whole of this early contest with the
Tegeans, the Lacedæmonians met with nothing but defeats; but
in the time of Crœsus, under the kings Anaxandrides and Aristo,
fortune had turned in their favour, in the manner which I will
now relate. Having been worsted in every engagement by their
enemy, they sent to Delphi, and inquired of the oracle what god
they must propitiate to prevail in the war against the Tegeans.
The answer of the Pythoness was, that before they could prevail,
they must remove to Sparta the bones of Orestes, the son of
Agamemnon. Unable to discover his burial-place, they sent a
second time, and asked the god where the body of the hero had
been laid. The following was the answer they received:–

Level and smooth is the plain where Arcadian Tegea standeth;
There two winds are ever, by strong necessity, blowing,
Counter-stroke answers stroke, and evil lies upon evil.
There all-teeming Earth doth harbour the son of Atrides;
Bring thou him to thy city, and then be Tegea's master.

After this reply, the Lacedæmonians were no nearer discovering the burial-place than before, though they continued to search
for it diligently; until at last a man named Lichas, one of the

---

1 Athena Alea was an Arcadian goddess. She was worshipped at Mantinea,
Manthyrea, and Alea, as well as at Tegea. Her temple at Tegea was particularly
magnificent. See the description in Pausanias (VIII. xlvii. § 1–2).

Spartans called Agathoërgi, found it. The Agathoërgi are citizens who have just served their time among the knights. The five eldest of the knights go out every year, and are bound during the year after their discharge, to go wherever the State sends them, and actively employ themselves in its service.

68. Lichas was one of this body when, partly by good luck, partly by his own wisdom, he discovered the burial-place. Intercourse between the two States existing just at this time, he went to Tegea, and, happening to enter into the workshop of a smith, he saw him forging some iron. As he stood marvelling at what he beheld,[1] he was observed by the smith who, leaving off his work, went up to him and said,

"Certainly, then, you Spartan stranger, you would have been wonderfully surprised if you had seen what I have, since you make a marvel even of the working in iron. I wanted to make myself a well in this room, and began to dig it, when what think you? I came upon a coffin seven cubits long. I had never believed that men were taller in the olden times than they are now, so I opened the coffin. The body inside was of the same length: I measured it, and filled up the hole again."

Such was the man's account of what he had seen. The other, on turning the matter over in his mind, conjectured that this was the body of Orestes, of which the oracle had spoken. He guessed so, because he observed that the smithy had two bellows, which he understood to be the two winds, and the hammer and anvil would do for the stroke and the counter-stroke, and the iron that was being wrought for the evil lying upon evil. This he imagined might be so because iron had been discovered to the hurt of man. Full of these conjectures, he sped back to Sparta and laid the whole matter before his countrymen. Soon after, by a concerted plan, they brought a charge against him, and began a prosecution. Lichas betook himself to Tegea, and on his arrival acquainted the smith with his misfortune, and proposed to rent his room of him. The smith refused for some time; but at last Lichas persuaded him, and took up his abode in it. Then he opened the grave, and collecting the bones, returned with them to Sparta. From henceforth, whenever the Spartans and the

1 Herodotus means to represent that the forging of *iron* was a novelty at the time. Brass was known to the Greeks before iron, as the Homeric poems sufficiently indicate.

Tegeans made trial of each other's skill in arms, the Spartans always had greatly the advantage; and by the time to which we are now come they were masters of most of the Peloponnese.

69. Crœsus, informed of all these circumstances, sent messengers to Sparta, with gifts in their hands, who were to ask the Spartans to enter into alliance with him. They received strict injunctions as to what they should say, and on their arrival at Sparta spake as follows:–

"Crœsus, king of the Lydians and of other nations, has sent us to speak thus to you; 'Oh! Lacedæmonians, the god has bidden me to make the Greek my friend; I therefore apply to you, in conformity with the oracle, knowing that you hold the first rank in Greece, and desire to become your friend and ally in all true faith and honesty.' "

Such was the message which Crœsus sent by his heralds. The Lacedæmonians, who were aware beforehand of the reply given him by the oracle, were full of joy at the coming of the messengers, and at once took the oaths of friendship and alliance: this they did the more readily as they had previously contracted certain obligations towards him. They had sent to Sardis on one occasion to purchase some gold, intending to use it on a statue of Apollo – the statue, namely, which remains to this day at Thornax in Laconia,[1] when Crœsus, hearing of the matter, gave them as a gift the gold which they wanted.

70. This was one reason why the Lacedæmonians were so willing to make the alliance: another was, because Crœsus had chosen them for his friends in preference to all the other Greeks. They therefore held themselves in readiness to come at his summons, and not content with so doing, they further had a huge vase made in bronze, covered with figures of animals all round the outside of the rim, and large enough to contain three hundred amphoræ, which they sent to Crœsus as a return for his presents to them. The vase, however, never reached Sardis. Its miscarriage is accounted for in two quite different ways. The Lacedæmonian story is, that when it reached Samos, on its way towards Sardis, the Samians having knowledge of it, put to sea in their ships of war and made it their prize. But the Samians declare, that the Lacedæmonians who had the vase in charge,

---

1 Pausanias declares that the gold obtained of Crœsus by the Lacedæmonians was used in fact upon a statue of Apollo at Amyclæ (III. x. § 10).

happening to arrive too late, and learning that Sardis had fallen and that Crœsus was a prisoner, sold it in their island, and the purchasers (who were, they say, private persons) made an offering of it at the shrine of Hera:[1] the sellers were very likely on their return to Sparta to have said that they had been robbed of it by the Samians. Such, then, was the fate of the vase.

71. Meanwhile Crœsus, taking the oracle in a wrong sense, led his forces into Cappadocia, fully expecting to defeat Cyrus and destroy the empire of the Persians. While he was still engaged in making preparations for his attack, a Lydian named Sandanis, who had always been looked upon as a wise man, but who after this obtained a very great name indeed among his countrymen, came forward and counselled the king in these words:

"Thou art about, oh! king, to make war against men who wear leathern trousers, and have all their other garments of leather;[2] who feed not on what they like, but on what they can get from a soil that is sterile and unkindly; who do not indulge in wine, but drink water; who possess no figs nor anything else that is good to eat. If, then, thou conquerest them, what canst thou get from them, seeing that they have nothing at all? But if they conquer thee, consider how much that is precious thou wilt lose: if they once get a taste of our pleasant things, they will keep such hold of them that we shall never be able to make them loose their grasp. For my part, I am thankful to the gods, that they have not put it into the hearts of the Persians to invade Lydia."

Crœsus was not persuaded by this speech, though it was true enough; for before the conquest of Lydia, the Persians possessed none of the luxuries or delights of life.

72. The Cappadocians are known to the Greeks by the name of Syrians.[3] Before the rise of the Persian power, they had been subject to the Medes; but at the present time they were within the empire of Cyrus, for the boundary between the Median and the Lydian empires was the river Halys. This stream, which rises in the mountain country of Armenia, runs first through Cilicia; afterwards it flows for a while with the Matiêni on the right,

---

1 Vide infra, ii. 182.

2 For a description of the Persian dress, see note on ch. 135.

3 Vide infra, vii. 72. The Cappadocians of Herodotus inhabit the country bounded by the Euxine on the north, the Halys on the west, the Armenians apparently on the east (from whom the Cappadocians are clearly distinguished, vii. 72–3), and the Matieni on the south.

and the Phrygians on the left: then, when they are passed, it proceeds with a northern course, separating the Cappadocian Syrians from the Paphlagonians, who occupy the left bank, thus forming the boundary of almost the whole of Lower Asia, from the sea opposite Cyprus to the Euxine. Just there is the neck of the peninsula, a journey of five days across for an active walker.[1]

73. There were two motives which led Crœsus to attack Cappadocia: firstly, he coveted the land, which he wished to add to his own dominions; but the chief reason was, that he wanted to revenge on Cyrus the wrongs of Astyages, and was made confident by the oracle of being able so to do: for the Astyages, son of Cyaxares and king of the Medes, who had been dethroned by Cyrus, son of Cambyses, was Crœsus' brother by marriage. This marriage had taken place under circumstances which I will now relate. A band of Scythian nomads, who had left their own land on occasion of some disturbance, had taken refuge in Media. Cyaxares, son of Phraortes, and grandson of Deïoces, was at that time king of the country. Recognising them as suppliants, he began by treating them with kindness, and coming presently to esteem them highly, he intrusted to their care a number of boys, whom they were to teach their language and to instruct in the use of the bow. Time passed, and the Scythians employed themselves, day after day, in hunting, and always brought home some game; but at last it chanced that one day they took nothing. On their return to Cyaxares with empty hands, that monarch, who was hot-tempered, as he showed upon the occasion, received them very rudely and insultingly. In consequence of this treatment, which they did not conceive themselves to have deserved, the Scythians determined to take one of the boys whom they had in charge, cut him in pieces, and then dressing the flesh as they were wont to dress that of the wild animals, serve it up to

---

1 Herodotus tells us in one place (iv. 101) that he reckons the day's journey at 200 stadia, that is at about 23 of our miles. If we regard this as the measure intended here, we must consider that Herodotus imagined the isthmus of Natolia to be but 115 miles across, 165 miles short of the truth. It must be observed, however, that the ordinary day's journey cannot be intended by the ὁδὸς εὐζώνῳ ἀνδρί. The ἀνὴρ εὔζωνος is not the mere common traveller. He is the lightly-equipped pedestrian, and his day's journey must be estimated at something considerably above 200 stades. Herodotus appears to speak not of any particular case or cases, but generally of all lightly-equipped pedestrians. He cannot therefore be rightly regarded as free from mistake in the matter. Probably he considered the isthmus at least 100 miles narrower than it really is.

Cyaxares as game: after which they resolved to convey themselves with all speed to Sardis, to the court of Alyattes, the son of Sadyattes. The plan was carried out: Cyaxares and his guests ate of the flesh prepared by the Scythians, and they themselves, having accomplished their purpose, fled to Alyattes in the guise of suppliants.

74. Afterwards, on the refusal of Alyattes to give up his suppliants when Cyaxares sent to demand them of him, war broke out between the Lydians and the Medes, and continued for five years, with various success. In the course of it the Medes gained many victories over the Lydians, and the Lydians also gained many victories over the Medes. Among their other battles there was one night engagement. As, however, the balance had not inclined in favour of either nation, another combat took place in the sixth year, in the course of which, just as the battle was growing warm, day was on a sudden changed into night. This event had been foretold by Thales, the Milesian, who forewarned the Ionians of it, fixing for it the very year in which it actually took place.[1] The Medes and Lydians, when they observed the change, ceased fighting, and were alike anxious to have terms of peace agreed on. Syennesis[2] of Cilicia,[3] and Labynetus[4] of Babylon, were the persons who mediated between the parties, who hastened the taking of the oaths, and brought

1 The prediction of this eclipse by Thales may fairly be classed with the prediction of a good olive-crop or of the fall of an aërolite. Thales, indeed, could only have obtained the requisite knowledge for predicting eclipses from the Chaldæans, and that the science of these astronomers, although sufficient for the investigation of lunar eclipses, did not enable them to calculate solar eclipses – dependent as such a calculation is, not only on the determination of the period of recurrence, but on the true projection also of the track of the sun's shadow along a particular line over the surface of the earth – may be inferred from our finding that in the astronomical canon of Ptolemy, which was compiled from the Chaldæan registers, the observations of the moon's eclipses are alone entered.

2 The name Syennesis is common to all the kings of Cilicia mentioned in history. It has been supposed not to be really a name, but, like Pharaoh, a title.

3 Cilicia had become an independent state, either by the destruction of Assyria, or in the course of her decline after the reign of Esarhaddon. Previously, she had been included in the dominions of the Assyrian kings.

4 The Babylonian monarch at this time was either Nabopolassar or Nebuchadnezzar. Neither of these names is properly Hellenised by Labynetus. Labynetus is undoubtedly the Nabunahid of the inscriptions, the Nabonadius of the Canon, the Nabonnedus of Berosus and Megasthenes.

about the exchange of espousals. It was they who advised that Alyattes should give his daughter Aryênis in marriage to Astyages the son of Cyaxares, knowing, as they did, that without some sure bond of strong necessity, there is wont to be but little security in men's covenants. Oaths are taken by these people in the same way as by the Greeks, except that they make a slight flesh wound in their arms, from which each sucks a portion of the other's blood.[1]

75. Cyrus had captured this Astyages, who was his mother's father, and kept him prisoner, for a reason which I shall bring forward in another part of my history. This capture formed the ground of quarrel between Cyrus and Crœsus, in consequence of which Crœsus sent his servants to ask the oracle if he should attack the Persians; and when an evasive answer came, fancying it to be in his favour, carried his arms into the Persian territory. When he reached the river Halys, he transported his army across it, as I maintain, by the bridges which exist there at the present day;[2] but, according to the general belief of the Greeks, by the aid of Thales the Milesian. The tale is, that Crœsus was in doubt how he should get his army across, as the bridges were not made at that time, and that Thales, who happened to be in the camp, divided the stream and caused it to flow on both sides of the army instead of on the left only. This he effected thus:– Beginning some distance above the camp, he dug a deep channel, which he brought round in a semicircle, so that it might pass to rearward of the camp; and that thus the river, diverted from its natural course into the new channel at the point where this left the stream, might flow by the station of the army, and afterwards fall again into the ancient bed. In this way the river was split into two streams, which were both easily fordable. It is said by some that the water was entirely drained off from the natural bed of the river. But I am of a different opinion; for I do not see how, in that case, they could have crossed it on their return.

1 Vide infra, iv. 70, and Tacit. Annal. xii. 47.

2 The Halys (*Kizil Irmak*) is fordable at no very great distance from its mouth, but bridges over it are not unfrequent. These are of a very simple construction, consisting of planks laid across a few slender beams, extending from bank to bank, without any parapet. Bridges with stone piers have existed at some former period, but they belong probably to Roman, and not to any earlier times. The ancient constructions mentioned by Herodotus are more likely to have been of the modern type.

76. Having passed the Halys with the forces under his command, Crœsus entered the district of Cappadocia which is called Pteria.[1] It lies in the neighbourhood of the city of Sinôpé[2] upon the Euxine, and is the strongest position in the whole country thereabouts. Here Crœsus pitched his camp, and began to ravage the fields of the Syrians. He besieged and took the chief city of the Pterians, and reduced the inhabitants to slavery: he likewise made himself master of the surrounding villages. Thus he brought ruin on the Syrians, who were guilty of no offence towards him. Meanwhile, Cyrus had levied an army and marched against Crœsus, increasing his numbers at every step by the forces of the nations that lay in his way. Before beginning his march he had sent heralds to the Ionians, with an invitation to them to revolt from the Lydian king: they, however, had refused compliance. Cyrus, notwithstanding, marched against the enemy, and encamped opposite them in the district of Pteria, where the trial of strength took place between the contending powers. The combat was hot and bloody, and upon both sides the number of the slain was great; nor had victory declared in favour of either party, when night came down upon the battle-field. Thus both armies fought valiantly.

77. Crœsus laid the blame of his ill success on the number of his troops, which fell very short of the enemy; and as on the next day Cyrus did not repeat the attack, he set off on his return to Sardis, intending to collect his allies and renew the contest in the spring. He meant to call on the Egyptians to send him aid, according to the terms of the alliance which he had concluded with Amasis,[3] previously to his league with the Lacedæmonians. He intended also to summon to his assistance the Babylonians, under their king Labynetus,[4] for they too were bound to him by

1 Pteria in Herodotus is a district, not a city.

2 Sinôpé, which recent events have once more made famous, was a colony of the Milesians, founded about B.C. 630 (infra, iv. 12). It occupied the neck of a small peninsula projecting into the Euxine towards the north-east, in lat. 42°, long. 35°, nearly. The ancient town has been completely ruined, and the modern is built of its fragments.

3 The treaty of Amasis with Crœsus would suffice to account for the hostility of the Persians against Egypt.

4 Undoubtedly the Nabonadius of the Canon, and the Nabunahid of the monuments. The fact that it was with this monarch that Crœsus made his treaty helps greatly to fix the date of the fall of Sardis; it proves that that event *cannot have happened earlier* than B.C. 554. For Nabunahid did not ascend the throne till

treaty: and further, he meant to send word to Sparta, and appoint a day for the coming of their succours. Having got together these forces in addition to his own, he would, as soon as the winter was past and springtime come, march once more against the Persians. With these intentions Crœsus, immediately on his return, despatched heralds to his various allies, with a request that they would join him at Sardis in the course of the fifth month from the time of the departure of his messengers. He then disbanded the army – consisting of mercenary troops – which had been engaged with the Persians and had since accompanied him to his capital, and let them depart to their homes, never imagining that Cyrus, after a battle in which victory had been so evenly balanced, would venture to march upon Sardis.

78. While Crœsus was still in this mind, all the suburbs of Sardis were found to swarm with snakes, on the appearance of which the horses left feeding in the pasture-grounds, and flocked to the suburbs to eat them. The king, who witnessed the unusual sight, regarded it very rightly as a prodigy. He therefore instantly sent messengers to the soothsayers of Telmessus,[1] to consult them upon the matter. His messengers reached the city, and obtained from the Telmessians an explanation of what the prodigy portended, but fate did not allow them to inform their lord; for ere they entered Sardis on their return, Crœsus was a prisoner. What the Telmessians had declared was, that Crœsus must look for the entry of an army of foreign invaders into his country, and that when they came they would subdue the native inhabitants; since the snake, said they, is a child of earth, and the horse a warrior and a foreigner. Crœsus was already a prisoner when the Telmessians thus answered his inquiry, but they had no knowledge of what was taking place at Sardis, or of the fate of the monarch.

79. Cyrus, however, when Crœsus broke up so suddenly from his quarters after the battle at Pteria, conceiving that he had marched away with the intention of disbanding his army, considered a little, and soon saw that it was advisable for him

---

B.C. 555, and a full year must be allowed between the conclusion of the treaty and the taking of the Lydian capital.

1 Three distinct cities of Asia Minor are called by this name. The *Lycian* Telmessus lay upon the coast occupying the site of the modern village of *Makri*, where are some curious remains, especially tombs, partly Greek, partly native Lycian.

to advance upon Sardis with all haste, before the Lydians could get their forces together a second time. Having thus determined, he lost no time in carrying out his plan. He marched forward with such speed that he was himself the first to announce his coming to the Lydian king. That monarch, placed in the utmost difficulty by the turn of events which had gone so entirely against all his calculations, nevertheless led out the Lydians to battle. In all Asia there was not at that time a braver or more warlike people. Their manner of fighting was on horseback; they carried long lances, and were clever in the management of their steeds.

80. The two armies met in the plain before Sardis. It is a vast flat, bare of trees, watered by the Hyllus and a number of other streams, which all flow into one larger than the rest, called the Hermus.[1] This river rises in the sacred mountain of the Dindymenian Mother,[2] and falls into the sea near the town of Phocæa.[3]

When Cyrus beheld the Lydians arranging themselves in order of battle on this plain, fearful of the strength of their cavalry, he adopted a device which Harpagus, one of the Medes, suggested to him. He collected together all the camels that had come in the train of his army to carry the provisions and the baggage, and taking off their loads, he mounted riders upon them accoutred as horsemen. These he commanded to advance in front of his other troops against the Lydian horse; behind them were to follow the foot soldiers, and last of all the cavalry. When his arrangements were complete, he gave his troops orders to slay all the other Lydians who came in their way without mercy, but to spare Crœsus and not kill him, even if he should be seized and offer resistance. The reason why Cyrus opposed his camels to the enemy's horse was, because the horse has a natural dread of the camel, and cannot abide either the sight or the smell of that animal. By this stratagem he hoped to make Crœsus's horse useless to him, the horse being what he chiefly depended on for victory. The two armies then joined battle, and immediately the

1 Sardis (the modern *Sart*) stood in the broad valley of the Hermus at a point where the hills approach each other more closely than in any other place. Some vestiges of the ancient town remain, but, except the ruins of the great temple of Cybêlé (infra, v. 102), they seem to be of a late date.

2 The Dindymenian mother was Cybêlé, the special deity of Phrygia.

3 The Hermus (*Ghiediz-Chai*) now falls into the sea very much nearer to Smyrna than to Phocæa. Its course is perpetually changing.

Lydian war-horses, seeing and smelling the camels, turned round and galloped off; and so it came to pass that all Crœsus's hopes withered away. The Lydians, however, behaved manfully. As soon as they understood what was happening, they leaped off their horses, and engaged with the Persians on foot. The combat was long; but at last, after a great slaughter on both sides, the Lydians turned and fled. They were driven within their walls, and the Persians laid siege to Sardis.

81. Thus the siege began. Meanwhile Crœsus, thinking that the place would hold out no inconsiderable time, sent off fresh heralds to his allies from the beleaguered town. His former messengers had been charged to bid them assemble at Sardis in the course of the fifth month; they whom he now sent were to say that he was already besieged, and to beseech them to come to his aid with all possible speed. Among his other allies Crœsus did not omit to send to Lacedæmon.

82. It chanced, however, that the Spartans were themselves just at this time engaged in a quarrel with the Argives about a place called Thyrea,[1] which was within the limits of Argolis, but had been seized on by the Lacedæmonians. Indeed, the whole country westward, as far as Cape Malea, belonged once to the Argives, and not only that entire tract upon the mainland, but also Cythêra, and the other islands. The Argives collected troops to resist the seizure of Thyrea, but before any battle was fought, the two parties came to terms, and it was agreed that three hundred Spartans and three hundred Argives should meet and fight for the place, which should belong to the nation with whom the victory rested. It was stipulated also that the other troops on each side should return home to their respective countries, and not remain to witness the combat, as there was danger, if the armies stayed, that either the one or the other, on seeing their countrymen undergoing defeat, might hasten to their assistance. These terms being agreed on, the two armies marched off, leaving three hundred picked men on each side to fight for the territory. The battle began, and so equal were the combatants, that at the close of the day, when night put a stop to the fight, of the whole six hundred only three men remained alive, two Argives, Alcanor and Chromius, and a single Spartan, Othryadas.

1 Thyrea was the chief town of the district called Cynuria, the border territory between Laconia and Argolis (cf. Thucyd. v. 41).

The two Argives, regarding themselves as the victors, hurried to Argos. Othryadas, the Spartan, remained upon the field, and, stripping the bodies of the Argives who had fallen, carried their armour to the Spartan camp. Next day the two armies returned to learn the result. At first they disputed, both parties claiming the victory, the one, because they had the greater number of survivors; the other, because their man remained on the field, and stripped the bodies of the slain, whereas the two men of the other side ran away; but at last they fell from words to blows, and a battle was fought, in which both parties suffered great loss, but at the end the Lacedæmonians gained the victory. Upon this the Argives, who up to that time had worn their hair long, cut it off close, and made a law, to which they attached a curse, binding themselves never more to let their hair grow, and never to allow their women to wear gold, until they should recover Thyrea. At the same time the Lacedæmonians made a law the very reverse of this, namely, to wear their hair long, though they had always before cut it close. Othryadas himself, it is said, the sole survivor of the three hundred, prevented by a sense of shame from returning to Sparta after all his comrades had fallen, laid violent hands upon himself in Thyrea.

83. Although the Spartans were engaged with these matters when the herald arrived from Sardis to entreat them to come to the assistance of the besieged king, yet, notwithstanding, they instantly set to work to afford him help. They had completed their preparations, and the ships were just ready to start, when a second message informed them that the place had already fallen, and that Crœsus was a prisoner. Deeply grieved at his misfortune, the Spartans ceased their efforts.

84. The following is the way in which Sardis was taken. On the fourteenth day of the siege Cyrus bade some horsemen ride about his lines, and make proclamation to the whole army that he would give a reward to the man who should first mount the wall. After this he made an assault, but without success. His troops retired, but a certain Mardian, Hyrœades by name, resolved to approach the citadel and attempt it at a place where no guards were ever set. On this side the rock was so precipitous, and the citadel (as it seemed) so impregnable, that no fear was entertained of its being carried in this place. Here was the only portion of the circuit round which their old king Meles did not carry the lion which his leman bore to him. For when the

Telmessians had declared that if the lion were taken round the defences, Sardis would be impregnable, and Meles, in consequence, carried it round the rest of the fortress where the citadel seemed open to attack, he scorned to take it round this side, which he looked on as a sheer precipice, and therefore absolutely secure. It is on that side of the city which faces Mount Tmolus. Hyrœades, however, having the day before observed a Lydian soldier descend the rock after a helmet that had rolled down from the top, and having seen him pick it up and carry it back, thought over what he had witnessed, and formed his plan. He climbed the rock himself, and other Persians followed in his track, until a large number had mounted to the top. Thus was Sardis taken,[1] and given up entirely to pillage.

85. With respect to Crœsus himself, this is what befell him at the taking of the town. He had a son, of whom I made mention above, a worthy youth, whose only defect was that he was deaf and dumb. In the days of his prosperity Crœsus had done the utmost that he could for him, and among other plans which he had devised, had sent to Delphi to consult the oracle on his behalf. The answer which he had received from the Pythoness ran thus:—

Lydian, wide-ruling monarch, thou wondrous simple Crœsus,
Wish not ever to hear in thy palace the voice thou hast prayed for,
Uttering intelligent sounds. Far better thy son should be silent!
Ah! woe worth the day when thine ear shall first list to his accents.

When the town was taken, one of the Persians was just going to kill Crœsus, not knowing who he was. Crœsus saw the man coming, but under the pressure of his affliction, did not care to avoid the blow, not minding whether or no he died beneath the stroke. Then this son of his, who was voiceless, beholding the Persian as he rushed towards Crœsus, in the agony of his fear and grief burst into speech, and said, "Man, do not kill Crœsus." This was the first time that he had ever spoken a word, but afterwards he retained the power of speech for the remainder of his life.

86. Thus was Sardis taken by the Persians, and Crœsus himself fell into their hands, after having reigned fourteen years, and

1 Sardis was taken a second time in almost exactly the same way by Lagoras, one of the generals of Antiochus the Great.

been besieged in his capital fourteen days; thus too did Crœsus fulfil the oracle, which said that he should destroy a mighty empire, – by destroying his own. Then the Persians who had made Crœsus prisoner brought him before Cyrus. Now a vast pile had been raised by his orders, and Crœsus, laden with fetters, was placed upon it, and with him twice seven of the sons of the Lydians. I know not whether Cyrus was minded to make an offering of the first-fruits to some god or other, or whether he had vowed a vow and was performing it, or whether, as may well be, he had heard that Crœsus was a holy man, and so wished to see if any of the heavenly powers would appear to save him from being burnt alive. However it might be, Cyrus was thus engaged, and Crœsus was already on the pile, when it entered his mind in the depth of his woe that there was a divine warning in the words which had come to him from the lips of Solon, "No one while he lives is happy." When this thought smote him he fetched a long breath, and breaking his deep silence, groaned out aloud, thrice uttering the name of Solon. Cyrus caught the sounds, and bade the interpreters inquire of Crœsus who it was he called on. They drew near and asked him, but he held his peace, and for a long time made no answer to their questionings, until at length, forced to say something, he exclaimed, "One I would give much to see converse with every monarch." Not knowing what he meant by this reply, the interpreters begged him to explain himself; and as they pressed for an answer, and grew to be troublesome, he told them how, a long time before, Solon, an Athenian, had come and seen all his splendour, and made light of it; and how whatever he had said to him had fallen out exactly as he foreshowed, although it was nothing that especially concerned him, but applied to all mankind alike, and most to those who seemed to themselves happy. Meanwhile, as he thus spoke, the pile was lighted, and the outer portion began to blaze. Then Cyrus, hearing from the interpreters what Crœsus had said, relented, bethinking himself that he too was a man, and that it was a fellow-man, and one who had once been as blessed by fortune as himself, that he was burning alive; afraid, moreover, of retribution, and full of the thought that whatever is human is insecure. So he bade them quench the blazing fire as quickly as they could, and take down Crœsus and the other Lydians, which they tried to do, but the flames were not to be mastered.

87. Then, the Lydians say that Crœsus, perceiving by the efforts made to quench the fire that Cyrus had relented, and seeing also that all was in vain, and that the men could not get the fire under, called with a loud voice upon the god Apollo, and prayed him, if he had ever received at his hands any acceptable gift, to come to his aid, and deliver him from his present danger. As thus with tears he besought the god, suddenly, though up to that time the sky had been clear and the day without a breath of wind,[1] dark clouds gathered, and the storm burst over their heads with rain of such violence, that the flames were speedily extinguished. Cyrus, convinced by this that Crœsus was a good man and a favourite of heaven, asked him after he was taken off the pile, "Who it was that had persuaded him to lead an army into his country, and so become his foe rather than continue his friend?" to which Crœsus made answer as follows: "What I did, oh! king, was to thy advantage and to my own loss. If there be blame, it rests with the god of the Greeks, who encouraged me to begin the war. No one is so foolish as to prefer war to peace, in which, instead of sons burying their fathers, fathers bury their sons. But the gods willed it so."[2]

88. Thus did Crœsus speak. Cyrus then ordered his fetters to be taken off, and made him sit down near himself, and paid him much respect, looking upon him, as did also the courtiers, with a sort of wonder. Crœsus, wrapped in thought, uttered no word. After a while, happening to turn and perceive the Persian soldiers engaged in plundering the town, he said to Cyrus, "May I now tell thee, oh! king, what I have in my mind, or is silence best?" Cyrus bade him speak his mind boldly. Then he put this question: "What is it, oh! Cyrus, which those men yonder are doing so busily?" "Plundering thy city," Cyrus answered, "and

1 The later romancers regarded this incident as over-marvellous, and softened down the miracle considerably.

2 Modern critics seem not to have been the first to object to this entire narrative, that the religion of the Persians did not allow the burning of human beings (vide infra, iii. 16). The objection had evidently been made before the time of Nicolas of Damascus, who meets it indirectly in his narrative. The Persians (he gives us to understand) had for some time before this neglected the precepts of Zoroaster, and allowed his ordinances with respect to fire to fall into desuetude. The miracle whereby Crœsus was snatched from the flames reminded them of their ancient creed, and induced them to re-establish the whole system of Zoroaster. It may be doubted, however, whether the system of Zoroaster was at this time any portion of the Persian religion.

carrying off thy riches." "Not my city," rejoined the other, "nor my riches. They are not mine any more. It is thy wealth which they are pillaging."

89. Cyrus, struck by what Crœsus had said, bade all the court to withdraw, and then asked Crœsus what he thought it best for him to do as regarded the plundering. Crœsus answered, "Now that the gods have made me thy slave, oh! Cyrus, it seems to me that it is my part, if I see anything to thy advantage, to show it to thee. Thy subjects, the Persians, are a poor people with a proud spirit. If then thou lettest them pillage and possess themselves of great wealth, I will tell thee what thou hast to expect at their hands. The man who gets the most, look to having him rebel against thee. Now then, if my words please thee, do thus, oh! king:— Let some of thy body-guards be placed as sentinels at each of the city gates, and let them take their booty from the soldiers as they leave the town, and tell them that they do so because the tenths are due to Zeus. So wilt thou escape the hatred they would feel if the plunder were taken away from them by force; and they, seeing that what is proposed is just, will do it willingly."

90. Cyrus was beyond measure pleased with this advice, so excellent did it seem to him. He praised Crœsus highly, and gave orders to his body-guard to do as he had suggested. Then, turning to Crœsus, he said, "Oh! Crœsus, I see that thou art resolved both in speech and act to show thyself a virtuous prince: ask me, therefore, whatever thou wilt as a gift at this moment." Crœsus replied, "Oh! my lord, if thou wilt suffer me to send these fetters to the god of the Greeks, whom I once honoured above all other gods, and ask him if it is his wont to deceive his benefactors, – that will be the highest favour thou canst confer on me." Cyrus upon this inquired what charge he had to make against the god. Then Crœsus gave him a full account of all his projects, and of the answers of the oracle, and of the offerings which he had sent, on which he dwelt especially, and told him how it was the encouragement given him by the oracle which had led him to make war upon Persia. All this he related, and at the end again besought permission to reproach the god with his behaviour. Cyrus answered with a laugh, "This I readily grant thee, and whatever else thou shalt at any time ask at my hands." Crœsus, finding his request allowed, sent certain Lydians to Delphi, enjoining them to lay his fetters upon the threshold of the temple, and ask the

god, "If he were not ashamed of having encouraged him, as the destined destroyer of the empire of Cyrus, to begin a war with Persia, of which such were the first-fruits?" As they said this they were to point to the fetters; and further they were to inquire, "if it was the wont of the Greek gods to be ungrateful?"

91. The Lydians went to Delphi and delivered their message, on which the Pythoness is said to have replied – "It is not possible even for a god to escape the decree of destiny. Crœsus has been punished for the sin of his fifth ancestor,[1] who, when he was one of the body-guard of the Heraclides, joined in a woman's fraud, and, slaying his master, wrongfully seized the throne. Apollo was anxious that the fall of Sardis should not happen in the lifetime of Crœsus, but be delayed to his son's days; he could not, however, persuade the Fates. All that they were willing to allow he took and gave to Crœsus. Let Crœsus know that Apollo delayed the taking of Sardis three full years, and that he is thus a prisoner three years later than was his destiny. Moreover it was Apollo who saved him from the burning pile. Nor has Crœsus any right to complain with respect to the oracular answer which he received. For when the god told him that, if he attacked the Persians, he would destroy a mighty empire, he ought, if he had been wise, to have sent again and inquired which empire was meant, that of Cyrus or his own; but if he neither understood what was said, nor took the trouble to seek for enlightenment, he has only himself to blame for the result. Besides, he had misunderstood the last answer which had been given him about the mule. Cyrus was that mule. For the parents of Cyrus were of different races, and of different conditions, – his mother a Median princess, daughter of King Astyages, and his father a Persian and a subject, who, though so far beneath her in all respects, had married his royal mistress."

Such was the answer of the Pythoness. The Lydians returned to Sardis and communicated it to Crœsus, who confessed, on hearing it, that the fault was his, not the god's. Such was the way in which Ionia was first conquered, and so was the empire of Crœsus brought to a close.

92. Besides the offerings which have been already mentioned, there are many others in various parts of Greece presented by

1 Vide supra, ch. 13.

Crœsus; as at Thebes in Bœotia, where there is a golden tripod, dedicated by him to Ismenian Apollo;[1] at Ephesus, where the golden heifers, and most of the columns are his gift; and at Delphi, in the temple of Pronaia,[2] where there is a huge shield in gold, which he gave. All these offerings were still in existence in my day; many others have perished: among them those which he dedicated at Branchidæ in Milesia, equal in weight, as I am informed, and in all respects like to those at Delphi. The Delphian presents, and those sent to Amphiaraüs, came from his own private property, being the first-fruits of the fortune which he inherited from his father; his other offerings came from the riches of an enemy, who, before he mounted the throne, headed a party against him, with the view of obtaining the crown of Lydia for Pantaleon. This Pantaleon was a son of Alyattes, but by a different mother from Crœsus; for the mother of Crœsus was a Carian woman, but the mother of Pantaleon an Ionian. When, by the appointment of his father, Crœsus obtained the kingly dignity,[3] he seized the man who had plotted against him, and broke him upon the wheel. His property, which he had previously devoted to the service of the gods, Crœsus applied in the way mentioned above. This is all I shall say about his offerings.

93. Lydia, unlike most other countries, scarcely offers any wonders for the historian to describe, except the gold-dust which is washed down from the range of Tmolus. It has, however, one structure of enormous size, only inferior to the monuments of Egypt[4] and

1 The river Ismênius washed the foot of the hill on which this temple stood (Paus. ix. 10, 2); hence the phrase "Ismenian Apollo."

2 The temple of Athena at Delphi stood in front of the great temple of Apollo. Hence the Delphian Athena was called Athena Pronaia ($\delta\iota\grave{\alpha}$ τo $\pi\grave{\rho}o$ $\tauo\mathring{\nu}$ $\nu\alpha o\mathring{\nu}$ $\iota\delta\rho\mathring{\nu}\sigma\theta\alpha\iota$, as Harpocration says). Vide infra, viii. 37. Pausanias mentions that the shield was no longer there in his day. It had been carried off by Philomêlus, the Phocian general in the Sacred War (Paus. x. viii. § 4).

3 This has been supposed to mean that Alyattes associated Crœsus with him in the government. But there are no sufficient grounds for such an opinion. Association, common enough in Egypt, was very rarely practised in the East until the time of the Sassanian princes; and does not seem ever to obtain unless where the succession is doubtful.

4 The colossal size of the monuments in Egypt is sufficiently known. They increased in size as the power of Egypt advanced. The taste for colossal statues is often supposed to be peculiarly Egyptian; but the Greeks had some as large as, and even larger than, any in Egypt.

Babylon. This is the tomb of Alyattes,¹ the father of Crœsus, the base of which is formed of immense blocks of stone, the rest being a vast mound of earth. It was raised by the joint labour of the tradesmen, handicraftsmen, and courtesans of Sardis, and had at the top five stone pillars, which remained to my day, with inscriptions cut on them, showing how much of the work was done by each class of workpeople. It appeared on measurement that the portion of the courtesans was the largest. The daughters of the common people in Lydia, one and all, pursue this traffic, wishing to collect money for their portions. They continue the practice till they marry; and are wont to contract themselves in marriage. The tomb is six stades and two plethra in circumference; its breadth is thirteen plethra. Close to the tomb is a large lake, which the Lydians say is never dry.² They call it the Lake Gygæa.

94. The Lydians have very nearly the same customs as the Greeks, with the exception that these last do not prostitute their daughters. So far as we have any knowledge, they were the first nation to introduce the use of gold and silver coin,³

---

1 The following account of the external appearance of this monument, which still exists on the north bank of the Hermus, near the ruins of the ancient Sardis, is given by Mr. Hamilton (Asia Minor, vol. i. pp. 145–6):– "One mile south of this spot we reached the principal tumulus, generally designated as the tomb of Halyattes. It took us about ten minutes to ride round its base, which would give it a circumference of nearly half a mile. Towards the north it consists of the natural rock, a white horizontally-stratified earthy limestone, cut away so as to appear as part of the structure. The upper portion is sand and gravel, apparently brought from the bed of the Hermus. Several deep ravines have been worn by time and weather in its sides, particularly on that to the south: we followed one of these as affording a better footing than the smooth grass, as we ascended to the summit. Here we found the remains of a foundation nearly eighteen feet square, on the north of which was a huge circular stone, ten feet in diameter, with a flat bottom and a raised edge or lip, evidently placed there as an ornament on the apex of the tumulus. Herodotus says that phalli were erected upon the summit of some of these tumuli, of which this may be one; but Mr. Strickland supposes that a rude representation of the human face might be traced on its weather-beaten surface. In consequence of the ground sloping to the south, this tumulus appears much higher when viewed from the side of Sardis than from any other. It rises at an angle of about 22°, and is a conspicuous object on all sides."

Besides the barrow of Alyattes there are a vast number of ancient tumuli on the shores of the Gygæan lake. Three or four of these are scarcely inferior in size to that of Alyattes.

2 This lake is still a remarkable feature in the scene.

3 It is probable that the Greeks derived their first knowledge of coined money from the Asiatics with whom they came into contact in Asia Minor.

and the first who sold goods by retail. They claim also the invention of all the games which are common to them with the Greeks. These they declare that they invented about the time when they colonised Tyrrhenia, an event of which they give the following account. In the days of Atys the son of Manes, there was great scarcity through the whole land of Lydia. For some time the Lydians bore the affliction patiently, but finding that it did not pass away, they set to work to devise remedies for the evil. Various expedients were discovered by various persons; dice, and huckle-bones, and ball,[1] and all such games were invented, except tables, the invention of which they do not claim as theirs. The plan adopted against the famine was to engage in games one day so entirely as not to feel any craving for food, and the next day to eat and abstain from games. In this way they passed eighteen years. Still the affliction continued and even became more grievous. So the king determined to divide the nation in half, and to make the two portions draw lots, the one to stay, the other to leave the land. He would continue to reign over those whose lot it should be to remain behind; the emigrants should have his son Tyrrhênus for their leader. The lot was cast, and they who had to emigrate went down to Smyrna, and built themselves ships, in which, after they had put on board all needful stores, they sailed away in search of new homes and better sustenance. After sailing past many countries they came to Umbria,[2] where they built cities for themselves, and fixed their residence. Their former name of Lydians they laid aside, and called themselves after the name of the king's son, who led the colony, Tyrrhenians.

95. Thus far I have been engaged in showing how the Lydians were brought under the Persian yoke. The course of my history now compels me to inquire who this Cyrus was by whom the Lydian empire was destroyed, and by what means the Persians had become the lords paramount of Asia. And herein I shall follow those Persian authorities whose object it appears to be not to magnify the exploits of Cyrus, but to relate the simple

1 The ball was a very old game, and it was doubtless invented in Egypt, as Plato says. It is mentioned by Homer (Od. viii. 372), and it was known in Egypt long before his time, in the twelfth dynasty.
2 The Umbria of Herodotus appears to include almost the whole of Northern Italy.

truth. I know besides three ways in which the story of Cyrus is told, all differing from my own narrative.

The Assyrians had held the Empire of Upper Asia for the space of five hundred and twenty years, when the Medes set the example of revolt from their authority. They took arms for the recovery of their freedom, and fought a battle with the Assyrians, in which they behaved with such gallantry as to shake off the yoke of servitude, and to become a free people. Upon their success the other nations also revolted and regained their independence.

96. Thus the nations over that whole extent of country obtained the blessing of self-government, but they fell again under the sway of kings, in the manner which I will now relate. There was a certain Mede named Deioces, son of Phraortes, a man of much wisdom, who had conceived the desire of obtaining to himself the sovereign power. In furtherance of his ambition, therefore, he formed and carried into execution the following scheme. As the Medes at that time dwelt in scattered villages without any central authority, and lawlessness in consequence prevailed throughout the land, Deioces, who was already a man of mark in his own village, applied himself with greater zeal and earnestness than ever before to the practice of justice among his fellows. It was his conviction that justice and injustice are engaged in perpetual war with one another. He therefore began this course of conduct, and presently the men of his village, observing his integrity, chose him to be the arbiter of all their disputes. Bent on obtaining the sovereign power, he showed himself an honest and an upright judge, and by these means gained such credit with his fellow-citizens as to attract the attention of those who lived in the surrounding villages. They had long been suffering from unjust and oppressive judgments; so that, when they heard of the singular uprightness of Deioces, and of the equity of his decisions, they joyfully had recourse to him in the various quarrels and suits that arose, until at last they came to put confidence in no one else.

97. The number of complaints brought before him continually increasing, as people learnt more and more the fairness of his judgments, Deioces, feeling himself now all important, announced that he did not intend any longer to hear causes, and appeared no more in the seat in which he had been accustomed to sit and administer justice. "It did not square with his

interests," he said, "to spend the whole day in regulating other men's affairs to the neglect of his own." Hereupon robbery and lawlessness broke out afresh, and prevailed through the country even more than heretofore; wherefore the Medes assembled from all quarters, and held a consultation on the state of affairs. The speakers, as I think, were chiefly friends of Deioces. "We cannot possibly," they said, "go on living in this country if things continue as they now are; let us therefore set a king over us, that so the land may be well governed, and we ourselves may be able to attend to our own affairs, and not be forced to quit our country on account of anarchy." The assembly was persuaded by these arguments, and resolved to appoint a king.

98. It followed to determine who should be chosen to the office. When this debate began the claims of Deioces and his praises were at once in every mouth; so that presently all agreed that he should be king. Upon this he required a palace to be built for him suitable to his rank, and a guard to be given him for his person. The Medes complied, and built him a strong and large palace,[1] on a spot which he himself pointed out, and likewise gave him liberty to choose himself a body-guard from the whole nation. Thus settled upon the throne, he further required them to build a single great city, and, disregarding the petty towns in which they had formerly dwelt, make the new capital the object of their chief attention. The Medes were again obedient, and built the city now called Agbatana,[2] the walls of which are of great size and strength, rising in circles one within the other. The plan of the place is, that each of the walls should out-top the one beyond it by the battlements. The nature of the ground, which is a gentle hill, favours this arrangement in some degree, but it was mainly effected by art. The number of the circles is seven, the royal palace and the treasuries standing within the last. The circuit of the outer wall is very nearly the same with that of Athens. Of this wall the battlements are white,[3] of

1 The royal palace at Agbatana is said by Polybius to have been 7 stades (more than four-fifths of a mile) in circumference.

2 There is every reason to believe that the original form of the name Hellenised as Ἀγβάτανα or Ἐκβάτανα was Hagmatán, and that it was of Arian etymology, having been first used by the Arian Medes. It would signify in the language of the country "the place of assemblage."

3 "This is manifestly a fable of Sabæan origin, the seven colours mentioned by Herodotus being precisely those employed by the Orientals to denote the

the next black, of the third scarlet, of the fourth blue, of the fifth orange; all these are coloured with paint. The two last have their battlements coated respectively with silver and gold.[1]

99. All these fortifications Deioces caused to be raised for himself and his own palace. The people were required to build their dwellings outside the circuit of the walls. When the town was finished, he proceeded to arrange the ceremonial. He allowed no one to have direct access to the person of the king, but made all communication pass through the hands of messengers, and forbade the king to be seen by his subjects. He also made it an offence for any one whatsoever to laugh or spit in the royal presence. This ceremonial, of which he was the first inventor, Deioces established for his own security, fearing that his compeers, who were brought up together with him, and were of as good family as he, and no whit inferior to him in manly qualities, if they saw him frequently would be pained at the sight, and would therefore be likely to conspire against him; whereas if they did not see him, they would think him quite a different sort of being from themselves.

100. After completing these arrangements, and firmly settling himself upon the throne, Deioces continued to administer justice with the same strictness as before. Causes were stated in writing, and sent in to the king, who passed his judgment upon the contents, and transmitted his decisions to the parties concerned: besides which he had spies and eavesdroppers in all parts of his dominions, and if he heard of any act of oppression, he sent for the guilty party, and awarded him the punishment meet for his offence.

101. Thus Deioces collected the Medes into a nation, and ruled over them alone. Now these are the tribes of which they consist: the Busæ, the Parêtacêni, the Struchates, the Arizanti, the Budii, and the Magi.

---

seven great heavenly bodies, or the seven climates in which they revolve. The great temple of Nebuchadnezzar at Borsippa (the modern *Birs-Nimrud*) was a building in seven platforms coloured in a similar way.

1 There is reason to believe that this account, though it may be greatly exaggerated, is not devoid of a foundation. The temple at Borsippa (see the preceding note) appears to have had its fourth and seventh stages actually coated with gold and silver respectively. And it seems certain that there was often in Oriental towns a most lavish display of the two precious metals.

102. Having reigned three-and-fifty years, Deioces was at his death succeeded by his son Phraortes. This prince, not satisfied with a dominion which did not extend beyond the single nation of the Medes, began by attacking the Persians; and marching an army into their country, brought them under the Median yoke before any other people. After this success, being now at the head of two nations, both of them powerful, he proceeded to conquer Asia, overrunning province after province. At last he engaged in war with the Assyrians – those Assyrians, I mean, to whom Nineveh belonged,[1] who were formerly the lords of Asia. At present they stood alone by the revolt and desertion of their allies, yet still their internal condition was as flourishing as ever. Phraortes attacked them, but perished in the expedition with the greater part of his army, after having reigned over the Medes two-and-twenty years.

103. On the death of Phraortes his son Cyaxares ascended the throne. Of him it is reported that he was still more warlike than any of his ancestors, and that he was the first who gave organisation to an Asiatic army, dividing the troops into companies, and forming distinct bodies of the spearmen, the archers, and the cavalry, who before his time had been mingled in one mass, and confused together. He it was who fought against the Lydians on the occasion when the day was changed suddenly into night, and who brought under his dominion the whole of Asia beyond the Halys.[2] This prince, collecting together all the nations which owned his sway, marched against Nineveh, resolved to avenge his father, and cherishing a hope that he might succeed in taking the town. A battle was fought, in which the Assyrians suffered a defeat, and Cyaxares had already begun the siege of the place, when a numerous horde of Scyths, under their king Madyes,[3] son of Prôtothyes, burst into Asia in pursuit of the Cimmerians whom they had driven out of Europe, and entered the Median territory.

104. The distance from the Palus Mæôtis to the river Phasis and the Colchians is thirty days' journey for a lightly-equipped

---

1 Herodotus intends here to distinguish the Assyrians of Assyria Proper from the Babylonians, whom he calls also Assyrians (i. 178, 188, etc.). Against the latter he means to say this expedition was not directed.

2 Vide supra, chapter 74.

3 According to Strabo, Madys, or Madyes, was a Cimmerian prince who drove the Treres out of Asia.

traveller.[1] From Colchis to cross into Media does not take long
– there is only a single intervening nation, the Saspirians,[2] passing whom you find yourself in Media. This however was not
the road followed by the Scythians, who turned out of the
straight course, and took the upper route, which is much longer,
keeping the Caucasus upon their right.[3] The Scythians, having
thus invaded Media, were opposed by the Medes, who gave them
battle, but, being defeated, lost their empire. The Scythians became masters of Asia.

105. After this they marched forward with the design of invading Egypt. When they had reached Palestine, however, Psammetichus the Egyptian king met them with gifts and prayers, and
prevailed on them to advance no further. On their return, passing through Ascalon, a city of Syria,[4] the greater part of them
went their way without doing any damage; but some few who
lagged behind pillaged the temple of Celestial Aphrodite.[5] I have
inquired and find that the temple at Ascalon is the most ancient
of all the temples to this goddess; for the one in Cyprus, as the
Cyprians themselves admit, was built in imitation of it; and that
in Cythêra was erected by the Phœnicians, who belong to this
part of Syria. The Scythians who plundered the temple were
punished by the goddess with the female sickness, which still
attaches to their posterity. They themselves confess that they are
afflicted with the disease for this reason, and travellers who visit

1 From the mouth of the Palus Mæotis, or Sea of Azof, to the river *Rion*,
(the ancient Phasis) is a distance of about 270 geographical miles, or but little
more than the distance (240 geog. miles) from the gulf of Issus to the Euxine,
which was called (ch. 72) "a journey of *five* days for a lightly-equipped traveller."
We may learn from this that Herodotus did not intend the day's journey for a
measure of length.

2 The Saspirians are mentioned again as lying north of Media (ch. 110), and
as separating Media from Colchis (iv. 37).

3 Herodotus, clearly, conceives the Cimmerians to have coasted the Black
Sea, and appears to have thought that the Scythians entered Asia by the route
of Daghestán, along the shores of the Caspian.

4 Ascalon was one of the most ancient cities of the Philistines (Judges
i. 18, xiv. 19, etc.). Ascalon is first mentioned in cuneiform inscriptions of the
time of Sennacherib, having been reduced by him in the famous campaign of
his third year.

5 Herodotus probably intends the Syrian goddess Atergatis or Dercĕto,
who was worshipped at Ascalon and elsewhere in Syria, under the form of a
mermaid, or figure half woman half fish. She may be identified with Astarté,
and therefore with the Aphrodite of the Greeks.

Scythia can see what sort of a disease it is. Those who suffer from it are called Enarees.

106. The dominion of the Scythians over Asia lasted eight-and-twenty years, during which time their insolence and oppression spread ruin on every side. For besides the regular tribute, they exacted from the several nations additional imposts, which they fixed at pleasure; and further, they scoured the country and plundered every one of whatever they could. At length Cyaxares and the Medes invited the greater part of them to a banquet, and made them drunk with wine, after which they were all massacred. The Medes then recovered their empire, and had the same extent of dominion as before. They took Nineveh—I will relate how in another history – and conquered all Assyria except the district of Babylonia. After this Cyaxares died, having reigned over the Medes, if we include the time of the Scythian rule, forty years.

107. Astyages, the son of Cyaxares, succeeded to the throne. He had a daughter who was named Mandané, concerning whom he had a wonderful dream. He dreamt that she urinated in such a quantity as not only to fill his capital, but to flood the whole of Asia. This vision he laid before such of the Magi as had the gift of interpreting dreams, who expounded its meaning to him in full, whereat he was greatly terrified. On this account, when his daughter was now of ripe age, he would not give her in marriage to any of the Medes who were of suitable rank, lest the dream should be accomplished; but he married her to a Persian of good family indeed,[1] but of a quiet temper, whom he looked on as much inferior to a Mede of even middle condition.

---

1 Cambyses, the father of Cyrus, appears to have been not only a man of good family, but of royal race – the hereditary monarch of his nation, which, when it became subject to the Medes, still retained its line of native kings, the descendants of Achæmenes (Hakhámanish). In the Behistun Inscription (col. I, par. 4) Darius carries up his genealogy to Achæmenes, and asserts that "eight of his race had been kings before himself – he was the ninth." Cambyses, the father of Cyrus, Cyrus himself, and Cambyses the son of Cyrus, are probably included in the eight. An inscription has been found upon a brick at *Senkereh* in lower Chaldæa, in which Cyrus the Great calls himself "the son of Cambyses, the powerful king." This then is decisive as to the royalty of the line of Cyrus the Great, and is confirmatory of the impression derived from other evidence, that when Darius speaks of eight Achæmenian kings having preceded him, he alludes to the ancestry of Cyrus the Great, and not to his own immediate paternal line.

108. Thus Cambyses (for so was the Persian called) wedded Mandané,[1] and took her to his home, after which, in the very first year, Astyages saw another vision. He fancied that a vine grew from the privy parts of his daughter, and overshadowed the whole of Asia. After this dream, which he submitted also to the interpreters, he sent to Persia and fetched away Mandané, who was now with child, and was not far from her time. On her arrival he set a watch over her, intending to destroy the child to which she should give birth; for the Magian interpreters had expounded the vision to foreshow that the offspring of his daughter would reign over Asia in his stead. To guard against this, Astyages, as soon as Cyrus was born, sent for Harpagus, a man of his own house and the most faithful of the Medes, to whom he was wont to entrust all his affairs, and addressed him thus – "Harpagus, I beseech thee neglect not the business with which I am about to charge thee; neither betray thou the interests of thy lord for others' sake, lest thou bring destruction on thine own head at some future time. Take the child born of Mandané my daughter; carry him with thee to thy home and slay him there. Then bury him as thou wilt." "Oh! king," replied the other, "never in time past did Harpagus disoblige thee in anything, and be sure that through all future time he will be careful in nothing to offend. If therefore it be thy will that this thing be done, it is for me to serve thee with all diligence."

109. When Harpagus had thus answered, the child was given into his hands, clothed in the garb of death, and he hastened weeping to his home. There on his arrival he found his wife, to whom he told all that Astyages had said. "What then," said she, "is it now in thy heart to do?" "Not what Astyages requires," he answered; "no, he may be madder and more frantic still than he is now, but I will not be the man to work his will, or lend a helping hand to such a murder as this. Many things forbid my slaying him. In the first place the boy is my own kith and kin; and next Astyages is old, and has no son.[2] If then when he dies the crown should go to his daughter – that daughter whose child

1 Whether there was really any connection of blood between Cyrus and Astyages, or whether they were no way related to one another, will perhaps never be determined.

2 Xenophon (Cyrop. I. iv. § 20) gives Astyages a son, whom he calls Cyaxares. The inscriptions tend to confirm Herodotus.

he now wishes to slay by my hand – what remains for me but danger of the fearfullest kind? For my own safety, indeed, the child must die; but some one belonging to Astyages must take his life, not I or mine."

110. So saying he sent off a messenger to fetch a certain Mitradates,[1] one of the herdsmen of Astyages, whose pasturages he knew to be the fittest for his purpose, lying as they did among mountains infested with wild beasts. This man was married to one of the king's female slaves, whose Median name was Spaco, which is in Greek Cyno, since in the Median tongue the word "Spaca" means a bitch. The mountains, on the skirts of which his cattle grazed, lie to the north of Agbatana, towards the Euxine. That part of Media which borders on the Saspirians is an elevated tract, very mountainous, and covered with forests, while the rest of the Median territory is entirely level ground. On the arrival of the herdsman, who came at the hasty summons, Harpagus said to him – "Astyages requires thee to take this child and lay him in the wildest part of the hills, where he will be sure to die speedily. And he bade me tell thee, that if thou dost not kill the boy, but anyhow allowest him to escape, he will put thee to the most painful of deaths. I myself am appointed to see the child exposed."

111. The herdsman on hearing this took the child in his arms, and went back the way he had come till he reached the folds. There, providentially, his wife, who had been expecting daily to be put to bed, had just, during the absence of her husband, been delivered of a child. Both the herdsman and his wife were uneasy on each other's account, the former fearful because his wife was so near her time, the woman alarmed because it was a new thing for her husband to be sent for by Harpagus. When therefore he came into the house upon his return, his wife, seeing him arrive so unexpectedly, was the first to speak, and begged to know why Harpagus had sent for him in such a hurry. "Wife," said he, "when I got to the town I saw and heard such things as I would to heaven I had never seen – such things as I would to heaven had never happened to our masters. Every one was weeping in

1 Ctesias seems to have called this person Atradates. Atradates may fairly be considered to be a mere Median synonym for the Persian Mitradates – the name signifying "given to the sun," and *Atra* or *Adar* (whence Atropatênê) being equivalent in Median, as a title of that luminary (or of fire, which was the usual emblem of his worship) to the Persian *Mitra* or *Mihr*.

Harpagus's house. It quite frightened me, but I went in. The moment I stepped inside, what should I see but a baby lying on the floor, panting and whimpering, and all covered with gold, and wrapped in clothes of such beautiful colours. Harpagus saw me, and directly ordered me to take the child in my arms and carry him off, and what was I to do with him, think you? Why, to lay him in the mountains, where the wild beasts are most plentiful. And he told me it was the king himself that ordered it to be done, and he threatened me with such dreadful things if I failed. So I took the child up in my arms, and carried him along. I thought it might be the son of one of the household slaves. I did wonder certainly to see the gold and the beautiful baby-clothes, and I could not think why there was such a weeping in Harpagus's house. Well, very soon, as I came along, I got at the truth. They sent a servant with me to show me the way out of the town, and to leave the baby in my hands; and he told me that the child's mother is the king's daughter Mandané, and his father Cambyses, the son of Cyrus; and that the king orders him to be killed; and look, here the child is."

112. With this the herdsman uncovered the infant, and showed him to his wife, who, when she saw him, and observed how fine a child and how beautiful he was, burst into tears, and clinging to the knees of her husband, besought him on no ac-count to expose the babe; to which he answered, that it was not possible for him to do otherwise, as Harpagus would be sure to send persons to see and report to him, and he was to suffer a most cruel death if he disobeyed. Failing thus in her first attempt to persuade her husband, the woman spoke a second time, saying, "If then there is no persuading thee, and a child must needs be seen exposed upon the mountains, at least do thus. The child of which I have just been delivered is still-born; take it and lay it on the hills, and let us bring up as our own the child of the daughter of Astyages. So shalt thou not be charged with unfaithfulness to thy lord, nor shall we have managed badly for ourselves. Our dead babe will have a royal funeral, and this living child will not be deprived of life."

113. It seemed to the herdsman that this advice was the best under the circumstances. He therefore followed it without loss of time. The child which he had intended to put to death he gave over to his wife, and his own dead child he put in the cradle wherein he had carried the other, clothing it first in all the other's

costly attire, and taking it in his arms he laid it in the wildest place of all the mountain-range. When the child had been three days exposed, leaving one of his helpers to watch the body, he started off for the city, and going straight to Harpagus's house, declared himself ready to show the corpse of the boy. Harpagus sent certain of his body-guard, on whom he had the firmest reliance, to view the body for him, and, satisfied with their seeing it, gave orders for the funeral. Thus was the herdsman's child buried, and the other child, who was afterwards known by the name of Cyrus, was taken by the herdsman's wife, and brought up under a different name.

114. When the boy was in his tenth year, an accident which I will now relate, caused it to be discovered who he was. He was at play one day in the village where the folds of the cattle were, along with the boys of his own age, in the street. The other boys who were playing with him chose the cowherd's son, as he was called, to be their king. He then proceeded to order them about – some he set to build him houses, others he made his guards, one of them was to be the king's eye, another had the office of carrying his messages, all had some task or other. Among the boys there was one, the son of Artembares, a Mede of distinction, who refused to do what Cyrus had set him. Cyrus told the other boys to take him into custody, and when his orders were obeyed, he chastised him most severely with the whip. The son of Artembares, as soon as he was let go, full of rage at treatment so little befitting his rank, hastened to the city and complained bitterly to his father of what had been done to him by Cyrus. He did not, of course, say "Cyrus," by which name the boy was not yet known, but called him the son of the king's cowherd. Artembares, in the heat of his passion, went to Astyages, accompanied by his son, and made complaint of the gross injury which had been done him. Pointing to the boy's shoulders, he exclaimed, "Thus, oh! king, has thy slave, the son of a cowherd, heaped insult upon us."

115. At this sight and these words Astyages, wishing to avenge the son of Artembares for his father's sake, sent for the cowherd and his boy. When they came together into his presence, fixing his eyes on Cyrus, Astyages said, "Hast thou then, the son of so mean a fellow as that, dared to behave thus rudely to the son of yonder noble, one of the first in my court?" "My lord," replied the boy, "I only treated him as he deserved. I was chosen king

in play by the boys of our village, because they thought me the best for it. He himself was one of the boys who chose me. All the others did according to my orders; but he refused, and made light of them, until at last he got his due reward. If for this I deserve to suffer punishment, here I am ready to submit to it."

116. While the boy was yet speaking Astyages was struck with a suspicion who he was. He thought he saw something in the character of his face like his own, and there was a nobleness about the answer he had made; besides which his age seemed to tally with the time when his grandchild was exposed. Astonished at all this, Astyages could not speak for a while. At last, recovering himself with difficulty, and wishing to be quit of Artembares, that he might examine the herdsman alone, he said to the former, "I promise thee, Artembares, so to settle this business that neither thou nor thy son shall have any cause to complain." Artembares retired from his presence, and the attendants, at the bidding of the king, led Cyrus into an inner apartment. Astyages then being left alone with the herdsman, inquired of him where he had got the boy, and who had given him to him; to which he made answer that the lad was his own child, begotten by himself, and that the mother who bore him was still alive, and lived with him in his house. Astyages remarked that he was very ill-advised to bring himself into such great trouble, and at the same time signed to his body-guard to lay hold of him. Then the herdsman, as they were dragging him to the rack, began at the beginning, and told the whole story exactly as it happened, without concealing anything, ending with entreaties and prayers to the king to grant him forgiveness.

117. Astyages, having got the truth of the matter from the herdsman, was very little further concerned about him, but with Harpagus he was exceedingly enraged. The guards were bidden to summon him into the presence, and on his appearance Astyages asked him, "By what death was it, Harpagus, that thou slewest the child of my daughter whom I gave into thy hands?" Harpagus, seeing the cowherd in the room, did not betake himself to lies, lest he should be confuted and proved false, but replied as follows:— "Sire, when thou gavest the child into my hands I instantly considered with myself how I could contrive to execute thy wishes, and yet, while guiltless of any unfaithfulness towards thee, avoid imbruing my hands in blood which was in truth thy daughter's and thine own. And this was how I

contrived it. I sent for this cowherd, and gave the child over to him, telling him that by the king's orders it was to be put to death. And in this I told no lie, for thou hadst so commanded. Moreover, when I gave him the child, I enjoined him to lay it somewhere in the wilds of the mountains, and to stay near and watch till it was dead; and I threatened him with all manner of punishment if he failed. Afterwards, when he had done according to all that I commanded him, and the child had died, I sent some of the most trustworthy of my eunuchs, who viewed the body for me, and then I had the child buried. This, sire, is the simple truth, and this is the death by which the child died."

118. Thus Harpagus related the whole story in a plain, straightforward way; upon which Astyages, letting no sign escape him of the anger that he felt, began by repeating to him all that he had just heard from the cowherd, and then concluded with saying, "So the boy is alive, and it is best as it is. For the child's fate was a great sorrow to me, and the reproaches of my daughter went to my heart. Truly fortune has played us a good turn in this. Go thou home then, and send thy son to be with the new comer, and to-night, as I mean to sacrifice thank-offerings for the child's safety to the gods to whom such honour is due, I look to have thee a guest at the banquet."

119. Harpagus, on hearing this, made obeisance, and went home rejoicing to find that his disobedience had turned out so fortunately, and that, instead of being punished, he was invited to a banquet given in honour of the happy occasion. The moment he reached home he called for his son, a youth of about thirteen, the only child of his parents, and bade him go to the palace, and do whatever Astyages should direct. Then, in the gladness of his heart, he went to his wife and told her all that had happened. Astyages, meanwhile, took the son of Harpagus, and slew him, after which he cut him in pieces, and roasted some portions before the fire, and boiled others; and when all were duly prepared, he kept them ready for use. The hour for the banquet came, and Harpagus appeared, and with him the other guests, and all sat down to the feast. Astyages and the rest of the guests had joints of meat served up to them; but on the table of Harpagus, nothing was placed except the flesh of his own son. This was all put before him, except the hands and feet and head, which were laid by themselves in a covered basket. When Harpagus seemed to have eaten his fill, Astyages called out to

him to know how he had enjoyed the repast. On his reply that he had enjoyed it excessively, they whose business it was brought him the basket, in which were the hands and feet and head of his son, and bade him open it, and take out what he pleased. Harpagus accordingly uncovered the basket, and saw within it the remains of his son. The sight, however, did not scare him, or rob him of his self-possession. Being asked by Astyages if he knew what beast's flesh it was that he had been eating, he answered that he knew very well, and that whatever the king did was agreeable. After this reply, he took with him such morsels of the flesh as were uneaten, and went home, intending, as I conceive, to collect the remains and bury them.

120. Such was the mode in which Astyages punished Harpagus: afterwards, proceeding to consider what he should do with Cyrus, his grandchild, he sent for the Magi, who formerly interpreted his dream in the way which alarmed him so much, and asked them how they had expounded it. They answered, without varying from what they had said before, that "the boy must needs be a king if he grew up, and did not die too soon." Then Astyages addressed them thus: "The boy has escaped, and lives; he has been brought up in the country, and the lads of the village where he lives have made him their king. All that kings commonly do he has done. He has had his guards, and his door-keepers, and his messengers, and all the other usual officers. Tell me, then, to what, think you, does all this tend?" The Magi answered, "If the boy survives, and has ruled as a king without any craft or contrivance, in that case we bid thee cheer up, and feel no more alarm on his account. He will not reign a second time. For we have found even oracles sometimes fulfilled in an unimportant way; and dreams, still oftener, have wondrously mean accomplishments." "It is what I myself most incline to think," Astyages rejoined; "the boy having been already king, the dream is out, and I have nothing more to fear from him. Nevertheless, take good heed and counsel me the best you can for the safety of my house and your own interests." "Truly," said the Magi in reply, "it very much concerns our interests that thy kingdom be firmly established; for if it went to this boy it would pass into foreign hands, since he is a Persian: and then we Medes should lose our freedom, and be quite despised by the Persians, as being foreigners. But so long as thou, our fellow-countryman, art on the throne all manner of honours are ours, and we are

even not without some share in the government. Much reason therefore have we to forecast well for thee and for thy sovereignty. If then we saw any cause for present fear, be sure we would not keep it back from thee. But truly we are persuaded that the dream has had its accomplishment in this harmless way; and so our own fears being at rest, we recommend thee to banish thine. As for the boy, our advice is, that thou send him away to Persia, to his father and mother."

121. Astyages heard their answer with pleasure, and calling Cyrus into his presence, said to him, "My child, I was led to do thee a wrong by a dream which has come to nothing: from that wrong thou wert saved by thy own good fortune. Go now with a light heart to Persia; I will provide thy escort. Go, and when thou gettest to thy journey's end, thou wilt behold thy father and thy mother, quite other people from Mitradates the cowherd and his wife."

122. With these words Astyages dismissed his grandchild. On his arrival at the house of Cambyses, he was received by his parents, who, when they learnt who he was, embraced him heartily, having always been convinced that he died almost as soon as he was born. So they asked him by what means he had chanced to escape; and he told them how that till lately he had known nothing at all about the matter, but had been mistaken – oh! so widely! – and how that he had learnt his history by the way, as he came from Media. He had been quite sure that he was the son of the king's cowherd, but on the road the king's escort had told him all the truth; and then he spoke of the cowherd's wife who had brought him up, and filled his whole talk with her praises; in all that he had to tell them about himself, it was always Cyno – Cyno was everything. So it happened that his parents, catching the name at his mouth, and wishing to persuade the Persians that there was a special providence in his preservation, spread the report that Cyrus, when he was exposed, was suckled by a bitch. This was the sole origin of the rumour.

123. Afterwards, when Cyrus grew to manhood, and became known as the bravest and most popular of all his compeers, Harpagus, who was bent on revenging himself upon Astyages, began to pay him court by gifts and messages. His own rank was too humble for him to hope to obtain vengeance without some foreign help. When therefore he saw Cyrus, whose wrongs were so similar to his own, growing up expressly (as it were) to be the

avenger whom he needed, he set to work to procure his support and aid in the matter. He had already paved the way for his designs, by persuading, severally, the great Median nobles, whom the harsh rule of their monarch had offended, that the best plan would be to put Cyrus at their head, and dethrone Astyages. These preparations made, Harpagus being now ready for revolt, was anxious to make known his wishes to Cyrus, who still lived in Persia; but as the roads between Media and Persia were guarded, he had to contrive a means of sending word secretly, which he did in the following way. He took a hare, and cutting open its belly without hurting the fur, he slipped in a letter containing what he wanted to say, and then carefully sewing up the paunch, he gave the hare to one of his most faithful slaves, disguising him as a hunter with nets, and sent him off to Persia to take the game as a present to Cyrus, bidding him tell Cyrus, by word of mouth, to paunch the animal himself, and let no one be present at the time.

124. All was done as he wished, and Cyrus, on cutting the hare open, found the letter inside, and read as follows:– "Son of Cambyses, the gods assuredly watch over thee, or never wouldst thou have passed through thy many wonderful adventures – now is the time when thou mayst avenge thyself upon Astyages, thy murderer. He willed thy death, remember; to the gods and to me thou owest that thou art still alive. I think thou art not ignorant of what he did to thee, nor of what I suffered at his hands because I committed thee to the cowherd, and did not put thee to death. Listen now to me, and obey my words, and all the empire of Astyages shall be thine. Raise the standard of revolt in Persia, and then march straight on Media. Whether Astyages appoint me to command his forces against thee, or whether he appoint any other of the princes of the Medes, all will go as thou couldst wish. They will be the first to fall away from him, and joining thy side, exert themselves to overturn his power. Be sure that on our part all is ready; wherefore do thou thy part, and that speedily."

125. Cyrus, on receiving the tidings contained in this letter, set himself to consider how he might best persuade the Persians to revolt. After much thought, he hit on the following as the most expedient course: he wrote what he thought proper upon a roll, and then calling an assembly of the Persians, he unfolded the roll, and read out of it that Astyages appointed him their

general. "And now," said he, "since it is so, I command you to go and bring each man his reaping-hook." With these words he dismissed the assembly.

Now the Persian nation is made up of many tribes.[1] Those which Cyrus assembled and persuaded to revolt from the Medes, were the principal ones on which all the others are dependent.[2] These are the Pasargadæ,[3] the Maraphians, and the Maspians, of whom the Pasargadæ are the noblest. The Achæmenidæ,[4] from which spring all the Perseid kings, is one of their clans. The rest of the Persian tribes are the following: the Panthialæans, the Derusiæans, the Germanians, who are engaged in husbandry; the Daans, the Mardians, the Dropicans, and the Sagartians, who are Nomads.[5]

126. When, in obedience to the orders which they had received, the Persians came with their reaping-hooks, Cyrus led them to a tract of ground, about eighteen or twenty furlongs each way, covered with thorns, and ordered them to clear it before the day was out. They accomplished their task; upon which he issued a second order to them, to take the bath the day following, and again come to him. Meanwhile he collected together all his father's flocks, both sheep and goats, and all his oxen, and slaughtered them, and made ready to give an entertainment to the entire Persian army. Wine, too, and bread of the

---

1 According to Xenophon the number of the Persian tribes was *twelve* (Cyrop. i. ii. § 5), according to Herodotus, ten.

2 The distinction of superior and inferior tribes is common among nomadic and semi-nomadic nations.

3 Pasargadæ was not only the name of the principal Persian tribe, but also of the ancient capital of the country (Strab. xv. p. 1035). It seems tolerably certain that the modern *Murg-aub* is the site of the ancient Pasargadæ. Its position with respect to Persepolis, its strong situation among the mountains, its remains bearing the marks of high antiquity, and, above all, the name and tomb of Cyrus, which have been discovered among the ruins, mark it for the capital of that monarch beyond all reasonable doubt.

4 The Achæmenidæ were the royal family of Persia, the descendants of Achæmenes (Hakhamanish), who was probably the leader under whom the Persians first settled in the country which has ever since borne their name. This Achæmenes is mentioned by Herodotus as the founder of the kingdom (iii. 75; vii. 11). Achæmenes continued to be used as a family name in after times. It was borne by one of the sons of Darius Hystaspes (infra, vii. 7).

5 Nomadic hordes must always be an important element in the population of Persia. Large portions of the country are only habitable at certain seasons of the year.

choicest kinds were prepared for the occasion. When the morrow came, and the Persians appeared, he bade them recline upon
the grass, and enjoy themselves. After the feast was over, he
requested them to tell him "which they liked best, to-day's work,
or yesterday's?" They answered that "the contrast was indeed
strong: yesterday brought them nothing but what was bad, to-day
everything that was good." Cyrus instantly seized on their reply,
and laid bare his purpose in these words: "Ye men of Persia,
thus do matters stand with you. If you choose to hearken to my
words, you may enjoy these and ten thousand similar delights,
and never condescend to any slavish toil; but if you will not
hearken, prepare yourselves for unnumbered toils as hard as
yesterday's. Now therefore follow my bidding, and be free. For
myself I feel that I am destined by Providence to undertake your
liberation; and you, I am sure, are no whit inferior to the Medes
in anything, least of all in bravery. Revolt, therefore, from
Astyages, without a moment's delay."

127. The Persians, who had long been impatient of the
Median dominion, now that they had found a leader, were delighted
to shake off the yoke. Meanwhile Astyages, informed of the
doings of Cyrus, sent a messenger to summon him to his
presence. Cyrus replied, "Tell Astyages that I shall appear in
his presence sooner than he will like." Astyages, when he
received this message, instantly armed all his subjects, and, as if
God had deprived him of his senses, appointed Harpagus to be
their general, forgetting how greatly he had injured him. So when
the two armies met and engaged, only a few of the Medes, who
were not in the secret, fought; others deserted openly to the
Persians; while the greater number counterfeited fear, and fled.

128. Astyages, on learning the shameful flight and dispersion
of his army, broke out into threats against Cyrus, saying, "Cyrus
shall nevertheless have no reason to rejoice;" and directly he
seized the Magian interpreters, who had persuaded him to allow
Cyrus to escape, and impaled them; after which, he armed all the
Medes who had remained in the city, both young and old; and
leading them against the Persians, fought a battle, in which he
was utterly defeated, his army being destroyed, and he himself
falling into the enemy's hands.

129. Harpagus then, seeing him a prisoner, came near, and
exulted over him with many jibes and jeers. Among other cutting
speeches which he made, he alluded to the supper where the

flesh of his son was given him to eat, and asked Astyages to answer *him* now, how he enjoyed being a slave instead of a king? Astyages looked in his face, and asked him in return, why he claimed as his own the achievements of Cyrus? "Because," said Harpagus, "it was my letter which made him revolt, and so I am entitled to all the credit of the enterprise." Then Astyages declared, that "in that case he was at once the silliest and the most unjust of men: the silliest, if when it was in his power to put the crown on his own head, as it must assuredly have been, if the revolt was entirely his doing, he had placed it on the head of another; the most unjust, if on account of that supper he had brought slavery on the Medes. For, supposing that he was obliged to invest another with the kingly power, and not retain it himself, yet justice required that a Mede, rather than a Persian, should receive the dignity. Now, however, the Medes, who had been no parties to the wrong of which he complained, were made slaves instead of lords, and slaves moreover of those who till recently had been their subjects."

130. Thus after a reign of thirty-five years, Astyages lost his crown, and the Medes, in consequence of his cruelty, were brought under the rule of the Persians. Their empire over the parts of Asia beyond the Halys had lasted one hundred and twenty-eight years, except during the time when the Scythians had the dominion.[1] Afterwards the Medes repented of their submission, and revolted from Darius, but were defeated in battle, and again reduced to subjection.[2] Now, however, in the time of Astyages, it was the Persians who under Cyrus revolted from the Medes, and became thenceforth the rulers of Asia. Cyrus kept Astyages at his court during the remainder of his life, without doing him any further injury. Such then were the circumstances of the birth and bringing up of Cyrus, and such were the steps by which he mounted the throne. It was at a later date that he was attacked by Crœsus, and overthrew him, as I have related in an earlier portion of this history. The overthrow of Crœsus made him master of the whole of Asia.

---

1 *i.e.* they ruled (128 − 28=) 100 years. This would make their rule begin in the twenty-third year of Deïoces.

2 In the great inscription of Darius at Behistun a long and elaborate account is given of a Median revolt which occurred in the third year of the reign of Darius, and was put down with difficulty.

131. The customs which I know the Persians to observe are the following. They have no images of the gods, no temples nor altars, and consider the use of them a sign of folly. This comes, I think, from their not believing the gods to have the same nature with men, as the Greeks imagine. Their wont, however, is to ascend the summits of the loftiest mountains, and there to offer sacrifice to Zeus, which is the name they give to the whole circuit of the firmament. They likewise offer to the sun and moon, to the earth, to fire, to water, and to the winds. These are the only gods whose worship has come down to them from ancient times. At a later period they began the worship of Urania, which they borrowed[1] from the Arabians and Assyrians. Mylitta is the name by which the Assyrians know this goddess, whom the Arabians call Alitta, and the Persians Mitra.[2]

132. To these gods the Persians offer sacrifice in the following manner: they raise no altar, light no fire, pour no libations; there is no sound of the flute, no putting on of chaplets, no consecrated barley-cake; but the man who wishes to sacrifice brings his victim to a spot of ground which is pure from pollution, and there calls upon the name of the god to whom he intends to offer. It is usual to have the turban encircled with a wreath, most commonly of myrtle. The sacrificer is not allowed to pray for blessings on himself alone, but he prays for the welfare of the king, and of the whole Persian people, among whom he is of necessity included. He cuts the victim in pieces,

1 The readiness of the Persians to adopt foreign customs, even in religion, is very remarkable. Perhaps the most striking instance is the adoption from the Assyrians of the well-known emblem consisting of a winged circle with or without a human figure rising from the circular space. This emblem is of Assyrian origin, appearing in the earliest sculptures of that country (Layard's Nineveh, vol. i. chap. v.). Its exact meaning is uncertain, but the conjecture is probable, that while in the human head we have the symbol of intelligence, the wings signify omnipresence, and the circle eternity. Thus the Persians were able, without the sacrifice of any principle, to admit it as a religious emblem, which we find them to have done, as early as the times of Darius, *universally* (see the sculptures at Persepolis, Nakhsh-i-Rustam, Behistun, etc.).

2 This identification is altogether a mistake. The Persians, like their Vedic brethren, worshipped the sun under the name of Mithra. This was a portion of the religion which they brought with them from the Indus, and was not adopted from any foreign nation. The name of Mithra does not indeed occur in the Achæmenian inscriptions until the time of Artaxerxes Mnemon, but there is no reason to question the antiquity of his worship in Persia. Xenophon is right in making it a part of the religion of Cyrus (Cyrop. VIII. iii. § 12, and vii. § 3).

and having boiled the flesh, he lays it out upon the tenderest herbage that he can find, trefoil especially. When all is ready, one of the Magi comes forward and chants a hymn, which they say recounts the origin of the gods. It is not lawful to offer sacrifice unless there is a Magus present. After waiting a short time the sacrificer carries the flesh of the victim away with him, and makes whatever use of it he may please.[1]

133. Of all the days in the year, the one which they celebrate most is their birthday. It is customary to have the board furnished on that day with an ampler supply than common. The richer Persians cause an ox, a horse, a camel, and an ass to be baked whole[2] and so served up to them: the poorer classes use instead the smaller kinds of cattle. They eat little solid food but abundance of dessert, which is set on table a few dishes at a time; this it is which makes them say that "the Greeks, when they eat, leave off hungry, having nothing worth mention served up to them after the meats; whereas, if they had more put before them, they would not stop eating." They are very fond of wine, and drink it in large quantities.[3] To vomit or obey natural calls in the presence of another, is forbidden among them. Such are their customs in these matters.

It is also their general practice to deliberate upon affairs of weight when they are drunk; and then on the morrow, when they are sober, the decision to which they came the night before is put before them by the master of the house in which it was made; and if it is then approved of, they act on it; if not, they set it aside. Sometimes, however, they are sober at their first deliberation, but in this case they always reconsider the matter under the influence of wine.[4]

---

1 At the secret meetings of the Ali Allahis of Persia, which in popular belief have attained an infamous notoriety, but which are in reality altogether innocent, are practised many ceremonies that bear a striking resemblance to the old Magian sacrifice.

2 It is a common custom in the East at the present day, to roast sheep whole, even for an ordinary repast; and on fête days it is done in Dalmatia and in other parts of Europe.

3 At the present day, among the "bons vivants" of Persia, it is usual to sit for hours before dinner drinking wine, and eating dried fruits, such as filberts, almonds, pistachio-nuts, melon seeds, etc. A party, indeed, often sits down at seven o'clock, and the dinner is not brought in till eleven.

4 Tacitus asserts that the Germans were in the habit of deliberating on peace and war under the influence of wine, reserving their determination for the morrow.

134. When they meet each other in the streets, you may know if the persons meeting are of equal rank by the following token; if they are, instead of speaking, they kiss each other on the lips. In the case where one is a little inferior to the other, the kiss is given on the cheek; where the difference of rank is great, the inferior prostrates himself upon the ground.[1] Of nations, they honour most their nearest neighbours, whom they esteem next to themselves; those who live beyond these they honour in the second degree; and so with the remainder, the further they are removed, the less the esteem in which they hold them. The reason is, that they look upon themselves as very greatly superior in all respects to the rest of mankind, regarding others as approaching to excellence in proportion as they dwell nearer to them; whence it comes to pass that those who are the farthest off must be the most degraded of mankind.[2] Under the dominion of the Medes, the several nations of the empire exercised authority over each other in this order. The Medes were lords over all, and governed the nations upon their borders, who in their turn governed the States beyond, who likewise bore rule over the nations which adjoined on them.[3] And this is the order which the Persians also follow in their distribution of honour; for that people, like the Medes, has a progressive scale of administration and government.

135. There is no nation which so readily adopts foreign customs as the Persians. Thus, they have taken the dress of the

1 The Persians are still notorious for their rigid attention to ceremonial and etiquette.

2 In an early stage of geographical knowledge each nation regards itself as occupying the centre of the earth. Herodotus tacitly assumes that Greece is the centre by his theory of ἐσχατίαι or "extremities" (iii. 115). Such was the view commonly entertained among the Greeks, and Delphi, as the centre of Greece, was called "the navel of the world."

3 It is quite inconceivable that there should have been any such system of government either in Media or Persia, as Herodotus here indicates. With respect to Persia, we know that the most distant satrapies were held as directly of the crown as the nearest. The utmost that can be said with truth is, that in the Persian and Median, as in the Roman empire, there were *three* grades; first, the ruling nation; secondly, the conquered provinces; thirdly, the nations on the frontier, governed by their own laws and princes, but owning the supremacy of the imperial power, and reckoned among its tributaries. This was the position in which the Ethiopians, Colchians, and Arabians, stood to Persia (Herod. iii. 97).

Medes,[1] considering it superior to their own; and in war they wear the Egyptian breastplate. As soon as they hear of any luxury, they instantly make it their own: and hence, among other novelties, they have learnt pederasty from the Greeks. Each of them has several wives, and a still larger number of concubines.

136. Next to prowess in arms, it is regarded as the greatest proof of manly excellence, to be the father of many sons. Every year the king sends rich gifts to the man who can show the largest number: for they hold that number is strength. Their sons are carefully instructed from their fifth to their twentieth year, in three things alone, – to ride, to draw the bow, and to speak the truth.[2] Until their fifth year they are not allowed to come into the sight of their father, but pass their lives with the women. This is done that, if the child die young, the father may not be afflicted by its loss.

137. To my mind it is a wise rule, as also is the following – that the king shall not put any one to death for a single fault, and that none of the Persians shall visit a single fault in a slave with any extreme penalty; but in every case the services of the offender shall be set against his misdoings; and, if the latter be found to outweigh the former, the aggrieved party shall then proceed to punishment.[3]

The Persians maintain that never yet did any one kill his own father or mother; but in all such cases they are quite sure that, if matters were sifted to the bottom, it would be found that the child was either a changeling or else the fruit of adultery; for it is not likely they say that the real father should perish by the hands of his child.

138. They hold it unlawful to talk of anything which it is unlawful to do. The most disgraceful thing in the world, they

1 It appears from ch. 71 that the old national dress of the Persians was a close-fitting tunic and trousers of leather. The Median costume, according to Xenophon (Cyrop. VIII. i. § 40) was of a nature to conceal the form, and give it an appearance of grandeur and elegance. It would seem therefore to have been a flowing robe.

2 The Persian regard for truth has been questioned by Larcher on the strength of the speech of Darius in Book iii. (chap. 72). This speech, however, is entirely unhistoric. The special estimation in which truth was held among the Persians is evidenced in a remarkable manner by the inscriptions of Darius, where *lying* is taken as the representative of all evil.

3 Vide infra, vii. 194.

think, is to tell a lie; the next worst, to owe a debt: because, among other reasons, the debtor is obliged to tell lies. If a Persian has the leprosy[1] he is not allowed to enter into a city, or to have any dealings with the other Persians; he must, they say, have sinned against the sun. Foreigners attacked by this disorder, are forced to leave the country: even white pigeons are often driven away, as guilty of the same offence. They never defile a river with the secretions of their bodies, nor even wash their hands in one; nor will they allow others to do so, as they have a great reverence for rivers.

139. There is another peculiarity, which the Persians themselves have never noticed, but which has not escaped my observation. Their names, which are expressive of some bodily or mental excellence, all end with the same letter – the letter which is called San by the Dorians, and Sigma by the Ionians. Any one who examines will find that the Persian names, one and all without exception, end with this letter.[2]

140. Thus much I can declare of the Persians with entire certainty, from my own actual knowledge. There is another custom which is spoken of with reserve, and not openly, concerning their dead. It is said that the body of a male Persian is never buried, until it has been torn either by a dog or a bird of prey.[3] That the Magi have this custom is beyond a doubt, for they practise it without any concealment. The dead bodies are covered with wax, and then buried in the ground.

The Magi are a very peculiar race, different entirely from the Egyptian priests, and indeed from all other men whatsoever. The Egyptian priests make it a point of religion not to kill any live animals except those which they offer in sacrifice. The Magi, on the contrary, kill animals of all kinds with their own hands, excepting dogs[4] and men. They even seem to take a delight in

1 With the Persian isolation of the leper, compare the Jewish practice (Lev. xiii. 46. 2 Kings vii. 3; xv. 5. Luke xvii. 12).

2 Here Herodotus was again mistaken. The Persian names of men which terminate with a consonant end indeed invariably with the letter *s*, or rather *sh*, as *Kurúsh* (Cyrus), *Dáryavush* (Darius). But a large number of Persian names of men were pronounced with a vowel termination, not expressed in writing, and in these the last consonant might be almost any letter.

3 Agathias and Strabo also mention this strange custom, which still prevails among the Parsees wherever they are found, whether in Persia or in India.

4 The dog is represented in the Zendavesta as the special animal of Ormazd, and is still regarded with peculiar reverence by the Parsees.

the employment, and kill, as readily as they do other animals, ants and snakes, and such like flying or creeping things. However, since this has always been their custom, let them keep to it. I return to my former narrative.

141. Immediately after the conquest of Lydia by the Persians, the Ionian and Æolian Greeks sent ambassadors to Cyrus at Sardis, and prayed to become his lieges on the footing which they had occupied under Crœsus. Cyrus listened attentively to their proposals, and answered them by a fable. "There was a certain piper," he said, "who was walking one day by the seaside, when he espied some fish; so he began to pipe to them, imagining they would come out to him upon the land. But as he found at last that his hope was vain, he took a net, and enclosing a great draught of fishes, drew them ashore. The fish then began to leap and dance; but the piper said, 'Cease your dancing now, as you did not choose to come and dance when I piped to you.'" Cyrus gave this answer to the Ionians and Æolians, because when he urged them by his messengers to revolt from Crœsus, they refused; but now, when his work was done, they came to offer their allegiance. It was in anger, therefore, that he made them this reply. The Ionians, on hearing it, set to work to fortify their towns, and held meetings at the Panionium, which were attended by all excepting the Milesians, with whom Cyrus had concluded a separate treaty, by which he allowed them the terms they had formerly obtained from Crœsus. The other Ionians resolved, with one accord, to send ambassadors to Sparta to implore assistance.

142. Now the Ionians of Asia, who meet at the Panionium, have built their cities in a region where the air and climate are the most beautiful in the whole world: for no other region is equally blessed with Ionia, neither above it nor below it, nor east nor west of it. For in other countries either the climate is over cold and damp, or else the heat and drought are sorely oppressive. The Ionians do not all speak the same language, but use in different places four different dialects. Towards the south their first city is Miletus, next to which lie Myus and Priênê;[1] all these three are in Caria and have the same dialect. Their cities in Lydia are the following: Ephesus, Colophon, Lebedus, Teos,

1 Miletus, Myus, and Priênê all lay near the mouth of the Mæander (the modern *Mendere*). At their original colonisation they were all maritime cities.

Clazomenæ, and Phocæa.[1] The inhabitants of these towns have none of the peculiarities of speech which belong to the three first-named cities, but use a dialect of their own. There remain three other Ionian towns, two situate in isles, namely, Samos and Chios; and one upon the mainland, which is Erythræ. Of these Chios and Erythræ have the same dialect, while Samos possesses a language peculiar to itself. Such are the four varieties of which I spoke.

143. Of the Ionians at this period, one people, the Milesians, were in no danger of attack, as Cyrus had received them into alliance. The islanders also had as yet nothing to fear, since Phœnicia was still independent of Persia, and the Persians themselves were not a seafaring people. The Milesians had separated from the common cause solely on account of the extreme weakness of the Ionians: for, feeble as the power of the entire Hellenic race was at that time, of all its tribes the Ionic was by far the feeblest and least esteemed, not possessing a single State of any mark excepting Athens. The Athenians and most of the other Ionic States over the world, went so far in their dislike of the name as actually to lay it aside; and even at the present day the greater number of them seem to me to be ashamed of it. But the twelve cities in Asia have always gloried in the appellation; they gave the temple which they built for themselves the name of the Panionium, and decreed that it should not be open to any of the other Ionic States; no State, however, except Smyrna, has craved admission to it.

144. In the same way the Dorians of the region which is now called the Pentapolis, but which was formerly known as the Doric Hexapolis, exclude all their Dorian neighbours from their temple, the Triopium:[2] nay, they have even gone so far as to shut out from it certain of their own body who were guilty of an offence against the customs of the place. In the games which were anciently celebrated in honour of the Triopian Apollo, the prizes given to the victors were tripods of brass; and the rule was that these tripods should not be carried away from the

1 These cities are enumerated in the order in which they stood, from south to north. Erythræ lay on the coast opposite Chios, between Teos and Clazomenæ.

2 The Triopium was built on a promontory of the same name within the territory of the Cnidians.

temple, but should then and there be dedicated to the god. Now a man of Halicarnassus, whose name was Agasicles, being declared victor in the games, in open contempt of the law, took the tripod home to his own house and there hung it against the wall. As a punishment for this fault, the five other cities, Lindus, Ialyssus, Cameirus, Cos, and Cnidus, deprived the sixth city, Halicarnassus, of the right of entering the temple.[1]

145. The Ionians founded twelve cities in Asia, and refused to enlarge the number, on account (as I imagine) of their having been divided into twelve States when they lived in the Peloponnese; just as the Achæans, who drove them out, are at the present day. The first city of the Achæans after Sicyon, is Pellênê, next to which are Ægeira, Ægæ upon the Crathis, a stream which is never dry, and from which the Italian Crathis[2] received its name, – Bura, Helicé – where the Ionians took refuge on their defeat by the Achæan invaders, – Ægium, Rhypes, Patreis, Phareis, Olenus on the Peirus, which is a large river, – Dymé and Tritæeis, all sea-port towns except the last two, which lie up the country.

146. These are the twelve divisions of what is now Achæa, and was formerly Ionia; and it was owing to their coming from a country so divided that the Ionians, on reaching Asia, founded their twelve States: for it is the height of folly to maintain that these Ionians are more Ionian than the rest, or in any respect better born, since the truth is that no small portion of them were Abantians from Eubœa, who are not even Ionians in name; and, besides, there were mixed up with the emigration, Minyæ from Orchomenus, Cadmeians, Dryopians, Phocians from the several cities of Phocis, Molossians, Arcadian Pelasgi, Dorians from Epidaurus, and many other distinct tribes. Even those who came from the Prytanêum of Athens,[3] and reckon themselves the

1 Lindus, Ialyssus, and Cameirus were in Rhodes; Cos was on the island of the same name, at the mouth of the Ceramic Gulf. Cnidus and Halicarnassus were on the mainland, the former near to the Triopium, the latter on the north shore of the Ceramic Gulf, on the site now occupied by *Boodroom.* These six cities formed an Amphictyony, which held its meetings at the temple of Apollo, called the Triopium, near Cnidus, the most central of the cities.

2 The Italian Crathis ran close by our author's adopted city, Thurium (infra, v. 45).

3 This expression alludes to the solemnities which accompanied the sending out of a colony. In the Prytanêum, or Government-house, of each state was preserved the sacred fire, which was never allowed to go out, whereon the life of the State was supposed to depend. When a colony took its departure, the

purest Ionians of all, brought no wives with them to the new country, but married Carian girls, whose fathers they had slain. Hence these women made a law, which they bound themselves by an oath to observe, and which they handed down to their daughters after them, "That none should ever sit at meat with her husband, or call him by his name;" because the invaders slew their fathers, their husbands, and their sons, and then forced them to become their wives. It was at Miletus that these events took place.

147. The kings, too, whom they set over them, were either Lycians, of the blood of Glaucus,[1] son of Hippolochus, or Pylian Caucons[2] of the blood of Codrus, son of Melanthus; or else from both those families. But since these Ionians set more store by the name than any of the others, let them pass for the pure-bred Ionians; though truly all are Ionians who have their origin from Athens, and keep the Apaturia.[3] This is a festival which all the Ionians celebrate, except the Ephesians and the Colophonians, whom a certain act of bloodshed excludes from it.

148. The Panionium[4] is a place in Mycalé, facing the north, which was chosen by the common voice of the Ionians and made sacred to Heliconian Poseidon.[5] Mycalé itself is a promontory of the mainland, stretching out westward towards Samos, in which the Ionians assemble from all their States to keep the feast

---

leaders went in solemn procession to the Prytanêum of the mother city, and took fresh fire from the sacred hearth, which was conveyed to the Prytanêum of the new settlement.

1 See Hom. Il. ii. 876.

2 The Caucons are reckoned by Strabo among the earliest inhabitants of Greece, and associated with the Pelasgi, Leleges, and Dryopes (vii. p. 465). Like their kindred tribes, they were very widely spread. Their chief settlements, however, appear to have been on the north coast of Asia Minor.

3 The Apaturia was the solemn annual meeting of the phratries, for the purpose of registering the children of the preceding year whose birth entitled them to citizenship. It took place in the month Pyanepsion (November), and lasted three days.

4 Under the name of Panionium are included both a tract of ground and a temple. It is the former of which Herodotus here speaks particularly, as the place in which the great Pan-Ionic festival was held. The spot was on the north side of the promontory of Mycalé. The Panionium was in the territory of Priêné, and consequently under the guardianship of that state.

5 Heliconian Poseidon was so called from Helicé, which is mentioned above among the ancient Ionian cities in the Peloponnese (ch. 145). This had been the central point of the old confederacy, and the temple there had been in old times their place of meeting.

of the Panionia.¹ The names of festivals, not only among the Ionians but among all the Greeks, end, like the Persian proper names, in one and the same letter.

149. The above-mentioned, then, are the twelve towns of the Ionians. The Æolic cities are the following:— Cymé, called also Phricônis, Larissa, Neonteichus, Temnus, Cilla, Notium, Ægiroëssa, Pitané, Ægææ, Myrina, and Gryneia. These are the eleven ancient cities of the Æolians. Originally, indeed, they had twelve cities upon the mainland, like the Ionians, but the Ionians deprived them of Smyrna, one of the number. The soil of Æolis is better than that of Ionia, but the climate is less agreeable.

150. The following is the way in which the loss of Smyrna happened. Certain men of Colophon had been engaged in a sedition there, and being the weaker party, were driven by the others into banishment. The Smyrnæans received the fugitives, who, after a time, watching their opportunity, while the inhabitants were celebrating a feast to Dionysus outside the walls, shut to the gates, and so got possession of the town. The Æolians of the other States came to their aid, and terms were agreed on between the parties, the Ionians consenting to give up all the moveables, and the Æolians making a surrender of the place. The expelled Smyrnæans were distributed among the other States of the Æolians, and were everywhere admitted to citizenship.

151. These, then, were all the Æolic cities upon the mainland, with the exception of those about Mount Ida, which made no part of this confederacy.² As for the islands, Lesbos contains five cities.³ Arisba, the sixth, was taken by the Methymnæans, their kinsmen, and the inhabitants reduced to slavery. Tenedos contains one city, and there is another which is built on what are called the Hundred Isles.⁴ The Æolians of Lesbos and Tenedos, like the Ionian islanders, had at this time nothing to fear. The

1 It is remarkable that Thucydides, writing so shortly after Herodotus, should speak of the Pan-Ionic festival at Mycalé as no longer of any importance, and regard it as practically superseded by the festival of the Ephesia, held near Ephesus (iii. 104). Still the old feast continued, and was celebrated as late as the time of Augustus.

2 The district here indicated, and commonly called the Troad, extended from Adramyttium on the south to Priapus on the north.

3 The five Lesbian cities were: Mytilêné, Methymna, Antissa, Eresus, and Pyrrha.

4 These islands lay off the promontory which separated the bay of Atarneus from that of Adramyttium, opposite to the northern part of the island of Lesbos.

other Æolians decided in their common assembly to follow the
Ionians, whatever course they should pursue.

152. When the deputies of the Ionians and Æolians, who had
journeyed with all speed to Sparta, reached the city, they chose
one of their number, Pythermus, a Phocæan, to be their spokesman. In order to draw together as large an audience as possible,
he clothed himself in a purple garment, and so attired stood forth
to speak. In a long discourse he besought the Spartans to come
to the assistance of his countrymen, but they were not to be
persuaded, and voted against sending any succour. The deputies
accordingly went their way, while the Lacedæmonians, notwithstanding the refusal which they had given to the prayer of the
deputation, despatched a penteconter[1] to the Asiatic coast with
certain Spartans on board, for the purpose, as I think, of watching
Cyrus and Ionia. These men, on their arrival at Phocæa, sent to
Sardis Lacrines, the most distinguished of their number, to pro-
hibit Cyrus, in the name of the Lacedæmonians, from offering
molestation to any city of Greece, since they would not allow it.

153. Cyrus is said, on hearing the speech of the herald, to
have asked some Greeks who were standing by, "Who these
Lacedæmonians were, and what was their number, that they
dared to send him such a notice?"[2] When he had received their
reply, he turned to the Spartan herald and said, "I have never
yet been afraid of any men, who have a set place in the middle
of their city, where they come together to cheat each other and
forswear themselves. If I live, the Spartans shall have troubles
enough of their own to talk of, without concerning themselves
about the Ionians." Cyrus intended these words as a reproach
against all the Greeks, because of their having market-places
where they buy and sell, which is a custom unknown to the
Persians, who never make purchases in open marts, and indeed
have not in their whole country a single market-place.[3]

1 Penteconters were ships with fifty rowers, twenty-five on a side, who sat
on a level, as is customary in rowboats at the present day.

2 Compare v. 73 and 105.

3 Markets in the strict sense of the word are still unknown in the East,
where the bazaars, which are collections of shops, take their place. The Persians
of the nobler class would neither buy nor sell at all, since they would be supplied
by their dependents and through presents with all that they required for the
common purposes of life. Those of lower rank would buy at the shops, which
were not allowed in the Forum, or public place of meeting.

After this interview Cyrus quitted Sardis, leaving the city under the charge of Tabalus, a Persian, but appointing Pactyas, a native, to collect the treasure belonging to Crœsus and the other Lydians, and bring it after him. Cyrus himself proceeded towards Agbatana, carrying Crœsus along with him, not regarding the Ionians as important enough to be his immediate object. Larger designs were in his mind. He wished to war in person against Babylon, the Bactrians, the Sacæ,[1] and Egypt; he therefore determined to assign to one of his generals the task of conquering the Ionians.

154. No sooner, however, was Cyrus gone from Sardis than Pactyas induced his countrymen to rise in open revolt against him and his deputy Tabalus. With the vast treasures at his disposal he then went down to the sea, and employed them in hiring mercenary troops, while at the same time he engaged the people of the coast to enrol themselves in his army. He then marched upon Sardis, where he besieged Tabalus, who shut himself up in the citadel.

155. When Cyrus, on his way to Agbatana, received these tidings, he turned to Crœsus and said, "Where will all this end, Crœsus, thinkest thou? It seemeth that these Lydians will not cease to cause trouble both to themselves and others. I doubt me if it were not best to sell them all for slaves. Methinks what I have now done is as if a man were to 'kill the father and then spare the child.' Thou, who wert something more than a father to thy people, I have seized and carried off, and to that people I have entrusted their city. Can I then feel surprise at their rebellion?" Thus did Cyrus open to Crœsus his thoughts; whereat the latter, full of alarm lest Cyrus should lay Sardis in ruins, replied as follows: "Oh! my king, thy words are reasonable; but do not, I beseech thee, give full vent to thy anger, nor doom to destruction an ancient city, guiltless alike of the past and of the present trouble. I caused the one, and in my own person now pay the forfeit. Pactyas has caused the other, he to whom thou gavest Sardis in charge; let him bear the punishment. Grant, then, forgiveness to the Lydians, and to make sure of their never rebelling against thee, or alarming thee more, send and forbid

1 Bactria may be regarded as fairly represented by the modern Balkh. The Sacæ (Scyths) are more difficult to locate; it only appears that their country bordered upon and lay beyond Bactria.

them to keep any weapons of war, command them to wear tunics under their cloaks, and to put buskins upon their legs, and make them bring up their sons to cithern-playing, harping, and shop-keeping. So wilt thou soon see them become women instead of men, and there will be no more fear of their revolting from thee."

156. Crœsus thought the Lydians would even so be better off than if they were sold for slaves, and therefore gave the above advice to Cyrus, knowing that, unless he brought forward some notable suggestion, he would not be able to persuade him to alter his mind. He was likewise afraid lest, after escaping the danger which now pressed, the Lydians at some future time might revolt from the Persians and so bring themselves to ruin. The advice pleased Cyrus, who consented to forego his anger and do as Crœsus had said. Thereupon he summoned to his presence a certain Mede, Mazares by name, and charged him to issue orders to the Lydians in accordance with the terms of Crœsus' discourse. Further, he commanded him to sell for slaves all who had joined the Lydians in their attack upon Sardis, and above aught else to be sure that he brought Pactyas with him alive on his return. Having given these orders Cyrus continued his journey towards the Persian territory.

157. Pactyas, when news came of the near approach of the army sent against him, fled in terror to Cymé. Mazares, therefore, the Median general, who had marched on Sardis with a detachment of the army of Cyrus, finding on his arrival that Pactyas and his troops were gone, immediately entered the town. And first of all he forced the Lydians to obey the orders of his master, and change (as they did from that time) their entire manner of living. Next, he despatched messengers to Cymé, and required to have Pactyas delivered up to him. On this the Cymæans resolved to send to Branchidæ and ask the advice of the god. Branchidæ[1] is situated in the territory of Miletus, above the port of Panormus. There was an oracle there, established in very ancient times, which both the Ionians and Æolians were wont often to consult.

1 The temple of Apollo at Branchidæ and the port Panormus still remain. The former is twelve miles from Miletus, nearly due south. It lies near the shore, about two miles inland from Cape *Monodendri.* It is a magnificent ruin of Ionic architecture. [See Frazer's *Pausanias,* vol. iv. 126 (E. H. B.).]

158. Hither therefore the Cymæans sent their deputies to make inquiry at the shrine, "What the gods would like them to do with the Lydian, Pactyas?" The oracle told them, in reply, to give him up to the Persians. With this answer the messengers returned, and the people of Cymé were ready to surrender him accordingly; but as they were preparing to do so, Aristodicus, son of Heraclides, a citizen of distinction, hindered them. He declared that he distrusted the response, and believed that the messengers had reported it falsely; until at last another embassy, of which Aristodicus himself made part, was despatched, to repeat the former inquiry concerning Pactyas.

159. On their arrival at the shrine of the god, Aristodicus, speaking on behalf of the whole body, thus addressed the oracle: "Oh! king, Pactyas the Lydian, threatened by the Persians with a violent death, has come to us for sanctuary, and lo, they ask him at our hands, calling upon our nation to deliver him up. Now, though we greatly dread the Persian power, yet have we not been bold to give up our suppliant, till we have certain knowledge of thy mind, what thou wouldst have us to do." The oracle thus questioned gave the same answer as before, bidding them surrender Pactyas to the Persians; whereupon Aristodicus, who had come prepared for such an answer, proceeded to make the circuit of the temple, and to take all the nests of young sparrows and other birds that he could find about the building. As he was thus employed, a voice, it is said, came forth from the inner sanctuary, addressing Aristodicus in these words: "Most impious of men, what is this thou hast the face to do? Dost thou tear my suppliants from my temple?" Aristodicus, at no loss for a reply, rejoined, "Oh, king, art thou so ready to protect thy suppliants, and dost thou command the Cymæans to give up a suppliant?" "Yes," returned the god, "I do command it, that so for the impiety you may the sooner perish, and not come here again to consult my oracle about the surrender of suppliants."

160. On the receipt of this answer the Cymæans, unwilling to bring the threatened destruction on themselves by giving up the man, and afraid of having to endure a siege if they continued to harbour him, sent Pactyas away to Mytilênê. On this Mazares despatched envoys to the Mytilenæans to demand the fugitive of them, and they were preparing to give him up for a reward (I cannot say with certainty how large, as the bargain was not

completed), when the Cymæans, hearing what the Mytilenæans
were about, sent a vessel to Lesbos, and conveyed away Pactyas
to Chios. From hence it was that he was surrendered. The
Chians dragged him from the temple of Athena Poliuchus[1] and
gave him up to the Persians, on condition of receiving the district of Atarneus, a tract of Mysia opposite to Lesbos,[2] as the
price of the surrender. Thus did Pactyas fall into the hands of
his pursuers, who kept a strict watch upon him, that they might
be able to produce him before Cyrus. For a long time afterwards
none of the Chians would use the barley of Atarneus to place
on the heads of victims, or make sacrificial cakes of the corn
grown there, but the whole produce of the land was excluded
from all their temples.

161. Meanwhile Mazares, after he had recovered Pactyas
from the Chians, made war upon those who had taken part in
the attack on Tabalus, and in the first place took Priêné and sold
the inhabitants for slaves, after which he overran the whole plain
of the Mæander and the district of Magnesia,[3] both of which he
gave up for pillage to the soldiery. He then suddenly sickened
and died.

162. Upon his death Harpagus was sent down to the coast
to succeed to his command. He also was of the race of the
Medes, being the man whom the Median king, Astyages, feasted
at the unholy banquet, and who lent his aid to place Cyrus upon
the throne. Appointed by Cyrus to conduct the war in these
parts, he entered Ionia, and took the cities by means of mounds.
Forcing the enemy to shut themselves up within their defences,
he heaped mounds of earth against their walls,[4] and thus carried
the towns. Phocæa was the city against which he directed his
first attack.

163. Now the Phocæans were the first of the Greeks who
performed long voyages, and it was they who made the Greeks
acquainted with the Adriatic and with Tyrrhenia, with Iberia, and

1 That is, "Athena, Guardian of the citadel."

2 Atarneus lay to the north of the Æolis of Herodotus, almost exactly
opposite to Mytilênê.

3 *Not* Magnesia *under Sipylus*, but Magnesia *on the Mæander*, one of the few
ancient Greek settlements situated far inland.

4 This plan seems not to have been known to the Lydians. The Persians
had learnt it, in all probability, from the Assyrians, by whom it had long been
practised. (2 Kings xix. 32. Isaiah xxxvii. 33.)

the city of Tartessus.¹ The vessel which they used in their voyages was not the round-built merchant-ship, but the long penteconter. On their arrival at Tartessus, the king of the country, whose name was Arganthônius, took a liking to them. This monarch reigned over the Tartessians for eighty years, and lived to be a hundred and twenty years old. He regarded the Phocæans with so much favour as, at first, to beg them to quit Ionia and settle in whatever part of his country they liked. Afterwards, finding that he could not prevail upon them to agree to this, and hearing that the Mede was growing great in their neighbourhood, he gave them money to build a wall about their town, and certainly he must have given it with a bountiful hand, for the town is many furlongs in circuit, and the wall is built entirely of great blocks of stone skilfully fitted together. The wall, then, was built by his aid.

164. Harpagus, having advanced against the Phocæans with his army, laid siege to their city, first, however, offering them terms. "It would content him," he said, "if the Phocæans would agree to throw down one of their battlements, and dedicate one dwelling-house to the king." The Phocæans, sorely vexed at the thought of becoming slaves, asked a single day to deliberate on the answer they should return, and besought Harpagus during that day to draw off his forces from the walls. Harpagus replied, "that he understood well enough what they were about to do, but nevertheless he would grant their request." Accordingly the troops were withdrawn, and the Phocæans forthwith took advantage of their absence to launch their pentecoters, and put on board their wives and children, their household goods, and even the images of their gods, with all the votive offerings from the fanes, except the paintings and the works in stone or brass, which were left behind. With the rest they embarked, and putting to sea, set sail for Chios. The Persians, on their return, took possession of an empty town.

165. Arrived at Chios, the Phocæans made offers for the purchase of the islands called the Œnussæ,² but the Chians

1 The Iberia of Herodotus is the Spanish Peninsula. Tartessus was a colony founded there very early by the Phœnicians. It was situated beyond the straits at the mouth of the Bætis (*Guadalquivir*), near the site of the modern Cadiz. Tarsus, Tartessus, Tarshish, are variants of the same word. [See Ulick Burke's *History of Spain*, vol. i. ch. i. (E. H. B.).]

2 The Œnussæ lay between Chios and the mainland, opposite the northern extremity of that island (Lat. 38° 33′).

refused to part with them, fearing lest the Phocæans should establish a factory there, and exclude their merchants from the commerce of those seas. On their refusal, the Phocæans, as Arganthônius was now dead, made up their minds to sail to Cyrnus (Corsica), where, twenty years before, following the direction of an oracle,[1] they had founded a city, which was called Alalia. Before they set out, however, on this voyage, they sailed once more to Phocæa, and surprising the Persian troops appointed by Harpagus to garrison the town, put them all to the sword. After this they laid the heaviest curses on the man who should draw back and forsake the armament; and having dropped a heavy mass of iron into the sea, swore never to return to Phocæa till that mass reappeared upon the surface. Nevertheless, as they were preparing to depart for Cyrnus, more than half of their number were seized with such sadness and so great a longing to see once more their city and their ancient homes, that they broke the oath by which they had bound themselves and sailed back to Phocæa.

166. The rest of the Phocæans, who kept their oath, proceeded without stopping upon their voyage, and when they came to Cyrnus established themselves along with the earlier settlers at Alalia and built temples in the place. For five years they annoyed their neighbours by plundering and pillaging on all sides, until at length the Carthaginians and Tyrrhenians[2] leagued against them, and sent each a fleet of sixty ships to attack the town. The Phocæans, on their part, manned all their vessels, sixty in number, and met their enemy on the Sardinian sea. In the engagement which followed the Phocæans were victorious, but their success was only a sort of Cadmeian victory.[3] They lost forty ships in the battle, and the twenty which remained came out of the engagement with beaks so bent and blunted as to be no longer serviceable. The Phocæans therefore sailed back again

1 A most important influence was exercised by the Greek oracles, especially that of Delphi, over the course of Hellenic colonisation. Further instances occur, iv. 155, 157, 159; v. 42.

2 The naval power of the Tyrrhenians was about this time at its height. Populonia and Cære (or Agylla) were the most important of their maritime towns. Like the Greeks at a somewhat earlier period (Thucyd. i. 5), the Tyrrhenians at this time and for some centuries afterwards were pirates.

3 A Cadmeian victory was one from which the victor received more hurt than profit.

to Alalia, and taking their wives and children on board, with such portion of their goods and chattels as the vessels could bear, bade adieu to Cyrnus and sailed to Rhegium.

167. The Carthaginians and Tyrrhenians, who had got into their hands many more than the Phocæans from among the crews of the forty vessels that were destroyed, landed their captives upon the coast after the fight, and stoned them all to death. Afterwards, when sheep, or oxen, or even men of the district of Agylla passed by the spot where the murdered Phocæans lay, their bodies became distorted, or they were seized with palsy, or they lost the use of some of their limbs. On this the people of Agylla sent to Delphi to ask the oracle how they might expiate their sin. The answer of the Pythoness required them to institute the custom, which they still observe, of honouring the dead Phocæans with magnificent funeral rites, and solemn games, both gymnic and equestrian. Such, then, was the fate that befell the Phocæan prisoners. The other Phocæans, who had fled to Rhegium, became after a while the founders of the city called Vela,[1] in the district of Œnotria. This city they colonised, upon the showing of a man of Posidonia,[2] who suggested that the oracle had not meant to bid them set up a town in Cyrnus the island, but set up the worship of Cyrnus the hero.[3]

168. Thus fared it with the men of the city of Phocæa in Ionia. They of Teos[4] did and suffered almost the same; for they too, when Harpagus had raised his mound to the height of their defences, took ship, one and all, and sailing across the sea to Thrace, founded there the city of Abdêra.[5] The site was one which Timêsius of Clazomenæ had previously tried to colonise, but without any lasting success, for he was expelled by the Thracians. Still the Teians of Abdêra worship him to this day as a hero.

169. Of all the Ionians these two states alone, rather than submit to slavery, forsook their fatherland. The others (I except

1 This is the town more commonly called Velia or Elea, where soon afterwards the great Eleatic school of philosophy arose.

2 This is the place now known as *Pæstum*, so famous for its beautiful ruins.

3 Cyrnus was a son of Heracles.

4 Teos was situated on the south side of the isthmus which joined the peninsula of Erythræ to the mainland, very nearly opposite Clazomenæ (Strab. xiv. p. 922). It was the birthplace of Anacreon, the lyric poet.

5 For the site of Abdêra, vide infra, vii. 109.

Miletus) resisted Harpagus no less bravely than those who fled their country, and performed many feats of arms, each fighting in their own defence, but one after another they suffered defeat; the cities were taken, and the inhabitants submitted, remaining in their respective countries, and obeying the behests of their new lords. Miletus, as I have already mentioned, had made terms with Cyrus, and so continued at peace. Thus was continental Ionia once more reduced to servitude; and when the Ionians of the islands saw their brethren upon the mainland subjugated, they also, dreading the like, gave themselves up to Cyrus.[1]

170. It was while the Ionians were in this distress, but still, amid it all, held their meetings, as of old, at the Panionium, that Bias of Priêné, who was present at the festival, recommended (as I am informed) a project of the very highest wisdom, which would, had it been embraced, have enabled the Ionians to become the happiest and most flourishing of the Greeks. He exhorted them "to join in one body, set sail for Sardinia, and there found a single Pan-Ionic city; so they would escape from slavery and rise to great fortune, being masters of the largest island in the world,[2] exercising dominion even beyond its bounds; whereas if they stayed in Ionia, he saw no prospect of their ever recovering their lost freedom." Such was the counsel which Bias gave the Ionians in their affliction. Before their misfortunes began, Thales, a man of Miletus, of Phœnician descent, had recommended a different plan. He counselled them to establish a single seat of government, and pointed out Teos as the fittest place for it; "for that," he said, "was the centre of Ionia. Their other cities might still continue to enjoy their own laws, just as if they were independent states." This also was good advice.

171. After conquering the Ionians, Harpagus proceeded to attack the Carians, the Caunians, and the Lycians. The Ionians and Æolians were forced to serve in his army. Now, of the above nations the Carians are a race who came into the mainland from the islands. In ancient times they were subjects of king Minos,

1 This statement appears to be too general. Samos certainly maintained her independence till the reign of Darius (vide infra, iii. 120).

2 Herodotus appears to have been entirely convinced that there was no island in the world so large as Sardinia. He puts the assertion into the mouth of Histiæus (v. 106), and again (vi. 2) repeats the statement, without expressing any doubt of the fact.

and went by the name of Leleges, dwelling among the isles, and, so far as I have been able to push my inquiries, never liable to give tribute to any man. They served on board the ships of king Minos whenever he required; and thus, as he was a great conqueror and prospered in his wars, the Carians were in his day the most famous by far of all the nations of the earth. They likewise were the inventors of three things, the use of which was borrowed from them by the Greeks; they were the first to fasten crests on helmets and to put devices on shields, and they also invented handles for shields. In the earlier times shields were without handles, and their wearers managed them by the aid of a leathern thong, by which they were slung round the neck and left shoulder.[1] Long after the time of Minos, the Carians were driven from the islands by the Ionians and Dorians, and so settled upon the mainland. The above is the account which the Cretans give of the Carians: the Carians themselves say very differently. They maintain that they are the aboriginal inhabitants of the part of the mainland where they now dwell,[2] and never had any other name than that which they still bear; and in proof of this they show an ancient temple of Carian Jove in the country of the Mylasians,[3] in which the Mysians and Lydians have the right of worshipping, as brother races to the Carians: for Lydus and Mysus, they say, were brothers of Car. These nations, therefore, have the aforesaid right; but such as are of a different race, even though they have come to use the Carian tongue, are excluded from this temple.

172. The Caunians,[4] in my judgment, are aboriginals; but by their own account they came from Crete. In their language, either they have approximated to the Carians, or the Carians to them – on this point I cannot speak with certainty. In their customs, however, they differ greatly from the Carians, and not only so, but from all other men. They think it a most honourable

1 Homer generally represents his heroes as managing their shields in this way (Il. ii. 388; iv. 796; xi. 38; xii. 401, etc). Sometimes, however, he speaks of shields with handles to them (viii. 193).

2 It seems probable that the Carians, who were a kindred nation to the Lydians and the Mysians, belonged originally to the Asiatic continent, and thence spread to the islands.

3 Mylasa was an inland town of Caria, about 20 miles from the sea. It was the capital of the later Carian kingdom (B.C. 385–334).

4 The Caunians occupied a small district on the coast.

practice for friends or persons of the same age, whether they be men, women, or children, to meet together in large companies, for the purpose of drinking wine. Again, on one occasion they determined that they would no longer make use of the foreign temples which had been long established among them, but would worship their own old ancestral gods alone. Then their whole youth took arms, and striking the air with their spears, marched to the Calyndic frontier,[1] declaring that they were driving out the foreign gods.

173. The Lycians are in good truth anciently from Crete; which island, in former days, was wholly peopled with barbarians. A quarrel arising there between the two sons of Europa, Sarpedon and Minos, as to which of them should be king, Minos, whose party prevailed, drove Sarpedon and his followers into banishment. The exiles sailed to Asia,[2] and landed on the Milyan territory. Milyas was the ancient name of the country now inhabited by the Lycians:[3] the Milyæ of the present day were, in those times, called Solymi.[4] So long as Sarpedon reigned, his followers kept the name which they brought with them from Crete, and were called Termilæ, as the Lycians still are by those who live in their neighbourhood. But after Lycus, the son of Pandion, banished from Athens by his brother Ægeus, had found a refuge with Sarpedon in the country of these Termilæ, they came, in course of time, to be called from him Lycians. Their customs are partly Cretan, partly Carian. They have, however, one singular custom in which they differ from every other nation in the world. They take the mother's and not the father's name. Ask a Lycian who he is, and he answers by giving his own name, that of his mother, and so on in the female line. Moreover, if a free woman marry a man who is a slave, their children are

---

1 Calynda was on the borders of Caria and Lycia.

2 It is doubtful whether there is any truth at all in this tale, which would connect the Greeks with Lycia. One thing is clear, namely, that the real Lycian people of history were an entirely distinct race from the Greeks.

3 Milyas continued to be a *district* of Lycia in the age of Augustus.

4 The Solymi were mentioned by Chærilus, who was contemporary with Herodotus and wrote a poem on the Persian War, as forming a part of the army of Xerxes. Their language, according to him, was Phœnician. That the Pisidians were Solymi is asserted by Pliny. The same people left their name in Lycia to Mount Solyma. Here we seem to have a trace of a Semitic occupation of these countries preceding the Indo-European. (Comp. Hom. Il. vi. 184.) [Acc. to Tacitus, *Hist.* v. 2, some made them the ancestors of the Jews (E. H. B.).]

full citizens; but if a free man marry a foreign woman, or live with a concubine, even though he be the first person in the State, the children forfeit all the rights of citizenship.

174. Of these nations, the Carians submitted to Harpagus without performing any brilliant exploits. Nor did the Greeks who dwelt in Caria behave with any greater gallantry. Among them were the Cnidians, colonists from Lacedæmon, who occupy a district facing the sea, which is called Triopium. This region adjoins upon the Bybassian Chersonese; and, except a very small space, is surrounded by the sea, being bounded on the north by the Ceramic Gulf, and on the south by the channel towards the islands of Symé and Rhodes. While Harpagus was engaged in the conquest of Ionia, the Cnidians, wishing to make their country an island, attempted to cut through this narrow neck of land, which was no more than five furlongs across from sea to sea. Their whole territory lay inside the isthmus; for where Cnidia ends towards the mainland, the isthmus begins which they were now seeking to cut through. The work had been commenced, and many hands were employed upon it, when it was observed that there seemed to be something unusual and unnatural in the number of wounds that the workmen received, especially about their eyes, from the splintering of the rock. The Cnidians, therefore, sent to Delphi, to inquire what it was that hindered their efforts; and received, according to their own account, the following answer from the oracle:—

> Fence not the isthmus off, nor dig it through —
> Jove would have made an island, had he wished.

So the Cnidians ceased digging, and when Harpagus advanced with his army, they gave themselves up to him without striking a blow.

175. Above Halicarnassus, and further from the coast, were the Pedasians.[1] With this people, when any evil is about to befall either themselves or their neighbours, the priestess of Athena grows an ample beard. Three times has this marvel happened. They alone, of all the dwellers in Caria, resisted Harpagus for a while, and gave him much trouble, maintaining themselves in a certain mountain called Lida, which they had fortified; but in course of time they also were forced to submit.

1 Pedasus was reckoned in Caria (infra, v. 121). Its exact site is uncertain.

176. When Harpagus, after these successes, led his forces into the Xanthian plain,[1] the Lycians of Xanthus[2] went out to meet him in the field: though but a small band against a numerous host, they engaged in battle, and performed many glorious exploits. Overpowered at last, and forced within their walls, they collected into the citadel their wives and children, all their treasures, and their slaves; and having so done, fired the building, and burnt it to the ground. After this, they bound themselves together by dreadful oaths, and sallying forth against the enemy, died sword in hand, not one escaping. Those Lycians who now claim to be Xanthians, are foreign immigrants, except eighty families, who happened to be absent from the country, and so survived the others. Thus was Xanthus taken by Harpagus,[3] and Caunus fell in like manner into his hands; for the Caunians in the main followed the example of the Lycians.

177. While the lower parts of Asia were in this way brought under by Harpagus, Cyrus in person subjected the upper regions, conquering every nation, and not suffering one to escape. Of these conquests I shall pass by the greater portion, and give an account of those only which gave him the most trouble, and are the worthiest of mention. When he had brought all the rest of the continent under his sway, he made war on the Assyrians.[4]

178. Assyria possesses a vast number of great cities,[5] whereof the most renowned and strongest at this time was Babylon, whither, after the fall of Nineveh, the seat of government had been removed. The following is a description of the place:— The city stands on a broad plain, and is an exact square, a hundred and twenty furlongs in length each way, so that the entire circuit is four hundred and eighty furlongs.[6] While such is its size, in

1 The Xanthian plain is to the south of the city, being in fact the alluvial deposit of the river Xanthus.

2 The real name of the city which the Greeks called Xanthus seems to have been Arna or Arīna. This is confirmed by the monuments of the country.

3 There is reason to believe that the government of Lycia remained in the family of Harpagus.

4 Herodotus includes Babylonia in Assyria (vide supra, ch. 106).

5 The large number of important cities in Assyria, especially if we include in it Babylonia, is one of the most remarkable features of Assyrian greatness.

6 The vast space enclosed within the walls of Babylon is noticed by Aristotle. (Polit. iii. 1, sub fin.).

magnificence there is no other city that approaches to it. It is surrounded, in the first place, by a broad and deep moat, full of water, behind which rises a wall fifty royal cubits in width, and two hundred in height.[1] (The royal cubit[2] is longer by three fingers' breadth than the common cubit.)[3]

179. And here I may not omit to tell the use to which the mould dug out of the great moat was turned, nor the manner wherein the wall was wrought. As fast as they dug the moat the soil which they got from the cutting was made into bricks, and when a sufficient number were completed they baked the bricks in kilns. Then they set to building, and began with bricking the borders of the moat, after which they proceeded to construct the wall itself, using throughout for their cement hot bitumen, and interposing a layer of wattled reeds at every thirtieth course of the bricks.[4] On the top, along the edges of the wall, they constructed buildings of a single chamber facing one another, leaving between them room for a four-horse chariot to turn. In the circuit of the wall are a hundred gates, all of brass, with brazen lintels and side-posts. The bitumen used in the work was brought to Babylon from the Is, a small stream which flows into the Euphrates at the point where the city of the same name stands, eight days' journey from Babylon. Lumps of bitumen are found in great abundance in this river.

180. The city is divided into two portions by the river which runs through the midst of it. This river is the Euphrates, a broad, deep, swift stream, which rises in Armenia, and empties itself into the Erythræan sea. The city wall is brought down on both sides to the edge of the stream: thence, from the corners of the wall, there is carried along each bank of the river a fence of burnt bricks. The houses are mostly three and four stories high; the streets all run in straight lines, not only those parallel to the river,

---

1 The great width and height of the walls are noticed in Scripture (Jerem. li. 53, 58). There can be no doubt that the Babylonians and Assyrians surrounded their cities with walls of a height which, to us, is astounding.

2 The Greek metrical system was closely connected with the Babylonian.

3 Assuming at present that the Babylonian foot nearly equalled the English, the common cubit would have been 1 foot 8 inches, and the Royal cubit 1 foot 10.4 inches.

4 Layers of reeds are found in some of the remains of brick buildings at present existing in Babylonia, but usually at much smaller intervals than here indicated.

but also the cross streets which lead down to the water-side. At the river end of these cross streets are low gates in the fence that skirts the stream, which are, like the great gates in the outer wall, of brass, and open on the water.

181. The outer wall is the main defence of the city. There is, however, a second inner wall, of less thickness than the first, but very little inferior to it in strength.[1] The centre of each division of the town was occupied by a fortress. In the one stood the palace of the kings,[2] surrounded by a wall of great strength and size: in the other was the sacred precinct of Zeus Bel,[3] a square enclosure two furlongs each way, with gates of solid brass; which was also remaining in my time. In the middle of the precinct there was a tower of solid masonry, a furlong in length and breadth, upon which was raised a second tower, and on that a third, and so on up to eight. The ascent to the top is on the outside, by a path which winds round all the towers. When one is about half-way up, one finds a resting-place and seats, where persons are wont to sit some time on their way to the summit. On the topmost tower there is a spacious temple, and inside the temple stands a couch of unusual size, richly adorned, with a golden table by its side. There is no statue of any kind set up in the place, nor is the chamber occupied of nights by any one but a single native woman, who, as the Chaldæans, the priests of this god,[4] affirm, is chosen for himself by the deity out of all the women of the land.

182. They also declare – but I for my part do not credit it – that the god comes down in person into this chamber, and sleeps upon the couch. This is like the story told by the Egyptians of

1 The "inner wall" here mentioned may have been the wall of Nebuchadnezzar's new city, which lay entirely within the ancient circuit.

2 This is the mass or mound still called the Kasr or Palace, "a square of 700 yards in length and breadth." (Rich, First Memoir, p. 22.) It is an immense pile of brickwork, chiefly of the finest kind.

3 The Babylonian worship of Bel is well known to us from Scripture (Isaiah xlvi. 1; Jerem. l. 2; Apoc. Dan. xii. 16). There is little doubt that he was (at least in the later times), the recognised head of the Babylonian Pantheon, and therefore properly identified by the Greeks with their Zeus or Jupiter.

4 The Chaldæans then appear to have been a branch of the great Hamite race of *Akkad*, which inhabited Babylonia from the earliest times. With this race originated the art of writing, the building of cities, the institution of a religious system, and the cultivation of all science, and of astronomy in particular.

what takes place in their city of Thebes,[1] where a woman always passes the night in the temple of the Theban Zeus.[2] In each case the woman is said to be debarred all intercourse with men. It is also like the custom of Patara, in Lycia, where the priestess who delivers the oracles, during the time that she is so employed – for at Patara there is not always an oracle,[3] – is shut up in the temple every night.

183. Below, in the same precinct, there is a second temple, in which is a sitting figure of Zeus, all of gold. Before the figure stands a large golden table, and the throne whereon it sits, and the base on which the throne is placed, are likewise of gold. The Chaldæans told me that all the gold together was eight hundred talents' weight. Outside the temple are two altars, one of solid gold, on which it is only lawful to offer sucklings; the other a common altar, but of great size, on which the full-grown animals are sacrificed. It is also on the great altar that the Chaldæans burn the frankincense, which is offered to the amount of a thousand talents' weight, every year, at the festival of the God. In the time of Cyrus there was likewise in this temple a figure of a man, twelve cubits high, entirely of solid gold. I myself did not see this figure, but I relate what the Chaldæans report concerning it. Darius, the son of Hystaspes, plotted to carry the statue off, but had not the hardihood to lay his hands upon it. Xerxes, however, the son of Darius, killed the priest who forbade him to move the statue, and took it away.[4] Besides the ornaments which I have mentioned, there are a large number of private offerings in this holy precinct.[5]

1 This fable of the god coming personally into his temple was contrary to the Egyptian belief in the nature of the gods. It was only a figurative expression, similar to that of the Jews, who speak of God visiting and dwelling in his holy hill, and was not intended to be taken literally.

2 The *Theban* Zeus, or god worshipped as the Supreme Being in the city of Thebes, was Ammon (Amun). Herodotus says the *Theban* rather than the Egyptian Zeus, because various gods were worshipped in various parts of Egypt as supreme.

3 Patara lay on the shore, a little to the east of the Xanthus.

4 There can be little doubt that this was done by Xerxes after the revolt of Babylon. Arrian relates that Xerxes not only plundered but *destroyed* the temple on his return from Greece.

5 The great temple of Babylon, regarding which the Greeks have left so many notices, is beyond all doubt to be identified with the enormous mound to which the Arabs universally apply the title of *Bâbil*. [For later information on the subject of this great temple, see Hilprecht, *Explorations in Bible Lands*, p. 19 sqq. (E. H. B.).]

184. Many sovereigns have ruled over this city of Babylon, and lent their aid to the building of its walls and the adornment of its temples, of whom I shall make mention in my Assyrian history. Among them two were women. Of these, the earlier, called Semiramis, held the throne five generations before the later princess. She raised certain embankments well worthy of inspection, in the plain near Babylon, to control the river, which, till then, used to overflow, and flood the whole country round about.

185. The later of the two queens, whose name was Nitocris, a wiser princess than her predecessor, not only left behind her, as memorials of her occupancy of the throne, the works which I shall presently describe, but also, observing the great power and restless enterprise of the Medes, who had taken so large a number of cities, and among them Nineveh, and expecting to be attacked in her turn, made all possible exertions to increase the defences of her empire. And first, whereas the river Euphrates, which traverses the city, ran formerly with a straight course to Babylon, she, by certain excavations which she made at some distance up the stream, rendered it so winding that it comes three several times in sight of the same village, a village in Assyria, which is called Ardericca; and to this day, they who would go from our sea to Babylon, on descending to the river touch three times, and on three different days, at this very place. She also made an embankment along each side of the Euphrates, wonderful both for breadth and height, and dug a basin for a lake a great way above Babylon, close alongside of the stream, which was sunk everywhere to the point where they came to water, and was of such breadth that the whole circuit measured four hundred and twenty furlongs. The soil dug out of this basin was made use of in the embankments along the waterside. When the excavation was finished, she had stones brought, and bordered with them the entire margin of the reservoir. These two things were done, the river made to wind, and the lake excavated, that the stream might be slacker by reason of the number of curves, and the voyage be rendered circuitous, and that at the end of the voyage it might be necessary to skirt the lake and so make a long round. All these works were on that side of Babylon where the passes lay, and the roads into Media were the straightest, and the aim of the queen in making them was to prevent the Medes from holding intercourse with the Babylonians, and so to keep them in ignorance of her affairs.

186. While the soil from the excavation was being thus used for the defence of the city, Nitocris engaged also in another undertaking, a mere by-work compared with those we have already mentioned. The city, as I said, was divided by the river into two distinct portions. Under the former kings, if a man wanted to pass from one of these divisions to the other, he had to cross in a boat; which must, it seems to me, have been very troublesome. Accordingly, while she was digging the lake, Nitocris bethought herself of turning it to a use which should at once remove this inconvenience, and enable her to leave another monument of her reign over Babylon. She gave orders for the hewing of immense blocks of stone, and when they were ready and the basin was excavated, she turned the entire stream of the Euphrates into the cutting, and thus for a time, while the basin was filling, the natural channel of the river was left dry. Forthwith she set to work, and in the first place lined the banks of the stream within the city with quays of burnt brick, and also bricked the landing-places opposite the river-gates, adopting throughout the same fashion of brickwork which had been used in the town wall; after which, with the materials which had been prepared, she built, as near the middle of the town as possible, a stone bridge, the blocks whereof were bound together with iron and lead. In the daytime square wooden platforms were laid along from pier to pier, on which the inhabitants crossed the stream; but at night they were withdrawn, to prevent people passing from side to side in the dark to commit robberies. When the river had filled the cutting, and the bridge was finished, the Euphrates was turned back again into its ancient bed; and thus the basin, transformed suddenly into a lake, was seen to answer the purpose for which it was made, and the inhabitants, by help of the basin, obtained the advantage of a bridge.

187. It was this same princess by whom a remarkable deception was planned. She had her tomb constructed in the upper part of one of the principal gateways of the city, high above the heads of the passers by, with this inscription cut upon it:— "If there be one among my successors on the throne of Babylon who is in want of treasure, let him open my tomb, and take as much as he chooses, – not, however, unless he be truly in want, for it will not be for his good." This tomb continued untouched until Darius came to the kingdom. To him it seemed a monstrous thing that he should be unable to use one of the gates of

the town, and that a sum of money should be lying idle, and moreover inviting his grasp, and he not seize upon it. Now he could not use the gate, because, as he drove through, the dead body would have been over his head. Accordingly he opened the tomb; but instead of money, found only the dead body, and a writing which said – "Hadst thou not been insatiate of pelf, and careless how thou gottest it, thou wouldst not have broken open the sepulchres of the dead."

188. The expedition of Cyrus was undertaken against the son of this princess, who bore the same name as his father Labynetus, and was king of the Assyrians. The Great King, when he goes to the wars, is always supplied with provisions carefully prepared at home, and with cattle of his own. Water too from the river Choaspes, which flows by Susa, is taken with him for his drink, as that is the only water which the kings of Persia taste.[1] Wherever he travels, he is attended by a number of four-wheeled cars drawn by mules, in which the Choaspes water, ready boiled for use, and stored in flagons of silver, is moved with him from place to place.

189. Cyrus on his way to Babylon came to the banks of the Gyndes,[2] a stream which, rising in the Matienian mountains, runs through the country of the Dardanians, and empties itself into the river Tigris. The Tigris, after receiving the Gyndes, flows on by the city of Opis, and discharges its waters into the Erythræan sea. When Cyrus reached this stream, which could only be passed in boats, one of the sacred white horses accompanying his march, full of spirit and high mettle, walked into the water, and tried to cross by himself; but the current seized him, swept him along with it, and drowned him in its depths. Cyrus, enraged at the insolence of the river, threatened so to break its strength that in future even women should cross it easily without wetting their knees. Accordingly he put off for a time his attack on Babylon, and, dividing his army into two parts, he marked out by ropes one hundred and eighty trenches on each side of the Gyndes, leading off from it in all directions, and setting his army to dig, some on one side of the river, some on the other, he accomplished his threat by the aid of so great a number of hands, but not without losing thereby the whole summer season.

1 This statement of Herodotus is echoed by various writers.
2 The Gyndes is undoubtedly the *Diyálah*.

190. Having, however, thus wreaked his vengeance on the Gyndes, by dispersing it through three hundred and sixty channels, Cyrus, with the first approach of the ensuing spring, marched forward against Babylon. The Babylonians, encamped without their walls, awaited his coming. A battle was fought at a short distance from the city, in which the Babylonians were defeated by the Persian king, whereupon they withdrew within their defences. Here they shut themselves up, and made light of his siege, having laid in a store of provisions for many years in preparation against this attack; for when they saw Cyrus conquering nation after nation, they were convinced that he would never stop, and that their turn would come at last.

191. Cyrus was now reduced to great perplexity, as time went on and he made no progress against the place. In this distress either some one made the suggestion to him, or he bethought himself of a plan, which he proceeded to put in execution. He placed a portion of his army at the point where the river enters the city, and another body at the back of the place where it issues forth, with orders to march into the town by the bed of the stream, as soon as the water became shallow enough: he then himself drew off with the unwarlike portion of his host, and made for the place where Nitocris dug the basin for the river, where he did exactly what she had done formerly: he turned the Euphrates by a canal into the basin, which was then a marsh, on which the river sank to such an extent that the natural bed of the stream became fordable. Hereupon the Persians who had been left for the purpose at Babylon by the river-side, entered the stream, which had now sunk so as to reach about midway up a man's thigh, and thus got into the town. Had the Babylonians been apprised of what Cyrus was about, or had they noticed their danger, they would never have allowed the Persians to enter the city, but would have destroyed them utterly; for they would have made fast all the street-gates which gave upon the river, and mounting upon the walls along both sides of the stream, would so have caught the enemy as it were in a trap. But, as it was, the Persians came upon them by surprise and so took the city. Owing to the vast size of the place, the inhabitants of the central parts (as the residents at Babylon declare) long after the outer portions of the town were taken, knew nothing of what had chanced, but as they were engaged in a festival, continued dancing and revelling until they learnt the capture but

too certainly. Such, then, were the circumstances of the first taking of Babylon.[1]

192. Among many proofs which I shall bring forward of the power and resources of the Babylonians, the following is of special account. The whole country under the dominion of the Persians, besides paying a fixed tribute, is parcelled out into divisions, which have to supply food to the Great King and his army during different portions of the year. Now out of the twelve months which go to a year, the district of Babylon furnishes food during four, the other regions of Asia during eight; by which it appears that Assyria, in respect of resources, is one-third of the whole of Asia. Of all the Persian governments, or satrapies as they are called by the natives, this is by far the best. When Tritantæchmes, son of Artabazus,[2] held it of the king, it brought him in an artaba of silver every day. The artaba is a Persian measure,[3] and holds three chœnixes more than the medimnus of the Athenians. He also had, belonging to his own private stud, besides war-horses, eight hundred stallions and six-teen thousand mares, twenty to each stallion. Besides which he kept so great a number of Indian hounds,[4] that four large villages of the plain were exempted from all other charges on condition of finding them in food.

193. But little rain falls in Assyria,[5] enough, however, to make the corn begin to sprout, after which the plant is nourished and

1 Herodotus intends to contrast this *first* capture with the *second* capture by Darius Hystaspes, of which he speaks in the latter portion of the third Book.

2 The name of Tritantæchmes is of considerable interest, because it points to the Vedic traditions which the Persians brought with them from the Indus, and of the currency of which in the time of Xerxes we have thus distinct evidence. The name means "strong as Tritan" – this title, which etymologically means "three-bodied," being the Sanscrit and Zend form of the famous Feridun of Persian romance, who divided the world between his three sons, Selm, Tur, and Erij.

3 This is the same name as the *ardeb* of modern Egypt, and, like the *medimnus*, is a corn measure. The *ardeb* is nearly five English bushels.

4 Models of favourite dogs are frequently found in excavating the cities of Babylonia. Some may be seen in the British Museum.

5 Rain is very rare in Babylonia during the summer months, and produc-tiveness depends entirely on irrigation. During the spring there are constant showers, and at other times of the year rain falls frequently, but irregularly, and never in great quantities. The heaviest is in December. In ancient times, when irrigation was carried to a far greater extent than it is at present, the meteorology of the country may probably have been different.

the ears formed by means of irrigation from the river.[1] For the river does not, as in Egypt, overflow the corn-lands of its own accord, but is spread over them by the hand, or by the help of engines.[2] The whole of Babylonia is, like Egypt, intersected with canals. The largest of them all, which runs towards the winter sun, and is impassable except in boats, is carried from the Euphrates into another stream, called the Tigris, the river upon which the town of Nineveh formerly stood. Of all the countries that we know there is none which is so fruitful in grain. It makes no pretension indeed of growing the fig, the olive, the vine, or any other tree of the kind; but in grain it is so fruitful as to yield commonly two-hundred-fold, and when the production is the greatest, even three-hundred-fold. The blade of the wheat-plant and barley-plant is often four fingers in breadth. As for the millet and the sesame, I shall not say to what height they grow, though within my own knowledge; for I am not ignorant that what I have already written concerning the fruitfulness of Babylonia must seem incredible to those who have never visited the country.[3] The only oil they use is made from the sesame-plant.[4] Palm-trees grow in great numbers over the whole of the flat country,[5] mostly of the kind which bears fruit, and this fruit supplies them with bread, wine, and honey. They are cultivated like the fig-tree in all respects, among others in this. The natives tie the fruit of the male-palms, as they are called by the Greeks, to the branches of the date-bearing palm, to let the gall-fly enter the dates and ripen them, and to prevent the fruit from falling

1 At the present day it is not usual to trust even the first sprouting of the corn to nature. The lands are laid under water for a few days before the corn is sown; the water is then withdrawn, and the seed scattered upon the moistened soil.

2 The engine intended by Herodotus seems to have been the common hand-swipe, to which alone the name of $\kappa\eta\lambda\omega\nu\acute{\eta}\ddot{\iota}o\nu$ would properly apply. The ordinary method of irrigation at the present day is by the help of oxen, which draw the water from the river to the top of the bank by means of ropes passed over a roller working between two upright posts.

3 The fertility of Babylonia is celebrated by a number of ancient writers.

4 This is still the case with respect to the people of the plains. The olive is cultivated on the flanks of Mount Zagros, but Babylonia did not extend so far.

5 There is reason to believe that anciently the country was very much more thickly wooded than it is at present. The palm will grow wherever water is brought. In ancient times the whole country between the rivers, and the greater portion of the tract intervening between the Tigris and the mountains, was artificially irrigated.

off. The male-palms, like the wild fig-trees, have usually the gall-fly in their fruit.

194. But that which surprises me most in the land, after the city itself, I will now proceed to mention. The boats which come down the river to Babylon are circular, and made of skins. The frames, which are of willow, are cut in the country of the Armenians above Assyria, and on these, which serve for hulls, a covering of skins is stretched outside, and thus the boats are made, without either stem or stern, quite round like a shield. They are then entirely filled with straw, and their cargo is put on board, after which they are suffered to float down the stream. Their chief freight is wine, stored in casks made of the wood of the palm-tree. They are managed by two men who stand upright in them, each plying an oar, one pulling and the other pushing.[1] The boats are of various sizes, some larger, some smaller; the biggest reach as high as five thousand talents' burthen. Each vessel has a live ass on board; those of larger size have more than one. When they reach Babylon, the cargo is landed and offered for sale; after which the men break up their boats, sell the straw and the frames, and loading their asses with the skins, set off on their way back to Armenia. The current is too strong to allow a boat to return up-stream, for which reason they make their boats of skins rather than wood. On their return to Armenia they build fresh boats for the next voyage.

195. The dress of the Babylonians is a linen tunic reaching to the feet, and above it another tunic made in wool, besides which they have a short white cloak thrown round them, and shoes of a peculiar fashion, not unlike those worn by the Bœotians. They have long hair, wear turbans on their heads, and anoint their whole body with perfumes.[2] Every one carries a

1 Boats of this kind, closely resembling coracles, are represented in the Nineveh sculptures, and still ply on the Euphrates.

2 The dress of the Babylonians appears on the cylinders to be a species of flounced robe, reaching from their neck to their feet. In some representations there is an appearance of a division into two garments; the upper one being a sort of short jacket or tippet, flounced like the under-robe or petticoat. The long hair of the Babylonians is very conspicuous on the cylinders. It either depends in lengthy tresses which fall over the back and shoulders, or is gathered into what seems a club behind. There are several varieties of head-dress; the most usual are a low cap or turban, from which two curved horns branch out, and a high crown or mitre, the appearance of which is very remarkable.

seal,[1] and a walking-stick, carved at the top into the form of an apple, a rose, a lily, an eagle, or something similar;[2] for it is not their habit to use a stick without an ornament.

196. Of their customs, whereof I shall now proceed to give an account, the following (which I understand belongs to them in common with the Illyrian tribe of the Eneti)[3] is the wisest in my judgment. Once a year in each village the maidens of age to marry were collected all together into one place; while the men stood round them in a circle. Then a herald called up the damsels one by one, and offered them for sale. He began with the most beautiful. When she was sold for no small sum of money, he offered for sale the one who came next to her in beauty. All of them were sold to be wives. The richest of the Babylonians who wished to wed bid against each other for the loveliest maidens, while the humbler wife-seekers, who were indifferent about beauty, took the more homely damsels with marriage-portions. For the custom was that when the herald had gone through the whole number of the beautiful damsels, he should then call up the ugliest – a cripple, if there chanced to be one – and offer her to the men, asking who would agree to take her with the smallest marriage-portion. And the man who offered to take the smallest sum had her assigned to him. The marriage-portions were furnished by the money paid for the beautiful damsels, and thus the fairer maidens portioned out the uglier. No one was allowed to give his daughter in marriage to the man of his choice, nor might any one carry away the damsel whom he had purchased without finding bail really and truly to make her his wife; if, however, it turned out that they did not agree, the money might be paid back. All who liked might come even from distant villages and bid for the women. This was the best of all their customs, but it has now fallen into disuse.[4] They have lately hit upon a very different plan to save their maidens from violence,

1 The Babylonian cylinders are undoubtedly the "seals" of Herodotus. Many impressions of them have been found upon clay-tablets.

2 Upon the cylinders the Babylonians are frequently, but not invariably, represented with sticks. In the Assyrian sculptures the officers of the court have always sticks, used apparently as staves of office.

3 The Eneti or Heneti are the same with the Venetians of later times (Liv. i. 1).

4 Writers of the Augustan age mention this custom as still existing in their day.

and prevent their being torn from them and carried to distant cities, which is to bring up their daughters to be courtesans. This is now done by all the poorer of the common people, who since the conquest have been maltreated by their lords, and have had ruin brought upon their families.

197. The following custom seems to me the wisest of their institutions next to the one lately praised. They have no physicians, but when a man is ill, they lay him in the public square, and the passers-by come up to him, and if they have ever had his disease themselves or have known any one who has suffered from it, they give him advice, recommending him to do whatever they found good in their own case, or in the case known to them; and no one is allowed to pass the sick man in silence without asking him what his ailment is.

198. They bury their dead in honey,[1] and have funeral lamentations like the Egyptians. When a Babylonian has consorted with his wife, he sits down before a censer of burning incense, and the woman sits opposite to him. At dawn of day they wash; for till they are washed they will not touch any of their common vessels. This practice is observed also by the Arabians.

199. The Babylonians have one most shameful custom. Every woman born in the country must once in her life go and sit down in the precinct of Aphrodite, and there consort with a stranger. Many of the wealthier sort, who are too proud to mix with the others, drive in covered carriages to the precinct, followed by a goodly train of attendants, and there take their station. But the larger number seat themselves within the holy enclosure with wreaths of string about their heads, – and here there is always a great crowd, some coming and others going; lines of cord mark out paths in all directions among the women, and the strangers pass along them to make their choice. A woman who has once taken her seat is not allowed to return home till one of the strangers throws a silver coin into her lap, and takes her with him beyond the holy ground. When he throws the coin he says these words – "The goddess Mylitta prosper thee." (Aphrodite is called Mylitta by the Assyrians.) The silver

1 Modern researches show two modes of burial to have prevailed in ancient Babylonia. *Ordinarily* the bodies seem to have been compressed into urns and baked, or burnt. Thousands of funeral urns are found on the sites of the ancient cities. Coffins are also found, but rarely.

coin may be of any size; it cannot be refused, for that is forbidden by the law, since once thrown it is sacred. The woman goes with the first man who throws her money, and rejects no one. When she has gone with him, and so satisfied the goddess, she returns home, and from that time forth no gift however great will prevail with her. Such of the women as are tall and beautiful are soon released, but others who are ugly have to stay a long time before they can fulfil the law. Some have waited three or four years in the precinct.¹ A custom very much like this is found also in certain parts of the island of Cyprus.

200. Such are the customs of the Babylonians generally. There are likewise three tribes among them who eat nothing but fish. These are caught and dried in the sun, after which they are brayed in a mortar, and strained through a linen sieve. Some prefer to make cakes of this material, while others bake it into a kind of bread.

201. When Cyrus had achieved the conquest of the Babylonians, he conceived the desire of bringing the Massagetæ under his dominion. Now the Massagetæ are said to be a great and warlike nation, dwelling eastward, toward the rising of the sun, beyond the river Araxes, and opposite the Issedonians. By many they are regarded as a Scythian race.

202. As for the Araxes, it is, according to some accounts, larger, according to others smaller than the Ister (Danube). It has islands in it, many of which are said to be equal in size to Lesbos. The men who inhabit them feed during the summer on roots of all kinds, which they dig out of the ground, while they store up the fruits, which they gather from the trees at the fitting season, to serve them as food in the winter-time. Besides the trees whose fruit they gather for this purpose, they have also a tree which bears the strangest produce. When they are met together in companies they throw some of it upon the fire round which they are sitting, and presently, by the mere smell of the fumes which it gives out in burning, they grow drunk, as the Greeks do with wine. More of the fruit is then thrown on the fire, and, their drunkenness increasing, they often jump up and begin to dance and sing. Such is the account which I have heard of this people.

¹ This unhallowed custom is mentioned among the abominations of the religion of the Babylonians in the book of Baruch (vi. 43).

The river Araxes, like the Gyndes, which Cyrus dispersed into three hundred and sixty channels, has its source in the country of the Matienians. It has forty mouths, whereof all, except one, end in bogs and swamps. These bogs and swamps are said to be inhabited by a race of men who feed on raw fish, and clothe themselves with the skins of seals. The other mouth of the river flows with a clear course into the Caspian Sea.[1]

203. The Caspian is a sea by itself, having no connection with any other.[2] The sea frequented by the Greeks, that beyond the Pillars of Heracles, which is called the Atlantic, and also the Erythræan, are all one and the same sea. But the Caspian is a distinct sea, lying by itself, in length fifteen days' voyage with a row-boat, in breadth, at the broadest part, eight days' voyage. Along its western shore runs the chain of the Caucasus, the most extensive and loftiest of all mountain-ranges.[3] Many and various are the tribes by which it is inhabited, most of whom live entirely on the wild fruits of the forest. In these forests certain trees are said to grow, from the leaves of which, pounded and mixed with water, the inhabitants make a dye, wherewith they paint upon their clothes the figures of animals; and the figures so impressed never wash out, but last as though they had been inwoven in the cloth from the first, and wear as long as the garment. And these people couple in the open, they say, like animals in herds.

204. On the west then, as I have said, the Caspian Sea is bounded by the range of Caucasus. On the east it is followed by a vast plain, stretching out interminably before the eye,[4] the greater portion of which is possessed by those Massagetæ, against whom Cyrus was now so anxious to make an expedition. Many strong motives weighed with him and urged him on – his birth especially, which seemed something more than human, and his good fortune in all his former wars, wherein he had always found, that against what country soever he turned his arms, it was impossible for that people to escape.

1 The geographical knowledge of Herodotus seems to be nowhere so much at fault as in his account of this river. He appears to have confused together the information which had reached him concerning two or three distinct streams.

2 Here the geographical knowledge of Herodotus was much in advance of his age.

3 This was true within the limits of our author's geographical knowledge. Peaks in the Caucasus attain the height of over 17,000 feet.

4 The deserts of Kharesm, Kizilkoum, etc., the most southern portion of the Steppe region.

205. At this time the Massagetæ were ruled by a queen, named Tomyris, who at the death of her husband, the late king, had mounted the throne. To her Cyrus sent ambassadors, with instructions to court her on his part, pretending that he wished to take her to wife. Tomyris, however, aware that it was her kingdom, and not herself, that he courted, forbade the men to approach. Cyrus, therefore, finding that he did not advance his designs by this deceit, marched towards the Araxes, and openly displaying his hostile intentions, set to work to construct a bridge on which his army might cross the river, and began building towers upon the boats which were to be used in the passage.

206. While the Persian leader was occupied in these labours, Tomyris sent a herald to him, who said, "King of the Medes, cease to press this enterprise, for thou canst not know if what thou art doing will be of real advantage to thee. Be content to rule in peace thy own kingdom, and bear to see us reign over the countries that are ours to govern. As, however, I know thou wilt not choose to hearken to this counsel, since there is nothing thou less desirest than peace and quietness, come now, if thou art so mightily desirous of meeting the Massagetæ in arms, leave thy useless toil of bridge-making; let us retire three days' march from the river bank, and do thou come across with thy soldiers; or, if thou likest better to give us battle on thy side the stream, retire thyself an equal distance." Cyrus, on this offer, called together the chiefs of the Persians, and laid the matter before them, requesting them to advise him what he should do. All the votes were in favour of his letting Tomyris cross the stream, and giving battle on Persian ground.

207. But Crœsus the Lydian, who was present at the meeting of the chiefs, disapproved of this advice; he therefore rose, and thus delivered his sentiments in opposition to it: "Oh! my king! I promised thee long since, that, as Jove had given me into thy hands, I would, to the best of my power, avert impending danger from thy house. Alas! my own sufferings, by their very bitterness, have taught me to be keen-sighted of dangers. If thou deemest thyself an immortal, and thine army an army of immortals, my counsel will doubtless be thrown away upon thee. But if thou feelest thyself to be a man, and a ruler of men, lay this first to heart, that there is a wheel on which the affairs of men revolve, and that its movement forbids the same man to be

always fortunate. Now concerning the matter in hand, my judgment runs counter to the judgment of thy other counsellors. For if thou agreest to give the enemy entrance into thy country, consider what risk is run! Lose the battle, and therewith thy whole kingdom is lost. For assuredly, the Massagetæ, if they win the fight, will not return to their homes, but will push forward against the states of thy empire. Or if thou gainest the battle, why, then thou gainest far less than if thou wert across the stream, where thou mightest follow up thy victory. For against thy loss, if they defeat thee on thine own ground, must be set theirs in like case. Rout their army on the other side of the river, and thou mayest push at once into the heart of their country. Moreover, were it not disgrace intolerable for Cyrus the son of Cambyses to retire before and yield ground to a woman? My counsel therefore is, that we cross the stream, and pushing forward as far as they shall fall back, then seek to get the better of them by stratagem. I am told they are unacquainted with the good things on which the Persians live, and have never tasted the great delights of life. Let us then prepare a feast for them in our camp; let sheep be slaughtered without stint, and the winecups be filled full of noble liquor, and let all manner of dishes be prepared: then leaving behind us our worst troops, let us fall back towards the river. Unless I very much mistake, when they see the good fare set out, they will forget all else and fall to. Then it will remain for us to do our parts manfully."

208. Cyrus, when the two plans were thus placed in contrast before him, changed his mind, and preferring the advice which Crœsus had given, returned for answer to Tomyris, that she should retire, and that he would cross the stream. She therefore retired, as she had engaged; and Cyrus, giving Crœsus into the care of his son Cambyses (whom he had appointed to succeed him on the throne), with strict charge to pay him all respect and treat him well, if the expedition failed of success; and sending them both back to Persia, crossed the river with his army.

209. The first night after the passage, as he slept in the enemy's country, a vision appeared to him. He seemed to see in his sleep the eldest of the sons of Hystaspes, with wings upon his shoulders, shadowing with the one wing Asia, and Europe with the other. Now Hystaspes, the son of Arsames, was of the

race of the Achæmenidæ,[1] and his eldest son, Darius, was at that time scarce twenty years old; wherefore, not being of age to go to the wars, he had remained behind in Persia. When Cyrus woke from his sleep, and turned the vision over in his mind, it seemed to him no light matter. He therefore sent for Hystaspes, and taking him aside said, "Hystaspes, thy son is discovered to be plotting against me and my crown. I will tell thee how I know it so certainly. The gods watch over my safety, and warn me beforehand of every danger. Now last night, as I lay in my bed, I saw in a vision the eldest of thy sons with wings upon his shoulders, shadowing with the one wing Asia, and Europe with the other. From this it is certain, beyond all possible doubt, that he is engaged in some plot against me. Return thou then at once to Persia, and be sure, when I come back from conquering the Massagetæ, to have thy son ready to produce before me, that I may examine him."

210. Thus Cyrus spoke, in the belief that he was plotted against by Darius; but he missed the true meaning of the dream, which was sent by God to forewarn him, that he was to die then and there, and that his kingdom was to fall at last to Darius.

Hystaspes made answer to Cyrus in these words:— "Heaven forbid, sire, that there should be a Persian living who would plot against thee! If such an one there be, may a speedy death overtake him! Thou foundest the Persians a race of slaves, thou hast made them free men: thou foundest them subject to others, thou hast made them lords of all. If a vision has announced that my son is practising against thee, lo, I resign him into thy hands to deal with as thou wilt." Hystaspes, when he had thus answered, recrossed the Araxes and hastened back to Persia, to keep a watch on his son Darius.

211. Meanwhile Cyrus, having advanced a day's march from the river, did as Crœsus had advised him, and, leaving the worthless portion of his army in the camp, drew off with his good troops towards the river. Soon afterwards, a detachment of the Massagetæ, one-third of their entire army, led by Spargapises, son of the queen Tomyris, coming up, fell upon the body which had been left behind by Cyrus, and on their resistance put them

---

1 It may be observed here that the inscriptions confirm Herodotus thus far. Darius was son of Hystaspes (Vashtáspa) and grandson of Arsames (Arsháma). He traced his descent through four ancestors to Achæmenes (Hakhámanish).

to the sword. Then, seeing the banquet prepared, they sat down and began to feast. When they had eaten and drunk their fill, and were now sunk in sleep, the Persians under Cyrus arrived, slaughtered a great multitude, and made even a larger number prisoners. Among these last was Spargapises himself.

212. When Tomyris heard what had befallen her son and her army, she sent a herald to Cyrus, who thus addressed the conqueror:– "Thou bloodthirsty Cyrus, pride not thyself on this poor success: it was the grape-juice – which, when ye drink it, makes you so mad, and as ye swallow it down brings up to your lips such bold and wicked words – it was this poison wherewith thou didst ensnare my child, and so overcamest him, not in fair open fight. Now hearken what I advise, and be sure I advise thee for thy good. Restore my son to me and get thee from the land unharmed, triumphant over a third part of the host of the Massagetæ. Refuse, and I swear by the sun, the sovereign lord of the Massagetæ, bloodthirsty as thou art, I will give thee thy fill of blood."

213. To the words of this message Cyrus paid no manner of regard. As for Spargapises, the son of the queen, when the wine went off, and he saw the extent of his calamity, he made request to Cyrus to release him from his bonds; then, when his prayer was granted, and the fetters were taken from his limbs, as soon as his hands were free, he destroyed himself.

214. Tomyris, when she found that Cyrus paid no heed to her advice, collected all the forces of her kingdom, and gave him battle. Of all the combats in which the barbarians have engaged among themselves, I reckon this to have been the fiercest. The following, as I understand, was the manner of it:– First, the two armies stood apart and shot their arrows at each other; then, when their quivers were empty, they closed and fought hand-to-hand with lances and daggers; and thus they continued fighting for a length of time, neither choosing to give ground. At length the Massagetæ prevailed. The greater part of the army of the Persians was destroyed and Cyrus himself fell, after reigning nine and twenty years. Search was made among the slain by order of the queen for the body of Cyrus, and when it was found she took a skin, and, filling it full of human blood, she dipped the head of Cyrus in the gore, saying, as she thus insulted the corse, "I live and have conquered thee in fight, and yet by thee am I ruined, for thou tookest my son with guile; but thus I make good my threat, and give thee thy fill of blood." Of the many different

accounts which are given of the death of Cyrus, this which I have followed appears to me most worthy of credit.[1]

215. In their dress and mode of living the Massagetæ resemble the Scythians. They fight both on horseback and on foot, neither method is strange to them: they use bows and lances, but their favourite weapon is the battle-axe.[2] Their arms are all either of gold or brass. For their spear-points, and arrow-heads, and for their battle-axes, they make use of brass; for head-gear, belts, and girdles, of gold. So too with the caparison of their horses, they give them breastplates of brass, but employ gold about the reins, the bit, and the cheek-plates. They use neither iron nor silver, having none in their country; but they have brass and gold in abundance.[3]

216. The following are some of their customs:— Each man has but one wife, yet all the wives are held in common; for this is a custom of the Massagetæ and not of the Scythians, as the Greeks wrongly say. For when a man of the Massagetæ desires a woman, he hangs up his quiver in front of her waggon, and lies with her without fear. Human life does not come to its natural close with this people; but when a man grows very old, all his kinsfolk collect together and offer him up in sacrifice; offering at the same time some cattle also. After the sacrifice they boil the flesh and feast on it; and those who thus end their days are reckoned the happiest. If a man dies of disease they do not eat him, but bury him in the ground, bewailing his ill-fortune that he did not come to be sacrificed. They sow no grain, but live on their herds, and on fish, of which there is great plenty in

1 It may be questioned whether the account, which out of many seemed to our author most worthy of credit, was ever really the most credible. Unwittingly Herodotus was drawn towards the most romantic and poetic version of each story, and what he admired most seemed to him the likeliest to be true. According to Xenophon, Cyrus died peacefully in his bed (Cyrop. VIII. vii.); according to Ctesias, he was severely wounded in a battle which he fought with the Derbices, and died in camp of his wounds. Of these two authors, Ctesias, perhaps, is the less untrustworthy. On his authority, conjoined with that of Herodotus, it may be considered certain, 1. That Cyrus died a violent death; and 2. That he received his death-wound in fight; but against what enemy must continue a doubtful point.

2 The σάγαρις is in all probability the *khanjar* of modern Persia, a short, curved, double-edged dagger, almost universally worn.

3 Both the Ural and the Altai mountains abound in gold. The richness of these regions in this metal is indicated (book iv. ch. 27) by the stories of the gold-guarding Grypes, and the Arimaspi who plunder them (book iii. ch. 116).

the Araxes. Milk is what they chiefly drink. The only god they worship is the sun, and to him they offer the horse in sacrifice; under the notion of giving to the swiftest of the gods the swiftest of all mortal creatures.[1]

1 Horse sacrifices are said to prevail among the modern Parsees.

BABYLON

[ADDED NOTE BY THE EDITOR]

For nearly 2000 years Babylon was the centre of the world's civilisation. Her script and her language were known in Egypt, and on the shores of the Mediterranean, and were the universal medium of communication between educated men. She was the bank and emporium of the East; and in the age of her splendour, with her daughter states about her, dominated the thoughts of mankind. What Rome has been, and London is, that Babylon was – "the glory of kingdoms, the beauty of the Chaldæans' pride" (Isaiah xiii. 7). Her ruins are still wonderful; but she has left us spiritual ruins too, and these are yet more strange. The debt of ancient Israel to Babylon was immense. The code of Khammurabi (circ. B.C. 2200) may well have influenced the Mosaic code; the angelology of later Jewish Scriptures was Babylonian in origin; the legends of Creation, the Fall, and the Deluge, are of Babylonian ancestry. Little wonder if, when the end came, and she fell, a cry went through the earth that had once feared her power, her pride, her universal empire – "Babylon is fallen, is fallen!" (Isaiah xxi. 9).

THE SECOND BOOK,
ENTITLED EUTERPÉ

1. ON the death of Cyrus, Cambyses his son by Cassandané daughter of Pharnaspes took the kingdom. Cassandané had died in the lifetime of Cyrus, who had made a great mourning for her at her death, and had commanded all the subjects of his empire to observe the like. Cambyses, the son of this lady and of Cyrus, regarding the Ionian and Æolian Greeks as vassals of his father, took them with him in his expedition against Egypt[1] among the other nations which owned his sway.

2. Now the Egyptians, before the reign of their king Psammetichus, believed themselves to be the most ancient of mankind.[2] Since Psammetichus, however, made an attempt to discover who were actually the primitive race, they have been of opinion that while they surpass all other nations, the Phrygians surpass them in antiquity. This king, finding it impossible to make out by dint of inquiry what men were the most ancient, contrived the following method of discovery:— He took two children of the common sort, and gave them over to a herdsman to bring up at his folds, strictly charging him to let no one utter a word in their presence, but to keep them in a sequestered cottage, and from time to time introduce goats to their apartment, see that they got their fill of milk, and in all other respects look after them. His object herein was to know, after the indistinct babblings of infancy were over, what word they would first articulate. It happened as he had anticipated. The herdsman obeyed his orders for two years, and at the end of that time, on his one day opening the door of their room and going in, the children both ran up to him with outstretched arms, and distinctly said "Becos." When this first happened the herdsman took no

1 The date of the expedition of Cambyses against Egypt cannot be fixed with absolute certainty. B.C. 525, which is the date ordinarily received, is, on the whole, the most probable.

2 This affectation of extreme antiquity is strongly put by Plato in his Timæus (p. 22. B), where the Greek nation is taxed by the Egyptians with being in its infancy as compared with them. The Egyptian claims to a high *relative* antiquity had, no doubt, a solid basis of truth.

notice; but afterwards when he observed, on coming often to see after them, that the word was constantly in their mouths, he informed his lord, and by his command brought the children into his presence. Psammetichus then himself heard them say the word, upon which he proceeded to make inquiry what people there was who called anything "becos," and hereupon he learnt that "becos" was the Phrygian name for bread. In consideration of this circumstance the Egyptians yielded their claims, and admitted the greater antiquity of the Phrygians.

3. That these were the real facts I learnt at Memphis from the priests of Hephaistos. The Greeks, among other foolish tales, relate that Psammetichus had the children brought up by women whose tongues he had previously cut out; but the priests said their bringing up was such as I have stated above. I got much other information also from conversation with these priests while I was at Memphis, and I even went to Heliopolis and to Thebes,[1] expressly to try whether the priests of those places would agree in their accounts with the priests at Memphis. The Heliopolitans have the reputation of being the best skilled in history of all the Egyptians.[2] What they told me concerning their religion it is not my intention to repeat, except the names of their deities, which I believe all men know equally. If I relate anything else concerning these matters, it will only be when compelled to do so by the course of my narrative.[3]

4. Now with regard to mere human matters, the accounts which they gave, and in which all agreed, were the following. The Egyptians, they said, were the first to discover the solar year, and to portion out its course into twelve parts. They obtained this knowledge from the stars. (To my mind they contrive their year much more cleverly than the Greeks, for these last every

---

1 The name of Thebes is almost always written in the plural by the Greeks and Romans – Θηβαι, Thebæ – but Pliny writes, "Thebe portarum centum nobilis fama." [This splendid city was for centuries the capital of Egypt. It was sacked by Asurbanipal (Sardanapalus) B.C. 663. Referred to in O. T. (Nahum iii. 8) as No-Amon. – E. H. B.]

2 Heliopolis ("City of the Sun") was the great seat of learning, and the university of Egypt.

3 For instances of the reserve which Herodotus here promises, see chapters 45, 46, 47, 48, 61, 62, 65, 81, 132, 170, and 171. The secrecy in matters of religion, which was no doubt enjoined upon Herodotus by the Egyptian priests, did not seem strange to a Greek, who was accustomed to it in the "mysteries" of his own countrymen.

other year intercalate a whole month,[1] but the Egyptians, dividing the year into twelve months of thirty days each, add every year a space of five days besides, whereby the circuit of the seasons is made to return with uniformity.)[2] The Egyptians, they went on to affirm, first brought into use the names of the twelve gods, which the Greeks adopted from them; and first erected altars, images, and temples to the gods; and also first engraved upon stone the figures of animals. In most of these cases they proved to me that what they said was true. And they told me that the first man[3] who ruled over Egypt was Mên, and that in his time all Egypt, except the Thebaic canton, was a marsh,[4] none of the land below lake Mœris then showing itself above the surface of the water. This is a distance of seven days' sail from the sea up the river.

5. What they said of their country seemed to me very reasonable. For any one who sees Egypt, without having heard a word about it before, must perceive, if he has only common powers of observation, that the Egypt to which the Greeks go in their ships is an acquired country, the gift of the river.[5] The same is true of the land above the lake, to the distance of three days' voyage, concerning which the Egyptians say nothing, but which is exactly the same kind of country.

The following is the general character of the region. In the first place, on approaching it by sea, when you are still a day's sail from the land, if you let down a sounding-line you will bring up mud, and find yourself in eleven fathoms' water, which

1 Vide supra, i. 32, and note ad loc.

2 This at once proves they intercalated the quarter day, making their year to consist of $365\frac{1}{4}$ days, without which the seasons could not return to the same periods. The fact of Herodotus not understanding their method of intercalation does not argue that the Egyptians were ignorant of it.

3 According to the chronological tables of the Egyptians the gods were represented to have reigned first, and after them Menes; and the same is found recorded in the Turin Papyrus of Kings, as well as in Manetho and other writers. [Menes (or Mena), perhaps a legendary figure. Some give his date as 3300 B.C., others much earlier. – E. H. B.]

4 Note, besides the improbability of such a change, the fact that Menes was the reputed founder of Memphis, which is far to the north of this lake; and that Busiris, near the coast (the reputed burial-place of Osiris), Buto, Pelusium, and other towns of the Delta, were admitted by the Egyptians to be of the earliest date.

5 Vide infra, ch. 10.

shows that the soil washed down by the stream extends to that distance.

6. The length of the country along shore, according to the bounds that we assign to Egypt, namely from the Plinthinêtic gulf[1] to lake Serbônis, which extends along the base of Mount Casius, is sixty schœnes.[2] The nations whose territories are scanty measure them by the fathom; those whose bounds are less confined, by the furlong; those who have an ample territory, by the parasang; but if men have a country which is very vast, they measure it by the schœne. Now the length of the parasang is thirty furlongs,[3] but the schœne, which is an Egyptian measure, is sixty furlongs.[4] Thus the coast-line of Egypt would extend a length of three thousand six hundred furlongs.

7. From the coast inland as far as Heliopolis the breadth of Egypt is considerable, the country is flat, without springs, and full of swamps.[5] The length of the route from the sea up to Heliopolis is almost exactly the same as that of the road which runs from the altar of the twelve gods at Athens[6] to the temple of Olympian Jove at Pisa.[7] If a person made a calculation he would find but a very little difference between the two routes, not more than about fifteen furlongs; for the road from Athens to Pisa falls short of fifteen hundred furlongs by exactly fifteen, whereas the distance of Heliopolis from the sea is just the round number.[8]

---

1 Plinthiné was a town near the Lake Mareotis.

2 The real length of the coast from the Bay of Plinthiné at Taposiris, or at Plinthiné, even to the *eastern* end of the Lake Serbonis, is by the shore little more than 300 English miles.

3 See note on Book v. ch. 53.

4 This would be more than 36,000 English feet, or nearly 7 miles. The Greek σχοῖνος, "rope," is the same word which signifies rush, of which ropes are still made in Egypt and in other countries.

5 Heliopolis stood on the edge of the desert, about $4\frac{1}{4}$ miles to the E. of the apex of the Delta; but the alluvial land of the Delta extended 5 miles farther to the eastward of that city.

6 The altar of the twelve gods at Athens stood in the Forum, and seems to have served, like the gilt pillar (*milliarium aureum*) in the Forum at Rome, as a central point from which to measure distances.

7 This mention of Pisa is curious, considering that it had been destroyed so long before (B.C. 572) by the Eleans (Pausan. VI. xxii. § 2), and that it had certainly not been rebuilt by the close of the Peloponnesian war. Probably Herodotus intends Olympia itself rather than the ancient town, which was six stades distant.

8 Fifteen hundred furlongs (stades), about equal to 173 English miles.

8. As one proceeds beyond Heliopolis[1] up the country, Egypt becomes narrow, the Arabian range of hills, which has a direction from north to south, shutting it in upon the one side, and the Libyan range upon the other. The former ridge runs on without a break, and stretches away to the sea called the Erythræan; it contains the quarries[2] whence the stone was cut for the pyramids of Memphis: and this is the point where it ceases its first direction, and bends away in the manner above indicated.[3] In its greatest length from east to west it is, as I have been informed, a distance of two months' journey; towards the extreme east its skirts produce frankincense. Such are the chief features of this range. On the Libyan side, the other ridge whereon the pyramids stand, is rocky and covered with sand; its direction is the same as that of the Arabian ridge in the first part of its course. Above Heliopolis, then, there is no great breadth of territory for such a country as Egypt, but during four days' sail Egypt is narrow;[4] the valley between the two ranges is a level plain, and seemed to me to be, at the narrowest point, not more than two hundred furlongs across from the Arabian to the Libyan hills. Above this point Egypt again widens.

9. From Heliopolis to Thebes is nine days' sail up the river; the distance is eighty-one schœnes, or 4860 furlongs.[5] If we now put together the several measurements of the country we shall find that the distance along shore is, as I stated above, 3600 furlongs, and the distance from the sea inland to Thebes 6120 furlongs. Further, it is a distance of eighteen hundred furlongs from Thebes to the place called Elephantiné.

1 The site of Heliopolis is still marked by the massive walls that surrounded it, and by a granite obelisk bearing the name of Osirtasen I. of the 12th dynasty, dating about 3900 years ago. It was one of two that stood before the entrance to the temple of the Sun. [The Biblical "ON," Gen. xli. 45; in Jeremiah called Bettashemesh ("house of the sun"): Hastings, *Dict. of Bible, s.v.* ON. – E. H. B.]

2 The quarries from which the stone for the casing of the pyramids was taken are in that part of the modern El-Mokuttum range of hills called by Strabo the "Trojan mountain," and now Gebel Māsarah or Toora Māsarah, from the two villages below them on the Nile.

3 That is, towards the Erythræan Sea, or Arabian Gulf.

4 That is, from Heliopolis southward; and he says it becomes broader again beyond that point. His 200 stadia are about $22\frac{1}{2}$ to 23 miles.

5 The nine days' sail, which Herodotus reckons at 4860 stadia, would give about 552 Eng. miles; but the distance is only about 421, even following the course of the river.

10. The greater portion of the country above described seemed to me to be, as the priests declared, a tract gained by the inhabitants. For the whole region above Memphis, lying between the two ranges of hills that have been spoken of, appeared evidently to have formed at one time a gulf of the sea. It resembles (to compare small things with great) the parts about Ilium and Teuthrania, Ephesus, and the plain of the Mæander.[1] In all these regions the land has been formed by rivers, whereof the greatest is not to compare for size with any one of the five mouths of the Nile.[2] I could mention other rivers also, far inferior to the Nile in magnitude, that have effected very great changes. Among these not the least is the Acheloüs, which, after passing through Acarnania, empties itself into the sea opposite the islands called Echinades,[3] and has already joined one-half of them to the continent.[4]

11. In Arabia, not far from Egypt, there is a long and narrow gulf running inland from the sea called the Erythræan,[5] of which I will here set down the dimensions. Starting from its innermost recess, and using a row-boat, you take forty days to reach the open main, while you may cross the gulf at its widest part in the space of half a day. In this sea there is an ebb and flow of the tide every day.[6] My opinion is, that Egypt was formerly very much such a gulf as this – one gulf penetrated from the sea that washes Egypt on the north,[7] and extended itself towards

1 In some of these places the gain of the land upon the sea has been very great. This is particularly the case at the mouth of the Mæander, where the alluvial plain has advanced in the historic times a distance of 12 or 13 miles.

2 This signifies the natural branches of the Nile; and when seven are reckoned, they include the two artificial ones.

3 These islands, which still bear the same name among the educated Greeks, consist of two clusters, linked together by the barren and rugged *Petalá*.

4 That the Acheloüs in ancient times formed fresh land at its mouth with very great rapidity is certain, from the testimony of various writers besides Herodotus.

5 The Greeks generally did not give the name Erythræan, or Red Sea, to the Arabian Gulf, but to all that part of the Indian Ocean reaching from the Persian Gulf to India (as in ii. 102; and iv. 39). It was also applied to the Persian Gulf (i. 1, 180, 189), and Herodotus sometimes gives it to the Arabian Gulf, and even the western branch between Mount Sinai and Egypt (ii. 158).

6 Herodotus is perfectly right in speaking of the tide in this gulf. At Suez it is from 5 to 6 feet, but much less to the southward.

7 The Mediterranean, called by the Arabs "the White Sea" as well as "the North Sea."

Ethiopia; another entered from the southern ocean, and stretched towards Syria; the two gulfs ran into the land so as almost to meet each other, and left between them only a very narrow tract of country. Now if the Nile should choose to divert his waters from their present bed into this Arabian gulf, what is there to hinder it from being filled up by the stream within, at the utmost, twenty thousand years? For my part, I think it would be filled in half the time. How then should not a gulf, even of much greater size, have been filled up in the ages that passed before I was born, by a river that is at once so large and so given to working changes?

12. Thus I give credit to those from whom I received this account of Egypt, and am myself, moreover, strongly of the same opinion, since I remarked that the country projects into the sea further than the neighbouring shores, and I observed that there were shells upon the hills, and that salt exuded from the soil to such an extent as even to injure the pyramids; and I noticed also that there is but a single hill in all Egypt where sand is found,¹ namely, the hill above Memphis; and further, I found the country to bear no resemblance either to its borderland Arabia, or to Libya² – nay, nor even to Syria, which forms the seaboard of Arabia; but whereas the soil of Libya is, we know, sandy and of a reddish hue, and that of Arabia and Syria inclines to stone and clay, Egypt has a soil that is black and crumbly, as being alluvial and formed of the deposits brought down by the river from Ethiopia.

13. One fact which I learnt of the priests is to me a strong evidence of the origin of the country. They said that when Mœris was king, the Nile overflowed all Egypt below Memphis, as soon as it rose so little as eight cubits. Now Mœris had not been dead 900 years at the time when I heard this of the priests;³ yet at the

1 The only mountain where sand abounds is certainly the African range.

2 It is perfectly true that neither in soil nor climate is Egypt like any other country. The soil is, as Herodotus says, "black and crumbly." The deposit of the Nile, when left on a rock and dried by the sun, resembles pottery in its appearance and by its fracture, from the silica it contains; but as long as it retains its moisture it has the appearance of clay, from its slimy and tenacious quality. It varies according to circumstances, sometimes being mixed with sand, but it is generally of a black colour, and Egypt is said to have been called hence "black," from the prevailing character of its soil.

3 This would make the date of Mœris about 1355 B.C.; but it neither agrees with the age of Amun-m'-he III. of the Labyrinth, nor of Thothmes III. The

present day, unless the river rise sixteen, or, at the very least, fifteen cubits, it does not overflow the lands. It seems to me, therefore, that if the land goes on rising and growing at this rate, the Egyptians who dwell below lake Mœris, in the Delta (as it is called) and elsewhere, will one day, by the stoppage of the inundations, suffer permanently the fate which they told me they expected would some time or other befall the Greeks. On hearing that the whole land of Greece is watered by rain from heaven, and not, like their own, inundated by rivers, they observed – "Some day the Greeks will be disappointed of their grand hope, and then they will be wretchedly hungry;" which was as much as to say, "If God shall some day see fit not to grant the Greeks rain, but shall afflict them with a long drought, the Greeks will be swept away by a famine, since they have nothing to rely on but rain from Jove, and have no other resource for water."

14. And certes, in thus speaking of the Greeks the Egyptians say nothing but what is true. But now let me tell the Egyptians how the case stands with themselves. If, as I said before, the country below Memphis, which is the land that is always rising, continues to increase in height at the rate at which it has risen in times gone by, how will it be possible for the inhabitants of that region to avoid hunger, when they will certainly have no rain,[1] and the river will not be able to overflow their corn-lands? At present, it must be confessed, they obtain the fruits of the field with less trouble than any other people in the world, the rest of the Egyptians included, since they have no need to break up the ground with the plough, nor to use the hoe, nor to do any of the work which the rest of mankind find necessary if they are to get a crop; but the husbandman waits till the river has of its own accord spread itself over the fields and withdrawn again

---

Mœris, however, *from whom these dates are calculated*, appears to have been Menophres, whose era was so remarkable, and was fixed as the Sothic period, B.C. 1322, which happened about 900 years before Herodotus' visit, only falling short of that sum by 33 years. It is reasonable to suppose that by Mœris he would refer to that king who was so remarkable for his attention to the levels of the Nile, shown by his making the lake called after him.

1 In Upper Egypt showers only occur about five or six times in the year, but every fifteen or twenty years heavy rain falls there, which will account for the deep ravines cut in the valleys of the Theban hills, about the Tombs of the Kings; in Lower Egypt rain is more frequent; and in Alexandria it is as abundant in winter as in the south of Europe.

to its bed, and then sows his plot of ground, and after sowing turns his swine into it — the swine tread in the corn[1] — after which he has only to await the harvest. The swine serve him also to thrash the grain,[2] which is then carried to the garner.

15. If then we choose to adopt the views of the Ionians concerning Egypt, we must come to the conclusion that the Egyptians had formerly no country at all. For the Ionians say that nothing is really Egypt[3] but the Delta, which extends along shore from the Watch-tower of Perseus,[4] as it is called, to the Pelusiac Salt-pans, a distance of forty schœnes, and stretches inland as far as the city of Cercasôrus, where the Nile divides into the two streams which reach the sea at Pelusium and Canôbus respectively. The rest of what is accounted Egypt belongs, they say, either to Arabia or Libya. But the Delta, as the Egyptians affirm, and as I myself am persuaded, is formed of the deposits of the river, and has only recently, if I may use the expression, come to light. If, then, they had formerly no territory at all, how came they to be so extravagant as to fancy themselves the most ancient race in the world? Surely there was no need of their making the experiment with the children to see what language they would first speak. But in truth I do not believe that the Egyptians came into being at the same time with the Delta, as the Ionians call it; I think they have always existed ever since the human race began; as the land went on increasing, part of the population came down into the new country, part remained in their old settlements. In ancient times the Thebaïs bore the name of Egypt, a district of which the entire circumference is but 6120 furlongs.

---

1 Plutarch, Ælian, and Pliny mention this custom of treading in the grain "with pigs" in Egypt; but no instance occurs of it in the tombs, though goats are sometimes so represented in the paintings. It is indeed more probable that pigs were turned in upon the land to eat up the weeds and roots.

2 The paintings show that oxen were commonly used to tread out the grain from the ear at harvest-time, and occasionally, though rarely, asses were so employed; but pigs not being sufficiently heavy for the purpose, are not likely to have been substituted for oxen.

3 There is no appearance of the name "Egypt" on the ancient monuments, where the country is called "Chemi." Egypt is said to have been called originally Aetia, and the Nile Aetos and Siris. Upper Egypt, or the Thebaïd, has even been confounded with, and called, Ethiopia.

4 This tower stood to the W. of the Canopic mouth.

16. If, then, my judgment on these matters be right, the Ionians are mistaken in what they say of Egypt. If, on the contrary, it is they who are right, then I undertake to show that neither the Ionians nor any of the other Greeks know how to count. For they all say that the earth is divided into three parts, Europe, Asia, and Libya, whereas they ought to add a fourth part, the Delta of Egypt, since they do not include it either in Asia or Libya.[1] For is it not their theory that the Nile separates Asia from Libya? As the Nile, therefore, splits in two at the apex of the Delta, the Delta itself must be a separate country, not contained in either Asia or Libya.

17. Here I take my leave of the opinions of the Ionians, and proceed to deliver my own sentiments on these subjects. I consider Egypt to be the whole country inhabited by the Egyptians, just as Cilicia is the tract occupied by the Cilicians, and Assyria that possessed by the Assyrians. And I regard the only proper boundary-line between Libya and Asia to be that which is marked out by the Egyptian frontier. For if we take the boundary-line commonly received by the Greeks,[2] we must regard Egypt as divided, along its whole length from Elephantiné and the Cataracts to Cercasôrus, into two parts, each belonging to a different portion of the world, one to Asia, the other to Libya; since the Nile divides Egypt in two from the Cataracts to the sea, running as far as the city of Cercasôrus in a single stream, but at that point separating into three branches, whereof the one which bends eastward is called the Pelusiac mouth, and that which slants to the west, the Canobic. Meanwhile the straight course of the stream, which comes down from the upper country and meets the apex of the Delta, continues on, dividing the Delta down the middle, and carries as large a body of water, as most of the others, the mouth called the Sebennytic. Besides these there are two other mouths which run out of the Sebennytic called respectively the Saitic and the Mendesian. The Bolbitine mouth, and the Bucolic, are not natural branches, but channels made by excavation.

18. My judgment as to the extent of Egypt is confirmed by an oracle delivered at the shrine of Ammon, of which I had no

1 Though Egypt really belongs to the continent of Africa, the inhabitants were certainly of Asiatic origin.
2 That is, the course of the Nile.

knowledge at all until after I had formed my opinion. It happened that the people of the cities Marea[1] and Apis, who live in the part of Egypt that borders on Libya, took a dislike to the religious usages of the country concerning sacrificial animals, and wished no longer to be restricted from eating the flesh of cows.[2] So, as they believed themselves to be Libyans and not Egyptians, they sent to the shrine to say that, having nothing in common with the Egyptians, neither inhabiting the Delta nor using the Egyptian tongue, they claimed to be allowed to eat whatever they pleased. Their request, however, was refused by the god, who declared in reply that Egypt was the entire tract of country which the Nile overspreads and irrigates, and the Egyptians were the people who lived below Elephantiné,[3] and drank the waters of that river.

19. So said the oracle. Now the Nile, when it overflows, floods not only the Delta, but also the tracts of country on both sides the stream which are thought to belong to Libya and Arabia, in some places reaching to the extent of two days' journey from its banks, in some even exceeding that distance, but in others falling short of it.

Concerning the nature of the river, I was not able to gain any information either from the priests or from others. I was particularly anxious to learn from them why the Nile, at the commencement of the summer solstice, begins to rise,[4] and continues to increase for a hundred days – and why, as soon as that number is past, it forthwith retires and contracts its stream, continuing low during the whole of the winter until the summer

1 The town of Marea stood near the lake to which it gave the name Mareotis. It was celebrated for the wine produced in its vicinity.

2 Though oxen were lawful food to the Egyptians, cows and heifers were forbidden to be killed, either for the altar or the table, being consecrated (not as Herodotus states, ch. 41, to Isis, but as Strabo says) to Athor, who was represented under the form of a spotted cow, and to whose temple at Atarbechis, "the city of Athor," as Herodotus afterwards shows, the bodies of those that died were carried (ch. 41).

3 Syene and Elephantiné were the real frontier of Egypt on the S.; Egypt extending "from the tower (Migdol) of Syene" to the sea (Ezek. xxix. 10).

4 Herodotus was surprised that the Nile should rise in the summer solstice and become low in winter. In the latitude of Memphis it begins to rise at the end of June, about the 10th of August it attains to the height requisite for cutting the canals and admitting it into the interior of the plain; and it is generally at its highest about the end of September. This makes from 92 to 100 days, as Herodotus states.

solstice comes round again. On none of these points could I obtain any explanation from the inhabitants,[1] though I made every inquiry, wishing to know what was commonly reported – they could neither tell me what special virtue the Nile has which makes it so opposite in its nature to all other streams, nor why, unlike every other river, it gives forth no breezes[2] from its surface.

20. Some of the Greeks, however, wishing to get a reputation for cleverness, have offered explanations of the phenomena of the river, for which they have accounted in three different ways. Two of these I do not think it worth while to speak of, further than simply to mention what they are. One pretends that the Etesian winds[3] cause the rise of the river by preventing the Nile-water from running off into the sea. But in the first place it has often happened, when the Etesian winds did not blow, that the Nile has risen according to its usual wont; and further, if the Etesian winds produced the effect, the other rivers which flow in a direction opposite to those winds ought to present the same phenomena as the Nile, and the more so as they are all smaller streams, and have a weaker current. But these rivers, of which there are many both in Syria[4] and Libya, are entirely unlike the Nile in this respect.

21. The second opinion is even more unscientific than the one just mentioned, and also, if I may so say, more marvellous. It is that the Nile acts so strangely, because it flows from the ocean, and that the ocean flows all round the earth.[5]

---

1 The cause of the inundation is the water that falls during the rainy season in Abyssinia; and the range of the tropical rains extends even as far N. as latitude 17° 43′.

2 If this signifies that breezes are not generated by, and do not rise from, the Nile, it is true; but not if it means that a current of air does not blow up the valley.

3 The annual N.W. winds blow from the Mediterranean during the inundation; but they are not the *cause* of the rise of the Nile, though they help in a small degree to impede its course northwards. For the navigation of the river they are invaluable.

4 It is possible to justify this statement, which at first sight seems untrue, by considering that the direction of the Etesian winds was *north-westerly* rather than north. This was natural, as they are caused by the rush of the air from the Mediterranean and Ægean, to fill up the vacuum caused by the rarefaction of the atmosphere over the desert lands in the neighbourhood of the sea.

5 That the Nile flowed from the ocean, and that the ocean flowed all round the earth, were certainly opinions of Hecatæus. It is probable, therefore, that his account of the inundation is here intended.

22. The third explanation, which is very much more plausible than either of the others, is positively the furthest from the truth; for there is really nothing in what it says, any more than in the other theories. It is, that the inundation of the Nile is caused by the melting of snows.[1] Now, as the Nile flows out of Libya,[2] through Ethiopia, into Egypt, how is it possible that it can be formed of melted snow, running, as it does, from the hottest regions of the world into cooler countries? Many are the proofs whereby any one capable of reasoning on the subject may be convinced that it is most unlikely this should be the case. The first and strongest argument is furnished by the winds, which always blow hot from these regions. The second is, that rain and frost are unknown there.[3] Now whenever snow falls, it must of necessity rain within five days;[4] so that, if there were snow, there must be rain also in those parts. Thirdly, it is certain that the natives of the country are black with the heat, that the kites and the swallows remain there the whole year, and that the cranes, when they fly from the rigours of a Scythian winter, flock thither to pass the cold season.[5] If then, in the country whence the Nile has its source, or in that through which it flows, there fell ever so little snow, it is absolutely impossible that any of these circumstances could take place.

23. As for the writer who attributes the phenomenon to the ocean,[6] his account is involved in such obscurity, that it is impossible to disprove it by argument. For my part I know of no

1 This was the opinion of Anaxagoras, as well as of his pupil Euripides and others. Herodotus is wrong in supposing snow could not be found on mountains in the hot climate of Africa; perpetual snow is not confined to certain latitudes; and ancient and modern discoveries prove that it is found in the ranges S. of Abyssinia.

2 That is, from Central Africa.

3 Herodotus was not aware of the rainy season in Sennár and the S.S.W. of Abyssinia, nor did he know of the Abyssinian snow.

4 I have found nothing in any writer, ancient or modern, to confirm, or so much as to explain, this assertion. In some parts of England there is a saying, that "three days of white frost are sure to bring rain."

5 Cranes and other wading birds are found in the winter, in Upper Egypt, but far more in Ethiopia. Kites remain all the winter, and swallows also, though in small numbers, even at Thebes. The swallow was always the harbinger of spring, as in Greece and the rest of Europe.

6 The person to whom Herodotus alludes is Hecatæus. He mentions it also as an opinion of the Greeks of Pontus, that the ocean flowed round the whole earth (B. iv. ch. 8).

river called Ocean, and I think that Homer, or one of the earlier poets, invented the name, and introduced it into his poetry.

24. Perhaps, after censuring all the opinions that have been put forward on this obscure subject, one ought to propose some theory of one's own. I will therefore proceed to explain what I think to be the reason of the Nile's swelling in the summer time. During the winter, the sun is driven out of his usual course by the storms, and removes to the upper parts of Libya. This is the whole secret in the fewest possible words; for it stands to reason that the country to which the Sun-god approaches the nearest, and which he passes most directly over, will be scantest of water, and that there the streams which feed the rivers will shrink the most.

25. To explain, however, more at length, the case is this. The sun, in his passage across the upper parts of Libya, affects them in the following way. As the air in those regions is constantly clear, and the country warm through the absence of cold winds, the sun in his passage across them acts upon them exactly as he is wont to act elsewhere in summer, when his path is in the middle of heaven – that is, he attracts the water. After attracting it, he again repels it into the upper regions, where the winds lay hold of it, scatter it, and reduce it to a vapour, whence it naturally enough comes to pass that the winds which blow from this quarter – the south and south-west – are of all winds the most rainy. And my own opinion is that the sun does not get rid of all the water which he draws year by year from the Nile, but retains some about him. When the winter begins to soften, the sun goes back again to his old place in the middle of the heaven, and proceeds to attract water equally from all countries. Till then the other rivers run big, from the quantity of rain-water which they bring down from countries where so much moisture falls that all the land is cut into gullies; but in summer, when the showers fail, and the sun attracts their water, they become low. The Nile, on the contrary, not deriving any of its bulk from rains, and being in winter subject to the attraction of the sun, naturally runs at that season, unlike all other streams, with a less burthen of water than in the summer time. For in summer it is exposed to attraction equally with all other rivers, but in winter it suffers alone. The sun, therefore, I regard as the sole cause of the phenomenon.

26. It is the sun also, in my opinion, which, by heating the space through which it passes, makes the air in Egypt so dry.

There is thus perpetual summer in the upper parts of Libya. Were the position of the heavenly regions reversed, so that the place where now the north wind and the winter have their dwelling became the station of the south wind and of the noon-day, while, on the other hand, the station of the south wind became that of the north, the consequence would be that the sun, driven from the mid-heaven by the winter and the northern gales, would betake himself to the upper parts of Europe, as he now does to those of Libya, and then I believe his passage across Europe would affect the Ister exactly as the Nile is affected at the present day.

27. And with respect to the fact that no breeze blows from the Nile, I am of opinion that no wind is likely to arise in very hot countries, for breezes love to blow from some cold quarter.

28. Let us leave these things, however, to their natural course, to continue as they are and have been from the beginning. With regard to the *sources* of the Nile,[1] I have found no one among all those with whom I have conversed, whether Egyptians, Libyans, or Greeks,[2] who professed to have any knowledge, except a single person. He was the scribe[3] who kept the register of the sacred treasures of Athena in the city of Saïs, and he did not seem to me to be in earnest when he said that he knew them perfectly well. His story was as follows:— "Between Syênê, a city of the Thebaïs, and Elephantiné, there are" (he said) "two hills with sharp conical tops; the name of the one is Crophi, of the other, Mophi. Midway between them are the fountains of the Nile, fountains which it is impossible to fathom. Half the water runs northward into Egypt, half to the south towards Ethiopia." The fountains were known to be unfathomable, he declared,

1 The sources of the great eastern branch of the Nile have long been discovered. They were first visited by the Portuguese Jesuit, Father Lobo, and afterwards by Bruce. Herodotus affirms that of all the persons he had consulted, none pretended to give him any information about the sources, except a scribe of the sacred treasury of Athena at Saïs, who said it rose from a certain abyss beneath two pointed hills between Syene and Elephantiné. This is an important passage in his narrative, as it involves the question of his having visited the Thebaïd.

2 This was one of the great problems of antiquity, as of later times.

3 The scribes had different offices and grades. The sacred scribes held a high post in the priesthood; and the royal scribes were the king's sons and military men of rank. There were also ordinary scribes or notaries, who were conveyancers, wrote letters on business, settled accounts, and performed different offices in the market.

because Psammetichus, an Egyptian king, had made trial of them. He had caused a rope to be made, many thousand fathoms in length, and had sounded the fountain with it, but could find no bottom. By this the scribe gave me to understand, if there was any truth at all in what he said, that in this fountain there are certain strong eddies, and a regurgitation, owing to the force wherewith the water dashes against the mountains, and hence a sounding-line cannot be got to reach the bottom of the spring.

29. No other information on this head could I obtain from any quarter. All that I succeeded in learning further of the more distant portions of the Nile, by ascending myself as high as Elephantiné, and making inquiries concerning the parts beyond, was the following:– As one advances beyond Elephantiné, the land rises.[1] Hence it is necessary in this part of the river to attach a rope to the boat on each side, as men harness an ox, and so proceed on the journey. If the rope snaps, the vessel is borne away down stream by the force of the current. The navigation continues the same for four days, the river winding greatly, like the Mæander,[2] and the distance traversed amounting to twelve schœnes. Here you come upon a smooth and level plain, where the Nile flows in two branches, round an island called Tachompso.[3] The country above Elephantiné is inhabited by the Ethiopians, who possess one-half of this island, the Egyptians occupying the other. Above the island there is a great lake, the shores of which are inhabited by Ethiopian nomads; after passing it, you come again to the stream of the Nile, which runs into the lake. Here you land, and travel for forty days along the banks of the river, since it is impossible to proceed further in a boat on account of the sharp peaks which jut out from the water, and the sunken rocks which abound in that part of the stream. When you have passed this portion of the river in the space of forty

---

1 This fact should have convinced Herodotus of the improbability of the story of the river flowing southwards into Ethiopia. That boats are obliged to be dragged by ropes in order to pass the rapids is true; and in performing this arduous duty great skill and agility are required.

2 The windings of the Mæander are perhaps at the present day still more remarkable than they were anciently, owing to the growth of the alluvial plain through which it flows.

3 The distances given by Herodotus are 4 days through the district of Dodecaschœnus to Tachompso Isle, then 40 days by land, then 12 days by boat to Meroë; altogether 56 days.

days, you go on board another boat and proceed by water for twelve days more, at the end of which time you reach a great city called Meroë, which is said to be the capital of the other Ethiopians. The only gods worshipped by the inhabitants are Zeus and Dionysus,[1] to whom great honours are paid. There is an oracle of Zeus in the city, which directs the warlike expeditions of the Ethiopians; when it commands they go to war,[2] and in whatever direction it bids them march, thither straightway they carry their arms.

30. On leaving this city, and again mounting the stream, in the same space of time which it took you to reach the capital from Elephantiné, you come to the Deserters,[3] who bear the name of Asmach. This word, translated into our language, means "the men who stand on the left hand of the king."[4] These Deserters are Egyptians of the warrior caste, who, to the number of two hundred and forty thousand, went over to the Ethiopians in the reign of king Psammetichus. The cause of their desertion was the following:— Three garrisons were maintained in Egypt at that time,[5] one in the city of Elephantiné against the Ethiopians,

1 Amun and Osiris answered to Zeus and Dionysus; and both the Amun of Thebes and the ram-headed Nou (or Kneph) were worshipped in Ethiopia. But it is this last deity to whom Herodotus alludes. [See Prof. W. Flinders Petrie, *Religion and Conscience in Ancient Egypt*, chap. iv. "The Egyptian Mythology." – E. H. B.]

2 The influence of the priests at Meroë, through the belief that they spoke the commands of the Deity, is more fully shown by Strabo and Diodorus, who say it was their custom to send to the king, when it pleased them, and order him to put an end to himself, in obedience to the will of the oracle imparted to them; and to such a degree had they contrived to enslave the understanding of those princes by superstitious fears, that they were obeyed without opposition. At length a king, called Ergamenes, a contemporary of Ptolemy Philadelphus, dared to disobey their orders, and having entered "the golden chapel" with his soldiers, caused them to be put to death in his stead, and abolished the custom.

3 The descendants of the 240,000 deserters from Psammetichus lived, according to Herodotus, 4 months' journey above Elephantiné (ch. 31), from which Meroë stood half-way.

4 Diodorus says that the reason of the Egyptian troops deserting from Psammetichus was his having placed them in the *left* wing, while the right was given to the strangers in his army, which is not only more probable than the reason assigned by Herodotus, but is strongly confirmed by the discovery of an inscription in Nubia, written apparently by the Greeks who accompanied Psammetichus when in pursuit of the deserters.

5 It was always the custom of the Egyptians to have a garrison stationed, as Herodotus states, on the frontier.

another in the Pelusiac Daphnæ, against the Syrians and Arabians, and a third, against the Libyans, in Marea. (The very same posts are to this day occupied by the Persians, whose forces are in garrison both in Daphnæ and in Elephantiné.) Now it happened, that on one occasion the garrisons were not relieved during the space of three years; the soldiers, therefore, at the end of that time, consulted together, and having determined by common consent to revolt, marched away towards Ethiopia. Psammetichus, informed of the movement, set out in pursuit, and coming up with them, besought them with many words not to desert the gods of their country, nor abandon their wives and children. "Nay, but," said one of the deserters with an unseemly gesture, "wherever we go, we are sure enough of finding wives and children." Arrived in Ethiopia, they placed themselves at the disposal of the king. In return, he made them a present of a tract of land which belonged to certain Ethiopians with whom he was at feud, bidding them expel the inhabitants and take possession of their territory. From the time that this settlement was formed, their acquaintance with Egyptian manners has tended to civilise the Ethiopians.[1]

31. Thus the course of the Nile is known, not only throughout Egypt, but to the extent of four months' journey either by land or water above the Egyptian boundary; for on calculation it will be found that it takes that length of time to travel from Elephantiné to the country of the Deserters. There the direction of the river is from west to east.[2] Beyond, no one has any certain knowledge of its course, since the country is uninhabited by reason of the excessive heat.

32. I did hear, indeed, what I will now relate, from certain natives of Cyrêné. Once upon a time, they said, they were on a visit to the oracular shrine of Ammon,[3] when it chanced that in the course of conversation with Etearchus, the Ammonian king, the talk fell upon the Nile, how that its sources were unknown to all men. Etearchus upon this mentioned that some

1 This would be a strong argument, if required, against the notion of civilisation having come from the Ethiopians to Egypt; but the monuments prove beyond all question that the Ethiopians borrowed from Egypt their religion and their habits of civilisation.

2 This only applies to the white river, or western branch of the Nile.

3 This was in the modern Oasis of See-wah (Siwah), where remains of the temple are still seen. The oracle long continued in great repute.

Nasamonians had once come to his court, and when asked if they could give any information concerning the uninhabited parts of Libya, had told the following tale. (The Nasamonians are a Libyan race who occupy the Syrtis, and a tract of no great size towards the east.)[1] They said there had grown up among them some wild young men, the sons of certain chiefs, who, when they came to man's estate, indulged in all manner of extravagancies, and among other things drew lots for five of their number to go and explore the desert parts of Libya, and try if they could not penetrate further than any had done previously. The coast of Libya along the sea which washes it to the north, throughout its entire length from Egypt to Cape Soloeis,[2] which is its furthest point, is inhabited by Libyans of many distinct tribes who possess the whole tract except certain portions which belong to the Phœnicians and the Greeks.[3] Above the coast-line and the country inhabited by the maritime tribes, Libya is full of wild beasts; while beyond the wild beast region there is a tract which is wholly sand, very scant of water, and utterly and entirely a desert. The young men therefore, despatched on this errand by their comrades with a plentiful supply of water and provisions, travelled at first through the inhabited region, passing which they came to the wild beast tract, whence they finally entered upon the desert, which they proceeded to cross in a direction from east to west. After journeying for many days over a wide extent of sand, they came at last to a plain where they observed trees growing; approaching them, and seeing fruit on them, they proceeded to gather it. While they were thus engaged, there came upon them some dwarfish men,[4] under the middle height, who seized them and carried them off. The Nasamonians could not understand a word of their language, nor had they any acquaintance with the language of the Nasamonians. They were led across extensive marshes, and finally came to a town, where all the men were of the height of their conductors, and black-

---

1 Vide infra, iv. 172, 173.

2 Cape *Spartel*, near Tangier.

3 That is, the Cyrenaica, and the possessions of the Phœnicians and Carthaginians, or more properly the Pœni, on the N. and W. coasts.

4 Men of diminutive size really exist in Africa, but the Nasamones probably only knew of some by report. The pigmies are mentioned by Homer (Il. iii. 6) and others, and often represented on Greek vases.

complexioned. A great river flowed by the town,[1] running from west to east, and containing crocodiles.

33. Here let me dismiss Etearchus the Ammonian, and his story, only adding that (according to the Cyrenæans) he declared that the Nasamonians got safe back to their country, and that the men whose city they had reached were a nation of sorcerers. With respect to the river which ran by their town, Etearchus conjectured it to be the Nile; and reason favours that view. For the Nile certainly flows out of Libya, dividing it down the middle, and as I conceive, judging the unknown from the known, rises at the same distance from its mouth as the Ister.[2] This latter river has its source in the country of the Celts near the city Pyrênê, and runs through the middle of Europe, dividing it into two portions. The Celts live beyond the pillars of Heracles, and border on the Cynesians,[3] who dwell at the extreme west of Europe. Thus the Ister flows through the whole of Europe before it finally empties itself into the Euxine at Istria,[4] one of the colonies of the Milesians.

34. Now as this river flows through regions that are inhabited, its course is perfectly well known; but of the sources of the Nile no one can give any account, since Libya, the country through which it passes, is desert and without inhabitants. As far as it was possible to get information by inquiry, I have given a description of the stream. It enters Egypt from the parts beyond. Egypt lies almost exactly opposite the mountainous portion of Cilicia,[5] whence a lightly-equipped traveller may reach Sinôpé on the Euxine in five days by the direct route.[6] Sinôpé lies opposite

---

1 It seems not improbable that we have here a mention of the river Niger, and of the ancient representative of the modern city of *Timbuctoo*.

2 Herodotus does not intend any exact correspondency between the Nile and the Danube. He is only speaking of the comparative *length* of the two streams, and conjectures that they are equal in this respect.

3 The Cynesians are mentioned again in iv. 49 as Cynêtes. They are a nation of whom nothing is known but their abode from very ancient times at the extreme S.W. of Europe.

4 If the Danube in the time of Herodotus entered the Euxine at Istria, it must have changed its course very greatly since he wrote.

5 Cilicia was divided into two portions, the eastern, or "Cilicia campestris," and the western, or "Cilicia aspera." Egypt does not really lie "opposite" – that is, in the same longitude with – the latter region. It rather faces Pamphylia, but Herodotus gives all Africa, as far as the Lesser Syrtis, too easterly a position.

6 Supra, i. 72, sub fin.

the place where the Ister falls into the sea.[1] My opinion therefore is that the Nile, as it traverses the whole of Libya, is of equal length with the Ister. And here I take my leave of this subject.

35. Concerning Egypt itself I shall extend my remarks to a great length, because there is no country that possesses so many wonders,[2] nor any that has such a number of works which defy description. Not only is the climate different from that of the rest of the world, and the rivers unlike any other rivers, but the people also, in most of their manners and customs, exactly reverse the common practice of mankind. The women attend the markets[3] and trade, while the men sit at home at the loom;[4] and here, while the rest of the world works the woof up the warp, the Egyptians work it down; the women likewise carry burthens upon their shoulders, while the men carry them upon their heads. The women urinate standing up, the men sitting down. They eat their food out of doors in the streets,[5] but retire for private purposes to their houses, giving as a reason that what

1 This of course is neither true, nor near the truth; and it is difficult to make out in what sense Herodotus meant to assert it. Perhaps he attached no very distinct geographical meaning to the word "opposite."

2 By this statement Herodotus prepares his readers for what he is about to relate; but the desire to tell of the wonders in which it differed from all other countries led Herodotus to indulge in his love of antithesis, so that in some cases he confines to one sex what was done by both (a singular instance being noted down by him as an invariable custom), and in others he has indulged in the marvellous at a sacrifice of truth. If, however, Herodotus had told us that the Egyptian women enjoyed greater liberty, confidence, and consideration than under the *hareem* system of the Greeks and Persians (Book i. ch. 136), he would have been fully justified, for the treatment of women in Egypt was far better than in Greece. In many cases where Herodotus tells improbable tales, they are on the authority of others, or mere hearsay reports, for which he at once declares himself not responsible, and he justly pleads that his history was not only a relation of facts, but the result of an "ἰστορία," or "inquiry," in which all he heard was inserted.

3 The market-place was originally outside the walls, generally in an open space, beneath what was afterwards the citadel or the acropolis.

4 The ancients generally seem to have believed the charge of effeminacy brought by Herodotus against the Egyptians.

5 That they sometimes ate in the street is not to be doubted; but this was only the poorer class, as in other parts of ancient and modern Europe, and could not be mentioned in contradistinction to a Greek custom. The Egyptians generally dined at a small round table, having one leg (similar to the mono-podium), at which one or more persons sat, and they ate with their fingers like the Greeks and the modern Arabs. Several dishes were placed upon the table, and before eating it was their custom to say grace.

is unseemly, but necessary, ought to be done in secret, but what has nothing unseemly about it, should be done openly. A woman cannot serve the priestly office,[1] either for god or goddess, but men are priests to both; sons need not support their parents unless they choose, but daughters must, whether they choose or no.[2]

36. In other countries the priests have long hair, in Egypt their heads are shaven;[3] elsewhere it is customary, in mourning, for near relations to cut their hair close: the Egyptians, who wear no hair at any other time, when they lose a relative, let their beards and the hair of their heads grow long. All other men pass their lives separate from animals, the Egyptians have animals always living with them;[4] others make barley and wheat their food; it is a disgrace to do so in Egypt,[5] where the grain they live on is spelt, which some call *zea*. Dough they knead with their feet; but they mix mud, and even take up dung, with their hands. They are the only people in the world – they at least, and such as have learnt the practice from them[6] – who use circumcision. Their men wear two garments apiece, their women but one.[7]

1 Though men held the priesthood in Egypt, as in other countries, women were not excluded from certain important duties in the temples, as Herodotus also shows (chs. 54, 56); the queens made offerings with the kings; and the monuments, as well as Diodorus, show that an order of women, chosen from the principal families, were employed in the service of the gods.

2 Of the daughters being forced to support their parents instead of the sons, it is difficult to decide; but the improbability of the custom is glaring. It is the son on whom the duty fell of providing for the services in honour of his deceased parent; and the law of debt mentioned by Herodotus (in ch. 136) contradicts his assertion here.

3 The custom of shaving the head as well as beard was not confined to the priests in Egypt, it was general among all classes; and all the men wore wigs or caps fitting close to their heads, except some of the poorest class. The custom of allowing the hair to grow in mourning was not confined to Egypt.

4 Their living with animals not only contradicts a previous assertion of their eating in the streets, but is contrary to fact.

5 Their considering it a "*disgrace*" to live on wheat and barley is equally extravagant.

6 Vide infra, ch. 104.

7 The men having two dresses, and the women one, gives an erroneous impression. The usual dress of men was a long upper robe and a short kilt beneath it, the former being laid aside when at work; while women had only the long robe. When an extra upper garment was worn over these the men had three, the women two; so that, instead of limiting the latter to one, he should have given to men always one more garment than the women.

They put on the rings and fasten the ropes to sails inside;[1] others put them outside. When they write[2] or calculate, instead of going, like the Greeks, from left to right, they move their hand from right to left; and they insist, notwithstanding, that it is they who go to the right, and the Greeks who go to the left. They have two quite different kinds of writing, one of which is called sacred, the other common.

37. They are religious to excess, far beyond any other race of men,[3] and use the following ceremonies:— They drink out of brazen cups,[4] which they scour every day: there is no exception to this practice. They wear linen garments, which they are specially careful to have always fresh washed.[5] They practise circumcision for the sake of cleanliness, considering it better to be cleanly than comely. The priests shave their whole body every other day, that no lice or other impure thing may adhere to them when they are engaged in the service of the gods. Their dress is entirely of linen,[6] and their shoes of the papyrus

1 The ancient custom of fastening the braces and sheets of the sails to rings within the gunwale fully agrees with that still adopted in the Nile boats.

2 The Egyptians wrote from right to left in hieratic and demotic (or enchorial), which are the two modes of *writing* here mentioned. The Greeks also in old times wrote from right to left, like the Phœnicians, from whom they borrowed their alphabet. This seems the natural mode of writing; for though we have always been accustomed to write from left to right, we invariably use our pencil, in shading a drawing, from right to left, in spite of all our previous habit.

3 The extreme religious views of the Egyptians became at length a gross superstition, and were naturally a subject for ridicule and contempt.

4 This, he says, is the universal custom, without exception; but we not only know that Joseph had a silver drinking-cup (Gen. xliv. 2, 5), but the sculptures show the wealthy Egyptians used glass, porcelain, and gold, sometimes inlaid with a coloured composition resembling enamel, or with precious stones. That persons who could not afford cups of more costly materials should have been contented with those of bronze is very probable.

5 Their attention to cleanliness was very remarkable, as is shown by their shaving the head and beard, and removing the hair from the whole body, by their frequent ablutions, and by the strict rules instituted to ensure it.

6 The dress of the priests consisted, as Herodotus states, of linen (ch. 81); but he does not say they were confined (as some have supposed) to a single robe; and whether walking abroad, or officiating in the temple, they were permitted to have more than one garment. The high priest styled *Sem* always wore a leopard-skin placed over the linen dress as his costume of office. The fine texture of the Egyptian linen is fully proved by its transparency, as represented in the paintings, and by the statements of ancient writers, sacred (Gen. xli. 42; and 2 Chron. i. 16) as well as profane.

plant:[1] it is not lawful for them to wear either dress or shoes of any other material. They bathe twice every day in cold water, and twice each night; besides which they observe, so to speak, thousands of ceremonies. They enjoy, however, not a few advantages.[2] They consume none of their own property, and are at no expense for anything;[3] but every day bread is baked for them of the sacred corn, and a plentiful supply of beef and of goose's flesh is assigned to each, and also a portion of wine made from the grape.[4] Fish they are not allowed to eat;[5] and beans, – which none of the Egyptians ever sow, or eat, if they come up of their own accord, either raw or boiled[6] – the priests will not even endure to look on, since they consider it an unclean kind of pulse. Instead of a single priest, each god has the attendance

1 Their sandals were made of the papyrus, an inferior quality being of matted palm-leaves; and they either slept on a simple skin stretched on the ground, or on a wicker bed, made of palm-branches.

2 The greatest of these was the paramount influence they exercised over the spiritual, and consequently over the temporal, concerns of the whole community, which was secured to them through their superior knowledge, by the dependence of all classes on them for the instruction they chose to impart, and by their exclusive right of possessing all the secrets of religion which were thought to place them far above the rest of mankind. Nor did their power over an individual cease with his life; it would even reach him after death; and their veto could prevent his being buried in his tomb, and consign his name to lasting infamy.

3 They were exempt from taxes, and were provided with a daily allowance of meat, corn, and wine; and when Pharaoh, by the advice of Joseph, took all the land of the Egyptians in lieu of corn (Gen. xlvii. 20, 22), the land of the priests was exempt, and the tax of the fifth part of the produce was not levied upon it.

4 Herodotus is quite right in saying they were allowed to drink wine, and the assertion of Plutarch that the kings (who were also of the priestly caste) were not permitted to drink it before the reign of Psammetichus is contradicted by the authority of the Bible (Gen. xl. 10, 13) and the sculptures.

5 Though fish were so generally eaten by the rest of the Egyptians, they were forbidden to the priests. The principal food of the priests was beef and goose, and the gazelle, ibex, oryx, and wild-fowl were not forbidden; but they "abstained from most sorts of pulse, from mutton, and swine's flesh, and in their more solemn purifications they even excluded salt from their meals." Garlick, leeks, onions, lentils, peas, and above all beans, are said to have been excluded from the tables of the priests.

6 Diodorus is more correct when he says that some only of the Egyptians abstained from beans, and it may be doubted if they grew in Egypt without being sown. The custom of forbidding beans to the priests was borrowed from Egypt by Pythagoras.

of a college, at the head of which is a chief priest;[1] when one of these dies, his son is appointed in his room.

38. Male kine are reckoned to belong to Epaphus,[2] and are therefore tested in the following manner:— One of the priests appointed for the purpose searches to see if there is a single black hair on the whole body, since in that case the beast is unclean. He examines him all over, standing on his legs, and again laid upon his back; after which he takes the tongue out of his mouth, to see if it be clean in respect of the prescribed marks (what they are I will mention elsewhere);[3] he also inspects the hairs of the tail, to observe if they grow naturally. If the animal is pronounced clean in all these various points, the priest marks him by twisting a piece of papyrus round his horns, and attaching thereto some sealing-clay, which he then stamps with his own signet-ring.[4] After this the beast is led away; and it is forbidden, under the penalty of death, to sacrifice an animal which has not been marked in this way.

39. The following is their manner of sacrifice:— They lead the victim, marked with their signet, to the altar where they are about to offer it, and setting the wood alight, pour a libation of wine upon the altar in front of the victim, and at the same time invoke the god. Then they slay the animal, and cutting off his head, proceed to flay the body. Next they take the head, and heaping imprecations on it, if there is a market-place and a body of Greek traders in the city, they carry it there and sell it instantly; if, however, there are no Greeks among them, they throw the head into the river. The imprecation is to this effect:— They pray that if any evil is impending either over those who sacrifice, or over universal Egypt, it may be made to fall upon that head. These practices, the imprecations upon the heads, and the libations of wine, prevail all over Egypt, and extend to victims of all sorts; and hence the Egyptians will never eat the head of any animal.

40. The disembowelling and burning are, however, different in different sacrifices. I will mention the mode in use with respect

---

1 This is fully confirmed by the sculptures.

2 Epaphus, Herodotus says (in ch. 153), is the Greek name of Apis.

3 Perhaps we have here, as in vii. 213, a promise that is unfulfilled.

4 The sanction given for sacrificing a bull was by a papyrus band tied by the priest round the horns, which he stamped with his signet on sealing-clay. Documents sealed with fine clay and impressed with a signet are very common; but the exact symbols impressed on it by the priest on this occasion are not known.

to the goddess whom they regard as the greatest,[1] and honour
with the chiefest festival. When they have flayed their steer they
pray, and when their prayer is ended they take the paunch of the
animal out entire, leaving the intestines and the fat inside the
body; they then cut off the legs, the ends of the loins, the shoulders, and the neck; and having so done, they fill the body of the
steer with clean bread, honey, raisins, figs, frankincense, myrrh,
and other aromatics.[2] Thus filled, they burn the body, pouring
over it great quantities of oil. Before offering the sacrifice they
fast, and while the bodies of the victims are being consumed
they beat themselves. Afterwards, when they have concluded this
part of the ceremony, they have the other parts of the victim
served up to them for a repast.

41. The male kine, therefore, if clean, and the male calves,
are used for sacrifice by the Egyptians universally; but the
females they are not allowed to sacrifice,[3] since they are sacred
to Isis. The statue of this goddess has the form of a woman but
with horns like a cow, resembling thus the Greek representations
of Io; and the Egyptians, one and all, venerate cows much more
highly than any other animal. This is the reason why no native
of Egypt, whether man or woman, will give a Greek a kiss,[4] or
use the knife of a Greek, or his spit, or his cauldron, or taste
the flesh of an ox, known to be pure, if it has been cut with a
Greek knife. When kine die, the following is the manner of their
sepulture:– The females are thrown into the river; the males are
buried in the suburbs of the towns, with one or both of their
horns appearing above the surface of the ground to mark the

1 Herodotus here evidently alludes to Isis, as he shows in chs. 59, 61, where
he speaks of her fête at Busiris; but he afterwards confounds her with Athor
(ch. 41). This is excusable in the historian, as the attributes of those two
goddesses are often so closely connected that it is difficult to distinguish them
in the sculptures, unless their names are specified. [In the *Book of the Dead*,
Hathor is identified with Isis. – E. H. B.]

2 The custom of filling the body with cakes and various things, and then
burning it all, calls to mind the Jewish burnt offering (Levit. viii. 25, 26).

3 In order to prevent the breed of cattle from being diminished: but some
mysterious reason being assigned for it, the people were led to respect an
ordonnance which might not otherwise have been attended to. This was the
general system, and the reason of many things being held sacred may be attributed to a necessary precaution.

4 The Egyptians considered all foreigners unclean, with whom they would
not eat, and particularly the Greeks. "The Egyptians might not eat bread with
the Hebrews, for that is an abomination unto the Egyptians" (Gen. xliii. 32).

place. When the bodies are decayed, a boat comes, at an appointed time, from the island called Prosôpitis,¹ – which is a portion of the Delta, nine schœnes in circumference, – and calls at the several cities in turn to collect the bones of the oxen. Prosôpitis is a district containing several cities; the name of that from which the boats come is Atarbêchis.² Aphrodite has a temple there of much sanctity. Great numbers of men go forth from this city and proceed to the other towns, where they dig up the bones, which they take away with them and bury together in one place. The same practice prevails with respect to the interment of all other cattle – the law so determining; they do not slaughter any of them.

42. Such Egyptians as possess a temple of the Theban Jove, or live in the Thebaïc canton, offer no sheep in sacrifice,³ but only goats; for the Egyptians do not all worship the same gods,⁴ excepting Isis and Osiris, the latter of whom they say is the Grecian Dionysus. Those, on the contrary, who possess a temple dedicated to Mendes,⁵ or belong to the Mendesian canton, abstain from offering goats, and sacrifice sheep instead. The Thebans, and such as imitate them in their practice, give the following account of the origin of the custom:– "Heracles," they say, "wished of all things to see Jove, but Jove did not choose to be seen of him. At length, when Heracles persisted, Jove hit on a device – to flay a ram, and, cutting off his head, hold the head before him, and cover himself with the fleece. In this guise he showed himself to Heracles." Therefore the Egyptians give their statues of Zeus the face of a ram:⁶ and from them the

1 The island was between the Canopic and Sebennytic branches, at the fork, and on the west side of the apex of the Delta. It was there that the Athenians, who came to assist the Egyptians against the Persians, were besieged, B.C. 460–458. (Thucyd. i. 109).

2 Athor being the Aphrodite of Egypt, Atarbechis was translated Aphroditopolis.

3 Sheep are never represented on the altar, or slaughtered for the table, at Thebes, though they were kept there for their wool.

4 Though each city had its presiding deity, many others of neighbouring and of distant towns were also admitted to its temples as contemplar gods, and none were positively excluded except some local divinities, and certain animals, whose sanctity was confined to particular places.

5 The mounds of *Ashmoun*, on the canal leading to *Ménzaleh*, mark the site of Mendes. The Greeks considered Pan to be both Mendes and Khem.

6 The god Noum (Nou, Noub, or Nef), with a ram's head, answered to Zeus (Jupiter). [See Renouf, *Lectures on Egyptian Religion* (1879), p. 199. – E. H. B.]

practice has passed to the Ammonians, who are a joint colony of Egyptians and Ethiopians, speaking a language between the two; hence also, in my opinion, the latter people took their name of Ammonians, since the Egyptian name for Zeus is Amun. Such, then, is the reason why the Thebans do not sacrifice rams, but consider them sacred animals. Upon one day in the year, however, at the festival of Zeus, they slay a single ram, and stripping off the fleece, cover with it the statue of that god, as he once covered himself, and then bring up to the statue of Jove an image of Heracles. When this has been done, the whole assembly beat their breasts in mourning for the ram, and afterwards bury him in a holy sepulchre.

43. The account which I received of this Heracles makes him one of the twelve gods.[1] Of the other Heracles, with whom the Greeks are familiar, I could hear nothing in any part of Egypt. That the Greeks, however (those I mean who gave the son of Amphitryon that name), took the name[2] from the Egyptians, and not the Egyptians from the Greeks,[3] is I think clearly proved, among other arguments, by the fact that both the parents of Heracles, Amphitryon as well as Alcmêna, were of Egyptian origin. Again, the Egyptians disclaim all knowledge of the names of Poseidon and the Dioscûri, and do not include them in the number of their gods; but had they adopted the name of any god from the Greeks, these would have been the likeliest to obtain notice, since the Egyptians, as I am well convinced, practised navigation at that time, and the Greeks also were some of them mariners, so that they would have been more likely to know the names of these gods than that of Heracles. But the Egyptian Heracles is one of their ancient gods. Seventeen thousand years before the reign of Amasis, the twelve gods were, they affirm, produced from the eight: and of these twelve, Heracles is one.

1 The Egyptian Heracles was the *abstract idea* of divine power, and it is not therefore surprising that Herodotus could learn nothing of the Greek Heracles, who was a hero unknown in Egypt.

2 Herodotus, who derived his knowledge of the Egyptian religion from the professional interpreters, seems to have regarded the *word* "Heracles" as Egyptian. It is scarcely necessary to say that no Egyptian god has a name from which that of Heracles can by any possibility have been formed.

3 The tendency of the Greeks to claim an indigenous origin for the deities they borrowed from strangers, and to substitute physical for abstract beings, readily led them to invent the story of Heracles, and every *dignus vindice nodus* was cut by the interposition of his marvellous strength.

44. In the wish to get the best information that I could on these matters, I made a voyage to Tyre in Phœnicia, hearing there was a temple of Heracles at that place,[1] very highly venerated. I visited the temple, and found it richly adorned with a number of offerings, among which were two pillars, one of pure gold, the other of emerald,[2] shining with great brilliancy at night. In a conversation which I held with the priests, I inquired how long their temple had been built, and found by their answer that they, too, differed from the Greeks. They said that the temple was built at the same time that the city was founded, and that the foundation of the city took place two thousand three hundred years ago. In Tyre I remarked another temple where the same god was worshipped as the Thasian Heracles. So I went on to Thasos,[3] where I found a temple of Heracles which had been built by the Phœnicians who colonised that island when they sailed in search of Europa. Even this was five generations earlier than the time when Heracles, son of Amphitryon, was born in Greece. These researches show plainly that there is an ancient god Heracles; and my own opinion is, that those Greeks act most wisely who build and maintain two temples of Heracles, in the one of which the Heracles worshipped is known by the name of Olympian, and has sacrifice offered to him as an immortal, while in the other the honours paid are such as are due to a hero.

45. The Greeks tell many tales without due investigation, and among them the following silly fable respecting Heracles:— "Heracles," they say, "went once to Egypt, and there the inhabitants took him, and putting a chaplet on his head, led him out in solemn procession, intending to offer him a sacrifice to Zeus. For a while he submitted quietly; but when they led him up to the altar and began the ceremonies, he put forth his strength and slew them all." Now to me it seems that such a story proves the Greeks to be utterly ignorant of the character and customs of the people. The Egyptians do not think it allowable even to

1 The temple of Heracles at Tyre was very ancient, and, according to Herodotus, as old as the city itself, or 2300 years before his time, i.e. about 2755 B.C. Heracles presided over it under the title of Melkarth, or Melek-Kartha, "king" (lord) of the city.

2 It was probably of glass, which is known to have been made in Egypt at least 3800 years ago, having been found bearing the name of a Pharaoh of the 18th dynasty.

3 Thasos, which still retains its name, is a small island off the Thracian coast.

sacrifice cattle, excepting sheep, and the male kine and calves, provided they be pure, and also geese. How, then, can it be believed that they would sacrifice men?[1] And again, how would it have been possible for Heracles alone, and, as they confess, a mere mortal, to destroy so many thousands? In saying thus much concerning these matters, may I incur no displeasure either of god or hero!

46. I mentioned above that some of the Egyptians abstain from sacrificing goats, either male or female. The reason is the following:— These Egyptians, who are the Mendesians, consider Pan to be one of the eight gods who existed before the twelve, and Pan is represented in Egypt by the painters and the sculptors, just as he is in Greece, with the face and legs of a goat. They do not, however, believe this to be his shape, or consider him in any respect unlike the other gods; but they represent him thus for a reason which I prefer not to relate. The Mendesians hold all goats in veneration, but the male more than the female, giving the goatherds of the males especial honour. One is venerated more highly than all the rest, and when he dies there is a great mourning throughout all the Mendesian canton. In Egyptian, the goat and Pan are both called Mendes. A marvel occurred in my time in this canton: a goat coupled openly with a woman, in full view. This was done as a public exhibition.

47. The pig is regarded among them as an unclean animal, so much so that if a man in passing accidentally touch a pig, he instantly hurries to the river, and plunges in with all his clothes on. Hence, too, the swineherds, notwithstanding that they are of pure Egyptian blood, are forbidden to enter into any of the temples, which are open to all other Egyptians; and further, no one will give his daughter in marriage to a swineherd, or take a wife from among them, so that the swineherds are forced to intermarry among themselves. They do not offer swine[2] in sacrifice to any of their gods, excepting Dionysus and the Moon,

1 Herodotus here denies, with reason, the possibility of a people with laws, and a character like those of the Egyptians, having human sacrifices. This very aptly refutes the idle tales of some ancient authors.

2 The pig is rarely represented in the sculptures of Thebes. The flesh was forbidden to the priests, and to all initiated in the mysteries, and it seems only to have been allowed to others once a year at the fête of the full moon, when it was sacrificed to the Moon. The reason of the meat not being eaten was its unwholesomeness, on which account it was forbidden to the Jews and Moslems; and the prejudice naturally extended from the animal to those who kept it.

whom they honour in this way at the same time, sacrificing pigs
to both of them at the same full moon, and afterwards eating of
the flesh. There is a reason alleged by them for their detestation
of swine at all other seasons, and their use of them at this
festival, with which I am well acquainted, but which I do not
think it proper to mention. The following is the mode in which
they sacrifice the swine to the Moon:— As soon as the victim is
slain, the tip of the tail, the spleen, and the caul are put together,
and having been covered with all the fat that has been found in
the animal's belly, are straightway burnt. The remainder of the
flesh is eaten on the same day that the sacrifice is offered, which
is the day of the full moon: at any other time they would not so
much as taste it. The poorer sort, who cannot afford live pigs,
form pigs of dough, which they bake and offer in sacrifice.

48. To Dionysus, on the eve of his feast, every Egyptian sacrifices a hog before the door of his house, which is then given back
to the swineherd by whom it was furnished, and by him carried
away. In other respects the festival is celebrated almost exactly as
Dionysiac festivals are in Greece, excepting that the Egyptians have
no choral dances. They also use instead of phalli another invention,
consisting of images a cubit high, pulled by strings, which the
women carry round to the villages. The genitals nod up and down
and are almost as large as the rest of the body. A piper goes in
front,[1] and the women follow, singing hymns in honour of Dionysus. They give a religious story for why the genitals are larger and
the only moveable part of the body.

49. Melampus, the son of Amytheon, cannot (I think) have
been ignorant of this ceremony – nay, he must, I should conceive, have been well acquainted with it. He it was who introduced into Greece the name of Dionysus, the ceremonial of his
worship, and the procession of the phallus. He did not, however,
so completely apprehend the whole doctrine as to be able to
communicate it entirely, but various sages since his time have
carried out his teaching to greater perfection. Still it is certain
that Melampus introduced the phallus, and that the Greeks learnt
from him the ceremonies which they now practise. I therefore
maintain that Melampus, who was a wise man, and had acquired
the art of divination, having become acquainted with the worship
of Dionysus through knowledge derived from Egypt, introduced

1 The instrument used was probably the double-pipe.

it into Greece, with a few slight changes, at the same time that he brought in various other practices. For I can by no means allow that it is by mere coincidence that the Dionysiac ceremonies in Greece are so nearly the same as the Egyptian – they would then have been more Greek in their character, and less recent in their origin. Much less can I admit that the Egyptians borrowed these customs, or any other, from the Greeks. My belief is that Melampus got his knowledge of them from Cadmus the Tyrian, and the followers whom he brought from Phœnicia into the country which is now called Bœotia.

50. Almost all the names of the gods came into Greece from Egypt.[1] My inquiries prove that they were all derived from a foreign source, and my opinion is that Egypt furnished the greater number. For with the exception of Poseidon and the Dioscûri, whom I mentioned above, and Hera, Hestia, Themis, the Graces, and the Nereids, the other gods have been known from time immemorial in Egypt. This I assert on the authority of the Egyptians themselves. The gods, with whose names they profess themselves unacquainted, the Greeks received, I believe, from the Pelasgi, except Poseidon. Of him they got their knowledge from the Libyans,[2] by whom he has been always honoured, and who were anciently the only people that had a god of the name. The Egyptians differ from the Greeks also in paying no divine honours to heroes.[3]

51. Besides these which have been here mentioned, there are many other practices whereof I shall speak hereafter, which the Greeks have borrowed from Egypt.[4] However the fashioning of

[1] There is no doubt that the Greeks borrowed sometimes the names, sometimes the attributes, of their deities from Egypt; but when Herodotus says the *names* of the Greek gods were always known in Egypt, it is evident that he does not mean they were the *same* as the Greek, since he gives in other places (chs. 42, 59, 138, 144, 156) the Egyptian name to which those very gods agree, whom he mentions in Egypt.

[2] Cf. iv. 188.

[3] No Egyptian god was supposed to have lived on earth as a mere man afterwards deified. The religion of the Egyptians was the worship of the Deity in all his attributes, and in those things which were thought to partake of his essence; but they did not transfer a mortal man to his place, though they allowed a king to pay divine honours to a deceased predecessor, or even to himself, his human doing homage to his divine nature.

[4] Herodotus expressly gives it as his opinion that nearly all the names of the gods were derived from Egypt, and shows that their ceremonies (chs. 81, 82) and science come from the same source.

statues of Hermes with the genitals erect they learnt not from
the Egyptians but from the Pelasgi; from them the Athenians
first adopted it, and afterwards it passed from the Athenians to
the other Greeks. For just at the time when the Athenians were
entering into the Hellenic body, the Pelasgi came to live with
them in their country,[1] whence it was that the latter came first
to be regarded as Greeks. Whoever has been initiated into the
mysteries of the Cabiri[2] will understand what I mean. The Samothracians received these mysteries from the Pelasgi, who, before
they went to live in Attica, were dwellers in Samothrace, and
imparted their religious ceremonies to the inhabitants. The Athenians, then, who were the first of all the Greeks to make their
statues of Hermes with genitals erect, learnt the practice from the
Pelasgians; and by this people a religious account of the matter
is given, which is explained in the Samothracian mysteries.

52. In early times the Pelasgi, as I know by information
which I got at Dodôna, offered sacrifices of all kinds, and prayed
to the gods, but had no distinct names or appellations for them,
since they had never heard of any. They called them gods
(θεοὶ, disposers), because they had disposed and arranged all
things in such a beautiful order.[3] After a long lapse of time the
names of the gods came to Greece from Egypt, and the Pelasgi
learnt them, only as yet they knew nothing of Dionysus, of
whom they first heard at a much later date. Not long after the
arrival of the names they sent to consult the oracle at Dodôna
about them. This is the most ancient oracle in Greece, and at
that time there was no other. To their question, "Whether they
should adopt the names that had been imported from the foreigners?" the oracle replied by recommending their use. Thenceforth in their sacrifices the Pelasgi made use of the names of the
gods, and from them the names passed afterwards to the Greeks.

1 The Pelasgi here intended are the Tyrrhenian Pelasgi, who are mentioned
again, iv. 145, and vi. 138.

2 Nothing is known for certain respecting the Cabiri. Most authorities agree
that they varied in number, and that their worship, which was very ancient in
Samothrace and in Phrygia, was carried to Greece from the former by the
Pelasgi. They were also worshipped at an early time in Lemnos and Imbros.

3 The same derivation is given by Eustathius and by Clement of Alexandria;
but the more general belief of the Greeks derived the word θεὸς from θεῖν,
"to run," because the gods first worshipped were the sun, moon, and stars. Both
these derivations are purely fanciful.

53. Whence the gods severally sprang, whether or no they had all existed from eternity, what forms they bore – these are questions of which the Greeks knew nothing until the other day, so to speak. For Homer and Hesiod were the first to compose Theogonies, and give the gods their epithets, to allot them their several offices and occupations, and describe their forms; and they lived but four hundred years before my time,[1] as I believe. As for the poets who are thought by some to be earlier than these,[2] they are, in my judgment, decidedly later writers. In these matters I have the authority of the priestesses of Dodôna for the former portion of my statements; what I have said of Homer and Hesiod is my own opinion.

54. The following tale is commonly told in Egypt concerning the oracle of Dodôna in Greece, and that of Ammon in Libya. My informants on the point were the priests of Zeus at Thebes. They said "that two of the sacred women were once carried off from Thebes by the Phœnicians,[3] and that the story went that one of them was sold into Libya, and the other into Greece, and these women were the first founders of the oracles in the two countries." On my inquiring how they came to know so exactly what became of the women, they answered, "that diligent search had been made after them at the time, but that it had not been found possible to discover where they were; afterwards, however, they received the information which they had given me."

55. This was what I heard from the priests at Thebes; at Dodôna, however, the women who deliver the oracles relate the matter as follows:– "Two black doves flew away from Egyptian Thebes, and while one directed its flight to Libya, the other came to them.[4] She alighted on an oak, and sitting there began to speak

1 The date of Homer has been variously stated. It is plain from the expressions which Herodotus here uses that in his time the general belief assigned to Homer an earlier date than that which he considered the true one. His date would place the poet about B.C. 880–830, which is very nearly the mean between the earliest and the latest epochs that are assigned to him. The time of Hesiod is even more doubtful, if possible, than that of his brother-poet. He was made before Homer, after him, and contemporary with him. Internal evidence and the weight of authority are in favour of the view which assigns him a comparatively late date.

2 The "poets thought by some to be earlier than Homer and Hesiod" are probably the mystic writers, Olen, Linus, Orpheus, Musæus, Pamphos, Olympus, etc., who were generally accounted by the Greeks anterior to Homer, but seen really to have belonged to a later age.

3 This carrying off priestesses from Thebes is of course a fable.

4 The idea of women giving out oracles is Greek, not Egyptian.

with a human voice, and told them that on the spot where she was, there should thenceforth be an oracle of Jove. They understood the announcement to be from heaven, so they set to work at once and erected the shrine. The dove which flew to Libya bade the Libyans to establish there the oracle of Ammon." This likewise is an oracle of Zeus. The persons from whom I received these particulars were three priestesses of the Dodonæans, the eldest Promeneia, the next Timareté, and the youngest Nicandra – what they said was confirmed by the other Dodonæans who dwell around the temple.[1]

56. My own opinion of these matters is as follows:– I think that, if it be true that the Phœnicians carried off the holy women, and sold them for slaves,[2] the one into Libya and the other into Greece, or Pelasgia (as it was then called), this last must have been sold to the Thesprotians. Afterwards, while undergoing servitude in those parts, she built under a real oak a temple to Zeus, her thoughts in her new abode reverting – as it was likely they would do, if she had been an attendant in a temple of Zeus at Thebes – to that particular god. Then, having acquired a knowledge of the Greek tongue, she set up an oracle. She also mentioned that her sister had been sold for a slave into Libya by the same persons as herself.

57. The Dodonæans called the women doves because they were foreigners, and seemed to them to make a noise like birds. After a while the dove spoke with a human voice, because the woman, whose foreign talk had previously sounded to them like the chattering of a bird, acquired the power of speaking what they could understand. For how can it be conceived possible that a dove should really speak with the voice of a man? Lastly, by calling the dove black the Dodonæans indicated that the woman was an Egyptian. And certainly the character of the oracles at Thebes and Dodôna is very similar. Besides this form of divination, the Greeks learnt also divination by means of victims from the Egyptians.

1 The Temple of Dodona was destroyed B.C. 219 by Dorimachus when, being chosen general of the Ætolians, he ravaged Epirus. (Polyb. iv. 67.) No remains of it now exist.

2 Cf. Joel iii. 6, where the Tyrians are said to have sold Jewish children "to the Grecians." [R.V. "Sons of the Grecians," *i.e.* men of Greek descent. – E. H. B.]

58. The Egyptians were also the first to introduce solemn assemblies,[1] processions, and litanies to the gods; of all which the Greeks were taught the use by them. It seems to me a sufficient proof of this, that in Egypt these practices have been established from remote antiquity, while in Greece they are only recently known.

59. The Egyptians do not hold a single solemn assembly, but several in the course of the year. Of these the chief, which is better attended than any other, is held at the city of Bubastis[2] in honour of Artemis.[3] The next in importance is that which takes place at Busiris, a city situated in the very middle of the Delta; it is in honour of Isis, who is called in the Greek tongue Demeter (Ceres). There is a third great festival in Saïs to Athena, a fourth in Heliopolis to the Sun, a fifth in Buto[4] to Leto, and a sixth in Paprêmis to Ares.

60. The following are the proceedings on occasion of the assembly at Bubastis:– Men and women come sailing all together, vast numbers in each boat, many of the women with castanets, which they strike, while some of the men pipe during the whole time of the voyage; the remainder of the voyagers, male and female, sing the while, and make a clapping with their hands. When they arrive opposite any of the towns upon the banks of the stream, they approach the shore, and, while some of the women continue to play and sing, others call aloud to the females of the place and load them with abuse, while a certain number dance, and some standing up uncover themselves. After proceeding in this way all along the river-course, they reach Bubastis, where they celebrate the feast with abundant sacrifices. More grape-wine[5] is consumed at this festival than in all the rest of the year besides. The number of those who attend, counting

1 "Solemn assemblies" were numerous in Egypt, and were of various kinds. The grand assemblies, or great panegyries, were held in the large halls of the principal temples, and the king presided at them in person. There were inferior panegyries in honour of different deities every day during certain months.

2 Bubastis, or Pasht, corresponded to the Greek Artemis. Remains of the temple and city of Bubastis, the "Pibeseth" (Pi-basth) of Ezekiel xxx. 17, are still seen at Tel Basta, "the mounds of Pasht." [See *Encyclopædia Biblica*, vol. iii., s.v. PIBESETH. Bubastis was the centre of Egyptian cat-worship. – E. H. B.]

3 Herodotus (infra, ch. 156) supposes her the daughter of Dionysus (Osiris) and Isis, which is, of course, an error, as Osiris had no daughter.

4 The Goddess mentioned at Bubastis should be Buto.

5 This is to be distinguished from beer, $οἶνος \ κρίθινος$, "barley-wine," both of which were made in great quantities in Egypt.

only the men and women and omitting the children, amounts, according to the native reports, to seven hundred thousand.

61. The ceremonies at the feast of Isis in the city of Busiris[1] have been already spoken of. It is there that the whole multitude, both of men and women, many thousands in number, beat themselves at the close of the sacrifice, in honour of a god, whose name a religious scruple forbids me to mention.[2] The Carian dwellers in Egypt proceed on this occasion to still greater lengths, even cutting their faces with their knives,[3] whereby they let it be seen that they are not Egyptians but foreigners.

62. At Saïs,[4] when the assembly takes place for the sacrifices, there is one night on which the inhabitants all burn a multitude of lights in the open air round their houses. They use lamps in the shape of flat saucers filled with a mixture of oil and salt,[5] on the top of which the wick floats. These burn the whole night, and give to the festival the name of the Feast of Lamps. The Egyptians who are absent from the festival observe the night of the sacrifice, no less than the rest, by a general lighting of lamps; so that the illumination is not confined to the city of Saïs, but extends over the whole of Egypt. And there is a religious reason assigned for the special honour paid to this night, as well as for the illumination which accompanies it.

63. At Heliopolis and Buto the assemblies are merely for the purpose of sacrifice; but at Paprêmis,[6] besides the sacrifices and other rites which are performed there as elsewhere, the following

1 There were several places called Busiris in Egypt. It signifies the burial place of Osiris. The Busiris mentioned by Herodotus stood in the Delta, a little to the S. of the modern *Abooseer*, the Coptic *Busiri*, of which nothing now remains but some granite blocks.

2 This was Osiris.

3 The custom of cutting themselves was not Egyptian; and it is therefore evident that the command in Leviticus (xix. 28; xxi. 5) against making "any cuttings in their flesh" was not directed against a custom derived from Egypt, but from Syria, where the worshippers of Baal "cut themselves after their manner with knives and lances," 1 Kings xviii. 28.

4 The site of Saïs is marked by lofty mounds, enclosing a space of great extent.

5 The oil floated on water mixed with salt.

6 Papremis is not known in the sculptures as the name of the Egyptian Ares; and it may only have been that of the city, the capital of a nome (ch. 165) which stood between the modern *Menzaleh* and *Damietta* in the Delta. It was here that Inaros routed the Persians (infra, iii. 12); and it is remarkable that in this very island, formed by the old Mendesian and the modern Damietta branches, the Crusaders were defeated in 1220, and again in 1249, when Louis IX. was taken prisoner.

custom is observed:– When the sun is getting low, a few only of the priests continue occupied about the image of the god, while the greater number, armed with wooden clubs, take their station at the portal of the temple. Opposite to them is drawn up a body of men, in number above a thousand, armed, like the others, with clubs, consisting of persons engaged in the performance of their vows. The image of the god, which is kept in a small wooden shrine covered with plates of gold, is conveyed from the temple into a second sacred building the day before the festival begins. The few priests still in attendance upon the image place it, together with the shrine containing it, on a four-wheeled car, and begin to drag it along; the others, stationed at the gateway of the temple, oppose its admission. Then the votaries come forward to espouse the quarrel of the god, and set upon the opponents, who are sure to offer resistance. A sharp fight with clubs ensues, in which heads are commonly broken on both sides. Many, I am convinced, die of the wounds that they receive, though the Egyptians insist that no one is ever killed.

The natives give the subjoined account of this festival. They say that the mother of the god Ares once dwelt in the temple. Brought up at a distance from his parent, when he grew to man's estate he conceived a wish to visit her. Accordingly he came, but the attendants, who had never seen him before, refused him entrance, and succeeded in keeping him out. So he went to another city and collected a body of men, with whose aid he handled the attendants very roughly, and forced his way in to his mother. Hence they say arose the custom of a fight with sticks in honour of Ares at this festival.

64. The Egyptians first made it a point of religion to have no converse with women in the sacred places, and not to enter them without washing, after such converse. Almost all other nations, except the Greeks and the Egyptians, do have converse in temples and enter temples unwashed after lying with a woman, regarding man as in this matter under no other law than the brutes. Many animals, they say, and various kinds of birds, may be seen to couple in the temples and the sacred precincts, which would certainly not happen if the gods were displeased at it. Such are the arguments by which they defend their practice, but I nevertheless can by no means approve of it. In these points the Egyptians are specially careful, as they are indeed in everything which concerns their sacred edifices.

65. Egypt, though it borders upon Libya, is not a region abounding in wild animals.[1] The animals that do exist in the country, whether domesticated or otherwise, are all regarded as sacred. If I were to explain why they are consecrated to the several gods, I should be led to speak of religious matters, which I particularly shrink from mentioning; the points whereon I have touched slightly hitherto have all been introduced from sheer necessity. Their custom with respect to animals is as follows:— For every kind there are appointed certain guardians, some male, some female,[2] whose business it is to look after them; and this honour is made to descend from father to son. The inhabitants of the various cities, when they have made a vow to any god, pay it to his animals in the way which I will now explain. At the time of making the vow they shave the head of the child,[3] cutting off all the hair, or else half, or sometimes a third part, which they then weigh in a balance against a sum of silver; and whatever sum the hair weighs is presented to the guardian of the animals, who thereupon cuts up some fish, and gives it to them for food — such being the stuff whereon they are fed. When a man has killed one of the sacred animals, if he did it with malice prepense, he is punished with death;[4] if unwittingly, he has to pay such a fine as the priests choose to impose. When an ibis, however, or a hawk is killed, whether it was done by accident or on purpose, the man must needs die.

1 This was thought to be extraordinary, because Africa abounded in wild animals (infra, iv. 191–2); but it was on the west and south, and not on the confines of Egypt, that they were numerous. Though Herodotus abstains from saying why the Egyptians held some animals sacred, he explains it in some degree by observing that Egypt did not abound in animals. It was therefore found necessary to ensure the preservation of some, as in the case of cows and sheep; others were sacred in consequence of their being unwholesome food, as swine, and certain fish; and others from their utility in destroying noxious reptiles, as the cat, ichneumon, ibis, vulture, and falcon tribe: or for some particular purpose, as the crocodile was sacred in places distant from the Nile, where the canals required keeping up.

2 Women were probably employed to give the food to many of the animals; but the curators appear to have been men of the sacerdotal class.

3 Though Egyptian men shaved their heads, boys had several tufts of hair left, as in modern Egypt and China. Princes also wore a long plaited lock, falling from near the top of the head, behind the ear, to the neck.

4 The law was, as Herodotus says, against a person killing them on purpose, but the prejudiced populace in after times did not always keep within the law.

66. The number of domestic animals in Egypt is very great, and would be still greater were it not for what befalls the cats. As the females, when they have kittened, no longer seek the company of the males, these last, to obtain once more their companionship, practise a curious artifice. They seize the kittens, carry them off, and kill them, but do not eat them afterwards. Upon this the females, being deprived of their young, and longing to supply their place, seek the males once more, since they are particularly fond of their offspring. On every occasion of a fire in Egypt the strangest prodigy occurs with the cats. The inhabitants allow the fire to rage as it pleases, while they stand about at intervals and watch these animals, which, slipping by the men or else leaping over them, rush headlong into the flames. When this happens, the Egyptians are in deep affliction. If a cat dies in a private house by a natural death, all the inmates of the house shave their eyebrows; on the death of a dog they shave the head and the whole of the body.

67. The cats on their decease are taken to the city of Bubastis,[1] where they are embalmed, after which they are buried in certain sacred repositories. The dogs are interred in the cities to which they belong, also in sacred burial-places. The same practice obtains with respect to the ichneumons;[2] the hawks and shrew-mice, on the contrary, are conveyed to the city of Buto for burial, and the ibises[3] to Hermopolis. The bears, which are scarce in Egypt,[4] and the wolves, which are not much bigger than foxes,[5] they bury wherever they happen to find them lying.

68. The following are the peculiarities of the crocodile:– During the four winter months they eat nothing;[6] they are

1 Cats were embalmed and buried where they died, except perhaps in the neighbourhood of Bubastis; for we find their mummies at Thebes and other Egyptian towns, and the same may be said of hawks and ibises.

2 The *viverra* ichneumon is still very common in Egypt.

3 These birds were sacred to Thoth, the god of letters.

4 It is very evident that bears were not natives of Egypt; they are not represented among the animals of the country; and no instance occurs of a bear in the sculptures, except as a curiosity brought by foreigners.

5 Herodotus is quite correct in saying that wolves in Egypt were scarcely larger than foxes. It is singular that he omits all mention of the hyæna, which is so common in the country, and which is represented in the sculptures of Upper and Lower Egypt.

6 If the crocodile rarely comes out of the river in the cold weather, because it finds the water warmer than the external air at that season, there is no reason

four-footed, and live indifferently on land or in the water. The female lays and hatches her eggs ashore, passing the greater portion of the day on dry land, but at night retiring to the river, the water of which is warmer than the night-air and the dew. Of all known animals this is the one which from the smallest size grows to be the greatest: for the egg of the crocodile is but little bigger than that of the goose, and the young crocodile is in proportion to the egg; yet when it is full grown, the animal measures frequently seventeen cubits and even more. It has the eyes of a pig, teeth large and tusk-like, of a size proportioned to its frame; unlike any other animal, it is without a tongue; it cannot move its under-jaw, and in this respect too it is singular, being the only animal in the world which moves the upper-jaw but not the under. It has strong claws and a scaly skin, impenetrable upon the back. In the water it is blind, but on land it is very keen of sight. As it lives chiefly in the river, it has the inside of its mouth constantly covered with leeches; hence it happens that, while all the other birds and beasts avoid it, with the trochilus it lives at peace, since it owes much to that bird: for the crocodile, when he leaves the water and comes out upon the land, is in the habit of lying with his mouth wide open, facing the western breeze: at such times the trochilus goes into his mouth and devours the leeches. This benefits the crocodile, who is pleased, and takes care not to hurt the trochilus.

69. The crocodile is esteemed sacred by some of the Egyptians, by others he is treated as an enemy. Those who live near Thebes, and those who dwell around Lake Mœris, regard them with especial veneration. In each of these places they keep one crocodile in particular, who is taught to be tame and tractable. They adorn his ears[1] with ear-rings of molten stone[2] or gold, and put bracelets on his fore-paws, giving him daily a set portion of

---

to believe it remains torpid all that time, though, like all the lizard tribe, it can exist a long time without eating, and I have known them live in a house for three months without food, sleeping most of the time. The story of the friendly offices of the Trochilus appears to be derived from that bird's uttering a shrill note as it flies away on the approach of man, and (quite unintentionally) warning the crocodile of danger.

1 The crocodile's ears are merely small openings without any flesh projecting beyond the head.

2 By molten stone seems to be meant glass, which was well known to the Egyptians.

bread, with a certain number of victims; and, after having thus treated him with the greatest possible attention while alive, they embalm him when he dies and bury him in a sacred repository. The people of Elephantiné, on the other hand, are so far from considering these animals as sacred that they even eat their flesh. In the Egyptian language they are not called crocodiles, but Champsæ. The name of crocodiles was given them by the Ionians, who remarked their resemblance to the lizards, which in Ionia live in the walls, and are called crocodiles.[1]

70. The modes of catching the crocodile are many and various. I shall only describe the one which seems to me most worthy of mention. They bait a hook with a chine of pork and let the meat be carried out into the middle of the stream, while the hunter upon the bank holds a living pig, which he belabours. The crocodile hears its cries, and, making for the sound, encounters the pork, which he instantly swallows down. The men on the shore haul, and when they have got him to land, the first thing the hunter does is to plaster his eyes with mud. This once accomplished, the animal is despatched with ease, otherwise he gives great trouble.

71. The hippopotamus,[2] in the canton of Paprêmis, is a sacred animal, but not in any other part of Egypt. It may be thus described:— It is a quadruped, cloven-footed, with hoofs like an ox, and a flat nose. It has the mane and tail of a horse, huge tusks which are very conspicuous, and a voice like a horse's neigh. In size it equals the biggest oxen, and its skin is so tough that when dried it is made into javelins.

72. Otters also are found in the Nile, and are considered sacred. Only two sorts of fish are venerated,[3] that called the lepidôtus and the eel. These are regarded as sacred to the Nile, as likewise among birds is the vulpanser, or fox-goose.[4]

---

1 Κροκόδειλος was the term given by the Ionians to lizards, as the Portuguese *al legato* "the lizard" is the origin of our alligator. The Ionians are here the descendants of the Ionian soldiers of Psammetichus.

2 This animal was formerly common in Egypt, but is now rarely seen as low as the second cataract. The description of the hippopotamus by Herodotus is far from correct.

3 The fish particularly sacred were the Oxyrhinchus, the Lepidotus, and the Phagrus or eel.

4 This goose of the Nile was an emblem of the God Seb, the father of Osiris; but it was not a sacred bird.

73. They have also another sacred bird called the phœnix, which I myself have never seen, except in pictures. Indeed it is a great rarity, even in Egypt, only coming there (according to the accounts of the people of Heliopolis) once in five hundred years, when the old phœnix dies. Its size and appearance, if it is like the pictures, are as follow:— The plumage is partly red, partly golden, while the general make and size are almost exactly that of the eagle. They tell a story of what this bird does, which does not seem to me to be credible: that he comes all the way from Arabia, and brings the parent bird, all plastered over with myrrh, to the temple of the Sun, and there buries the body. In order to bring him, they say, he first forms a ball of myrrh as big as he finds that he can carry; then he hollows out the ball, and puts his parent inside, after which he covers over the opening with fresh myrrh, and the ball is then of exactly the same weight as at first; so he brings it to Egypt, plastered over as I have said, and deposits it in the temple of the Sun. Such is the story they tell of the doings of this bird.

74. In the neighbourhood of Thebes there are some sacred serpents[1] which are perfectly harmless.[2] They are of small size, and have two horns growing out of the top of the head. These snakes, when they die, are buried in the temple of Zeus, the god to whom they are sacred.

75. I went once to a certain place in Arabia, almost exactly opposite the city of Buto, to make inquiries concerning the winged serpents.[3] On my arrival I saw the back-bones and ribs of serpents in such numbers as it is impossible to describe: of the ribs there were a multitude of heaps, some great, some small, some middle-sized. The place where the bones lie is at the entrance of a narrow gorge between steep mountains, which there open upon a spacious plain communicating with the great plain of Egypt. The story goes, that with the spring the winged snakes

1 The horned snake, *vipera cerastes*, is common in Upper Egypt and throughout the deserts. It is very poisonous, and its habit of burying itself in the sand renders it particularly dangerous.

2 The bite of the cerastes or horned snake is deadly; but of the many serpents in Egypt, three only are poisonous – the cerastes, the asp or naia, and the common viper.

3 The winged serpents of Herodotus have puzzled many persons from the time of Pausanias to the present day. Isaiah (xxx. 6) mentions the "fiery flying serpent."

come flying from Arabia towards Egypt, but are met in this gorge by the birds called ibises, who forbid their entrance and destroy them all. The Arabians assert, and the Egyptians also admit, that it is on account of the service thus rendered that the Egyptians hold the ibis in so much reverence.

76. The ibis is a bird of a deep-black colour, with legs like a crane; its beak is strongly hooked, and its size is about that of the landrail. This is a description of the black ibis which contends with the serpents. The commoner sort, for there are two quite distinct species,[1] has the head and the whole throat bare of feathers; its general plumage is white, but the head and neck are jet black, as also are the tips of the wings and the extremity of the tail; in its beak and legs it resembles the other species. The winged serpent is shaped like the water-snake. Its wings are not feathered, but resemble very closely those of the bat. And thus I conclude the subject of the sacred animals.

77. With respect to the Egyptians themselves, it is to be remarked that those who live in the corn country,[2] devoting themselves, as they do, far more than any other people in the world, to the preservation of the memory of past actions, are the best skilled in history of any men that I have ever met. The following is the mode of life habitual to them:— For three successive days in each month they purge the body by means of emetics and clysters, which is done out of a regard for their health, since they have a persuasion that every disease to which men are liable is occasioned by the substances whereon they

1 The great services the ibis rendered by destroying snakes and noxious insects were the cause of its being in such esteem in Egypt. The stork was honoured for the same reason in Thessaly. The ibis was sacred to Thoth, the Egyptian Hermes.

2 This is in contradistinction to the marsh-lands, and signifies Upper Egypt; but when he says they have no vines in the country and only drink beer, his statement is opposed to fact, and to the ordinary habits of the Egyptians. In the neighbourhood of Memphis, at Thebes, and the places between those two cities, as well as at Eileithyias, all corn-growing districts, they ate wheaten bread and cultivated the vine. Herodotus may, therefore, have had in view the corn-country, in the interior of the broad Delta, where the alluvial soil was not well suited to the vine. Wine was universally used by the rich throughout Egypt, and beer supplied its place at the tables of the poor, not because "they had no vines in their country," but because it was cheaper. And that wine was known in Lower as well as Upper Egypt is shown by the Israelites mentioning the desert as a place which had "no figs, or *vines*, or pomegranates" in contradistinction to Egypt (Gen. xl. 10; Numb. xx. 5).

feed. Apart from any such precautions, they are, I believe, next to the Libyans,[1] the healthiest people in the world — an effect of their climate, in my opinion, which has no sudden changes. Diseases almost always attack men when they are exposed to a change, and never more than during changes of the weather. They live on bread made of spelt, which they form into loaves called in their own tongue *cyllêstis*. Their drink is a wine which they obtain from barley,[2] as they have no vines in their country. Many kinds of fish they eat raw, either salted or dried in the sun.[3] Quails also, and ducks and small birds, they eat uncooked, merely first salting them. All other birds and fishes, excepting those which are set apart as sacred, are eaten either roasted or boiled.

78. In social meetings among the rich, when the banquet is ended, a servant carries round to the several guests a coffin, in which there is a wooden image of a corpse,[4] carved and painted to resemble nature as nearly as possible, about a cubit or two cubits in length. As he shows it to each guest in turn, the servant says, "Gaze here, and drink and be merry; for when you die, such will you be."

79. The Egyptians adhere to their own national customs, and adopt no foreign usages. Many of these customs are worthy of note: among others their song, the Linus,[5] which is sung under various names not only in Egypt but in Phœnicia, in Cyprus, and in other places; and which seems to be exactly the same as that in use among the Greeks, and by them called Linus. There were very many things in Egypt which filled me with astonishment, and this was one of them. Whence could the Egyptians have got the Linus? It appears to have been sung by them from the very earliest times. For the Linus in Egyptian is called Manerôs; and they told me that Manerôs was the only son of their first king, and that on his untimely death he was honoured by the

1 Their health was attributable to their living in the dry atmosphere of the desert, where sickness is rarely known.

2 This is the οἶνος κρίθινος of Xenophon.

3 The custom of drying fish is frequently represented in the sculptures of Upper and Lower Egypt. Fishing was a favourite amusement of the Egyptians.

4 The figure introduced at supper was of a mummy in the usual form of Osiris, either standing, or lying on a bier, intended to warn the guests of their mortality.

5 This song had different names in Egypt, in Phœnicia, in Cyprus, and other places. In Greece it was called Linus, in Egypt Maneros. The stories told of Linus, the inventor of melody, and of his death, are mere fables.

Egyptians with these dirgelike strains, and in this way they got their first and only melody.

80. There is another custom in which the Egyptians resemble a particular Greek people, namely the Lacedæmonians. Their young men, when they meet their elders in the streets, give way to them and step aside;[1] and if an elder come in where young men are present, these latter rise from their seats. In a third point they differ entirely from all the nations of Greece. Instead of speaking to each other when they meet in the streets, they make an obeisance, sinking the hand to the knee.

81. They wear a linen tunic fringed about the legs, and called *calasiris*; over this they have a white woollen garment thrown on afterwards. Nothing of woollen, however, is taken into their temples or buried with them, as their religion forbids it. Here their practice resembles the rites called Orphic and Dionysiac, but which are in reality Egyptian and Pythagorean; for no one initiated in these mysteries can be buried in a woollen shroud, a religious reason being assigned for the observance.

82. The Egyptians likewise discovered to which of the gods each month and day is sacred;[2] and found out from the day of a man's birth, what he will meet with in the course of his life,[3] and how he will end his days, and what sort of man he will be — discoveries whereof the Greeks engaged in poetry have made a use. The Egyptians have also discovered more prognostics than all the rest of mankind besides. Whenever a prodigy takes place, they watch and record the result; then, if anything similar ever happens again, they expect the same consequences.

83. With respect to divination, they hold that it is a gift which no mortal possesses, but only certain of the gods:[4] thus they have an oracle of Heracles, one of Apollo, of Athena, of Artemis, of

1 A similar respect is paid to age by the Chinese and Japanese, and even by the modern Egyptians. In this the Greeks, except the Lacedæmonians, were wanting. The Jews were commanded to "rise up before the hoary head and honour the face of the old man" (Levit. xix. 32).

2 The Romans also made their twelve gods preside over the months; and the days of the week, when introduced in late times, received the names of the sun and moon and five planets, which have been retained to the present day.

3 Horoscopes were of very early use in Egypt, as well as the interpretation of dreams; and Cicero speaks of the Egyptians and Chaldees predicting future events, as well as a man's destiny at his birth, by their observations of the stars.

4 Yet the Egyptians sought "to the idols, and to the charmers, and to them that had familiar spirits, and to the wizards" (Is. xix. 3). Herodotus probably

Ares, and of Zeus. Besides these, there is the oracle of Leto at Buto, which is held in much higher repute than any of the rest. The mode of delivering the oracles is not uniform, but varies at the different shrines.

84. Medicine is practised among them[1] on a plan of separation; each physician treats a single disorder, and no more:[2] thus the country swarms with medical practitioners, some undertaking to cure diseases of the eye, others of the head, others again of the teeth, others of the intestines, and some those which are not local.

85. The following is the way in which they conduct their mournings[3] and their funerals:— On the death in any house of a man of consequence, forthwith the women of the family beplaster their heads, and sometimes even their faces, with mud; and then, leaving the body indoors, sally forth and wander through the city, with their dress fastened by a band, and their bosoms bare, beating themselves as they walk. All the female relations join them and do the same. The men too, similarly begirt, beat

---

means that none but oracles gave the real answer of the deity; and this would not prevent the "prophets" and "magicians" pretending to this art, like the μάντεις of Greece. To the Israelites it was particularly forbidden "to use divination, to be an observer of times, or an enchanter, or a witch, or a charmer, or a consulter with familiar spirits, or a wizard, or a necromancer."

1 Not only was the study of medicine of very early date in Egypt, but medical men there were in such repute that they were sent for at various times from other countries. Their knowledge of medicine is celebrated by Homer (Od. iv. 229), who describes Polydamna, the wife of Thonis, as giving medicinal plants "to Helen, in Egypt, a country producing an infinite number of drugs ... where each physician possesses knowledge above all other men." "O virgin daughter of Egypt," says Jeremiah (lxvi. II), "in vain shalt thou use many medicines." Cyrus and Darius both sent to Egypt for medical men (Her. iii. I, 132); and Pliny (xix. 5) says *post-mortem* examinations were made in order to discover the nature of maladies. [Cf. Erman, *Life in Ancient Egypt*, pp. 377 sqq. — E. H. B.]

2 The medical profession being so divided (as is the custom in modern Europe), indicates a great advancement of civilisation, as well as of medicinal knowledge. The Egyptian doctors were of the sacerdotal order, like the embalmers, who are called (in Genesis l. 2) "Physicians," and were "commanded by Joseph to embalm his father."

3 The custom of weeping, and throwing dust on their heads, is often represented on the monuments; when the men and women have their dresses fastened by a band round the waist, the breast being bare, as described by Herodotus. For seventy days (Gen. l. 3), or, according to some, seventy-two days, the family mourned at home, singing the funeral dirge.

their breasts separately. When these ceremonies are over, the body is carried away to be embalmed.

86. There are a set of men in Egypt who practise the art of embalming, and make it their proper business. These persons, when a body is brought to them, show the bearers various models of corpses,[1] made in wood, and painted so as to resemble nature. The most perfect is said to be after the manner of him whom I do not think it religious to name in connection with such a matter; the second sort is inferior to the first, and less costly; the third is the cheapest of all. All this the embalmers explain, and then ask in which way it is wished that the corpse should be prepared. The bearers tell them, and having concluded their bargain, take their departure, while the embalmers, left to themselves, proceed to their task. The mode of embalming, according to the most perfect process, is the following:– They take first a crooked piece of iron,[2] and with it draw out the brain through the nostrils, thus getting rid of a portion, while the skull is cleared of the rest by rinsing with drugs; next they make a cut along the flank with a sharp Ethiopian stone,[3] and take out the whole contents of the abdomen, which they then cleanse, washing it thoroughly with palm wine, and again frequently with an infusion of pounded aromatics. After this they fill the cavity with the purest bruised myrrh, with cassia, and every other sort of spicery[4]

---

1 These were in the form of Osiris, and not only those of the best kind, but all the mummies were put up in the same position, representing the deceased as a figure of Osiris, those only excepted which were of the very poor people, and which were merely wrapped up in mats, or some other common covering. Even the small earthenware and other figures of the dead were in the same form of that Deity, whose name Herodotus, as usual, had scruples about mentioning, from having been admitted to a participation of the secrets of the lesser Mysteries.

2 The mummies afford ample evidence of the brain having been extracted through the nostrils; and the "drugs" were employed to clear out what the instrument could not touch.

3 Ethiopian stone either is *black* flint, or an Ethiopian agate, the use of which was the remnant of a very primitive custom. [An embalming knife, used for this one purpose only: see King and Hall's *Egypt and W. Asia in the Light of Modern Discoveries*, p. 14. – E. H. B.]

4 The "spicery, and balm, and myrrh," carried by the Ishmaelites (or Arabs) to Egypt were principally for the embalmers, who were doubtless supplied regularly with them. (Gen. xxxvii. 25.) Other caravans, like the Midianite merchantmen (Gen. xxxvii. 28), visited Egypt for trade; and "the spice merchants" are noticed (1 Kings x. 15) in Solomon's time.

except frankincense, and sew up the opening. Then the body is placed in natrum[1] for seventy days, and covered entirely over. After the expiration of that space of time, which must not be exceeded, the body is washed, and wrapped round, from head to foot, with bandages of fine linen cloth,[2] smeared over with gum, which is used generally by the Egyptians in the place of glue, and in this state it is given back to the relations, who enclose it in a wooden case which they have had made for the purpose, shaped into the figure of a man. Then fastening the case, they place it in a sepulchral chamber, upright against the wall. Such is the most costly way of embalming the dead.

87. If persons wish to avoid expense, and choose the second process, the following is the method pursued:– Syringes are filled with oil made from the cedar-tree, which is then, without any incision[3] or disembowelling, injected into the abdomen. The passage by which it might be likely to return is stopped, and the body laid in natrum the prescribed number of days. At the end of the time the cedar-oil is allowed to make its escape; and such is its power that it brings with it the whole stomach and intestines in a liquid state. The natrum meanwhile has dissolved the flesh, and so nothing is left of the dead body but the skin and the bones. It is returned in this condition to the relatives, without any further trouble being bestowed upon it.

88. The third method of embalming, which is practised in the case of the poorer classes, is to clear out the intestines with a clyster, and let the body lie in natrum the seventy days, after which it is at once given to those who come to fetch it away.

89. The wives of men of rank are not given to be embalmed immediately after death, nor indeed are any of the more beautiful and valued women. It is not till they have been dead three or four days that they are carried to the embalmers. This is done to prevent indignities from being offered them. It is said that once a case of this kind occurred: the man was detected by the information of his fellow-workman.

1 *i.e.* subcarbonate of soda, which abounds at the natron lakes in the Libyan desert.

2 Not cotton. The microscope has decided (what no one ever doubted in Egypt) that the mummy-cloths are linen.

3 Second-class mummies without any incision are found in the tombs; but the opening in the side was made in many of them, and occasionally even in those of an inferior quality; so that it was not exclusively confined to mummies of the first class. There were, in fact, many gradations in each class.

90. Whensoever any one, Egyptian or foreigner, has lost his life by falling a prey to a crocodile, or by drowning in the river, the law compels the inhabitants of the city near which the body is cast up to have it embalmed, and to bury it in one of the sacred repositories with all possible magnificence.[1] No one may touch the corpse, not even any of the friends or relatives, but only the priests of the Nile, who prepare it for burial with their own hands — regarding it as something more than the mere body of a man — and themselves lay it in the tomb.

91. The Egyptians are averse to adopt Greek customs, or, in a word, those of any other nation. This feeling is almost universal among them. At Chemmis,[2] however, which is a large city in the Thebaïc canton, near Neapolis,[3] there is a square enclosure sacred to Perseus, son of Danaë. Palm trees grow all round the place, which has a stone gateway of an unusual size, surmounted by two colossal statues,[4] also in stone. Inside this precinct is a temple, and in the temple an image of Perseus. The people of Chemmis say that Perseus often appears to them, sometimes within the sacred enclosure, sometimes in the open country: one of the sandals which he has worn is frequently found — two cubits in length, as they affirm — and then all Egypt flourishes greatly. In the worship of Perseus Greek ceremonies are used; gymnastic games are celebrated in his honour, comprising every kind of contest, with prizes of cattle, cloaks, and skins. I made inquiries of the Chemmites why it was that Perseus appeared to them and not elsewhere in Egypt, and how they came to celebrate gymnastic contests unlike the rest of the Egyptians: to which they answered, "that Perseus belonged to their city by descent. Danaüs and Lynceus were Chemmites before they set sail for Greece, and from them Perseus was descended," they said, tracing the genealogy; "and he, when he came to Egypt for

1 The law which obliged the people to embalm the body of any one found dead, and to bury it in the most expensive manner, was a police, as well as a sanatory, regulation.

2 Khem, the god of Chemmis, or Khemmo, being supposed to answer to Pan, this city was called Panopolis by the Greeks and Romans.

3 The "*neighbouring* Neapolis" is at least ninety miles further up the river, and sixty in a direct line. It has been succeeded by the modern *Keneh*, a name taken from the Greek καινὴ πόλις, the "Newtown" of those days.

4 The court planted with trees seems to be the "grove" mentioned in the Bible. [Uncertain: see *Encyclopædia Biblica, s.v.* ASHERAH. — E. H. B.]

the purpose" (which the Greeks also assign) "of bringing away from Libya the Gorgon's head, paid them a visit, and acknowledged them for his kinsmen – he had heard the name of their city from his mother before he left Greece – he bade them institute a gymnastic contest in his honour, and that was the reason why they observed the practice."

92. The customs hitherto described are those of the Egyptians who live above the marsh-country. The inhabitants of the marshes have the same customs as the rest, as well in those matters which have been mentioned above as in respect of marriage, each Egyptian taking to himself, like the Greeks, a single wife;[1] but for greater cheapness of living the marsh-men practise certain peculiar customs, such as these following. They gather the blossoms of a certain water-lily, which grows in great abundance all over the flat country at the time when the Nile rises and floods the regions along its banks – the Egyptians call it the lotus[2] – they gather, I say, the blossoms of this plant and dry them in the sun, after which they extract from the centre of each blossom a substance like the head of a poppy, which they crush and make into bread. The root of the lotus is likewise eatable, and has a pleasant sweet taste: it is round, and about the size of an apple. There is also another species of the lily in Egypt, which grows, like the lotus, in the river, and resembles the rose. The fruit springs up side by side with the blossom, on a separate stalk, and has almost exactly the look of the comb made by wasps. It contains a number of seeds, about the size of an olive-stone, which are good to eat: and these are eaten both green and dried. The byblus[3] (papyrus), which grows year after year in the marshes, they pull up, and, cutting the plant in two, reserve the upper portion for other purposes, but take the lower, which is about a cubit long, and either eat it or else sell it. Such as wish

1 There is no instance on the monuments of Egypt of a man having more than one wife at a time.

2 This Nymphæa Lotus grows in ponds and small channels in the Delta during the inundation, which are dry during the rest of the year; but it is not found in the Nile itself. It is nearly the same as our white water-lily. The lotus flower was always presented to guests at an Egyptian party; and garlands were put round their heads and necks.

3 The use of the pith of its triangular stalk for paper made it a very valuable plant; and the right of growing the best quality, and of selling the papyrus made from it, belonged to the Government.

to enjoy the byblus in full perfection bake it first in a closed vessel, heated to a glow. Some of these folk, however, live entirely on fish, which are gutted as soon as caught, and then hung up in the sun: when dry, they are used as food.

93. Gregarious fish are not found in any numbers in the rivers; they frequent the lagunes, whence, at the season of breeding, they proceed in shoals towards the sea. The males lead the way, and drop their milt as they go, while the females, following close behind, eagerly swallow it down. From this they conceive,[1] and when, after passing some time in the sea, they begin to be in spawn, the whole shoal sets off on its return to its ancient haunts. Now, however, it is no longer the males, but the females, who take the lead: they swim in front in a body, and do exactly as the males did before, dropping, little by little, their grains of spawn as they go, while the males in the rear devour the grains, each one of which is a fish.[2] A portion of the spawn escapes and is not swallowed by the males, and hence come the fishes which grow afterwards to maturity. When any of this sort of fish are taken on their passage to the sea, they are found to have the left side of the head scarred and bruised; while if taken on their return, the marks appear on the right. The reason is, that as they swim down the Nile seaward, they keep close to the bank of the river upon their left, and returning again up stream they still cling to the same side, hugging it and brushing against it constantly, to be sure that they miss not their road through the great force of the current. When the Nile begins to rise, the hollows in the land and the marshy spots near the river are flooded before any other places by the percolation of the water through the river-banks;[3] and these, almost as soon as they become pools, are found to be full of numbers of little fishes. I think that I understand how it is this comes to pass. On the subsidence of the Nile the year before, though the fish retired with the retreating waters, they had first deposited their spawn in the mud upon the

1 Aristotle shows the absurdity of this statement.

2 The male fish deposits the milt *after* the female has deposited the spawn, and thus renders it prolific. The swallowing of the spawn is simply the act of any hungry fish, male or female, who happens to find it. The bruised heads are a fable.

3 The sudden appearance of the young fish in the ponds was simply owing to these being supplied by the canals from the river, or by its overflowing its banks.

banks; and so, when at the usual season the water returns, small fry are rapidly engendered out of the spawn of the preceding year. So much concerning the fish.

94. The Egyptians who live in the marshes[1] use for the anointing of their bodies an oil made from the fruit of the sillicyprium,[2] which is known among them by the name of "kiki." To obtain this they plant the sillicyprium (which grows wild in Greece) along the banks of the rivers and by the sides of the lakes, where it produces fruit in great abundance, but with a very disagreeable smell. This fruit is gathered, and then bruised and pressed, or else boiled down after roasting: the liquid which comes from it is collected and is found to be unctuous, and as well suited as olive-oil for lamps, only that it gives out an unpleasant odour.

95. The contrivances which they use against gnats, wherewith the country swarms, are the following. In the parts of Egypt above the marshes the inhabitants pass the night upon lofty towers,[3] which are of great service, as the gnats are unable to fly to any height on account of the winds. In the marsh-country, where there are no towers, each man possesses a net instead. By day it serves him to catch fish, while at night he spreads it over the bed in which he is to rest, and creeping in, goes to sleep underneath. The gnats, which, if he rolls himself up in his dress or in a piece of muslin, are sure to bite through the covering, do not so much as attempt to pass the net.

96. The vessels used in Egypt for the transport of merchandise are made of the Acantha (Thorn), a tree which in its growth is very like the Cyrenaïc lotus, and from which there exudes a gum. They cut a quantity of planks about two cubits in length from this tree, and then proceed to their ship-building, arranging the planks like bricks, and attaching them by ties to a number of long stakes or poles till the hull is complete, when they lay the cross-planks on the top from side to side. They give the boats no ribs, but caulk the seams with papyrus on the inside.

1 The intimate acquaintance of Herodotus with the inhabitants of the marsh-region is probably owing to the important position occupied by that region in the revolt of Inaros, which the Athenians, whom Herodotus probably accompanied, went to assist.

2 This was the *Ricinus communis*, the Castor-oil plant.

3 A similar practice is found in the valley of the Indus. The custom of sleeping on the flat roofs of their houses is still common in Egypt.

Each has a single rudder, which is driven straight through the keel. The mast is a piece of acantha-wood, and the sails are made of papyrus. These boats cannot make way against the current unless there is a brisk breeze; they are, therefore, towed up-stream from the shore: down-stream they are managed as follows. There is a raft belonging to each, made of the wood of the tamarisk, fastened together with a wattling of reeds; and also a stone bored through the middle about two talents in weight. The raft is fastened to the vessel by a rope, and allowed to float down the stream in front, while the stone is attached by another rope astern.[1] The result is, that the raft, hurried forward by the current, goes rapidly down the river, and drags the "baris" (for so they call this sort of boat) after it; while the stone, which is pulled along in the wake of the vessel, and lies deep in the water, keeps the boat straight. There are a vast number of these vessels in Egypt, and some of them are of many thousand talents' burthen.

97. When the Nile overflows, the country is converted into a sea, and nothing appears but the cities, which look like the islands in the Ægean.[2] At this season boats no longer keep the course of the river, but sail right across the plain. On the voyage from Naucratis to Memphis at this season, you pass close to the pyramids, whereas the usual course is by the apex of the Delta, and the city of Cercasôrus. You can sail also from the maritime town of Canôbus across the flat to Naucratis, passing by the cities of Anthylla and Archandropolis.

98. The former of these cities, which is a place of note, is assigned expressly to the wife of the ruler of Egypt for the time being, to keep her in shoes. Such has been the custom ever since Egypt fell under the Persian yoke. The other city seems to me to have got its name of Archandropolis from Archander the Phthian, son of Achæus, and son-in-law of Danaus. There might certainly have been another Archander; but, at any rate, the name is not Egyptian.

99. Thus far I have spoken of Egypt from my own observation, relating what I myself saw, the ideas that I formed, and the results of my own researches. What follows rests on the accounts given me by the Egyptians, which I shall now repeat, adding thereto some particulars which fell under my own notice.

---

1 A similar practice prevails to this day on the Euphrates.
2 This still happens in those years when the inundation is very high.

The priests said that Mên was the first king of Egypt,[1] and that it was he who raised the dyke which protects Memphis from the inundations of the Nile. Before his time the river flowed entirely along the sandy range of hills which skirts Egypt on the side of Libya. He, however, by banking up the river at the bend which it forms about a hundred furlongs south of Memphis, laid the ancient channel dry, while he dug a new course for the stream half-way between the two lines of hills. To this day, the elbow which the Nile forms at the point where it is forced aside into the new channel is guarded with the greatest care by the Persians, and strengthened every year; for if the river were to burst out at this place, and pour over the mound, there would be danger of Memphis being completely overwhelmed by the flood. Mên, the first king, having thus, by turning the river, made the tract where it used to run, dry land, proceeded in the first place to build the city now called Memphis, which lies in the narrow part of Egypt; after which he further excavated a lake outside the town, to the north and west, communicating with the river, which was itself the eastern boundary. Besides these works,[2] he also, the priests said, built the temple of Hephaistos which stands within the city, a vast edifice, very worthy of mention.

100. Next, they read me from a papyrus, the names of three hundred and thirty monarchs,[3] who (they said) were his successors upon the throne. In this number of generations there were eighteen Ethiopian kings,[4] and one queen who was a native; all the rest were kings and Egyptians. The queen bore the same name as the Babylonian princes, namely, Nitocris.[5] They said that she succeeded her brother; he had been king of Egypt, and was

1 Manetho, Eratosthenes, and other writers, agree with Herodotus that Mên or Menes (the Mna, or Mænai, of the monuments) was the first Egyptian king. [As I have already noted, Menes is not an historical figure. Possibly Aha and Narmer − first conquerors of the North and unifiers of the kingdom − were the originals of the legendary king. Since Rawlinson wrote, the spade of the archæologist has unearthed a vast mass of material bearing on Egyptian history; and a new chapter in the history of the world has been recovered. − E. H. B.]

2 Neither Menes nor his immediate successors have left any monuments.

3 That is, from Menes to Mœris.

4 The intermarriages of the Egyptian and Ethiopian royal families may be inferred from the sculptures.

5 The fact of Nitocris having been an early Egyptian queen is proved in her name, Neitakri, occurring in the Turin Papyrus.

put to death by his subjects, who then placed her upon the throne. Bent on avenging his death, she devised a cunning scheme by which she destroyed a vast number of Egyptians. She constructed a spacious underground chamber, and, on pretence of inaugurating it, contrived the following:— Inviting to a banquet those of the Egyptians whom she knew to have had the chief share in the murder of her brother, she suddenly, as they were feasting, let the river in upon them, by means of a secret duct of large size. This, and this only, did they tell me of her, except that, when she had done as I have said, she threw herself into an apartment full of ashes, that she might escape the vengeance whereto she would otherwise have been exposed.

101. The other kings, they said, were personages of no note or distinction,[1] and left no monuments of any account, with the exception of the last, who was named Mœris.[2] He left several memorials of his reign – the northern gateway of the temple of Hephaistos, the lake excavated by his orders, whose dimensions I shall give presently,[3] and the pyramids built by him in the lake, the size of which will be stated when I describe the lake itself wherein they stand. Such were his works: the other kings left absolutely nothing.

102. Passing over these monarchs, therefore, I shall speak of the king who reigned next, whose name was Sesostris.[4] He, the priests said, first of all proceeded in a fleet of ships of war from the Arabian gulf along the shores of the Erythræan sea, subduing the nations as he went, until he finally reached a sea which could not be navigated by reason of the shoals. Hence he returned to Egypt, where, they told me, he collected a vast armament, and made a progress by land across the continent, conquering every people which fell in his way. In the countries where the natives withstood his attack, and fought gallantly for their liberties, he

1 Their obscurity was owing to Egypt being part of the time under the dominion of the Shepherds, who, finding Egypt divided into several kingdoms, or principalities, invaded the country, and succeeded at length in dispossessing the Memphite kings of their territories.

2 See chs. 13 and 100.

3 Infra, ch. 149.

4 The original Sesostris was the first king of the 12th dynasty, Osirtasen I., who was the first great Egyptian conqueror; but when Osirei or Sethi (Sethos), and his son Rameses II. surpassed the exploits of their predecessor, the name of Sesostris became confounded with Sethos, and the conquests of that king, and his still greater son, were ascribed to the original Sesostris.

erected pillars,[1] on which he inscribed his own name and country, and how that he had here reduced the inhabitants to subjection by the might of his arms: where, on the contrary, they submitted readily and without a struggle, he inscribed on the pillars, in addition to these particulars, the female genitalia to mark that they were a nation of women, that is, unwarlike and effeminate.

103. In this way he traversed the whole continent of Asia, whence he passed on into Europe, and made himself master of Scythia and of Thrace, beyond which countries I do not think that his army extended its march. For thus far the pillars which he erected are still visible, but in the remoter regions they are no longer found. Returning to Egypt from Thrace, he came, on his way, to the banks of the river Phasis. Here I cannot say with any certainty what took place. Either he of his own accord detached a body of troops from his main army and left them to colonise the country, or else a certain number of his soldiers, wearied with their long wanderings, deserted, and established themselves on the banks of this stream.

104. There can be no doubt that the Colchians are an Egyptian race. Before I heard any mention of the fact from others, I had remarked it myself. After the thought had struck me, I made inquiries on the subject both in Colchis and in Egypt, and I found that the Colchians had a more distinct recollection of the Egyptians, than the Egyptians had of them. Still the Egyptians said that they believed the Colchians to be descended from the army of Sesostris. My own conjectures were founded, first, on the fact that they are black-skinned and have woolly hair,[2] which certainly amounts to but little, since several other nations are so too; but further and more especially, on the circumstance that the Colchians, the Egyptians, and the Ethiopians, are the only nations who have practised circumcision from the earliest times.

---

1 These memorials, which belong to Rameses II., are found in Syria, on the rocks above the mouth of the Lycus (now *Nahr el Kelb*).

2 Herodotus also alludes in ch. 57 to the black colour of the Egyptians; but not only do the paintings pointedly distinguish the Egyptians from the blacks of Africa, and even from the copper-coloured Ethiopians, both of whom are shown to have been of the same hue as their descendants: but the mummies prove that the Egyptians were *neither black nor woolly-haired*, and the formation of the head at once decides that they are of Asiatic, and not of African, origin. Egypt was called Chemi, "black," from the colour of the rich soil, not from that of the people.

The Phœnicians and the Syrians of Palestine[1] themselves confess that they learnt the custom of the Egyptians; and the Syrians who dwell about the rivers Thermôdon and Parthenius,[2] as well as their neighbours the Macronians, say that they have recently adopted it from the Colchians. Now these are the only nations who use circumcision, and it is plain that they all imitate herein the Egyptians.[3] With respect to the Ethiopians, indeed, I cannot decide whether they learnt the practice of the Egyptians, or the Egyptians of them — it is undoubtedly of very ancient date in Ethiopia — but that the others derived their knowledge of it from Egypt is clear to me, from the fact that the Phœnicians, when they come to have commerce with the Greeks, cease to follow the Egyptians in this custom, and allow their children to remain uncircumcised.

105. I will add a further proof to the identity of the Egyptians and the Colchians. These two nations weave their linen in exactly the same way, and this is a way entirely unknown to the rest of the world; they also in their whole mode of life and in their language resemble one another. The Colchian linen[4] is called by the Greeks Sardinian, while that which comes from Egypt is known as Egyptian.

106. The pillars which Sesostris erected in the conquered countries have for the most part disappeared; but in the part of Syria called Palestine, I myself saw them still standing, with the writing above-mentioned, and the emblem distinctly visible. In Ionia also, there are two representations of this prince engraved upon rocks,[5] one on the road from Ephesus to Phocæa, the other between Sardis and Smyrna. In each case the figure is that of a man, four cubits and a span high, with a spear in his right hand and a bow in his left, the rest of his costume being likewise half Egyptian, half Ethiopian. There is an inscription across the breast from shoulder to shoulder, in the sacred character of Egypt, which says, "With my own shoulders I conquered this

1 Herodotus apparently alludes to the Jews.
2 The Syrians here intended are undoubtedly the Cappadocians.
3 Circumcision was not practised by the Philistines (1 Sam. xiv. 6; xvii. 26; xviii. 27; 2 Sam. i. 20; 1 Chron. x. 4), nor by the generality of the Phœnicians.
4 Colchis was famous for its linen.
5 A figure, which seems certainly to be one of the two here mentioned by Herodotus, has been discovered at *Ninfi*, on what appears to have been the ancient road from Sardis to Smyrna.

land." The conqueror does not tell who he is, or whence he comes, though elsewhere Sesostris records these facts. Hence it has been imagined by some of those who have seen these forms, that they are figures of Memnon;[1] but such as think so err very widely from the truth.

107. This Sesostris, the priests went on to say, upon his return home, accompanied by vast multitudes of the people whose countries he had subdued,[2] was received by his brother,[3] whom he had made viceroy of Egypt on his departure, at Daphnæ near Pelusium, and invited by him to a banquet, which he attended, together with his sons. Then his brother piled a quantity of wood all round the building, and having so done set it alight. Sesostris, discovering what had happened, took counsel instantly with his wife, who had accompanied him to the feast, and was advised by her to lay two of their six sons upon the fire, and so make a bridge across the flames, whereby the rest might effect their escape. Sesostris did as she recommended, and thus while two of his sons were burnt to death, he himself and his other children were saved.

108. The king then returned to his own land and took vengeance upon his brother, after which he proceeded to make use of the multitudes whom he had brought with him from the conquered countries, partly to drag the huge masses of stone which were moved in the course of his reign to the temple of Hephaistos – partly to dig the numerous canals with which the whole of Egypt is intersected. By these forced labours the entire face of the country was changed; for whereas Egypt had formerly been

1 Herodotus shows his discrimination in rejecting the notion of his being Memnon, which had already become prevalent among the Greeks, who saw Memnon everywhere in Egypt merely because he was mentioned in Homer. A similar error is made at the present day in expecting to find a reference to Jewish history on the monuments, though it is obviously not the custom of any people to record their misfortunes to posterity in painting or sculpture.

2 It was the custom of the Egyptian kings to bring their prisoners to Egypt, and to employ them in public works, as the sculptures abundantly prove, and as Herodotus states (ch. 108). The Jews were employed in the same way: for though at first they obtained grazing-lands for their cattle in the land of Goshen (Gen. xlvi. 34), or the Bucolia, where they tended the king's herds (Gen. xlvii. 6, 27), they were afterwards forced to perform various services, like ordinary prisoners of war.

3 This at once shows that the conqueror here mentioned is not the early Sesostris of the 12th dynasty, but the great king of the 19th dynasty.

a region suited both for horses and carriages, henceforth it became entirely unfit for either.[1] Though a flat country throughout its whole extent, it is now unfit for either horse or carriage, being cut up by the canals, which are extremely numerous and run in all directions. The king's object was to supply Nile water to the inhabitants of the towns situated in the mid-country, and not lying upon the river; for previously they had been obliged, after the subsidence of the floods, to drink a brackish water which they obtained from wells.[2]

109. Sesostris also, they declared, made a division of the soil of Egypt among the inhabitants, assigning square plots of ground of equal size to all, and obtaining his chief revenue from the rent which the holders were required to pay him year by year. If the river carried away any portion of a man's lot, he appeared before the king, and related what had happened; upon which the king sent persons to examine, and determine by measurement the exact extent of the loss; and thenceforth only such a rent was demanded of him as was proportionate to the reduced size of his land. From this practice, I think, geometry first came to be known in Egypt, whence it passed into Greece. The sun-dial, however, and the gnomon[3] with the division of the day into twelve parts, were received by the Greeks from the Babylonians.

110. Sesostris was king not only of Egypt, but also of Ethiopia. He was the only Egyptian monarch who ever ruled over the latter country.[4] He left, as memorials of his reign, the stone statues which stand in front of the temple of Hephaistos, two

1 It is very possible that the number of canals may have increased in the time of Rameses II.: and this, like the rest of Herodotus' account, shows that this king is the Sesostris whose actions he is describing.

2 The water filtrates through the alluvial soil to the inland wells, where it is sweet, though sometimes hard.

3 The gnomon was of course part of every dial. Herodotus, however, is correct in making a difference between the γνώμων and the πόλος. The former, called also στοιχεῖον, was a perpendicular rod, whose shadow indicated noon, and also by its length a particular part of the day, being longest at sunrise and sunset. The πόλος was an improvement, and a real dial, on which the division of the day was set off by lines, and indicated by the shadow of its gnomon.

4 This cannot apply to any one Egyptian king in particular, as many ruled in Ethiopia; and though Osirtasen I. (the original Sesostris) may have been the *first*, the monuments show that his successors of the 12th dynasty, and others, ruled and erected buildings in Ethiopia. The Egyptians evidently overran all Ethiopia, and part of the interior of Africa, in the time of the 18th and 19th dynasties, and had long before conquered Negro tribes.

of which, representing himself and his wife, are thirty cubits in height, while the remaining four, which represent his sons, are twenty cubits. These are the statues, in front of which the priest of Hephaistos, very many years afterwards, would not allow Darius the Persian[1] to place a statue of himself; "because," he said, "Darius had not equalled the achievements of Sesostris the Egyptian: for while Sesostris had subdued to the full as many nations as ever Darius had brought under, he had likewise conquered the Scythians, whom Darius had failed to master. It was not fair, therefore, that he should erect his statue in front of the offerings of a king, whose deeds he had been unable to surpass." Darius, they say, pardoned the freedom of this speech.

111. On the death of Sesostris, his son Pheron, the priests said, mounted the throne. He undertook no warlike expeditions; being struck with blindness, owing to the following circumstance. The river had swollen to the unusual height of eighteen cubits, and had overflowed all the fields, when, a sudden wind arising, the water rose in great waves. Then the king, in a spirit of impious violence, seized his spear, and hurled it into the strong eddies of the stream. Instantly he was smitten with disease of the eyes, from which after a little while he became blind,[2] continuing without the power of vision for ten years. At last, in the eleventh year, an oracular announcement reached him from the city of Buto, to the effect, that "the time of his punishment had run out, and he should recover his sight by washing his eyes with urine. He must find a woman who had been faithful to her husband, and had never preferred to him another man." The king, therefore, first of all made trial of his wife, but to no purpose – he continued as blind as before. So he made the experiment with other women, until at length he succeeded, and in this way recovered his sight. Hereupon he assembled all the women, except the last, and bringing them to the city which now

1 The name of Darius occurs in the sculptures. He seems to have treated the Egyptians with far more uniform lenity than the other Persian kings.

2 This is one of the Greek ciceroni tales. A Greek poet might make a graceful story of Achilles and a Trojan stream, but the prosaic Egyptians would never represent one of their kings performing a feat so opposed to his habits, and to all their religious notions. The story about the women is equally un-Egyptian; but the mention of a remedy which is still used in Egypt for ophthalmia, shows that some simple fact has been converted into a wholly improbable tale.

bears the name of Erythrabôlus (Red-soil), he there burnt them all, together with the place itself. The woman to whom he owed his cure, he married, and after his recovery was complete, he presented offerings to all the temples of any note, among which the best worthy of mention are the two stone obelisks which he gave to the temple of the Sun.[1] These are magnificent works; each is made of a single stone, eight cubits broad, and a hundred cubits in height.

112. Pheron, they said, was succeeded by a man of Memphis, whose name, in the language of the Greeks, was Proteus. There is a sacred precinct of this king in Memphis, which is very beautiful, and richly adorned, situated south of the great temple of Hephaistos. Phœnicians from the city of Tyre dwell all round this precinct, and the whole place is known by the name of "the camp of the Tyrians." Within the enclosure stands a temple, which is called that of Aphrodite the Stranger.[2] I conjecture the building to have been erected to Helen, the daughter of Tyndarus; first, because she, as I have heard say, passed some time at the court of Proteus; and secondly, because the temple is dedicated to Aphrodite *the Stranger*; for among all the many temples of Aphrodite there is no other where the goddess bears this title.

113. The priests, in answer to my inquiries on the subject of Helen,[3] informed me of the following particulars. When Alexander had carried off Helen from Sparta, he took ship and sailed homewards. On his way across the Ægean a gale arose, which drove him from his course and took him down to the sea of

1 They were therefore most probably at Heliopolis. The height of 100 cubits, at least 150 feet, far exceeds that of any found in Egypt, the highest being less than 100 feet. The mode of raising an obelisk seems to have been by tilting it from an inclined plane into a pit, at the bottom of which the pedestal was placed to receive it, a wheel or roller of wood being fastened on each side to the end of the obelisk, which enabled it to run down the wall opposite the inclined plane to its proper position. During this operation it was dragged by ropes up the inclined plane, and then gradually lowered into the pit as soon as it had been tilted.

2 This was evidently Astarté, the Aphrodite of the Phœnicians and Syrians.

3 The eagerness of the Greeks to "inquire" after events mentioned by Homer, and the readiness of the Egyptians to take advantage of it, are shown in this story related to Herodotus. The fact of Homer having believed that Helen went to Egypt, only proves that the story was not invented in Herodotus' time, but was current long before.

Egypt; hence, as the wind did not abate, he was carried on to the coast, when he went ashore, landing at the Salt-Pans, in that mouth of the Nile which is now called the Canobic.[1] At this place there stood upon the shore a temple, which still exists, dedicated to Heracles. If a slave runs away from his master, and taking sanctuary at this shrine gives himself up to the god, and receives certain sacred marks upon his person,[2] whosoever his master may be, he cannot lay hand on him. This law still remained unchanged to my time. Hearing, therefore, of the custom of the place, the attendants of Alexander deserted him, and fled to the temple, where they sat as suppliants. While there, wishing to damage their master, they accused him to the Egyptians, narrating all the circumstances of the rape of Helen and the wrong done to Menelaus. These charges they brought, not only before the priests, but also before the warden of that mouth of the river, whose name was Thônis.

114. As soon as he received the intelligence, Thônis sent a message to Proteus, who was at Memphis, to this effect: "A stranger is arrived from Greece; he is by race a Teucrian, and has done a wicked deed in the country from which he is come. Having beguiled the wife of the man whose guest he was, he carried her away with him, and much treasure also. Compelled by stress of weather, he has now put in here. Are we to let him depart as he came, or shall we seize what he has brought?" Proteus replied, "Seize the man, be he who he may, that has dealt thus wickedly with his friend, and bring him before me, that I may hear what he will say for himself."

115. Thônis, on receiving these orders, arrested Alexander, and stopped the departure of his ships; then, taking with him Alexander, Helen, the treasures, and also the fugitive slaves, he went up to Memphis. When all were arrived, Proteus asked Alexander, "who he was, and whence he had come?" Alexander replied by giving his descent, the name of his country, and a true account of his late voyage. Then Proteus questioned him as to how he got possession of Helen. In his reply Alexander became confused, and diverged from the truth, whereon the slaves

1 This branch of the Nile entered the sea a little to the E. of the town of Canopus, close to Heracleum.

2 Showing they were dedicated to the service of the Deity. To set a mark on any one as a protection was a very ancient custom. Cp. Gen. iv. 15.

interposed, confuted his statements, and told the whole history of the crime. Finally, Proteus delivered judgment as follows: "Did I not regard it as a matter of the utmost consequence that no stranger driven to my country by adverse winds should ever be put to death, I would certainly have avenged the Greek by slaying thee. Thou basest of men, – after accepting hospitality, to do so wicked a deed! First, thou didst seduce the wife of thy own host – then, not content therewith, thou must violently excite her mind, and steal her away from her husband. Nay, even so thou wert not satisfied, but on leaving, thou must plunder the house in which thou hadst been a guest. Now then, as I think it of the greatest importance to put no stranger to death, I suffer thee to depart; but the woman and the treasures I shall not permit to be carried away. Here they must stay, till the Greek stranger comes in person and takes them back with him. For thyself and thy companions, I command thee to begone from my land within the space of three days – and I warn you, that otherwise at the end of that time you will be treated as enemies."

116. Such was the tale told me by the priests concerning the arrival of Helen at the court of Proteus. It seems to me that Homer was acquainted with this story, and while discarding it, because he thought it less adapted for epic poetry than the version which he followed, showed that it was not unknown to him. This is evident from the travels which he assigns to Alexander in the Iliad – and let it be borne in mind that he has nowhere else contradicted himself – making him be carried out of his course on his return with Helen, and after divers wanderings come at last to Sidon[1] in Phœnicia. The passage is in the Bravery of Diomed,[2] and the words are as follows:–

"There were the robes, many-coloured, the work of Sidonian
        women:
    They from Sidon had come, what time god-shaped Alexander
    Over the broad sea brought, that way, the high-born Helen."

1 Herodotus very properly ranks the Sidonians before the Tyrians (viii. 67), and Isaiah calls Tyre daughter of Sidon (xxiii. 12), having been founded by the Sidonians. Sidon is in Genesis (x. 19), but no Tyre; and Homer only mentions Sidon and not "Tyre," as Strabo observes. It may be "doubtful which was the metropolis of Phœnicia," in later times; Sidon, however, appears to be the older city.

2 Il. vi. 290–2.

In the Odyssey also the same fact is alluded to, in these words:[1] –

"Such, so wisely prepared, were the drugs that her stores afforded,
Excellent; gift which once Polydamna, partner of Thônis,
Gave her in Egypt, where many the simples that grow in the
    meadows,
Potent to cure in part, in part as potent to injure."

Menelaus too, in the same poem, thus addresses Telemachus:[2] –

"Much did I long to return, but the Gods still kept me in Egypt–
Angry because I had failed to pay them their hecatombs duly."

In these places Homer shows himself acquainted with the voyage of Alexander to Egypt, for Syria borders on Egypt, and the Phœnicians, to whom Sidon belongs, dwell in Syria.

117. From these various passages, and from that about Sidon especially, it is clear that Homer did not write the Cypria.[3] For there it is said that Alexander arrived at Ilium with Helen on the third day after he left Sparta, the wind having been favourable, and the sea smooth; whereas in the Iliad, the poet makes him wander before he brings her home. Enough, however, for the present of Homer and the Cypria.

118. I made inquiry of the priests, whether the story which the Greeks tell about Ilium is a fable, or no. In reply they related the following particulars, of which they declared that Menelaus had himself informed them. After the rape of Helen, a vast army of Greeks, wishing to render help to Menelaus, set sail for the Teucrian territory; on their arrival they disembarked, and formed their camp, after which they sent ambassadors to Ilium, of whom Menelaus was one. The embassy was received within the walls, and demanded the restoration of Helen with the treasures which Alexander had carried off, and likewise required satisfaction for the wrong done. The Teucrians gave at once the answer in which they persisted ever afterwards, backing their assertions sometimes even with oaths, to wit, that neither Helen, nor the treasures claimed, were in their possession, – both the one and the

---

1 Odyss. iv. 227–230.
2 Ibid. iv. 351–2.
3 The criticism here is better than the argument. There can be no doubt that Homer was not the author of the rambling epic called "The Cypria."

other had remained, they said, in Egypt; and it was not just to come upon them for what Proteus, king of Egypt, was detaining. The Greeks, imagining that the Teucrians were merely laughing at them, laid siege to the town, and never rested until they finally took it. As, however, no Helen was found, and they were still told the same story, they at length believed in its truth, and despatched Menelaus to the court of Proteus.

119. So Menelaus travelled to Egypt, and on his arrival sailed up the river as far as Memphis, and related all that had happened. He met with the utmost hospitality, received Helen back unharmed, and recovered all his treasures. After this friendly treatment Menelaus, they said, behaved most unjustly towards the Egyptians; for as it happened that at the time when he wanted to take his departure, he was detained by the wind being contrary, and as he found this obstruction continue, he had recourse to a most wicked expedient. He seized, they said, two children of the people of the country, and offered them up in sacrifice.[1] When this became known, the indignation of the people was stirred, and they went in pursuit of Menelaus, who, however, escaped with his ships to Libya, after which the Egyptians could not say whither he went. The rest they knew full well, partly by the inquiries which they had made, and partly from the circumstances having taken place in their own land, and therefore not admitting of doubt.

120. Such is the account given by the Egyptian priests, and I am myself inclined to regard as true all that they say of Helen from the following considerations:— If Helen had been at Troy, the inhabitants would, I think, have given her up to the Greeks, whether Alexander consented to it or no. For surely neither Priam, nor his family, could have been so infatuated as to endanger their own persons, their children, and their city, merely that Alexander might possess Helen. At any rate, if they determined to refuse at first, yet afterwards when so many of the Trojans fell on every encounter with the Greeks, and Priam too

---

1 · This story recalls the "Sanguine placâstis ventos, et virgine cæsâ," Virg. Æn. ii. 116; and Herodotus actually records human sacrifices in Achaia, or Phthiotis (vii. 197). Some have attributed human sacrifices to the Egyptians; and Virgil says "Quis illaudati nescit Busiridis aras?" (Georg. iii. 5); but it must be quite evident that such a custom was inconsistent with the habits of the civilised Egyptians, and Herodotus has disproved the probability of human sacrifices in Egypt by his judicious remarks in ch. 45.

in each battle lost a son, or sometimes two, or three, or even more, if we may credit the epic poets, I do not believe that even if Priam himself had been married to her he would have declined to deliver her up, with the view of bringing the series of calamities to a close. Nor was it as if Alexander had been heir to the crown, in which case he might have had the chief management of affairs, since Priam was already old. Hector, who was his elder brother, and a far braver man, stood before him, and was the heir to the kingdom on the death of their father Priam. And it could not be Hector's interest to uphold his brother in his wrong, when it brought such dire calamities upon himself and the other Trojans. But the fact was that they had no Helen to deliver, and so they told the Greeks, but the Greeks would not believe what they said – Divine Providence, as I think, so willing, that by their utter destruction it might be made evident to all men that when great wrongs are done, the gods will surely visit them with great punishments. Such, at least, is my view of the matter.

121. (1.) When Proteus died, Rhampsinitus,[1] the priests informed me, succeeded to the throne. His monuments were, the western gateway of the temple of Hephaistos, and the two statues which stand in front of this gateway, called by the Egyptians, the one Summer, the other Winter, each twenty-five cubits in height. The statue of Summer, which is the northernmost of the two, is worshipped by the natives, and has offerings made to it; that of Winter, which stands towards the south, is treated in exactly the contrary way. King Rhampsinitus was possessed, they said, of great riches in silver, – indeed to such an amount, that none of the princes, his successors, surpassed or even equalled his wealth. For the better custody of this money, he proposed to build a vast chamber of hewn stone, one side of which was to form a part of the outer wall of his palace. The builder, therefore, having designs upon the treasures, contrived, as he was making the building, to insert in this wall a stone, which could easily be removed from its place by two men, or even by one. So the chamber was finished, and the king's money stored away in it. Time passed, and the builder fell sick, when finding his end approaching, he called for his two sons, and related to them the contrivance he had made in the king's treasure-cham-

---

1 This is evidently the name of a Rameses, and not of a king of an early dynasty.

ber, telling them it was for their sakes he had done it, that so they might always live in affluence. Then he gave them clear directions concerning the mode of removing the stone, and communicated the measurements, bidding them carefully keep the secret, whereby they would be Comptrollers of the Royal Exchequer so long as they lived. Then the father died, and the sons were not slow in setting to work: they went by night to the palace, found the stone in the wall of the building, and having removed it with ease, plundered the treasury of a round sum.

(2.) When the king next paid a visit to the apartment, he was astonished to see that the money was sunk in some of the vessels wherein it was stored away. Whom to accuse, however, he knew not, as the seals were all perfect, and the fastenings of the room secure. Still each time that he repeated his visits, he found that more money was gone. The thieves in truth never stopped, but plundered the treasury ever more and more. At last the king determined to have some traps made, and set near the vessels which contained his wealth. This was done, and when the thieves came, as usual, to the treasure-chamber, and one of them entering through the aperture, made straight for the jars, suddenly he found himself caught in one of the traps. Perceiving that he was lost, he instantly called his brother, and telling him what had happened, entreated him to enter as quickly as possible and cut off his head, that when his body should be discovered it might not be recognised, which would have the effect of bringing ruin upon both. The other thief thought the advice good, and was persuaded to follow it;– then, fitting the stone into its place, he went home, taking with him his brother's head.

(3.) When day dawned, the king came into the room, and marvelled greatly to see the body of the thief in the trap without a head, while the building was still whole, and neither entrance nor exit was to be seen anywhere. In this perplexity he commanded the body of the dead man to be hung up outside the palace wall, and set a guard to watch it, with orders that if any persons were seen weeping or lamenting near the place, they should be seized and brought before him. When the mother heard of this exposure of the corpse of her son, she took it sorely to heart, and spoke to her surviving child, bidding him devise some plan or other to get back the body, and threatening, that if he did not exert himself, she would go herself to the king, and denounce him as the robber.

(4.) The son said all he could to persuade her to let the matter rest, but in vain; she still continued to trouble him, until at last he yielded to her importunity, and contrived as follows:– Filling some skins with wine, he loaded them on donkeys, which he drove before him till he came to the place where the guards were watching the dead body, when pulling two or three of the skins towards him, he untied some of the necks which dangled by the asses' sides. The wine poured freely out, whereupon he began to beat his head, and shout with all his might, seeming not to know which of the donkeys he should turn to first. When the guards saw the wine running, delighted to profit by the occasion, they rushed one and all into the road, each with some vessel or other, and caught the liquor as it was spilling. The driver pretended anger, and loaded them with abuse; whereon they did their best to pacify him, until at last he appeared to soften, and recover his good humour, drove his asses aside out of the road, and set to work to rearrange their burthens; meanwhile, as he talked and chatted with the guards, one of them began to rally him, and make him laugh, whereupon he gave them one of the skins as a gift. They now made up their minds to sit down and have a drinking-bout where they were, so they begged him to remain and drink with them. Then the man let himself be persuaded, and stayed. As the drinking went on, they grew very friendly together, so presently he gave them another skin, upon which they drank so copiously that they were all overcome with the liquor, and growing drowsy lay down, and fell asleep on the spot. The thief waited till it was the dead of the night, and then took down the body of his brother; after which, in mockery, he shaved off the right side of all the soldiers' beards,[1] and so left them. Laying his brother's body upon the asses, he carried it home to his mother, having thus accomplished the thing that she had required of him.

(5.) When it came to the king's ears that the thief's body was stolen away, he was sorely vexed. Wishing, therefore, whatever

---

1 This is a curious mistake for any one to make who had been in Egypt, since the soldiers had no beards, and it was the custom of all classes to shave. This we know from ancient authors, and, above all, from the sculptures, where the only persons who have beards are foreigners. Herodotus even allows that the Egyptians shaved their heads and beards (ch. 36; cp. Gen. xli. 4). Joseph, when sent for from prison by Pharaoh, "shaved himself and changed his raiment." Herodotus could not have learnt this story from the Egyptians, and it is evidently from a Greek source.

it might cost, to catch the man who had contrived the trick, he had recourse (the priests said) to an expedient, which I can scarcely credit. He sent his own daughter[1] to the common stews, with orders to admit all comers, but to require every man to tell her what was the cleverest and wickedest thing he had done in the whole course of his life. If any one in reply told her the story of the thief, she was to lay hold of him and not allow him to get away. The daughter did as her father willed, whereon the thief, who was well aware of the king's motive, felt a desire to outdo him in craft and cunning. Accordingly he contrived the following plan:– He procured the corpse of a man lately dead, and cutting off one of the arms at the shoulder, put it under his dress, and so went to the king's daughter. When she put the question to him as she had done to all the rest, he replied, that the wickedest thing he had ever done was cutting off the head of his brother when he was caught in a trap in the king's treasury, and the cleverest was making the guards drunk and carrying off the body. As he spoke, the princess caught at him, but the thief took advantage of the darkness to hold out to her the hand of the corpse. Imagining it to be his own hand, she seized and held it fast; while the thief, leaving it in her grasp, made his escape by the door.

. (6.) The king, when word was brought him of this fresh success, amazed at the sagacity and boldness of the man, sent messengers to all the towns in his dominions to proclaim a free pardon for the thief, and to promise him a rich reward, if he came and made himself known. The thief took the king at his word, and came boldly into his presence; whereupon Rhampsinitus, greatly admiring him, and looking on him as the most knowing of men, gave him his daughter in marriage. "The Egyptians," he said, "excelled all the rest of the world in wisdom, and this man excelled all other Egyptians."

122. The same king, I was also informed by the priests, afterwards descended alive into the region which the Greeks call Hades,[2] and there played at dice with Demeter, sometimes winning and sometimes suffering defeat. After a while he returned

---

1 This in a country where social ties were so much regarded, and where the distinction of royal and noble classes was more rigidly maintained than in the most exclusive community of modern Europe, shows that the story was of foreign origin.

2 Hades was called in Egyptian Ament or Amenti, over which Osiris presided as judge of the dead.

to earth, and brought with him a golden napkin, a gift which he had received from the goddess. From this descent of Rhampsinitus into Hades, and return to earth again, the Egyptians, I was told, instituted a festival, which they certainly celebrated in my day. On what occasion it was that they instituted it, whether upon this or upon any other, I cannot determine. The following are the ceremonies:– On a certain day in the year the priests weave a mantle, and binding the eyes of one of their number with a fillet, they put the mantle upon him, and take him with them into the roadway conducting to the temple of Demeter, when they depart and leave him to himself. Then the priest, thus blindfolded, is led (they say) by two wolves to the temple of Demeter, distant twenty furlongs from the city, where he stays awhile, after which he is brought back from the temple by the wolves, and left upon the spot where they first joined him.

123. Such as think the tales told by the Egyptians credible are free to accept them for history. For my own part, I propose to myself throughout my whole work faithfully to record the traditions of the several nations. The Egyptians maintain that Demeter and Dionysus preside in the realms below. They were also the first to broach the opinion, that the soul of man is immortal,[1] and that, when the body dies, it enters into the form of an animal[2] which is born at the moment, thence passing on from one animal into another, until it has circled through the forms of all the creatures which tenant the earth, the water, and the air, after which it enters again into a human frame, and is born anew. The whole period of the transmigration is (they say) three thousand years. There are Greek writers, some of an earlier, some of a later date,[3] who have borrowed this doctrine from the Egyptians, and put it forward as their own. I could mention their names, but I abstain from doing so.

1 This was the great doctrine of the Egyptians, and their belief in it is everywhere proclaimed in the paintings of the tombs. But the souls of wicked men alone appear to have suffered the disgrace of entering the body of an animal, when, "weighed in the balance" before the tribunal of Osiris, they were pronounced unworthy to enter the abode of the blessed.

2 [As a matter of fact we can find no trace in Egyptian religion of this doctrine of "metempsychosis," – at least in the form in which Herodotus gives it. – E. H. B.]

3 Pythagoras is supposed to be included among the later writers. Herodotus, with more judgment and fairness, and on better information, than some modern writers, allows that the Greeks borrowed their early lessons of philosophy and science from Egypt.

124. Till the death of Rhampsinitus, the priests said, Egypt was excellently governed, and flourished greatly; but after him Cheops succeeded to the throne, and plunged into all manner of wickedness. He closed the temples, and forbade the Egyptians to offer sacrifice, compelling them instead to labour, one and all, in his service. Some were required to drag blocks of stone down to the Nile from the quarries in the Arabian range of hills; others received the blocks after they had been conveyed in boats across the river, and drew them to the range of hills called the Libyan.[1] A hundred thousand men laboured constantly, and were relieved every three months by a fresh lot. It took ten years' oppression of the people to make the causeway[2] for the conveyance of the stones, a work not much inferior, in my judgment, to the pyramid itself. This causeway is five furlongs in length, ten fathoms wide, and in height, at the highest part, eight fathoms. It is built of polished stone, and is covered with carvings of animals. To make it took ten years, as I said – or rather to make the causeway, the works on the mound[3] where the pyramid stands, and the underground chambers, which Cheops intended as vaults for his own use: these last were built on a sort of island, surrounded by water introduced from the Nile by a canal.[4] The Pyramid itself was twenty years in building. It is a square, eight hundred feet each way,[5] and the height the same, built entirely of polished stone, fitted together with the utmost care. The stones of which it is composed are none of them less than thirty feet in length.[6]

1 The western hills being specially appropriated to tombs in all the places where pyramids were built will account for these monuments being on that side of the Nile. The abode of the dead was supposed to be the West, the land of darkness where the sun ended his course.

2 The remains of two causeways still exist – the northern one, which is the largest, corresponding with the great pyramid, as the other does with the third.

3 This was levelling the top of the hill to form a platform. A piece of rock was also left in the centre as a nucleus on which the pyramid was built.

4 There is no trace of a canal, nor is there any probability of its having existed.

5 The dimensions of the great pyramid were – each face, 756 ft., now reduced to 732 ft.; original height when entire, 480 ft. 9 in., now 460 ft. 9 in.; angles at the base, 51° 50'; angle at the apex, 76° 20'; it covered an area of 571,536 square feet, now 535,824 square feet. Herodotus' measurement of eight plethra, or 800 ft., for each face, is not very far from the truth as a round number; but the height, which he says was the same, is far from correct.

6 The size of the stones varies. Herodotus alludes to those of the outer surface, which are now gone.

125. The pyramid was built in steps,[1] battlement-wise, as it is called, or, according to others, altar-wise. After laying the stones for the base, they raised the remaining stones to their places by means of machines[2] formed of short wooden planks. The first machine raised them from the ground to the top of the first step. On this there was another machine, which received the stone upon its arrival, and conveyed it to the second step, whence a third machine advanced it still higher. Either they had as many machines as there were steps in the pyramid, or possibly they had but a single machine, which, being easily moved, was transferred from tier to tier as the stone rose – both accounts are given, and therefore I mention both. The upper portion of the pyramid was finished first, then the middle, and finally the part which was lowest and nearest the ground. There is an inscription in Egyptian characters[3] on the pyramid which records the quantity of radishes, onions, and garlick consumed by the labourers who constructed it; and I perfectly well remember that the interpreter who read the writing to me said that the money expended in this way was 1600 talents of silver. If this then is a true record, what a vast sum must have been spent on the iron tools[4] used in the work, and on the feeding and clothing of the labourers, considering the length of time the work lasted, which has already been stated, and the additional time – no small space, I imagine – which must have been occupied by the quarrying of the stones, their conveyance, and the formation of the underground apartments.

1 These steps, or successive stages, had their faces nearly perpendicular, or at an angle of about 75°, and the triangular space, formed by each projecting considerably beyond the one immediately above it, was afterwards filled in, thus completing the general form of the pyramid. It is a curious question if the Egyptians brought with them the idea of the pyramid, or sepulchral mound, when they migrated into the valley of the Nile, and if it originated in the same idea as the tower, built also in stages, of Assyria, and the pagoda of India.

2 The notion of Diodorus that machines were not yet invented is sufficiently disproved by common sense and by the assertion of Herodotus. The position of these pyramids is very remarkable in being placed so exactly facing the four cardinal points that the variation of the compass may be ascertained from them. This accuracy would imply some astronomical knowledge and careful observations at that time.

3 This must have been in hieroglyphics, the monumental character. The outer stones being gone, it is impossible to verify, or disprove, the assertion of Herodotus.

4 Iron was known in Egypt at a very early time.

126. The wickedness of Cheops reached to such a pitch that, when he had spent all his treasures and wanted more, he sent his daughter to the stews, with orders to procure him a certain sum — how much I cannot say, for I was not told; she procured it, however, and at the same time, bent on leaving a monument which should perpetuate her own memory, she required each man to make her a present of a stone towards the works which she contemplated. With these stones she built the pyramid which stands midmost of the three that are in front of the great pyramid, measuring along each side a hundred and fifty feet.[1]

127. Cheops reigned, the Egyptians said, fifty years, and was succeeded at his demise by Chephren, his brother.

Chephren imitated the conduct of his predecessor, and, like him, built a pyramid, which did not, however, equal the dimensions of his brother's. Of this I am certain, for I measured them both myself.[2] It has no subterraneous apartments, nor any canal from the Nile to supply it with water, as the other pyramid has. In that, the Nile water, introduced through an artificial duct, surrounds an island, where the body of Cheops is said to lie. Chephren built his pyramid close to the great pyramid of Cheops, and of the same dimensions, except that he lowered the height forty feet. For the basement he employed the many-coloured stone of Ethiopia.[3] These two pyramids stand both on the same hill, an elevation not far short of a hundred feet in height. The reign of Chephren lasted fifty-six years.

1 The story of the daughter of Cheops is on a par with that of the daughter of Rhampsinitus; and we may be certain that Herodotus never received it from "the priests," whose language he did not understand, but from some of the Greek "interpreters," by whom he was so often misled.

2 The measurements of the Second Pyramid are:— present base, 690 ft.; former base (according to Colonel Howard Vyse), 707 ft. 9 in.; present perpendicular height (calculating the angle 52° 20'), 446 ft. 9 in.; former height, 454 ft. 3 in. Herodotus supposes it was 40 feet less in height than the Great Pyramid, but the real difference was only 24 ft. 6 in. It is singular that Herodotus takes no notice of the sphinx, which was made at least as early as the 18th dynasty, as it bears the name of Thothmes IV.

3 This was red granite of Syene; and Herodotus appears to be correct in saying that the lower tier was of that stone, or at least the casing, which was all that he could see; and the numbers of fragments of granite lying about this pyramid show that it has been partly faced with it. The casing which remains on the upper part is of the limestone of the eastern hills. All the pyramids were opened by the Arab caliphs in the hopes of finding treasure.

128. Thus the affliction of Egypt endured for the space of one hundred and six years, during the whole of which time the temples were shut up and never opened. The Egyptians so detest the memory of these kings that they do not much like even to mention their names. Hence they commonly call the pyramids after Philition,[1] a shepherd who at that time fed his flocks about the place.

129. After Chephren, Mycerinus (they said), son of Cheops, ascended the throne. This prince disapproved the conduct of his father, re-opened the temples, and allowed the people, who were ground down to the lowest point of misery, to return to their occupations, and to resume the practice of sacrifice. His justice in the decision of causes was beyond that of all the former kings. The Egyptians praise him in this respect more highly than any of their other monarchs, declaring that he not only gave his judgments with fairness, but also, when any one was dissatisfied with his sentence, made compensation to him out of his own purse, and thus pacified his anger. Mycerinus had established his character for mildness, and was acting as I have described, when the stroke of calamity fell on him. First of all his daughter died, the only child that he possessed. Experiencing a bitter grief at this visitation, in his sorrow he conceived the wish to entomb his child in some unusual way. He therefore caused a cow to be made of wood, and after the interior had been hollowed out, he had the whole surface coated with gold; and in this novel tomb laid the dead body of his daughter.

130. The cow was not placed under ground, but continued visible to my times: it was at Saïs, in the royal palace, where it occupied a chamber richly adorned. Every day there are burnt before it aromatics of every kind; and all night long a lamp is kept burning in the apartment. In an adjoining chamber are statues which the priests at Saïs declared to represent the various concubines of Mycerinus. They are colossal figures in wood, of the number of about twenty, and are represented naked. Whose images they really are, I cannot say – I can only repeat the account which was given to me.

1 This can have no connection with the invasion, or the memory, of the Shepherd-kings, at least as founders of the pyramids, for those monuments were raised long before the rule of the Shepherd-kings in Egypt. In the mind of the Egyptians two periods of oppression may have gradually come to be confounded, and they may have ascribed to the tyranny of the Shepherd-kings what in reality belonged to a far earlier time of misrule.

131. Concerning these colossal figures and the sacred cow, there is also another tale narrated, which runs thus: "Mycerinus was enamoured of his daughter, and offered her violence – the damsel for grief hanged herself, and Mycerinus entombed her in the cow. Then her mother cut off the hands of all her tiring-maids, because they had sided with the father, and betrayed the child; and so the statues of the maids have no hands." All this is mere fable in my judgment, especially what is said about the hands of the colossal statues. I could plainly see that the figures had only lost their hands through the effect of time. They had dropped off, and were still lying on the ground about the feet of the statues.

132. As for the cow, the greater portion of it is hidden by a scarlet coverture; the head and neck, however, which are visible, are coated very thickly with gold, and between the horns there is a representation in gold of the orb of the sun. The figure is not erect, but lying down, with the limbs under the body; the dimensions being fully those of a large animal of the kind. Every year it is taken from the apartment where it is kept, and exposed to the light of day – this is done at the season when the Egyptians beat themselves in honour of one of their gods, whose name I am unwilling to mention in connection with such a matter.[1] They say that the daughter of Mycerinus requested her father in her dying moments to allow her once a year to see the sun.

133. After the death of his daughter, Mycerinus was visited with a second calamity, of which I shall now proceed to give an account. An oracle reached him from the town of Buto, which said, "Six years only shalt thou live upon the earth, and in the seventh thou shalt end thy days." Mycerinus, indignant, sent an angry message to the oracle, reproaching the god with his injustice – "My father and uncle," he said, "though they shut up the temples, took no thought of the gods, and destroyed multitudes of men, nevertheless enjoyed a long life; I, who am pious, am to die so soon!" There came in reply a second message from the oracle – "For this very reason is thy life brought so quickly to a close – thou hast not done as it behoved thee. Egypt was fated to suffer affliction one hundred and fifty years – the two kings who preceded thee upon the throne understood this – thou hast not understood it." Mycerinus, when this answer reached him,

1 This was Osiris.

perceiving that his doom was fixed, had lamps prepared, which he lighted every day at eventime, and feasted and enjoyed himself unceasingly both day and night, moving about in the marsh-country and the woods, and visiting all the places that he heard were agreeable sojourns. His wish was to prove the oracle false, by turning the nights into days, and so living twelve years in the space of six.

134. He too left a pyramid, but much inferior in size to his father's. It is a square, each side of which falls short of three plethra by twenty feet, and is built for half its height of the stone of Ethiopia. Some of the Greeks call it the work of Rhodôpis the courtesan, but they report falsely. It seems to me that these persons cannot have any real knowledge who Rhodôpis was; otherwise they would scarcely have ascribed to her a work on which uncounted treasures, so to speak, must have been expended. Rhodôpis also lived during the reign of Amasis, not of Mycerinus, and was thus very many years later than the time of the kings who built the pyramids. She was a Thracian by birth, and was the slave of Iadmon, son of Hephæstopolis, a Samian. Æsop, the fable-writer, was one of her fellow-slaves. That Æsop belonged to Iadmon is proved by many facts — among others, by this. When the Delphians, in obedience to the command of the oracle, made proclamation that if any one claimed compensation for the murder of Æsop he should receive it, the person who at last came forward was Iadmon, grandson of the former Iadmon, and he received the compensation. Æsop therefore must certainly have been the former Iadmon's slave.

135. Rhodôpis really arrived in Egypt under the conduct of Xantheus the Samian; she was brought there to exercise her trade, but was redeemed for a vast sum by Charaxus, a Mytil-enæan, the son of Scamandrônymus, and brother of Sappho the poetess.[1] After thus obtaining her freedom, she remained in Egypt, and, as she was very beautiful, amassed great wealth, for a person in her condition; not, however, enough to enable her to erect such a work as this pyramid. Any one who likes may go and see to what the tenth part of her wealth amounted, and he will thereby learn that her riches must not be imagined to have been very wonderfully great. Wishing to leave a memorial of

1 Charaxus, the brother of Sappho, traded in wine from Lesbos, which he was in the habit of taking to Naucratis, the entrepot of all Greek merchandise.

herself in Greece, she determined to have something made the like of which was not to be found in any temple, and to offer it at the shrine at Delphi. So she set apart a tenth of her possessions, and purchased with the money a quantity of iron spits, such as are fit for roasting oxen whole, whereof she made a present to the oracle. They are still to be seen there, lying of a heap, behind the altar which the Chians dedicated, opposite the sanctuary. Naucratis seems somehow to be the place where such women are most attractive. First there was this Rhodôpis of whom we have been speaking, so celebrated a person that her name came to be familiar to all the Greeks; and, afterwards, there was another, called Archidicé, renowned throughout Greece, though not so much talked of as her predecessor. Charaxus, after ransoming Rhodôpis, returned to Mytilene, and was often lashed by Sappho in her poetry. But enough has been said on the subject of this courtesan.

136. After Mycerinus, the priests said, Asychis[1] ascended the throne. He built the eastern gateway[2] of the temple of Hephaistos, which in size and beauty far surpasses the other three. All the four gateways have figures graven on them, and a vast amount of architectural ornament, but the gateway of Asychis is by far the most richly adorned. In the reign of this king, money being scarce and commercial dealings straitened, a law was passed that the borrower might pledge his father's body to raise the sum whereof he had need. A proviso was appended to this law, giving the lender authority over the entire sepulchre of the borrower, so that a man who took up money under this pledge, if he died without paying the debt, could not obtain burial either in his own ancestral tomb, or in any other, nor could he during his lifetime bury in his own tomb any member of his family. The same king, desirous of eclipsing all his predecessors upon the throne, left as a monument of his reign a pyramid of brick.[3] It

1 It is probable that he was Shishak, of the 22nd dynasty.
2 The lofty pyramidal towers forming the façades of the courts, or vestibules, of the temple.
3 The use of crude brick was general in Egypt, for dwelling-houses, tombs, and ordinary buildings, the walls of towns, fortresses, and of the sacred enclosures of temples, and for all purposes where stone was not required, which last was nearly confined to temples, quays, and reservoirs. Even some small ancient temples were of crude bricks, which were merely baked in the sun, and never burnt in early Pharaonic times. A great number of people were employed in

bears an inscription, cut in stone, which runs thus:— "Despise me not in comparison with the stone pyramids; for I surpass them all, as much as Jove surpasses the other gods. A pole was plunged into a lake, and the mud which clave thereto was gathered; and bricks were made of the mud, and so I was formed." Such were the chief actions of this prince.

137. He was succeeded on the throne, they said, by a blind man, a native of Anysis, whose own name also was Anysis. Under him Egypt was invaded by a vast army of Ethiopians, led by Sabacôs,[1] their king. The blind Anysis fled away to the marsh-country, and the Ethiopian was lord of the land for fifty years, during which his mode of rule was the following:— When an Egyptian was guilty of an offence, his plan was not to punish him with death: instead of so doing, he sentenced him, according to the nature of his crime, to raise the ground to a greater or a less extent in the neighbourhood of the city to which he belonged. Thus the cities came to be even more elevated than they were before. As early as the time of Sesostris, they had been raised by those who dug the canals in his reign; this second elevation of the soil under the Ethiopian king gave them a very lofty position. Among the many cities which thus attained to a great elevation, none (I think) was raised so much as the town called Bubastis, where there is a temple of the goddess Bubastis, which well deserves to be described. Other temples may be grander, and may have cost more in the building, but there is none so pleasant to the eye as this of Bubastis. The Bubastis of the Egyptians is the same as the Artemis (Diana) of the Greeks.

138. The following is a description of this edifice:[2] — Excepting the entrance, the whole forms an island. Two artificial

---

this extensive manufacture; it was an occupation to which many prisoners of war were condemned, who, like the Jews, worked for the king, bricks being a government monopoly.

1 Herodotus mentions only one Sabaco, but the monuments and Manetho notice two, the Sabakôn and Sebichôs (Sevêchos) of Manetho, called Shebek in the hieroglyphics. One of these is the same as So (Savá), the contemporary of Hosea, King of Israel, who is said (in 2 Kings xvii. 4) to have made a treaty with the King of Egypt, and to have refused the annual tribute to Shalmanezer, King of Assyria.

2 This account of the position of the temple of Bubastis is very accurate. The height of the mound, the site of the temple in a low space beneath the houses, from which you look down upon it, are the very peculiarities any one would remark on visiting the remains at Tel Basta.

channels from the Nile, one on either side of the temple, encompass the building, leaving only a narrow passage by which it is approached. These channels are each a hundred feet wide, and are thickly shaded with trees. The gateway is sixty feet in height, and is ornamented with figures cut upon the stone, six cubits high and well worthy of notice. The temple stands in the middle of the city, and is visible on all sides as one walks round it; for as the city has been raised up by embankment, while the temple has been left untouched in its original condition, you look down upon it wheresoever you are. A low wall runs round the enclosure, having figures engraved upon it, and inside there is a grove of beautiful tall trees growing round the shrine, which contains the image of the goddess. The enclosure is a furlong in length, and the same in breadth. The entrance to it is by a road paved with stone for a distance of about three furlongs, which passes straight through the market-place with an easterly direction, and is about four hundred feet in width. Trees of an extraordinary height grow on each side the road, which conducts from the temple of Bubastis to that of Hermes.

139. The Ethiopian finally quitted Egypt, the priests said, by a hasty flight under the following circumstances. He saw in his sleep a vision:— a man stood by his side, and counselled him to gather together all the priests of Egypt and cut every one of them asunder. On this, according to the account which he himself gave, it came into his mind that the gods intended hereby to lead him to commit an act of sacrilege, which would be sure to draw down upon him some punishment either at the hands of gods or men. So he resolved not to do the deed suggested to him, but rather to retire from Egypt, as the time during which it was fated that he should hold the country had now (he thought) expired. For before he left Ethiopia he had been told by the oracles which are venerated there, that he was to reign fifty years over Egypt. The years were now fled, and the dream had come to trouble him; he therefore of his own accord withdrew from the land.

140. As soon as Sabacôs was gone, the blind king left the marshes, and resumed the government. He had lived in the marsh-region the whole time, having formed for himself an island there by a mixture of earth and ashes. While he remained, the natives had orders to bring him food unbeknown to the Ethiopian, and latterly, at his request, each man had brought

him, with the food, a certain quantity of ashes. Before Amyrtæus,[1] no one was able to discover the site of this island,[2] which
continued unknown to the kings of Egypt who preceded him on
the throne for the space of seven hundred years and more.[3] The
name which it bears is Elbo. It is about ten furlongs across in
each direction.

141. The next king, I was told, was a priest of Hephaistos,
called Sethôs. This monarch despised and neglected the warrior
class of the Egyptians, as though he did not need their services.
Among other indignities which he offered them, he took from
them the lands which they had possessed under all the previous
kings, consisting of twelve acres of choice land for each warrior.
Afterwards, therefore, when Sanacharib, king of the Arabians[4]
and Assyrians, marched his vast army into Egypt, the warriors
one and all refused to come to his aid. On this the monarch,
greatly distressed, entered into the inner sanctuary, and, before
the image of the god, bewailed the fate which impended over
him. As he wept he fell asleep, and dreamed that the god came
and stood at his side, bidding him be of good cheer, and go
boldly forth to meet the Arabian host, which would do him no
hurt, as he himself would send those who should help him.
Sethôs, then, relying on the dream, collected such of the Egyptians as were willing to follow him, who were none of them
warriors, but traders, artisans, and market people; and with these
marched to Pelusium, which commands the entrance into Egypt,

1 See Book iii. ch. 15.

2 This island appears to have stood at the S.E. corner of the lake of Buto.

3 Niebuhr proposes to read 300 for 700 (T or Ṫ for Ψ), remarking that
these signs are often confounded. It certainly does seem almost incredible that
Herodotus should have committed the gross chronological error involved in
the text as it stands, especially as his date for Psammetichus is so nearly correct.

4 It is curious to find Sennacherib called the "king of *the Arabians* and
Assyrians" – an order of words which seems even to regard him as *rather* an
Arabian than an Assyrian king. In the same spirit his army is termed afterwards
"the Arabian host." It is impossible altogether to defend the view which Herodotus here discloses, but we may understand how such a mistake was possible,
if we remember how Arabians were mixed up with other races in Lower Mesopotamia and what an extensive influence a great Assyrian king would exercise
over the tribes of the desert, especially those bordering on Mesopotamia. The
ethnic connection of the two great Semitic races would render union between
them comparatively easy; and so we find Arabian kings at one time paramount
over Assyria, while now apparently the case was reversed, and an Assyrian
prince bore sway over some considerable number of the Arab tribes.

and there pitched his camp. As the two armies lay here opposite one another, there came in the night a multitude of field-mice, which devoured all the quivers and bowstrings of the enemy, and ate the thongs by which they managed their shields. Next morning they commenced their flight, and great multitudes fell, as they had no arms with which to defend themselves. There stands to this day in the temple of Hephaistos, a stone statue of Sethôs, with a mouse in his hand,[1] and an inscription to this effect — "Look on me, and learn to reverence the gods."

142. Thus far I have spoken on the authority of the Egyptians and their priests. They declare that from their first king to this last-mentioned monarch, the priest of Hephaistos, was a period of three hundred and forty-one generations; such, at least, they say, was the number both of their kings, and of their high-priests, during this interval. Now three hundred generations of men make ten thousand years, three generations filling up the century; and the remaining forty-one generations make thirteen hundred and forty years. Thus the whole number of years is eleven thousand, three hundred and forty; in which entire space, they said, no god had ever appeared in a human form; nothing of this kind had happened either under the former or under the later Egyptian kings. The sun, however, had within this period of time, on four several occasions, moved from his wonted course, twice rising where he now sets, and twice setting where he now rises. Egypt was in no degree affected by these changes; the productions of the land, and of the river, remained the same; nor was there anything unusual either in the diseases or the deaths.

143. When Hecatæus the historian[2] was at Thebes, and, discoursing of his genealogy, traced his descent to a god in the

---

1 If any particular reverence was paid to mice at Memphis, it probably arose from some other mysterious reason. They were emblems of the generating and perhaps of the producing principle; and some thought them to be endued with prophetic power (a merit attributed now in some degree to rats on certain occasions). The people of Troas are said to have revered mice "because they gnawed the bowstrings of their enemies," and Apollo, who was called Smintheus (from σμίνθος, a "mouse"), was represented on coins of Alexandria Troas with a mouse in his hand.

2 This is the first distinct mention of Hecatæus, who has been glanced at more than once. (Vide supra, chs. 21, 23.) He had flourished from about B.C. 520 to B.C. 475, and had done far more than any other writer to pave the way for Herodotus. His works were of two kinds, geographical and historical. Under the former head he wrote a description of the known world (Γῆς περίοδος),

person of his sixteenth ancestor, the priests of Zeus did to him exactly as they afterwards did to me, though I made no boast of my family. They led me into the inner sanctuary, which is a spacious chamber, and showed me a multitude of colossal statues, in wood, which they counted up, and found to amount to the exact number they had said; the custom being for every high-priest during his lifetime to set up his statue in the temple. As they showed me the figures and reckoned them up, they assured me that each was the son of the one preceding him; and this they repeated throughout the whole line, beginning with the representation of the priest last deceased, and continuing till they had completed the series. When Hecatæus, in giving his genealogy, mentioned a god as his sixteenth ancestor, the priests opposed their genealogy to his, going through this list, and refusing to allow that any man was ever born of a god. Their colossal figures were each, they said, a Pirômis, born of a Pirômis, and the number of them was three hundred and forty-five; through the whole series Pirômis followed Pirômis, and the line did not run up either to a god or a hero. The word *Pirômis* may be rendered "gentleman."

144. Of such a nature were, they said, the beings represented by these images — they were very far indeed from being gods. However, in the times anterior to them it was otherwise; then Egypt had gods for its rulers, who dwelt upon the earth with men, one being always supreme above the rest. The last of these was Horus, the son of Osiris, called by the Greeks Apollo. He deposed Typhon,[1] and ruled over Egypt as its last god-king. Osiris is named Dionysus by the Greeks.

145. The Greeks regard Heracles, Dionysus, and Pan as the youngest of the gods. With the Egyptians, contrariwise, Pan is exceedingly ancient, and belongs to those whom they call "the eight gods," who existed before the rest. Heracles is one of the gods of the second order, who are known as "the twelve;" and

chiefly the result of his own travels, which must have been of considerable service to our author. Under the latter he wrote his genealogies, which were for the most part mythical, but contained occasionally important history (vide infra, vi. 137). The political influence of Hecatæus is noticed by Herodotus in two passages (v. 35, 125). He is the only prose-writer whom Herodotus mentions by name.

1 Typhon, or rather Seth, the brother of Osiris, was the abstract idea of "evil," as Osiris was of "good."

Dionysus belongs to the gods of the third order, whom the twelve produced. I have already mentioned how many years intervened according to the Egyptians between the birth of Heracles and the reign of Amasis.[1] From Pan to this period they count a still longer time; and even from Dionysus, who is the youngest of the three, they reckon fifteen thousand years to the reign of that king. In these matters they say they cannot be mistaken, as they have always kept count of the years, and noted them in their registers. But from the present day to the time of Dionysus, the reputed son of Semelé, daughter of Cadmus, is a period of not more than sixteen hundred years; to that of Heracles, son of Alcmêna, is about nine hundred; while to the time of Pan, son of Penelopé (Pan, according to the Greeks, was her child by Hermes), is a shorter space than to the Trojan war, eight hundred years or thereabouts.

146. It is open to all to receive whichever he may prefer of these two traditions; my own opinion about them has been already declared. If indeed these gods had been publicly known, and had grown old in Greece, as was the case with Heracles, son of Amphitryon, Dionysus, son of Semelé, and Pan, son of Penelopé, it might have been said that the last-mentioned personages were men who bore the names of certain previously existing deities. But Dionysus, according to the Greek tradition, was no sooner born than he was sewn up in Zeus's thigh, and carried off to Nysa, above Egypt, in Ethiopia; and as to Pan, they do not even profess to know what happened to him after his birth. To me, therefore, it is quite manifest that the names of these gods became known to the Greeks after those of their other deities, and that they count their birth from the time when they first acquired a knowledge of them. Thus far my narrative rests on the accounts given by the Egyptians.

147. In what follows I have the authority, not of the Egyptians only, but of others also who agree with them. I shall speak likewise in part from my own observation. When the Egyptians regained their liberty after the reign of the priest of Hephaistos, unable to continue any while without a king, they divided Egypt into twelve districts, and set twelve kings over them. These twelve kings, united together by intermarriages, ruled Egypt in peace, having entered into engagements with one another not to

1 Supra, ch. 43.

depose any of their number, nor to aim at any aggrandisement of one above the rest, but to dwell together in perfect amity. Now the reason why they made these stipulations, and guarded with care against their infraction, was, because at the very first establishment of the twelve kingdoms, an oracle had declared — "That he among them who should pour in Hephaistos's temple a libation from a cup of bronze, would become monarch of the whole land of Egypt." Now the twelve held their meetings at all the temples.

148. To bind themselves yet more closely together, it seemed good to them to leave a common monument. In pursuance of this resolution they made the Labyrinth which lies a little above Lake Mœris, in the neighbourhood of the place called the city of Crocodiles.[1] I visited this place, and found it to surpass description; for if all the walls and other great works of the Greeks could be put together in one, they would not equal, either for labour or expense, this Labyrinth;[2] and yet the temple of Ephesus is a building worthy of note,[3] and so is the temple of Samos.[4] The pyramids likewise surpass description, and are severally equal to a number of the greatest works of the Greeks, but the Labyrinth surpasses the pyramids. It has twelve courts, all of them roofed, with gates exactly opposite one another, six looking to the north, and six to the south. A single wall surrounds the entire building. There are two different sorts of chambers throughout — half under ground, half above ground, the latter built upon the former; the whole number of these chambers is three thousand, fifteen hundred of each kind. The upper cham-

1 Afterwards called Arsinoë, from the wife and sister of Ptolemy Philadelphus, like the port on the Red Sea (now Suez).

2 The admiration expressed by Herodotus for the Labyrinth is singular, when there were so many far more magnificent buildings at Thebes, of which he takes no notice. It was probably the beauty of the stone, the richness of its decoration, and the peculiarity of its plan that struck him so much.

3 The original temple of Artemis at Ephesus seems to have been destroyed by the Cimmerians. The temple which Herodotus saw was then begun to be built by Chersiphron of Cnossus and his son Metagenes. These architects did not live to complete their work, which was finished by Demetrius and Peonius of Ephesus, the rebuilder of the temple of Apollo at Branchidæ. The architecture of the temple of Chersiphron was Ionic. After its destruction by Eratostratus in the year of Alexander's birth, the temple of Artemis was rebuilt with greater magnificence, and probably on a larger scale, than before.

4 Vide infra, iii. 60.

bers I myself passed through and saw, and what I say concerning them is from my own observation; of the underground chambers I can only speak from report: for the keepers of the building could not be got to show them, since they contained (as they said) the sepulchres of the kings who built the Labyrinth, and also those of the sacred crocodiles. Thus it is from hearsay only that I can speak of the lower chambers. The upper chambers, however, I saw with my own eyes, and found them to excel all other human productions; for the passages through the houses, and the varied windings of the paths across the courts, excited in me infinite admiration, as I passed from the courts into chambers, and from the chambers into colonnades, and from the colonnades into fresh houses, and again from these into courts unseen before. The roof was throughout of stone, like the walls; and the walls were carved all over with figures; every court was surrounded with a colonnade, which was built of white stones, exquisitely fitted together. At the corner of the Labyrinth stands a pyramid, forty fathoms high, with large figures engraved on it; which is entered by a subterranean passage.

149. Wonderful as is the Labyrinth, the work called the Lake of Mœris, which is close by the Labyrinth, is yet more astonishing. The measure of its circumference is sixty schœnes, or three thousand six hundred furlongs, which is equal to the entire length of Egypt along the sea-coast. The lake stretches in its longest direction from north to south, and in its deepest parts is of the depth of fifty fathoms. It is manifestly an artificial excavation, for nearly in the centre there stand two pyramids,[1] rising to the height of fifty fathoms above the surface of the water, and extending as far beneath, crowned each of them with a colossal statue sitting upon a throne. Thus these pyramids are one hundred fathoms high, which is exactly a furlong (stadium) of six hundred feet: the fathom being six feet in length, or four cubits, which is the same thing, since a cubit measures six, and a foot four, palms. The water of the lake does not come out of the ground, which is here excessively dry,[2] but is introduced by a canal from the Nile. The

1 No traces remain of these pyramids.
2 This is the nature of the basin on which the alluvial soil has been deposited; but it resembles the whole valley of the Nile in being destitute of springs, which are only met with in two or three places. The wells are all formed by the filtration of water from the river.

current sets for six months into the lake from the river, and for the next six months into the river from the lake. While it runs outward it returns a talent of silver daily to the royal treasury from the fish that are taken,[1] but when the current is the other way the return sinks to one-third of that sum.

150. The natives told me that there was a subterranean passage from this lake to the Libyan Syrtis, running westward into the interior by the hills above Memphis. As I could not anywhere see the earth which had been taken out when the excavation was made, and I was curious to know what had become of it, I asked the Egyptians who live closest to the lake where the earth had been put. The answer that they gave me I readily accepted as true, since I had heard of the same thing being done at Nineveh of the Assyrians. There, once upon a time, certain thieves, having formed a plan to get into their possession the vast treasures of Sardanapalus, the Ninevite king, which were laid up in subterranean treasuries, proceeded to tunnel a passage from the house where they lived into the royal palace, calculating the distance and the direction. At nightfall they took the earth from the excavation and carried it to the river Tigris, which ran by Nineveh, continuing to get rid of it in this manner until they had accomplished their purpose. It was exactly in the same way that the Egyptians disposed of the mould from their excavation, except that they did it by day and not by night; for as fast as the earth was dug, they carried it to the Nile, which they knew would disperse it far and wide. Such was the account which I received of the formation of this lake.

151. The twelve kings for some time dealt honourably by one another, but at length it happened that on a certain occasion, when they had met to worship in the temple of Hephaistos, the high-priest on the last day of the festival, in bringing forth the golden goblets from which they were wont to pour the libations, mistook the number, and brought eleven goblets only for the twelve princes. Psammetichus was standing last, and, being left without a cup, he took his helmet, which was of bronze,[2] from

---

1 A great quantity of fish is caught even at the present day at the mouths of the canals, when they are closed and the water is prevented from returning to the Nile.

2 Bronze armour was of very early date in Egypt, and was therefore no novelty in the reign of Psammetichus.

off his head, stretched it out to receive the liquor, and so made his libation. All the kings were accustomed to wear helmets, and all indeed wore them at this very time. Nor was there any crafty design in the action of Psammetichus. The eleven, however, when they came to consider what had been done, and bethought them of the oracle which had declared "that he who, of the twelve, should pour a libation from a cup of bronze, the same would be king of the whole land of Egypt," doubted at first if they should not put Psammetichus to death. Finding, however, upon examination, that he had acted in the matter without any guilty intent, they did not think it would be just to kill him; but determined, instead, to strip him of the chief part of his power and to banish him to the marshes, forbidding him to leave them or to hold any communication with the rest of Egypt.

152. This was the second time that Psammetichus had been driven into banishment. On a former occasion he had fled from Sabacôs the Ethiopian, who had put his father Necôs to death; and had taken refuge in Syria, from whence, after the retirement of the Ethiop in consequence of his dream, he was brought back by the Egyptians of the Saïtic canton. Now it was his ill-fortune to be banished a second time by the eleven kings, on account of the libation which he had poured from his helmet; on this occasion he fled to the marshes. Feeling that he was an injured man, and designing to avenge himself upon his persecutors, Psammetichus sent to the city of Buto, where there is an oracle of Leto, the most veracious of all the oracles of the Egyptians, and having inquired concerning means of vengeance, received for answer, that "Vengeance would come from the sea, when brazen men should appear." Great was his incredulity when this answer arrived, for never, he thought, would brazen men arrive to be his helpers. However, not long afterwards certain Carians and Ionians, who had left their country on a voyage of plunder, were carried by stress of weather to Egypt, where they disembarked, all equipped in their brazen armour, and were seen by the natives, one of whom carried the tidings to Psammetichus, and, as he had never before seen men clad in brass, he reported that brazen men had come from the sea and were plundering the plain. Psammetichus, perceiving at once that the oracle was accomplished, made friendly advances to the strangers, and engaged them, by splendid promises, to enter into his service. He

then, with their aid and that of the Egyptians who espoused his cause, attacked the eleven and vanquished them.[1]

153. When Psammetichus had thus become sole monarch of Egypt, he built the southern gateway of the temple of Hephaistos in Memphis, and also a court for Apis, in which Apis is kept whenever he makes his appearance in Egypt. This court is opposite the gateway of Psammetichus, and is surrounded with a colonnade and adorned with a multitude of figures. Instead of pillars, the colonnade rests upon colossal statues, twelve cubits in height. The Greek name for Apis is Epaphus.

154. To the Ionians and Carians who had lent him their assistance Psammetichus assigned as abodes two places opposite to each other, one on either side of the Nile, which received the name of "the Camps." He also made good all the splendid promises by which he had gained their support; and further, he intrusted to their care certain Egyptian children, whom they were to teach the language of the Greeks. These children, thus instructed, became the parents of the entire class of interpreters in Egypt. The Ionians and Carians occupied for many years the places assigned them by Psammetichus, which lay near the sea, a little below the city of Bubastis, on the Pelusiac mouth of the Nile.[2] King Amasis, long afterwards, removed the Greeks hence, and settled them at Memphis to guard him against the native Egyptians. From the date of the original settlement of these persons in Egypt, we Greeks, through our intercourse with them, have acquired an accurate knowledge of the several events in Egyptian history, from the reign of Psammetichus downwards; but before his time no foreigners had ever taken up their residence in that land. The docks where their vessels were laid up, and the ruins of their habitations, were still to be seen in my day at the place where they dwelt originally, before they were removed by Amasis. Such was the mode by which Psammetichus became master of Egypt.

155. I have already made mention more than once of the Egyptian oracle,[3] and, as it well deserves notice, I shall now

1 The improbability of a few Ionian and Carian pirates having enabled Psammetichus to obtain possession of the throne is sufficiently obvious. The Egyptians may not have been willing to inform Herodotus how long their kings had employed Greek mercenary troops before the Persian invasion.

2 The site chosen for the Greek camps shows that they were thought necessary as a defence against foreign invasion from the eastward.

3 Supra, chs. 83, 133, and 152. There were several other oracles, but that of Buto, or Leto, was held in the highest repute. (See ch. 83.)

proceed to give an account of it more at length. It is a temple of Leto,[1] situated in the midst of a great city on the Sebennytic mouth of the Nile, at some distance up the river from the sea. The name of the city, as I have before observed, is Buto; and in it are two other temples also, one of Apollo and one of Artemis. Leto's temple, which contains the oracle, is a spacious building with a gateway ten fathoms in height.[2] The most wonderful thing that was actually to be seen about this temple was a chapel in the enclosure made of a single stone, the length and height of which were the same, each wall being forty cubits square, and the whole a single block! Another block of stone formed the roof, and projected at the eaves to the extent of four cubits.

156. This, as I have said, was what astonished me the most, of all the things that were actually to be seen about the temple. The next greatest marvel was the island called Chemmis. This island lies in the middle of a broad and deep lake close by the temple, and the natives declare that it floats. For my own part I did not see it float, or even move; and I wondered greatly, when they told me concerning it, whether there be really such a thing as a floating island. It has a grand temple of Apollo built upon it, in which are three distinct altars. Palm-trees grow on it in great abundance, and many other trees, some of which bear fruit, while others are barren. The Egyptians tell the following story in connection with this island, to explain the way in which it first came to float:— "In former times, when the isle was still fixed and motionless, Leto, one of the eight gods of the first order, who dwelt in the city of Buto, where now she has her oracle, received Apollo as a sacred charge from Isis, and saved him by hiding him in what is now called the floating island. Typhon meanwhile was searching everywhere in hopes of finding the child of Osiris." (According to the Egyptians, Apollo and Artemis are the children of Dionysus and Isis;[3] while Leto is their nurse and their preserver. They call Apollo, in their language, Horus; Demeter they call Isis; Artemis, Bubastis. From this Egyptian

1 Herodotus says that this goddess was one of the great deities (ch. 156).

2 This is the height of the pyramidal towers of the propylæum, or court of entrance.

3 Apollo was Horus, the son of Isis and Osiris (Demeter and Dionysus); but he had no sister in Egyptian mythology, and Artemis was Bubastis or Pasht, who appears to be one of the great deities.

tradition, and from no other, it must have been that Æschylus, the son of Euphorion, took the idea, which is found in none of the earlier poets, of making Artemis the daughter of Demeter.) The island, therefore, in consequence of this event, was first made to float. Such at least is the account which the Egyptians give.

157. Psammetichus ruled Egypt for fifty-four years, during twenty-nine of which he pressed the siege of Azôtus[1] without intermission, till finally he took the place. Azôtus is a great town in Syria. Of all the cities that we know, none ever stood so long a siege.

158. Psammetichus left a son called Necôs, who succeeded him upon the throne. This prince was the first to attempt the construction of the canal to the Red Sea — a work completed afterwards by Darius the Persian — the length of which is four days' journey, and the width such as to admit of two triremes being rowed along it abreast. The water is derived from the Nile, which the canal leaves a little above the city of Bubastis,[2] near Patûmus, the Arabian town,[3] being continued thence until it joins the Red Sea. At first it is carried along the Arabian side of the Egyptian plain, as far as the chain of hills opposite Memphis, whereby the plain is bounded, and in which lie the great stone quarries; here it skirts the base of the hills running in a direction from west to east; after which it turns, and enters a narrow pass, trending southwards from this point, until it enters the Arabian Gulf. From the northern sea to that which is called the southern or Erythræan, the shortest and quickest passage, which is from Mount Casius, the boundary between Egypt and Syria, to the Gulf of Arabia, is a distance of exactly one thousand furlongs. But the way by the canal is very much longer, on account of the crookedness of its course. A hundred and twenty thousand of the Egyptians, employed upon the work in the reign of Necôs, lost their lives in making the excavation. He at length desisted from his undertaking, in consequence of an oracle which warned

1 Azotus is Ashdod of sacred Scripture. This shows how much the Egyptian power had declined when Psammetichus was obliged to besiege a city near the confines of Egypt for so long a time as twenty-nine years.

2 The commencement of the Red Sea canal was in different places at various periods. In the time of Herodotus it left the Pelusiac branch a little above Bubastis.

3 Patumus was not near the Red Sea, but at the commencement of the canal, and was the Pithom mentioned in Exod. i. 11.

him "that he was labouring for the barbarian."[1] The Egyptians call by the name of barbarians all such as speak a language different from their own.

159. Necôs, when he gave up the construction of the canal, turned all his thoughts to war, and set to work to build a fleet of triremes, some intended for service in the northern sea, and some for the navigation of the Erythræan. These last were built in the Arabian Gulf, where the dry docks in which they lay are still visible. These fleets he employed wherever he had occasion; while he also made war by land upon the Syrians, and defeated them in a pitched battle at Magdolus,[2] after which he made himself master of Cadytis,[3] a large city of Syria. The dress which he wore on these occasions he sent to Branchidæ in Milesia, as an offering to Apollo.[4] After having reigned in all sixteen years,[5] Necôs died, and at his death bequeathed the throne to his son Psammis.

160. In the reign of Psammis, ambassadors from Elis[6] arrived in Egypt, boasting that their arrangements for the conduct of the Olympic games were the best and fairest that could be devised, and fancying that not even the Egyptians, who surpassed all other nations in wisdom, could add anything to their perfection.

---

1 This was owing to the increasing power of the Asiatic nations.

2 The place here intended seems to be Megiddo, where Josiah lost his life, between Gilgal and Mount Carmel, on the road through Syria northwards, and not Migdol ($M\alpha\gamma\delta\omega\lambda\acute{o}\varsigma$), which was in Egypt. The similarity of the two names easily led to the mistake (2 Chron. xxxv. 22).

3 After the defeat and death of Josiah, Neco proceeded to Carchemish, and on his return, finding that the Jews had put Jehoahaz, his son, on the throne, "he made him a prisoner at Riblah, in the land of Hamath, and, after having imposed a tribute of 100 talents of silver and a talent of gold upon Jerusalem, he made his brother Eliakim (whose name he changed to Jehoiakim) king in his stead, carrying Jehoahaz captive to Egypt, where he died" (2 Kings xxiii. 29).

4 For an account of the temple of Apollo at Branchidæ, see Bk. i. ch. 157.

5 The reverses which soon afterwards befell the Egyptians were not mentioned to Herodotus. Neco was defeated at Carchemish by Nebuchadnezzar, in the 4th year of Jehoiakim (Jer. xlvi. 2), and lost all the territory which it had been so long the object of the Pharaohs to possess. For "the king of Babylon took, from the river of Egypt unto the river Euphrates, all that pertained to the king of Egypt" (2 Kings xxiv. 7). This river of Egypt was the small torrent-bed that formed the boundary of the country on the N.E. side by the modern El Aréesh. Jerusalem was afterwards taken by Nebuchadnezzar.

6 This shows the great repute of the Egyptians for learning, even at this time, when they had greatly declined as a nation.

When these persons reached Egypt, and explained the reason of their visit, the king summoned an assembly of all the wisest of the Egyptians. They met, and the Eleans having given them a full account of all their rules and regulations with respect to the contests, said that they had come to Egypt for the express purpose of learning whether the Egyptians could improve the fairness of their regulations in any particular. The Egyptians considered awhile, and then made inquiry, "If they allowed their own citizens to enter the lists?" The Eleans answered, "That the lists were open to all Greeks, whether they belonged to Elis or to any other state." Hereupon the Egyptians observed, "That if this were so, they departed from justice very widely, since it was impossible but that they would favour their own countrymen, and deal unfairly by foreigners. If therefore they really wished to manage the games with fairness, and if this was the object of their coming to Egypt, they advised them to confine the contests to strangers, and allow no native of Elis to be a candidate." Such was the advice which the Egyptians gave to the Eleans.

161. Psammis reigned only six years. He attacked Ethiopia, and died almost directly afterwards. Apries, his son,[1] succeeded him upon the throne, who, excepting Psammetichus, his great-grandfather, was the most prosperous of all the kings that ever ruled over Egypt. The length of his reign was twenty-five years, and in the course of it he marched an army to attack Sidon, and fought a battle with the king of Tyre by sea. When at length the time came that was fated to bring him woe, an occasion arose which I shall describe more fully in my Libyan history, only touching it very briefly here. An army despatched by Apries to attack Cyrênê, having met with a terrible reverse, the Egyptians laid the blame on him, imagining that he had, of *malice prepense*, sent the troops into the jaws of destruction. They believed he had wished a vast number of them to be slain, in order that he himself might reign with more security over the rest of the Egyptians. Indignant therefore at this usage, the soldiers who returned and the friends of the slain broke instantly into revolt.

162. Apries, on learning these circumstances, sent Amasis to the rebels, to appease the tumult by persuasion. Upon his arrival, as he was seeking to restrain the malcontents by his exhortations, one of them, coming behind him, put a helmet on his head,

---

1 Apries is the Pharaoh-Hophra of Jeremiah (xliv. 30).

saying, as he put it on, that he thereby crowned him king. Amasis was not altogether displeased at the action, as his conduct soon made manifest: for no sooner had the insurgents agreed to make him actually their king, than he prepared to march with them against Apries. That monarch, on tidings of these events reaching him, sent Patarbêmis, one of his courtiers, a man of high rank, to Amasis, with orders to bring him alive into his presence. Patarbêmis, on arriving at the place where Amasis was, called on him to come back with him to the king, whereupon Amasis broke a coarse jest, and said, "Prythee take that back to thy master." When the envoy, notwithstanding this reply, persisted in his request, exhorting Amasis to obey the summons of the king, he made answer, "that this was exactly what he had long been intending to do; Apries would have no reason to complain of him on the score of delay; he would shortly come himself to the king, and bring others with him."[1] Patarbêmis, upon this, comprehending the intention of Amasis, partly from his replies, and partly from the preparations which he saw in progress, departed hastily, wishing to inform the king with all speed of what was going on. Apries, however, when he saw him approaching without Amasis, fell into a paroxysm of rage; and not giving himself time for reflection, commanded the nose and ears of Patarbêmis to be cut off. Then the rest of the Egyptians, who had hitherto espoused the cause of Apries, when they saw a man of such note among them so shamefully outraged, without a moment's hesitation went over to the rebels, and put themselves at the disposal of Amasis.

163. Apries, informed of this new calamity, armed his mercenaries, and led them against the Egyptians: this was a body of Carians and Ionians,[2] numbering thirty thousand men, which was now with him at Saïs, where his palace stood – a vast building, well worthy of notice. The army of Apries marched out to attack the host of the Egyptians, while that of Amasis went forth to fight the strangers; and now both armies drew near the city of Momemphis,[3] and prepared for the coming fight.

---

1 Compare the answer of Cyrus to Astyages (i. 127), which shows that this was a commonplace – the answer supposed to be proper for a powerful rebel.

2 The Greek troops continued in the pay of the king. The state of Egypt, and the dethronement of Apries, are predicted in Isa. xix. 2, and in Jer. xliv. 30.

3 Momemphis was on the edge of the desert, near the mouth of the Lycus canal.

164. The Egyptians are divided into seven distinct classes[1] – these are, the priests, the warriors, the cowherds, the swineherds, the tradesmen, the interpreters, and the boatmen. Their titles indicate their occupations. The warriors consist of Hermotybians and Calasirians, who come from different cantons,[2] the whole of Egypt being parcelled out into districts bearing this name.

165. The following cantons furnish the Hermotybians:– The cantons of Busiris, Saïs, Chemmis, Paprêmis, that of the island called Prosôpitis,[3] and half of Natho. They number, when most numerous, a hundred and sixty thousand. None of them ever practises a trade, but all are given wholly to war.

166. The cantons of the Calasirians are different – they include the following:– The cantons of Thebes, Bubastis, Aphthis, Tanis,[4] Mendes, Sebennytus, Athribis, Pharbæthus, Thmuis, Onuphis, Anysis, and Myecphoris – this last canton consists of an island which lies over against the town of Bubastis. The Calasirians, when at their greatest number, have amounted to two hundred and fifty thousand. Like the Hermotybians, they are forbidden to pursue any trade, and devote themselves entirely to warlike exercises, the son following the father's calling.

167. Whether the Greeks borrowed from the Egyptians their notions about trade, like so many others, I cannot say for certain. I have remarked that the Thracians, the Scyths, the Persians, the Lydians, and almost all other barbarians, hold the citizens who practise trades, and their children, in less repute than the rest, while they esteem as noble those who keep aloof from handicrafts, and especially honour such as are given wholly to war. These ideas prevail throughout the whole of Greece, particularly among the Lacedæmonians. Corinth is the place where mechanics are least despised.[5]

---

1 These classes, rather than *castes*, were, according to Herodotus – 1. The sacerdotal. 2. The military. 3. The herdmen. 4. Swineherds. 5. Shopkeepers. 6. Interpreters. 7. Boatmen.

2 The number of the nomes or cantons varied at different times. Each nome was governed by a Nomarch, to whom was entrusted the levying of taxes, and various duties connected with the administration of the province.

3 Of Busiris, see ch. 61.

4 The city of Tanis is the Zoan of Scripture. [Cf. *Encycl. Biblica*, vol. iv. *s.v.* – E. H. B.]

5 The situation of Corinth led so naturally to extensive trade, and thence to that splendour and magnificence of living by which the useful and ornamental arts are most encouraged, that, in spite of Dorian pride and exclusiveness,

168. The warrior class in Egypt had certain special privileges in which none of the rest of the Egyptians participated, except the priests. In the first place each man had twelve *arurœ*[1] of land assigned him free from tax. (The *arura* is a square of a hundred Egyptian cubits, the Egyptian cubit being of the same length as the Samian.) All the warriors enjoyed this privilege together; but there were other advantages which came to each in rotation, the same man never obtaining them twice. A thousand Calasirians, and the same number of Hermotybians, formed in alternate years the body-guard of the king; and during their year of service these persons, besides their *arurœ*, received a daily portion of meat and drink, consisting of five pounds of baked bread, two pounds of beef, and four cups of wine.

169. When Apries, at the head of his mercenaries, and Amasis, in command of the whole native force of the Egyptians, encountered one another near the city of Momemphis, an engagement presently took place. The foreign troops fought bravely, but were overpowered by numbers, in which they fell very far short of their adversaries. It is said that Apries believed that there was not a god who could cast him down from his eminence, so firmly did he think that he had established himself in his kingdom. But at this time the battle went against him; and, his army being worsted, he fell into the enemy's hands, and was brought back a prisoner to Saïs, where he was lodged in what had been his own house, but was now the palace of Amasis. Amasis treated him with kindness, and kept him in the palace for a while; but finding his conduct blamed by the Egyptians, who charged him with acting unjustly in preserving a man who had shown himself so bitter an enemy both to them and him, he gave Apries over into the hands of his former subjects, to deal with as they chose. Then the Egyptians took him and strangled him, but having so done they buried him in the sepulchre of his fathers. This tomb is in the temple of Athena, very

---

the mechanic's occupation came soon to be regarded with a good deal of favour. As early as the time of Cypselus elaborate works of art proceeded from the Corinthian workshops, as the golden statue of Zeus at Olympia. Later, Corinth became noted for the peculiar composition of its bronze, which was regarded as better suited for works of art than any other, and which under the name of Æs Corinthiacum was celebrated throughout the world.

1 The arura was a little more than three-fourths of an English acre; and was only a land measure.

near the sanctuary, on the left hand as one enters. The Saïtes buried all the kings who belonged to their canton inside this temple; and thus it even contains the tomb of Amasis, as well as that of Apries and his family. The latter is not so close to the sanctuary as the former, but still it is within the temple. It stands in the court, and is a spacious cloister, built of stone, and adorned with pillars carved so as to resemble palm-trees,[1] and with other sumptuous ornaments. Within the cloister is a chamber with folding doors, behind which lies the sepulchre of the king.

170. Here too, in this same precinct of Athena at Saïs, is the burial-place of one whom I think it not right to mention in such a connection.[2] It stands behind the temple, against the back-wall, which it entirely covers. There are also some large stone obelisks in the enclosure, and there is a lake[3] near them, adorned with an edging of stone. In form it is circular, and in size, as it seemed to me, about equal to the lake in Delos called "the Hoop."[4]

171. On this lake it is that the Egyptians represent by night his sufferings[5] whose name I refrain from mentioning, and this representation they call their Mysteries.[6] I know well the whole

1 They are common in Egyptian temples, particularly in the Delta where they are often of granite.

2 This was Osiris.

3 This lake still remains at Saïs, the modern *Sa-el-Hagar*. The stone casing, which always lined the sides of these sacred lakes (and which may be seen at Thebes, Hermonthes, and other places), is entirely gone; but the extent of the main enclosure, which included within it the lake and temple, is very evident; and the massive crude brick walls are standing to a great height. They are about seventy feet thick, and have layers of reeds and rushes at intervals, to serve as binders. The lake is still supplied by a canal from the river.

4 The Delian lake was a famous feature of the great temple or sacred enclosure of Apollo, which was the chief glory of that island.

5 The Egyptians and the Syrians had each the myth of a dying God; but they selected a different phenomenon for its basis; the former the Nile, the Syrians, the aspect of nature, or, as Macrobius shows, the sun; which, during one part of the year manifesting its vivifying effects on the earth's surface, seemed to die on the approach of winter; and hence the notion of a God who was both mortal and immortal. In the religion of Greece we trace this more obscurely; but the Cretans believed that Zeus had died, and even showed his tomb. This belief was perhaps borrowed from Egypt or from Syria; for the Greeks derided the notion of a God dying.

6 The sufferings and death of Osiris were the great mystery of the Egyptian religion; and some traces of it are perceptible among other people of antiquity. His being the divine goodness, and the abstract idea of "good," his manifestation upon earth (like an Indian God), his death, and resurrection, and his office

course of the proceedings in these ceremonies,[1] but they shall not pass my lips. So too, with regard to the mysteries of Demeter, which the Greeks term "the Thesmophoria," I know them, but I shall not mention them, except so far as may be done without impiety. The daughters of Danaus brought these rites from Egypt, and taught them to the Pelasgic women of the Peloponnese. Afterwards, when the inhabitants of the peninsula were driven from their homes by the Dorians, the rites perished. Only in Arcadia, where the natives remained and were not compelled to migrate,[2] their observance continued.

172. After Apries had been put to death in the way that I have described above, Amasis reigned over Egypt. He belonged

---

as judge of the dead in a future state, look like the early revelation of a future manifestation of the deity converted into a mythological fable. Osiris may be said rather to have presided over the judgment of the dead, than to have judged them; he gave admission, to those who were found worthy, to the abode of happiness. He was not the avenging deity; he did not punish, nor could he show mercy, or subvert the judgment pronounced. It was a simple question of fact. If wicked they were destined to suffer punishment. A man's actions were balanced in the scales against justice or truth, and if found wanting he was excluded from future happiness. Thus, though the Egyptians are said to believe the gods were capable of influencing destiny (Euseb. Pr. Ev. iii. 4), it is evident that Osiris (like the Greek Zeus) was bound by it; and the wicked were punished, not because he rejected them, but because they *were* wicked. Each man's conscience, released from the sinful body, was his own judge; and self-condemnation hereafter followed up the γνῶθι and αἰσχύνεο σεαυτὸν enjoined on earth.

1 These mysteries of Osiris, Herodotus says, were introduced into Greece by the daughters of Danaus. The fables of antiquity had generally several meanings; they were either historical, physical, or religious. The less instructed were led to believe Osiris represented some natural phenomenon; as the inundation of the Nile, which disappearing again, and losing its effects in the sea, was construed into the manifestation and death of the deity, destroyed by Typhon; and the story of his body having been carried to Byblus, and that of the head which went annually from Egypt to that place, swimming on the sea (Lucian, de Deâ Syriâ) for seven days, were the allegory of the water of the Nile carried by the currents to the Syrian coast; though Pausanias (x. 12) says they lamented Osiris, "when the Nile began to rise." His fabulous history was also thought by the Greeks to be connected with the sun; but it was not so viewed in early times by the Egyptians; and this was rather an Asiatic notion, and an instance of the usual adaptation of deities to each other in different mythologies. Least of all was he thought to be a man deified. The portion of the mysteries imparted to strangers, as to Herodotus, Plutarch, and others, and even to Pythagoras, was limited; and the more important secrets were not even revealed to all "the priests, but to those only who were the most approved." [See J. G. Frazer's *Adonis, Attis, Osiris* (1907). – E. H. B.]

2 Compare viii. 73.

to the canton of Saïs, being a native of the town called Siouph. At first his subjects looked down on him and held him in small esteem, because he had been a mere private person, and of a house of no great distinction; but after a time Amasis succeeded in reconciling them to his rule, not by severity, but by cleverness. Among his other splendour he had a golden foot-pan, in which his guests and himself were wont upon occasion to wash their feet. This vessel he caused to be broken in pieces, and made of the gold an image of one of the gods, which he set up in the most public place in the whole city; upon which the Egyptians flocked to the image, and worshipped it with the utmost reverence. Amasis, finding this was so, called an assembly, and opened the matter to them, explaining how the image had been made of the foot-pan, wherein they had been wont formerly to wash their feet and to put all manner of filth, yet now it was greatly reverenced. "And truly," he went on to say, "it had gone with him as with the foot-pan. If he was a private person formerly, yet now he had come to be their king. And so he bade them honour and reverence him." Such was the mode in which he won over the Egyptians, and brought them to be content to do him service.

173. The following was the general habit of his life:– From early dawn to the time when the forum is wont to fill,[1] he sedulously transacted all the business that was brought before him; during the remainder of the day he drank and joked with his guests, passing the time in witty and, sometimes, scarce seemly conversation. It grieved his friends that he should thus demean himself, and accordingly some of them chid him on the subject, saying to him, – "Oh! king, thou dost but ill guard thy royal dignity whilst thou allowest thyself in such levities. Thou shouldest sit in state upon a stately throne, and busy thyself with affairs the whole day long. So would the Egyptians feel that a great man rules them, and thou wouldst be better spoken of. But now thou conductest thyself in no kingly fashion." Amasis answered them thus:– "Bowmen bend their bows when they wish to shoot; unbrace them when the shooting is over.

---

1 In early times the Greeks divided the day into three parts. The division, according to Dio Chrysostomus, was πρωὶ, sunrise, or early morn; περὶ πλήθουσαν ἀγορὰν, market time or forenoon, the third hour; μεσημβρία, midday; δείλη, or περὶ δείλην, afternoon, or the ninth hour; and ἑσπέρα, evening, or sunset. These are very like the Arabic divisions at the present time, for each of which they have a stated number of prayers.

Were they kept always strung they would break, and fail the archer in time of need. So it is with men. If they give themselves constantly to serious work, and never indulge awhile in pastime or sport, they lose their senses, and become mad or moody. Knowing this, I divide my life between pastime and business." Thus he answered his friends.

174. It is said that Amasis, even while he was a private man, had the same tastes for drinking and jesting, and was averse to engaging in any serious employment. He lived in constant feasts and revelries, and whenever his means failed him, he roamed about and robbed people. On such occasions the persons from whom he had stolen would bring him, if he denied the charge, before the nearest oracle; sometimes the oracle would pronounce him guilty of the theft, at other times it would acquit him. When afterwards he came to be king, he neglected the temples of such gods as had declared that he was not a thief, and neither contributed to their adornment, nor frequented them for sacrifice; since he regarded them as utterly worthless, and their oracles as wholly false: but the gods who had detected his guilt he considered to be true gods whose oracles did not deceive, and these he honoured exceedingly.

175. First of all, therefore, he built the gateway[1] of the temple of Athena at Saïs, which is an astonishing work, far surpassing all other buildings of the same kind both in extent and height, and built with stones of rare size and excellency. In the next place, he presented to the temple a number of large colossal statues, and several prodigious andro-sphinxes,[2] besides certain stones for the repairs, of a most extraordinary size. Some of these he got from the quarries over against Memphis, but the largest were brought from Elephantiné,[3] which is twenty days' voyage from Saïs. Of all these wonderful masses that which I most admire is a chamber made of a single stone, which was quarried at Elephantiné. It took three years to convey this block from the quarry to Saïs; and in the conveyance were employed no fewer than two thousand labourers, who were all from the class of boatmen. The length of this chamber on the outside is

---

1 Not a "portico," but the lofty towers of the Area, or Court of Entrance.

2 The usual sphinxes of the *dromos*, or avenue, leading to the entrance of the large temples.

3 These were granite blocks.

twenty-one cubits, its breadth fourteen cubits, and its height eight. The measurements inside are the following:— The length, eighteen cubits and five-sixths; the breadth, twelve cubits; and the height, five. It lies near the entrance of the temple, where it was left in consequence of the following circumstance:— It happened that the architect, just as the stone had reached the spot where it now stands, heaved a sigh, considering the length of time that the removal had taken, and feeling wearied with the heavy toil. The sigh was heard by Amasis, who, regarding it as an omen, would not allow the chamber to be moved forward any further. Some, however, say that one of the workmen engaged at the levers was crushed and killed by the mass, and that this was the reason of its being left where it now stands.

176. To the other temples of much note Amasis also made magnificent offerings — at Memphis, for instance, he gave the recumbent colossus[1] in front of the temple of Hephaistos, which is seventy-five feet long. Two other colossal statues stand on the same base, each twenty feet high, carved in the stone of Ethiopia, one on either side of the temple. There is also a stone colossus of the same size at Saïs, recumbent like that at Memphis. Amasis finally built the temple of Isis at Memphis, a vast structure, well worth seeing.

177. It is said that the reign of Amasis was the most prosperous time that Egypt ever saw,[2] — the river was more liberal to the land, and the land brought forth more abundantly for the service of man than had ever been known before; while the number of inhabited cities was not less than twenty thousand. It was this king Amasis who established the law that every Egyptian should appear once a year before the governor of his canton,[3] and show his means of living; or, failing to do so, and to prove that he got an honest livelihood, should be put to death. Solon the Athenian borrowed this law from the Egyptians, and imposed it on his countrymen, who have observed it ever since. It is indeed an excellent custom.

1 It was an unusual position for an Egyptian statue; and this, as well as the other at Memphis, and the monolith, may have been left on the ground, in consequence of the troubles which came upon Egypt at the time; and which the Egyptians concealed from Herodotus.

2 This can only relate to the internal state of the country; and what Herodotus afterwards says shows this was his meaning.

3 Each nome, or canton, was governed by a nomarch.

178. Amasis was partial to the Greeks,[1] and, among other favours which he granted them, gave to such as liked to settle in Egypt the city of Naucratis[2] for their residence. To those who only wished to trade upon the coast, and did not want to fix their abode in the country, he granted certain lands where they might set up altars and erect temples to the gods. Of these temples the grandest and most famous, which is also the most frequented, is that called "the Hellenium." It was built conjointly by the Ionians, Dorians, and Æolians, the following cities taking part in the work:— the Ionian states of Chios, Teos, Phocæa, and Clazomenæ; Rhodes, Cnidus, Halicarnassus, and Phasêlis[3] of the Dorians; and Mytilêne of the Æolians. These are the states to whom the temple belongs, and they have the right of appointing the governors of the factory; the other cities which claim a share in the building, claim what in no sense belongs to them. Three nations, however, consecrated for themselves separate temples – the Eginetans one to Zeus, the Samians to Hera, and the Milesians to Apollo.[4]

179. In ancient times there was no factory but Naucratis in the whole of Egypt; and if a person entered one of the other mouths of the Nile, he was obliged to swear that he had not come there of his own free will. Having so done, he was bound to sail in his ship to the Canobic mouth, or, were that impossible owing to contrary winds, he must take his wares by boat all round the Delta, and so bring them to Naucratis, which had an exclusive privilege.

180. It happened in the reign of Amasis that the temple of Delphi had been accidentally burnt,[5] and the Amphictyons[6] had contracted to have it rebuilt for three hundred talents, of which

---

1 Amasis had reason to be hostile to the Greeks, who had assisted Apries, but, perceiving the value of their aid, he became friendly to them, and granted them many privileges, which had the effect of inducing many to settle in Egypt, and afterwards led them to assist the Egyptians in freeing their country from the Persians.

2 This was "formerly" the only commercial entrepôt for Greek merchandise, and was established for the first time by Amasis.

3 Phasêlis lay on the east coast of Lycia, directly at the base of Mount Solyma (*Takhtalu*).

4 That is, to the gods specially worshipped in their respective countries.

5 The temple at Delphi was burnt in the year B.C. 548, consequently in the 21st year of Amasis.

6 See Book vii. ch. 200.

sum one-fourth was to be furnished by the Delphians. Under these circumstances the Delphians went from city to city begging contributions, and among their other wanderings came to Egypt and asked for help. From few other places did they obtain so much – Amasis gave them a thousand talents of alum,[1] and the Greek settlers twenty minæ.[2]

181. A league was concluded by Amasis with the Cyrenæans, by which Cyrênê and Egypt became close friends and allies. He likewise took a wife from that city, either as a sign of his friendly feeling, or because he had a fancy to marry a Greek woman. However this may be, certain it is that he espoused a lady of Cyrênê, by name Ladicé, daughter, some say, of Battus or Arcesilaüs, the king – others, of Critobûlus, one of the chief citizens. When the time came to complete the contract, Amasis was struck with weakness and he used his other women. Astonished hereat the king thus addressed his bride: "Woman, thou hast certainly bewitched me – now therefore be sure thou shalt perish more miserably than ever woman perished yet." Ladicé protested her innocence, but in vain; Amasis was not softened. Hereupon she made a vow internally, that if he re-covered within the day (for no longer time was allowed her), she would present a statue to the temple of Aphrodite at Cyrênê. Immediately she obtained her wish, and the king's weakness disappeared. Amasis loved her greatly ever after, and Ladicé per-formed her vow. The statue which she caused to be made, and sent to Cyrênê, continued there to my day, standing with its face looking outwards from the city. Ladicé herself, when Cambyses conquered Egypt, suffered no wrong; for Cambyses, on learning of her who she was, sent her back unharmed to her country.

182. Besides the marks of favour already mentioned, Amasis also enriched with offerings many of the Greek temples. He sent to Cyrênê a statue of Athena covered with plates of gold,[3] and a painted likeness[4] of himself. To the Athena of Lindus he gave

---

1 That of Egypt was celebrated.

2 Twenty minæ would be somewhat more than £80 of our money. The entire sum which the Delphians had to collect exceeded £18,000.

3 Statues of this kind were not uncommon (infra, vi. 118). The most famous was that of Athena [Minerva] at Delphi, which the Athenians dedicated from the spoils of their victory at the Eurymedon.

4 The Egyptians had actual portraits of their kings at a very remote period; and those in the sculptures were real likenesses. There are some portraits

two statues in stone, and a linen corslet[1] well worth inspection. To the Samian Hera he presented two statues of himself, made in wood,[2] which stood in the great temple to my day, behind the doors. Samos was honoured with these gifts on account of the bond of friendship subsisting between Amasis and Polycrates, the son of Æaces:[3] Lindus, for no such reason, but because of the tradition that the daughters of Danaus[4] touched there in their flight from the sons of Ægyptus, and built the temple of Athena. Such were the offerings of Amasis. He likewise took Cyprus, which no man had ever done before,[5] and compelled it to pay him a tribute.[6]

---

painted on wood and affixed to mummy cases, but these are of Greek and Roman time, and an innovation not Egyptian.

1 It has been conjectured that the "tree-wool" of Herodotus was silk; but cotton is commonly used for embroidery even at the present day.

2 Pausanias (ii. 19) says "all ancient statues were of wood, especially those of the Egyptians."

3 Vide infra, iii. 39–43.

4 The flight of Danaus from Egypt to Greece is not only mentioned by Herodotus, but by Manetho and others, and was credited both by Greeks and Egyptians.

5 According to Greek tradition, the conquest was effected by a certain Cinyras, a Syrian king, whom Homer makes contemporary with Agamemnon. (Il. xi. 20.) His capital was Paphos.

6 Neco had made Egypt a naval power (supra, ch. 159), which she thenceforth continued to be.

ADDED NOTES BY THE EDITOR

(1.) *The Pyramids.* – The Pyramids divide themselves into seven large groups, the two largest (at Gizeh) being the work of the old kings, while the five smaller were probably built in the Vth and VIth dynasties. On being investigated, the chambers within several of these structures were found to be covered with hieroglyphic signs. They are among the very oldest literary monuments of Egypt. The pyramid texts are religious, and contain hymns, prayers, and magical formulæ, reflecting the popular ideas of life after death. Most of them are in poetical language. Large and important finds of gems and treasure were dug up in the under chambers, as well as of reliefs, granite figures, and the like.

(2.) Among recent discoveries in Egypt the *Tel-el-Amarna* tablets are the most important. These clay tablets, in cuneiform character, enable us to get a singularly helpful understanding not only of the civilisation of the period (about 1400 B.C.), but also of the political status of Egypt at the time. They prove the prevalence of Babylonian influence and civilising power in Western Asia in a hitherto unexpected fashion. Even Egyptian kings wrote to their Syrian subjects in Babylonian.

(3.) The *Labyrinth* was probably a temple, though (so far) no architectural plan of the building has been obtained.

The discovery by Dr. A. J. Evans of a huge, many-chambered building in Cnossus (Crete), on the traditional site of the palace of Minos, has suggested to him the idea that this Cretan structure was the original labyrinth. Its huge size and complexity caused the name to be used in its conventional meaning; but originally the word seems to mean "house of the double-axe" (*labrys*).

Every excavation made proves the extraordinarily high state of civilisation which had been attained in ancient Egypt.

THE THIRD BOOK,
ENTITLED THALIA

1. THE above-mentioned Amasis was the Egyptian king against whom Cambyses, son of Cyrus, made his expedition; and with him went an army composed of the many nations under his rule, among them being included both Ionic and Æolic Greeks. The reason of the invasion was the following.[1] Cambyses, by the advice of a certain Egyptian, who was angry with Amasis for having torn him from his wife and children, and given him over to the Persians, had sent a herald to Amasis to ask his daughter in marriage. His adviser was a physician, whom Amasis, when Cyrus had requested that he would send him the most skilful of all the Egyptian eye-doctors,[2] singled out as the best from the whole number. Therefore the Egyptian bore Amasis a grudge, and his reason for urging Cambyses to ask the hand of the king's daughter was, that if he complied, it might cause him annoyance; if he refused, it might make Cambyses his enemy. When the message came, Amasis, who much dreaded the power of the Persians, was greatly perplexed whether to give his daughter or no; for that Cambyses did not intend to make her his wife, but would only receive her as his concubine, he knew for certain. He therefore cast the matter in his mind, and finally resolved what he would do. There was a daughter of the late king Apries, named Nitêtis,[3] a tall and beautiful woman, the last survivor of that royal house. Amasis took this woman, and, decking her out with gold and costly garments, sent her to Persia as if she had been his own child. Some time afterwards, Cambyses, as he gave

1 Herodotus had already told us that the subjugation of Egypt was among the designs of Cyrus (i. 153). Indeed, two motives of a public character, each by itself enough to account for the attack, urged the Persian arms in this direction; viz., revenge, and the lust of conquest. Grote has noticed the "impulse of aggrandisement," which formed the predominant characteristic of the Persian nation at this period.

2 Vide supra, ii. 84. Egyptians first, and afterwards Greeks, were the court physicians of the Achæmenidæ.

3 This account, which Herodotus says was that of the Persians, is utterly inadmissible.

her an embrace, happened to call her by her father's name, whereupon she said to him, "I see, O king, thou knowest not how thou hast been cheated by Amasis; who took me, and, tricking me out with gauds, sent me to thee as his own daughter. But I am in truth the child of Apries, who was his lord and master, until he rebelled against him, together with the rest of the Egyptians, and put him to death." It was this speech, and the cause of quarrel it disclosed, which roused the anger of Cambyses, son of Cyrus, and brought his arms upon Egypt. Such is the Persian story.

2. The Egyptians, however, claim Cambyses as belonging to them, declaring that he was the son of this Nitêtis. It was Cyrus, they say, and not Cambyses, who sent to Amasis for his daughter. But here they mis-state the truth. Acquainted as they are beyond all other men with the laws and customs of the Persians, they cannot but be well aware, first, that it is not the Persian wont to allow a bastard to reign when there is a legitimate heir; and next, that Cambyses was the son of Cassandané, the daughter of Pharnaspes, an Achæmenian, and not of this Egyptian. But the fact is, that they pervert history, in order to claim relationship with the house of Cyrus. Such is the truth of this matter.

3. I have also heard another account, which I do not at all believe, – that a Persian lady came to visit the wives of Cyrus, and seeing how tall and beautiful were the children of Cassandané, then standing by, broke out into loud praise of them, and admired them exceedingly. But Cassandané, wife of Cyrus, answered, "Though such the children I have borne him, yet Cyrus slights me and gives all his regard to the new-comer from Egypt." Thus did she express her vexation on account of Nitêtis: whereupon Cambyses, the eldest of her boys, exclaimed, "Mother, when I am a man, I will turn Egypt upside down for you." He was but ten years old, as the tale runs, when he said this, and astonished all the women, yet he never forgot it afterwards; and on this account, they say, when he came to be a man, and mounted the throne, he made his expedition against Egypt.

4. There was another matter, quite distinct, which helped to bring about the expedition. One of the mercenaries of Amasis,[1]

---

1 The Carian and Ionian mercenaries mentioned repeatedly in the second Book (chs. 152, 154, 163, etc.).

a Halicarnassian, Phanes by name, a man of good judgment, and a brave warrior, dissatisfied for some reason or other with his master, deserted the service, and, taking ship, fled to Cambyses, wishing to get speech with him. As he was a person of no small account among the mercenaries, and one who could give very exact intelligence about Egypt, Amasis, anxious to recover him, ordered that he should be pursued. He gave the matter in charge to one of the most trusty of the eunuchs, who went in quest of the Halicarnassian in a vessel of war. The eunuch caught him in Lycia, but did not contrive to bring him back to Egypt, for Phanes outwitted him by making his guards drunk, and then escaping into Persia. Now it happened that Cambyses was meditating his attack on Egypt, and doubting how he might best pass the desert, when Phanes arrived, and not only told him all the secrets of Amasis, but advised him also how the desert might be crossed. He counselled him to send an ambassador to the king of the Arabs,[1] and ask him for safe-conduct through the region.

5. Now the only entrance into Egypt is by this desert: the country from Phœnicia to the borders of the city Cadytis[2] belongs to the people called the Palæstine Syrians;[3] from Cadytis, which it appears to me is a city almost as large as Sardis, the marts upon the coast till you reach Jenysus are the Arabian king's; after Jenysus the Syrians again come in, and extend to Lake Serbônis, near the place where Mount Casius juts out into the sea. At Lake Serbônis, where the tale goes that Typhon hid himself, Egypt begins. Now the whole tract between Jenysus on the one side, and Lake Serbônis and Mount Casius on the other, and this is no small space, being as much as three days' journey, is a dry desert without a drop of water.

6. I shall now mention a thing of which few of those who sail to Egypt are aware. Twice a year wine is brought into Egypt from every part of Greece, as well as from Phœnicia, in earthen jars;[4] and yet in the whole country you will nowhere see, as I

1 Herodotus appears to have thought that the Arabs were united under the government of a single king.

2 That is, Gaza.

3 Palestine Syria means properly "the Syria of the Philistines," who were in ancient times by far the most powerful race of *southern* Syria (cf. Gen. xxi. 32–4, xxvi. 14–8; Ex. xiii. 17, etc.).

4 Besides the quantity of wine made in Egypt, a great supply was annually imported from Greece, after the trade was opened with that country.

may say, a single jar. What then, every one will ask, becomes of the jars? This, too, I will clear up. The burgomaster of each town has to collect the wine-jars within his district, and to carry them to Memphis, where they are all filled with water by the Memphians, who then convey them to this desert tract of Syria. And so it comes to pass that all the jars which enter Egypt year by year, and are there put up to sale, find their way into Syria, whither all the old jars have gone before them.

7. This way of keeping the passage into Egypt fit for use by storing water there, was begun by the Persians so soon as they became masters of that country. As, however, at the time of which we speak the tract had not yet been so supplied, Cambyses took the advice of his Halicarnassian guest, and sent messengers to the Arabian to beg a safe-conduct through the region. The Arabian granted his prayer, and each pledged faith to the other.

8. The Arabs keep such pledges more religiously than almost any other people.[1] They plight faith with the forms following. When two men would swear a friendship, they stand on each side of a third: he with a sharp stone makes a cut on the inside of the hand of each near the middle finger, and, taking a piece from their dress, dips it in the blood of each, and moistens therewith seven stones[2] lying in the midst, calling the while on Dionysus and Urania. After this, the man who makes the pledge commends the stranger (or the citizen, if citizen he be) to all his friends, and they deem themselves bound to stand to the engagement. They have but these two gods, to wit, Dionysus and Urania;[3] and they say that in their mode of cutting the hair, they follow Dionysus. Now their practice is to cut it in a ring, away from the temples. Dionysus they call in their language Orotal, and Urania, Alilat.

9. When, therefore, the Arabian had pledged his faith to the messengers of Cambyses, he straightway contrived as follows:—

1 The fidelity of the Arabs to their engagements is noticed by all travellers. Mr. Kinglake remarks, "It is not of the Bedouins that travellers are afraid, for the safe-conduct granted by the Chief of the ruling tribe is never, I believe, violated." (Eothen.)

2 Events were often recorded in the East by stones. Comp. the 12 stones placed in the bed of the Jordan, Joshua iv. 9. The number 7 had an important meaning (as in the Bible frequently), as well as 4. The former was the fortunate number. It was also a sacred number with the Persians.

3 There can be little doubt that the religion of the Arabians in the time of Herodotus was *astral* – "the worship of the host of heaven."

he filled a number of camels' skins with water, and loading therewith all the live camels that he possessed, drove them into the desert, and awaited the coming of the army. This is the more likely of the two tales that are told. The other is an improbable story, but, as it is related, I think that I ought not to pass it by. There is a great river in Arabia, called the Corys, which empties itself into the Erythræan sea. The Arabian king, they say, made a pipe of the skins of oxen and other beasts, reaching from this river all the way to the desert, and so brought the water to certain cisterns which he had had dug in the desert to receive it. It is a twelve days' journey from the river to this desert tract. And the water, they say, was brought through three different pipes to three separate places.

10. Psammenitus, son of Amasis, lay encamped at the mouth of the Nile, called the Pelusiac, awaiting Cambyses. For Cambyses, when he went up against Egypt, found Amasis no longer in life: he had died after ruling Egypt forty and four years, during all which time no great misfortune had befallen him. When he died, his body was embalmed, and buried in the tomb which he had himself caused to be made in the temple.[1] After his son Psammenitus had mounted the throne, a strange prodigy occurred in Egypt:– Rain fell at Egyptian Thebes, a thing which never happened before, and which, to the present time, has never happened again, as the Thebans themselves testify. In Upper Egypt it does not usually rain at all; but on this occasion, rain fell at Thebes in small drops.

11. The Persians crossed the desert, and, pitching their camp close to the Egyptians, made ready for battle. Hereupon the mercenaries in the pay of Psammenitus, who were Greeks and Carians, full of anger against Phanes for having brought a foreign army upon Egypt, bethought themselves of a mode whereby they might be revenged on him. Phanes had left sons in Egypt. The mercenaries took these, and leading them to the camp, displayed them before the eyes of their father; after which they brought out a bowl, and, placing it in the space between the two hosts, they led the sons of Phanes, one by one, to the vessel, and slew them over it.[2] When the last was dead, water and wine were poured into the bowl, and all the soldiers tasted

---

1 The temple of Athena at Saïs. (Vide supra, ii. 169.)
2 This was a mode of making an oath binding.

of the blood, and so they went to the battle. Stubborn was the fight which followed, and it was not till vast numbers had been slain upon both sides, that the Egyptians turned and fled.

12. On the field where this battle was fought I saw a very wonderful thing which the natives pointed out to me. The bones of the slain lie scattered upon the field in two lots, those of the Persians in one place by themselves, as the bodies lay at the first – those of the Egyptians in another place apart from them: If, then, you strike the Persian skulls, even with a pebble, they are so weak, that you break a hole in them; but the Egyptian skulls are so strong, that you may smite them with a stone and you will scarcely break them in. They gave me the following reason for this difference, which seemed to me likely enough:– The Egyptians (they said) from early childhood have the head shaved, and so by the action of the sun the skull becomes thick and hard. The same cause prevents baldness in Egypt, where you see fewer bald men than in any other land. Such, then, is the reason why the skulls of the Egyptians are so strong. The Persians, on the other hand, have feeble skulls, because they keep themselves shaded from the first,[1] wearing turbans upon their heads. What I have here mentioned I saw with my own eyes, and I observed also the like at Paprêmis, in the case of the Persians who were killed with Achæmenes, the son of Darius, by Inarus the Libyan.[2]

13. The Egyptians who fought in the battle, no sooner turned their backs upon the enemy, than they fled away in complete disorder to Memphis, where they shut themselves up within the walls. Hereupon Cambyses sent a Mytilenæan vessel, with a Persian herald on board, who was to sail up the Nile to Memphis, and invite the Egyptians to a surrender. They, however, when they saw the vessel entering the town, poured forth in crowds from the castle, destroyed the ship, and, tearing the crew limb from limb, so bore them into the fortress. After this Memphis was besieged, and in due time surrendered. Hereon the Libyans who bordered upon Egypt, fearing the fate of that country, gave themselves up to Cambyses without a battle, made an agreement to pay tribute to him, and forthwith sent him gifts.[3]

---

1 Propably the shading by the turban is alone meant.
2 Vide infra, vii. 7. The revolt of Inarus is fixed by Clinton to the year B.C. 460, the fifth year of Artaxerxes.
3 Vide infra, iv. 165. Arcesilaüs III. was king of Cyrene at this time.

The Cyrenæans too, and the Barcæans, having the same fear as the Libyans, immediately did the like. Cambyses received the Libyan presents very graciously, but not so the gifts of the Cyrenæans. They had sent no more than five hundred *minæ*[1] of silver, which Cambyses, I imagine, thought too little. He therefore snatched the money from them, and with his own hands scattered it among his soldiers.

14. Ten days after the fort had fallen, Cambyses resolved to try the spirit of Psammenitus, the Egyptian king, whose whole reign had been but six months. He therefore had him set in one of the suburbs, and many other Egyptians with him, and there subjected him to insult. First of all he sent his daughter out from the city, clothed in the garb of a slave, with a pitcher to draw water. Many virgins, the daughters of the chief nobles, accompanied her, wearing the same dress. When the damsels came opposite the place where their fathers sate, shedding tears and uttering cries of woe, the fathers, all but Psammenitus, wept and wailed in return, grieving to see their children in so sad a plight; but he, when he had looked and seen, bent his head towards the ground. In this way passed by the water-carriers. Next to them came Psammenitus' son, and two thousand Egyptians of the same age with him – all of them having ropes round their necks and bridles in their mouths – and they too passed by on their way to suffer death for the murder of the Mytilenæans who were destroyed, with their vessel, in Memphis. For so had the royal judges given their sentence – "for each Mytilenæan ten of the noblest Egyptians must forfeit life." King Psammenitus saw the train pass on, and knew his son was being led to death, but, while the other Egyptians who sate around him wept and were sorely troubled, he showed no further sign than when he saw his daughter. And now, when they too were gone, it chanced that one of his former boon-companions, a man advanced in years, who had been stripped of all that he had and was a beggar, came where Psammenitus, son of Amasis, and the rest of the Egyptians were, asking alms from the soldiers. At this sight the king burst into tears, and, weeping out aloud, called his friend by his name, and smote himself on the head. Now there were some who had been set to watch Psammenitus and see what he would

---

1 If Attic minæ are intended, as is probable, the value of the Cyrenæan contribution would be little more than £2000 of our money.

do as each train went by; so these persons went and told Cambyses of his behaviour. Then he, astonished at what was done, sent a messenger to Psammenitus, and questioned him, saying, "Psammenitus, thy lord Cambyses asketh thee why, when thou sawest thy daughter brought to shame, and thy son on his way to death, thou didst neither utter cry nor shed tear, while to a beggar, who is, he hears, a stranger to thy race, thou gavest those marks of honour." To this question Psammenitus made answer, "O son of Cyrus, my own misfortunes were too great for tears; but the woe of my friend deserved them. When a man falls from splendour and plenty into beggary at the threshold of old age, one may well weep for him." When the messenger brought back this answer, Cambyses owned it was just; Crœsus, likewise, the Egyptians say, burst into tears − for he too had come into Egypt with Cambyses − and the Persians who were present wept. Even Cambyses himself was touched with pity, and he forthwith gave an order, that the son of Psammenitus should be spared from the number of those appointed to die, and Psammenitus himself brought from the suburb into his presence.

15. The messengers were too late to save the life of Psammenitus' son, who had been cut in pieces the first of all; but they took Psammenitus himself and brought him before the king. Cambyses allowed him to live with him, and gave him no more harsh treatment; nay, could he have kept from intermeddling with affairs, he might have recovered Egypt, and ruled it as governor. For the Persian wont is to treat the sons of kings with honour, and even to give their fathers' kingdoms to the children of such as revolt from them.[1] There are many cases from which one may collect that this is the Persian rule, and especially those of Pausiris and Thannyras. Thannyras was son of Inarus the Libyan, and was allowed to succeed his father, as was also Pausiris, son of Amyrtæus; yet certainly no two persons ever did the Persians more damage than Amyrtæus and Inarus. In this case Psammenitus plotted evil, and received his reward accordingly. He was discovered to be stirring up revolt in Egypt, wherefore Cambyses, when his guilt clearly appeared, compelled him to

1 It appears from the Jewish history that this was a general Oriental practice in ancient times. When Pharaoh-Necho deposed Jehoahaz, he made Eliakim (Jehoiakim), his brother, king over Judah (2 Kings xxiii. 34). And when Nebuchadnezzar deposed Jehoiachin (2 Kings xxiv. 17), he set Mattaniah (Zedekiah), his uncle, upon the throne.

drink bull's blood,[1] which presently caused his death. Such was the end of Psammenitus.

16. After this Cambyses left Memphis, and went to Saïs, wishing to do that which he actually did on his arrival there. He entered the palace of Amasis, and straightway commanded that the body of the king should be brought forth from the sepulchre. When the attendants did according to his commandment, he further bade them scourge the body, and prick it with goads, and pluck the hair from it,[2] and heap upon it all manner of insults. The body, however, having been embalmed, resisted, and refused to come apart, do what they would to it; so the attendants grew weary of their work; whereupon Cambyses bade them take the corpse and burn it. This was truly an impious command to give, for the Persians hold fire to be a god,[3] and never by any chance burn their dead. Indeed this practice is unlawful, both with them and with the Egyptians – with them for the reason above mentioned, since they deem it wrong to give the corpse of a man to a god; and with the Egyptians, because they believe fire to be a live animal, which eats whatever it can seize, and then, glutted with the food, dies with the matter which it feeds upon. Now to give a man's body to be devoured by beasts is in no wise agreeable to their customs, and indeed this is the very reason why they embalm their dead; namely, to prevent them from being eaten in the grave by worms. Thus Cambyses commanded what both nations accounted unlawful.[4] According to the Egyptians, it was not Amasis who was thus treated, but another of their nation who was of about the same height. The Persians, believing this man's body to be the king's, abused it in the fashion described above. Amasis, they say, was warned by an oracle of what would happen to him after his death: in order, therefore, to prevent the impending fate, he buried the body,

---

1 There seems to have been a wide-spread belief among the ancients that bull's blood was poisonous.

2 This is evidently a Greek statement, and not derived from the Egyptian priests. There was no hair to pluck out, the "head and all the body" of the kings and priests being shaved. The whole story may be doubted.

3 On this point see above, i. 131.

4 The Egyptians were averse to burning a body, not only because burning was considered the punishment of the wicked, but because it was opposed to all their prejudices in favour of its preservation. If they really believed in the return of the soul to the body, this would be an additional reason.

which afterwards received the blows, inside his own tomb near the entrance, commanding his son to bury him, when he died, in the furthest recess of the same sepulchre. For my own part I do not believe that these orders were ever given by Amasis; the Egyptians, as it seems to me, falsely assert it, to save their own dignity.

17. After this Cambyses took counsel with himself, and planned three expeditions. One was against the Carthaginians, another against the Ammonians, and a third against the long-lived Ethiopians, who dwelt in that part of Libya which borders upon the southern sea.[1] He judged it best to despatch his fleet against Carthage and to send some portion of his land army to act against the Ammonians, while his spies went into Ethiopia, under the pretence of carrying presents to the king, but in reality to take note of all they saw, and especially to observe whether there was really what is called "the table of the Sun" in Ethiopia.

18. Now the table of the Sun according to the accounts given of it may be thus described:— It is a meadow in the skirts of their city full of the boiled flesh[2] of all manner of beasts, which the magistrates are careful to store with meat every night, and where whoever likes may come and eat during the day. The people of the land say that the earth itself brings forth the food. Such is the description which is given of this table.

19. When Cambyses had made up his mind that the spies should go, he forthwith sent to Elephantiné for certain of the Icthyophagi who were acquainted with the Ethiopian tongue; and, while they were being fetched, issued orders to his fleet to sail against Carthage. But the Phœnicians said they would not go, since they were bound to the Carthaginians by solemn oaths, and since besides it would be wicked in them to make war on their own children. Now when the Phœnicians refused, the rest of the fleet was unequal to the undertaking; and so it was that the Carthaginians escaped, and were not enslaved by the

1 Not only in this passage, but again, infra, ch. 114, they are said to dwell towards the south, *at the furthest limits of Africa*. Their country must have lain, therefore, beyond the Straits of Babel-mandeb.

2 This was less common in early times, and as Athenæus says, the heroes in Homer seldom "boil their meat, or dress it with sauces;" but in Egypt as well as in Ethiopia boiled meat was eaten, though the Egyptians more frequently roasted it, and boiled their fish. With the Arabs the custom of boiling meat seems to be very ancient.

Persians. Cambyses thought not right to force the war upon the Phœnicians, because they had yielded themselves to the Persians,[1] and because upon the Phœnicians all his sea-service depended. The Cyprians had also joined the Persians of their own accord, and took part with them in the expedition against Egypt.

20. As soon as the Icthyophagi arrived from Elephantiné, Cambyses, having told them what they were to say, forthwith despatched them into Ethiopia with these following gifts: to wit, a purple robe,[2] a gold chain for the neck, armlets, an alabaster box of myrrh, and a cask of palm wine. The Ethiopians to whom this embassy was sent, are said to be the tallest[3] and handsomest men in the whole world. In their customs they differ greatly from the rest of mankind, and particularly in the way they choose their kings; for they find out the man who is the tallest of all the citizens, and of strength equal to his height, and appoint him to rule over them.

21. The Icthyophagi on reaching this people, delivered the gifts to the king of the country, and spoke as follows:— "Cambyses, king of the Persians, anxious to become thy ally and sworn friend, has sent us to hold converse with thee, and to bear thee the gifts thou seest, which are the things wherein he himself delights the most." Hereon the Ethiopian, who knew they came as spies, made answer:— "The king of the Persians sent you not with these gifts because he much desired to become my sworn friend — nor is the account which ye give of yourselves true, for ye are come to search out my kingdom. Also your king is not a just man — for were he so, he had not coveted a land which is not his own, nor brought slavery on a people who never did him any wrong. Bear him this bow, and say, — 'The king of the Ethiops thus advises the king of the Persians — when the Persians can pull a bow of this strength thus easily, then let him come with an army of superior strength against the long-lived

1 It has been usual to ascribe the conquest of Phœnicia to Cyrus. But, *according to Herodotus*, the acquisition belongs to the reign of Cambyses.

2 Various opinions have been held about the origin of the Tyrian purple. The murex is generally supposed to have given it. A shell-fish (Helix Ianthina) is found on the coast, about Tyre and Beyroot, which is remarkable for its throwing out a quantity of purple liquid when approached, in order (like the sepia) to conceal itself.

3 Vide infra, iii. 114; and compare Isaiah xlv. 14.

Ethiopians – till then, let him thank the gods that they have not put it into the heart of the sons of the Ethiops to covet countries which do not belong to them.'"

22. So speaking, he unstrung the bow, and gave it into the hands of the messengers. Then, taking the purple robe, he asked them what it was, and how it had been made. They answered truly, telling him concerning the purple, and the art of the dyer – whereat he observed, "that the men were deceitful, and their garments also." Next he took the neck-chain and the armlets, and asked about them. So the Icthyophagi explained their use as ornaments. Then the king laughed, and fancying they were fetters, said, "the Ethiopians had much stronger ones." Thirdly, he inquired about the myrrh, and when they told him how it was made and rubbed upon the limbs, he said the same as he had said about the robe. Last of all he came to the wine, and having learnt their way of making it, he drank a draught, which greatly delighted him; whereupon he asked what the Persian king was wont to eat, and to what age the longest-lived of the Persians had been known to attain. They told him that the king ate bread, and described the nature of wheat – adding that eighty years was the longest term of man's life among the Persians. Hereat he remarked, "It did not surprise him, if they fed on dirt, that they died so soon; indeed he was sure they never would have lived so long as eighty years, except for the refreshment they got from that drink (meaning the wine), wherein he confessed the Persians surpassed the Ethiopians."

23. The Icthyophagi then in their turn questioned the king concerning the term of life, and diet of his people, and were told that most of them lived to be a hundred and twenty years old, while some even went beyond that age – they ate boiled flesh, and had for their drink nothing but milk. When the Icthyophagi showed wonder at the number of the years, he led them to a fountain, wherein when they had washed, they found their flesh all glossy and sleek, as if they had bathed in oil – and a scent came from the spring like that of violets. The water was so weak, they said, that nothing would float in it, neither wood, nor any lighter substance, but all went to the bottom. If the account of this fountain be true, it would be their constant use of the water from it which makes them so long-lived. When they quitted the fountain the king led them to a prison, where the prisoners were all of them bound with fetters of gold. Among these Ethiopians

copper is of all metals the most scarce and valuable. After they had seen the prison, they were likewise shown what is called "the table of the Sun."

24. Also, last of all, they were allowed to behold the coffins of the Ethiopians, which are made (according to report) of crystal, after the following fashion:– When the dead body has been dried, either in the Egyptian, or in some other manner, they cover the whole with gypsum, and adorn it with painting until it is as like the living man as possible. Then they place the body in a crystal pillar which has been hollowed out to receive it, crystal being dug up in great abundance in their country, and of a kind very easy to work. You may see the corpse through the pillar within which it lies; and it neither gives out any unpleasant odour, nor is it in any respect unseemly; yet there is no part that is not as plainly visible as if the body was bare. The next of kin keep the crystal pillar in their houses for a full year from the time of the death, and give it the first fruits continually, and honour it with sacrifice. After the year is out they bear the pillar forth, and set it up near the town.

25. When the spies had now seen everything, they returned back to Egypt, and made report to Cambyses, who was stirred to anger by their words. Forthwith he set out on his march against the Ethiopians without having made any provision for the sustenance of his army, or reflected that he was about to wage war in the uttermost parts of the earth. Like a senseless madman as he was, no sooner did he receive the report of the Icthyophagi than he began his march, bidding the Greeks who were with his army remain where they were, and taking only his land force with him. At Thebes, which he passed through on his way, he detached from his main body some fifty thousand men, and sent them against the Ammonians with orders to carry the people into captivity, and burn the oracle of Zeus. Meanwhile he himself went on with the rest of his forces against the Ethiopians. Before, however, he had accomplished one-fifth part of the distance, all that the army had in the way of provisions failed; whereupon the men began to eat the sumpter beasts, which shortly failed also. If then, at this time, Cambyses, seeing what was happening, had confessed himself in the wrong, and led his army back, he would have done the wisest thing that he could after the mistake made at the outset; but as it was, he took no manner of heed, but continued to march forwards. So long

as the earth gave them anything, the soldiers sustained life by eating the grass and herbs; but when they came to the bare sand, a portion of them were guilty of a horrid deed: by tens they cast lots for a man, who was slain to be the food of the others. When Cambyses heard of these doings, alarmed at such cannibalism, he gave up his attack on Ethiopia, and retreating by the way he had come, reached Thebes, after he had lost vast numbers of his soldiers. From Thebes he marched down to Memphis, where he dismissed the Greeks, allowing them to sail home. And so ended the expedition against Ethiopia.[1]

26. The men sent to attack the Ammonians, started from Thebes, having guides with them, and may be clearly traced as far as the city Oasis,[2] which is inhabited by Samians, said to be of the tribe Æschrionia. The place is distant from Thebes seven days' journey across the sand, and is called in our tongue "the Island of the Blessed." Thus far the army is known to have made its way; but thenceforth nothing is to be heard of them, except what the Ammonians, and those who get their knowledge from them, report. It is certain they neither reached the Ammonians, nor even came back to Egypt. Further than this, the Ammonians relate as follows:— That the Persians set forth from Oasis across the sand, and had reached about half way between that place and themselves, when, as they were at their midday meal, a wind arose from the south, strong and deadly, bringing with it vast columns of whirling sand, which entirely covered up the troops, and caused them wholly to disappear. Thus, according to the Ammonians, did it fare with this army.

27. About the time when Cambyses arrived at Memphis, Apis appeared to the Egyptians. Now Apis is the god whom the Greeks call Epaphus.[3] As soon as he appeared, straightway all the Egyptians arrayed themselves in their gayest garments, and fell to feasting and jollity: which when Cambyses saw, making sure that these rejoicings were on account of his own ill success,

1 The communication between Egypt and Ethiopia was such as to render the expedition easy. Its chief object would be the conquest of Meroë.

2 The city Oasis is taken, with much reason, for the modern *El Khargeh*, the chief town of what is called the great Oasis. This is distant, by one road 42, by another 52 hours (6 and $7\frac{1}{2}$ days' journey respectively), from ancient Thebes. The Egyptians in the time of Herodotus may have given the name Oasis to the city, as well as to the tract surrounding it.

3 Vide supra, ii. 153.

he called before him the officers who had charge of Memphis, and demanded of them, – "Why, when he was in Memphis before, the Egyptians had done nothing of this kind, but waited until now, when he had returned with the loss of so many of his troops?" The officers made answer, "That one of their gods had appeared to them, a god who at long intervals of time had been accustomed to show himself in Egypt – and that always on his appearance the whole of Egypt feasted and kept jubilee." When Cambyses heard this, he told them that they lied, and as liars he condemned them all to suffer death.

28. When they were dead, he called the priests to his presence, and questioning them received the same answer; whereupon he observed, "That he would soon know whether a tame god had really come to dwell in Egypt" – and straightway, without another word, he bade them bring Apis to him. So they went out from his presence to fetch the god. Now this Apis, or Epaphus, is the calf of a cow which is never afterwards able to bear young. The Egyptians say that fire comes down from heaven upon the cow, which thereupon conceives Apis. The calf which is so called has the following marks:– He is black, with a square spot of white upon his forehead, and on his back the figure of an eagle; the hairs in his tail are double, and there is a beetle upon his tongue.[1]

29. When the priests returned bringing Apis with them, Cambyses, like the harebrained person that he was, drew his dagger, and aimed at the belly of the animal, but missed his mark, and stabbed him in the thigh. Then he laughed, and said thus to the priests:– "Oh! blockheads, and think ye that gods become like this, of flesh and blood, and sensible to steel? A fit god indeed for Egyptians, such an one! But it shall cost you dear that you have made me your laughing-stock." When he had so spoken, he ordered those, whose business it was,[2] to scourge the priests,

[1] Apis was supposed to be the image of the soul of Osiris, and he was the sacred emblem of that God; but he is sometimes figured as a man with a bull's head.

[2] Like the Turks, and other orientals, the Persians had certain persons whose duty it was to inflict the bastinado and other punishments. The conduct of the Egyptians to their enemies contrasts favourably with that of the Eastern people of antiquity; for they only cut off the hands of the *dead*, and laid them in "heaps" before the king (cp. 1 Kings x. 8, and 1 Sam. xviii. 27), as returns of the enemy's killed; and if their captives were obliged to work, this was only the condition on which life was preserved in early times; and we see no systematic

and if they found any of the Egyptians keeping festival to put them to death. Thus was the feast stopped throughout the land of Egypt, and the priests suffered punishment. Apis, wounded in the thigh, lay some time pining in the temple; at last he died of his wound, and the priests buried him secretly without the knowledge of Cambyses.

30. And now Cambyses, who even before had not been quite in his right mind, was forthwith, as the Egyptians say, smitten with madness[1] for this crime. The first of his outrages was the slaying of Smerdis, his full brother,[2] whom he had sent back to Persia from Egypt out of envy, because he drew the bow brought from the Ethiopians by the Icthyophagi (which none of the other Persians were able to bend) the distance of two fingers' breadth.[3] When Smerdis was departed into Persia, Cambyses had a vision in his sleep – he thought a messenger from Persia came to him with tidings that Smerdis sat upon the royal throne, and with his head touched the heavens. Fearing therefore for himself, and thinking it likely that his brother would kill him, and rule in his stead, Cambyses sent into Persia Prexaspes, whom he trusted beyond all the other Persians, bidding him put Smerdis to death. So this Prexaspes went up to Susa[4] and slew Smerdis. Some say he killed him as they hunted together, others, that he took him down to the Erythræan Sea, and there drowned him.[5]

31. This, it is said, was the first outrage which Cambyses committed. The second was the slaying of his sister, who had accompanied him into Egypt, and lived with him as his wife, though she was his full sister,[6] the daughter both of his father

tortures inflicted, and no cruelties beyond accidental harsh treatment by some ignorant soldier, not unknown in the wars of Christian Europe.

1 The madness of Cambyses has been generally accepted by our writers. But, as Heeren long ago observed, "we ought to be particularly on our guard against the evil that is related of Cambyses, inasmuch as our information is derived entirely from his enemies, the Egyptian priests."

2 In the original, "both of the same father and of the same mother."

3 This is contradicted by the Inscription, which records that Smerdis was put to death *before Cambyses started for Egypt.*

4 From this passage, as well as from several others (chs. 65, 70, etc.) it would appear that Susa had become the chief residence of the Persian court as early as the time of Cambyses.

5 The Inscription expressly confirms the fact of the putting to death of Smerdis by his brother, and also states that the death was not generally known.

6 The Egyptians were permitted to marry their sisters by the same father and mother. Both were forbidden by the Levitical law; but in Patriarchal times

and his mother. The way wherein he had made her his wife was the following:– It was not the custom of the Persians, before his time, to marry their sisters – but Cambyses, happening to fall in love with one of his, and wishing to take her to wife, as he knew that it was an uncommon thing, called together the royal judges, and put it to them, "whether there was any law which allowed a brother, if he wished, to marry his sister?" Now the royal judges are certain picked men among the Persians, who hold their office for life, or until they are found guilty of some misconduct. By them justice is administered in Persia, and they are the interpreters of the old laws, all disputes being referred to their decision. When Cambyses, therefore, put his question to these judges, they gave him an answer which was at once true and safe – "they did not find any law," they said, "allowing a brother to take his sister to wife, but they found a law, that the king of the Persians might do whatever he pleased." And so they neither warped the law through fear of Cambyses, nor ruined themselves by over stiffly maintaining the law; but they brought another quite distinct law to the king's help, which allowed him to have his wish.[1] Cambyses, therefore, married the object of his love,[2] and no long time afterwards he took to wife another sister. It was the younger of these who went with him into Egypt, and there suffered death at his hands.

32. Concerning the manner of her death, as concerning that of Smerdis,[3] two different accounts are given. The story which the Greeks tell, is, that Cambyses had set a young dog to fight the cub of a lioness – his wife looking on at the time. Now the dog was getting the worse, when a pup of the same litter broke his chain, and came to his brother's aid – then the two dogs together fought the lion, and conquered him. The thing greatly pleased Cambyses, but his sister who was sitting by shed tears. When Cambyses saw this, he asked her why she wept: whereon she told him, that seeing the young dog come to his brother's

---

a man was permitted to marry a sister, the daughter of his father only (Gen. xx. 12). The Egyptian custom is one of those pointed at in Levit. xviii. 3.

1 It is scarcely necessary to point out the agreement between the view of Persian law here disclosed, and that furnished by Dan. ch. vi. – "The law of the Medes and Persians alters not."

2 This was Atossa, the mother of Xerxes (vide infra, iii. 88), who was the wife successively of Cambyses, the Pseudo-Smerdis, and Darius Hystaspes.

3 Vide supra, ch. 30, sub fin.

aid made her think of Smerdis, whom there was none to help. For this speech, the Greeks say, Cambyses put her to death. But the Egyptians tell the story thus:— The two were sitting at table, when the sister took a lettuce, and stripping the leaves off, asked her brother "when he thought the lettuce looked the prettiest — when it had all its leaves on, or now that it was stripped?" He answered, "When the leaves were on." "But thou," she rejoined, "hast done as I did to the lettuce, and made bare the house of Cyrus." Then Cambyses was wroth, and sprang fiercely upon her, though she was with child at the time. And so it came to pass that she miscarried and died.

33. Thus mad was Cambyses upon his own kindred, and this either from his usage of Apis, or from some other among the many causes from which calamities are wont to arise. They say that from his birth he was afflicted with a dreadful disease, the disorder which some call "the sacred sickness."[1] It would be by no means strange, therefore, if his mind were affected in some degree, seeing that his body laboured under so sore a malady.

34. He was mad also upon others besides his kindred; among the rest, upon Prexaspes, the man whom he esteemed beyond all the rest of the Persians, who carried his messages, and whose son held the office — an honour of no small account in Persia — of his cupbearer. Him Cambyses is said to have once addressed as follows:— "What sort of man, Prexaspes, do the Persians think me? What do they say of me?" Prexaspes answered, "Oh! sire, they praise thee greatly in all things but one — they say thou art too much given to love of wine."[2] Such Prexaspes told him was the judgment of the Persians; whereupon Cambyses, full of rage, made answer, "What? they say now that I drink too much wine, and so have lost my senses, and am gone out of my mind! Then their former speeches about me were untrue." For once, when the Persians were sitting with him, and Crœsus was by, he had asked them, "What sort of man they thought him compared to his father Cyrus?" Hereon they had answered, "That he surpassed his father, for he was lord of all that his father ever ruled,

1 That the disease known under this name was epilepsy appears from the book of Hippocrates, "On the Sacred Sickness." The Italians still call it "mal benedetto." Its sudden and terrible character caused it to be regarded as a divine visitation.

2 The drinking propensities of the Persians generally have been already noticed by Herodotus (i. 133).

and further had made himself master of Egypt, and the sea." Then Crœsus, who was standing near, and misliked the comparison, spoke thus to Cambyses: "In my judgment, O son of Cyrus, thou art not equal to thy father, for thou hast not yet left behind thee such a son as he." Cambyses was delighted when he heard this reply, and praised the judgment of Crœsus.

35. Recollecting these answers, Cambyses spoke fiercely to Prexaspes, saying, "Judge now thyself, Prexaspes, whether the Persians tell the truth, or whether it is not they who are mad for speaking as they do. Look there now at thy son standing in the vestibule – if I shoot and hit him right in the middle of the heart, it will be plain the Persians have no grounds for what they say: if I miss him, then I allow that the Persians are right, and that I am out of my mind." So speaking he drew his bow to the full, and struck the boy, who straightway fell down dead. Then Cambyses ordered the body to be opened, and the wound examined; and when the arrow was found to have entered the heart, the king was quite overjoyed, and said to the father with a laugh, "Now thou seest plainly, Prexaspes, that it is not I who am mad, but the Persians who have lost their senses. I pray thee tell me, sawest thou ever mortal man send an arrow with a better aim?" Prexaspes, seeing that the king was not in his right mind, and fearing for himself, replied, "Oh! my lord, I do not think that God himself could shoot so dexterously." Such was the outrage which Cambyses committed at this time: at another, he took twelve of the noblest Persians, and, without bringing any charge worthy of death against them, buried them all up to the neck.

36. Hereupon Crœsus the Lydian thought it right to admonish Cambyses, which he did in these words following:– "Oh! king, allow not thyself to give way entirely to thy youth, and the heat of thy temper, but check and control thyself. It is well to look to consequences, and in forethought is true wisdom. Thou layest hold of men, who are thy fellow-citizens, and, without cause of complaint, slayest them – thou even puttest children to death – bethink thee now, if thou shalt often do things like these, will not the Persians rise in revolt against thee? It is by thy father's wish that I offer thee advice; he charged me strictly to give thee such counsel as I might see to be most for thy good." In thus advising Cambyses, Crœsus meant nothing but what was friendly. But Cambyses answered him, "Dost thou presume to offer me advice? Right well thou ruledst thy own country when

thou wert a king, and right sage advice thou gavest my father
Cyrus, bidding him cross the Araxes and fight the Massagetæ in
their own land, when they were willing to have passed over into
ours. By thy misdirection of thine own affairs thou broughtest
ruin upon thyself, and by thy bad counsel, which he followed,
thou broughtest ruin upon Cyrus, my father. But thou shalt not
escape punishment now, for I have long been seeking to find
some occasion against thee." As he thus spoke, Cambyses took
up his bow to shoot at Crœsus; but Crœsus ran hastily out, and
escaped. So when Cambyses found that he could not kill him
with his bow, he bade his servants seize him, and put him to
death. The servants, however, who knew their master's humour,
thought it best to hide Crœsus; that so, if Cambyses relented,
and asked for him, they might bring him out, and get a reward
for having saved his life — if, on the other hand, he did not relent,
or regret the loss, they might then despatch him. Not long afterwards, Cambyses did in fact regret the loss of Crœsus, and the
servants, perceiving it, let him know that he was still alive. "I am
glad," said he, "that Crœsus lives, but as for you who saved him,
ye shall not escape my vengeance, but shall all of you be put to
death." And he did even as he had said.

37. Many other wild outrages of this sort did Cambyses commit, both upon the Persians and the allies, while he still stayed
at Memphis; among the rest he opened the ancient sepulchres,
and examined the bodies that were buried in them. He likewise
went into the temple of Hephaistos, and made great sport of the
image. For the image of Hephaistos[1] is very like the Patæci[2] of
the Phœnicians, wherewith they ornament the prows of their
ships of war. If persons have not seen these, I will explain in a
different way — it is a figure resembling that of a pigmy. He went
also into the temple of the Cabiri,[3] which it is unlawful for any
one to enter except the priests, and not only made sport of the
images, but even burnt them. They are made like the statue of
Hephaistos, who is said to have been their father.

1 The deformed figure of the Pthah of Memphis doubtless gave rise to the
fable of the lameness of the Greek Hephaistus or Vulcan.

2 They were dwarf figures of gods, apparently of *any* gods, placed, according to Herodotus, at the prow, according to Hesychius and Suidas, at the poop
of a galley. They were probably intended to protect the ship from harm.

3 The Cabiri were Pelasgic gods. [The word is connected with the Semitic
Kebîr = great. — E. H. B.]

38. Thus it appears certain to me, by a great variety of proofs, that Cambyses was raving mad; he would not else have set himself to make a mock of holy rites and long-established usages. For if one were to offer men to choose out of all the customs in the world such as seemed to them the best, they would examine the whole number, and end by preferring their own;[1] so convinced are they that their own usages far surpass those of all others. Unless, therefore, a man was mad, it is not likely that he would make sport of such matters. That people have this feeling about their laws may be seen by very many proofs: among others, by the following. Darius, after he had got the kingdom, called into his presence certain Greeks who were at hand, and asked – "What he should pay them to eat the bodies of their fathers when they died?" To which they answered, that there was no sum that would tempt them to do such a thing. He then sent for certain Indians, of the race called Callatians, men who eat their fathers,[2] and asked them, while the Greeks stood by, and knew by the help of an interpreter all that was said – "What he should give them to burn the bodies of their fathers at their decease?" The Indians exclaimed aloud, and bade him forbear such language. Such is men's wont herein; and Pindar was right, in my judgment, when he said, "Law is the king o'er all."

39. While Cambyses was carrying on this war in Egypt, the Lacedæmonians likewise sent a force to Samos against Polycrates, the son of Æaces, who had by insurrection made himself master of that island.[3] At the outset he divided the state into three parts, and shared the kingdom with his brothers, Pantagnôtus and Syloson; but later, having killed the former and banished the latter, who was the younger of the two, he held the whole island. Hereupon he made a contract of friendship with Amasis the Egyptian king, sending him gifts, and receiving from him others in return. In a little while his power so greatly increased, that the fame of it went abroad throughout Ionia and the rest of Greece. Wherever he turned his arms, success waited

---

1 This just remark of Herodotus is one of many tending to show how unprejudiced and sensible his opinions were; and we may readily absolve him from the folly of believing many of the strange stories he relates, against which indeed he guards himself by saying he merely reports what he hears without giving credit to all himself, or expecting others to do so.

2 Vide infra, iii. 99, and compare the custom of the Issedonians, iv. 26.

3 See below, ch. 120.

on him. He had a fleet of a hundred penteconters, and bowmen to the number of a thousand.[1] Herewith he plundered all, without distinction of friend or foe; for he argued that a friend was better pleased if you gave him back what you had taken from him, than if you spared him at the first. He captured many of the islands, and several towns upon the mainland. Among his other doings he overcame the Lesbians in a sea-fight, when they came with all their forces to the help of Miletus, and made a number of them prisoners. These persons, laden with fetters, dug the moat which surrounds the castle at Samos.[2]

40. The exceeding good fortune of Polycrates did not escape the notice of Amasis, who was much disturbed thereat. When therefore his successes continued increasing, Amasis wrote him the following letter, and sent it to Samos. "Amasis to Polycrates thus sayeth: It is a pleasure to hear of a friend and ally prospering, but thy exceeding prosperity does not cause me joy, forasmuch as I know that the gods are envious. My wish for myself, and for those whom I love, is, to be now successful, and now to meet with a check; thus passing through life amid alternate good and ill, rather than with perpetual good fortune. For never yet did I hear tell of any one succeeding in all his undertakings, who did not meet with calamity at last, and come to utter ruin. Now, therefore, give ear to my words, and meet thy good luck in this way: bethink thee which of all thy treasures thou valuest most and canst least bear to part with; take it, whatsoever it be, and throw it away, so that it may be sure never to come any more into the sight of man. Then, if thy good fortune be not thenceforth chequered with ill, save thyself from harm by again doing as I have counselled."

41. When Polycrates read this letter, and perceived that the advice of Amasis was good, he considered carefully with himself which of the treasures that he had in store it would grieve him most to lose. After much thought he made up his mind that it was a signet-ring which he was wont to wear, an emerald set in gold,[3] the workmanship of Theodore, son of Têlecles, a Samian. So he determined to throw this away; and, manning a pente-

1 These bowmen were Samians.

2 The *town* Samos, not the island, is of course here meant. The islands of the Egean almost all derived their name from their chief city.

3 The story of the fisherman and the ring has been adopted by the Arabs with variations. [Cf. Macculloch, *The Childhood of Fiction*, p. 201. – E. H. B.]

conter, he went on board, and bade the sailors put out into the open sea. When he was now a long way from the island, he took the ring from his finger, and, in the sight of all those who were on board, flung it into the deep. This done, he returned home, and gave vent to his sorrow.

42. Now it happened five or six days afterwards that a fisherman caught a fish so large and beautiful that he thought it well deserved to be made a present of to the king. So he took it with him to the gate of the palace, and said that he wanted to see Polycrates. Then Polycrates allowed him to come in, and the fisherman gave him the fish with these words following – "Sir king, when I took this prize, I thought I would not carry it to market, though I am a poor man who live by my trade. I said to myself, it is worthy of Polycrates and his greatness; and so I brought it here to give it to you." The speech pleased the king, who thus spoke in reply:– "Thou didst right well, friend, and I am doubly indebted, both for the gift, and for the speech. Come now, and sup with me." So the fisherman went home, esteeming it a high honour that he had been asked to sup with the king. Meanwhile the servants, on cutting open the fish, found the signet of their master in its belly. No sooner did they see it than they seized upon it, and, hastening to Polycrates with great joy, restored it to him, and told him in what way it had been found. The king, who saw something providential in the matter, forthwith wrote a letter to Amasis, telling him all that had happened, what he had himself done, and what had been the upshot – and despatched the letter to Egypt.

43. When Amasis had read the letter of Polycrates, he perceived that it does not belong to man to save his fellow-man from the fate which is in store for him; likewise he felt certain that Polycrates would end ill, as he prospered in everything, even finding what he had thrown away. So he sent a herald to Samos, and dissolved the contract of friendship. This he did, that when the great and heavy misfortune came, he might escape the grief which he would have felt if the sufferer had been his bond-friend.

44. It was with this Polycrates, so fortunate in every undertaking, that the Lacedæmonians now went to war. Certain Samians, the same who afterwards founded the city of Cydonia in Crete,[1] had earnestly intreated their help. For Polycrates, at

1 Infra, ch. 59.

the time when Cambyses, son of Cyrus, was gathering together an armament against Egypt, had sent to beg him not to omit to ask aid from Samos; whereupon Cambyses with much readiness despatched a messenger to the island, and made request that Polycrates would give some ships to the naval force which he was collecting against Egypt. Polycrates straightway picked out from among the citizens such as he thought most likely to stir revolt against him, and manned with them forty triremes, which he sent to Cambyses, bidding him keep the men safe, and never allow them to return home.

45. Now some accounts say that these Samians did not reach Egypt; for that when they were off Carpathus,[1] they took counsel together and resolved to sail no further. But others maintain that they did go to Egypt, and, finding themselves watched, deserted, and sailed back to Samos. There Polycrates went out against them with his fleet, and a battle was fought and gained by the exiles; after which they disembarked upon the island and engaged the land forces of Polycrates, but were defeated, and so sailed off to Lacedæmon. Some relate that the Samians from Egypt overcame Polycrates, but it seems to me untruly; for had the Samians been strong enough to conquer Polycrates by themselves, they would not have needed to call in the aid of the Lacedæmonians. And moreover, it is not likely that a king who had in his pay so large a body of foreign mercenaries, and maintained likewise such a force of native bowmen, would have been worsted by an army so small as that of the returned Samians. As for his own subjects, to hinder them from betraying him and joining the exiles, Polycrates shut up their wives and children in the sheds built to shelter his ships, and was ready to burn sheds and all in case of need.

46. When the banished Samians reached Sparta, they had audience of the magistrates, before whom they made a long speech, as was natural with persons greatly in want of aid. Accordingly at this first sitting the Spartans answered them, that they had forgotten the first half of their speech, and could make nothing of the remainder. Afterwards the Samians had another audience, whereat they simply said, showing a bag which they had brought with them, "The bag wants flour." The Spartans

1 Carpathus, the modern *Scarpanto*, half-way between Rhodes and Crete, would lie directly in the passage from Samos to Egypt.

answered that they did not need to have said "the bag;" however, they resolved to give them aid.

47. Then the Lacedæmonians made ready and set forth to the attack of Samos, from a motive of gratitude, if we may believe the Samians, because the Samians had once sent ships to their aid against the Messenians; but as the Spartans themselves say, not so much from any wish to assist the Samians who begged their help, as from a desire to punish the people who had seized the bowl which they sent to Crœsus,[1] and the corselet which Amasis, king of Egypt, sent as a present to them. The Samians made prize of this corselet the year before they took the bowl – it was of linen, and had a vast number of figures of animals inwoven into its fabric, and was likewise embroidered with gold and tree-wool.[2] What is most worthy of admiration in it is, that each of the twists, although of fine texture, contains within it three hundred and sixty threads, all of them clearly visible. The corselet which Amasis gave to the temple of Athena in Lindus is just such another.[3]

48. The Corinthians likewise right willingly lent a helping hand towards the expedition against Samos; for a generation earlier, about the time of the seizure of the wine-bowl,[4] they too had suffered insult at the hands of the Samians. It happened that Periander, son of Cypselus, had taken three hundred boys, children of the chief nobles among the Corcyræans, and sent them to Alyattes for eunuchs; the men who had them in charge touched at Samos on their way to Sardis; whereupon the Samians, having found out what was to become of the boys when they reached that city, first prompted them to take sanctuary at the temple of Artemis; and after this, when the Corinthians, as they were forbidden to tear the suppliants from the holy place, sought to cut off from them all supplies of food, invented a festival in their behoof, which they celebrate to this day with the self-same rites. Each evening, as night closed in, during the whole time that the boys continued there, choirs of youths and virgins were placed about the temple, carrying in their hands

1 Vide supra, i. 70.

2 This is the name by which Herodotus designates "cotton," as is plain from ch. 106 of this Book, and from Book vii. ch. 65.

3 Vide supra, ii. 182.

4 On the strength of this passage and another (v. 94), I should think it probable that Periander's reign came down at least as low as B.C. 567.

cakes made of sesame and honey, in order that the Corcyræan boys might snatch the cakes, and so get enough to live upon.

49. And this went on for so long, that at last the Corinthians who had charge of the boys gave them up, and took their departure, upon which the Samians conveyed them back to Corcyra. If now, after the death of Periander, the Corinthians and Corcyræans had been good friends, it is not to be imagined that the former would ever have taken part in the expedition against Samos for such a reason as this; but as, in fact, the two people have always, ever since the first settlement of the island, been enemies to one another, this outrage was remembered, and the Corinthians bore the Samians a grudge for it. Periander had chosen the youths from among the first families in Corcyra, and sent them a present to Alyattes, to revenge a wrong which he had received. For it was the Corcyræans who began the quarrel and injured Periander by an outrage of a horrid nature.

50. After Periander had put to death his wife Melissa, it chanced that on this first affliction a second followed of a different kind. His wife had borne him two sons, and one of them had now reached the age of seventeen, the other of eighteen years, when their mother's father, Procles, tyrant of Epidaurus, asked them to his court. They went, and Procles treated them with much kindness, as was natural, considering they were his own daughter's children. At length, when the time for parting came, Procles, as he was sending them on their way, said, "Know you now, my children, who it was that caused your mother's death?" The elder son took no account of this speech, but the younger, whose name was Lycophron, was sorely troubled at it — so much so, that when he got back to Corinth, looking upon his father as his mother's murderer, he would neither speak to him, nor answer when spoken to, nor utter a word in reply to all his questionings. So Periander at last, growing furious at such behaviour, banished him from his house.

51. The younger son gone, he turned to the elder and asked him, "what it was that their grandfather had said to them?" Then he related in how kind and friendly a fashion he had received them; but, not having taken any notice of the speech which Procles had uttered at parting, he quite forgot to mention it. Periander insisted that it was not possible this should be all — their grandfather must have given them some hint or other — and he went on pressing him, till at last the lad remembered the

parting speech and told it. Periander, after he had turned the whole matter over in his thoughts, and felt unwilling to give way at all, sent a messenger to the persons who had opened their houses to his outcast son, and forbade them to harbour him. Then the boy, when he was chased from one friend, sought refuge with another, but was driven from shelter to shelter by the threats of his father, who menaced all those that took him in, and commanded them to shut their doors against him. Still, as fast as he was forced to leave one house he went to another, and was received by the inmates; for his acquaintance, although in no small alarm, yet gave him shelter, as he was Periander's son.

52. At last Periander made proclamation that whoever harboured his son or even spoke to him, should forfeit a certain sum of money to Apollo. On hearing this no one any longer liked to take him in, or even to hold converse with him, and he himself did not think it right to seek to do what was forbidden; so, abiding by his resolve, he made his lodging in the public porticos. When four days had passed in this way, Periander, seeing how wretched his son was, that he neither washed nor took any food, felt moved with compassion towards him; wherefore, foregoing his anger, he approached him, and said, "Which is better, oh! my son, to fare as now thou farest, or to receive my crown and all the good things that I possess, on the one condition of submitting thyself to thy father? See, now, though my own child, and lord of this wealthy Corinth, thou hast brought thyself to a beggar's life, because thou must resist and treat with anger him whom it least behoves thee to oppose. If there has been a calamity, and thou bearest me ill will on that account, bethink thee that I too feel it, and am the greatest sufferer, in as much as it was by me that the deed was done. For thyself, now that thou knowest how much better a thing it is to be envied than pitied, and how dangerous it is to indulge anger against parents and superiors, come back with me to thy home." With such words as these did Periander chide his son; but the son made no reply, except to remind his father that he was indebted to the god in the penalty for coming and holding converse with him. Then Periander knew that there was no cure for the youth's malady, nor means of overcoming it; so he prepared a ship and sent him away out of his sight to Corcyra, which island at that time belonged to him. As for Procles, Periander,

regarding him as the true author of all his present troubles, went to war with him as soon as his son was gone, and not only made himself master of his kingdom Epidaurus, but also took Procles himself, and carried him into captivity.

53. As time went on, and Periander came to be old, he found himself no longer equal to the oversight and management of affairs. Seeing, therefore, in his eldest son no manner of ability, but knowing him to be dull and blockish, he sent to Corcyra and recalled Lycophron to take the kingdom. Lycophron, however, did not even deign to ask the bearer of this message a question. But Periander's heart was set upon the youth, so he sent again to him, this time by his own daughter, the sister of Lycophron, who would, he thought, have more power to persuade him than any other person. Then she, when she reached Corcyra, spoke thus with her brother:— "Dost thou wish the kingdom, brother, to pass into strange hands, and our father's wealth to be made a prey, rather than thyself return to enjoy it? Come back home with me, and cease to punish thyself. It is scant gain, this obstinacy. Why seek to cure evil by evil? Mercy, remember, is by many set above justice. Many, also, while pushing their mother's claims have forfeited their father's fortune. Power is a slippery thing — it has many suitors; and he is old and stricken in years — let not thy own inheritance go to another." Thus did the sister, who had been tutored by Periander what to say, urge all the arguments most likely to have weight with her brother. He however made answer, "That so long as he knew his father to be still alive, he would never go back to Corinth." When the sister brought Periander this reply, he sent to his son a third time by a herald, and said he would come himself to Corcyra, and let his son take his place at Corinth as heir to his kingdom. To these terms Lycophron agreed; and Periander was making ready to pass into Corcyra and his son to return to Corinth, when the Corcyræans, being informed of what was taking place, to keep Periander away, put the young man to death.[1] For this reason it was that Periander took vengeance on the Corcyræans.

54. The Lacedæmonians arrived before Samos with a mighty armament, and forthwith laid siege to the place. In one of the

1 The Scholiast on Thucyd. i. 13, states that the naval battle there spoken of as the earliest upon record, took place in a war between Corinth and Corcyra arising out of this murder.

assaults upon the walls, they forced their way to the top of the tower which stands by the sea on the side where the suburb is, but Polycrates came in person to the rescue with a strong force, and beat them back. Meanwhile at the upper tower, which stood on the ridge of the hill, the besieged, both mercenaries and Samians, made a sally; but after they had withstood the Lacedæmonians a short time, they fled backwards, and the Lacedæmonians, pressing upon them, slew numbers.

55. If now all who were present had behaved that day like Archias and Lycôpas, two of the Lacedæmonians, Samos might have been taken. For these two heroes, following hard upon the flying Samians, entered the city along with them, and, being all alone, and their retreat cut off, were slain within the walls of the place. I myself once fell in with the grandson of this Archias, a man named Archias like his grandsire, and the son of Samius, whom I met at Pitana, to which canton he belonged. He respected the Samians beyond all other foreigners, and he told me that his father was called Samius, because his grandfather Archias died in Samos so gloriously, and that the reason why he respected the Samians so greatly was, that his grandsire was buried with public honours by the Samian people.

56. The Lacedæmonians besieged Samos during forty days, but not making any progress before the place, they raised the siege at the end of that time, and returned home to the Peloponnese. There is a silly tale told, that Polycrates struck a quantity of the coin of his country in lead, and, coating it with gold, gave it to the Lacedæmonians, who on receiving it took their departure.[1]

This was the first expedition into Asia of the Lacedæmonian Dorians.[2]

---

1 This tale may have been false, yet it is not without its value. It shows the general opinion of the corruptibility of the Spartans. The peculiar attractions possessed by the *vetitum nefas* may account for the greater openness of the Spartans to bribery than the other Greeks. Traces of this national characteristic appear in other parts of Herodotus's History; for instance, in the story of Mæandrius (iii. 148), in that of Cleomenes (v. 51), and in that of Leotychidas (vi. 72).

2 These words are emphatic. They mark the place which this expedition occupies in the mind of Herodotus. It is an aggression of the Greeks upon Asia, and therefore a passage in the history of the great quarrel between Persia and Greece, for all Asia is the King's (i. 4).

57. The Samians who had fought against Polycrates, when they knew that the Lacedæmonians were about to forsake them, left Samos themselves, and sailed to Siphnos.¹ They happened to be in want of money; and the Siphnians at that time were at the height of their greatness, no islanders having so much wealth as they. There were mines of gold and silver in their country, and of so rich a yield, that from a tithe of the ores the Siphnians furnished out a treasury at Delphi which was on a par with the grandest there. What the mines yielded was divided year by year among the citizens. At the time when they formed the treasury, the Siphnians consulted the oracle, and asked whether their good things would remain to them many years. The Pythoness made answer as follows:—

"When the Prytanies' seat shines white² in the island of Siphnos,
  White-browed all the forum – need then of a true seer's wisdom –
  Danger will threat from a wooden host, and a herald in scarlet."

Now about this time the forum of the Siphnians and their town-hall or prytaneum had been adorned with Parian marble.³

58. The Siphnians, however, were unable to understand the oracle, either at the time when it was given, or afterwards on the arrival of the Samians. For these last no sooner came to anchor off the island than they sent one of their vessels, with an ambassage on board, to the city. All ships in these early times were painted with vermilion;⁴ and this was what the Pythoness had

1 Siphnos (the modern *Sifanto*) is one of the western Cyclades.

2 The mention of whiteness here, and the expression "*then*," show that the attack was to be made before the Siphnians had had time to colour their buildings. In Herodotus's time they were evidently painted, but "*then*" they had merely the natural hue of the white marble. The Greek custom of painting their monuments was common from the earliest to the latest times, and traces of colour are found on the Parthenon and other buildings. At first they were covered with painted stucco; and when marble took its place it received the same coloured ornaments, for which it was as well suited as its less durable predecessor.

3 This is the first known instance of the use of Parian marble in ornamental building.

4 Yet Homer almost invariably speaks of "black ships" (νηες μέλαιναι). Perhaps, however, there is no contradiction here. For Homer's ships are "crimson-cheeked," or "*vermilion*-cheeked." It would seem that while the hull of the vessel was in the main black, being probably covered with pitch or some similar substance, the sides above the water, which Homer called the "cheeks" of the ship, were red. Herodotus may not mean more than this.

meant when she told them to beware of danger "from a wooden host, and a herald in scarlet." So the ambassadors came ashore and besought the Siphnians to lend them ten talents; but the Siphnians refused, whereupon the Samians began to plunder their lands. Tidings of this reached the Siphnians, who straightway sallied forth to save their crops; then a battle was fought, in which the Siphnians suffered defeat, and many of their number were cut off from the city by the Samians, after which these latter forced the Siphnians to give them a hundred talents.

59. With this money they bought of the Hermionians the island of Hydrea,[1] off the coast of the Peloponnese, and this they gave in trust to the Trœzenians, to keep for them, while they themselves went on to Crete, and founded the city of Cydonia. They had not meant, when they set sail, to settle there, but only to drive out the Zacynthians from the island. However they rested at Cydonia,[2] where they flourished greatly for five years. It was they who built the various temples that may still be seen at that place, and among them the fane of Dictyna.[3] But in the sixth year they were attacked by the Eginetans, who beat them in a sea-fight, and, with the help of the Cretans, reduced them all to slavery. The beaks of their ships, which carried the figure of a wild boar, they sawed off, and laid them up in the temple of Athena in Egina. The Eginetans took part against the Samians on account of an ancient grudge, since the Samians had first, when Amphicrates was king of Samos, made war on them and done great harm to their island, suffering, however, much damage also themselves. Such was the reason which moved the Eginetans to make this attack.

60. I have dwelt the longer on the affairs of the Samians, because three of the greatest works in all Greece were made by them. One is a tunnel, under a hill one hundred and fifty fathoms high, carried entirely through the base of the hill, with a mouth at either end. The length of the cutting is seven furlongs – the height and width are each eight feet. Along the whole course

1 An island about twelve miles long, and only two or three broad, off the coast of the Argolic peninsula.

2 Cydonia lay on the northern coast of Crete, towards the western end of the island.

3 Dictyna, or Dictynna, was the same as Britomartis, an ancient goddess of the Cretans. The Greeks usually regarded her as identical with their Artemis (Diana).

there is a second cutting, twenty cubits deep and three feet broad, whereby water is brought, through pipes, from an abundant source into the city. The architect of this tunnel was Eupalinus, son of Naustrophus, a Megarian. Such is the first of their great works; the second is a mole in the sea, which goes all round the harbour, near twenty fathoms deep, and in length above two furlongs. The third is a temple; the largest of all the temples known to us,[1] whereof Rhœcus, son of Phileus, a Samian, was first architect. Because of these works I have dwelt the longer on the affairs of Samos.

61. While Cambyses, son of Cyrus, after losing his senses, still lingered in Egypt, two Magi, brothers, revolted against him. One of them had been left in Persia by Cambyses as comptroller of his household; and it was he who began the revolt. Aware that Smerdis was dead, and that his death was hid, and known to few of the Persians, while most believed that he was still alive, he laid his plan, and made a bold stroke for the crown. He had a brother – the same of whom I spoke before as his partner in the revolt – who happened greatly to resemble Smerdis the son of Cyrus, whom Cambyses his brother had put to death. And not only was this brother of his like Smerdis in person, but he also bore the selfsame name, to wit Smerdis. Patizeithes, the other Magus, having persuaded him that he would carry the whole business through, took him and made him sit upon the royal throne. Having so done, he sent heralds through all the land, to Egypt and elsewhere, to make proclamation to the troops that henceforth they were to obey Smerdis the son of Cyrus, and not Cambyses.

62. The other heralds therefore made proclamation as they were ordered, and likewise the herald whose place it was to proceed into Egypt. He, when he reached Agbatana in Syria, finding Cambyses and his army there, went straight into the middle of the host, and standing forth before them all, made the proclamation which Patizeithes the Magus had commanded. Cambyses no sooner heard him, than believing that what the herald said was true, and imagining that he had been betrayed by Prexaspes (who, he supposed, had not put Smerdis to death when sent into Persia for that purpose), he turned his eyes full

1 Herodotus means no doubt "the largest *Greek* temple," since the Egyptian temples were of much greater size.

upon Prexaspes, and said, "Is this the way, Prexaspes, that thou didst my errand?" "Oh! my liege," answered the other, "there is no truth in the tidings that Smerdis thy brother has revolted against thee, nor hast thou to fear in time to come any quarrel, great or small, with that man. With my own hands I wrought thy will on him, and with my own hands I buried him. If of a truth the dead can leave their graves, expect Astyages the Mede to rise and fight against thee; but if the course of nature be the same as formerly, then be sure no ill will ever come upon thee from this quarter. Now therefore my counsel is, that we send in pursuit of the herald, and strictly question him who it was that charged him to bid us obey king Smerdis."

63. When Prexaspes had so spoken, and Cambyses had approved his words, the herald was forthwith pursued, and brought back to the king. Then Prexaspes said to him, "Sirrah, thou bear'st us a message, sayst thou, from Smerdis, son of Cyrus. Now answer truly, and go thy way scathless. Did Smerdis have thee to his presence and give thee thy orders, or hadst thou them from one of his officers?" The herald answered, "Truly I have not set eyes on Smerdis son of Cyrus, since the day when king Cambyses led the Persians into Egypt. The man who gave me my orders was the Magus that Cambyses left in charge of the household; but he said that Smerdis son of Cyrus sent you the message." In all this the herald spoke nothing but the strict truth. Then Cambyses said thus to Prexaspes:– "Thou art free from all blame, Prexaspes, since, as a right good man, thou hast not failed to do the thing which I commanded. But tell me now, which of the Persians can have taken the name of Smerdis, and revolted from me?" "I think, my liege," he answered, "that I apprehend the whole business. The men who have risen in revolt against thee are the two Magi, Patizeithes, who was left comptroller of thy household, and his brother, who is named Smerdis."

64. Cambyses no sooner heard the name of Smerdis than he was struck with the truth of Prexaspes' words, and the fulfilment of his own dream – the dream, I mean, which he had in former days, when one appeared to him in his sleep and told him that Smerdis sate upon the royal throne, and with his head touched the heavens.[1] So when he saw that he had needlessly slain his brother Smerdis, he wept and bewailed his loss: after which,

---

1 Supra, ch. 30.

smarting with vexation as he thought of all his ill luck, he sprang hastily upon his steed, meaning to march his army with all haste to Susa against the Magus. As he made his spring, the button of his sword-sheath fell off, and the bared point entered his thigh, wounding him exactly where he had himself once wounded the Egyptian god Apis.[1] Then Cambyses, feeling that he had got his death-wound, inquired the name of the place where he was, and was answered, "Agbatana." Now before this it had been told him by the oracle at Buto that he should end his days at Agbatana. He, however, had understood the Median Agbatana, where all his treasures were, and had thought that he should die there in a good old age; but the oracle meant Agbatana in Syria. So when Cambyses heard the name of the place, the double shock that he had received, from the revolt of the Magus and from his wound, brought him back to his senses. And he understood now the true meaning of the oracle, and said, "Here then Cambyses, son of Cyrus, is doomed to die."

65. At this time he said no more; but twenty days afterwards he called to his presence all the chief Persians who were with the army, and addressed them as follows:— "Persians, needs must I tell you now what hitherto I have striven with the greatest care to keep concealed. When I was in Egypt I saw in my sleep a vision, which would that I had never beheld! I thought a messenger came to me from my home, and told me that Smerdis sate upon the royal throne, and with his head touched the heavens. Then I feared to be cast from my throne by Smerdis my brother, and I did what was more hasty than wise. Ah! truly, do what they may, it is impossible for men to turn aside the coming fate. I, in my folly, sent Prexaspes to Susa to put my brother to death. So this great woe was accomplished, and I then lived without fear, never imagining that, after Smerdis was dead, I need dread revolt from any other. But herein I had quite mistaken what was about to happen, and so I slew my brother without any need, and nevertheless have lost my crown. For it was Smerdis the Magus, and not Smerdis my brother, of whose rebellion God forewarned me by the vision. The deed is done, however, and Smerdis, son of Cyrus, be sure is lost to you. The Magi have the

1 The details here are suspicious, since they evidently come from the Egyptian priests, who wish to represent the death of Cambyses as a judgment upon him for his impiety.

royal power – Patizeithes, whom I left at Susa to overlook my household, and Smerdis his brother. There was one who would have been bound beyond all others to avenge the wrongs I have suffered from these Magians, but he, alas! has perished by a horrid fate, deprived of life by those nearest and dearest to him. In his default, nothing now remains for me but to tell you, O Persians, what I would wish to have done after I have breathed my last. Therefore, in the name of the Gods that watch over our royal house, I charge you all, and specially such of you as are Achæmenids, that ye do not tamely allow the kingdom to go back to the Medes. Recover it one way or another, by force or fraud; by fraud, if it is by fraud that they have seized on it; by force, if force has helped them in their enterprise. Do this, and then may your land bring you forth fruit abundantly, and your wives bear children, and your herds increase, and freedom be your portion for ever: but do it not – make no brave struggle to regain the kingdom – and then my curse be on you, and may the opposite of all these things happen to you – and not only so, but may you, one and all, perish at the last by such a fate as mine!" Then Cambyses, when he left speaking, bewailed his whole misfortune from beginning to end.

66. Whereupon the Persians, seeing their king weep, rent the garments that they had on, and uttered lamentable cries; after which, as the bone presently grew carious, and the limb gangrened, Cambyses, son of Cyrus, died. He had reigned in all seven years and five months,[1] and left no issue behind him, male or female. The Persians who had heard his words, put no faith in anything that he said concerning the Magi having the royal power; but believed that he spoke out of hatred towards Smerdis, and had invented the tale of his death to cause the whole Persian race to rise up in arms against him. Thus they were convinced that it was Smerdis the son of Cyrus who had rebelled and now sate on the throne. For Prexaspes stoutly denied that he had slain Smerdis, since it was not safe for him, after Cambyses was dead, to allow that a son of Cyrus had met with death at his hands.

67. Thus then Cambyses died, and the Magus now reigned in security, and passed himself off for Smerdis the son of Cyrus. And so went by the seven months which were wanting to

---

1 Vide infra. ch. 67.

complete the eighth year of Cambyses. His subjects, while his reign lasted, received great benefits from him, insomuch that, when he died, all the dwellers in Asia mourned his loss exceedingly, except only the Persians. For no sooner did he come to the throne than forthwith he sent round to every nation under his rule, and granted them freedom from war-service and from taxes for the space of three years.

68. In the eighth month, however, it was discovered who he was in the mode following. There was a man called Otanes, the son of Pharnaspes, who for rank and wealth was equal to the greatest of the Persians. This Otanes was the first to suspect that the Magus was not Smerdis the son of Cyrus, and to surmise moreover who he really was. He was led to guess the truth by the king never quitting the citadel,[1] and never calling before him any of the Persian noblemen. As soon, therefore, as his suspicions were aroused he adopted the following measures:– One of his daughters, who was called Phædima, had been married to Cambyses, and was taken to wife, together with the rest of Cambyses' wives, by the Magus. To this daughter Otanes sent a message, and inquired of her "who it was whose bed she shared, – was it Smerdis the son of Cyrus, or was it some other man?" Phædima in reply declared she did not know – Smerdis the son of Cyrus she had never seen, and so she could not tell whose bed she shared. Upon this Otanes sent a second time, and said, "If thou dost not know Smerdis son of Cyrus thyself, ask queen Atossa who it is with whom ye both live – she cannot fail to know her own brother." To this the daughter made answer, "I can neither get speech with Atossa, nor with any of the women who lodge in the palace. For no sooner did this man, be he who he may, obtain the kingdom, than he parted us from one another, and gave us all separate chambers."

69. This made the matter seem still more plain to Otanes. Nevertheless he sent a third message to his daughter in these words following:– "Daughter, thou art of noble blood – thou wilt not shrink from a risk which thy father bids thee encounter. If this fellow be not Smerdis the son of Cyrus, but the man

---

1 By the citadel (ἀκρόπολις) it is uncertain whether Herodotus means the citadel proper, or the only royal palace *at Susa* (v. infr. ch. 70), called by the Greeks "the Memnonium," which he speaks of below (v. 54), and which was no doubt strongly fortified.

whom I think him to be, his boldness in taking thee to be his wife, and lording it over the Persians, must not be allowed to pass unpunished. Now therefore do as I command – when next he passes the night with thee, wait till thou art sure he is fast asleep, and then feel for his ears. If thou findest him to have ears, then believe him to be Smerdis the son of Cyrus, but if he has none, know him for Smerdis the Magian." Phædima returned for answer, "It would be a great risk. If he was without ears, and caught her feeling for them, she well knew he would make away with her – nevertheless she would venture." So Otanes got his daughter's promise that she would do as he desired. Now Smerdis the Magian had had his ears cut off in the lifetime of Cyrus son of Cambyses, as a punishment for a crime of no slight heinousness.[1] Phædima therefore, Otanes' daughter, bent on accomplishing what she had promised her father, when her turn came, and she was taken to the bed of the Magus (in Persia a man's wives sleep with him in their turns),[2] waited till he was sound asleep, and then felt for his ears. She quickly perceived that he had no ears; and of this, as soon as day dawned, she sent word to her father.

70. Then Otanes took to him two of the chief Persians, Aspathines and Gobryas,[3] men whom it was most advisable to trust in such a matter, and told them everything. Now they had already of themselves suspected how the matter stood. When Otanes therefore laid his reasons before them they at once came into his views; and it was agreed that each of the three should take as companion in the work the Persian in whom he placed the greatest confidence. Then Otanes chose Intaphernes, Gobryas Megabyzus, and Aspathines Hydarnes.[4] After the number had thus become six, Darius, the son of Hystaspes, arrived at Susa from Persia, whereof his father was governor.[5] On his coming it seemed good to the six to take him likewise into their counsels.

1 See, below, the story of Zopyrus, which implies that such mutilation was an ordinary punishment (infra, chs. 154–158).

2 Compare Esther ii. 12.

3 Gobryas appears to have been the bow-bearer of Darius. Such an office might, I think, have been held by a Persian of very exalted rank.

4 He was employed by Darius on occasion of the Median revolt, and gained a great victory over the Medes in their own country.

5 The curious fact, that Darius became king in his father's lifetime, is confirmed by the Behistun Inscription.

71. After this, the men, being now seven in all, met together to exchange oaths, and hold discourse with one another. And when it came to the turn of Darius to speak his mind, he said as follows:— "Methought no one but I knew that Smerdis, the son of Cyrus, was not now alive, and that Smerdis the Magian ruled over us; on this account I came hither with speed, to compass the death of the Magian. But as it seems the matter is known to you all, and not to me only, my judgment is that we should act at once, and not any longer delay. For to do so were not well." Otanes spoke upon this:— "Son of Hystaspes," said he, "thou art the child of a brave father, and seemest likely to show thyself as bold a gallant as he. Beware, however, of rash haste in this matter; do not hurry so, but proceed with soberness. We must add to our number ere we adventure to strike the blow." "Not so," Darius rejoined; "for let all present be well assured, that if the advice of Otanes guide our acts, we shall perish most miserably. Some one will betray our plot to the Magians for lucre's sake. Ye ought to have kept the matter to yourselves, and so made the venture; but as ye have chosen to take others into your secret, and have opened the matter to me, take my advice and make the attempt to-day — or if not, if a single day be suffered to pass by, be sure that I will let no one betray me to the Magian. I myself will go to him, and plainly denounce you all."

72. Otanes, when he saw Darius so hot, replied, "But if thou wilt force us to action, and not allow a day's delay, tell us, I pray thee, how we shall get entrance into the palace, so as to set upon them. Guards are placed everywhere, as thou thyself well knowest — for if thou hast not seen, at least thou hast heard tell of them. How are we to pass these guards, I ask thee?" "Otanes," answered Darius, "there are many things easy enough in act, which by speech it is hard to explain. There are also things concerning which speech is easy, but no noble action follows when the speech is done. As for these guards, ye know well that we shall not find it hard to make our way through them. Our rank alone would cause them to allow us to enter, — shame and fear alike forbidding them to say us nay. But besides, I have the fairest plea that can be conceived for gaining admission. I can say that I have just come from Persia, and have a message to deliver to the king from my father. An untruth must be spoken, where need requires. For whether men lie, or say true,

it is with one and the same object. Men lie, because they think to gain by deceiving others; and speak the truth, because they expect to get something by their true speaking, and to be trusted afterwards in more important matters. Thus, though their conduct is so opposite, the end of both is alike. If there were no gain to be got, your true-speaking man would tell untruths as much as your liar, and your liar would tell the truth as much as your true-speaking man. The doorkeeper, who lets us in readily, shall have his guerdon some day or other; but woe to the man who resists us, he must forthwith be declared an enemy. Forcing our way past him, we will press in and go straight to our work."

73. After Darius had thus said, Gobryas spoke as follows:— "Dear friends, when will a fitter occasion offer for us to recover the kingdom, or, if we are not strong enough, at least die in the attempt? Consider that we Persians are governed by a Median Magus, and one, too, who has had his ears cut off! Some of you were present when Cambyses lay upon his death-bed — such, doubtless, remember what curses he called down upon the Persians if they made no effort to recover the kingdom. Then, indeed, we paid but little heed to what he said, because we thought he spoke out of hatred, to set us against his brother. Now, however, my vote is, that we do as Darius has counselled — march straight in a body to the palace from the place where we now are, and forthwith set upon the Magian." So Gobryas spake, and the others all approved.

74. While the seven were thus taking counsel together, it so chanced that the following events were happening:— The Magi had been thinking what they had best do, and had resolved for many reasons to make a friend of Prexaspes. They knew how cruelly he had been outraged by Cambyses, who slew his son with an arrow;[1] they were also aware that it was by his hand that Smerdis the son of Cyrus fell, and that he was the only person privy to that prince's death; and they further found him to be held in the highest esteem by all the Persians. So they called him to them, made him their friend, and bound him by a promise and by oaths to keep silence about the fraud which they were practising upon the Persians, and not discover it to any one; and they pledged themselves that in this case they would give him

1 Vide supra, ch. 35.

thousands of gifts of every sort and kind.¹ So Prexaspes agreed; and the Magi, when they found that they had persuaded him so far, went on to another proposal, and said they would assemble the Persians at the foot of the palace wall, and he should mount one of the towers and harangue them from it, assuring them that Smerdis the son of Cyrus, and none but he, ruled the land. This they bade him do, because Prexaspes was a man of great weight with his countrymen, and had often declared in public that Smerdis the son of Cyrus was still alive, and denied being his murderer.

75. Prexaspes said he was quite ready to do their will in the matter; so the Magi assembled the people, and placed Prexaspes upon the top of the tower, and told him to make his speech. Then this man, forgetting of set purpose all that the Magi had intreated him to say, began with Achæmenes, and traced down the descent of Cyrus; after which, when he came to that king, he recounted all the services that had been rendered by him to the Persians, from whence he went on to declare the truth, which hitherto he had concealed, he said, because it would not have been safe for him to make it known, but now necessity was laid on him to disclose the whole. Then he told how, forced to it by Cambyses, he had himself taken the life of Smerdis, son of Cyrus, and how that Persia was now ruled by the Magi. Last of all, with many curses upon the Persians if they did not recover the kingdom, and wreak vengeance on the Magi, he threw himself headlong from the tower into the abyss below. Such was the end of Prexaspes, a man all his life of high repute among the Persians.

76. And now the seven Persians, having resolved that they would attack the Magi without more delay, first offered prayers to the gods and then set off for the palace, quite unacquainted with what had been done by Prexaspes. The news of his doings reached them upon their way, when they had accomplished about half the distance. Hereupon they turned aside out of the road, and consulted together. Otanes and his party said they must certainly put off the business, and not make the attack when affairs were in such a ferment. Darius, on the other hand, and his friends, were against any change of plan, and wished to go straight on, and not lose a moment. Now, as they strove

1 Literally, "ten thousand of every thing;" that is, of every thing which it was customary to give. Similar expressions occur elsewhere in their strict proper sense (see i. 50, iv. 88, ix. 81, etc.); but here the phrase can only be a strong hyperbole.

together, suddenly there came in sight two pairs of vultures, and seven pairs of hawks, pursuing them, and the hawks tore the vultures both with their claws and bills. At this sight the seven with one accord came in to the opinion of Darius, and encouraged by the omen hastened on towards the palace.

77. At the gate they were received as Darius had foretold. The guards, who had no suspicion that they came for any ill purpose, and held the chief Persians in much reverence, let them pass without difficulty – it seemed as if they were under the special protection of the gods – none even asked them any question. When they were now in the great court they fell in with certain of the eunuchs, whose business it was to carry the king's messages, who stopped them and asked what they wanted, while at the same time they threatened the doorkeepers for having let them enter. The seven sought to press on, but the eunuchs would not suffer them. Then these men, with cheers encouraging one another, drew their daggers, and stabbing those who strove to withstand them, rushed forward to the apartment of the males.

78. Now both the Magi were at this time within, holding counsel upon the matter of Prexaspes. So when they heard the stir among the eunuchs, and their loud cries, they ran out themselves, to see what was happening. Instantly perceiving their danger, they both flew to arms; one had just time to seize his bow, the other got hold of his lance; when straightway the fight began. The one whose weapon was the bow found it of no service at all; the foe was too near, and the combat too close to allow of his using it. But the other made a stout defence with his lance, wounding two of the seven, Aspathines in the leg, and Intaphernes in the eye. This wound did not kill Intaphernes, but it cost him the sight of that eye. The other Magus, when he found his bow of no avail, fled into a chamber which opened out into the apartment of the males, intending to shut to the doors. But two of the seven entered the room with him, Darius and Gobryas. Gobryas seized the Magus and grappled with him, while Darius stood over them, not knowing what to do; for it was dark,[1] and he was afraid that if he struck a blow he might

1 The Persian, like the Assyrian palaces, consisted of one or more central halls or courts, probably open to the sky, on which adjoined a number of ceiled chambers of small size, without windows, and only lighted through the doorway, which opened into the court.

kill Gobryas. Then Gobryas, when he perceived that Darius stood doing nothing, asked him, "why his hand was idle?" "I fear to hurt thee," he answered. "Fear not," said Gobryas; "strike, though it be through both." Darius did as he desired, drove his dagger home, and by good hap killed the Magus.

79. Thus were the Magi slain; and the seven, cutting off both the heads, and leaving their own wounded in the palace, partly because they were disabled, and partly to guard the citadel, went forth from the gates with the heads in their hands, shouting and making an uproar. They called out to all the Persians that they met, and told them what had happened, showing them the heads of the Magi, while at the same time they slew every Magus who fell in their way. Then the Persians, when they knew what the seven had done, and understood the fraud of the Magi, thought it but just to follow the example set them, and, drawing their daggers, they killed the Magi wherever they could find any. Such was their fury, that, unless night had closed in, not a single Magus would have been left alive. The Persians observe this day with one accord, and keep it more strictly than any other in the whole year. It is then that they hold the great festival, which they call the Magophonia. No Magus may show himself abroad during the whole time that the feast lasts; but all must remain at home the entire day.

80. And now when five days were gone, and the hubbub had settled down, the conspirators met together to consult about the situation of affairs. At this meeting speeches were made, to which many of the Greeks give no credence, but they were made nevertheless.[1] Otanes recommended that the management of public affairs should be entrusted to the whole nation. "To me," he said, "it seems advisable, that we should no longer have a single man to rule over us – the rule of one is neither good nor pleasant. Ye cannot have forgotten to what lengths Cambyses went in his haughty tyranny, and the haughtiness of the Magi ye have yourselves experienced. How indeed is it possible that monarchy should be a well-adjusted thing, when it allows a man to do as he likes without being answerable? Such licence is enough to stir strange and unwonted thoughts in the heart of the

1 The incredulity of the Greeks is again alluded to (infra, vi. 43). No doubt Herodotus had Persian authority for his tale; but it is so utterly at variance with Oriental notions as to be absolutely incredible.

worthiest of men. Give a person this power, and straightway his manifold good things puff him up with pride, while envy is so natural to human kind that it cannot but arise in him. But pride and envy together include all wickedness – both of them leading on to deeds of savage violence. True it is that kings, possessing as they do all that heart can desire, ought to be void of envy; but the contrary is seen in their conduct towards the citizens. They are jealous of the most virtuous among their subjects, and wish their death; while they take delight in the meanest and basest, being ever ready to listen to the tales of slanderers. A king, besides, is beyond all other men inconsistent with himself. Pay him court in moderation, and he is angry because you do not show him more profound respect – show him profound respect, and he is offended again, because (as he says) you fawn on him. But the worst of all is, that he sets aside the laws of the land, puts men to death without trial, and subjects women to violence. The rule of the many, on the other hand, has, in the first place, the fairest of names, to wit, *isonomy*;[1] and further it is free from all those outrages which a king is wont to commit. There, places are given by lot, the magistrate is answerable for what he does, and measures rest with the commonalty. I vote, therefore, that we do away with monarchy, and raise the people to power. For the people are all in all."

81. Such were the sentiments of Otanes. Megabyzus spoke next, and advised the setting up of an oligarchy:– "In all that Otanes has said to persuade you to put down monarchy," he observed, "I fully concur; but his recommendation that we should call the people to power seems to me not the best advice. For there is nothing so void of understanding, nothing so full of wantonness, as the unwieldy rabble. It were folly not to be borne, for men, while seeking to escape the wantonness of a tyrant, to give themselves up to the wantonness of a rude unbridled mob. The tyrant, in all his doings, at least knows what is he about, but a mob is altogether devoid of knowledge; for how should there be any knowledge in a rabble, untaught, and with no natural sense of what is right and fit? It rushes wildly into state affairs with all the fury of a stream swollen in the

---

1 Modern languages have no single word to express the Greek ἰσονομία, which signified that perfect equality of all civil and political rights which was the fundamental notion of the Greek democracy.

winter, and confuses everything. Let the enemies of the Persians be ruled by democracies; but let us choose out from the citizens a certain number of the worthiest, and put the government into their hands. For thus both we ourselves shall be among the governors, and power being entrusted to the best men, it is likely that the best counsels will prevail in the state."

82. This was the advice which Megabyzus gave, and after him Darius came forward, and spoke as follows:– "All that Megabyzus said against democracy was well said, I think; but about oligarchy he did not speak advisedly; for take these three forms of government – democracy, oligarchy, and monarchy – and let them each be at their best, I maintain that monarchy far surpasses the other two. What government can possibly be better than that of the very best man in the whole state? The counsels of such a man are like himself, and so he governs the mass of the people to their hearts' content; while at the same time his measures against evil-doers are kept more secret than in other states. Contrariwise, in oligarchies, where men vie with each other in the service of the commonwealth, fierce enmities are apt to arise between man and man, each wishing to be leader, and to carry his own measures; whence violent quarrels come, which lead to open strife, often ending in bloodshed. Then monarchy is sure to follow; and this too shows how far that rule surpasses all others. Again, in a democracy, it is impossible but that there will be malpractices: these malpractices, however, do not lead to enmities, but to close friendships, which are formed among those engaged in them, who must hold well together to carry on their villainies. And so things go on until a man stands forth as champion of the commonalty, and puts down the evil-doers. Straightway the author of so great a service is admired by all, and from being admired soon comes to be appointed king; so that here too it is plain that monarchy is the best government. Lastly, to sum up all in a word, whence, I ask, was it that we got the freedom which we enjoy? – did democracy give it us, or oligarchy, or a monarch? As a single man recovered our freedom for us, my sentence is that we keep to the rule of one. Even apart from this, we ought not to change the laws of our forefathers when they work fairly; for to do so is not well."

83. Such were the three opinions brought forward at this meeting; the four other Persians voted in favour of the last. Otanes, who wished to give his countrymen a democracy, when

he found the decision against him, arose a second time, and spoke thus before the assembly:– "Brother conspirators, it is plain that the king who is to be chosen will be one of ourselves, whether we make the choice by casting lots for the prize, or by letting the people decide which of us they will have to rule over them, or in any other way. Now, as I have neither a mind to rule nor to be ruled, I shall not enter the lists with you in this matter. I withdraw, however, on one condition – none of you shall claim to exercise rule over me or my seed for ever." The six agreed to these terms, and Otanes withdrew and stood aloof from the contest. And still to this day the family of Otanes continues to be the only free family in Persia; those who belong to it submit to the rule of the king only so far as they themselves choose; they are bound, however, to observe the laws of the land like the other Persians.

84. After this the six took counsel together, as to the fairest way of setting up a king: and first, with respect to Otanes, they resolved, that if any of their own number got the kingdom, Otanes and his seed after him should receive year by year, as a mark of special honour, a Median robe,[1] and all such other gifts as are accounted the most honourable in Persia. And these they resolved to give him, because he was the man who first planned the outbreak, and who brought the seven together. These privileges, therefore, were assigned specially to Otanes. The following were made common to them all:– It was to be free to each, whenever he pleased, to enter the palace unannounced, unless the king were in the company of one of his wives; and the king was to be bound to marry into no family excepting those of the conspirators.[2] Concerning the appointment of a king, the resolve to which they came was the following:– They would ride out together next morning into the skirts of the city, and he whose steed first neighed after the sun was up should have the kingdom.

85. Now Darius had a groom, a sharp-witted knave, called Œbares. After the meeting had broken up, Darius sent for him, and said, "Œbares, this is the way in which the king is to be

---

1 Garments have at all times been gifts of honour in the East. (Gen. xlv. 22; 2 Kings v. 5; 2 Chron. ix. 24, etc.) The practice continues in the *kaftan* of the present day.

2 So far as can be traced, this rule was always observed.

chosen – we are to mount our horses, and the man whose horse first neighs after the sun is up is to have the kingdom. If then you have any cleverness, contrive a plan whereby the prize may fall to us, and not go to another." "Truly, master," Œbares answered, "if it depends on this whether thou shalt be king or no, set thine heart at ease, and fear nothing: I have a charm which is sure not to fail." "If thou hast really aught of the kind," said Darius, "hasten to get it ready. The matter does not brook delay, for the trial is to be to-morrow." So Œbares when he heard that, did as follows:– When night came, he took one of the mares, the chief favourite of the horse which Darius rode, and tethering it in the suburb, brought his master's horse to the place; then, after leading him round and round the mare several times, nearer and nearer at each circuit, he ended by letting them come together.

86. And now, when the morning broke, the six Persians, according to agreement, met together on horseback, and rode out to the suburb. As they went along they neared the spot where the mare was tethered the night before, whereupon the horse of Darius sprang forward and neighed. Just at the same time, though the sky was clear and bright, there was a flash of lightning, followed by a thunder-clap. It seemed as if the heavens conspired with Darius, and hereby inaugurated him king: so the five other nobles leaped with one accord from their steeds, and bowed down before him and owned him for their king.

87. This is the account which some of the Persians gave of the contrivance of Œbares; but there are others who relate the matter differently. They say that in the morning he stroked the mare with his hand, which he then hid in his trousers until the sun rose and the horses were about to start, when he suddenly drew his hand forth and put it to the nostrils of his master's horse, which immediately snorted and neighed.

88. Thus was Darius, son of Hystaspes, appointed king; and, except the Arabians, all they of Asia were subject to him; for Cyrus, and after him Cambyses,[1] had brought them all under. The Arabians were never subject as slaves to the Persians, but had a league of friendship with them from the time when they brought Cambyses on his way as he went into Egypt; for had

1 The Phœnicians and Cyprians would be here alluded to – perhaps also the Cilicians.

they been unfriendly the Persians could never have made their invasion.

And now Darius contracted marriages[1] of the first rank, according to the notions of the Persians: to wit, with two daughters of Cyrus, Atossa and Artystône; of whom, Atossa had been twice married before, once to Cambyses, her brother, and once to the Magus, while the other, Artystône, was a virgin. He married also Parmys, daughter of Smerdis, son of Cyrus; and he likewise took to wife the daughter of Otanes, who had made the discovery about the Magus. And now when his power was established firmly throughout all the kingdoms, the first thing that he did was to set up a carving in stone, which showed a man mounted upon a horse, with an inscription in these words following:— "Darius, son of Hystaspes, by aid of his good horse" (here followed the horse's name), "and of his good groom Œbares, got himself the kingdom of the Persians."

89. This he set up in Persia; and afterwards he proceeded to establish twenty governments of the kind which the Persians call satrapies, assigning to each its governor, and fixing the tribute which was to be paid him by the several nations. And generally he joined together in one satrapy the nations that were neighbours, but sometimes he passed over the nearer tribes, and put in their stead those which were more remote. The following is an account of these governments, and of the yearly tribute which they paid to the king:— Such as brought their tribute in silver were ordered to pay according to the Babylonian talent; while the Euboic was the standard measure for such as brought gold. Now the Babylonian talent contains seventy Euboic minæ.[2] During all the reign of Cyrus, and afterwards when Cambyses ruled, there were no fixed tributes, but the nations severally brought gifts to the king. On account of this and other like doings, the Persians say that Darius was a huckster, Cambyses a master, and Cyrus a father; for Darius looked to making a gain in everything;

1 Darius had married a daughter of Gobryas before his accession (vii. 2). He also took to wife his niece, Phratagûne, the daughter of his brother Artanes (vii. 224).

2 Standards of weight probably passed into Greece from Asia, whence the word *mina* (μνᾶ) seems certainly to have been derived. That the standard known to the Greeks as the Euboic was an Asiatic one, is plain from this passage. If the (later) Attic talent was worth £243 15s. of our money, the Euboic (silver) talent would be £250 8s. 5d., and the Babylonian £292 3s. 3d.

Cambyses was harsh and reckless; while Cyrus was gentle, and procured them all manner of goods.

90. The Ionians, the Magnesians of Asia,[1] the Æolians, the Carians, the Lycians, the Milyans,[2] and the Pamphylians, paid their tribute in a single sum, which was fixed at four hundred talents of silver. These formed together the first satrapy.

The Mysians, Lydians, Lasonians,[3] Cabalians, and Hygennians paid the sum of five hundred talents. This was the second satrapy.

The Hellespontians, of the right coast as one enters the straits, the Phrygians, the Asiatic Thracians, the Paphlagonians, the Mariandynians, and the Syrians[4] paid a tribute of three hundred and sixty talents. This was the third satrapy.

The Cilicians gave three hundred and sixty white horses, one for each day in the year,[5] and five hundred talents of silver. Of this sum one hundred and forty talents went to pay the cavalry which guarded the country, while the remaining three hundred and sixty were received by Darius. This was the fourth satrapy.

91. The country reaching from the city of Posideïum[6] (built by Amphilochus, son of Amphiaraüs, on the confines of Syria and Cilicia) to the borders of Egypt, excluding therefrom a district which belonged to Arabia, and was free from tax,[7] paid a tribute of three hundred and fifty talents. All Phœnicia, Palestine Syria, and Cyprus, were herein contained. This was the fifth satrapy.

From Egypt, and the neighbouring parts of Libya, together with the towns of Cyrênê and Barca, which belonged to the Egyptian satrapy, the tribute which came in was seven hundred talents. These seven hundred talents did not include the profits of the fisheries of Lake Mœris, nor the corn furnished to the troops at Memphis. Corn was supplied to 120,000 Persians, who dwelt at Memphis in the quarter called the White Castle, and to a number of auxiliaries. This was the sixth satrapy.

1 There were two towns of the name of Magnesia in Asia Minor, Magnesia under Sipylus and Magnesia on the Mæander.

2 Vide supra, i. 173.

3 In the Seventh Book (ch. 77) Herodotus identifies the Cabalians and the Lasonians.

4 That is, the Cappadocians. (Vide supra, i. 72.)

5 Compare i. 32, and ii. 4.

6 Posideïum lay about 12 miles south of the embouchure of the Orontes.

7 The district here spoken of is that between Gaza (Cadytis) and Jenysus (vide supra, ch. 5), which Cambyses traversed on his road to Egypt. Concerning the exemption of the Arabs from tribute, vide infra, ch. 97.

The Sattagydians, the Gandarians, the Dadicæ, and the Aparytæ, who were all reckoned together, paid a tribute of a hundred and seventy talents. This was the seventh satrapy.

Susa, and the other parts of Cissia, paid three hundred talents. This was the eighth satrapy.

92. From Babylonia, and the rest of Assyria, were drawn a thousand talents of silver, and five hundred boy-eunuchs. This was the ninth satrapy.

Agbatana, and the other parts of Media, together with the Paricanians and Orthocorybantes, paid in all four hundred and fifty talents. This was the tenth satrapy.

The Caspians, Pausicæ, Pantimathi, and Daritæ, were joined in one government, and paid the sum of two hundred talents. This was the eleventh satrapy.

From the Bactrian tribes as far as the Ægli, the tribute received was three hundred and sixty talents. This was the twelfth satrapy.

93. From Pactyïca, Armenia, and the countries reaching thence to the Euxine, the sum drawn was four hundred talents. This was the thirteenth satrapy.

The Sagartians, Sarangians, Thamanæans, Utians, and Mycians, together with the inhabitants of the islands in the Erythræan sea, where the king sends those whom he banishes, furnished altogether a tribute of six hundred talents. This was the fourteenth satrapy.

The Sacans and Caspians gave two hundred and fifty talents. This was the fifteenth satrapy.

The Parthians, Chorasmians, Sogdians, and Arians, gave three hundred. This was the sixteenth satrapy.

94. The Paricanians and Ethiopians of Asia furnished a tribute of four hundred talents. This was the seventeenth satrapy.

The Matienians, Saspeires, and Alarodians were rated to pay two hundred talents. This was the eighteenth satrapy.

The Moschi, Tibareni, Macrones, Mosynœci, and Mares had to pay three hundred talents. This was the nineteenth satrapy.

The Indians, who are more numerous than any other nation with which we are acquainted, paid a tribute exceeding that of every other people, to wit, three hundred and sixty talents of gold-dust. This was the twentieth satrapy.

95. If the Babylonian money here spoken of be reduced to the Euboic scale, it will make nine thousand five hundred and

forty such talents; and if the gold be reckoned at thirteen times
the worth of silver,[1] the Indian gold-dust will come to four
thousand six hundred and eighty talents. Add those two amounts
together, and the whole revenue which came in to Darius year
by year will be found to be in Euboic money fourteen thousand
five hundred and sixty talents, not to mention parts of a talent.[2]

96. Such was the revenue which Darius derived from Asia
and a small part of Libya. Later in his reign the sum was increased by the tribute of the islands, and of the nations of Europe as far as Thessaly. The great king stores away the tribute
which he receives after this fashion − he melts it down, and,
while it is in a liquid state, runs it into earthen vessels, which are
afterwards removed, leaving the metal in a solid mass. When
money is wanted, he coins as much of this bullion as the occasion requires.

97. Such then were the governments, and such the amounts
of tribute at which they were assessed respectively. Persia alone
has not been reckoned among the tributaries − and for this
reason, because the country of the Persians is altogether exempt
from tax. The following peoples paid no settled tribute, but
brought gifts to the king: first, the Ethiopians bordering upon
Egypt,[3] who were reduced by Cambyses when he made war on
the long-lived Ethiopians, and who dwell about the sacred city
of Nysa, and have festivals in honour of Dionysus. The grain on
which they and their next neighbours feed is the same as that
used by the Calantian Indians. Their dwelling-houses are under
ground.[4] Every third year these two nations brought − and they
still bring to my day − two chœnices[5] of virgin gold, two hundred
logs of ebony, five Ethiopian boys, and twenty elephant tusks.
The Colchians, and the neighbouring tribes who dwell between

1 In Greece the relative value of gold varied at different times. Herodotus
says gold was to silver as 13 to 1, afterwards in Plato and Xenophon's time
(and more than 100 years after the death of Alexander) it was 10 to 1, owing
to the quantity of gold brought in through the Persian war. It long continued
at 10 to 1 (Liv. xxxviii. 11) except when an accident altered the proportion of
those metals.

2 It is impossible to reconcile Herodotus's numbers, and equally impossible
to say where the mistake lies.

3 These were the inhabitants of Lower Ethiopia and Nubia.

4 This notion probably arose from their having mud huts, so common in
central Africa.

5 [That is, about two quarts. − E. H. B.]

them and the Caucasus – for so far the Persian rule reaches, while north of the Caucasus no one fears them any longer – undertook to furnish a gift, which in my day was still brought every fifth year, consisting of a hundred boys, and the same number of maidens. The Arabs brought every year a thousand talents of frankincense. Such were the gifts which the king received over and above the tribute-money.

98. The way in which the Indians get the plentiful supply of gold, which enables them to furnish year by year so vast an amount of gold-dust to the king, is the following:– Eastward of India lies a tract which is entirely sand. Indeed of all the inhabitants of Asia, concerning whom anything certain is known, the Indians dwell the nearest to the east, and the rising of the sun. Beyond them the whole country is desert on account of the sand.[1] The tribes of Indians are numerous, and do not all speak the same language[2] – some are wandering tribes, others not. They who dwell in the marshes along the river live on raw fish, which they take in boats made of reeds, each formed out of a single joint. These Indians wear a dress of sedge, which they cut in the river and bruise; afterwards they weave it into mats, and wear it as we wear a breast-plate.

99. Eastward of these Indians are another tribe, called Padæans, who are wanderers, and live on raw flesh. This tribe is said to have the following customs:– If one of their number be ill, man or woman, they take the sick person, and if he be a man, the men of his acquaintance proceed to put him to death, because, they say, his flesh would be spoilt for them if he pined and wasted away with sickness. The man protests he is not ill in the least; but his friends will not accept his denial – in spite of all he can say, they kill him, and feast themselves on his body. So also if a woman be sick, the women, who are her friends, take her and do with her exactly the same as the men. If one of them reaches to old age, about which there is seldom any

1 The India of Herodotus is the true *ancient* India, the region about the Upper Indus, best known to us at present under the name of the Punjab. Herodotus knows nothing of the great southern peninsula.

2 The Hindoo races are supposed to have been settled in India as early as 1200 B.C.; which is the date assigned to the Vedas, though these appear not to be all of one period. The aborigines are still found in Ceylon and in Southern India as well as in the hill-country in other parts; and their customs differ as much as their languages from those of the Hindoos.

question, as commonly before that time they have had some disease or other, and so have been put to death – but if a man, notwithstanding, comes to be old, then they offer him in sacrifice to their gods, and afterwards eat his flesh.[1]

100. There is another set of Indians whose customs are very different. They refuse to put any live animal to death,[2] they sow no corn, and have no dwelling-houses. Vegetables are their only food. There is a plant which grows wild in their country, bearing seed, about the size of millet-seed, in a calyx: their wont is to gather this seed and having boiled it, calyx and all, to use it for food. If one of them is attacked with sickness, he goes forth into the wilderness, and lies down to die; no one has the least concern either for the sick or for the dead.

101. All the tribes which I have mentioned mate together in the open like the brute beasts: they have also all the same tint of skin, which approaches that of the Ethiopians. Their seed which enters into the women, is not white like that of other men, but black like their skin. The seed of the Ethiopians is also black. Their country is a long way from Persia towards the south: nor had king Darius ever any authority over them.

102. Besides these, there are Indians of another tribe, who border on the city of Caspatyrus,[3] and the country of Pactyïca; these people dwell northward of all the rest of the Indians, and follow nearly the same mode of life as the Bactrians. They are more warlike than any of the other tribes, and from them the men are sent forth who go to procure the gold. For it is in this part of India that the sandy desert lies. Here, in this desert, there live amid the sand great ants, in size somewhat less than dogs, but bigger than foxes. The Persian king has a number of them, which have been caught by the hunters in the land whereof we are speaking. Those ants make their dwellings under ground, and like the Greek ants, which they very much resemble in shape, throw up sand-heaps as they burrow. Now the sand which they throw up is full of gold.[4] The Indians, when they go into

1 Vide supra, ch. 38. The same custom is said to have prevailed among the Massagetæ (i. 216) and the Issedonians (iv. 26).

2 The repugnance of true Brahmins to take away life is well known.

3 [Some say "Kabul," others "Kashmere"; but we have no means of ascertaining the site of Caspatyrus. – E. H. B.]

4 Modern research has not discovered anything very satisfactory either with respect to the animal intended, or the habits ascribed to it. Perhaps the most

the desert to collect this sand, take three camels and harness them together, a female in the middle and a male on either side, in a leading-rein. The rider sits on the female, and they are particular to choose for the purpose one that has but just dropped her young; for their female camels can run as fast as horses, while they bear burthens very much better.

103. As the Greeks are well acquainted with the shape of the camel, I shall not trouble to describe it; but I shall mention what seems to have escaped their notice. The camel has in its hind legs four thigh-bones and four knee-joints and its genitalia are turned towards the tail between its hind legs.[1]

104. When the Indians therefore have thus equipped themselves they set off in quest of the gold, calculating the time so that they may be engaged in seizing it during the most sultry part of the day, when the ants hide themselves to escape the heat. The sun in those parts shines fiercest in the morning, not, as elsewhere, at noonday; the greatest heat is from the time when he has reached a certain height, until the hour at which the market closes. During this space he burns much more furiously than at midday in Greece, so that the men there are said at that time to drench themselves with water. At noon his heat is much the same in India as in other countries, after which, as the day declines, the warmth is only equal to that of the morning sun elsewhere. Towards evening the coolness increases, till about sunset it becomes very cold.[2]

105. When the Indians reach the place where the gold is, they fill their bags with the sand, and ride away at their best speed: the ants, however, scenting them, as the Persians say, rush forth in pursuit. Now these animals are, they declare, so swift, that there is nothing in the world like them: if it were not, therefore, that the Indians get a start while the ants are mustering, not a single gold-gatherer could escape. During the flight the male camels, which are not so fleet as the females, grow tired, and

---

plausible conjecture is that which identifies it with the Pengolin, or Ant-eater, which burrows on the sandy plains of northern India.

1 This is of course untrue, and it is difficult to understand how Herodotus could entertain such a notion. There is no *real* difference, as regards the anatomy of the leg, between the horse and the camel.

2 Herodotus is apparently narrating *what he had heard*, and it belongs to his simplicity not to mix up his own speculations with the relations which he had received from others.

begin to drag, first one, and then the other; but the females recollect the young which they have left behind, and never give way or flag.[1] Such, according to the Persians, is the manner in which the Indians get the greater part of their gold; some is dug out of the earth, but of this the supply is more scanty.[2]

106. It seems as if the extreme regions of the earth were blessed by nature with the most excellent productions, just in the same way that Greece enjoys a climate more excellently tempered than any other country. In India, which, as I observed lately, is the furthest region of the inhabited world towards the east, all the four-footed beasts and the birds are very much bigger than those found elsewhere, except only the horses, which are surpassed by the Median breed called the Nisæan. Gold too is produced there in vast abundance, some dug from the earth, some washed down by the rivers, some carried off in the mode which I have but now described. And further, there are trees which grow wild there, the fruit whereof is a wool exceeding in beauty and goodness that of sheep. The natives make their clothes of this tree-wool.[3]

107. Arabia is the last of inhabited lands towards the south, and it is the only country which produces frankincense, myrrh, cassia, cinnamon, and ladanum.[4] The Arabians[5] do not get any of these, except the myrrh,[6] without trouble. The frankincense they procure by means of the gum styrax,[7] which the Greeks obtain from the Phœnicians; this they burn, and thereby obtain the spice. For the trees which bear the frankincense are guarded by winged serpents, small in size, and of varied colours, whereof vast numbers hang about every tree. They are of the same kind as the serpents that invade Egypt;[8] and there is nothing but the smoke of the styrax which will drive them from the trees.

1 Marco Polo relates that, when the Tatars make incursions into the country lying to the north of them, they adopt the same device.

2 The whole of this region of Central Asia is in the highest degree auriferous.

3 Vide supra, ch. 47. "Tree-wool" is exactly the German name for cotton (*Baumwolle*).

4 Lêdanon or ladanon, a resin or gum.

5 The Arabs supplied Egypt with various spices and gums which were required for embalming and other purposes. In Genesis xxxvii. 25, the Ishmaelites or Arabs were going to Egypt from "Gilead with their camels bearing spicery, and balm, and myrrh."

6 Smyrna, the Greek name of *myrrh*, is the same as that of the city.

7 This is the "gum storax" of modern commerce.

8 Vide supra, ii. 75. If serpents, they should be oviparous.

108. The Arabians say that the whole world would swarm with these serpents, if they were not kept in check in the way in which I know that vipers are. Of a truth Divine Providence does appear to be, as indeed one might expect beforehand, a wise contriver. For timid animals which are a prey to others are all made to produce young abundantly, that so the species may not be entirely eaten up and lost; while savage and noxious creatures are made very unfruitful. The hare, for instance, which is hunted alike by beasts, birds, and men, breeds so abundantly as even to superfetate, a thing which is true of no other animal. You find in a hare's belly, at one and the same time, some of the young all covered with fur, others quite naked, others again just fully formed in the womb, while the hare perhaps has lately conceived afresh. The lioness, on the other hand, which is one of the strongest and boldest of brutes, brings forth young but once in her lifetime,[1] and then a single cub;[2] she cannot possibly conceive again, since she loses her womb at the same time that she drops her young. The reason of this is, that as soon as the cub begins to stir inside the dam, his claws, which are sharper than those of any other animal, scratch the womb; as the time goes on, and he grows bigger, he tears it ever more and more; so that at last, when the birth comes, there is not a morsel in the whole womb that is sound.

109. Now with respect to the vipers and the winged snakes of Arabia, if they increased as fast as their nature would allow, impossible were it for man to maintain himself upon the earth. Accordingly it is found that when the male and female come together, at the very moment of impregnation, the female seizes the male by the neck, and having once fastened, cannot be brought to leave go till she has bit the neck entirely through. And so the male perishes; but after a while he is revenged upon the female by means of the young, which, while still unborn, gnaw a passage through the womb, and then through the belly of their mother, and so make their entrance into the world. Contrariwise, other snakes, which are harmless, lay eggs, and hatch a vast number of young. Vipers are found in all parts of the world, but the winged serpents are nowhere seen except in

---

1 The fabulous character of the whole of this account was known to Aristotle.
2 According to travellers, it is not uncommon for the lioness to have three or four cubs at a birth.

Arabia, where they are all congregated together. This makes them appear so numerous.

110. Such, then, is the way in which the Arabians obtain their frankincense; their manner of collecting the cassia[1] is the following:– They cover all their body and their face with the hides of oxen and other skins, leaving only holes for the eyes, and thus protected go in search of the cassia, which grows in a lake of no great depth. All round the shores and in the lake itself there dwell a number of winged animals, much resembling bats, which screech horribly, and are very valiant. These creatures they must keep from their eyes all the while that they gather the cassia.

111. Still more wonderful is the mode in which they collect the cinnamon. Where the wood grows, and what country produces it, they cannot tell – only some, following probability, relate that it comes from the country in which Dionysus was brought up.[2] Great birds, they say, bring the sticks which we Greeks, taking the word from the Phœnicians, call cinnamon, and carry them up into the air to make their nests. These are fastened with a sort of mud to a sheer face of rock, where no foot of man is able to climb. So the Arabians, to get the cinnamon, use the following artifice. They cut all the oxen and asses and beasts of burthen that die in their land into large pieces, which they carry with them into those regions, and place near the nests: then they withdraw to a distance, and the old birds, swooping down, seize the pieces of meat and fly with them up to their nests; which, not being able to support the weight, break off and fall to the ground.[3] Hereupon the Arabians return and collect the cinnamon, which is afterwards carried from Arabia into other countries.

112. Ledanum, which the Arabs call *ladanum*, is procured in a yet stranger fashion. Found in a most inodorous place, it is the sweetest-scented of all substances. It is gathered from the beards of he-goats, where it is found sticking like gum, having come

1 Cassia and cinnamon, according to Larcher (note ad loc.), are from the same tree, the only difference being that cinnamon is properly the branch with the bark on; cassia is the bark without the branch.

2 Ethiopia probably.

3 The story evidently belongs to a whole class of Eastern tales, wherein an important part is played by great birds. Compare the *rocs* in the story of Sindbad the Sailor in the Arabian Nights, and the tale related by Marco Polo [Travels, p. 393 of the "Everyman's Library" edit.] of the mines of Golconda.

from the bushes on which they browse. It is used in many sorts of unguents, and is what the Arabs burn chiefly as incense.

113. Concerning the spices of Arabia let no more be said. The whole country is scented with them, and exhales an odour marvellously sweet. There are also in Arabia two kinds of sheep worthy of admiration, the like of which is nowhere else to be seen; the one kind has long tails, not less than three cubits in length, which, if they were allowed to trail on the ground, would be bruised and fall into sores. As it is, all the shepherds know enough of carpentering to make little trucks for their sheep's tails. The trucks are placed under the tails, each sheep having one to himself, and the tails are then tied down upon them. The other kind has a broad tail, which is a cubit across sometimes.

114. Where the south declines towards the setting sun lies the country called Ethiopia, the last inhabited land in that direction. There gold is obtained in great plenty,[1] huge elephants abound, with wild trees of all sorts, and ebony; and the men are taller, handsomer, and longer lived than anywhere else.

115. Now these are the furthest regions of the world in Asia and Libya. Of the extreme tracts of Europe towards the west I cannot speak with any certainty; for I do not allow that there is any river, to which the barbarians give the name of Eridanus, emptying itself into the northern sea, whence (as the tale goes) amber is procured;[2] nor do I know of any islands called the Cassiterides[3] (Tin Islands), whence the tin comes which we use. For in the first place the name Eridanus is manifestly not a barbarian word at all, but a Greek name, invented by some poet or other; and secondly, though I have taken vast pains, I have never been able to get an assurance from an eye-witness that

1 Vide supra, ch. 22.
2 Here Herodotus is over-cautious, and rejects as fable what we can see to be truth. The amber district upon the northern sea is the coast of the Baltic about the Gulf of Dantzig, and the mouths of the Vistula and Niemen, which is still one of the best amber regions in the world. The very name, Eridanus, lingers there in the Rhodaune, the small stream which washes the west side of the town of Dantzig. The word Eridanus (= Rhodanus) seems to have been applied, by the early inhabitants of Europe, especially to great and strong-running rivers.
3 This name was applied to the Selinæ, or Scilly Isles; and the imperfect information respecting the site of the mines of tin led to the belief that they were there, instead of on the mainland (of Cornwall).

there is any sea on the further side of Europe. Nevertheless, tin and amber do certainly come to us from the ends of the earth.[1]

116. The northern parts of Europe are very much richer in gold than any other region: but how it is procured I have no certain knowledge. The story runs, that the one-eyed Arimaspi purloin it from the griffins; but here too I am incredulous, and cannot persuade myself that there is a race of men born with one eye, who in all else resemble the rest of mankind. Nevertheless it seems to be true that the extreme regions of the earth, which surround and shut up within themselves all other countries, produce the things which are the rarest, and which men reckon the most beautiful.

117. There is a plain in Asia which is shut in on all sides by a mountain-range, and in this mountain-range are five openings. The plain lies on the confines of the Chorasmians, Hyrcanians, Parthians, Sarangians, and Thamanæans, and belonged formerly to the first-mentioned of those peoples. Ever since the Persians, however, obtained the mastery of Asia, it has been the property of the Great King. A mighty river, called the Aces,[2] flows from the hills inclosing the plain; and this stream, formerly splitting into five channels, ran through the five openings in the hills, and watered the lands of the five nations which dwell around. The Persian came, however, and conquered the region, and then it went ill with the people of these lands. The Great King blocked up all the passages between the hills with dykes and flood-gates, and so prevented the water from flowing out. Then the plain within the hills became a sea, for the river kept rising, and the water could find no outlet. From that time the five nations which were wont formerly to have the use of the stream, losing their accustomed supply of water, have been in great distress. In winter, indeed, they have rain from heaven like the rest of the world, but in summer, after sowing their millet and their sesame, they always stood in need of water from the river. When,

1 [For a brief account of the *amber* and *tin* trades in antiquity, see Tozer, *History of Ancient Geography*, pp. 32 sqq., and for a note on amber, W. Ridgeway's art. in *Encyclopædia Biblica*, cols. 134–136. – E. H. B.]

2 The plain and the five openings are probably a fable; but the origin of the tale may be found in the distribution by the Persian Government of the waters (most likely) of the Heri-rud, which is capable of being led through the hills into the low country north of the range, or of being prolonged westward along the range, or finally of being turned southward into the desert.

therefore, they suffer from this want, hastening to Persia, men and women alike, they take their station at the gate of the king's palace, and wail aloud. Then the king orders the flood-gates to be opened towards the country whose need is greatest, and lets the soil drink until it has had enough; after which the gates on this side are shut, and others are unclosed for the nation which, of the remainder, needs it most. It has been told me that the king never gives the order to open the gates till the suppliants have paid him a large sum of money over and above the tribute.

118. Of the seven Persians who rose up against the Magus, one, Intaphernes, lost his life very shortly after the outbreak, for an act of insolence. He wished to enter the palace and transact a certain business with the king. Now the law was that all those who had taken part in the rising against the Magus might enter unannounced into the king's presence, unless he happened to be in private with his wife.[1] So Intaphernes would not have any one announce him, but, as he belonged to the seven, claimed it as his right to go in. The doorkeeper, however, and the chief usher forbade his entrance, since the king, they said, was with his wife. But Intaphernes thought they told lies; so, drawing his scymitar, he cut off their noses and their ears,[2] and, hanging them on the bridle of his horse, put the bridle round their necks, and so let them go.

119. Then these two men went and showed themselves to the king, and told him how it had come to pass that they were thus treated. Darius trembled lest it was by the common consent of the six that the deed had been done; he therefore sent for them all in turn, and sounded them to know if they approved the conduct of Intaphernes. When he found by their answers that there had been no concert between him and them, he laid hands on Intaphernes, his children, and all his near kindred; strongly suspecting that he and his friends were about to raise a revolt. When all had been seized and put in chains, as malefactors condemned to death, the wife of Intaphernes came and stood continually at the palace-gates, weeping and wailing sore. So Darius after a while, seeing that she never ceased to stand

---

1 Supra, ch. 84.

2 This mode of punishment has always been common in the East. Its infliction by the revolted Sepoys on our own countrymen and countrywomen during the Mutiny in 1857 will occur to all readers.

and weep, was touched with pity for her, and bade a messenger go to her and say, "Lady, king Darius gives thee as a boon the life of one of thy kinsmen – choose which thou wilt of the prisoners." Then she pondered awhile before she answered, "If the king grants me the life of one alone, I make choice of my brother." Darius, when he heard the reply, was astonished, and sent again, saying, "Lady, the king bids thee tell him why it is that thou passest by thy husband and thy children, and preferrest to have the life of thy brother spared. He is not so near to thee as thy children, nor so dear as thy husband." She answered, "O king, if the gods will, I may have another husband and other children when these are gone. But as my father and my mother are no more, it is impossible that I should have another brother. This was my thought when I asked to have my brother spared." Then it seemed to Darius that the lady spoke well, and he gave her, besides the life that she had asked, the life also of her eldest son, because he was greatly pleased with her. But he slew all the rest. Thus one of the seven died, in the way I have described, very shortly after the insurrection.

120. About the time of Cambyses' last sickness, the following events happened. There was a certain Orœtes, a Persian, whom Cyrus had made governor of Sardis. This man conceived a most unholy wish. He had never suffered wrong or had an ill word from Polycrates the Samian – nay, he had not so much as seen him in all his life; yet, notwithstanding, he conceived the wish to seize him and put him to death. This wish, according to the account which the most part give, arose from what happened one day as he was sitting with another Persian in the gate of the king's palace. The man's name was Mitrobates, and he was ruler of the satrapy of Dascyleium.[1] He and Orœtes had been talking together, and from talking they fell to quarrelling and comparing their merits; whereupon Mitrobates said to Orœtes reproachfully, "Art thou worthy to be called a man, when, near as Samos lies to thy government, and easy as it is to conquer, thou hast omitted to bring it under the dominion of the king? Easy to conquer, said I? Why, a mere common citizen, with the help of fifteen men-at-arms, mastered the island, and is still king of it." Orœtes, they say, took this reproach greatly to heart; but, instead

1 Dascyleium was the capital city of the great northern satrapy, which at this time (according to Herodotus, supra, ch. 90) included the whole of Phrygia.

of seeking to revenge himself on the man by whom it was uttered, he conceived the desire of destroying Polycrates, since it was on Polycrates' account that the reproach had fallen on him.

121. Another less common version of the story is that Orœtes sent a herald to Samos to make a request, the nature of which is not stated; Polycrates was at the time reclining in the apartment of the males, and Anacreon the Teian was with him; when therefore the herald came forward to converse, Polycrates, either out of studied contempt for the power of Orœtes, or it may be merely by chance, was lying with his face turned away towards the wall; and so he lay all the time that the herald spake, and when he ended, did not even vouchsafe him a word.

122. Such are the two reasons alleged for the death of Polycrates; it is open to all to believe which they please. What is certain is, that Orœtes, while residing at Magnesia on the Mæander, sent a Lydian, by name Myrsus, the son of Gyges,[1] with a message to Polycrates at Samos, well knowing what that monarch designed. For Polycrates entertained a design which no other Greek, so far as we know, ever formed before him, unless it were Minos the Cnossian, and those (if there were any such) who had the mastery of the Ægean at an earlier time — Polycrates, I say, was the first of mere human birth who conceived the design of gaining the empire of the sea, and aspired to rule over Ionia and the islands. Knowing then that Polycrates was thus minded, Orœtes sent his message, which ran as follows:—

"Orœtes to Polycrates thus sayeth: I hear thou raisest thy thoughts high, but thy means are not equal to thy ambition. Listen then to my words, and learn how thou mayest at once serve thyself and preserve me. King Cambyses is bent on my destruction — of this I have warning from a sure hand. Come thou, therefore, and fetch me away, me and all my wealth — share my wealth with me, and then, so far as money can aid, thou mayest make thyself master of the whole of Greece. But if thou doubtest of my wealth, send the trustiest of thy followers, and I will show my treasures to him."

123. Polycrates, when he heard this message, was full of joy, and straightway approved the terms; but, as money was what he chiefly desired, before stirring in the business he sent his

<hr />

1 Vide infra, v. 121.

secretary, Mæandrius, son of Mæandrius,[1] a Samian, to look into the matter. This was the man who, not very long afterwards, made an offering at the temple of Hera of all the furniture which had adorned the male apartments in the palace of Polycrates, an offering well worth seeing. Orœtes learning that one was coming to view his treasures, contrived as follows:— he filled eight great chests almost brimful of stones, and then covering over the stones with gold, corded the chests, and so held them in readiness.[2] When Mæandrius arrived, he was shown this as Orœtes' treasure, and having seen it returned to Samos.

124. On hearing his account, Polycrates, notwithstanding many warnings given him by the soothsayers, and much dissuasion of his friends, made ready to go in person. Even the dream which visited his daughter failed to check him. She had dreamed that she saw her father hanging high in air, washed by Jove, and anointed by the sun. Having therefore thus dreamed, she used every effort to prevent her father from going; even as he went on board his penteconter crying after him with words of evil omen. Then Polycrates threatened her that, if he returned in safety, he would keep her unmarried many years. She answered, "Oh! that he might perform his threat; far better for her to remain long unmarried than to be bereft of her father!"

125. Polycrates, however, making light of all the counsel offered him, set sail and went to Orœtes. Many friends accompanied him; among the rest, Democêdes, the son of Calliphon, a native of Crotona, who was a physician, and the best skilled in his art of all men then living. Polycrates, on his arrival at Magnesia, perished miserably, in a way unworthy of his rank and of his lofty schemes. For, if we except the Syracusans,[3] there has never been one of the Greek tyrants who was to be compared with Polycrates for magnificence. Orœtes, however, slew him in a mode which is not fit to be described, and then hung his dead body upon a cross. His Samian followers Orœtes let go free, bidding them thank him that they were allowed their liberty; the rest, who were in part slaves, in part free foreigners, he alike treated as his slaves by conquest. Then

1 This is the only instance in Herodotus of a Greek bearing the name of his father.

2 Compare the similar artifice by which Hannibal [when in Crete] deceived the Gortynians. [Cf. Nepos, *Life of Hannibal*, chap. ix. — E. H. B.]

3 Gelo, Hiero, and Thrasybulus, three brothers, who successively ruled over Syracuse from B.C. 485 to B.C. 466.

was the dream of the daughter of Polycrates fulfilled; for Polycrates, as he hung upon the cross, and rain fell on him, was washed by Zeus; and he was anointed by the sun, when his own moisture overspread his body. And so the vast good fortune of Polycrates came at last to the end which Amasis the Egyptian king had prophesied in days gone by.

126. It was not long before retribution for the murder of Polycrates overtook Orœtes. After the death of Cambyses, and during all the time that the Magus sat upon the throne, Orœtes remained in Sardis, and brought no help to the Persians, whom the Medes had robbed of the sovereignty. On the contrary, amid the troubles of this season, he slew Mitrobates, the satrap of Dascyleium, who had cast the reproach upon him in the matter of Polycrates; and he slew also Mitrobates' son, Cranaspes, – both men of high repute among the Persians. He was likewise guilty of many other acts of insolence; among the rest, of the following:– There was a courier sent to him by Darius whose message was not to his mind – Orœtes had him waylaid and murdered on his road back to the king; the man and his horse both disappeared, and no traces were left of either.

127. Darius therefore was no sooner settled upon the throne than he longed to take vengeance upon Orœtes for all his misdoings, and especially for the murder of Mitrobates and his son. To send an armed force openly against him, however, he did not think advisable, as the whole kingdom was still unsettled, and he too was but lately come to the throne, while Orœtes, as he understood, had a great power. In truth a thousand Persians attended on him as a body-guard, and he held the satrapies of Phrygia, Lydia, and Ionia. Darius therefore proceeded by artifice. He called together a meeting of all the chief of the Persians, and thus addressed them:– "Who among you, O Persians, will undertake to accomplish me a matter by skill without force or tumult? Force is misplaced where the work wants skilful management. Who, then, will undertake to bring me Orœtes alive, or else to kill him? He never did the Persians any good in his life, and he has wrought us abundant injury. Two of our number, Mitrobates and his son, he has slain; and when messengers go to recall him, even though they have their mandate from me, with an insolence which is not to be endured, he puts them to death.[1] We must

---

[1] Turkish pashas and Persian governors have often had recourse to similar stratagems.

kill this man, therefore, before he does the Persians any greater hurt."

128. Thus spoke Darius; and straightway thirty of those present came forward and offered themselves for the work. As they strove together, Darius interfered, and bade them have recourse to the lot. Accordingly lots were cast, and the task fell to Bagæus, son of Artontes. Then Bagæus caused many letters to be written on divers matters, and sealed them all with the king's signet; after which he took the letters with him, and departed for Sardis. On his arrival he was shown into the presence of Orœtes, when he uncovered the letters one by one, and giving them to the king's secretary – every satrap has with him a king's secretary – commanded him to read their contents. Herein his design was to try the fidelity of the body-guard, and to see if they would be likely to fall away from Orœtes. When therefore he saw that they showed the letters all due respect, and even more highly reverenced their contents, he gave the secretary a paper in which was written, "Persians, king Darius forbids you to guard Orœtes." The soldiers at these words laid aside their spears. So Bagæus, finding that they obeyed this mandate, took courage, and gave into the secretary's hands the last letter, wherein it was written, "King Darius commands the Persians who are in Sardis to kill Orœtes." Then the guards drew their swords and slew him upon the spot. Thus did retribution for the murder of Polycrates the Samian overtake Orœtes the Persian.

129. Soon after the treasures of Orœtes had been conveyed to Susa[1] it happened that king Darius, as he leaped from his horse during the chase, sprained his foot. The sprain was one of no common severity, for the ankle-bone was forced quite out of the socket. Now Darius already had at his court certain Egyptians whom he reckoned the best-skilled physicians in all the world;[2] to their aid, therefore, he had recourse; but they twisted the foot so clumsily, and used such violence, that they only made the mischief greater. For seven days and seven nights the king lay without sleep, so grievous was the pain he suffered. On the eighth day of his indisposition, one who had heard before leaving Sardis of the skill of Democêdes the Crotoniat, told Darius,

1 In the East the disgrace of a governor, or other great man, has always involved the forfeiture of his property to the crown.

2 On the celebrity of the Egyptians as physicians, see Book ii. ch. 84.

who commanded that he should be brought with all speed into his presence. When, therefore, they had found him among the slaves of Orœtes, quite uncared for by any one, they brought him just as he was, clanking his fetters, and all clothed in rags, before the king.

130. As soon as he was entered into the presence, Darius asked him if he knew medicine – to which he answered "No," for he feared that if he made himself known he would lose all chance of ever again beholding Greece. Darius, however, perceiving that he dealt deceitfully, and really understood the art, bade those who had brought him to the presence go fetch the scourges and the pricking-irons.[1] Upon this Democêdes made confession, but at the same time said, that he had no thorough knowledge of medicine – he had but lived some time with a physician, and in this way had gained a slight smattering of the art. However, Darius put himself under his care, and Democêdes, by using the remedies customary among the Greeks, and exchanging the violent treatment of the Egyptians for milder means, first enabled him to get some sleep, and then in a very little time restored him altogether, after he had quite lost the hope of ever having the use of his foot. Hereupon the king presented Democêdes with two sets of fetters wrought in gold; so Democêdes asked if he meant to double his sufferings because he had brought him back to health? Darius was pleased at the speech, and bade the eunuchs take Democêdes to see his wives, which they did accordingly, telling them all that this was the man who had saved the king's life. Then each of the wives dipped with a saucer into a chest of gold, and gave so bountifully to Democêdes, that a slave named Sciton, who followed him, and picked up the staters[2] which fell from the saucers, gathered together a great heap of gold.

131. This Democêdes left his country and became attached to Polycrates in the following way:– His father, who dwelt at Crotona, was a man of a savage temper, and treated him cruelly. When, therefore, he could no longer bear such constant ill-usage,

---

1 In ancient, as in modern times, putting out the eyes has been a Persian punishment. [See the story of Zedekiah, *Jeremiah*, xxxix. 8. – E. H. B.]

2 By staters we must here understand Darics, the earliest gold coin of Persia. Herodotus in another place calls them Daric staters (vii. 28). These were of very nearly the same value as the staters principally current in Greece [*i.e.* rather over a guinea. – E. H. B.].

Democêdes left his home, and sailed away to Egina. There he set up in business, and succeeded the first year in surpassing all the best-skilled physicians of the place, notwithstanding that he was without instruments, and had with him none of the appliances needful for the practice of his art. In the second year the state of Egina hired his services at the price of a talent; in the third the Athenians engaged him at a hundred minæ; and in the fourth Polycrates at two talents.[1] So he went to Samos, and there took up his abode. It was in no small measure from his success that the Crotoniats came to be reckoned such good physicians; for about this period the physicians of Crotona had the name of being the best, and those of Cyrênê the second best, in all Greece. The Argives, about the same time, were thought to be the first musicians in Greece.

132. After Democêdes had cured Darius at Susa, he dwelt there in a large house, and feasted daily at the king's table, nor did he lack anything that his heart desired, excepting liberty to return to his country. By interceding for them with Darius, he saved the lives of the Egyptian physicians who had had the care of the king before he came, when they were about to be impaled because they had been surpassed by a Greek; and further, he succeeded in rescuing an Elean soothsayer,[2] who had followed the fortunes of Polycrates, and was lying in utter neglect among his slaves. In short there was no one who stood so high as Democêdes in the favour of the king.

133. Moreover, within a little while it happened that Atossa, the daughter of Cyrus, who was married to Darius, had a boil form upon her breast, which, after it burst, began to spread and increase. Now so long as the sore was of no great size, she hid it through shame and made no mention of it to any one; but when it became worse, she sent at last for Democêdes, and showed it to him. Democêdes said that he would make her well, but she must first promise him with an oath that if he cured her she would grant him whatever request he might prefer; assuring her at the same time that it should be nothing which she could blush to hear.

---

1 Herodotus, where he mentions no standard, must be regarded as intending the Attic, which was in general use throughout Greece in his own day. The salary of Democêdes will therefore be:— 1st year, 60 *minæ*, or £243 15s.; 2nd year, 100 *minæ*, or £406 5s.; 3rd year, 120 *minæ*, or £487 10s.

2 Elis about this time appears to have furnished soothsayers to all Greece.

134. On these terms Democêdes applied his art, and soon cured the abscess; and Atossa, when she had heard his request, spake thus one night to Darius:–

"It seemeth to me strange, my lord, that, with the mighty power which is thine, thou sittest idle, and neither makest any conquest, nor advancest the power of the Persians. Methinks that one who is so young, and so richly endowed with wealth, should perform some noble achievement to prove to the Persians that it is a man who governs them. Another reason, too, should urge thee to attempt some enterprise. Not only does it befit thee to show the Persians that a man rules them, but for thy own peace thou shouldest waste their strength in wars lest idleness breed revolt against thy authority. Now, too, whilst thou art still young, thou mayest well accomplish some exploit; for as the body grows in strength the mind too ripens, and as the body ages, the mind's powers decay, till at last it becomes dulled to everything."

So spake Atossa, as Democêdes had instructed her. Darius answered:– "Dear lady, thou hast uttered the very thoughts that occupy my brain. I am minded to construct a bridge which shall join our continent with the other, and so carry war into Scythia. Yet a brief space and all will be accomplished as thou desirest."

But Atossa rejoined:– "Look now, this war with Scythia were best reserved awhile – for the Scythians may be conquered at any time. Prithee, lead me thy host first into Greece. I long to be served by some of those Lacedæmonian maids of whom I have heard so much. I want also Argive, and Athenian, and Corinthian women. There is now at the court a man who can tell thee better than any one else in the whole world whatever thou wouldst know concerning Greece, and who might serve thee right well as guide; I mean him who performed the cure on thy foot."

"Dear lady," Darius answered, "since it is thy wish that we try first the valour of the Greeks, it were best, methinks, before marching against them, to send some Persians to spy out the land; they may go in company with the man thou mentionest, and when they have seen and learnt all, they can bring us back a full report. Then, having a more perfect knowledge of them, I will begin the war."

135. Darius, having so spoke, put no long distance between the word and the deed, but as soon as day broke he summoned

to his presence fifteen Persians of note, and bade them take Democêdes for their guide, and explore the sea-coasts of Greece. Above all, they were to be sure to bring Democêdes back with them, and not suffer him to run away and escape. After he had given these orders, Darius sent for Democêdes, and besought him to serve as guide to the Persians, and when he had shown them the whole of Greece to come back to Persia. He should take, he said, all the valuables he possessed as presents to his father and his brothers, and he should receive on his return a far more abundant store. Moreover, the king added, he would give him, as his contribution towards the presents, a merchant-ship laden with all manner of precious things, which should accompany him on his voyage. Now I do not believe that Darius, when he made these promises, had any guile in his heart: Democêdes, however, who suspected that the king spoke to try him, took care not to snatch at the offers with any haste; but said, "he would leave his own goods behind to enjoy upon his return – the merchant-ship which the king proposed to grant him to carry gifts to his brothers, that he would accept at the king's hands." So when Darius had laid his orders upon Democêdes, he sent him and the Persians away to the coast.

136. The men went down to Phœnicia, to Sidon, the Phœnician town, where straightway they fitted out two triremes and a trading-vessel,[1] which they loaded with all manner of precious merchandise; and, everything being now ready, they set sail for Greece. When they had made the land, they kept along the shore and examined it, taking notes of all that they saw; and in this way they explored the greater portion of the country, and all the most famous regions, until at last they reached Tarentum in Italy. There Aristophilides, king of the Tarentines, out of kindness to Democêdes, took the rudders off the Median ships, and detained their crews as spies. Meanwhile Democêdes escaped to Crotona, his native city,[2] whereupon Aristophilides released the Persians from prison, and gave their rudders back to them.

137. The Persians now quitted Tarentum, and sailed to Crotona in pursuit of Democêdes; they found him in the market-place, where they straightway laid violent hands on him. Some

1 Literally, "a *round*-built vessel." It may be remarked that the Greek writers use γαῦλος specially, if not solely, for a Phœnician merchant-ship.
2 Crotona was distant about 150 miles along shore from Tarentum (*Taranto*).

of the Crotoniats, who greatly feared the power of the Persians, were willing to give him up; but others resisted, held Democêdes fast, and even struck the Persians with their walking-sticks. They, on their part, kept crying out, "Men of Crotona, beware what you do. It is the king's runaway slave that you are rescuing. Think you Darius will tamely submit to such an insult? Think you, that if you carry off the man from us, it will hereafter go well with you? Will you not rather be the first persons on whom we shall make war? Will not your city be the first we shall seek to lead away captive?" Thus they spake, but the Crotoniats did not heed them; they rescued Democêdes, and seized also the trading-ship which the Persians had brought with them from Phœnicia. Thus robbed, and bereft of their guide, the Persians gave up all hope of exploring the rest of Greece, and set sail for Asia. As they were departing, Democêdes sent to them and begged they would inform Darius that the daughter of Milo was affianced to him as his bride. For the name of Milo the wrestler was in high repute with the king.[1] My belief is, that Democêdes hastened his marriage by the payment of a large sum of money for the purpose of showing Darius that he was a man of mark in his own country.

138. The Persians weighed anchor and left Crotona, but, being wrecked on the coast of Iapygia,[2] were made slaves by the inhabitants. From this condition they were rescued by Gillus, a banished Tarentine, who ransomed them at his own cost, and took them back to Darius. Darius offered to repay this service by granting Gillus whatever boon he chose to ask; whereupon Gillus told the king of his misfortune, and begged to be restored to his country. Fearing, however, that he might bring trouble on Greece if a vast armament were sent to Italy on his account, he added that it would content him if the Cnidians undertook to obtain his recall. Now the Cnidians were close friends of the Tarentines, which made him think there was no likelier means of procuring his return. Darius promised and performed his part; for he sent a messenger to Cnidus, and commanded the Cnidians to restore Gillus. The Cnidians did as he wished, but found

1 Milo is said to have carried off the prize for wrestling, six times at the Olympic, and seven times at the Pythian, games. Grote remarks with justice that "gigantic muscular force" would be appreciated in Persia much more than intellectual ability.

2 The Iapygian promontory (*Capo di Leuca*) was always difficult to double.

themselves unable to persuade the Tarentines, and were too weak to attempt force. Such then was the course which this matter took. These were the first Persians who ever came from Asia to Greece;[1] and they were sent to spy out the land for the reason which I have before mentioned.

139. After this, king Darius besieged and took Samos, which was the first city, Greek or Barbarian, that he conquered. The cause of his making war upon Samos was the following:– At the time when Cambyses, son of Cyrus, marched against Egypt, vast numbers of Greeks flocked thither; some, as might have been looked for, to push their trade; others, to serve in his army; others again, merely to see the land: among these last was Syloson, son of Æaces, and brother of Polycrates, at that time an exile from Samos.[2] This Syloson, during his stay in Egypt, met with a singular piece of good fortune. He happened one day to put on a scarlet cloak, and thus attired to go into the market-place at Memphis, when Darius, who was one of Cambyses' body-guard, and not at that time a man of any account,[3] saw him, and taking a strong liking to the dress, went up and offered to purchase it. Syloson perceived how anxious he was, and by a lucky inspiration answered: "There is no price at which I would sell my cloak; but I will give it thee for nothing, if it must needs be thine." Darius thanked him, and accepted the garment.

140. Poor Syloson felt at the time that he had fooled away his cloak in a very simple manner; but afterwards, when in the course of years Cambyses died, and the seven Persians rose in revolt against the Magus, and Darius was the man chosen out of the seven to have the kingdom, Syloson learnt that the person to whom the crown had come was the very man who had coveted his cloak in Egypt, and to whom he had freely given it. So he made his way to Susa, and seating himself at the portal of the royal palace, gave out that he was a benefactor of the king.[4]

---

1 Compare the conclusion of ch. 56. In the mind of Herodotus this voyage is of the greatest importance. It is the first step towards the invasion of Greece, and so a chief link in the chain of his History. Whether Darius attached much importance to it is a different matter.

2 Vide supra, ch. 39.

3 This could not be true, yet it is a necessary feature in the story.

4 The king's benefactors were a body of persons whose names were formally enregistered in the royal archives (vide infra, viii. 85). Syloson makes a claim to be put on this list.

Then the doorkeeper went and told Darius. Amazed at what he heard, the king said thus within himself:– "What Greek can have been my benefactor, or to which of them do I owe anything, so lately as I have got the kingdom? Scarcely a man of them all has been here, not more than one or two certainly, since I came to the throne. Nor do I remember that I am in the debt of any Greek. However, bring him in, and let me hear what he means by his boast." So the doorkeeper ushered Syloson into the presence, and the interpreters asked him who he was, and what he had done that he should call himself a benefactor of the king. Then Syloson told the whole story of the cloak, and said that it was he who had made Darius the present. Hereupon Darius exclaimed, "Oh! thou most generous of men, art thou indeed he who, when I had no power at all, gavest me something, albeit little? Truly the favour is as great as a very grand present would be nowadays. I will therefore give thee in return gold and silver without stint, that thou mayest never repent of having rendered a service to Darius, son of Hystaspes." "Give me not, O king," replied Syloson, "either silver or gold, but recover me Samos, my native land, and let that be thy gift to me. It belongs now to a slave of ours, who, when Orœtes put my brother Polycrates to death, became its master. Give me Samos, I beg; but give it unharmed, with no bloodshed – no leading into captivity."

141. When he heard this, Darius sent off an army, under Otanes, one of the seven, with orders to accomplish all that Syloson had desired. And Otanes went down to the coast and made ready to cross over.

142. The government of Samos was held at this time by Mæandrius, son of Mæandrius,[1] whom Polycrates had appointed as his deputy. This person conceived the wish to act like the justest of men, but it was not allowed him to do so. On receiving tidings of the death of Polycrates, he forthwith raised an altar to Jove the Protector of Freedom, and assigned it the piece of ground which may still be seen in the suburb. This done, he assembled all the citizens, and spoke to them as follows:–

"Ye know, friends, that the sceptre of Polycrates, and all his power, has passed into my hands, and if I choose I may rule over you. But what I condemn in another I will, if I may, avoid myself. I never approved the ambition of Polycrates to lord it

1 Vide supra, ch. 123.

over men as good as himself, nor looked with favour on any of
those who have done the like. Now therefore, since he has
fulfilled his destiny, I lay down my office, and proclaim equal
rights. All that I claim in return is six talents from the treasures
of Polycrates, and the priesthood of Jove the Protector of Freedom, for myself and my descendants for ever. Allow me this, as
the man by whom his temple has been built, and by whom ye
yourselves are now restored to liberty." As soon as Mæandrius
had ended, one of the Samians rose up and said, "As if thou
wert fit to rule us, base-born[1] and rascal as thou art! Think rather
of accounting for the monies which thou hast fingered."

143. The man who thus spoke was a certain Telesarchus, one
of the leading citizens. Mæandrius, therefore, feeling sure that if
he laid down the sovereign power some one else would become
tyrant in his room, gave up the thought of relinquishing it. Withdrawing to the citadel, he sent for the chief men one by one,
under pretence of showing them his accounts, and as fast as they
came arrested them and put them in irons. So these men were
bound; and Mæandrius within a short time fell sick: whereupon
Lycarêtus,[2] one of his brothers, thinking that he was going to
die, and wishing to make his own accession to the throne the
easier, slew all the prisoners. It seemed that the Samians did not
choose to be a free people.

144. When the Persians whose business it was to restore
Syloson reached Samos, not a man was found to lift up his hand
against them. Mæandrius and his partisans expressed themselves
willing to quit the island upon certain terms, and these terms
were agreed to by Otanes. After the treaty was made, the most
distinguished of the Persians had their thrones[3] brought, and
seated themselves over against the citadel.

145. Now the king Mæandrius had a lightheaded brother –
Charilaüs by name – whom for some offence or other he had
shut up in prison: this man heard what was going on, and peering
through his bars, saw the Persians sitting peacefully upon their

1 Mæandrius had been the secretary (γραμματιστὴς) of Polycrates (supra,
ch. 123), which would indicate a humble origin.

2 For the ultimate fate of Lycarêtus, see below, Book v. ch. 27.

3 For a representation of the Persian throne, see note on Book vii. ch. 15.
Darius is mentioned as sitting upon a throne at the siege of Babylon (infra,
ch. 155), and Xerxes at Thermopylæ (vii. 211, ad fin.), and Salamis (viii. 90). So
Sennacherib is represented in the Assyrian sculptures.

seats, whereupon he exclaimed aloud, and said he must speak with Mæandrius. When this was reported to him, Mæandrius gave orders that Charilaüs should be released from prison and brought into his presence. No sooner did he arrive than he began reviling and abusing his brother, and strove to persuade him to attack the Persians. "Thou meanest-spirited of men," he said, "thou canst keep me, thy brother, chained in a dungeon, notwithstanding that I have done nothing worthy of bonds; but when the Persians come and drive thee forth a houseless wanderer from thy native land, thou lookest on, and hast not the heart to seek revenge, though they might so easily be subdued. If thou, however, art afraid, lend me thy soldiers, and I will make them pay dearly for their coming here. I engage too to send thee first safe out of the island."

146. So spake Charilaüs, and Mæandrius gave consent; not (I believe) that he was so void of sense as to imagine that his own forces could overcome those of the king, but because he was jealous of Syloson, and did not wish him to get so quietly an unharmed city. He desired therefore to rouse the anger of the Persians against Samos, that so he might deliver it up to Syloson with its power at the lowest possible ebb; for he knew well that if the Persians met with a disaster they would be furious against the Samians, while he himself felt secure of a retreat at any time that he liked, since he had a secret passage under ground[1] leading from the citadel to the sea. Mæandrius accordingly took ship and sailed away from Samos; and Charilaüs, having armed all the mercenaries, threw open the gates, and fell upon the Persians, who looked for nothing less, since they supposed that the whole matter had been arranged by treaty. At the first onslaught therefore all the Persians of most note, men who were in the habit of using litters, were slain by the mercenaries; the rest of the army, however, came to the rescue, defeated the mercenaries, and drove them back into the citadel.

147. Then Otanes, the general, when he saw the great calamity which had befallen the Persians, made up his mind to forget the orders which Darius had given him, "not to kill or enslave a single Samian, but to deliver up the island unharmed to Syloson," and gave the word to his army that they should slay

---

1 That the art of tunnelling was known at Samos is evident from what is said above (ch. 60), and from the remains which have been found in the island.

the Samians, both men and boys, wherever they could find them. Upon this some of his troops laid siege to the citadel, while others began the massacre, killing all they met, some outside, some inside the temples.

148. Mæandrius fled from Samos to Lacedæmon, and conveyed thither all the riches which he had brought away from the island, after which he acted as follows. Having placed upon his board all the gold and silver vessels that he had, and bade his servants employ themselves in cleaning them, he himself went and entered into conversation with Cleomenes, son of Anaxandridas, king of Sparta, and as they talked brought him along to his house. There Cleomenes, seeing the plate, was filled with wonder and astonishment; whereon the other begged that he would carry home with him any of the vessels that he liked. Mæandrius said this two or three times; but Cleomenes here displayed surpassing honesty.[1] He refused the gift, and thinking that if Mæandrius made the same offers to others he would get the aid he sought, the Spartan king went straight to the ephors and told them "it would be best for Sparta that the Samian stranger should be sent away from the Peloponnese; for otherwise he might perchance persuade himself or some other Spartan to be base." The ephors took his advice, and let Mæandrius know by a herald that he must leave the city.

149. Meanwhile the Persians netted[2] Samos, and delivered it up to Syloson, stripped of all its men. After some time, however, this same general Otanes was induced to repeople it by a dream which he had, and a loathsome disease that seized on him.

150. After the armament of Otanes had set sail for Samos, the Babylonians revolted,[3] having made every preparation for defence. During all the time that the Magus was king, and while the seven were conspiring, they had profited by the troubles, and had made themselves ready against a siege. And it happened

1 It was rarely that the Spartan kings, or indeed their other leaders, could resist a bribe.

2 For the description of this process see below, Book vi. ch. 31. Samos does not appear to have suffered very greatly by these transactions, since in the Ionian revolt, not twenty years afterwards, she was able to furnish sixty ships (vi. 8). The severities exercised by the Persians are probably exaggerated.

3 It has been already mentioned that Babylon revolted *twice* from Darius, once in the first, and a second time in the fourth year of his reign. It cannot be determined which of these two revolts Herodotus intended to describe.

somehow or other that no one perceived what they were doing. At last when the time came for rebelling openly, they did as follows:— having first set apart their mothers, each man chose besides out of his whole household one woman, whomsoever he pleased; these alone were allowed to live, while all the rest were brought to one place and strangled. The women chosen were kept to make bread for the men;[1] while the others were strangled that they might not consume the stores.

151. When tidings reached Darius of what had happened, he drew together all his power, and began the war by marching straight upon Babylon, and laying siege to the place. The Babylonians, however, cared not a whit for his siege.[2] Mounting upon the battlements that crowned their walls, they insulted and jeered at Darius and his mighty host. One even shouted to them and said, "Why sit ye there, Persians? why do ye not go back to your homes? Till mules foal ye will not take our city." This was said by a Babylonian who thought that a mule would never foal.

152. Now when a year and seven months had passed, Darius and his army were quite wearied out, finding that they could not anyhow take the city. All stratagems and all arts had been used, and yet the king could not prevail — not even when he tried the means by which Cyrus made himself master of the place. The Babylonians were ever upon the watch, and he found no way of conquering them.

153. At last, in the twentieth month, a marvellous thing happened to Zopyrus, son of the Megabyzus who was among the seven men that overthrew the Magus. One of his sumpter-mules gave birth to a foal. Zopyrus, when they told him, not thinking that it could be true, went and saw the colt with his own eyes; after which he commanded his servants to tell no one what had come to pass, while he himself pondered the matter. Calling to mind then the words of the Babylonian at the beginning of the siege, "Till mules foal ye shall not take our city" — he thought, as he reflected on this speech, that Babylon might now be taken. For it seemed to him that there was a divine providence in the man having used the phrase, and then his mule having foaled.

---

1 The "bread-maker" had not merely to mix and bake the bread, but to grind the flour. (Cf. Exodus xi. 5; Matt. xxiv. 41.)

2 Compare their confidence when besieged by Cyrus (supra, i. 190).

154. As soon therefore as he felt within himself that Babylon was fated to be taken, he went to Darius and asked him if he set a very high value on its conquest. When he found that Darius did indeed value it highly, he considered further with himself how he might make the deed his own, and be the man to take Babylon. Noble exploits in Persia are ever highly honoured and bring their authors to greatness. He therefore reviewed all ways of bringing the city under, but found none by which he could hope to prevail, unless he maimed himself and then went over to the enemy. To do this seeming to him a light matter, he mutilated himself in a way that was utterly without remedy. For he cut off his own nose and ears, and then, clipping his hair close and flogging himself with a scourge, he came in this plight before Darius.

155. Wrath stirred within the king at the sight of a man of his lofty rank in such a condition; leaping down from his throne, he exclaimed aloud, and asked Zopyrus who it was that had disfigured him, and what he had done to be so treated. Zopyrus answered, "There is not a man in the world, but thou, O king, that could reduce me to such a plight – no stranger's hands have wrought this work on me, but my own only. I maimed myself because I could not endure that the Assyrians should laugh at the Persians." "Wretched man," said Darius, "thou coverest the foulest deed with the fairest possible name, when thou sayest thy maiming is to help our siege forward. How will thy disfigurement, thou simpleton, induce the enemy to yield one day the sooner? Surely thou hadst gone out of thy mind when thou didst so misuse thyself." "Had I told thee," rejoined the other, "what I was bent on doing, thou wouldest not have suffered it; as it is, I kept my own counsel, and so accomplished my plans. Now, therefore, if there be no failure on thy part, we shall take Babylon. I will desert to the enemy as I am, and when I get into their city I will tell them that it is by thee I have been thus treated. I think they will believe my words, and entrust me with a command of troops. Thou, on thy part, must wait till the tenth day after I am entered within the town, and then place near to the gates of Semiramis a detachment of thy army, troops for whose loss thou wilt care little, a thousand men. Wait, after that, seven days, and post me another detachment, two thousand strong, at the Nineveh gates; then let twenty days pass, and at the end of that time station near the Chaldæan gates a body of four

thousand. Let neither these nor the former troops be armed with any weapons but their swords – those thou mayest leave them. After the twenty days are over, bid thy whole army attack the city on every side, and put me two bodies of Persians, one at the Belian, the other at the Cissian gates; for I expect that, on account of my successes, the Babylonians will entrust everything, even the keys of their gates,[1] to me. Then it will be for me and my Persians to do the rest."[2]

156. Having left these instructions, Zopyrus fled towards the gates of the town, often looking back, to give himself the air of a deserter. The men upon the towers, whose business it was to keep a look-out, observing him, hastened down, and setting one of the gates slightly ajar, questioned him who he was, and on what errand he had come. He replied that he was Zopyrus, and had deserted to them from the Persians. Then the doorkeepers, when they heard this, carried him at once before the Magistrates. Introduced into the assembly, he began to bewail his misfortunes, telling them that Darius had maltreated him in the way they could see, only because he had given advice that the siege should be raised, since there seemed no hope of taking the city. "And now," he went on to say, "my coming to you, Babylonians, will prove the greatest gain that you could possibly receive, while to Darius and the Persians it will be the severest loss. Verily he by whom I have been so mutilated shall not escape unpunished. And truly all the paths of his counsels are known to me." Thus did Zopyrus speak.

157. The Babylonians, seeing a Persian of such exalted rank in so grievous a plight, his nose and ears cut off, his body red with marks of scourging and with blood, had no suspicion but that he spoke the truth, and was really come to be their friend and helper. They were ready, therefore, to grant him anything that he asked; and on his suing for a command, they entrusted to him a body of troops, with the help of which he proceeded to do as he had arranged with Darius. On the tenth day after his flight he led out his detachment, and surrounding the thousand

1 Properly "bolt-drawers," which were very like those now used in the East – a straight piece of wood, with upright pins, corresponding with those that fall down into the bolt, and which are pushed up by this key so as to enable the bolt to be drawn back.

2 The stratagem of Zopyrus has small claims to be considered an historic fact.

men, whom Darius according to agreement had sent first, he fell upon them and slew them all. Then the Babylonians, seeing that his deeds were as brave as his words, were beyond measure pleased, and set no bounds to their trust. He waited, however, and when the next period agreed on had elapsed, again with a band of picked men he sallied forth, and slaughtered the two thousand. After this second exploit, his praise was in all mouths. Once more, however, he waited till the interval appointed had gone by, and then leading the troops to the place where the four thousand were, he put them also to the sword. This last victory gave the finishing stroke to his power, and made him all in all with the Babylonians: accordingly they committed to him the command of their whole army, and put the keys of their city into his hands.

158. Darius now, still keeping to the plan agreed upon, attacked the walls on every side, whereupon Zopyrus played out the remainder of his stratagem. While the Babylonians, crowding to the walls, did their best to resist the Persian assault, he threw open the Cissian and the Belian gates, and admitted the enemy. Such of the Babylonians as witnessed the treachery, took refuge in the temple of Bel;[1] the rest, who did not see it, kept at their posts, till at last they too learnt that they were betrayed.

159. Thus was Babylon taken for the second[2] time. Darius having become master of the place, destroyed the wall,[3] and tore down all the gates; for Cyrus had done neither the one nor the other when he took Babylon. He then chose out near three thousand of the leading citizens, and caused them to be crucified, while he allowed the remainder still to inhabit the city. Further, wishing to prevent the race of the Babylonians from becoming extinct, he provided wives for them in the room of those whom

1 [Bel was the name of the sun-god worshipped by the Babylonians. The city-god of Babylon was Marduk; but, as that city became the capital of the country, he became identified with Bel (cf. *Baal*), the "lord." Cf. Sayce, *The Religions of Ancient Egypt and Babylonia*, p. 267. – E. H. B.]

2 [The first capture, by Cyrus, is described in Book i. chs. 190, 191. – E. H. B.]

3 It is probable that Darius contented himself with breaking breaches in the great wall, instead of undertaking the enormous and useless labour of levelling the immense mounds which begirt Babylon. The walls must have been tolerably complete when Babylon stood a siege against the forces of Xerxes.

(as I explained before) they strangled, to save their stores. These he levied from the nations bordering on Babylonia, who were each required to send so large a number to Babylon, that in all there were collected no fewer than fifty thousand. It is from these women that the Babylonians of our times are sprung.

160. As for Zopyrus, he was considered by Darius to have surpassed, in the greatness of his achievements, all other Persians, whether of former or of later times, except only Cyrus — with whom no Persian ever yet thought himself worthy to compare. Darius, as the story goes, would often say that "he had rather Zopyrus were unmaimed, than be master of twenty more Babylons." And he honoured Zopyrus greatly; year by year he presented him with all the gifts which are held in most esteem among the Persians;[1] he gave him likewise the government of Babylon for his life, free from tribute; and he also granted him many other favours. Megabyzus, who held the command in Egypt against the Athenians and their allies,[2] was a son of this Zopyrus. And Zopyrus, who fled from Persia to Athens,[3] was a son of this Megabyzus.

Even in the time of Herodotus, so much was left that he could speak of the wall as still *encircling* the city (i. 178).

1 Ctesias mentioned as the chief of these presents a golden hand-mill, weighing six talents, and worth somewhat more than £3000. This, according to him, was the most honourable gift that a Persian subject could receive.

2 Megabyzus married Amytis, daughter of Xerxes, was one of the six superior generals of the Persian army in the Greek campaign, drove the Athenians out of Egypt, and put down the Egyptian revolt; revolted himself against Artaxerxes for not observing the terms granted to Inarus, was reconciled with him, and died in Persia at an advanced age.

3 This is probably the latest event recorded by Herodotus. It is mentioned by Ctesias almost immediately before the death of Artaxerxes, and so belongs most likely to the year B.C. 426 or 425.

ADDED NOTE BY THE EDITOR

With the capture of Babylon by Cyrus, the history of the Babylonians as an independent nation came to an end. Henceforth it became a province subject to the various powers which succeeded one another in the hegemony of western Asia. Under Cambyses, and still more under Darius Hystaspis, there were many manifestations of discontent, which broke out into open revolt soon after the accession of the latter king. A similar revolt took place in Xerxes' reign; but both these insurrectionary movements were stamped out. The people of Babylonia were, as a whole, content to serve their foreign masters. The country remained subject to Persian domination until the conquests of Alexander the Great brought it under Greek control; this subsequently giving way to Parthian supremacy. The impoverishment of the country, in these later days, led to the gradual extinction of the great priestly tradition which had so long maintained itself. The knowledge of the ancient writings and speech was gradually lost, and not recovered till the epoch-marking discoveries of Sir Henry Rawlinson and other scholars in the middle of the nineteenth century. But now every year sees fresh light thrown upon the history and religion of a once mighty, and long-forgotten, empire. And the end is not yet.

THE FOURTH BOOK,
ENTITLED MELPOMENE

1. AFTER the taking of Babylon, an expedition was led by Darius into Scythia. Asia abounding in men, and vast sums flowing into the treasury, the desire seized him to exact vengeance from the Scyths, who had once in days gone by invaded Media, defeated those who met them in the field, and so begun the quarrel. During the space of eight-and-twenty years, as I have before mentioned,[1] the Scyths continued lords of the whole of Upper Asia. They entered Asia in pursuit of the Cimmerians, and overthrew the empire of the Medes, who till they came possessed the sovereignty. On their return to their homes after the long absence of twenty-eight years, a task awaited them little less troublesome than their struggle with the Medes. They found an army of no small size prepared to oppose their entrance. For the Scythian women, when they saw that time went on, and their husbands did not come back, had intermarried with their slaves.

2. Now the Scythians blind all their slaves, to use them in preparing their milk. The plan they follow is to thrust tubes made of bone, not unlike our musical pipes, up the vulva of the mare,[2] and then to blow into the tubes with their mouths, some milking while the others blow. They say that they do this because when the veins of the animal are full of air, the udder is forced down. The milk thus obtained is poured into deep wooden casks, about which the blind slaves are placed, and then the milk is stirred round.[3] That which rises to the top is drawn off, and considered the best part; the under portion is of less account. Such is the reason why the Scythians blind all those whom they take in war; it arises from their not being tillers of the ground, but a pastoral race.

1 Vide supra, i. 103–106.

2 Mares' milk constituted the chief food of the ancient Scythians. It is still the principal support of the Calmuck hordes which wander over the vast steppes north and west of the Caspian.

3 It is apparent from this circumstance that it was *koumiss*, and not cream, on which the Scythians lived. *Koumiss* is still prepared from mares' milk by the Calmucks.

3. When therefore the children sprung from these slaves and the Scythian women grew to manhood, and understood the circumstances of their birth, they resolved to oppose the army which was returning from Media. And, first of all, they cut off a tract of country from the rest of Scythia by digging a broad dyke[1] from the Tauric mountains to the vast lake of the Mæotis. Afterwards, when the Scythians tried to force an entrance, they marched out and engaged them. Many battles were fought, and the Scythians gained no advantage, until at last one of them thus addressed the remainder: "What are we doing, Scythians? We are fighting our slaves, diminishing our own number when we fall, and the number of those that belong to us when they fall by our hands. Take my advice – lay spear and bow aside,[2] and let each man fetch his horsewhip,[3] and go boldly up to them. So long as they see us with arms in our hands, they imagine themselves our equals in birth and bravery; but let them behold us with no other weapon but the whip, and they will feel that they are our slaves, and flee before us."

4. The Scythians followed this counsel, and the slaves were so astounded, that they forgot to fight, and immediately ran away. Such was the mode in which the Scythians, after being for a time the lords of Asia, and being forced to quit it by the Medes, returned and settled in their own country. This inroad of theirs it was that Darius was anxious to avenge, and such was the purpose for which he was now collecting an army to invade them.

5. According to the account which the Scythians themselves give, they are the youngest of all nations.[4] Their tradition is as follows. A certain Targitaüs was the first man who ever lived in their country, which before his time was a desert without inhabitants. He was a child – I do not believe the tale, but it is told nevertheless – of Jove and a daughter of the Borysthenes.

---

1 On the position of this dyke, vide infra, ch. 20.

2 The spear and the bow were the national weapons of the European Scyths, the bow on the whole being regarded as the more essential. The spear used was short, apparently not more than five feet in length.

3 The ancient Scythian whip seems to have closely resembled the *nogaik* of the modern Cossacks.

4 We must understand by the Scyths of Herodotus in this place, the single nation of European Scyths with which the Greeks of the Pontus were acquainted.

Targitaüs, thus descended, begat three sons, Leipoxais, Arpoxais, and Colaxais, who was the youngest born of the three. While they still ruled the land, there fell from the sky four implements, all of gold, – a plough, a yoke, a battle-axe, and a drinking-cup. The eldest of the brothers perceived them first, and approached to pick them up; when lo! as he came near, the gold took fire, and blazed. He therefore went his way, and the second coming forward made the attempt, but the same thing happened again. The gold rejected both the eldest and the second brother. Last of all the youngest brother approached, and immediately the flames were extinguished; so he picked up the gold, and carried it to his home. Then the two elder agreed together, and made the whole kingdom over to the youngest born.

6. From Leipoxais sprang the Scythians of the race called Auchatæ; from Arpoxais, the middle brother, those known as the Catiari and Traspians; from Colaxais, the youngest, the Royal Scythians, or Paralatæ. All together they are named Scoloti, after one of their kings: the Greeks, however, call them Scythians.

7. Such is the account which the Scythians give of their origin. They add that from the time of Targitaüs, their first king, to the invasion of their country by Darius, is a period of one thousand years, neither less nor more. The Royal Scythians guard the sacred gold with most especial care, and year by year offer great sacrifices in its honour. At this feast, if the man who has the custody of the gold should fall asleep in the open air, he is sure (the Scythians say) not to outlive the year. His pay therefore is as much land as he can ride round on horseback in a day. As the extent of Scythia is very great, Colaxais gave each of his three sons a separate kingdom, one of which was of ampler size than the other two: in this the gold was preserved. Above, to the northward of the furthest dwellers in Scythia, the country is said to be concealed from sight and made impassable by reason of the feathers which are shed abroad abundantly. The earth and air are alike full of them, and this it is which prevents the eye from obtaining any view of the region.[1]

8. Such is the account which the Scythians give of themselves, and of the country which lies above them. The Greeks who dwell about the Pontus tell a different story. According to

[1] Vide infra, ch. 31, where Herodotus explains that the so-called feathers are snow-flakes.

them, Heracles, when he was carrying off the cows of Geryon, arrived in the region which is now inhabited by the Scyths, but which was then a desert. Geryon lived outside the Pontus, in an island called by the Greeks Erytheia,[1] near Gades, which is beyond the Pillars of Heracles[2] upon the Ocean. Now some say that the Ocean begins in the east, and runs the whole way round the world; but they give no proof that this is really so. Heracles came from thence into the region now called Scythia, and, being overtaken by storm and frost, drew his lion's skin about him, and fell fast asleep. While he slept, his mares, which he had loosed from his chariot to graze, by some wonderful chance disappeared.

9. On waking, he went in quest of them, and, after wandering over the whole country, came at last to the district called "the Woodland," where he found in a cave a strange being, between a maiden and a serpent, whose form from the waist upwards was like that of a woman, while all below was like a snake. He looked at her wonderingly; but nevertheless inquired, whether she had chanced to see his strayed mares anywhere. She answered him, "Yes, and they were now in her keeping; but never would she consent to give them back, unless he took her for his mistress." So Heracles, to get his mares back, agreed; but afterwards she put him off and delayed restoring the mares, since she wished to keep him with her as long as possible. He, on the other hand, was only anxious to secure them and to get away. At last, when she gave them up, she said to him, "When thy mares strayed hither, it was I who saved them for thee: now thou hast paid their salvage; for lo! I bear in my womb three sons of thine. Tell me therefore when thy sons grow up, what must I do with them? Wouldst thou wish that I should settle them here in this land, whereof I am mistress, or shall I send them to thee?" Thus questioned, they say, Heracles answered, "When the lads have grown to manhood, do thus, and assuredly thou wilt not err. Watch them, and when thou seest one of them bend this bow as I now bend it, and gird himself with this girdle thus, choose *him* to remain in the land. Those who fail in the trial, send away. Thus wilt thou at once please thyself and obey me."

10. Hereupon he strung one of his bows — up to that time he had carried two — and showed her how to fasten the belt.

1 Cadiz.
2 By the Pillars of Heracles we must understand the Straits of Gibraltar.

Then he gave both bow and belt into her hands. Now the belt had a golden goblet attached to its clasp. So after he had given them to her, he went his way; and the woman, when her children grew to manhood, first gave them severally their names. One she called Agathyrsus, one Gelônus, and the other, who was the youngest, Scythes. Then she remembered the instructions she had received from Heracles, and, in obedience to his orders, she put her sons to the test. Two of them, Agathyrsus and Gelô-nus, proving unequal to the task enjoined, their mother sent them out of the land; Scythes, the youngest, succeeded, and so he was allowed to remain. From Scythes, the son of Heracles, were descended the after kings of Scythia; and from the circumstance of the goblet which hung from the belt, the Scythians to this day wear goblets at their girdles. This was the only thing which the mother of Scythes did for him. Such is the tale told by the Greeks who dwell around the Pontus.

11. There is also another different story, now to be related, in which I am more inclined to put faith than in any other. It is that the wandering Scythians once dwelt in Asia, and there warred with the Massagetæ, but with ill success; they therefore quitted their homes, crossed the Araxes,[1] and entered the land of Cimmeria. For the land which is now inhabited by the Scyths was formerly the country of the Cimmerians.[2] On their coming, the natives, who heard how numerous the invading army was, held a council. At this meeting opinion was divided, and both parties stiffly maintained their own view; but the counsel of the Royal tribe was the braver. For the others urged that the best thing to be done was to leave the country, and avoid a contest with so vast a host; but the Royal tribe advised remaining and fighting for the soil to the last. As neither party chose to give way, the one determined to retire without a blow and yield their lands to the invaders; but the other, remembering the good things which they had enjoyed in their homes, and picturing to themselves the evils which they had to expect if they gave them up, resolved not to flee, but rather to die and at least be buried in their fatherland. Having thus decided, they drew apart in two bodies, the one as numerous as the other, and fought together.

---

[1] It seems impossible that the Araxes can here represent any river but the Volga.

[2] Their name is still found in the modern name, Crimea.

All of the Royal tribe were slain, and the people buried them near the river Tyras, where their grave is still to be seen. Then the rest of the Cimmerians departed, and the Scythians, on their coming, took possession of a deserted land.

12. Scythia still retains traces of the Cimmerians; there are Cimmerian castles, and a Cimmerian ferry, also a tract called Cimmeria, and a Cimmerian Bosphorus. It appears likewise that the Cimmerians, when they fled into Asia to escape the Scyths, made a settlement in the peninsula where the Greek city of Sinôpé was afterwards built. The Scyths, it is plain, pursued them, and missing their road, poured into Media. For the Cimmerians kept the line which led along the sea-shore, but the Scyths in their pursuit held the Caucasus upon their right, thus proceeding inland, and falling upon Media. This account is one which is common both to Greeks and barbarians.

13. Aristeas also, son of Caÿstrobius, a native of Proconnêsus,[1] says in the course of his poem that rapt in Dionysiac fury he went as far as the Issedones. Above them dwelt the Arimaspi, men with one eye; still further, the gold-guarding Griffins;[2] and beyond these, the Hyperboreans, who extended to the sea. Except the Hyperboreans, all these nations, beginning with the Arimaspi, were continually encroaching upon their neighbours. Hence it came to pass that the Arimaspi drove the Issedonians from their country, while the Issedonians dispossessed the Scyths; and the Scyths, pressing upon the Cimmerians, who dwelt on the shores of the Southern Sea,[3] forced them to leave their land.[4] Thus even Aristeas does not agree in his account of this region with the Scythians.

14. The birthplace of Aristeas, the poet who sung of these things, I have already mentioned. I will now relate a tale which I heard concerning him both at Proconnêsus and at Cyzicus. Aristeas, they said, who belonged to one of the noblest families in the island, had entered one day into a fuller's shop, when he

1 Proconnêsus is the island now called *Marmora*, which gives its modern appellation to the Propontis (Sea of Marmora).

2 Vide supra, iii. 116.

3 That is, the Euxine.

4 The poem of Aristeas indicated an important general fact, viz., the perpetual pressure on one another of the nomadic hordes which from time immemorial have occupied the vast steppes of Central and Northern Asia, and of Eastern Europe.

suddenly dropt down dead. Hereupon the fuller shut up his shop, and went to tell Aristeas' kindred what had happened. The report of the death had just spread through the town, when a certain Cyzicenian, lately arrived from Artaca,[1] contradicted the rumour, affirming that he had met Aristeas on his road to Cyzicus, and had spoken with him. This man, therefore, strenuously denied the rumour; the relations, however, proceeded to the fuller's shop with all things necessary for the funeral, intending to carry the body away. But on the shop being opened, no Aristeas was found, either dead or alive. Seven years afterwards he reappeared, they told me, in Proconnêsus, and wrote the poem called by the Greeks "The Arimaspeia," after which he disappeared a second time. This is the tale current in the two cities above mentioned.

15. What follows I know to have happened to the Metapontines of Italy, three hundred and forty years[2] after the second disappearance of Aristeas, as I collect by comparing the accounts given me at Proconnêsus and Metapontum.[3] Aristeas then, as the Metapontines affirm, appeared to them in their own country, and ordered them to set up an altar in honour of Apollo, and to place near it a statue to be called that of Aristeas the Proconnêsian. "Apollo," he told them, "had come to their country once, though he had visited no other Italiots; and he had been with Apollo at the time, not however in his present form, but in the shape of a crow."[4] Having said so much, he vanished. Then the Metapontines, as they relate, sent to Delphi, and inquired of the god, in what light they were to regard the appearance of this ghost of a man. The Pythoness, in reply, bade them attend to what the spectre said, "for so it would go best with them." Thus advised, they did as they had been directed and there is now a statue bearing the name of Aristeas, close by the image of Apollo in the market-place of Metapontum, with bay-trees standing around it. But enough has been said concerning Aristeas.

1 The name remains in the modern *Erdek*, which has taken the place of Cyzicus (*Bal Kiz*), now in ruins, and is the see of an archbishop.

2 This date must certainly be wrong. The date usually assigned to Aristeas is about B.C. 580.

3 Metapontum (the modern *Basiento*), was distant about 50 miles from Thurii, where Herodotus lived during his later years.

4 Natural superstition first regarded the croak of the crow or raven as an omen; after which it was natural to attach the bird to the God of Prophecy. The crow is often called the companion or attendant of Apollo.

16. With regard to the regions which lie above the country whereof this portion of my history treats, there is no one who possesses any exact knowledge. Not a single person can I find who professes to be acquainted with them by actual observation. Even Aristeas, the traveller of whom I lately spoke, does not claim – and he is writing poetry – to have reached any farther than the Issedonians. What he relates concerning the regions beyond is, he confesses, mere hearsay, being the account which the Issedonians gave him of those countries. However, I shall proceed to mention all that I have learnt of these parts by the most exact inquiries which I have been able to make concerning them.

17. Above the mart of the Borysthenites, which is situated in the very centre of the whole sea-coast of Scythia, the first people who inhabit the land are the Callipedæ, a Græco-Scythic race. Next to them, as you go inland, dwell the people called the Alazonians. These two nations in other respects resemble the Scythians in their usages, but sow and eat corn, also onions, garlic, lentils, and millet.[1] Beyond the Alazonians reside Scythian cultivators, who grow corn, not for their own use, but for sale.[2] Still higher up are the Neuri.[3] Northwards of the Neuri the continent, as far as it is known to us, is uninhabited. These are the nations along the course of the river Hypanis,[4] west of the Borysthenes.[5]

18. Across the Borysthenes, the first country after you leave the coast is Hylæa (the Woodland).[6] Above this dwell the Scythian Husbandmen, whom the Greeks living near the Hypanis call Borysthenites, while they call themselves Olbiopolites. These Husbandmen extend eastward a distance of three days' journey to a river bearing the name of Panticapes,[7] while northward the country

1 Millet is still largely cultivated in these regions. It forms almost the only cereal food of the Nogais.

2 The corn-trade of the Scythians appears to have been chiefly, if not exclusively, with the Greeks.

3 Vide infra, ch. 105.

4 The modern *Bug* or *Boug*.

5 The modern *Dnieper*.

6 Portions of this country are still thickly wooded, and contrast remarkably with the general bare and arid character of the steppe.

7 Here the description of Herodotus, which has been hitherto excellent, begins to fail. There is at present no river which at all corresponds with his Panticapes. Either the face of the country must have greatly altered since his time, or he must have obtained a confused and incorrect account.

is theirs for eleven days' sail up the course of the Borysthenes. Further inland there is a vast tract which is uninhabited. Above this desolate region dwell the Cannibals, who are a people apart, much unlike the Scythians. Above them the country becomes an utter desert; not a single tribe, so far as we know, inhabits it.

19. Crossing the Panticapes, and proceeding eastward of the Husbandmen, we come upon the wandering Scythians, who neither plough nor sow. Their country, and the whole of this region, except Hylæa, is quite bare of trees.[1] They extend towards the east a distance of fourteen[2] days' journey, occupying a tract which reaches to the river Gerrhus.[3]

20. On the opposite side of the Gerrhus is the Royal district, as it is called: here dwells the largest and bravest of the Scythian tribes, which looks upon all the other tribes in the light of slaves.[4] Its country reaches on the south to Taurica,[5] on the east to the trench dug by the sons of the blind slaves, the mart upon the Palus Mæotis, called Cremni (the Cliffs), and in part to the river Tanais.[6] North of the country of the Royal Scythians are the Melanchlæni (Black-Robes),[7] a people of quite a different race from the Scythians. Beyond them lie marshes and a region without inhabitants, so far as our knowledge reaches.

21. When one crosses the Tanais, one is no longer in Scythia; the first region on crossing is that of the Sauromatæ,[8] who, beginning at the upper end of the Palus Mæotis, stretch northward a distance of fifteen days' journey, inhabiting a country which is entirely bare of trees, whether wild or cultivated.[9] Above them, possessing the second region, dwell the Budini,[10] whose territory is thickly wooded with trees of every kind.

22. Beyond the Budini, as one goes northward, first there is a desert, seven days' journey across; after which, if one inclines

1 The general treeless character of the steppes is noticed by all travellers.

2 Rennell proposes to read "four days' journey" – and indeed without some such alteration the geography of this part of Scythia is utterly inexplicable.

3 Vide infra, ch. 56.

4 The analogous case of the Golden Horde among the Mongols has been adduced by many writers.

5 Taurica appears here to be nothing but the high tract along the southern coast of the Crimea.

6 Now the *Don*.   7 Vide infra, ch. 107.   8 Vide infra, ch. 110.

9 The ancient country of the Sauromatæ or Sarmatæ (Sarmatians) appears to have been nearly identical with that of the modern Don Cossacks.

10 Vide infra, ch. 108.

somewhat to the east, the Thyssagetæ are reached, a numerous nation quite distinct from any other, and living by the chase. Adjoining them, and within the limits of the same region, are the people who bear the name of Iyrcæ; they also support themselves by hunting, which they practise in the following manner. The hunter climbs a tree, the whole country abounding in wood, and there sets himself in ambush; he has a dog at hand, and a horse, trained to lie down upon its belly, and thus make itself low; the hunter keeps watch, and when he sees his game, lets fly an arrow; then mounting his horse, he gives the beast chase, his dog following hard all the while. Beyond these people, a little to the east, dwells a distinct tribe of Scyths, who revolted once from the Royal Scythians, and migrated into these parts.

23. As far as their country, the tract of land whereof I have been speaking is all a smooth plain, and the soil deep; beyond you enter on a region which is rugged and stony. Passing over a great extent of this rough country, you come to a people dwelling at the foot of lofty mountains,[1] who are said to be all – both men and women – bald from their birth, to have flat noses, and very long chins. These people speak a language of their own, but the dress which they wear is the same as the Scythian. They live on the fruit of a certain tree, the name of which is Ponticum;[2] in size it is about equal to our fig-tree, and it bears a fruit like a bean, with a stone inside. When the fruit is ripe, they strain it through cloths; the juice which runs off is black and thick, and is called by the natives "aschy." They lap this up with their tongues, and also mix it with milk for a drink; while they make the lees, which are solid, into cakes, and eat them instead of meat; for they have but few sheep in their country, in which there is no good pasturage. Each of them dwells under a tree, and they cover the tree in winter with a cloth of thick white felt, but take off the covering in the summer-time. No one harms these people, for they are looked upon as sacred, – they do not even possess any warlike weapons. When their neighbours fall out, they make up the quarrel; and when one flies to them for refuge, he is safe from all hurt. They are called the Argippæans.

24. Up to this point the territory of which we are speaking is very completely explored, and all the nations between the

1 The chain of the Ural.
2 A species of cherry, which is eaten by the Calmucks of the present day in almost the same manner.

coast and the bald-headed men are well known to us. For some of the Scythians are accustomed to penetrate as far, of whom inquiry may easily be made, and Greeks also go there from the mart on the Borysthenes, and from the other marts along the Euxine. The Scythians who make this journey communicate with the inhabitants by means of seven interpreters and seven languages.

25. Thus far therefore the land is known; but beyond the bald-headed men lies a region of which no one can give any exact account. Lofty and precipitous mountains, which are never crossed, bar further progress.[1] The bald men say, but it does not seem to me credible, that the people who live in these mountains have feet like goats; and that after passing them you find another race of men, who sleep during one half of the year. This latter statement appears to me quite unworthy of credit. The region east of the bald-headed men is well known to be inhabited by the Issedonians, but the tract that lies to the north of these two nations is entirely unknown, except by the accounts which they give of it.

26. The Issedonians are said to have the following customs. When a man's father dies, all the near relatives bring sheep to the house; which are sacrificed, and their flesh cut in pieces, while at the same time the dead body undergoes the like treatment. The two sorts of flesh are afterwards mixed together, and the whole is served up at a banquet. The head of the dead man is treated differently: it is stripped bare, cleansed, and set in gold.[2] It then becomes an ornament on which they pride themselves, and is brought out year by year at the great festival which sons keep in honour of their fathers' death, just as the Greeks keep their Genesia. In other respects the Issedonians are reputed to be observers of justice: and it is to be remarked that their women have equal authority with the men.[3] Thus our knowledge extends as far as this nation.

1 Heeren considers the mountains here spoken of to be the Altai; but to me it seems that Herodotus in these chapters speaks only of a single mountain-chain, and that is the Ural.

2 Compare the Scythian custom with respect to the skulls of enemies (infra, ch. 65). A similar practice to theirs is ascribed by Livy to the Boii, a tribe of Gauls (xxiii. 24).

3 And among the Nairs of Malabar the institutions all incline to a gyno-cracy, each woman having several husbands, and property passing through the female line in preference to the male.

27. The regions beyond are known only from the accounts of the Issedonians, by whom the stories are told of the one-eyed race of men and the gold-guarding griffins. These stories are received by the Scythians from the Issedonians, and by them passed on to us Greeks: whence it arises that we give the one-eyed race the Scythian name of Arimaspi, "*arima*" being the Scythic word for "one," and "*spû*" for "the eye."

28. The whole district whereof we have here discoursed has winters of exceeding rigour. During eight months the frost is so intense that water poured upon the ground does not form mud, but if a fire be lighted on it mud is produced. The sea freezes, and the Cimmerian Bosphorus is frozen over. At that season the Scythians who dwell inside the trench make warlike expeditions upon the ice, and even drive their waggons across to the country of the Sindians. Such is the intensity of the cold during eight months out of the twelve; and even in the remaining four the climate is still cool.[1] The character of the winter likewise is unlike that of the same season in any other country; for at that time, when the rains ought to fall in Scythia, there is scarcely any rain worth mentioning, while in summer it never gives over raining; and thunder, which elsewhere is frequent then, in Scythia is unknown in that part of the year, coming only in summer, when it is very heavy. Thunder in the winter-time is there accounted a prodigy; as also are earthquakes, whether they happen in winter or summer. Horses bear the winter well, cold as it is, but mules and asses are quite unable to bear it; whereas in other countries mules and asses are found to endure the cold, while horses, if they stand still, are frost-bitten.

29. To me it seems that the cold may likewise be the cause which prevents the oxen in Scythia from having horns. There is a line of Homer's in the Odyssey which gives a support to my opinion:—

"Lybia too, where horns bud quick on the foreheads of lambkins."[2]

He means to say, what is quite true, that in warm countries the horns come early. So too in countries where the cold is

1 The clearing of forests and the spread of agriculture have tended to render the climate of these regions less severe than in the time of Herodotus. Still, even at the present day, the south of Russia has a six months' winter, lasting from October to April. From November to March the cold is, ordinarily, very intense. The summer is now intensely hot.   2 Odyss. iv. 85.

severe animals either have no horns, or grow them with difficulty – the cold being the cause in this instance.

30. Here I must express my wonder – additions being what my work always from the very first affected – that in Elis, where the cold is not remarkable, and there is nothing else to account for it, mules are never produced. The Eleans say it is in consequence of a curse;[1] and their habit is, when the breeding-time comes, to take their mares into one of the adjoining countries, and there keep them till they are in foal, when they bring them back again into Elis.

31. With respect to the feathers which are said by the Scythians to fill the air,[2] and to prevent persons from penetrating into the remoter parts of the continent, or even having any view of those regions, my opinion is, that in the countries above Scythia it always snows – less, of course, in the summer than in the winter-time. Now snow when it falls looks like feathers, as every one is aware who has seen it come down close to him. These northern regions, therefore, are uninhabitable, by reason of the severity of the winter; and the Scythians, with their neighbours, call the snow-flakes feathers because, I think, of the likeness which they bear to them. I have now related what is said of the most distant parts of this continent whereof any account is given.

32. Of the Hyperboreans nothing is said either by the Scythians or by any of the other dwellers in these regions, unless it be the Issedonians. But in my opinion, even the Issedonians are silent concerning them; otherwise the Scythians would have repeated their statements, as they do those concerning the one-eyed men. Hesiod, however, mentions them, and Homer also in the Epigoni, if that be really a work of his.[3]

33. But the persons who have by far the most to say on this subject are the Delians. They declare that certain offerings, packed in wheaten straw, were brought from the country of the Hyperboreans[4] into Scythia, and that the Scythians received them

1 According to Plutarch, Œnomaüs, king of Elis, out of his love for horses, laid heavy curses on the breeding of mules in that country.

2 Supra, ch. 7, ad fin.

3 An epic poem, in hexameter verse, on the subject of the second siege of Thebes by the sons of those killed in the first siege. It was a sequel to another very ancient epic, the Thebaïs, which was upon the first Theban war.

4 Very elaborate accounts have been given of the Hyperboreans both in ancient and modern times. They are, however, in reality not an historical, but

and passed them on to their neighbours upon the west, who continued to pass them on until at last they reached the Adriatic. From hence they were sent southward, and when they came to Greece, were received first of all by the Dodonæans. Thence they descended to the Maliac Gulf, from which they were carried across into Eubœa, where the people handed them on from city to city, till they came at length to Carystus. The Carystians took them over to Tenos, without stopping at Andros; and the Tenians brought them finally to Delos. Such, according to their own account, was the road by which the offerings reached the Delians. Two damsels, they say, named Hyperoché and Laodicé, brought the first offerings from the Hyperboreans; and with them the Hyperboreans sent five men, to keep them from all harm by the way; these are the persons whom the Delians call "Perpherees," and to whom great honours are paid at Delos. Afterwards the Hyperboreans, when they found that their messengers did not return, thinking it would be a grievous thing always to be liable to lose the envoys they should send, adopted the following plan:— they wrapped their offerings in the wheaten straw, and bearing them to their borders, charged their neighbours to send them forward from one nation to another, which was done accordingly, and in this way the offerings reached Delos. I myself know of a practice like this, which obtains with the women of Thrace and Pæonia. They in their sacrifices to the queenly Artemis bring wheaten straw always with their offerings. Of my own knowledge I can testify that this is so.

34. The damsels sent by the Hyperboreans died in Delos; and in their honour all the Delian girls and youths are wont to cut off their hair. The girls, before their marriage-day, cut off a curl, and twining it round a distaff, lay it upon the grave of the strangers. This grave is on the left as one enters the precinct of Artemis, and has an olive-tree growing on it. The youths wind some of their hair round a kind of grass, and, like the girls, place it upon the tomb. Such are the honours paid to these damsels by the Delians.

35. They add that, once before, there came to Delos by the same road as Hyperoché and Laodicé, two other virgins from

---

an ideal nation. The North Wind being given a local seat in certain mountains called Rhipæan (from ριπή, "a blast"), it was supposed there must be a country above the north wind, which would not be cold, and which would have inhabitants. Ideal perfections were gradually ascribed to this region.

the Hyperboreans, whose names were Argé and Opis. Hyperoché and Laodicé came to bring to Eileithyia the offering which they had laid upon themselves, in acknowledgment of their quick labours; but Argé and Opis came at the same time as the gods of Delos,[1] and are honoured by the Delians in a different way. For the Delian women make collections in these maidens' names, and invoke them in the hymn which Olen, a Lycian, composed for them; and the rest of the islanders, and even the Ionians, have been taught by the Delians to do the like. This Olen, who came from Lycia, made the other old hymns also which are sung in Delos. The Delians add, that the ashes from the thigh-bones burnt upon the altar are scattered over the tomb of Opis and Argé. Their tomb lies behind the temple of Artemis, facing the east, near the banqueting-hall of the Ceians. Thus much then, and no more, concerning the Hyperboreans.

36. As for the tale of Abaris, who is said to have been a Hyperborean, and to have gone with his arrow all round the world without once eating, I shall pass it by in silence. Thus much, however, is clear: if there are Hyperboreans, there must also be Hypernotians. For my part, I cannot but laugh when I see numbers of persons drawing maps of the world without having any reason to guide them; making, as they do, the ocean-stream to run all round the earth, and the earth itself to be an exact circle, as if described by a pair of compasses,[2] with Europe and Asia just of the same size. The truth in this matter I will now proceed to explain in a very few words, making it clear what the real size of each region is, and what shape should be given them.

37. The Persians inhabit a country upon the southern or Erythræan sea; above them, to the north, are the Medes; beyond the Medes, the Saspirians; beyond them, the Colchians, reaching to the northern sea, into which the Phasis empties itself. These four nations fill the whole space from one sea to the other.

38. West of these nations there project into the sea two tracts which I will now describe; one, beginning at the river Phasis on the north, stretches along the Euxine and the Hellespont to

---

1 Apollo and Artemis.
2 The belief which Herodotus ridicules is not that of the world's spherical form, which had not yet been suspected by the Greeks, but a false notion of the configuration of the land on the earth's surface.

Sigeum in the Troas; while on the south it reaches from the Myriandrian gulf,[1] which adjoins Phœnicia, to the Triopic promontory. This is one of the tracts, and is inhabited by thirty different nations.

39. The other starts from the country of the Persians, and stretches into the Erythræan sea, containing first Persia, then Assyria, and after Assyria, Arabia. It ends, that is to say it is considered to end, though it does not really come to a termination,[2] at the Arabian gulf – the gulf whereinto Darius conducted the canal which he made from the Nile.[3] Between Persia and Phœnicia lies a broad and ample tract of country, after which the region I am describing skirts our sea,[4] stretching from Phœnicia along the coast of Palestine-Syria till it comes to Egypt, where it terminates. This entire tract contains but three nations.[5] The whole of Asia west of the country of the Persians is comprised in these two regions.

40. Beyond the tract occupied by the Persians, Medes, Saspirians, and Colchians, towards the east and the region of the sunrise, Asia is bounded on the south by the Erythræan sea, and on the north by the Caspian and the river Araxes, which flows towards the rising sun. Till you reach India the country is peopled; but further east it is void of inhabitants, and no one can say what sort of region it is. Such then is the shape, and such the size of Asia.

41. Libya belongs to one of the above-mentioned tracts, for it adjoins on Egypt. In Egypt the tract is at first a narrow neck, the distance from our sea to the Erythræan not exceeding a hundred thousand fathoms, or, in other words, a thousand furlongs;[6] but from the point where the neck ends, the tract which bears the name of Libya is of very great breadth.

42. For my part I am astonished that men should ever have divided Libya, Asia, and Europe as they have, for they are

1 Or Bay of Issus [a city in the S.E. extremity of Cilicia, in Asia Minor. – E. H. B.].

2 Since Egypt adjoins Arabia.

3 This was the completion of the canal which Neco found it prudent to desist from re-opening, through fear of the growing power of Babylon. It was originally a canal of Rameses II., which had been filled up by the sand.

4 The Mediterranean. (See Book i. ch. 185.)

5 The Assyrians (among whom the Palestine *Syrians* were included), the Arabians, and the Phœnicians.

6 Modern surveys show that the direct distance across the isthmus is not so much as 80 miles.

exceedingly unequal. Europe extends the entire length of the other two, and for breadth will not even (as I think) bear to be compared to them. As for Libya, we know it to be washed on all sides by the sea, except where it is attached to Asia. This discovery was first made by Necôs,[1] the Egyptian king, who on desisting from the canal which he had begun between the Nile and the Arabian Gulf,[2] sent to sea a number of ships manned by Phœnicians, with orders to make for the Pillars of Heracles,[3] and return to Egypt through them, and by the Mediterranean. The Phœnicians took their departure from Egypt by way of the Erythræan Sea, and so sailed into the southern ocean. When autumn came, they went ashore, wherever they might happen to be, and having sown a tract of land with corn, waited until the grain was fit to cut. Having reaped it, they again set sail; and thus it came to pass that two whole years went by, and it was not till the third year that they doubled the Pillars of Heracles, and made good their voyage home. On their return, they declared – I for my part do not believe them, but perhaps others may – that in sailing round Libya they had the sun upon their right hand.[4] In this way was the extent of Libya first discovered.

43. Next to these Phœnicians the Carthaginians, according to their own accounts, made the voyage. For Sataspes, son of Teaspes the Achæmenian, did not circumnavigate Libya, though he was sent to do so; but, fearing the length and desolateness of the journey, he turned back and left unaccomplished the task which had been set him by his mother. This man had used violence towards a maiden, the daughter of Zopyrus, son of Megabyzus,[5] and King Xerxes was about to impale him for the offence, when his mother, who was a sister of Darius, begged

1 We may infer, from Neco's ordering the Phœnicians to come round by the "Pillars of Heracles," that the form of Africa was *already* known, and that this was not the first expedition which had gone round it.

2 Vide supra, ii. 158.

3 They were so called, not from the Greek hero, but from the Tyrian deity, whose worship was always introduced by the Phœnicians in their settlements.

4 Here the faithful reporting of what he did not himself imagine true has stood our author in good stead. Few would have believed the Phœnician circumnavigation of Africa had it not been vouched for by this discovery. When Herodotus is blamed for repeating the absurd stories which he had been told, it should be considered what we must have lost had he made it a rule to reject from his History all that he thought unlikely.

5 Vide supra, iii. 160.

him off, undertaking to punish his crime more heavily than the
king himself had designed. She would force him, she said, to sail
round Libya and return to Egypt by the Arabian Gulf. Xerxes
gave his consent; and Sataspes went down to Egypt, and there
got a ship and crew, with which he set sail for the Pillars of
Heracles. Having passed the Straits, he doubled the Libyan headland, known as Cape Soloeis,[1] and proceeded southward. Following this course for many months over a vast stretch of sea,
and finding that more water than he had crossed still lay ever
before him, he put about, and came back to Egypt. Thence
proceeding to the court, he made report to Xerxes, that at the
farthest point to which he had reached, the coast was occupied
by a dwarfish race,[2] who wore a dress made from the palm-tree.
These people, whenever he landed, left their towns and fled away
to the mountains; his men, however, did them no wrong, only
entering into their cities and taking some of their cattle. The
reason why he had not sailed quite round Libya was, he said,
because the ship stopped, and would not go any further. Xerxes,
however, did not accept this account for true; and so Sataspes,
as he had failed to accomplish the task set him, was impaled by
the king's orders in accordance with the former sentence.[3] One
of his eunuchs, on hearing of his death, ran away with a great
portion of his wealth, and reached Samos, where a certain
Samian seized the whole. I know the man's name well, but I shall
willingly forget it here.

44. Of the greater part of Asia Darius was the discoverer.
Wishing to know where the Indus (which is the only river save
one[4] that produces crocodiles) emptied itself into the sea, he sent
a number of men, on whose truthfulness he could rely, and
among them Scylax of Caryanda,[5] to sail down the river. They
started from the city of Caspatyrus,[6] in the region called Pactyïca,
and sailed down the stream in an easterly direction[7] to the sea.
Here they turned westward, and, after a voyage of thirty months,

---

1 The modern Cape Spartel.
2 This is the second mention of a dwarfish race in Africa (see above, ii. 32).
3 The fate of Sir Walter Raleigh furnishes a curious parallel to this.
4 That is, the Nile. Vide supra, ii. 67.
5 Caryanda was a place on or near the Carian coast.
6 Vide supra, iii. 102.
7 The real course of the Indus is somewhat *west* of south. The error of Herodotus arose perhaps from the Cabul river being mistaken for the true Indus.

reached the place from which the Egyptian king, of whom I spoke above, sent the Phœnicians to sail round Libya.[1] After this voyage was completed, Darius conquered the Indians,[2] and made use of the sea in those parts. Thus all Asia, except the eastern portion, has been found to be similarly circumstanced with Libya.[3]

45. But the boundaries of Europe are quite unknown, and there is not a man who can say whether any sea girds it round either on the north[4] or on the east, while in length it undoubtedly extends as far as both the other two. For my part I cannot conceive why three names, and women's names especially, should ever have been given to a tract which is in reality one, nor why the Egyptian Nile and the Colchian Phasis (or according to others the Mæotic Tanais and Cimmerian ferry) should have been fixed upon for the boundary lines;[5] nor can I even say who gave the three tracts their names, or whence they took the epithets. According to the Greeks in general, Libya was so called after a certain Libya, a native woman, and Asia after the wife of Prometheus. The Lydians, however, put in a claim to the latter name, which, thy declare, was not derived from Asia the wife of Prometheus, but from Asies, the son of Cotys, and grandson of Manes, who also gave name to the tribe Asias at Sardis. As for Europe, no one can say whether it is surrounded by the sea or not, neither is it known whence the name of Europe was derived, nor who gave it name, unless we say that Europe was so called after the Tyrian Europé, and before her time was nameless, like the other divisions. But it is certain that Europé was an Asiatic, and never even set foot on the land which the Greeks now call Europe, only sailing from Phœnicia to Crete, and from Crete to Lycia. However let us quit these matters. We shall ourselves continue to use the names[6] which custom sanctions.

1 Vide supra, ch. 42.

2 The conquest of the Indians, by which we are to understand the reduction of the Punjab, and perhaps (though this is not certain) of Scinde, preceded (as may be proved by the Inscriptions) the Scythian expedition.

3 Limited, that is, and circumscribed by fixed boundaries.

4 See Book iii. ch. 115, sub. fin.

5 The earliest Greek geographers divided the world into two portions only, Europe and Asia, in the latter of which they included Libya.

6 There are grounds for believing Europe and Asia to have originally signified "the west" and "the east" respectively. Both are Semitic terms, and probably passed to the Greeks from the Phœnicians.

46. The Euxine sea, where Darius now went to war, has nations dwelling around it, with the one exception of the Scythians, more unpolished than those of any other region that we know of. For, setting aside Anacharsis[1] and the Scythian people, there is not within this region a single nation which can be put forward as having any claims to wisdom, or which has produced a single person of any high repute. The Scythians indeed have in one respect, and that the very most important of all those that fall under man's control, shown themselves wiser than any nation upon the face of the earth. Their customs otherwise are not such as I admire.[2] The one thing of which I speak, is the contrivance whereby they make it impossible for the enemy who invades them to escape destruction, while they themselves are entirely out of his reach, unless it please them to engage with him. Having neither cities nor forts, and carrying their dwellings with them wherever they go; accustomed, moreover, one and all of them, to shoot from horseback; and living not by husbandry but on their cattle, their waggons the only houses that they possess,[3] how can they fail of being unconquerable, and unassailable even?

47. The nature of their country, and the rivers by which it is intersected, greatly favour this mode of resisting attacks. For the land is level, well watered, and abounding in pasture;[4] while the rivers which traverse it are almost equal in number to the canals of Egypt. Of these I shall only mention the most famous and such as are navigable to some distance from the sea. They are, the Ister, which has five mouths; the Tyras, the Hypanis, the Borysthenes, the Panticapes, the Hypacyris, the Gerrhus, and the Tanais. The courses of these streams I shall now proceed to describe.

48. The Ister is of all the rivers with which we are acquainted the mightiest. It never varies in height, but continues at the same

1 Concerning Anacharsis, see below, ch. 76.

2 It was a fashion among the Greeks to praise the simplicity and honesty of the nomad races, who were less civilised than themselves. Herodotus intends to mark his dissent from such views.

3 It may be doubted whether the ancient Scythians really lived entirely in their waggons. More probably their waggons carried a tent, consisting of a light framework of wood covered with felt or matting, which could be readily transferred from the wheels to the ground, and *vice versa*.

4 The pasture is now not good, excepting in the immediate vicinity of the rivers; otherwise the picture drawn of the country accords exactly with the accounts given by modern travellers.

level summer and winter. Counting from the west it is the first
of the Scythian rivers, and the reason of its being the greatest is,
that it receives the waters of several tributaries. Now the tributaries which swell its flood are the following: first, on the side
of Scythia, these five – the stream called by the Scythians Porata,
and by the Greeks Pyretus, the Tiarantus, the Ararus, the
Naparis, and the Ordessus. The first mentioned is a great stream,
and is the easternmost of the tributaries. The Tiarantus is of less
volume, and more to the west. The Ararus, Naparis, and Ordessus fall into the Ister between these two. All the above mentioned are genuine Scythian rivers, and go to swell the current
of the Ister.

49. From the country of the Agathyrsi comes down another
river, the Maris, which empties itself into the same; and from
the heights of Hæmus descend with a northern course three
mighty streams, the Atlas, the Auras, and the Tibisis, and pour
their waters into it. Thrace gives it three tributaries, the Athrys,
the Noës, and the Artanes, which all pass through the country
of the Crobyzian Thracians. Another tributary is furnished by
Pæonia, namely, the Scius; this river, rising near Mount Rhodopé, forces its way through the chain of Hæmus,[1] and so
reaches the Ister. From Illyria comes another stream, the Angrus,
which has a course from south to north, and after watering the
Triballian plain, falls into the Brongus, which falls into the Ister.[2]
So the Ister is augmented by these two streams, both considerable. Besides all these, the Ister receives also the waters of the
Carpis[3] and the Alpis,[4] two rivers running in a northerly direction
from the country above the Umbrians. For the Ister flows
through the whole extent of Europe, rising in the country of the
Celts (the most westerly of all the nations of Europe, excepting
the Cynetians), and thence running across the continent till it
reaches Scythia, whereof it washes the flanks.

1 This is untrue. No stream forces its way through this chain.

2 The Angrus is either the western *Morava* or the *Ibar*, most probably the
latter. The Brongus is the eastern or Bulgarian *Morava*. The Triballian plain is
thus the modern Servia.

3 As Herodotus plunges deeper into the European continent, his knowledge is less exact. He knows the fact that the Danube receives two great
tributaries from the south (the Drave and the Save) in the upper part of its
course, but he does not any longer know the true direction of the streams.

4 It is interesting to find in Herodotus this first trace of the word *Alp*, by
which, from the time of Polybius, the great European chain has been known.

50. All these streams, then, and many others, add their waters to swell the flood of the Ister, which thus increased becomes the mightiest of rivers; for undoubtedly if we compare the stream of the Nile with the *single* stream of the Ister, we must give the preference to the Nile,[1] of which no tributary river, nor even rivulet, augments the volume. The Ister remains at the same level both summer and winter – owing to the following reasons, as I believe. During the winter it runs at its natural height, or a very little higher, because in those countries there is scarcely any rain in winter, but constant snow. When summer comes, this snow, which is of great depth, begins to melt, and flows into the Ister, which is swelled at that season, not only by this cause but also by the rains, which are heavy and frequent at that part of the year. Thus the various streams which go to form the Ister are higher in summer than in winter, and just so much higher as the sun's power and attraction are greater; so that these two causes counteract each other, and the effect is to produce a balance, whereby the Ister remains always at the same level.[2]

51. This, then, is one of the great Scythian rivers; the next to it is the Tyras, which rises from a great lake separating Scythia from the land of the Neuri, and runs with a southerly course to the sea. Greeks dwell at the mouth of the river, who are called Tyritæ.

52. The third river is the Hypanis.[3] This stream rises within the limits of Scythia, and has its source in another vast lake, around which wild white horses graze. The lake is called, properly enough, the Mother of the Hypanis.[4] The Hypanis, rising here, during the distance of five days' navigation is a shallow stream, and the water sweet and pure; thence, however, to the sea, which is a distance of four days, it is exceedingly bitter. This change is caused by its receiving into it at that point a brook the waters of which are so bitter that, although it is but a tiny rivulet, it

1 The lengths of the two rivers are – of the Nile, 4000 miles; of the Danube, 1760 miles.

2 The "balance" of which Herodotus speaks is caused by the increased volume of the southern tributaries during the summer (which is caused by the melting of the snows along the range of the Alps), being just sufficient to compensate for the diminished volume of the northern tributaries, which in winter are swelled by the rains.

3 The Hypanis is undoubtedly a main tributary of the Dnieper.

4 Compare below, ch. 86.

nevertheless taints the entire Hypanis, which is a large stream among those of the second order. The source of this bitter spring is on the borders of the Scythian Husbandmen, where they adjoin upon the Alazonians; and the place where it rises is called in the Scythic tongue *Exampæus*, which means in our language, "The Sacred Ways." The spring itself bears the same name. The Tyras and the Hypanis approach each other in the country of the Alazonians,[1] but afterwards separate, and leave a wide space between their streams.

53. The fourth of the Scythian rivers is the Borysthenes.[2] Next to the Ister, it is the greatest of them all; and, in my judgment, it is the most productive river, not merely in Scythia, but in the whole world, excepting only the Nile, with which no stream can possibly compare. It has upon its banks the loveliest and most excellent pasturages for cattle; it contains abundance of the most delicious fish; its water is most pleasant to the taste; its stream is limpid, while all the other rivers near it are muddy; the richest harvests spring up along its course, and where the ground is not sown, the heaviest crops of grass; while salt forms in great plenty about its mouth without human aid,[3] and large fish are taken in it of the sort called Antacæi, without any prickly bones, and good for pickling.[4] Nor are these the whole of its marvels. As far inland as the place named Gerrhus, which is distant forty days' voyage from the sea, its course is known, and its direction is from north to south; but above this no one has traced it, so as to say through what countries it flows. It enters the territory of the Scythian Husbandmen after running for some time across a desert region, and continues for ten days' navigation to pass through the land which they inhabit. It is the only river besides the Nile the sources of which are unknown to me, as they are also (I believe) to all the other Greeks. Not long before it reaches the sea, the Borysthenes is joined by the Hypanis, which pours its waters into the same lake. The land

1 That is, between the 47th and 48th parallels. The fact here noticed by Herodotus strongly proves his actual knowledge of the geography of these countries.

2 The Borysthenes is the Dnieper.

3 The salines of *Kinburn*, at the extremity of the promontory which forms the southern shore of the *liman* of the Dnieper, are still of the greatest importance to Russia, and supply vast tracts of the interior.

4 The sturgeon of the Dnieper have to this day a great reputation.

that lies between them, a narrow point like the beak of a ship, is called Cape Hippolaüs. Here is a temple dedicated to Demeter, and opposite the temple upon the Hypanis is the dwelling-place of the Borysthenites. But enough has been said of these streams.

54. Next in succession comes the fifth river, called the Panticapes, which has, like the Borysthenes, a course from north to south, and rises from a lake. The space between this river and the Borysthenes is occupied by the Scythians who are engaged in husbandry. After watering their country, the Panticapes flows through Hylæa, and empties itself into the Borysthenes.

55. The sixth stream is the Hypacyris, a river rising from a lake, and running directly through the middle of the Nomadic Scythians. It falls into the sea near the city of Carcinitis, leaving Hylæa and the course of Achilles[1] to the right.

56. The seventh river is the Gerrhus, which is a branch thrown out by the Borysthenes at the point where the course of that stream first begins to be known, to wit, the region called by the same name as the stream itself, viz. Gerrhus. This river on its passage towards the sea divides the country of the Nomadic from that of the Royal Scyths. It runs into the Hypacyris.

57. The eighth river is the Tanais, a stream which has its source, far up the country, in a lake of vast size,[2] and which empties itself into another still larger lake, the Palus Mæotis, whereby the country of the Royal Scythians is divided from that of the Sauromatæ. The Tanais receives the waters of a tributary stream, called the Hyrgis.[3]

58. Such then are the rivers of chief note in Scythia. The grass which the land produces is more apt to generate gall in the beasts that feed on it than any other grass which is known to us, as plainly appears on the opening of their carcases.

59. Thus abundantly are the Scythians provided with the most important necessaries. Their manners and customs come now to be described. They worship only the following gods,

---

1 This is the modern *Kosa Tendra* and *Kosa Djarilgatch*, a long and narrow strip of sandy beach extending about 80 miles from nearly opposite *Kalantchak* to a point about 12 miles south of the promontory of *Kinburn* and attached to the continent only in the middle by an isthmus about 12 miles across.

2 The Tanais (the modern *Don*) rises from a *small* lake, the lake of *Ivan-Ozero*, in lat. 54°2′, long. 38° 3′. The Volga flows in part from the *great* lake of Onega.

3 Dean Blakesley regards it as the *Seviersky*, in which he finds "some vestige of the ancient title."

namely, Hestia, whom they reverence beyond all the rest, Zeus, and Gē (Earth), whom they consider to be the wife of Zeus; and after these Apollo, Celestial Aphrodite, Heracles, and Ares. These gods are worshipped by the whole nation: the Royal Scythians offer sacrifice likewise to Poseidon. In the Scythic tongue Hestia is called *Tabiti*, Zeus (very properly, in my judgment) *Papæus*, Gē *Apia*, Apollo *Œtosyrus*, Celestial Aphrodite *Artimpasa*, and Poseidon *Thamimasadas*. They use no images, altars, or temples, except in the worship of Ares; but in his worship they do use them.

60. The manner of their sacrifices is everywhere and in every case the same; the victim stands with its two fore-feet bound together by a cord, and the person who is about to offer, taking his station behind the victim, gives the rope a pull, and thereby throws the animal down; as it falls he invokes the god to whom he is offering; after which he puts a noose round the animal's neck, and, inserting a small stick, twists it round, and so strangles him. No fire is lighted, there is no consecration, and no pouring out of drink-offerings; but directly that the beast is strangled the sacrificer flays him, and then sets to work to boil the flesh.

61. As Scythia, however, is utterly barren of firewood, a plan has had to be contrived for boiling the flesh, which is the following. After flaying the beasts, they take out all the bones, and (if they possess such gear) put the flesh into boilers made in the country, which are very like the cauldrons of the Lesbians, except that they are of a much larger size; then placing the bones of the animals beneath the cauldron, they set them alight, and so boil the meat.[1] If they do not happen to possess a cauldron, they make the animal's paunch hold the flesh, and pouring in at the same time a little water, lay the bones under and light them. The bones burn beautifully; and the paunch easily contains all the flesh when it is stript from the bones, so that by this plan your ox is made to boil himself, and other victims also to do the like. When the meat is all cooked, the sacrificer offers a portion of the flesh and of the entrails, by casting it on the ground before him. They sacrifice all sorts of cattle, but most commonly horses.[2]

1 It may be gathered from Ezekiel (xxiv. 5) that a similar custom prevailed among the Jews.

2 Vide supra, ch. i. 216, where the same is related of the Massagetæ. Horses have always abounded in the steppes, and perhaps in ancient times were more common than any other animal.

62. Such are the victims offered to the other gods, and such is the mode in which they are sacrificed; but the rites paid to Ares are different. In every district, at the seat of government, there stands a temple of this god, whereof the following is a description. It is a pile of brushwood, made of a vast quantity of fagots, in length and breadth three furlongs; in height somewhat less,[1] having a square platform upon the top, three sides of which are precipitous, while the fourth slopes so that men may walk up it. Each year a hundred and fifty waggon-loads of brushwood are added to the pile, which sinks continually by reason of the rains. An antique iron sword is planted on the top of every such mound, and serves as the image of Ares: yearly sacrifices of cattle and of horses are made to it, and more victims are offered thus than to all the rest of their gods. When prisoners are taken in war, out of every hundred men they sacrifice one, not however with the same rites as the cattle, but with different. Libations of wine are first poured upon their heads, after which they are slaughtered over a vessel; the vessel is then carried up to the top of the pile, and the blood poured upon the scymitar. While this takes place at the top of the mound, below, by the side of the temple, the right hands and arms of the slaughtered prisoners are cut off, and tossed on high into the air. Then the other victims are slain, and those who have offered the sacrifice depart, leaving the hands and arms where they may chance to have fallen, and the bodies also, separate.

63. Such are the observances of the Scythians with respect to sacrifice. They never use swine for the purpose, nor indeed is it their wont to breed them in any part of their country.

64. In what concerns war, their customs are the following. The Scythian soldier drinks the blood of the first man he overthrows in battle. Whatever number he slays, he cuts off all their heads, and carries them to the king; since he is thus entitled to a share of the booty, whereto he forfeits all claim if he does not produce a head. In order to strip the skull of its covering, he makes a cut round the head above the ears, and, laying hold of the scalp, shakes the skull out; then with the rib of an ox he scrapes the scalp clean of flesh, and softening it by rubbing between the hands, uses it thenceforth as a napkin. The Scyth is proud of these scalps, and hangs them from his bridle-rein; the

1 These measures are utterly incredible.

greater the number of such napkins that a man can show, the more highly is he esteemed among them. Many make themselves cloaks, like the capotes of our peasants, by sewing a quantity of these scalps together. Others flay the right arms of their dead enemies, and make of the skin, which is stripped off with the nails hanging to it, a covering for their quivers. Now the skin of a man is thick and glossy, and would in whiteness surpass almost all other hides. Some even flay the entire body of their enemy, and stretching it upon a frame carry it about with them wherever they ride. Such are the Scythian customs with respect to scalps and skins.

65. The skulls of their enemies, not indeed of all, but of those whom they most detest, they treat as follows. Having sawn off the portion below the eyebrows, and cleaned out the inside, they cover the outside with leather. When a man is poor, this is all that he does; but if he is rich, he also lines the inside with gold: in either case the skull is used as a drinking-cup. They do the same with the skulls of their own kith and kin if they have been at feud with them, and have vanquished them in the presence of the king. When strangers whom they deem of any account come to visit them, these skulls are handed round, and the host tells how that these were his relations who made war upon him, and how that he got the better of them; all this being looked upon as proof of bravery.

66. Once a year the governor of each district, at a set place in his own province, mingles a bowl of wine, of which all Scythians have a right to drink by whom foes have been slain; while they who have slain no enemy are not allowed to taste of the bowl, but sit aloof in disgrace. No greater shame than this can happen to them. Such as have slain a very large number of foes, have two cups instead of one, and drink from both.

67. Scythia has an abundance of soothsayers, who foretell the future by means of a number of willow wands. A large bundle of these wands is brought and laid on the ground. The soothsayer unties the bundle, and places each wand by itself, at the same time uttering his prophecy: then, while he is still speaking, he gathers the rods together again, and makes them up once more into a bundle. This mode of divination is of home growth in Scythia.[1] The Enarees, or woman-like men, have another

1 It was not, however, confined to Scythia. There is distinct allusion to such a mode of divination in Hosea (ii. 12): "My people ask counsel of their stocks, *and their staff declareth unto them.*"

method, which they say Aphrodite taught them. It is done with
the inner bark of the linden-tree. They take a piece of this bark,
and, splitting it into three strips, keep twining the strips about
their fingers, and untwining them, while they prophesy.

68. Whenever the Scythian king falls sick, he sends for the
three soothsayers of most renown at the time, who come and
make trial of their art in the mode above described. Generally
they say that the king is ill, because such or such a person,
mentioning his name, has sworn falsely by the royal hearth. This
is the usual oath among the Scythians, when they wish to swear
with very great solemnity. Then the man accused of having for-
sworn himself is arrested and brought before the king. The
soothsayers tell him that by their art it is clear he has sworn a
false oath by the royal hearth, and so caused the illness of the
king – he denies the charge, protests that he has sworn no false
oath, and loudly complains of the wrong done to him. Upon this
the king sends for six new soothsayers, who try the matter by
soothsaying. If they too find the man guilty of the offence,
straightway he is beheaded by those who first accused him, and
his goods are parted among them: if, on the contrary, they acquit
him, other soothsayers, and again others, are sent for, to try the
case. Should the greater number decide in favour of the man's
innocence, then they who first accused him forfeit their lives.

69. The mode of their execution is the following: a waggon
is loaded with brushwood, and oxen are harnessed to it;[1] the
soothsayers, with their feet tied together, their hands bound behind their backs, and their mouths gagged, are thrust into the
midst of the brushwood; finally the wood is set alight, and the
oxen, being startled, are made to rush off with the waggon. It
often happens that the oxen and the soothsayers are both consumed together, but sometimes the pole of the waggon is burnt
through, and the oxen escape with a scorching. Diviners – lying
diviners, they call them – are burnt in the way described, for
other causes besides the one here spoken of. When the king puts
one of them to death, he takes care not to let any of his sons
survive: all the male offspring are slain with the father, only the
females being allowed to live.

70. Oaths among the Scyths are accompanied with the following ceremonies: a large earthen bowl is filled with wine, and

1 We learn from this that the ancient Scythians, like the modern Calmucks
and Nogais, used oxen and not horses to draw their waggons.

the parties to the oath, wounding themselves slightly with a knife or an awl, drop some of their blood into the wine; then they plunge into the mixture a scymitar, some arrows, a battle-axe, and a javelin, all the while repeating prayers; lastly the two contracting parties drink each a draught from the bowl, as do also the chief men among their followers.[1]

71. The tombs of their kings are in the land of the Gerrhi, who dwell at the point where the Borysthenes is first navigable. Here, when the king dies, they dig a grave, which is square in shape, and of great size. When it is ready, they take the king's corpse, and, having opened the belly, and cleaned out the inside, fill the cavity with a preparation of chopped cypress, frankincense, parsley-seed, and anise-seed, after which they sew up the opening, enclose the body in wax, and, placing it on a waggon, carry it about through all the different tribes. On this procession each tribe, when it receives the corpse, imitates the example which is first set by the Royal Scythians; every man chops off a piece of his ear, crops his hair close, and makes a cut all round his arm, lacerates his forehead and his nose, and thrusts an arrow through his left hand. Then they who have the care of the corpse carry it with them to another of the tribes which are under the Scythian rule, followed by those whom they first visited. On completing the circuit of all the tribes under their sway, they find themselves in the country of the Gerrhi, who are the most remote of all, and so they come to the tombs of the kings. There the body of the dead king is laid in the grave prepared for it, stretched upon a mattress; spears are fixed in the ground on either side of the corpse, and beams stretched across above it to form a roof, which is covered with a thatching of osier twigs. In the open space around the body of the king they bury one of his concubines, first killing her by strangling, and also his cup-bearer, his cook, his groom, his lacquey, his messenger, some of his horses, firstlings of all his other possessions, and some golden cups; for they use neither silver nor brass. After this they set to work, and raise a vast mound above the grave, all of them vying with each other and seeking to make it as tall as possible.

---

1 Modified forms of the same ceremony are ascribed to the Lydians and Assyrians by Herodotus (i. 74), and to the Armenians and Iberians by Tacitus (Ann. xii. 47). The Arab practice (iii. 8) is somewhat different. In Southern Africa a custom very like the Scythian prevails to this day.

72. When a year is gone by, further ceremonies take place. Fifty of the best of the late king's attendants are taken, all native Scythians – for as bought slaves are unknown in the country, the Scythian kings choose any of their subjects that they like, to wait on them – fifty of these are taken and strangled, with fifty of the most beautiful horses. When they are dead, their bowels are taken out, and the cavity cleaned, filled full of chaff, and straightway sewn up again. This done, a number of posts are driven into the ground, in sets of two pairs each, and on every pair half the felly of a wheel is placed archwise; then strong stakes are run lengthways through the bodies of the horses from tail to neck, and they are mounted up upon the fellies, so that the felly in front supports the shoulders of the horses, while that behind sustains the belly and quarters, the legs dangling in mid-air; each horse is furnished with a bit and bridle, which latter is stretched out in front of the horse, and fastened to a peg.[1] The fifty strangled youths are then mounted severally on the fifty horses. To effect this, a second stake is passed through their bodies along the course of the spine to the neck; the lower end of which projects from the body, and is fixed into a socket, made in the stake that runs lengthwise down the horse. The fifty riders are thus ranged in a circle round the tomb, and so left.

73. Such, then, is the mode in which the kings are buried: as for the people, when any one dies, his nearest of kin lay him upon a waggon and take him round to all his friends in succession: each receives them in turn and entertains them with a banquet, whereat the dead man is served with a portion of all that is set before the others; this is done for forty days, at the end of which time the burial takes place. After the burial, those engaged in it have to purify themselves, which they do in the following way. First they well soap and wash their heads; then, in order to cleanse their bodies, they act as follows: they make a booth by fixing in the ground three sticks inclined towards one another,[2] and stretching around them woollen felts, which they arrange so as to fit as close as possible: inside the booth a dish is placed upon the ground, into which they put a number of red-hot stones, and then add some hemp-seed.

---

1 The practice of impaling horses seems to have ceased in these regions. It was found, however, among the Tatars so late as the fourteenth century.

2 Here we see tent-making in its infancy. The tents of the wandering tribes of the steppes are now of a much more elaborate construction.

74. Hemp grows in Scythia: it is very like flax; only that it is a much coarser and taller plant: some grows wild about the country, some is produced by cultivation:[1] the Thracians make garments of it which closely resemble linen; so much so, indeed, that if a person has never seen hemp he is sure to think they are linen, and if he has, unless he is very experienced in such matters, he will not know of which material they are.

75. The Scythians, as I said, take some of this hemp-seed, and, creeping under the felt coverings, throw it upon the red-hot stones; immediately it smokes, and gives out such a vapour as no Grecian vapour-bath can exceed; the Scyths, delighted, shout for joy, and this vapour serves them instead of a waterbath; for they never by any chance wash their bodies with water. Their women make a mixture of cypress, cedar, and frankincense wood, which they pound into a paste upon a rough piece of stone, adding a little water to it. With this substance, which is of a thick consistency, they plaster their faces all over, and indeed their whole bodies. A sweet odour is thereby imparted to them, and when they take off the plaster on the day following, their skin is clean and glossy.

76. The Scythians have an extreme hatred of all foreign customs, particularly of those in use among the Greeks, as the instances of Anacharsis, and, more lately, of Scylas, have fully shown. The former, after he had travelled over a great portion of the world, and displayed wherever he went many proofs of wisdom, as he sailed through the Hellespont on his return to Scythia touched at Cyzicus. There he found the inhabitants celebrating with much pomp and magnificence a festival to the Mother of the Gods,[2] and was himself induced to make a vow to the goddess, whereby he engaged, if he got back safe and sound to his home, that he would give her a festival and a night-procession in all respects like those which he had seen in Cyzicus. When, therefore, he arrived in Scythia, he betook himself to the district called the Woodland,[3] which lies opposite the Course of Achilles, and is covered with trees of all manner of

---

1 Hemp is not now cultivated in these regions. It forms, however, an item of some importance among the exports of Southern Russia.

2 Cybelé or Rhea, whose worship (common throughout Asia) passed from the Phrygians to the Ionian Greeks, and thence to their colonies.

3 Vide supra, chs. 18, 19, and 54.

different kinds, and there went through all the sacred rites with the tabour in his hand, and the images tied to him. While thus employed, he was noticed by one of the Scythians, who went and told king Saulius what he had seen. Then king Saulius came in person, and when he perceived what Anacharsis was about, he shot at him with an arrow and killed him. To this day, if you ask the Scyths about Anacharsis, they pretend ignorance of him, because of his Grecian travels and adoption of the customs of foreigners. I learnt, however, from Timnes, the steward of Ariapithes, that Anacharsis was paternal uncle to the Scythian king Idanthyrsus, being the son of Gnurus, who was the son of Lycus and the grandson of Spargapithes. If Anacharsis were really of this house, it must have been by his own brother that he was slain, for Idanthyrsus was a son of the Saulius who put Anacharsis to death.[1]

77. I have heard, however, another tale, very different from this, which is told by the Peloponnesians: they say, that Anacharsis was sent by the king of the Scyths to make acquaintance with Greece – that he went, and on his return home reported that the Greeks were all occupied in the pursuit of every kind of knowledge, except the Lacedæmonians; who, however, alone knew how to converse sensibly. A silly tale this, which the Greeks have invented for their amusement! There is no doubt that Anacharsis suffered death in the mode already related, on account of his attachment to foreign customs, and the intercourse which he held with the Greeks.

78. Scylas, likewise, the son of Ariapithes, many years later, met with almost the very same fate. Ariapithes, the Scythian king, had several sons, among them this Scylas, who was the child, not of a native Scyth, but of a woman of Istria.[2] Bred up by her, Scylas gained an acquaintance with the Greek language and letters. Some time afterwards, Ariapithes was treacherously slain by Spargapithes, king of the Agathyrsi; whereupon Scylas succeeded to the throne, and married one of his father's wives,[3] a woman

---

1 Herodotus is the earliest writer who mentions Anacharsis. There is no sufficient reason to doubt the fact of his travels.

2 Istria, Ister, or Istropolis, at the mouth of the Danube or Ister, was a colony of the Milesians.

3 Compare Adonijah's request to be given one of his father's (David's) wives (1 Kings ii. 17–25). Such marriages were forbidden by the Jewish law (Lev. xviii. 8, etc.), but they were no doubt common among other nations.

named Opœa. This Opœa was a Scythian by birth, and had brought Ariapithes a son called Oricus. Now when Scylas found himself king of Scythia, as he disliked the Scythic mode of life, and was attached, by his bringing up, to the manners of the Greeks, he made it his usual practice, whenever he came with his army to the town of the Borysthenites, who, according to their own account, are colonists of the Milesians, – he made it his practice, I say, to leave the army before the city, and, having entered within the walls by himself, and carefully closed the gates, to exchange his Scythian dress for Grecian garments, and in this attire to walk about the forum, without guards or retinue. The Borysthenites kept watch at the gates, that no Scythian might see the king thus apparelled. Scylas, meanwhile, lived exactly as the Greeks, and even offered sacrifices to the Gods according to the Grecian rites. In this way he would pass a month, or more, with the Borysthenites, after which he would clothe himself again in his Scythian dress, and so take his departure. This he did repeatedly, and even built himself a house in Borysthenes, and married a wife there who was a native of the place.

79. But when the time came that was ordained to bring him woe, the occasion of his ruin was the following. He wanted to be initiated in the Dionysiac mysteries, and was on the point of obtaining admission to the rites, when a most strange prodigy occurred to him. The house which he possessed, as I mentioned a short time back, in the city of the Borysthenites, a building of great extent and erected at a vast cost, round which there stood a number of sphinxes and griffins carved in white marble, was struck by lightning from on high, and burnt to the ground. Scylas, nevertheless, went on and received the initiation. Now the Scythians are wont to reproach the Greeks with their Dionysiac rage, and to say that it is not reasonable to imagine there is a god who impels men to madness. No sooner, therefore, was Scylas initiated in the Dionysiac mysteries than one of the Borysthenites went and carried the news to the Scythians – "You Scyths laugh at us," he said, "because we rave when the god seizes us. But now our god has seized upon your king, who raves like us, and is maddened by the influence. If you think I do not tell you true, come with me, and I will show him to you." The chiefs of the Scythians went with the man accordingly, and the Borysthenite, conducting them into the city, placed them secretly

on one of the towers. Presently Scylas passed by with the band of revellers, raving like the rest, and was seen by the watchers. Regarding the matter as a very great misfortune they instantly departed, and came and told the army what they had witnessed.

80. When, therefore, Scylas, after leaving Borysthenes, was about returning home, the Scythians broke out into revolt. They put at their head Octamasadas, grandson (on the mother's side) of Teres. Then Scylas, when he learned the danger with which he was threatened, and the reason of the disturbance, made his escape to Thrace. Octamasadas, discovering whither he had fled, marched after him, and had reached the Ister, when he was met by the forces of the Thracians. The two armies were about to engage, but before they joined battle, Sitalces[1] sent a message to Octamasadas to this effect – "Why should there be trial of arms betwixt thee and me? Thou art my own sister's son, and thou hast in thy keeping my brother. Surrender him into my hands, and I will give thy Scylas back to thee. So neither thou nor I will risk our armies." Sitalces sent this message to Octamasadas, by a herald, and Octamasadas, with whom a brother of Sitalces[2] had formerly taken refuge, accepted the terms. He surrendered his own uncle to Sitalces, and obtained in exchange his brother Scylas. Sitalces took his brother with him and withdrew; but Octamasadas beheaded Scylas upon the spot. Thus rigidly do the Scythians maintain their own customs, and thus severely do they punish such as adopt foreign usages.

81. What the population of Scythia is, I was not able to learn with certainty; the accounts which I received varied from one another. I heard from some that they were very numerous indeed; others made their numbers but scanty for such a nation as the Scyths. Thus much, however, I witnessed with my own eyes. There is a tract called Exampæus between the Borysthenes and the Hypanis. I made some mention of it in a former place, where I spoke of the bitter stream which rising there flows into the Hypanis, and renders the water of that river undrinkable.[3] Here then stands a brazen bowl, six times as big as that at the entrance of the Euxine, which Pausanias, the son of Cleombrotus, set up.

1 Vide infra, vii. 137. Sitalces was contemporary with Herodotus. He died B.C. 424 (Thucyd. iv. 101).
2 Perhaps Sparadocus, the father of Seuthes.
3 Vide supra, ch. 52.

Such as have never seen that vessel may understand me better if I say that the Scythian bowl holds with ease six hundred amphoræ,[1] and is of the thickness of six fingers' breadth. The natives gave me the following account of the manner in which it was made. One of their kings, by name Ariantas, wishing to know the number of his subjects, ordered them all to bring him, on pain of death, the point off one of their arrows. They obeyed; and he collected thereby a vast heap of arrow-heads, which he resolved to form into a memorial that might go down to posterity. Accordingly he made of them this bowl, and dedicated it at Exampæus. This was all that I could learn concerning the number of the Scythians.

82. The country has no marvels except its rivers, which are larger and more numerous than those of any other land. These, and the vastness of the great plain, are worthy of note, and one thing besides, which I am about to mention. They show a foot-mark of Heracles, impressed on a rock, in shape like the print of a man's foot, but two cubits in length. It is in the neighbourhood of the Tyras. Having described this, I return to the subject on which I originally proposed to discourse.

83. The preparations of Darius against the Scythians had begun, messengers had been despatched on all sides with the king's commands, some being required to furnish troops, others to supply ships, others again to bridge the Thracian Bosphorus, when Artabanus, son of Hystaspes and brother of Darius, entreated the king to desist from his expedition, urging on him the great difficulty of attacking Scythia.[2] Good, however, as the advice of Artabanus was, it failed to persuade Darius. He therefore ceased his reasonings; and Darius, when his preparations were complete, led his army forth from Susa.

84. It was then that a certain Persian, by name Œobazus, the father of three sons, all of whom were to accompany the army, came and prayed the king that he would allow one of his sons to remain with him. Darius made answer, as if he regarded him in the light of a friend who had urged a moderate request, "that he would allow them all to remain." Œobazus was overjoyed,

1 The Greek *amphora* ($\dot{\alpha}\mu\phi o\rho\epsilon\grave{\nu}\varsigma$) contained nearly nine of our gallons; whence it appears that this bowl would have held about 5,400 gallons, or above 85 hogsheads. (The "Great Tun" at Heidelberg holds above 800 hogsheads.)

2 The cautious temper of Artabanus again appears, vii. 10.

expecting that all his children would be excused from serving; the king however bade his attendants take the three sons of Œobazus and forthwith put them to death. Thus they were all left behind, but not till they had been deprived of life.[1]

85. When Darius, on his march from Susa, reached the territory of Chalcedon[2] on the shores of the Bosphorus, where the bridge had been made, he took ship and sailed thence to the Cyanean islands,[3] which, according to the Greeks, once floated. He took his seat also in the temple[4] and surveyed the Pontus, which is indeed well worthy of consideration. There is not in the world any other sea so wonderful: it extends in length eleven thousand one hundred furlongs, and its breadth, at the widest part, is three thousand three hundred.[5] The mouth is but four furlongs wide; and this strait, called the Bosphorus, and across which the bridge of Darius had been thrown, is a hundred and twenty furlongs in length, reaching from the Euxine to the Propontis. The Propontis is five hundred furlongs across, and fourteen hundred long.[6] Its waters flow into the Hellespont, the length of which is four hundred furlongs, and the width no more than seven.[7] The Hellespont opens into the wide sea called the Ægean.

86. The mode in which these distances have been measured is the following. In a long day a vessel generally accomplishes about seventy thousand fathoms, in the night sixty thousand. Now from the mouth of the Pontus to the river Phasis, which is the extreme length of this sea, is a voyage of nine days and eight nights, which makes the distance one million one hundred and ten thousand fathoms, or eleven thousand one hundred furlongs. Again, from Sindica, to Themiscyra on the river Thermôdon,

1 Compare the similar story told of Xerxes, infra, vii. 39.

2 Chalcedon was situated on the Asiatic side, at the point where the Bosphorus opens into the Sea of Marmora.

3 Otherwise called the Symplegades [which, in Greek myth, crushed all vessels that tried to pass between them. Milton speaks of these "justling rocks," in reference to the story of Jason and the Argonauts (P. L. ii. 1017, 8). – E. H. B.].

4 The temple at the mouth of the strait mentioned below, ch. 87.

5 These measurements are extremely incorrect.

6 By the length of the Propontis we must understand here the distance from the lower mouth of the Bosphorus to the upper end of the Hellespont.

7 The length of the Dardanelles is, as nearly as possible, 40 miles. Its breadth at the narrowest part is about one mile.

where the Pontus is wider than at any other place,[1] is a sail of three days and two nights; which makes three hundred and thirty thousand fathoms, or three thousand three hundred furlongs. Such is the plan on which I have measured the Pontus, the Bosphorus, and the Hellespont, and such is the account which I have to give of them. The Pontus has also a lake belonging to it, not very much inferior to itself in size. The waters of this lake run into the Pontus: it is called the Mæotis, and also the Mother of the Pontus.

87. Darius, after he had finished his survey, sailed back to the bridge, which had been constructed for him by Mandrocles, a Samian. He likewise surveyed the Bosphorus, and erected upon its shores two pillars of white marble, whereupon he inscribed the names of all the nations which formed his army – on the one pillar in Greek, on the other in Assyrian characters.[2] Now his army was drawn from all the nations under his sway; and the whole amount, without reckoning the naval forces, was seven hundred thousand men, including cavalry. The fleet consisted of six hundred ships. Some time afterwards the Byzantines removed these pillars to their own city, and used them for an altar which they erected to Orthosian Artemis.[3] One block remained behind: it lay near the temple of Dionysus at Byzantium, and was covered with Assyrian writing. The spot where Darius bridged the Bosphorus was, I think, but I speak only from conjecture, half-way between the city of Byzantium and the temple at the mouth of the strait.

88. Darius was so pleased with the bridge thrown across the strait by the Samian Mandrocles, that he not only bestowed upon him all the customary presents, but gave him ten of every kind. Mandrocles, by way of offering first-fruits from these presents, caused a picture to be painted which showed the whole of the bridge, with King Darius sitting in a seat of honour, and his army engaged in the passage. This painting he dedicated in the temple of Hera at Samos, attaching to it the inscription following:—

---

1 This is a mistake. It is possible that the Palus Mæotis (= Sea of Azov) may have been very greatly larger in the time of Herodotus than it is at present. [See Tozer, *History of Ancient Geography*, p. 81. – E. H. B.]

2 It was natural that the Persians, who set up trilingual inscriptions in the central provinces for the benefit of their Arian, Semitic, and Tatar populations, should leave bilingual records in other places.

3 That is, Artemis, who had established or *preserved* their city. (Compare the Latin "*Jupiter Stator.*")

"The fish-fraught Bosphorus bridged, to Hera's fane
        Did Mandrocles this proud memorial bring;
    When for himself a crown he'd skill to gain,
        For Samos praise, contenting the Great King."

Such was the memorial of his work which was left by the architect of the bridge.

89. Darius, after rewarding Mandrocles, passed into Europe,
while he ordered the Ionians to enter the Pontus, and sail to the
mouth of the Ister. There he bade them throw a bridge across
the stream and await his coming. The Ionians, Æolians, and
Hellespontians were the nations which furnished the chief
strength of his navy. So the fleet, threading the Cyanean Isles,
proceeded straight to the Ister, and, mounting the river to the
point where its channels separate,¹ a distance of two days' voyage
from the sea, yoked the neck of the stream. Meantime Darius,
who had crossed the Bosphorus by the bridge over it, marched
through Thrace; and happening upon the sources of the Tearus,
pitched his camp and made a stay of three days.

90. Now the Tearus is said by those who dwell near it, to be
the most healthful of all streams, and to cure, among other
diseases, the scab either in man or beast. Its sources, which are
eight and thirty in number, all flowing from the same rock, are
in part cold, in part hot. They lie at an equal distance from the
town of Heræum near Perinthus,² and Apollonia on the Euxine,
a two days' journey from each. This river, the Tearus, is a tributary of the Contadesdus, which runs into the Agrianes, and that
into the Hebrus.³ The Hebrus empties itself into the sea near the
city of Ænus.⁴

91. Here then, on the banks of the Tearus, Darius stopped
and pitched his camp. The river charmed him so, that he caused
a pillar to be erected in this place also, with an inscription to the
following effect: "The fountains of the Tearus afford the best and
most beautiful water of all rivers: they were visited, on his march

1 The Danube divides at present near *Isatcha*, between *Brailow* and *Ismail;*
but we cannot be certain that the division was always at this place.
2 Perinthus (afterwards Heraclea) lay upon the Propontis, in lat. 41°, long.
28°, nearly. Its site is marked by the modern *Erekli* (vide infra, v. 1).
3 The Agrianes is undoubtedly the modern *Erkene*, which runs into the
Maritza (Hebrus) to the north of the range of Rhodope (*Despoto Dagh*). The
Contadesdus is the river of *Karishtiran.*
4 Concerning the site of Ænus, vide infra, vii. 58.

into Scythia, by the best and most beautiful of men, Darius, son of Hystaspes, king of the Persians, and of the whole continent."[1] Such was the inscription which he set up at this place.

92. Marching thence, he came to a second river, called the Artiscus, which flows through the country of the Odrysians.[2] Here he fixed upon a certain spot, where every one of his soldiers should throw a stone as he passed by. When his orders were obeyed, Darius continued his march, leaving behind him great hills formed of the stones cast by his troops.

93. Before arriving at the Ister,[3] the first people whom he subdued were the Getæ,[4] who believe in their immortality. The Thracians of Salmydessus, and those who dwelt above the cities of Apollonia and Mesembria – the Scyrmiadæ and Nipsæans, as they are called – gave themselves up to Darius without a struggle; but the Getæ obstinately defending themselves, were forthwith enslaved, notwithstanding that they are the noblest as well as the most just of all the Thracian tribes.

94. The belief of the Getæ in respect of immortality is the following. They think that they do not really die, but that when they depart this life they go to Zalmoxis, who is called also Gebeleïzis by some among them. To this god every five years they send a messenger, who is chosen by lot out of the whole nation, and charged to bear him their several requests. Their mode of sending him is this. A number of them stand in order, each holding in his hand three darts; others take the man who is to be sent to Zalmoxis, and swinging him by his hands and feet, toss him into the air so that he falls upon the points of the weapons. If he is pierced and dies, they think that the god is propitious to them; but if not, they lay the fault on the messenger, who (they say) is a wicked man: and so they choose another to send away. The messages are given while the man is still alive. This same people, when it lightens and thunders, aim their arrows at the sky, uttering threats against the god;[5] and they do not believe that there is any god but their own.

1 Vide supra, i. 4.

2 The country of the Odrysæ was the great plain in the centre of which now stands the city of Adrianople.

3 It is not quite clear by which route Darius crossed the Balkans.

4 The identity of the Getæ with the Goths of later times is more than a plausible conjecture.

5 Compare the customs of the Calyndians (i. 172), and the Psylli (iv. 173).

95. I am told by the Greeks who dwell on the shores of the Hellespont and the Pontus, that this Zalmoxis was in reality a man, that he lived at Samos, and while there was the slave[1] of Pythagoras son of Mnesarchus. After obtaining his freedom he grew rich, and leaving Samos, returned to his own country. The Thracians at that time lived in a wretched way, and were a poor ignorant race; Zalmoxis, therefore, who by his commerce with the Greeks, and especially with one who was by no means their most contemptible philosopher, Pythagoras to wit, was acquainted with the Ionic mode of life and with manners more refined than those current among his countrymen, had a chamber built, in which from time to time he received and feasted all the principal Thracians, using the occasion to teach them that neither he, nor they, his boon companions, nor any of their posterity would ever perish, but that they would all go to a place where they would live for aye in the enjoyment of every conceivable good. While he was acting in this way, and holding this kind of discourse, he was constructing an apartment underground, into which, when it was completed, he withdrew, vanishing suddenly from the eyes of the Thracians, who greatly regretted his loss, and mourned over him as one dead. He meanwhile abode in his secret chamber three full years, after which he came forth from his concealment, and showed himself once more to his countrymen, who were thus brought to believe in the truth of what he had taught them. Such is the account of the Greeks.

96. I for my part neither put entire faith in this story of Zalmoxis and his underground chamber, nor do I altogether discredit it: but I believe Zalmoxis to have lived long before the time of Pythagoras. Whether there was ever really a man of the name, or whether Zalmoxis is nothing but a native god of the Getæ, I now bid him farewell. As for the Getæ themselves, the people who observe the practices described above, they were now reduced by the Persians, and accompanied the army of Darius.

97. When Darius, with his land forces, reached the Ister, he made his troops cross the stream, and after all were gone over gave orders to the Ionians to break the bridge, and follow him with the whole naval force in his land march. They were about

---

1 Thracian slaves were very numerous in Greece.

to obey his command, when the general of the Mytilenæans, Coës son of Erxander, having first asked whether it was agreeable to the king to listen to one who wished to speak his mind, addressed him in the words following:– "Thou art about, Sire, to attack a country no part of which is cultivated, and wherein there is not a single inhabited city. Keep this bridge, then, as it is, and leave those who built it to watch over it. So if we come up with the Scythians and succeed against them as we could wish, we may return by this route; or if we fail of finding them, our retreat will still be secure. For I have no fear lest the Scythians defeat us in battle, but my dread is lest we be unable to discover them, and suffer loss while we wander about their territory. And now, mayhap, it will be said, I advise thee thus in the hope of being myself allowed to remain behind; but in truth I have no other design than to recommend the course which seems to me the best; nor will I consent to be among those left behind, but my resolve is, in any case, to follow thee." The advice of Coës pleased Darius highly, who thus replied to him:– "Dear Lesbian, when I am safe home again in my palace, be sure thou come to me, and with good deeds will I recompense thy good words of to-day."

98. Having so said, the king took a leathern thong, and tying sixty knots in it, called together the Ionian tyrants, and spoke thus to them:– "Men of Ionia, my former commands to you concerning the bridge are now withdrawn. See, here is a thong: take it, and observe my bidding with respect to it. From the time that I leave you to march forward into Scythia, untie every day one of the knots. If I do not return before the last day to which the knots will hold out, then leave your station, and sail to your several homes. Meanwhile, understand that my resolve is changed, and that you are to guard the bridge with all care, and watch over its safety and preservation. By so doing ye will oblige me greatly." When Darius had thus spoken, he set out on his march with all speed.

99. Before you come to Scythia, on the sea-coast, lies Thrace. The land here makes a sweep, and then Scythia begins, the Ister falling into the sea at this point with its mouth facing the east. Starting from the Ister I shall now describe the measurements of the sea-shore of Scythia. Immediately that the Ister is crossed, Old Scythia begins, and continues as far as the city called Carcinitis, fronting towards the south wind and the mid-day. Here

upon the same sea, there lies a mountainous tract[1] projecting into the Pontus, which is inhabited by the Tauri, as far as what is called the Rugged Chersonese,[2] which runs out into the sea upon the east. For the boundaries of Scythia extend on two sides to two different seas, one upon the south, and the other towards the east, as is also the case with Attica. And the Tauri occupy a position in Scythia like that which a people would hold in Attica, who, being foreigners and not Athenians, should inhabit the high land of Sunium, from Thoricus to the township of Anaphlystus, if this tract projected into the sea somewhat further than it does. Such, to compare great things with small, is the Tauric territory. For the sake of those who may not have made the voyage round these parts of Attica, I will illustrate in another way. It is as if in Iapygia a line were drawn from Port Brundusium[3] to Tarentum, and a people different from the Iapygians inhabited the promontory. These two instances may suggest a number of others where the shape of the land closely resembles that of Taurica.

100. Beyond this tract, we find the Scythians again in possession of the country above the Tauri and the parts bordering on the eastern sea, as also of the whole district lying west of the Cimmerian Bosphorus and the Palus Mæotis, as far as the river Tanais, which empties itself into that lake at its upper end. As for the inland boundaries of Scythia, if we start from the Ister, we find it enclosed by the following tribes, first the Agathyrsi, next the Neuri, then the Androphagi, and last of all, the Melanchlæni.

101. Scythia then, which is square in shape, and has two of its sides reaching down to the sea, extends inland to the same distance that it stretches along the coast, and is equal every way. For it is a ten days' journey from the Ister[4] to the Borysthenes, and ten more from the Borysthenes to the Palus Mæotis, while the distance from the coast inland to the country of the Melanchlæni, who dwell above Scythia, is a journey of twenty days. I reckon the day's journey at two hundred furlongs. Thus the two sides which run straight inland are four thousand furlongs

1 The mountains lie only along the southern coast of the Crimea. All the rest of the peninsula belongs to the steppes.

2 By the "rough" or "rugged" Chersonese, Herodotus plainly intends the eastern part of the Crimea.

3 Brindisi.

4 [See Macan's *Herodotus*, vol. ii. p. 32. – E. H. B.]

each, and the transverse sides at right angles to these are also of the same length, which gives the full size of Scythia.

102. The Scythians, reflecting on their situation, perceived that they were not strong enough by themselves to contend with the army of Darius in open fight. They, therefore, sent envoys to the neighbouring nations, whose kings had already met, and were in consultation upon the advance of so vast a host. Now they who had come together were the kings of the Tauri, the Agathyrsi, the Neuri, the Androphagi, the Melanchlæni, the Gelôni, the Budini, and the Sauromatæ.

103. The Tauri have the following customs. They offer in sacrifice to the Virgin all shipwrecked persons, and all Greeks compelled to put into their ports by stress of weather. The mode of sacrifice is this. After the preparatory ceremonies, they strike the victim on the head with a club. Then, according to some accounts, they hurl the trunk from the precipice whereon the temple stands, and nail the head to a cross. Others grant that the head is treated in this way, but deny that the body is thrown down the cliff – on the contrary, they say, it is buried. The goddess to whom these sacrifices are offered the Tauri themselves declare to be Iphigenia[1] the daughter of Agamemnon. When they take prisoners in war they treat them in the following way. The man who has taken a captive cuts off his head, and carrying it to his home, fixes it upon a tall pole, which he elevates above his house, most commonly over the chimney. The reason that the heads are set up so high, is (it is said) in order that the whole house may be under their protection. These people live entirely by war and plundering.

104. The Agathyrsi are a race of men very luxurious, and very fond of wearing gold on their persons. They have wives in common, that so they may be all brothers,[2] and, as members of one family, may neither envy nor hate one another. In other respects their customs approach nearly to those of the Thracians.

105. The Neurian customs are like the Scythian. One generation before the attack of Darius they were driven from their land

1 The virgin goddess of the Tauri was more generally identified by the Greeks with their own Artemis. The legend of Iphigenia is probably a mere Greek fancy, having the Tauric custom of offering human sacrifices as its basis.

2 This anticipation of the theory of Plato (Rep. v.) is curious. Was Plato indebted to Herodotus?

by a huge multitude of serpents which invaded them. Of these some were produced in their own country, while others, and those by far the greater number, came in from the deserts on the north. Suffering grievously beneath this scourge, they quitted their homes, and took refuge with the Budini. It seems that these people are conjurers: for both the Scythians and the Greeks who dwell in Scythia say, that every Neurian once a year becomes a wolf[1] for a few days, at the end of which time he is restored to his proper shape.[2] Not that I believe this, but they constantly affirm it to be true, and are even ready to back their assertion with an oath.

106. The manners of the Androphagi[3] are more savage than those of any other race. They neither observe justice, nor are governed by any laws. They are nomads, and their dress is Scythian; but the language which they speak is peculiar to themselves. Unlike any other nation in these parts, they are cannibals.

107. The Melanchlæni[4] wear, all of them, black cloaks, and from this derive the name which they bear. Their customs are Scythic.

108. The Budini are a large and powerful nation: they have all deep blue eyes, and bright red hair. There is a city in their territory, called Gelônus, which is surrounded with a lofty wall, thirty furlongs each way, built entirely of wood. All the houses in the place and all the temples are of the same material. Here are temples built in honour of the Grecian gods, and adorned after the Greek fashion with images, altars, and shrines, all in wood. There is even a festival, held every third year in honour of Dionysus, at which the natives fall into the Dionysiac fury. For the fact is that the Gelôni were anciently Greeks, who, being driven out of the factories along the coast, fled to the Budini and took up their abode with them. They still speak a language half Greek, half Scythian.

109. The Budini, however, do not speak the same language as the Gelôni, nor is their mode of life the same. They are the aboriginal people of the country, and are nomads; unlike any of

1 The story recalls the loup-garou of France. [The were-wolf constantly appears in modern folk-lore. – E. H. B.]

2 As Herodotus recedes from the sea his accounts become more mythic and less trustworthy.

3 Or "Men-eaters."

4 Or "Black-cloaks." This is probably a translation of the native name.

the neighbouring races, they eat lice. The Gelôni, on the contrary, are tillers of the soil, eat bread, have gardens, and both in shape and complexion are quite different from the Budini. The Greeks notwithstanding call these latter Gelôni; but it is a mistake to give them the name. Their country is thickly planted with trees of all manner of kinds. In the very woodiest part is a broad deep lake, surrounded by marshy ground with reeds growing on it. Here otters are caught, and beavers, with another sort of animal which has a square face. With the skins of this last the natives border their capotes:[1] and they also get from them a remedy, which is of virtue in diseases of the womb.

110. It is reported of the Sauromatæ, that when the Greeks fought with the Amazons,[2] whom the Scythians call *Oior-pata* or "man-slayers," as it may be rendered, *Oior* being Scythic for "man," and *pata* for "to slay" — it is reported, I say, that the Greeks after gaining the battle of the Thermôdon, put to sea, taking with them on board three of their vessels all the Amazons whom they had made prisoners; and that these women upon the voyage rose up against the crews, and massacred them to a man. As however they were quite strange to ships, and did not know how to use either rudder, sails, or oars, they were carried, after the death of the men, where the winds and the waves listed. At last they reached the shores of the Palus Mæotis and came to a place called Cremni or "the Cliffs," which is in the country of the free Scythians. Here they went ashore, and proceeded by land towards the inhabited regions; the first herd of horses which they fell in with they seized, and mounting upon their backs, fell to plundering the Scythian territory.

111. The Scyths could not tell what to make of the attack upon them — the dress, the language, the nation itself, were alike unknown — whence the enemy had come even, was a marvel. Imagining, however, that they were all men of about the same age,[3] they went out against them, and fought a battle. Some of the bodies of the slain fell into their hands, whereby they discovered the truth. Hereupon they deliberated, and made a resolve

---

1 A border of fur is commonly seen to edge the coat worn by the Scythians on the sepulchral vases and other remains.

2 Some Amazons were supposed to live in Asia, others in Africa.

3 That is to say, as they were all alike beardless, they took them for an army of youths.

to kill no more of them, but to send against them a detachment of their youngest men, as near as they could guess equal to the women in number, with orders to encamp in their neighbourhood, and do as they saw them do — when the Amazons advanced against them, they were to retire, and avoid a fight — when they halted, the young men were to approach and pitch their camp near the camp of the enemy. All this they did on account of their strong desire to obtain children from so notable a race.

112. So the youths departed, and obeyed the orders which had been given them. The Amazons soon found out that they had not come to do them any harm; and so they on their part ceased to offer the Scythians any molestation. And now day after day the camps approached nearer to one another; both parties led the same life, neither having anything but their arms and horses, so that they were forced to support themselves by hunting and pillage.

113. But the Amazons towards noonday used to do the following: they would scatter in ones and twos, moving away from each other to relieve themselves. When the Scythians realised this, they did likewise. One of the young men approached one of the women who was alone, and the Amazon did not reject him but allowed him to enjoy her favours. She bade him by signs (for they did not understand each other's language) to bring a friend the next day to the spot where they had met — promising on her part to bring with her another woman. He did so, and the woman kept her word. When the rest of the youths heard what had taken place, they also sought and gained the favour of the other Amazons.

114. The two camps were then joined in one, the Scythians living with the Amazons as their wives; and the men were unable to learn the tongue of the women, but the women soon caught up the tongue of the men. When they could thus understand one another, the Scyths addressed the Amazons in these words, — "We have parents, and properties, let us therefore give up this mode of life, and return to our nation, and live with them. You shall be our wives there no less than here, and we promise you to have no others." But the Amazons said — "We could not live with your women — our customs are quite different from theirs. To draw the bow, to hurl the javelin, to bestride the horse, these are our arts — of womanly employments we know nothing. Your women, on the contrary, do none of these things; but stay at home in their waggons, engaged in womanish tasks, and never go out to hunt, or to do anything. We should never agree together.

But if you truly wish to keep us as your wives, and would conduct yourselves with strict justice towards us, go you home to your parents, bid them give you your inheritance, and then come back to us, and let us and you live together by ourselves."

115. The youths approved of the advice, and followed it. They went and got the portion of goods which fell to them, returned with it, and rejoined their wives, who then addressed them in these words following:— "We are ashamed, and afraid to live in the country where we now are. Not only have we stolen you from your fathers, but we have done great damage to Scythia by our ravages. As you like us for wives, grant the request we make of you. Let us leave this country together, and go and dwell beyond the Tanais." Again the youths complied.

116. Crossing the Tanais they journeyed eastward a distance of three days' march from that stream, and again northward a distance of three days' march from the Palus Mæotis. Here they came to the country where they now live, and took up their abode in it. The women of the Sauromatæ have continued from that day to the present to observe their ancient customs,[1] frequently hunting on horseback with their husbands, sometimes even unaccompanied; in war taking the field; and wearing the very same dress as the men.

117. The Sauromatæ speak the language of Scythia, but have never talked it correctly, because the Amazons learnt it imperfectly at the first. Their marriage-law lays it down that no girl shall wed till she has killed a man in battle. Sometimes it happens that a woman dies unmarried at an advanced age, having never been able in her whole lifetime to fulfil the condition.

118. The envoys of the Scythians, on being introduced into the presence of the kings of these nations, who were assembled to deliberate, made it known to them, that the Persian, after subduing the whole of the other continent, had thrown a bridge over the strait of the Bosphorus, and crossed into the continent of Europe, where he had reduced the Thracians, and was now making a bridge over the Ister, his aim being to bring under his sway all Europe also. "Stand ye not aloof then from this contest," they went on to say, "look not on tamely while we are perishing — but make common cause with us, and together let

---

1 This is of course the origin of the myth narrated above. That the Sarmatian women had these habits seems to be a certain fact.

us meet the enemy. If ye refuse, we must yield to the pressure, and either quit our country, or make terms with the invaders. For what else is left for us to do, if your aid be withheld from us? The blow, be sure, will not light on you more gently upon this account. The Persian comes against you no less than against us: and will not be content, after we are conquered, to leave you in peace. We can bring strong proof of what we here advance. Had the Persian leader indeed come to avenge the wrongs which he suffered at our hands when we enslaved his people, and to war on us only, he would have been bound to march straight upon Scythia, without molesting any nation by the way.[1] Then it would have been plain to all that Scythia alone was aimed at. But now, what has his conduct been? From the moment of his entrance into Europe, he has subjugated without exception every nation that lay in his path. All the tribes of the Thracians have been brought under his sway, and among them even our next neighbours, the Getæ."

119. The assembled princes of the nations, after hearing all that the Scythians had to say, deliberated. At the end opinion was divided — the kings of the Gelôni, Budini, and Sauromatæ were of accord, and pledged themselves to give assistance to the Scythians; but the Agathyrsian and Neurian princes, together with the sovereigns of the Androphagi, the Melanchlæni, and the Tauri, replied to their request as follows:— "If you had not been the first to wrong the Persians, and begin the war, we should have thought the request you make just; we should then have complied with your wishes, and joined our arms with yours. Now, however, the case stands thus — you, independently of us, invaded the land of the Persians, and so long as God gave you the power, lorded it over them: raised up now by the same God, they are come to do to you the like. We, on our part, did no wrong to these men in the former war, and will not be the first to commit wrong now. If they invade our land, and begin aggressions upon us, we will not suffer them; but, till we see this come to pass, we will remain at home. For we believe that the Persians are not come to attack us, but to punish those who are guilty of first injuring them."

120. When this reply reached the Scythians, they resolved, as the neighbouring nations refused their alliance, that they would

---

1 Alluding to the Scythian invasion of Asia in the time of Cyaxares. See Book i. chs. 103–105, and supra, ch. 1.

not openly venture on any pitched battle with the enemy, but would retire before them, driving off their herds, choking up all the wells and springs as they retreated, and leaving the whole country bare of forage. They divided themselves into three bands, one of which, namely that commanded by Scopasis, it was agreed should be joined by the Sauromatæ, and if the Persians advanced in the direction of the Tanais, should retreat along the shores of the Palus Mæotis and make for that river; while if the Persians retired, they should at once pursue and harass them. This was one division of the royal forces, and this the route it was instructed to take. The two other divisions, the principal one under the command of Idanthyrsus, and the third, of which Taxacis was king, were to unite in one, and, joined by the detachments of the Gelôni and Budini, were, like the others, to keep at the distance of a day's march from the Persians, falling back as they advanced, and doing the same as the others. And first, they were to take the direction of the nations which had refused to join the alliance, and were to draw the war upon them: that so, if they would not of their own free will engage in the contest, they might by these means be forced into it. Afterwards, it was agreed that they should retire into their own land, and, should it on deliberation appear to them expedient, join battle with the enemy.

121. When these measures had been determined on, the Scythians went out to meet the army of Darius, sending on in front as scouts the fleetest of their horsemen. Their waggons, wherein their women and their children lived, and all their cattle, except such a number as was wanted for food, which they kept with them, were made to precede them in their retreat, and departed, with orders to keep marching, without change of course, to the north.

122. The scouts of the Scythians found the Persian host advanced three days' march from the Ister, and immediately took the lead of them at the distance of a day's march, encamping from time to time, and destroying all that grew on the ground. The Persians no sooner caught sight of the Scythian horse than they pursued upon their track, while the enemy retired before them. The pursuit of the Persians was directed towards the single division of the Scythian army,[1] and thus their line of march was eastward toward the Tanais. The Scyths crossed the river, and the Persians after them, still in pursuit. In this way they passed

---

1 The division of Scopasis (supra, ch. 120).

through the country of the Sauromatæ, and entered that of the Budini.

123. As long as the march of the Persian army lay through the countries of the Scythians and Sauromatæ, there was nothing which they could damage, the land being waste and barren; but on entering the territories of the Budini, they came upon the wooden fortress above mentioned,[1] which was deserted by its inhabitants and left quite empty of everything. This place they burnt to the ground; and having so done, again pressed forward on the track of the retreating Scythians, till, having passed through the entire country of the Budini, they reached the desert, which has no inhabitants,[2] and extends a distance of seven days' journey above the Budinian territory. Beyond this desert dwell the Thyssagetæ, out of whose land four great streams flow. These rivers all traverse the country of the Mæotians, and fall into the Palus Mæotis. Their names are the Lycus, the Oarus, the Tanais, and the Syrgis.[3]

124. When Darius reached the desert, he paused from his pursuit, and halted his army upon the Oarus. Here he built eight large forts, at an equal distance from one another, sixty furlongs apart or thereabouts, the ruins of which were still remaining in my day.[4] During the time that he was so occupied, the Scythians whom he had been following made a circuit by the higher regions, and re-entered Scythia. On their complete disappearance, Darius, seeing nothing more of them, left his forts half finished, and returned towards the west. He imagined that the Scythians whom he had seen were the entire nation, and that they had fled in that direction.

125. He now quickened his march, and entering Scythia, fell in with the two combined divisions of the Scythian army,[5] and instantly gave them chase. They kept to their plan of retreating before him at the distance of a day's march; and, he still following them hotly, they led him, as had been previously settled, into the territories of the nations that had refused to become their

---

1 That is, the town Gelônus. Vide supra, ch. 108.

2 Mentioned above, ch. 22.

3 This appears to be the stream called the Hyrgis in ch. 57.

4 The conjecture is probable that these supposed "forts" were ruined barrows – perhaps of larger size and better material than common. Herodotus would hear of them from the Greek traders.

5 The divisions of Idanthyrsus and Taxacis (supra, ch. 120).

allies, and first of all into the country of the Melanchlæni. Great disturbance was caused among this people by the invasion of the Scyths first, and then of the Persians. So, having harassed them after this sort, the Scythians led the way into the land of the Androphagi, with the same result as before; and thence passed onwards into Neuris, where their coming likewise spread dismay among the inhabitants. Still retreating they approached the Agathyrsi; but this people, which had witnessed the flight and terror of their neighbours, did not wait for the Scyths to invade them, but sent a herald to forbid them to cross their borders, and to forewarn them, that, if they made the attempt, it would be resisted by force of arms. The Agathyrsi then proceeded to the frontier, to defend their country against the invaders. As for the other nations, the Melanchlæni, the Androphagi, and the Neuri, instead of defending themselves, when the Scyths and Persians overran their lands, they forgot their threats and fled away in confusion to the deserts lying towards the north. The Scythians, when the Agathyrsi forbade them to enter their country, refrained; and led the Persians back from the Neurian district into their own land.

126. This had gone on so long, and seemed so interminable, that Darius at last sent a horseman to Idanthyrsus, the Scythian king, with the following message:– "Thou strange man, why dost thou keep on flying before me, when there are two things thou mightest do so easily? If thou deemest thyself able to resist my arms, cease thy wanderings and come, let us engage in battle. Or if thou art conscious that my strength is greater than thine – even so thou shouldest cease to run away – thou hast but to bring thy lord earth and water, and to come at once to a conference."

127. To this message Idanthyrsus, the Scythian king, replied:– "This is my way, Persian. I never fear men or fly from them. I have not done so in times past, nor do I now fly from thee. There is nothing new or strange in what I do; I only follow my common mode of life in peaceful years. Now I will tell thee why I do not at once join battle with thee. We Scythians have neither towns nor cultivated lands, which might induce us, through fear of their being taken or ravaged, to be in any hurry to fight with you. If, however, you must needs come to blows with us speedily, look you now, there are our fathers' tombs[1] – seek them out,

---

1 The tombs of the *kings* seem to be meant.

and attempt to meddle with them – then ye shall see whether or no we will fight with you. Till ye do this, be sure we shall not join battle, unless it pleases us. This is my answer to the challenge to fight. As for lords, I acknowledge only Jove my ancestor,[1] and Hestia, the Scythian queen. Earth and water, the tribute thou askedst, I do not send, but thou shalt soon receive more suitable gifts. Last of all, in return for thy calling thyself my lord, I say to thee, 'Go weep.' " (This is what men mean by the Scythian mode of speech.) So the herald departed, bearing this message to Darius.

128. When the Scythian kings heard the name of slavery they were filled with rage, and despatched the division under Scopasis to which the Sauromatæ were joined, with orders that they should seek a conference with the Ionians, who had been left at the Ister to guard the bridge. Meanwhile the Scythians who remained behind resolved no longer to lead the Persians hither and thither about their country, but to fall upon them whenever they should be at their meals. So they waited till such times, and then did as they had determined. In these combats the Scythian horse always put to flight the horse of the enemy; these last, however, when routed, fell back upon their foot, who never failed to afford them support; while the Scythians, on their side, as soon as they had driven the horse in, retired again, for fear of the foot. By night too the Scythians made many similar attacks.

129. There was one very strange thing which greatly advantaged the Persians, and was of equal disservice to the Scyths, in these assaults on the Persian camp. This was the braying of the asses and the appearance of the mules. For, as I observed before, the land of the Scythians produces neither ass nor mule, and contains no single specimen of either animal, by reason of the cold. So, when the asses brayed, they frightened the Scythian cavalry; and often, in the middle of a charge, the horses, hearing the noise made by the asses, would take fright and wheel round, pricking up their ears, and showing astonishment. This was owing to their having never heard the noise, or seen the form, of the animal before: and it was not without some little influence on the progress of the war.

130. The Scythians, when they perceived signs that the Persians were becoming alarmed, took steps to induce them not to

1 Supra, ch. 5.

quit Scythia, in the hope, if they stayed, of inflicting on them the greater injury, when their supplies should altogether fail. To effect this, they would leave some of their cattle exposed with the herdsmen, while they themselves moved away to a distance: the Persians would make a foray, and take the beasts, whereupon they would be highly elated.

131. This they did several times, until at last Darius was at his wits' end; hereon the Scythian princes, understanding how matters stood, despatched a herald to the Persian camp with presents for the king: these were, a bird, a mouse, a frog, and five arrows. The Persians asked the bearer to tell them what these gifts might mean, but he made answer that he had no orders except to deliver them, and return again with all speed. If the Persians were wise, he added, they would find out the meaning for themselves. So when they heard this, they held a council to consider the matter.

132. Darius gave it as his opinion, that the Scyths intended a surrender of themselves and their country, both land and water, into his hands. This he conceived to be the meaning of the gifts, because the mouse is an inhabitant of the earth, and eats the same food as man, while the frog passes his life in the water; the bird bears a great resemblance to the horse, and the arrows might signify the surrender of all their power. To the explanation of Darius, Gobryas, one of the seven conspirators against the Magus, opposed another which was as follows:— "Unless, Persians, ye can turn into birds and fly up into the sky, or become mice and burrow under the ground, or make yourselves frogs, and take refuge in the fens, ye will never make escape from this land, but die pierced by our arrows." Such were the meanings which the Persians assigned to the gifts.

133. The single division of the Scyths, which in the early part of the war had been appointed to keep guard about the Palus Mæotis, and had now been sent to get speech of the Ionians stationed at the Ister, addressed them, on reaching the bridge, in these words:— "Men of Ionia, we bring you freedom, if ye will only do as we recommend. Darius, we understand, enjoined you to keep your guard here at this bridge just sixty days; then, if he did not appear, you were to return home. Now, therefore, act so as to be free from blame, alike in his sight, and in ours. Tarry here the appointed time, and at the end go your ways." Having said this, and received a promise from the Ionians to do

as they desired, the Scythians hastened back with all possible speed.

134. After the sending of the gifts to Darius, the part of the Scythian army, which had not marched to the Ister, drew out in battle array horse and foot[1] against the Persians, and seemed about to come to an engagement. But as they stood in battle array, it chanced that a hare started up between them and the Persians, and set to running; when immediately all the Scyths who saw it, rushed off in pursuit, with great confusion and loud cries and shouts. Darius, hearing the noise, inquired the cause of it, and was told that the Scythians were all engaged in hunting a hare. On this he turned to those with whom he was wont to converse, and said:— "These men do indeed despise us utterly: and now I see that Gobryas was right about the Scythian gifts. As, therefore, his opinion is now mine likewise, it is time we form some wise plan, whereby we may secure ourselves a safe return to our homes." "Ah! sire," Gobryas rejoined, "I was well nigh sure, ere I came here, that this was an impracticable race – since our coming I am yet more convinced of it, especially now that I see them making game of us. My advice is, therefore, that, when night falls, we light our fires as we are wont to do at other times, and leaving behind us on some pretext that portion of our army which is weak and unequal to hardship, taking care also to leave our asses tethered, retreat from Scythia, before our foes march forward to the Ister and destroy the bridge, or the Ionians come to any resolution which may lead to our ruin."

135. So Gobryas advised; and when night came, Darius followed his counsel, and leaving his sick soldiers, and those whose loss would be of least account, with the asses also tethered about the camp, marched away. The asses were left that their noise might be heard: the men, really because they were sick and useless, but under the pretence that he was about to fall upon the Scythians with the flower of his troops, and that they meanwhile were to guard his camp for him. Having thus declared his plans to the men whom he was deserting, and having caused the fires to be lighted, Darius set forth, and marched hastily towards the Ister. The asses, aware of the departure of the host, brayed

---

1 We now hear for the first time of the Scythians having infantry. It is scarcely possible that they really possessed any such force. The nomad nations of these countries have always lived on horseback, and are utterly helpless on foot.

louder than ever; and the Scythians, hearing the sound, entertained no doubt of the Persians being still in the same place.

136. When day dawned, the men who had been left behind, perceiving that they were betrayed by Darius, stretched out their hands towards the Scythians, and spoke as befitted their situation. The enemy no sooner heard, than they quickly joined all their troops in one, and both portions of the Scythian army, – alike that which consisted of a single division, and that made up of two,[1] – accompanied by all their allies, the Sauromatæ, the Budini, and the Gelôni, set off in pursuit, and made straight for the Ister. As, however, the Persian army was chiefly foot, and had no knowledge of the routes, which are not cut out in Scythia; while the Scyths were all horsemen and well acquainted with the shortest way; it so happened that the two armies missed one another, and the Scythians, getting far ahead of their adversaries, came first to the bridge. Finding that the Persians were not yet arrived, they addressed the Ionians, who were aboard their ships, in these words:– "Men of Ionia, the number of your days is out, and ye do wrong to remain. Fear doubtless has kept you here hitherto: now, however, you may safely break the bridge, and hasten back to your homes, rejoicing that you are free, and thanking for it the gods and the Scythians. Your former lord and master we undertake so to handle, that he will never again make war upon any one."

137. The Ionians now held a council. Miltiades the Athenian, who was king of the Chersonesites upon the Hellespont,[2] and their commander at the Ister, recommended the other generals to do as the Scythians wished, and restore freedom to Ionia. But Histiæus the Milesian opposed this advice. "It is through Darius," he said, "that we enjoy our thrones in our several states. If his power be overturned, I cannot continue lord of Miletus, nor ye of your cities. For there is not one of them which will not prefer democracy to kingly rule." Then the other captains, who, till Histiæus spoke, were about to vote with Miltiades, changed their minds, and declared in favour of the last speaker.

138. The following were the voters on this occasion – all of them men who stood high in the esteem of the Persian king: the

1 Vide supra, ch. 120.
2 Concerning the mode in which this sovereignty came into the family of Miltiades, vide infra, Book vi. chs. 34–36.

tyrants of the Hellespont, – Daphnis of Abydos, Hippoclus of Lampsacus, Herophantus of Parium, Metrodôrus of Proconnêsus, Aristagoras of Cyzicus, and Ariston of Byzantium;[1] the Ionian princes – Strattis of Chios, Æaces of Samos, Laodamas of Phocæa, and Histiæus of Miletus, the man who had opposed Miltiades. Only one Æolian of note was present, to wit, Aristagoras[2] of Cymé.

139. Having resolved to follow the advice of Histiæus, the Greek leaders further determined to speak and act as follows. In order to appear to the Scythians to be doing something, when in fact they were doing nothing of consequence, and likewise to prevent them from forcing a passage across the Ister by the bridge, they resolved to break up the part of the bridge which abutted on Scythia, to the distance of a bowshot from the river bank; and to assure the Scythians, while the demolition was proceeding, that there was nothing which they would not do to pleasure them. Such were the additions made to the resolution of Histiæus; and then Histiæus himself stood forth and made answer to the Scyths in the name of all the Greeks:– "Good is the advice which ye have brought us, Scythians, and well have ye done to come here with such speed. Your efforts have now put us into the right path; and our efforts shall not be wanting to advance your cause. Your own eyes see that we are engaged in breaking the bridge; and, believe us, we will work zealously to procure our own freedom. Meantime, while we labour here at our task, be it your business to seek them out, and, when found, for our sakes, as well as your own, to visit them with the vengeance which they so well deserve."

140. Again the Scyths put faith in the promises of the Ionian chiefs, and retraced their steps, hoping to fall in with the Persians. They missed, however, the enemy's whole line of march; their own former acts being to blame for it. Had they not ravaged all the pasturages of that region, and filled in all the wells, they would have easily found the Persians whenever they chose. But, as it turned out, the measures which seemed to them so wisely planned were exactly what caused their failure. They took a route where water was to be found and fodder could be got for their horses, and on this track sought their adversaries,

---

1 Except Byzantium, all these places are on the Asiatic side.
2 Of whom we hear again, infra, v. 37–8.

expecting that they too would retreat through regions where these things were to be obtained. The Persians, however, kept strictly to the line of their former march, never for a moment departing from it; and even so gained the bridge with difficulty. It was night when they arrived, and their terror, when they found the bridge broken up, was great; for they thought that perhaps the Ionians had deserted them.

141. Now there was in the army of Darius a certain man, an Egyptian, who had a louder voice than any other man in the world. This person was bid by Darius to stand at the water's edge, and call Histiæus the Milesian. The fellow did as he was bid; and Histiæus, hearing him at the very first summons, brought the fleet to assist in conveying the army across, and once more made good the bridge.

142. By these means the Persians escaped from Scythia, while the Scyths sought for them in vain, again missing their track.[1] And hence the Scythians are accustomed to say of the Ionians, by way of reproach, that, if they be looked upon as freemen, they are the basest and most dastardly of all mankind — but if they be considered as under servitude, they are the faithfullest of slaves, and the most fondly attached to their lords. Such were the Scythian taunts against the Ionians.

143. Darius, having passed through Thrace, reached Sestos in the Chersonese, whence he crossed by the help of his fleet into Asia, leaving a Persian, named Megabazus, commander on the European side. This was the man on whom Darius once conferred special honour by a compliment which he paid him before all the Persians. He was about to eat some pomegranates, and had opened the first, when his brother Artabanus asked him "what he would like to have in as great plenty as the seeds of the pomegranate?" Darius answered — "Had I as many men like Megabazus as there are seeds here, it would please me better than to be lord of Greece." Such was the compliment wherewith Darius honoured the general to whom at this time he gave the command of the troops left in Europe, amounting in all to some eighty thousand men.

144. This same Megabazus got himself an undying remembrance among the Hellespontians, by a certain speech which he made. It came to his knowledge, while he was staying at Byzantium,

1 That Darius led an expedition into Scythia, across the Canal of Constantinople and the Danube, may be regarded as historically certain.

that the Chalcedonians made their settlement seventeen years earlier than the Byzantines. "Then," said he, "the Chalcedonians must at that time have been labouring under blindness – otherwise, when so far more excellent a site was open to them, they would never have chosen one so greatly inferior." Megabazus now, having been appointed to take the command upon the Hellespont, employed himself in the reduction of all those states which had not of their own accord joined the Medes.

145. About this very time another great expedition was undertaken against Libya,[1] on a pretext which I will relate when I have premised certain particulars. The descendants of the Argonauts in the third generation,[2] driven out of Lemnos by the Pelasgi who carried off the Athenian women from Brauron,[3] took ship and went to Lacedæmon, where, seating themselves on Mount Taÿgetum,[4] they proceeded to kindle their fires. The Lacedæmonians, seeing this, sent a herald to inquire of them "who they were, and from what region they had come;" whereupon they made answer, "that they were Minyæ,[5] sons of the heroes by whom the ship Argo was manned; for these persons had stayed awhile in Lemnos, and had there become their progenitors." On hearing this account of their descent, the Lacedæmonians sent to them a second time, and asked, "what was their object in coming to Lacedæmon, and there kindling their fires?" They answered, "that, driven from their own land by the Pelasgi, they had come, as was most reasonable, to their fathers;[6] and their wish was to dwell with them in their country, partake their privileges, and obtain allotments of land." It seemed

1 Vide infra, ch. 167.

2 The myth ran, that in Lemnos at the time of the Argonautic expedition there were no males, the women having revenged their ill-treatment upon the men by murdering them all. The Argonauts touched at the island, and were received with great favour. They stayed some months, and the subsequent population of the island was the fruit of this visit. Hypsipylé, the queen, had twin sons by Jason.

3 Vide infra, vi. 138.

4 Taÿgetum or Taÿgetus (Pliny) is the high mountain-range west of the valley of the Eurotas, the modern *Pentadactylon*.

5 The Argonauts generally were called Minyæ.

6 According to some, Heracles himself was one of the Argonauts and accompanied the expedition beyond Lemnos. But the reference here is evidently to Castor and Pollux, the two great heroes of Sparta, who are always enumerated among the companions of Jason.

good to the Lacedæmonians to receive the Minyæ among them on their own terms; to assign them lands, and enrol them in their tribes. What chiefly moved them to this was the consideration that the sons of Tyndarus[1] had sailed on board the Argo. The Minyæ, on their part, forthwith married Spartan wives, and gave the wives, whom they had married in Lemnos, to Spartan husbands.

146. However, before much time had elapsed, the Minyæ began to wax wanton, demanded to share the throne, and committed other impieties: whereupon the Lacedæmonians passed on them sentence of death, and, seizing them, cast them into prison. Now the Lacedæmonians never put criminals to death in the daytime, but always at night. When the Minyæ, accordingly, were about to suffer, their wives, who were not only citizens, but daughters of the chief men among the Spartans, entreated to be allowed to enter the prison, and have some talk with their lords; and the Spartans, not expecting any fraud from such a quarter, granted their request. The women entered the prison, gave their own clothes to their husbands, and received theirs in exchange: after which the Minyæ, dressed in their wives' garments, and thus passing for women, went forth. Having effected their escape in this manner, they seated themselves once more upon Taÿgetum.

147. It happened that at this very time Theras, son of Autesion (whose father Tisamenus was the son of Thersander, and grandson of Polynices), was about to lead out a colony from Lacedæmon. This Theras, by birth a Cadmeian, was uncle on the mother's side to the two sons of Aristodêmus, Procles and Eurysthenes, and, during their infancy, administered in their right the royal power. When his nephews, however, on attaining to man's estate, took the government, Theras, who could not bear to be under the authority of others after he had wielded authority so long himself, resolved to leave Sparta, and cross the sea to join his kindred. There were in the island now called Thera,[2] but at that time Callisté, certain descendants of Membliarus, the son of Pœciles, a Phœnician. (For Cadmus, the son of Agenor, when he was sailing in search of Europé, made a landing on this island; and, either because the country pleased him, or because he had

---

1 Castor and Pollux.
2 Thera is the island, or group of islands, now known by the name of *Santorin*, lying to the south of the other Cyclades.

a purpose in so doing,¹ left there a number of Phœnicians, and with them his own kinsman Membliarus. Callisté had been inhabited by this race for eight generations of men, before the arrival of Theras from Lacedæmon.)

148. Theras now, having with him a certain number of men from each of the tribes, was setting forth on his expedition hitherward. Far from intending to drive out the former inhabitants, he regarded them as his near kin, and meant to settle among them. It happened that just at this time the Minyæ, having escaped from their prison, had taken up their station upon Mount Taÿgetum; and the Lacedæmonians, wishing to destroy them, were considering what was best to be done, when Theras begged their lives, undertaking to remove them from the territory. His prayer being granted, he took ship, and sailed, with three triaconters,² to join the descendants of Membliarus. He was not, however, accompanied by all the Minyæ, but only by some few of them. The greater number fled to the land of the Paroreats, and Caucons, whom they drove out, themselves occupying the region in six bodies, by which were afterwards built the towns of Lepreum, Macistus, Phryxæ, Pyrgus, Epium, and Nudium; whereof the greater part were in my day demolished by the Eleans.

149. The island was called Thera after the name of its founder. This same Theras had a son, who refused to cross the sea with him; Theras therefore left him behind, "a sheep," as he said, "among wolves." From this speech his son came to be called Œolycus, a name which afterwards grew to be the only one by which he was known. This Œolycus was the father of Ægeus, from whom sprang the Ægîdæ, a great tribe in Sparta. The men of this tribe lost at one time all their children, whereupon they were bidden by an oracle to build a temple to the furies of Laïus and Œdipus; they complied, and the mortality ceased. The same thing happened in Thera to the descendants of these men.

150. Thus far the history is delivered without variation both by the Theræans and the Lacedæmonians; but from this point

1 It is conjectured that the real "purpose" was to found a settlement *for dyeing*, as the *murex*, which furnished the precious Tyrian purple, was plentiful in that part of the Mediterranean.

2 Triaconters were vessels of 30 oars, 15 on each side, in which the rowers all sat upon the same level. Compare the account given of penteconters (supra, i. 152).

we have only the Theræan narrative. Grinus (they say), the son of Æsanius, a descendant of Theras, and king of the island of Thera, went to Delphi to offer a hecatomb on behalf of his native city. He was accompanied by a large number of the citizens, and among the rest by Battus, the son of Polymnestus, who belonged to the Minyan family of the Euphemidæ. On Grinus consulting the oracle about sundry matters, the Pythoness gave him for answer, "that he should found a city in Libya." Grinus replied to this: "I, O king! am too far advanced in years, and too inactive, for such a work. Bid one of these youngsters undertake it." As he spoke, he pointed towards Battus; and thus the matter rested for that time. When the embassy returned to Thera, small account was taken of the oracle by the Theræans, as they were quite ignorant where Libya was, and were not so venturesome as to send out a colony in the dark.

151. Seven years passed from the utterance of the oracle, and not a drop of rain fell in Thera: all the trees in the island, except one, were killed with the drought. The Theræans upon this sent to Delphi, and were reminded reproachfully, that they had never colonised Libya. So, as there was no help for it, they sent messengers to Crete, to inquire whether any of the Cretans, or of the strangers sojourning among them, had ever travelled as far as Libya: and these messengers of theirs, in their wanderings about the island, among other places visited Itanus,[1] where they fell in with a man, whose name was Corôbius, a dealer in purple. In answer to their inquiries, he told them that contrary winds had once carried him to Libya, where he had gone ashore on a certain island which was named Platea.[2] So they hired this man's services, and took him back with them to Thera. A few persons then sailed from Thera to reconnoitre. Guided by Corôbius to the island of Platea, they left him there with provisions for a certain number of months, and returned home with all speed to give their countrymen an account of the island.

152. During their absence, which was prolonged beyond the time that had been agreed upon, Corôbius' provisions failed him. He was relieved, however, after a while by a Samian vessel, under the command of a man named Colæus, which, on its way to

1 Itanus lay at the eastern extremity of Crete.
2 There can be little doubt that Platea is the small island of *Bomba*, which lies off the African coast in the gulf of the same name, lat. 32° 20′, long. 23° 15′.

Egypt, was forced to put in at Platea. The crew, informed by Corôbius of all the circumstances, left him sufficient food for a year. They themselves quitted the island; and, anxious to reach Egypt, made sail in that direction, but were carried out of their course by a gale of wind from the east. The storm not abating, they were driven past the Pillars of Heracles, and at last, by some special guiding providence, reached Tartessus. This trading town was in those days a virgin port, unfrequented by the merchants. The Samians, in consequence, made by the return-voyage a profit greater than any Greeks before their day, excepting Sostratus, son of Laodamas, an Eginetan, with whom no one else can compare. From the tenth part of their gains, amounting to six talents,[1] the Samians made a brazen vessel, in shape like an Argive wine-bowl, adorned with the heads of griffins standing out in high relief.[2] This bowl, supported by three kneeling colossal figures in bronze, of the height of seven cubits, was placed as an offering in the temple of Hera at Samos. The aid given to Corôbius was the original cause of that close friendship which afterwards united the Cyrenæans and Theræans with the Samians.

153. The Theræans who had left Corôbius at Platea, when they reached Thera, told their countrymen that they had colonised an island on the coast of Libya. They of Thera, upon this, resolved that men should be sent to join the colony from each of their seven districts, and that the brothers in every family should draw lots to determine who were to go. Battus was chosen to be king and leader of the colony. So these men departed for Platea on board of two penteconters.

154. Such is the account which the Theræans give. In the sequel of the history their accounts tally with those of the people of Cyrênê; but in what they relate of Battus these two nations differ most widely. The following is the Cyrenaic story. There was once a king named Etearchus, who ruled over Axus, a city in Crete, and had a daughter named Phronima. This girl's mother having died, Etearchus married a second wife; who no sooner took up her abode in his house than she proved a true stepmother to poor Phronima, always vexing her, and contriving

---

1 About £1460 of our money. The entire profit was therefore between £14,000 and £15,000.
2 Concerning the eminence of Samos in the arts, vide supra, Bk. iii. ch. 60.

against her every sort of mischief. At last she taxed her with light conduct; and Etearchus, persuaded by his wife that the charge was true, bethought himself of a most barbarous mode of punishment. There was a certain Theræan, named Themison, a merchant, living at Axus. This man Etearchus invited to be his friend and guest, and then induced him to swear that he would do him any service he might require.[1] No sooner had he given the promise, than the king fetched Phronima, and, delivering her into his hands, told him to carry her away and throw her into the sea. Hereupon Themison, full of indignation at the fraud whereby his oath had been procured, dissolved forthwith the friendship, and, taking the girl with him, sailed away from Crete. Having reached the open main, to acquit himself of the obligation under which he was laid by his oath to Etearchus, he fastened ropes about the damsel, and, letting her down into the sea, drew her up again, and so made sail for Thera.

155. At Thera, Polymnêstus, one of the chief citizens of the place, took Phronima to be his concubine. The fruit of this union was a son, who stammered and had a lisp in his speech. According to the Cyrenæans and Theræans, the name given to the boy was Battus: in my opinion, however, he was called at the first something else, and only got the name of Battus after his arrival in Libya, assuming it either in consequence of the words addressed to him by the Delphian oracle, or on account of the office which he held. For, in the Libyan tongue, the word "Battus" means "a king." And this, I think, was the reason why the Pythoness addressed him as she did: she knew he was to be a king in Libya, and so she used the Libyan word in speaking to him. For after he had grown to man's estate, he made a journey to Delphi, to consult the oracle about his voice; when, upon his putting his question, the Pythoness thus replied to him:—

"Battus, thou camest to ask of thy voice; but Phœbus Apollo
   Bids thee establish a city in Libya, abounding in fleeces;"

which was as if she had said in her own tongue, "King, thou camest to ask of thy voice." Then he replied, "Mighty lord, I did indeed come hither to consult thee about my voice, but thou speakest to me of quite other matters, bidding me colonise Libya — an impossible thing! what power have I? what followers?"

---

[1] Of this practice we have another instance, infra, vi. 62.

Thus he spake, but he did not persuade the Pythoness to give him any other response; so, when he found that she persisted in her former answer, he left her speaking, and set out on his return to Thera.

156. After a while, everything began to go wrong both with Battus and with the rest of the Theræans, whereupon these last, ignorant of the cause of their sufferings, sent to Delphi to inquire for what reason they were afflicted. The Pythoness in reply told them, "that if they and Battus would make a settlement at Cyrêné in Libya, things would go better with them." Upon this the Theræans sent out Battus with two penteconters, and with these he proceeded to Libya, but within a little time, not knowing what else to do, the men returned and arrived off Thera. The Theræans, when they saw the vessels approaching, received them with showers of missiles, would not allow them to come near the shore, and ordered the men to sail back from whence they came. Thus compelled to return, they settled on an island near the Libyan coast, which (as I have already said) was called Platea. In size it is reported to have been about equal to the city of Cyrêné, as it now stands.

157. In this place they continued two years, but at the end of that time, as their ill luck still followed them, they left the island to the care of one of their number, and went in a body to Delphi, where they made complaint at the shrine, to the effect that, notwithstanding they had colonised Libya, they prospered as poorly as before. Hereon the Pythoness made them the following answer:—

"Knowest thou better than I, fair Libya abounding in fleeces?
 Better the stranger than he who has trod it? Oh! clever Theræans!"

Battus and his friends, when they heard this, sailed back to Platea: it was plain the god would not hold them acquitted of the colony till they were absolutely in Libya. So, taking with them the man whom they had left upon the island, they made a settlement on the mainland directly opposite Platea, fixing themselves at a place called Aziris, which is closed in on both sides by the most beautiful hills, and on one side is washed by a river.[1]

158. Here they remained six years, at the end of which time the Libyans induced them to move, promising that they would

1 If Platea is *Bomba*, the Aziris of Herodotus must be sought in the valley of the *Temimeh*, the ancient Paliurus.

lead them to a better situation.¹ So the Greeks left Aziris and were conducted by the Libyans towards the west, their journey being so arranged, by the calculation of their guides, that they passed in the night the most beautiful district of that whole country, which is the region called Irasa. The Libyans brought them to a spring, which goes by the name of Apollo's fountain, and told them – "Here, Grecians, is the proper place for you to settle; for here the sky leaks."

159. During the lifetime of Battus, the founder of the colony, who reigned forty years, and during that of his son Arcesilaüs, who reigned sixteen, the Cyrenæans continued at the same level, neither more nor fewer in number than they were at the first. But in the reign of the third king, Battus, surnamed the Happy, the advice of the Pythoness brought Greeks from every quarter into Libya, to join the settlement. The Cyrenæans had offered to all comers a share in their lands; and the oracle had spoken as follows:–

"He that is backward to share in the pleasant Libyan acres,²
Sooner or later, I warn him, will feel regret at his folly."

Thus a great multitude were collected together to Cyrênê, and the Libyans of the neighbourhood found themselves stripped of large portions of their lands. So they, and their king Adicran, being robbed and insulted by the Cyrenæans, sent messengers to Egypt, and put themselves under the rule of Apries, the Egyptian monarch; who, upon this, levied a vast army of Egyptians, and sent them against Cyrênê. The inhabitants of that place left their walls and marched out in force to the district of Irasa, where, near the spring called Thesté, they engaged the Egyptian host, and defeated it. The Egyptians, who had never before made trial of the prowess of the Greeks, and so thought but meanly of them, were routed with such slaughter that but a very few of them ever got back home. For this reason, the subjects of Apries, who laid the blame of the defeat on him, revolted from his authority.³

160. This Battus left a son called Arcesilaüs, who, when he came to the throne, had dissensions with his brothers, which

¹ The friendly terms on which the Greeks stand towards the natives *at the first*, is here very apparent. Their position resembles that of the first English settlers in America.

² The beauty and fertility of the Cyrenaica are celebrated by all who visit it.

³ Vide supra, ii. 161.

ended in their quitting him and departing to another region of
Libya,[1] where, after consulting among themselves, they founded
the city, which is still called by the name then given to it, Barca.
At the same time they endeavoured to induce the Libyans to
revolt from Cyrêné. Not long afterwards Arcesilaüs made an expedition against the Libyans who had received his brothers and
been prevailed upon to revolt; and they, fearing his power, fled
to their countrymen who dwelt towards the east. Arcesilaüs pursued, and chased them to a place called Leucon, which is in Libya,
where the Libyans resolved to risk a battle. Accordingly they
engaged the Cyrenæans, and defeated them so entirely that as
many as seven thousand of their heavy-armed were slain in the
fight. Arcesilaüs, after this blow, fell sick, and, whilst he was under
the influence of a draught which he had taken, was strangled by
Learchus, one of his brothers. This Learchus was afterwards en-
trapped by Eryxo, the widow of Arcesilaüs, and put to death.

161. Battus, Arcesilaüs' son, succeeded to the kingdom, a
lame man, who limped in his walk. Their late calamities now
induced the Cyrenæans to send to Delphi and inquire of the god
what form of government they had best set up to secure themselves prosperity. The Pythoness answered by recommending
them to fetch an arbitrator from Mantinea in Arcadia.[2] Accordingly they sent; and the Mantineans gave them a man named
Demônax,[3] a person of high repute among the citizens; who, on
his arrival at Cyrêné, having first made himself acquainted with
all the circumstances, proceeded to enrol the people in three
tribes. One he made to consist of the Theræans and their vassals;
another of the Peloponnesians and Cretans; and a third of the
various islanders.[4] Besides this, he deprived the king Battus of
his former privileges, only reserving for him certain sacred
lands and offices;[5] while, with respect to the powers which had

1 There is no difficulty in determining the exact site of Cyrêné. The Arabic
name *Grennah* (Κυρήνη, or in the Doric Greek of the place, Κυράνα, sounded
Kyrána) is sufficiently close to mark the identity of the ruined city, which is so
called, with the Cyrêné of former times. The country around Grennah is celebrated for its fertility.

2 Mantinea was situated near the eastern frontier of Arcadia.

3 Demônax, the Mantinean lawgiver.

4 Who would be principally Ionians.

5 The early kings of the various Grecian states, like those of Rome, were
uniformly priests likewise.

hitherto been exercised by the king, he gave them all into the hands of the people.

162. Thus matters rested during the lifetime of this Battus, but when his son Arcesilaüs came to the throne, great disturbance arose about the privileges. For Arcesilaüs, son of Battus the lame and Pheretima, refused to submit to the arrangements of Demônax the Mantinean, and claimed all the powers of his forefathers. In the contention which followed Arcesilaüs was worsted, whereupon he fled to Samos, while his mother took refuge at Salamis in the island of Cyprus. Salamis was at that time ruled by Evelthon, the same who offered at Delphi the censer which is in the treasury of the Corinthians, a work deserving of admiration. Of him Pheretima made request, that he would give her an army, whereby she and her son might regain Cyrêné. But Evelthon, preferring to give her anything rather than an army, made her various presents. Pheretima accepted them all, saying, as she took them: "Good is this too, O king! but better were it to give me the army which I crave at thy hands." Finding that she repeated these words each time that he presented her with a gift, Evelthon at last sent her a golden spindle and distaff, with the wool ready for spinning. Again she uttered the same speech as before, whereupon Evelthon rejoined – "These are the gifts I present to women, not armies."

163. At Samos, meanwhile, Arcesilaüs was collecting troops by the promise of granting them lands. Having in this way drawn together a vast host, he sent to Delphi to consult the oracle about his restoration. The answer of the Pythoness was this: "Loxias grants thy race to rule over Cyrêné, till four kings Battus, four Arcesilaüs by name, have passed away. Beyond this term of eight generations of men, he warns you not to seek to extend your reign. Thou, for thy part, be gentle, when thou art restored. If thou findest the oven full of jars, bake not the jars; but be sure to speed them on their way. If, however, thou heatest the oven, then avoid the island – else thou wilt die thyself, and with thee the most beautiful bull."

164. So spake the Pythoness. Arcesilaüs upon this returned to Cyrêné, taking with him the troops which he had raised in Samos. There he obtained possession of the supreme power; whereupon, forgetful of the oracle, he took proceedings against those who had driven him into banishment. Some of them fled from him and quitted the country for good; others fell into his

hands and were sent to suffer death in Cyprus. These last happening on their passage to put in through stress of weather at Cnidus, the Cnidians rescued them, and sent them off to Thera. Another body found a refuge in the great tower of Aglômachus, a private edifice, and were there destroyed by Arcesilaüs, who heaped wood around the place, and burnt them to death. Aware, after the deed was done, that this was what the Pythoness meant when she warned him, if he found the jars in the oven, not to bake them, he withdrew himself of his own accord from the city of Cyrênê, believing that to be the island of the oracle,[1] and fearing to die as had been prophesied. Being married to a relation of his own, a daughter of Alazir, at that time king of the Barcæans, he took up his abode with him. At Barca, however, certain of the citizens, together with a number of Cyrenæan exiles, recognising him as he walked in the forum, killed him; they slew also at the same time Alazir, his father-in-law. So Arcesilaüs, wittingly or unwittingly, disobeyed the oracle, and thereby fulfilled his destiny.

165. Pheretima, the mother of Arcesilaüs, during the time that her son, after working his own ruin, dwelt at Barca, continued to enjoy all his privileges at Cyrênê, managing the government, and taking her seat at the council-board. No sooner, however, did she hear of the death of her son at Barca, than leaving Cyrênê, she fled in haste to Egypt. Arcesilaüs had claims for service done to Cambyses, son of Cyrus; since it was by him that Cyrênê was put under the Persian yoke, and a rate of tribute agreed upon.[2] Pheretima therefore went straight to Egypt, and presenting herself as a suppliant before Aryandes, entreated him to avenge her wrongs. Her son, she said, had met his death on account of his being so well affected towards the Medes.

166. Now Aryandes had been made governor of Egypt by Cambyses. He it was who in after times was punished with death by Darius for seeking to rival him. Aware, by report and also by his own eyesight, that Darius wished to leave a memorial of himself, such as no king had ever left before, Aryandes resolved to follow his example, and did so, till he got his reward. Darius had refined gold to the last perfection of purity in order to have

1 It is not very easy to see how either Cyrênê or Barca could be regarded as islands.
2 Vide supra, iii. 13 and 91.

coins struck of it: Aryandes, in his Egyptian government, did the very same with silver, so that to this day there is no such pure silver anywhere as the Aryandic. Darius, when this came to his ears, brought another charge, a charge of rebellion, against Aryandes, and put him to death.

167. At the time of which we are speaking Aryandes, moved with compassion for Pheretima, granted her all the forces which there were in Egypt, both land and sea. The command of the army he gave to Amasis, a Maraphian;[1] while Badres, one of the tribe of the Pasargadæ, was appointed to lead the fleet. Before the expedition, however, left Egypt, he sent a herald to Barca to inquire who it was that had slain king Arcesilaüs. The Barcæans replied "that they, one and all, acknowledged the deed – Arcesilaüs had done them many and great injuries." After receiving this reply, Aryandes gave the troops orders to march with Pheretima. Such was the cause which served as a pretext for this expedition: its real object was, I believe, the subjugation of Libya. For Libya is inhabited by many and various races, and of these but a very few were subjects of the Persian king, while by far the larger number held Darius in no manner of respect.

168. The Libyans dwell in the order which I will now describe. Beginning on the side of Egypt, the first Libyans are the Adyrmachidæ. These people have, in most points, the same customs as the Egyptians, but use the costume of the Libyans. Their women wear on each leg a ring made of bronze; they let their hair grow long, and when they catch any vermin on their persons, bite it and throw it away. In this they differ from all the other Libyans. They are also the only tribe with whom the custom obtains of bringing all women about to become brides before the king, that he might deflower the one who seemed to him most agreeable.[2] The Adyrmachidæ extend from the borders of Egypt to the harbour called Port Plynus.

169. Next to the Adyrmachidæ are the Gilligammæ, who inhabit the country westward as far as the island of Aphrodisias. Off this tract is the island of Platea, which the Cyrenæans colonised. Here too, upon the mainland, are Port Menelaüs, and

1 The Maraphians were the Persian tribe next in dignity to the Pasargadæ. (Vide supra, i. 125.)
2 Compare the middle age *droit de cuissage* ["jus primæ noctis." – E. H. B.].

Aziris, where the Cyrenæans once lived. The Silphium¹ begins to grow in this region, extending from the island of Platea on the one side to the mouth of the Syrtis on the other. The customs of the Gilligammæ are like those of the rest of their countrymen.

170. The Asbystæ² adjoin the Gilligammæ upon the west. They inhabit the regions above Cyrênê, but do not reach to the coast, which belongs to the Cyrenæans. Four-horse chariots are in more common use among them than among any other Libyans. In most of their customs they ape the manners of the Cyrenæans.³

171. Westward of the Asbystæ dwell the Auschisæ, who possess the country above Barca, reaching, however, to the sea at the place called Euesperides. In the middle of their territory is the little tribe of the Cabalians, which touches the coast near Tauchira,⁴ a city of the Barcæans. Their customs are like those of the Libyans above Cyrênê.

172. The Nasamonians,⁵ a numerous people, are the western neighbours of the Auschisæ. In summer they leave their flocks and herds upon the sea-shore, and go up the country to a place called Augila,⁶ where they gather the dates from the palms, which in those parts grow thickly, and are of great size, all of them being of the fruit-bearing kind. They also chase the locusts, and, when caught, dry them in the sun, after which they grind them to powder, and, sprinkling this upon their milk, so drink it. Each man among them has several wives, in their intercourse with whom they resemble the Massagetæ; when a man has set up a staff, he is lying with a woman. When a Nasamonian first marries a woman, the custom is that the bride on the first night lies with all the guests in turn; as each lies with her, he gives her a gift which he has brought from his house. The following are their customs in the swearing of oaths and the practice of augury. The

1 This famous plant, the *laserpitium* of the Romans, which is figured upon most of the Cyrenæan and Barcæan coins, was celebrated both as an article of food and also for its medicinal virtues. It formed an important element in the ancient commerce of Cyrênê.

2 The Asbystæ, being neighbours of the Cyrenæans, were well known to the Greeks.

3 The Cyrenæans were famous for their skill in chariot-driving.

4 Tauchira retains its name as *Taukra*, *Tokrah*, or *Terkera*. Considerable ruins mark the site.

5 They dwelt around the shores of the Greater Syrtis (vide supra, ii. 32).

6 This place retains its name unchanged. It lies on the great route from Egypt to Fezzan.

man, as he swears, lays his hand upon the tomb of some one considered to have been pre-eminently just and good, and so doing swears by his name. For divination they betake themselves to the sepulchres of their own ancestors, and, after praying, lie down to sleep upon their graves; by the dreams which then come to them they guide their conduct. When they pledge their faith to one another, each gives the other to drink out of his hand; if there be no liquid to be had, they take up dust from the ground,[1] and put their tongues to it.

173. On the country of the Nasamonians borders that of the Psylli, who were swept away under the following circumstances. The south-wind had blown for a long time and dried up all the tanks in which their water was stored. Now the whole region within the Syrtis is utterly devoid of springs. Accordingly the Psylli took counsel among themselves, and by common consent made war upon the south-wind — so at least the Libyans say, I do but repeat their words — they went forth and reached the desert; but there the south-wind rose and buried them under heaps of sand: whereupon, the Psylli being destroyed, their lands passed to the Nasamonians.

174. Above the Nasamonians, towards the south, in the district where the wild beasts abound, dwell the Garamantians, who avoid all society or intercourse with their fellow-men, have no weapon of war, and do not know how to defend themselves.

175. These border the Nasamonians on the south: westward along the sea-shore their neighbours are the Macæ, who, by letting the locks about the crown of their head grow long, while they clip them close everywhere else, make their hair resemble a crest. In war these people use the skins of ostriches for shields.[2] The river Cinyps[3] rises among them from the height called "the Hill of the Graces," and runs from thence through their country to the sea. The Hill of the Graces is thickly covered with wood, and is thus very unlike the rest of Libya, which is bare. It is distant two hundred furlongs from the sea.

176. Adjoining the Macæ are the Gindanes, whose women wear on their legs anklets of leather. Each lover that a woman has gives her one; and she who can show the most is the best

1 So the Mahometan law of ablution allows sand to be used where water cannot be procured.

2 Compare vii. 70.

3 Perhaps the *Wad' el Kháhan* has the best right to be considered the ancient Cinyps.

esteemed, as she appears to have been loved by the greatest number of men.

177. A promontory jutting out into the sea from the country of the Gindanes is inhabited by the Lotophagi,[1] who live entirely on the fruit of the lotus-tree.[2] The lotus fruit is about the size of the lentisk berry, and in sweetness resembles the date. The Lotophagi even succeed in obtaining from it a sort of wine.[3]

178. The sea-coast beyond the Lotophagi is occupied by the Machlyans, who use the lotus to some extent, though not so much as the people of whom we last spoke. The Machlyans reach as far as the great river called the Triton, which empties itself into the great lake Tritônis. Here, in this lake, is an island called Phla, which it is said the Lacedæmonians were to have colonised, according to an oracle.

179. The following is the story as it is commonly told. When Jason had finished building the Argo at the foot of Mount Pelion, he took on board the usual hecatomb, and moreover a brazen tripod. Thus equipped, he set sail, intending to coast round the Peloponnese, and so to reach Delphi. The voyage was prosperous as far as Malea; but at that point a gale of wind from the north came on suddenly, and carried him out of his course to the coast of Libya; where, before he discovered the land, he got among the shallows of Lake Tritônis. As he was turning it in his mind how he should find his way out, Triton (they say) appeared to him, and offered to show him the channel, and secure him a safe retreat, if he would give him the tripod. Jason complying, was shown by Triton the passage through the shallows; after which the god took the tripod, and, carrying it to his own temple, seated himself upon it, and, filled with prophetic fury, delivered to Jason and his companions a long prediction. "When a descendant," he said, "of one of the Argo's crew should seize and carry off the brazen tripod, then by inevitable

1 The country of the Lotophagi is evidently the Peninsula of *Zarzis* which is the only tract projecting from this part of the coast. They are thus brought into the position usually assigned them, the neighbourhood of the Lesser Syrtis, or Gulf of *Khabs*.

2 The lotus is evidently the *Rhamnus*, now called in Arabic *Sidr*, the fruit *Nebk*. It looks and tastes rather like a bad crab-apple. It has a single stone within it. To Ulysses it was as inconvenient as modern "gold-diggings" to ship captains, since he had the greatest difficulty in keeping his sailors to the ship when they had once tasted it (Hom. Od. ix. 84 to 96).

3 Perhaps this is the origin of the Homeric myth (Od. ix. 74 et seqq.).

fate would a hundred Grecian cities be built around Lake Tritônis." The Libyans of that region, when they heard the words of this prophecy, took away the tripod and hid it.

180. The next tribe beyond the Machlyans is the tribe of the Auseans. Both these nations inhabit the borders of Lake Tritônis, being separated from one another by the river Triton. Both also wear their hair long, but the Machlyans let it grow at the back of the head, while the Auseans have it long in front. The Ausean maidens keep year by year a feast in honour of Athena, whereat their custom is to draw up in two bodies, and fight with stones and clubs. They say that these are rites which have come down to them from their fathers, and that they honour with them their native goddess, who is the same as the Athena (Minerva) of the Grecians. If any of the maidens die of the wounds they receive, the Auseans declare that such are false maidens. Before the fight is suffered to begin, they have another ceremony. One of the virgins, the loveliest of the number, is selected from the rest; a Corinthian helmet and a complete suit of Greek armour are publicly put upon her; and, thus adorned, she is made to mount into a chariot, and led around the whole lake in a procession. What arms they used for the adornment of their damsels before the Greeks came to live in their country, I cannot say. I imagine they dressed them in Egyptian armour, for I maintain that both the shield and the helmet came into Greece from Egypt. The Auseans declare that Athena is the daughter of Poseidon and the Lake Tritônis[1] – they say she quarrelled with her father, and applied to Zeus, who consented to let her be his child; and so she became his adopted daughter. These people do not marry or live in families, but dwell together like the gregarious beasts. When their children are full-grown, they are brought before the assembly of the men, which is held every third month, and assigned to those whom they most resemble.

181. Such are the tribes of wandering Libyans dwelling upon the sea-coast. Above them inland is the wild-beast tract: and beyond that, a ridge of sand, reaching from Egyptian Thebes to the Pillars of Heracles. Throughout this ridge, at the distance of about ten days' journey from one another, heaps of salt in large lumps lie upon hills. At the top of every hill there gushes forth from the middle of the salt a stream of water, which is both cold

1 This is the earliest form of the legend, and hence the epithet Τριτογένεια, so frequently applied to this goddess.

and sweet.[1] Around dwell men who are the last inhabitants of Libya on the side of the desert, living, as they do, more inland than the wild-beast district. Of these nations the first is that of the Ammonians, who dwell at a distance of ten days' journey from Thebes,[2] and have a temple derived from that of the Theban Zeus. For at Thebes likewise, as I mentioned above,[3] the image of Zeus has a face like that of a ram. The Ammonians have another spring besides that which rises from the salt. The water of this stream is lukewarm at early dawn; at the time when the market fills it is much cooler; by noon it has grown quite cold; at this time, therefore, they water their gardens. As the afternoon advances the coldness goes off, till, about sunset, the water is once more lukewarm; still the heat increases, and at midnight it boils furiously. After this time it again begins to cool, and grows less and less hot till morning comes. This spring is called "the Fountain of the Sun."

182. Next to the Ammonians, at the distance of ten days' journey along the ridge of sand, there is a second salt-hill like the Ammonian, and a second spring. The country round is inhabited, and the place bears the name of Augila.[4] Hither it is that the Nasamonians come to gather in the dates.

183. Ten days' journey from Augila there is again a salt-hill and a spring; palms of the fruitful kind grow here abundantly, as they do also at the other salt-hills. This region is inhabited by a nation called the Garamantians,[5] a very powerful people, who cover the salt with mould, and then sow their crops. From thence is the shortest road to the Lotophagi, a journey of thirty days. In the Garamantian country are found the oxen which, as they graze, walk backwards. This they do because their horns curve outwards in front of their heads, so that it is not possible for them when grazing to move forwards, since in that case their

1 In the Oases salt is in great abundance, and sometimes a large space is covered with an incrustation of it, which breaks like frozen mud or shallow water, under the feet. Springs frequently rise from the sand in that desert, and sometimes on the top of hillocks of sand; where the water, as Herodotus says, is always cool and sweet; the coolness being caused by the evaporation.

2 *Siwah*, which is undoubtedly where the temple of Ammon stood (vide supra, iii. 26), lies at the distance of 400 geographical miles, or not less than 20 days' journey, from Thebes.

3 Vide supra, ii. 42.

4 [It still bears the name of Aujileh. – E. H. B.].

5 The modern Fezzan.

horns would become fixed in the ground. Only herein do they differ from other oxen, and further in the thickness and hardness of their hides. The Garamantians have four-horse chariots, in which they chase the Troglodyte Ethiopians,[1] who of all the nations whereof any account has reached our ears are by far the swiftest of foot. The Troglodytes feed on serpents, lizards, and other similar reptiles. Their language is unlike that of any other people; it sounds like the screeching of bats.

184. At the distance of ten days' journey from the Garamantians there is again another salt-hill and spring of water; around which dwell a people, called the Atarantians, who alone of all known nations are destitute of names. The title of Atarantians is borne by the whole race in common; but the men have no particular names of their own. The Atarantians, when the sun rises high in the heaven, curse him, and load him with reproaches, because (they say) he burns and wastes both their country and themselves. Once more at the distance of ten days' journey there is a salt-hill, a spring, and an inhabited tract. Near the salt is a mountain called Atlas, very taper and round; so lofty, moreover, that the top (it is said) cannot be seen, the clouds never quitting it either summer or winter.[2] The natives call this mountain "the Pillar of Heaven;" and they themselves take their name from it, being called Atlantes. They are reported not to eat any living thing, and never to have any dreams.

185. As far as the Atlantes the names of the nations inhabiting the sandy ridge are known to me; but beyond them my knowledge fails. The ridge itself extends as far as the Pillars of Heracles, and even further than these;[3] and throughout the

1 Perhaps it would be better to translate "the Ethiopians who dwell in holes." Troglodytes have always abounded in Africa.

2 The earlier writers (Homer, Hesiod, etc.) intended by that name the Peak of Teneriffe, of which they had some indistinct knowledge derived from Phœnician sources. The later, unacquainted with the great Western Ocean, placed Atlas in Africa, first regarding it as a single mountain, and then, as their geographical knowledge increased, they found there was no very remarkable mountain in North-western Africa, as a mountain chain. Herodotus is a writer of the transition period. His description is only applicable to the Peak, while his locality is Africa – not, however, the western coast, but an inland tract, probably south-eastern Algeria. Thus his mountain, if it is to be considered as having any foundation at all on fact, must represent the eastern, not the western, extremity of the Atlas chain.

3 Herodotus, it should be observed, knows that the African coast *projects* beyond the Pillars.

whole distance, at the end of every ten days' journey, there is a salt-mine, with people dwelling round it who all of them build their houses with blocks of the salt. No rain falls in these parts of Libya; if it were otherwise, the walls of these houses could not stand.[1] The salt quarried is of two colours, white and purple.[2] Beyond the ridge, southwards, in the direction of the interior, the country is a desert,[3] with no springs, no beasts, no rain, no wood, and altogether destitute of moisture.

186. Thus from Egypt as far as Lake Tritônis Libya is inhabited by wandering tribes,[4] whose drink is milk and their food the flesh of animals. Cow's flesh however none of these tribes ever taste, but abstain from it for the same reason as the Egyptians, neither do they any of them breed swine. Even at Cyrênê, the women think it wrong to eat the flesh of the cow, honouring in this Isis, the Egyptian goddess, whom they worship both with fasts and festivals. The Barcæan women abstain, not from cow's flesh only, but also from the flesh of swine.

187. West of Lake Tritônis the Libyans are no longer wanderers, nor do they practise the same customs as the wandering people, or treat their children in the same way. For the wandering Libyans, many of them at any rate, if not all — concerning which I cannot speak with certainty — when their children come to the age of four years, burn the veins at the top of their heads with a flock from the fleece of a sheep: others burn the veins about the temples.[5] This they do to prevent them from being plagued in their after lives by a flow of rheum from the head; and such they declare is the reason why they are so much more healthy than other men. Certainly the Libyans are the healthiest men that I know;[6] but whether this is what makes them so, or not, I cannot positively say — the healthiest certainly they are. If when the children are being burnt convulsions come on, there

1 They have been found in the Oasis of Ammon, and in the western part of Fezzan.

2 The rock-salt of Africa is, in fact, of *three* colours.

3 He alludes to the great Sáhara.

4 Herodotus here indicates that he is about to resume the account of the sea-coast tribes, which was broken off at the end of ch. 180.

5 Burning with a red-hot iron is still practised in these countries for the cure of diseases.

6 Vide supra, ii. 77. The Tuaregs have, of all existing tribes, the best right to be regarded as the descendants of Herodotus's Libyans.

is a remedy of which they have made discovery. It is to sprinkle goat's water upon the child, who thus treated, is sure to recover. In all this I only repeat what is said by the Libyans.

188. The rites which the wandering Libyans use in sacrificing are the following. They begin with the ear of the victim, which they cut off and throw over their house: this done, they kill the animal by twisting the neck. They sacrifice to the Sun and Moon, but not to any other god. This worship is common to all the Libyans. The inhabitants of the parts about Lake Tritônis worship in addition Triton, Poseidon,[1] and Athena, the last especially.

189. The dress wherewith Athena's statues are adorned, and her Ægis, were derived by the Greeks from the women of Libya. For, except that the garments of the Libyan women are of leather, and their fringes made of leathern thongs instead of serpents, in all else the dress of both is exactly alike. The name too itself shows that the mode of dressing the Pallas-statues came from Libya. For the Libyan women wear over their dress goat-skins stript of the hair, fringed at their edges, and coloured with vermilion;[2] and from these goat-skins the Greeks get their word Ægis (goat-harness). I think for my part that the loud cries uttered in our sacred rites came also from thence; for the Libyan women are greatly given to such cries and utter them very sweetly. Likewise the Greeks learnt from the Libyans to yoke four horses to a chariot.[3]

190. All the wandering tribes bury their dead according to the fashion of the Greeks, except the Nasamonians. They bury them sitting, and are right careful when the sick man is at the point of giving up the ghost, to make him sit and not let him die lying down.[4] The dwellings of these people are made of the stems of the asphodel, and of rushes wattled together. They can be carried from place to place. Such are the customs of the afore-mentioned tribes.

1 Vide supra, ii. 50.

2 Vermilion is abundant in North Africa. Red shoes are commonly worn at Tripoli. Red shawls and mantles are frequent in the interior. The African nations, too, continue to excel in the dressing and dyeing of leather.

3 Can Herodotus intend to assert a connection between Greece and Libya Proper in the ante-Homeric times?

4 The ancient Britons often buried their dead in a sitting posture, the hands raised to the neck, and the elbows close to the knees.

191. Westward of the river Triton and adjoining upon the Auseans,[1] are other Libyans who till the ground, and live in houses: these people are named the Maxyans. They let the hair grow long on the right side of their heads, and shave it close on the left; they besmear their bodies with red paint; and they say that they are descended from the men of Troy. Their country and the remainder of Libya towards the west is far fuller of wild beasts, and of wood, than the country of the wandering people. For the eastern side of Libya, where the wanderers dwell, is low and sandy, as far as the river Triton; but westward of that the land of the husbandmen is very hilly, and abounds with forests and wild beasts. For this is the tract in which the huge serpents are found, and the lions, the elephants, the bears, the aspicks, and the horned asses.[2] Here too are the dog-faced creatures, and the creatures without heads, whom the Libyans declare to have their eyes in their breasts; and also the wild men, and wild women, and many other far less fabulous beasts.

192. Among the wanderers are none of these, but quite other animals; as antelopes, gazelles, buffaloes, and asses, not of the horned sort, but of a kind which does not need to drink;[3] also oryxes, whose horns are used for the curved sides of citherns, and whose size is about that of the ox; foxes, hyænas, porcupines, wild rams, dictyes,[4] jackals, panthers, boryes,[5] land-crocodiles about three cubits in length,[6] very like lizards, ostriches, and little snakes, each with a single horn. All these animals are found here, and likewise those belonging to other countries, except the stag and the wild-boar; but neither stag nor wild-boar are found in any part of Libya. There are, however, three sorts of mice in these parts; the first are called two-footed;[7]

1 Vide supra, ch. 180. Herodotus here proceeds in his enumeration of the tribes of the coast.

2 Elephants are not now found in the countries north of the desert. It is uncertain what animal Herodotus intends by his "horned ass;" probably some kind of antelope.

3 The wild ass can live in the worst parts of the desert and needs probably less water than almost any animal. Still, however, there are no doubt times when "the wild asses quench their thirst." (Ps. civ. 11.)

4 It is impossible to say what animal is here intended.

5 Herodotus does not mention the camel, which may have been introduced later.

6 This immense lizard, or monitor, is very common in parts of Africa.

7 The jerboa (*Dipus jaculus* of Linnæus) is undoubtedly intended.

the next, zegeries, which is a Libyan word meaning "hills;" and the third, urchins. Weasels also are found in the Silphium-region, much like the Tartessian. So many, therefore, are the animals belonging to the land of the wandering Libyans, in so far at least as my researches have been able to reach.

193. Next to the Maxyan Libyans are the Zavecians, whose wives drive their chariots to battle.

194. On them border the Gyzantians; in whose country a vast deal of honey is made by bees; very much more, however, by the skill of men. The people all paint themselves red, and eat monkeys, whereof there is inexhaustible store in the hills.

195. Off their coast, as the Carthaginians report, lies an is-land, by name Cyraunis, the length of which is two hundred furlongs, its breadth not great, and which is soon reached from the mainland. Vines and olive-trees cover the whole of it, and there is in the island a lake, from which the young maidens of the country draw up gold-dust, by dipping into the mud birds' feathers smeared with pitch. If this be true, I know not; I but write what is said. It may be even so, however; since I myself have seen pitch drawn up out of the water from a lake in Zacynthus. At the place I speak of there are a number of lakes; but one is larger than the rest, being seventy feet every way, and two fathoms in depth. Here they let down a pole into the water, with a bunch of myrtle tied to one end, and when they raise it again, there is pitch sticking to the myrtle, which in smell is like to bitumen, but in all else is better than the pitch of Pieria. This they pour into a trench dug by the lake's side; and when a good deal has thus been got together, they draw it off and put it up in jars. Whatever falls into the lake passes underground, and comes up in the sea, which is no less than four furlongs distant. So then what is said of the island off the Libyan coast is not without likelihood.

196. The Carthaginians also relate the following:— There is a country in Libya, and a nation, beyond the Pillars of Heracles,[1] which they are wont to visit, where they no sooner arrive but forthwith they unlade their wares, and, having disposed them after an orderly fashion along the beach, leave them, and, return-ing aboard their ships, raise a great smoke. The natives, when

1 The trade of the Carthaginians with the western coast of Africa (outside the Straits of Gibraltar) has been fully proved.

they see the smoke, come down to the shore, and, laying out to view so much gold as they think the worth of the wares, withdraw to a distance. The Carthaginians upon this come ashore and look. If they think the gold enough, they take it and go their way; but if it does not seem to them sufficient, they go aboard ship once more, and wait patiently. Then the others approach and add to their gold, till the Carthaginians are content. Neither party deals unfairly by the other: for they themselves never touch the gold till it comes up to the worth of their goods, nor do the natives ever carry off the goods till the gold is taken away.

197. These be the Libyan tribes whereof I am able to give the names; and most of these cared little then, and indeed care little now, for the king of the Medes. One thing more also I can add concerning this region, namely, that, so far as our knowledge reaches, four nations, and no more, inhabit it; and two of these nations are indigenous, while two are not. The two indigenous are the Libyans and Ethiopians, who dwell respectively in the north and the south of Libya. The Phœnicians and the Greek are in-comers.[1]

198. It seems to me that Libya is not to compare for goodness of soil with either Asia or Europe, except the Cinyps-region, which is named after the river that waters it. This piece of land is equal to any country in the world for cereal crops, and is in nothing like the rest of Libya. For the soil here is black, and springs of water abound; so that there is nothing to fear from drought; nor do heavy rains (and it rains in that part of Libya) do any harm when they soak the ground. The returns of the harvest come up to the measure which prevails in Babylonia.[2] The soil is likewise good in the country of the Euesperites;[3] for there the land brings forth in the best years a hundred-fold. But the Cinyps-region yields three hundred-fold.

199. The country of the Cyrenæans, which is the highest tract within the part of Libya inhabited by the wandering tribes,[4] has

---

1 The Egyptians are omitted, because Egypt is reckoned to Asia (supra, ii. 17, iv. 39 and 41).

2 Vide supra, i. 193.

3 The Euesperites are the inhabitants of a town situated at the eastern extremity of the Greater Syrtis, between the Borean or Northern Promontory (*Cape Tejones*) and Tauchira. The Ptolemies changed its name to Berenice, which has since been corrupted into *Benghazi*.

4 Kiepert gives the height of the upper plateau of Cyrênê at 1700 feet.

three seasons that deserve remark. First the crops along the sea-coast begin to ripen, and are ready for the harvest and the vintage; after they have been gathered in, the crops of the middle tract above the coast-region (the hill-country, as they call it) need harvesting; while about the time when this middle crop is housed, the fruits ripen and are fit for cutting in the highest tract of all. So that the produce of the first tract has been all eaten and drunk by the time that the last harvest comes in. And the harvest-time of the Cyrenæans continues thus for eight full months. So much concerning these matters.

200. When the Persians sent from Egypt by Aryandes to help Pheretima reached Barca, they laid siege to the town, calling on those within to give up the men who had been guilty of the murder of Arcesilaüs. The townspeople, however, as they had one and all taken part in the deed, refused to entertain the proposition. So the Persians beleaguered Barca for nine months, in the course of which they dug several mines from their own lines to the walls, and likewise made a number of vigorous assaults. But their mines were discovered by a man who was a worker in brass, who went with a brazen shield all round the fortress, and laid it on the ground inside the city. In other places the shield, when he laid it down, was quite dumb; but where the ground was undermined, there the brass of the shield rang. Here, therefore, the Barcæans countermined, and slew the Persian diggers. Such was the way in which the mines were discovered; as for the assaults, the Barcæans beat them back.

201. When much time had been consumed, and great numbers had fallen on both sides, nor had the Persians lost fewer than their adversaries, Amasis, the leader of the land-army, perceiving that, although the Barcæans would never be conquered by force, they might be overcome by fraud, contrived as follows. One night he dug a wide trench, and laid light planks of wood across the opening, after which he brought mould and placed it upon the planks, taking care to make the place level with the surrounding ground. At dawn of day he summoned the Barcæans to a parley: and they gladly hearkening, the terms were at length agreed upon. Oaths were interchanged upon the ground over the hidden trench, and the agreement ran thus – "So long as the ground beneath our feet stands firm, the oath shall abide unchanged; the people of Barca agree to pay a fair sum to the king, and the Persians promise to cause no further trouble to the

people of Barca." After the oath, the Barcæans, relying upon its terms, threw open all their gates, went out themselves beyond the walls, and allowed as many of the enemy as chose to enter. Then the Persians broke down their secret bridge, and rushed at speed into the town – their reason for breaking the bridge being, that so they might observe what they had sworn; for they had promised the Barcæans that the oath should continue "so long as the ground whereon they stood was firm." When, therefore, the bridge was once broken down, the oath ceased to hold.

202. Such of the Barcæans as were most guilty the Persians gave up to Pheretima, who nailed them to crosses all round the walls of the city.[1] She also cut off the breasts of their wives, and fastened them likewise about the walls. The remainder of the people she gave as booty to the Persians, except only the Battiadæ, and those who had taken no part in the murder, to whom she handed over the possession of the town.

203. The Persians now set out on their return home, carrying with them the rest of the Barcæans, whom they had made their slaves. On their way they came to Cyrênê; and the Cyrenæans, out of regard for an oracle, let them pass through the town. During the passage, Bares, the commander of the fleet, advised to seize the place; but Amasis, the leader of the land-force, would not consent; "because," he said, "they had only been charged to attack the one Greek city of Barca."[2] When, however, they had passed through the town, and were encamped upon the hill of Lycæan Jove, it repented them that they had not seized Cyrênê, and they endeavoured to enter it a second time. The Cyrenæans, however, would not suffer this; whereupon, though no one appeared to offer them battle, yet a panic came upon the Persians, and they ran a distance of full sixty furlongs before they pitched their camp. Here as they lay, a messenger came to them from Aryandes, ordering them home. Then the Persians besought the men of Cyrênê to give them provisions for the way, and, these consenting, they set off on their return to Egypt. But the Libyans now beset them, and, for the sake of their clothes and harness, slew all who dropped behind and straggled, during the whole march homewards.

1 Compare the punishment of the Babylonians by Darius (supra, iii. 159).
2 This whole account of the danger and escape of Cyrênê is exceedingly improbable.

204. The furthest point of Libya reached by this Persian host was the city of Euesperides. The Barcæans carried into slavery were sent from Egypt to the king; and Darius assigned them a village in Bactria for their dwelling-place. To this village they gave the name of Barca, and it was to my time an inhabited place in Bactria.

205. Nor did Pheretima herself end her days happily. For on her return to Egypt from Libya, directly after taking vengeance on the people of Barca, she was overtaken by a most horrid death. Her body swarmed with worms, which ate her flesh while she was still alive.[1] Thus do men, by over-harsh punishments, draw down upon themselves the anger of the gods. Such then, and so fierce, was the vengeance which Pheretima, daughter of Battus, took upon the Barcæans.

---

1 The manner of her death cannot fail to recall the end of Herod Agrippa (Acts xii. 23).

THE FIFTH BOOK,
ENTITLED TERPSICHORE

1. THE Persians left behind by King Darius in Europe, who had Megabazus for their general,[1] reduced, before any other Hellespontine state, the people of Perinthus,[2] who had no mind to become subjects of the king. Now the Perinthians had ere this been roughly handled by another nation, the Pæonians. For the Pæonians from about the Strymon were once bidden by an oracle to make war upon the Perinthians, and if these latter, when the camps faced one another, challenged them by name to fight, then to venture on a battle, but if otherwise, not to make the hazard. The Pæonians followed the advice. Now the men of Perinthus drew out to meet them in the skirts of their city; and a threefold single combat was fought on challenge given. Man to man, and horse to horse, and dog to dog, was the strife waged; and the Perinthians, winners of two combats out of the three, in their joy had raised the pæan; when the Pæonians, struck by the thought that this was what the oracle had meant, passed the word one to another, saying, "Now of a surety has the oracle been fulfilled for us; now our work begins." Then the Pæonians set upon the Perinthians in the midst of their pæan, and defeated them utterly, leaving but few of them alive.

2. Such was the affair of the Pæonians, which happened a long time previously. At this time the Perinthians, after a brave struggle for freedom, were overcome by numbers, and yielded to Megabazus and his Persians. After Perinthus had been brought under, Megabazus led his host through Thrace, subduing to the dominion of the king all the towns and all the nations of those parts.[3] For the king's command to him was, that he should conquer Thrace.

3. The Thracians are the most powerful people in the world, except, of course, the Indians;[4] and if they had one head, or were

---

1 Vide supra, iv. 143.
2 The modern *Erekli*, a place of some consequence on the sea of Marmora.
3 The conquests of Megabazus were confined to the tracts along the coast.
4 Alluding to what he had said before (Bk. iii. ch. 94).

agreed among themselves, it is my belief that their match could not be found anywhere, and that they would very far surpass all other nations. But such union is impossible for them, and there are no means of ever bringing it about. Herein therefore consists their weakness. The Thracians bear many names in the different regions of their country, but all of them have like usages in every respect, excepting only the Getæ,[1] the Trausi, and those who dwell above the people of Creston.[2]

4. Now the manners and customs of the Getæ, who believe in their immortality, I have already spoken of.[3] The Trausi in all else resemble the other Thracians, but have customs at births and deaths which I will now describe. When a child is born all its kindred sit round about it in a circle and weep for the woes it will have to undergo now that it is come into the world, making mention of every ill that falls to the lot of humankind; when, on the other hand, a man has died, they bury him with laughter and rejoicings, and say that now he is free from a host of sufferings, and enjoys the completest happiness.

5. The Thracians who live above the Crestonæans observe the following customs. Each man among them has several wives; and no sooner does a man die than a sharp contest ensues among the wives upon the question, which of them all the husband loved most tenderly; the friends of each eagerly plead on her behalf, and she to whom the honour is adjudged, after receiving the praises both of men and women, is slain over the grave by the hand of her next of kin, and then buried with her husband. The others are sorely grieved, for nothing is considered such a disgrace.[4]

6. The Thracians who do not belong to these tribes have the customs which follow. They sell their children to traders. On their maidens they keep no watch, but allow them to enjoy any men they wished, while on the conduct of their wives they keep a most strict watch. Brides are purchased of their parents for large sums of money. Tattooing among them marks noble birth, and the want of it low birth. To be idle is accounted the most honourable

---

1 Concerning the Getæ, vide supra, Bk. iv. ch. 93.
2 Concerning Creston, vide supra, i. 57.
3 Supra, iv. 94.
4 [Analogous to this custom is the Indian *Suttee*, in which two distinct motives were combined: Lyall, *Asiatic Studies*, vol. ii. p. 313.– E. H. B.]

thing, and to be a tiller of the ground the most dishonourable. To live by war and plunder is of all things the most glorious. These are the most remarkable of their customs.

7. The gods which they worship are but three, Ares, Dionysus, and Artemis.[1] Their kings, however, unlike the rest of the citizens, worship Hermes more than any other god, always swearing by his name, and declaring that they are themselves sprung from him.

8. Their wealthy ones are buried in the following fashion. The body is laid out for three days; and during this time they kill victims of all kinds, and feast upon them, after first bewailing the departed. Then they either burn the body[2] or else bury it in the ground. Lastly, they raise a mound over the grave, and hold games of all sorts, wherein the single combat is awarded the highest prize. Such is the mode of burial among the Thracians.

9. As regards the region lying north of this country no one can say with any certainty what men inhabit it. It appears that you no sooner cross the Ister than you enter on an interminable wilderness.[3] The only people of whom I can hear as dwelling beyond the Ister are the race named Sigynnæ, who wear, they say, a dress like the Medes, and have horses which are covered entirely with a coat of shaggy hair, five fingers in length. They are a small breed, flat-nosed, and not strong enough to bear men on their backs; but when yoked to chariots, they are among the swiftest known, which is the reason why the people of that country use chariots. Their borders reach down almost to the Eneti upon the Adriatic Sea, and they call themselves colonists of the Medes; but how they can be colonists of the Medes I for my part cannot imagine. Still nothing is impossible in the long lapse of ages. Sigynnæ is the name which the Ligurians who dwell above Massilia[4] give to traders, while among the Cyprians the word means spears.

10. According to the account which the Thracians give, the country beyond the Ister is possessed by bees, on account of

1 War, drinking, and the chase – the principal delights of a nation in the condition of the Thracians – had, it would seem, their respective deities, which the Greeks identified with their Ares, Dionysus, and Artemis.

2 Cremation was the mode in which the Indo-European nations most usually disposed of their dead. [So in Homer; but inhumation was normal in the Mycenæan age in Greece. – E. H. B.]

3 Hungary and Austria.

4 The modern Marseilles.

which it is impossible to penetrate farther.¹ But in this they seem to me to say what has no likelihood; for it is certain that those creatures are very impatient of cold. I rather believe that it is on account of the cold that the regions which lie under the Bear are without inhabitants. Such then are the accounts given of this country, the sea-coast whereof Megabazus was now employed in subjecting to the Persians.

11. King Darius had no sooner crossed the Hellespont and reached Sardis, than he bethought himself of the good deed of Histiæus the Milesian,² and the good counsel of the Mytilenean Coës.³ He therefore sent for both of them to Sardis, and bade them each crave a boon at his hands. Now Histiæus, as he was already king of Miletus, did not make request for any government besides, but asked Darius to give him Myrcinus of the Edonians, where he wished to build him a city. Such was the choice that Histiæus made. Coës, on the other hand, as he was a mere burgher, and not a king, requested the sovereignty of Mytilênê. Both alike obtained their requests, and straightway betook themselves to the places which they had chosen.

12. It chanced in the meantime that King Darius saw a sight which determined him to bid Megabazus remove the Pæonians from their seats in Europe and transport them to Asia. There were two Pæonians, Pigres and Mantyes, whose ambition it was to obtain the sovereignty over their countrymen. As soon therefore as ever Darius crossed into Asia, these men came to Sardis, and brought with them their sister, who was a tall and beautiful woman. Having so done, they waited till a day came when the king sat in state in the suburb of the Lydians; and then dressing their sister in the richest gear they could, sent her to draw water for them. She bore a pitcher upon her head, and with one arm led a horse, while all the way as she went she span flax. Now as she passed by where the king was, Darius took notice of her; for it was neither like the Persians nor the Lydians, nor any of the dwellers in Asia, to do as she did. Darius accordingly noted her, and ordered some of his guard to follow her steps, and watch to see what she would do with the horse. So the spearmen went; and the woman, when she came to the river, first watered the horse, and then filling the pitcher, came back the same way she had gone, with the pitcher of water upon her

1 Mosquitoes.   2 Supra, iv. 137.   3 Supra, iv. 97.

head, and the horse dragging upon her arm, while she still kept twirling the spindle.

13. King Darius was full of wonder both at what they who had watched the woman told him, and at what he had himself seen. So he commanded that she should be brought before him. And the woman came; and with her appeared her brothers, who had been watching everything a little way off. Then Darius asked them of what nation the woman was; and the young men replied that they were Pæonians, and she was their sister. Darius rejoined by asking, "Who the Pæonians were, and in what part of the world they lived? and, further, what business had brought the young men to Sardis?" Then the brothers told him they had come to put themselves under his power, and Pæonia was a country upon the river Strymon, and the Strymon was at no great distance from the Hellespont. The Pæonians, they said, were colonists of the Teucrians from Troy. When they had thus answered his questions, Darius asked if all the women of their country worked so hard? Then the brothers eagerly answered, Yes; for this was the very object with which the whole thing had been done.

14. So Darius wrote letters to Megabazus, the commander whom he had left behind in Thrace,[1] and ordered him to remove the Pæonians from their own land, and bring them into his presence, men, women, and children. And straightway a horseman took the message, and rode at speed to the Hellespont; and, crossing it, gave the paper to Megabazus. Then Megabazus, as soon as he had read it, and procured guides from Thrace, made war upon Pæonia.

15. Now when the Pæonians heard that the Persians were marching against them, they gathered themselves together, and marched down to the sea-coast, since they thought the Persians would endeavour to enter their country on that side. Here then they stood in readiness to oppose the army of Megabazus. But the Persians, who knew that they had collected, and were gone to keep guard at the pass near the sea, got guides, and taking the inland route before the Pæonians were aware, poured down upon their cities, from which the men had all marched out; and finding them empty, easily got possession of them. Then the men, when they heard that all their towns were taken, scattered

---

1 Supra, iv. 143; and v. 1.

this way and that to their homes, and gave themselves up to the Persians. And so these tribes of the Pæonians, to wit, the Siro-pæonians, the Pæoplians, and all the others as far as Lake Prasias, were torn from their seats and led away into Asia.

16. They on the other hand who dwelt about Mount Pan-gæum[1] and in the country of the Dobêres, the Agrianians, and the Odomantians, and they likewise who inhabited Lake Prasias, were not conquered by Megabazus. He sought indeed to subdue the dwellers upon the lake, but could not effect his purpose. Their manner of living is the following. Platforms supported upon tall piles stand in the middle of the lake, which are ap-proached from the land by a single narrow bridge.[2] At the first the piles which bear up the platforms were fixed in their places by the whole body of the citizens, but since that time the custom which has prevailed about fixing them is this:— they are brought from a hill called Orbêlus, and every man drives in three for each wife that he marries. Now the men have all many wives apiece; and this is the way in which they live. Each has his own hut, wherein he dwells, upon one of the platforms, and each has also a trap-door giving access to the lake beneath; and their wont is to tie their baby children by the foot with a string, to save them from rolling into the water. They feed their horses and their other beasts upon fish, which abound in the lake to such a degree that a man has only to open his trap-door and to let down a basket by a rope into the water, and then to wait a very short time, when he draws it up quite full of them. The fish are of two kinds, which they call the paprax and the tilon.

17. The Pæonians[3] therefore – at least such of them as had been conquered – were led away into Asia. As for Megabazus, he no sooner brought the Pæonians under, than he sent into Macedonia an embassy of Persians, choosing for the purpose the seven men of most note in all the army after himself. These

1 The range which runs parallel to the coast between the valley of the *Anghista* and the high road from *Orfano to Pravista.*

2 Discoveries in the lakes of central Europe, particularly those of Switzer-land, have confirmed in the most remarkable way this whole description of Herodotus. A similar mode of life to that here described, and apparently prac-tised by the early inhabitants of Switzerland, is found among the natives of New Guinea [Borneo, Celebes, and among the Ainus of Japan. – E. H. B.]

3 Pæonia in ancient times appears to have consisted of two distinct tracts. Herodotus seems to have known only of the Strymonic Pæonia.

persons were to go to Amyntas, and require him to give earth and water to King Darius. Now there is a very short cut from the lake Prasias across to Macedonia. Quite close to the lake is the mine which yielded afterwards a talent of silver a day to Alexander; and from this mine you have only to cross the mountain called Dysôrum to find yourself in the Macedonian territory.

18. So the Persians sent upon this errand, when they reached the court, and were brought into the presence of Amyntas, required him to give earth and water to King Darius. And Amyntas not only gave them what they asked, but also invited them to come and feast with him; after which he made ready the board with great magnificence, and entertained the Persians in right friendly fashion. Now when the meal was over, and they were all set to the drinking, the Persians said –

"Dear Macedonian, we Persians have a custom when we make a great feast to bring with us to the board our wives and concubines, and make them sit beside us.[1] Now then, as thou hast received us so kindly, and feasted us so handsomely, and givest moreover earth and water to King Darius, do also after our custom in this matter."

Then Amyntas answered – "O, Persians! we have no such custom as this; but with us men and women are kept apart. Nevertheless, since you, who are our lords, wish it, this also shall be granted to you."

When Amyntas had thus spoken, he bade some go and fetch the women. And the women came at his call and took their seats in a row over against the Persians. Then, when the Persians saw that the women were fair and comely, they spoke again to Amyntas and said, that "what had been done was not wise; for it had been better for the women not to have come at all, than to come in this way, and not sit by their sides, but remain over against them, the torment of their eyes." So Amyntas was forced to bid the women sit side by side with the Persians. The women did as he ordered; and then the Persians, who had drunk more than they ought, began to put their hands on them, and one even tried to give the woman next him a kiss.

19. King Amyntas saw, but he kept silence, although sorely grieved, for he greatly feared the power of the Persians.

---

1 The seclusion of the women was as much practised by the Persians as by any other Orientals.

Alexander, however, Amyntas' son, who was likewise there and witnessed the whole, being a young man and unacquainted with suffering, could not any longer restrain himself. He therefore, full of wrath, spake thus to Amyntas:— "Dear father, thou art old and shouldest spare thyself. Rise up from table and go take thy rest; do not stay out the drinking. I will remain with the guests and give them all that is fitting."

Amyntas, who guessed that Alexander would play some wild prank, made answer:— "Dear son, thy words sound to me as those of one who is well nigh on fire, and I perceive thou sendest me away that thou mayest do some wild deed. I beseech thee make no commotion about these men, lest thou bring us all to ruin, but bear to look calmly on what they do. For myself, I will e'en withdraw as thou biddest me."

20. Amyntas, when he had thus besought his son, went out; and Alexander said to the Persians, "Look on these ladies as your own, dear strangers, all or any of them – only tell us your wishes. But now, as the evening wears, and I see you have all had wine enough, let them, if you please, retire, and when they have bathed they shall come back again." To this the Persians agreed, and Alexander, having got the women away, sent them off to the harem, and made ready in their room an equal number of beardless youths, whom he dressed in the garments of the women, and then, arming them with daggers, brought them in to the Persians, saying as he introduced them, "Methinks, dear Persians, that your entertainment has fallen short in nothing. We have set before you all that we had ourselves in store, and all that we could anywhere find to give you – and now, to crown the whole, we make over to you our sisters and our mothers, that you may perceive yourselves to be entirely honoured by us, even as you deserve to be – and also that you may take back word to the king who sent you here, that there was one man, a Greek, the satrap of Macedonia, by whom you were both feasted and lodged handsomely." So speaking, Alexander set by the side of each Persian one of those whom he had called Macedonian women, but who were in truth men. And these men, when the Persians began to be rude, despatched them with their daggers.

21. So the ambassadors perished by this death, both they and also their followers. For the Persians had brought a great train with them, carriages, and attendants, and baggage of every kind – all of which disappeared at the same time as the men

themselves. Not very long afterwards the Persians made strict search for their lost embassy; but Alexander, with much wisdom, hushed up the business, bribing those sent on the errand, partly with money, and partly with the gift of his own sister Gygæa,[1] whom he gave in marriage to Bubares,[2] a Persian, the chief leader of the expedition which came in search of the lost men. Thus the death of these Persians was hushed up, and no more was said of it.

22. Now that the men of this family are Greeks, sprung from Perdiccas, as they themselves affirm, is a thing which I can declare of my own knowledge, and which I will hereafter make plainly evident.[3] That they are so has been already adjudged by those who manage the Pan-Hellenic contest at Olympia. For when Alexander wished to contend in the games, and had come to Olympia with no other view, the Greeks who were about to run against him would have excluded him from the contest — saying that Greeks only were allowed to contend, and not barbarians. But Alexander proved himself to be an Argive, and was distinctly adjudged a Greek; after which he entered the lists for the foot-race, and was drawn to run in the first pair. Thus was this matter settled.

23. Megabazus, having reached the Hellespont with the Pæonians, crossed it, and went up to Sardis. He had become aware while in Europe that Histiæus the Milesian was raising a wall at Myrcinus — the town upon the Strymon which he had obtained from King Darius as his guerdon for keeping the bridge. No sooner therefore did he reach Sardis with the Pæonians than he said to Darius, "What mad thing is this that thou hast done, sire, to let a Greek, a wise man and a shrewd, get hold of a town in Thrace, a place too where there is abundance of timber fit for shipbuilding, and oars in plenty, and mines of silver,[4] and about which are many dwellers both Greek and barbarian, ready enough to take him for their chief, and by day and night to do

---

1 Vide infra, viii. 136.

2 Bubares was the son of Megabazus. He was afterwards overseer of the workmen at Athos (infra, vii. 22).

3 Vide infra, viii. 137.

4 Histiæus showed excellent judgment in selecting this site. The vicinity of the rich and extensive Strymonic plain, the abundance of timber, the neighbourhood of gold and silver mines, the ready access to the sea, were all points of the utmost importance to a new settlement.

his bidding! I pray thee make this man cease his work, if thou wouldest not be entangled in a war with thine own followers. Stop him, but with a gentle message, only bidding him to come to thee. Then when thou once hast him in thy power, be sure thou take good care that he never get back to Greece again."

24. With these words Megabazus easily persuaded Darius, who thought he had shown true foresight in this matter. Darius therefore sent a messenger to Myrcinus, who said, "These be the words of the king to thee, O Histiæus! I have looked to find a man well affectioned towards me and towards my greatness; and I have found none whom I can trust like thee. Thy deeds, and not thy words only, have proved thy love for me. Now then, since I have a mighty enterprise in hand, I pray thee come to me, that I may show thee what I purpose!"

Histiæus, when he heard this, put faith in the words of the messenger; and, as it seemed to him a grand thing to be the king's counsellor, he straightway went up to Sardis. Then Darius, when he was come, said to him, "Dear Histiæus, hear why I have sent for thee. No sooner did I return from Scythia, and lose thee out of my sight, than I longed, as I have never longed for aught else, to behold thee once more, and to interchange speech with thee. Right sure I am there is nothing in all the world so precious as a friend who is at once wise and true: both which thou art, as I have had good proof in what thou hast already done for me. Now then 'tis well thou art come; for look, I have an offer to make to thee. Let go Miletus and thy newly-founded town in Thrace, and come with me up to Susa; share all that I have; live with me, and be my counsellor."[1]

25. When Darius had thus spoken he made Artaphernes, his brother by the father's side, governor of Sardis, and taking Histiæus with him, went up to Susa. He left as general of all the troops upon the sea-coast Otanes, son of Sisamnes,[2] whose father King Cambyses slew and flayed,[3] because that he, being of the number of the royal judges, had taken money to give an unrighteous sentence. Therefore Cambyses slew and flayed Sisamnes, and cutting his skin into strips, stretched them across the seat of the throne whereon he had been wont to sit when

---

1 Compare, for this Oriental practice, 2 Sam. ix. 7, 11; xix. 33; 1 Kings ii. 7.
2 *Not* the conspirator, who was Otanes, son of *Pharnaspes* (iii. 68).
3 In later times the Persians seem to have flayed their criminals *alive*.

he heard causes. Having so done Cambyses appointed the son of Sisamnes to be judge in his father's room, and bade him never forget in what way his seat was cushioned.

26. Accordingly this Otanes, who had occupied so strange a throne, became the successor of Megabazus in his command, and took first of all Byzantium and Chalcêdon,[1] then Antandrus[2] in the Troas, and next Lampônium. This done, he borrowed ships of the Lesbians, and took Lemnos and Imbrus, which were still inhabited by Pelasgians.[3]

27. Now the Lemnians stood on their defence, and fought gallantly; but they were brought low in course of time. Such as outlived the struggle were placed by the Persians under the government of Lycarêtus, the brother of that Mæandrius[4] who was tyrant of Samos. (This Lycarêtus died afterwards in his government.) The cause which Otanes alleged for conquering and enslaving all these nations was, that some had refused to join the king's army against Scythia, while others had molested the host on its return. Such were the exploits which Otanes performed in his command.

28. Afterwards, but for no long time,[5] there was a respite from suffering. Then from Naxos and Miletus troubles gathered anew about Ionia. Now Naxos at this time surpassed all the other islands in prosperity;[6] and Miletus had reached the height of her power, and was the glory of Ionia. But previously for two generations the Milesians had suffered grievously from civil disorders, which were composed by the Parians, whom the Milesians chose before all the rest of the Greeks to rearrange their government.[7]

29. Now the way in which the Parians healed their differences was the following. A number of the chief Parians came to Miletus, and when they saw in how ruined a condition the Milesians

---

1 Vide supra, iv. 144.

2 Antandrus lay on the sea-coast of the gulf of *Adramyti*, a short distance west of Adramyttium. The name remains in the *Antandro* of the present day.

3 Vide supra, iv. 145.

4 Supra, iii. 142–148.

5 Perhaps Clinton is not far wrong in reckoning it "a tranquillity of two years."

6 The fertility of Naxos was proverbial in ancient times.

7 Concerning the practice of calling in foreigners to settle the domestic differences of a state, vide supra, iv. 161.

were, they said that they would like first to go over their country. So they went through all Milesia, and on their way, whenever they saw in the waste and desolate country any land that was well farmed, they took down the names of the owners in their tablets; and having thus gone through the whole region, and obtained after all but few names, they called the people together on their return to Miletus, and made proclamation that they gave the government into the hands of those persons whose lands they had found well farmed; for they thought it likely (they said) that the same persons who had managed their own affairs well would likewise conduct aright the business of the state. The other Milesians, who in time past had been at variance, they placed under the rule of these men. Thus was the Milesian government set in order by the Parians.

30. It was, however, from the two cities above mentioned that troubles began now to gather again about Ionia; and this is the way in which they arose. Certain of the rich men had been banished from Naxos by the commonalty, and, upon their banishment, had fled to Miletus. Aristagoras, son of Molpagoras, the nephew and likewise the son-in-law of Histiæus, son of Lysagoras, who was still kept by Darius at Susa, happened to be regent of Miletus at the time of their coming. For the kingly power belonged to Histiæus; but he was at Susa when the Naxians came. Now these Naxians had in times past been bond-friends of Histiæus; and so on their arrival at Miletus they addressed themselves to Aristagoras, and begged him to lend them such aid as his ability allowed, in hopes thereby to recover their country. Then Aristagoras, considering with himself that, if the Naxians should be restored by his help, he would be lord of Naxos, put forward the friendship with Histiæus to cloak his views, and spoke as follows:–

"I cannot engage to furnish you with such a power as were needful to force you, against their will, upon the Naxians who hold the city; for I know they can bring into the field eight thousand bucklers, and have also a vast number of ships of war. But I will do all that lies in my power to get you some aid, and I think I can manage it in this way. Artaphernes happens to be my friend. Now he is a son of Hystaspes, and brother to King Darius. All the sea-coast of Asia is under him,[1] and he has a

1 This is evidently an exaggeration.

numerous army and numerous ships. I think I can prevail on him to do what we require."

When the Naxians heard this, they empowered Aristagoras to manage the matter for them as well as he could, and told him to promise gifts and pay for the soldiers, which (they said) they would readily furnish, since they had great hope that the Naxians, so soon as they saw them returned, would render them obedience, and likewise the other islanders.[1] For at that time not one of the Cyclades was subject to King Darius.

31. So Aristagoras went to Sardis and told Artaphernes that Naxos was an island of no great size, but a fair land and fertile,[2] lying near Ionia,[3] and containing much treasure and a vast number of slaves. "Make war then upon this land (he said) and reinstate the exiles; for if thou wilt do this, first of all, I have very rich gifts in store for thee (besides the cost of the armament, which it is fair that we who are the authors of the war should pay); and, secondly, thou wilt bring under the power of the king not only Naxos but the other islands which depend on it, as Paros, Andros, and all the rest of the Cyclades. And when thou hast gained these, thou mayest easily go on against Euboea, which is a large and wealthy island not less in size than Cyprus,[4] and very easy to bring under. A hundred ships were quite enough to subdue the whole." The other answered – "Truly thou art the author of a plan which may much advantage the house of the king, and thy counsel is good in all points except the number of the ships. Instead of a hundred, two hundred shall be at thy disposal when the spring comes. But the king himself must first approve the undertaking."

32. When Aristagoras heard this he was greatly rejoiced, and went home in good heart to Miletus. And Artaphernes, after he had sent a messenger to Susa to lay the plans of Aristagoras before the king, and received his approval of the undertaking, made ready a fleet of two hundred triremes and a vast army of

1 Naxos would appear by this to have exercised a species of sovereignty over some of the other Cyclades.

2 Naxos is considerably larger than Jersey, but not more than half the size of the Isle of Wight.

3 Naxos is distant from the Ionian coast at least 80 miles. From Samos, however, which was now in the possession of the Persians, it is not more than 65 miles, and in clear weather is *visible*.

4 Cyprus is really more than twice the size of Euboea (*Negropont*).

Persians and their confederates. The command of these he gave to a Persian named Megabates, who belonged to the house of the Achæmenids, being nephew both to himself and to King Darius. It was to a daughter of this man that Pausanias the Lacedæmonian, the son of Cleombrotus (if at least there be any truth in the tale[1]), was affianced many years afterwards, when he conceived the desire of becoming tyrant of Greece. Artaphernes now, having named Megabates to the command, sent forward the armament to Aristagoras.

33. Megabates set sail, and, touching at Miletus, took on board Aristagoras with the Ionian troops and the Naxians; after which he steered, as he gave out, for the Hellespont; and when he reached Chios, he brought the fleet to anchor off Caucasa, being minded to wait there for a north wind, and then sail straight to Naxos. The Naxians however were not to perish at this time; and so the following events were brought about. As Megabates went his rounds to visit the watches on board the ships, he found a Myndian vessel upon which there was none set. Full of anger at such carelessness, he bade his guards to seek out the captain, one Scylax by name, and thrusting him through one of the holes in the ship's side,[2] to fasten him there in such a way that his head might show outside the vessel, while his body remained within. When Scylax was thus fastened, one went and informed Aristagoras that Megabates had bound his Myndian friend and was entreating him shamefully. So he came and asked Megabates to let the man off; but the Persian refused him; whereupon Aristagoras went himself and set Scylax free. When Megabates heard this he was still more angry than before, and spoke hotly to Aristagoras. Then the latter said to him –

"What hast thou to do with these matters? Wert thou not sent here by Artaphernes to obey me, and to sail whithersoever I ordered? Why dost meddle so?"

Thus spake Aristagoras. The other, in high dudgeon at such language, waited till the night, and then despatched a boat to Naxos, to warn the Naxians of the coming danger.

34. Now the Naxians up to this time had not had any suspicion that the armament was directed against them; as soon, therefore,

---

1 For the true account of these proceedings of Pausanias, cf. Thucyd. i. 128–130.

2 The "holes in the side" of a Greek vessel were, of course, for the oars.

as the message reached them, forthwith they brought within their walls all that they had in the open field, and made themselves ready against a siege by provisioning their town both with food and drink. Thus was Naxos placed in a posture of defence; and the Persians, when they crossed the sea from Chios, found the Naxians fully prepared for them. However they sat down before the place, and besieged it for four whole months. When at length all the stores which they had brought with them were exhausted, and Aristagoras had likewise spent upon the siege no small sum from his private means, and more was still needed to insure success, the Persians gave up the attempt, and first building certain forts, wherein they left the banished Naxians, withdrew to the mainland, having utterly failed in their undertaking.

35. And now Aristagoras found himself quite unable to make good his promises to Artaphernes; nay, he was even hard pressed to meet the claims whereto he was liable for the pay of the troops; and at the same time his fear was great, lest, owing to the failure of the expedition and his own quarrel with Megabates, he should be ousted from the government of Miletus. These manifold alarms had already caused him to contemplate raising a rebellion, when the man with the marked head came from Susa, bringing him instructions on the part of Histiæus to revolt from the king. For Histiæus, when he was anxious to give Aristagoras orders to revolt, could find but one safe way, as the roads were guarded, of making his wishes known; which was by taking the trustiest of his slaves, shaving all the hair from off his head, and then pricking letters upon the skin, and waiting till the hair grew again. Thus accordingly he did; and as soon as ever the hair was grown, he despatched the man to Miletus, giving him no other message than this – "When thou art come to Miletus, bid Aristagoras shave thy head, and look thereon." Now the marks on the head, as I have already mentioned, were a command to revolt. All this Histiæus did because it irked him greatly to be kept at Susa, and because he had strong hopes that, if troubles broke out, he would be sent down to the coast to quell them, whereas, if Miletus made no movement, he did not see a chance of his ever again returning thither.

36. Such, then, were the views which led Histiæus to despatch his messenger; and it so chanced that all these several motives to revolt were brought to bear upon Aristagoras at one and the same time.

Accordingly, at this conjuncture Aristagoras held a council of his trusty friends, and laid the business before them, telling them both what he had himself purposed, and what message had been sent him by Histiæus. At this council all his friends were of the same way of thinking, and recommended revolt, except only Hecatæus the historian. He, first of all, advised them by all means to avoid engaging in war with the king of the Persians, whose might he set forth, and whose subject nations he enumerated. As however he could not induce them to listen to this counsel, he next advised that they should do all that lay in their power to make themselves masters of the sea. "There was one only way," he said, "so far as he could see, of their succeeding in this. Miletus was, he knew, a weak state – but if the treasures in the temple at Branchidæ,[1] which Crœsus the Lydian gave to it, were seized, he had strong hopes that the mastery of the sea might be thereby gained; at least it would give them money to begin the war, and would save the treasures from falling into the hands of the enemy." Now these treasures were of very great value, as I showed in the first part of my History.[2] The assembly, however, rejected the counsel of Hecatæus, while, nevertheless, they resolved upon a revolt. One of their number, it was agreed, should sail to Myus,[3] where the fleet had been lying since its return from Naxos, and endeavour to seize the captains who had gone there with the vessels.

37. Iatragoras accordingly was despatched on this errand, and he took with guile Oliatus the son of Ibanôlis the Mylassian,[4] and Histiæus the son of Tymnes[5] the Termerean, – Coës likewise, the son of Erxander, to whom Darius gave Mytilênê,[6] and Aristagoras the son of Heraclides the Cymæan, and also many others. Thus Aristagoras revolted openly from Darius; and now he set to work to scheme against him in every possible way. First of all, in order to induce the Milesians to join heartily in the revolt, he gave out, that he laid down his own lordship over

1 [For a note on the Temple of Apollo at Branchidæ (near Miletus), see Frazer's *Pausanias*, vol. iv. pp. 125, 126. – E. H. B.]

2 Supra, i. 92.

3 Myus was one of the twelve cities of Ionia (supra, i. 142).

4 Mylasa or Mylassa was, like Termera, a town of Caria.

5 This Histiæus afterwards accompanied the expedition of Xerxes (infra, vii. 98).

6 Supra, ch. 11.

Miletus, and in lieu thereof established a commonwealth: after which, throughout all Ionia he did the like; for from some of the cities he drove out their tyrants, and to others, whose goodwill he hoped thereby to gain, he handed theirs over, thus giving up all the men whom he had seized at the Naxian fleet, each to the city whereto he belonged.

38. Now the Mytileneans had no sooner got Coës into their power, than they led him forth from the city and stoned him; the Cymæans, on the other hand, allowed their tyrant to go free; as likewise did most of the others. And so this form of government ceased throughout all the cities. Aristagoras the Milesian, after he had in this way put down the tyrants, and bidden the cities choose themselves captains in their room, sailed away himself on board a trireme to Lacedæmon; for he had great need of obtaining the aid of some powerful ally.

39. At Sparta, Anaxandridas the son of Leo was no longer king: he had died, and his son Cleomenes had mounted the throne, not however by right of merit, but of birth. Anaxandridas took to wife his own sister's daughter,[1] and was tenderly attached to her; but no children came from the marriage. Hereupon the Ephors[2] called him before them, and said – "If thou hast no care for thine own self, nevertheless *we* cannot allow this, nor suffer the race of Eurysthenes to die out from among us. Come then, as thy present wife bears thee no children, put her away, and wed another. So wilt thou do what is well-pleasing to the Spartans." Anaxandridas however refused to do as they required, and said it was no good advice the Ephors gave, to bid him put away his wife when she had done no wrong, and take to himself another. He therefore declined to obey them.

40. Then the Ephors and Elders[3] took counsel together, and laid this proposal before the king:– "Since thou art so fond, as we see thee to be, of thy present wife, do what we now advise, and gainsay us not, lest the Spartans make some unwonted decree concerning thee. We ask thee not now to put away thy

1 Marriages of this kind were common at Sparta. Leonidas married his niece, Gorgo (infra, vii. 239); Archidamus his aunt, Lampito (infra, vi. 71).

2 Concerning the Ephors at Sparta, vide supra, i. 65. This passage is very important, as marking their power over the kings.

3 The council of twenty-eight, mentioned, with the Ephors, in Book i. ch. 65, and again spoken of in Book vi. ch. 57. It seems that, when the Ephors and the Elders agreed together, the king had no power to withstand them.

wife to whom thou art married – give her still the same love and honour as ever, – but take thee another wife beside, who may bear thee children."

When he heard this offer, Anaxandridas gave way – and henceforth he lived with two wives in two separate houses, quite against all Spartan custom.

41. In a short time, the wife whom he had last married bore him a son, who received the name of Cleomenes; and so the heir to the throne was brought into the world by her. After this, the first wife also, who in time past had been barren, by some strange chance conceived, and came to be with child. Then the friends of the second wife, when they heard a rumour of the truth, made a great stir, and said it was a false boast, and she meant, they were sure, to bring forward as her own a supposititious child. So they raised an outcry against her; and therefore, when her full time was come, the Ephors, who were themselves incredulous, sat round her bed, and kept a strict watch on the labour.[1] At this time then she bore Dorieus, and after him, quickly, Leonidas, and after him, again quickly, Cleombrotus. Some even say that Leonidas and Cleombrotus were twins. On the other hand, the second wife, the mother of Cleomenes (who was a daughter of Prinetadas, the son of Demarmenus), never gave birth to a second child.

42. Now Cleomenes, it is said, was not right in his mind; indeed he verged upon madness; while Dorieus surpassed all his co-mates, and looked confidently to receiving the kingdom on the score of merit. When, therefore, after the death of Anaxandridas, the Spartans kept to the law, and made Cleomenes, his eldest son, king in his room, Dorieus, who had imagined that he should be chosen, and who could not bear the thought of having such a man as Cleomenes to rule over him, asked the Spartans to give him a body of men, and left Sparta with them in order to found a colony. However, he neither took counsel of the oracle at Delphi as to the place whereto he should go,[2] nor observed any of

1 Compare with this, the practice in our own country of summoning the great officers of state to the queen's apartments at the birth of a prince or princess. With the Spartans there was a religious motive at work, in addition to the political one which alone obtains with ourselves. It was necessary for them, in a religious point of view, to preserve the purity of the blood of Heracles.

2 The sanction of some oracle or other was required for every colony; the sanction of the oracle at Delphi, when the colony was Dorian.

the customary usages; but left Sparta in dudgeon, and sailed away to Libya, under the guidance of certain men who were Theræans.[1] These men brought him to Cinyps, where he colonised a spot, which has not its equal in all Libya, on the banks of a river:[2] but from this place he was driven in the third year by the Macians, the Libyans, and the Carthaginians.

43. Dorieus returned to the Peloponnese; whereupon Antichares the Eleônian gave him a counsel (which he got from the oracles of Laïus[3]), to "found the city of Heraclea in Sicily; the whole country of Eryx[4] belonged," he said, "to the Heracleids, since Heracles himself conquered it." On receiving this advice, Dorieus went to Delphi to inquire of the oracle whether he would take the place to which he was about to go. The Pythoness prophesied that he would; whereupon Dorieus went back to Libya, took up the men who had sailed with him at the first, and proceeded upon his way along the shores of Italy.

44. Just at this time, the Sybarites[5] say, they and their king Têlys were about to make war upon Crotôna, and the Crotoniats, greatly alarmed, besought Dorieus to lend them aid. Dorieus was prevailed upon, bore part in the war against Sybaris, and had a share in taking the town. Such is the account which the Sybarites give of what was done by Dorieus and his companions. The Crotoniats, on the other hand, maintain that no foreigner lent them aid in their war against the Sybarites, save and except Callias the Elean, a soothsayer of the race of the Iamidæ; and he only forsook Têlys the Sybaritic king, and deserted to their side, when he found on sacrificing that the victims were not favourable to an attack on Crotôna. Such is the account which each party gives of these matters.

45. Both parties likewise adduce testimonies to the truth of what they say. The Sybarites show a temple and sacred precinct

---

1 The connection of Thera with Cyrênê (iv. 150–159) would explain the choice of Cinyps as a settlement.

2 This place, which Herodotus regarded as the most fertile spot in Africa, has been already described (iv. 198; compare ch. 175).

3 We may understand "oracles *given* to Laïus."

4 It lay at the western point of the island, a little to the north of Drepanum, the modern *Trapani*.

5 Sybaris was one of the most important towns of Magna Græcia. Its luxury is proverbial (cf. vi. 127). It was taken (B.C. 510) after a siege of 70 days by the Crotoniats: who turned the river upon the town, and so destroyed it — [an event which preluded the decadence of Magna Græcia. – E. H. B.]

near the dry stream of the Crastis, which they declare that Dorieus, after taking their city, dedicated to Athena Crastias. And further, they bring forward the death of Dorieus as the surest proof; since he fell, they say, because he disobeyed the oracle. For had he in nothing varied from the directions given him, but confined himself to the business on which he was sent, he would assuredly have conquered the Erycian territory, and kept possession of it, instead of perishing with all his followers. The Crotoniats, on the other hand, point to the numerous allotments within their borders which were assigned to Callias the Elean by their countrymen, and which to my day remained in the possession of his family; while Dorieus and his descendants (they remark) possess nothing. Yet if Dorieus had really helped them in the Sybaritic war, he would have received very much more than Callias. Such are the testimonies which are adduced on either side; it is open to every man to adopt whichever view he deems the best.

46. Certain Spartans accompanied Dorieus on his voyage as co-founders, to wit, Thessalus, Paræbates, Celeas, and Euryleon. These men and all the troops under their command reached Sicily; but there they fell in a battle wherein they were defeated by the Egesteans and Phœnicians, only one, Euryleon, surviving the disaster. He then, collecting the remnants of the beaten army, made himself master of Minôa, the Selinusian colony, and helped the Selinusians to throw off the yoke of their tyrant Peithagoras. Having upset Peithagoras, he sought to become tyrant in his room, and he even reigned at Selinus for a brief space – but after a while the Selinusians rose up in revolt against him, and though he fled to the altar of Zeus Agoræus,[1] they notwithstanding put him to death.

47. Another man who accompanied Dorieus, and died with him, was Philip the son of Butacidas, a man of Crotôna; who, after he had been betrothed to a daughter of Têlys the Sybarite, was banished from Crotôna, whereupon his marriage came to nought; and he in his disappointment took ship and sailed to Cyrênê. From thence he became a follower of Dorieus, furnishing to the fleet a trireme of his own, the crew of which he supported at his own charge. This Philip was an Olympian victor, and the

---

1 That is, "Protector of the Forum" ($\dot{\alpha}\gamma o\rho\dot{\alpha}$). It probably stood in the market-place.

handsomest Greek of his day. His beauty gained him honours at the hands of the Egestæans which they never accorded to any one else; for they raised a hero-temple over his grave, and they still worship him with sacrifices.

48. Such then was the end of Dorieus, who if he had brooked the rule of Cleomenes, and remained in Sparta, would have been king of Lacedæmon; since Cleomenes, after reigning no great length of time, died without male offspring, leaving behind him an only daughter, by name Gorgo.[1]

49. Cleomenes, however, was still king when Aristagoras, tyrant of Miletus, reached Sparta. At their interview, Aristagoras, according to the report of the Lacedæmonians, produced a bronze tablet, whereupon the whole circuit of the earth was engraved, with all its seas and rivers. Discourse began between the two; and Aristagoras addressed the Spartan king in these words following:– "Think it not strange, O King Cleomenes, that I have been at the pains to sail hither; for the posture of affairs, which I will now recount unto thee, made it fitting. Shame and grief is it indeed to none so much as to us, that the sons of the Ionians should have lost their freedom, and come to be the slaves of others; but yet it touches you likewise, O Spartans, beyond the rest of the Greeks, inasmuch as the pre-eminence over all Greece appertains to you. We beseech you, therefore, by the common gods of the Grecians, deliver the Ionians, who are your own kinsmen, from slavery. Truly the task is not difficult; for the barbarians are an unwarlike people; and you are the best and bravest warriors in the whole world. Their mode of fighting is the following:– they use bows and arrows and a short spear; they wear trousers in the field, and cover their heads with turbans.[2] So easy are they to vanquish! Know too that the dwellers in these parts have more good things than all the rest of the world put together – gold, and silver, and brass, and embroidered garments, beasts of burthen, and bondservants – all which, if you only wish it, you may soon have for your own. The nations border on one another, in the order which I will now explain. Next to these Ionians" (here he pointed with his finger to the map of the world which was engraved upon the

---

1 She became the wife of Leonidas, her uncle, according to a usual Spartan custom (infra, vii. 239).
2 Vide infra, vii. 61.

tablet that he had brought with him) "these Lydians dwell; their soil is fertile, and few people are so rich in silver. Next to them," he continued, "come these Phrygians, who have more flocks and herds than any race that I know,[1] and more plentiful harvests. On them border the Cappadocians, whom we Greeks know by the name of Syrians: they are neighbours to the Cilicians, who extend all the way to this sea, where Cyprus (the island which you see here) lies. The Cilicians pay the king a yearly tribute of five hundred talents.[2] Next to them come the Armenians, who live here – they too have numerous flocks and herds. After them come the Matiêni, inhabiting this country; then Cissia, this province, where you see the river Choaspes marked, and likewise the town Susa upon its banks, where the Great King holds his court,[3] and where the treasuries are in which his wealth is stored.[4] Once masters of this city, you may be bold to vie with Zeus himself for riches. In the wars which ye wage with your rivals of Messenia, with them of Argos likewise and of Arcadia, about paltry boundaries and strips of land not so remarkably good,[5] ye contend with those who have no gold, nor silver even, which often give men heart to fight and die. Must ye wage such wars, and when ye might so easily be lords of Asia, will ye decide otherwise?" Thus spoke Aristagoras; and Cleomenes replied to him, – "Milesian stranger, three days hence I will give thee an answer."

50. So they proceeded no further at that time. When, however, the day appointed for the answer came, and the two once more met, Cleomenes asked Aristagoras, "how many days' journey it was from the sea of the Ionians to the king's residence?" Hereupon Aristagoras, who had managed the rest so cleverly, and succeeded in deceiving the king, tripped in his speech and blundered; for instead of concealing the truth, as he ought to have done if he wanted to induce the Spartans to cross into Asia,

---

1 The high table-land of Phrygia is especially adapted for pasturage.

2 Supra, iii. 90.

3 Susa had by this time certainly become the Persian capital. The Choaspes is at present a mile and a half to the west of the town. The magnificent palace of Susa had a great fame in antiquity (infra, ch. 53). [See A. H. Sayce in Hastings' *Dict. of Bible*, vol. iv. p. 511. – E. H. B.]

4 When Susa was entered by Alexander the Great, the silver captured amounted to 50,000 talents, or more than twelve millions sterling.

5 Cf. i. 66–68, and 82.

he said plainly that it was a journey of three months. Cleomenes caught at the words, and, preventing Aristagoras from finishing what he had begun to say concerning the road, addressed him thus:— "Milesian stranger, quit Sparta before sunset. This is no good proposal that thou makest to the Lacedæmonians, to conduct them a distance of three months' journey from the sea." When he had thus spoken, Cleomenes went to his home.

51. But Aristagoras took an olive-bough in his hand, and hastened to the king's house, where he was admitted by reason of his suppliant's guise. Gorgo, the daughter of Cleomenes, and his only child, a girl of about eight or nine years of age, happened to be there, standing by her father's side. Aristagoras, seeing her, requested Cleomenes to send her out of the room before he began to speak with him; but Cleomenes told him to say on, and not mind the child. So Aristagoras began with a promise of ten talents if the king would grant him his request, and when Cleomenes shook his head, continued to raise his offer till it reached fifty talents; whereupon the child spoke:— "Father," she said, "get up and go, or the stranger will certainly corrupt thee." Then Cleomenes, pleased at the warning of his child, withdrew and went into another room. Aristagoras quitted Sparta for good, not being able to discourse any more concerning the road which led up to the king.

52. Now the true account of the road in question is the following:— Royal stations[1] exist along its whole length, and excellent caravanserais; and throughout, it traverses an inhabited tract, and is free from danger. In Lydia and Phrygia there are twenty stations within a distance of $94\frac{1}{2}$ parasangs. On leaving Phrygia the Halys has to be crossed; and here are gates through which you must needs pass ere you can traverse the stream. A strong force guards this post. When you have made the passage, and are come into Cappadocia, 28 stations and 104 parasangs bring you to the borders of Cilicia, where the road passes through two sets of gates, at each of which there is a guard posted. Leaving these behind, you go on through Cilicia, where you find three stations in a distance of $15\frac{1}{2}$ parasangs. The boundary between Cilicia and Armenia is the river Euphrates,

1 By "royal stations" are to be understood the abodes of the king's "couriers," who conveyed despatches from their own station to the next, and then returned (infra, viii. 98).

which it is necessary to cross in boats. In Armenia the resting-places are 15 in number, and the distance is $56\frac{1}{2}$ parasangs. There is one place where a guard is posted. Four large streams intersect this district, all of which have to be crossed by means of boats. The first of these is the Tigris; the second and the third have both of them the same name,[1] though they are not only different rivers, but do not even run from the same place.[2] For the one which I have called the first of the two has its source in Armenia, while the other flows afterwards out of the country of the Matienians. The fourth of the streams is called the Gyndes, and this is the river which Cyrus dispersed by digging for it three hundred and sixty channels. Leaving Armenia and entering the Matienian country, you have four stations; these passed you find yourself in Cissia, where eleven stations and $42\frac{1}{2}$ parasangs bring you to another navigable stream, the Choaspes, on the banks of which the city of Susa is built. Thus the entire number of the stations is raised to one hundred and eleven; and so many are in fact the resting-places that one finds between Sardis and Susa.

53. If then the royal road be measured aright, and the parasang equals, as it does, thirty furlongs,[3] the whole distance from Sardis to the palace of Memnon (as it is called), amounting thus to 450 parasangs, would be 13,500 furlongs. Travelling then at the rate of 150 furlongs a day,[4] one will take exactly ninety days to perform the journey.

54. Thus when Aristagoras the Milesian told Cleomenes the Lacedæmonian that it was a three months' journey from the sea up to the king, he said no more than the truth. The exact distance (if any one desires still greater accuracy) is somewhat more; for the journey from Ephesus to Sardis must be added to the foregoing account; and this will make the whole distance

1 Undoubtedly the two Zabs, the Greater and the Lesser.

2 What Herodotus here states is exactly true of the two Zabs.

3 Supra, ii. 6. This was the ordinary estimate of the Greeks. Strabo, however, tells us that it was not universally agreed upon, since there were some who considered the parasang to equal 40, and others 60 stades. The truth is, that the ancient parasang, like the modern farsakh, was originally a measure of time (an hour), not a measure of distance. In passing from the one meaning to the other, it came to mark a different length in different places, according to the nature of the country traversed.

4 Herodotus takes here the rate at which an army would be likely to move. Elsewhere (iv. 101) he reckons the journey of the ordinary pedestrian at 200 stades (about 23 miles).

between the Greek Sea and Susa (or the city of Memnon, as it is called[1]) 14,040 furlongs; since Ephesus is distant from Sardis 540 furlongs. This would add three days to the three months' journey.

55. When Aristagoras left Sparta he hastened to Athens which had got quit of its tyrants in the way that I will now describe. After the death of Hipparchus (the son of Pisistratus, and brother of the tyrant Hippias), who, in spite of the clear warning he had received concerning his fate in a dream, was slain by Harmodius and Aristogeiton (men both of the race of the Gephyræans), the oppression of the Athenians continued by the space of four years;[2] and they gained nothing, but were worse used than before.

56. Now the dream of Hipparchus was the following:— The night before the Panathenaic festival, he thought he saw in his sleep a tall and beautiful man, who stood over him, and read him the following riddle:—

"Bear thou unbearable woes with the all-bearing heart of a lion;
Never, be sure, shall wrong-doer escape the reward of wrong-doing."

As soon as day dawned he sent and submitted his dream to the interpreters, after which he offered the averting sacrifices, and then went and led the procession in which he perished.

57. The family of the Gephyræans, to which the murderers of Hipparchus belonged, according to their own account, came originally from Eretria. My inquiries, however, have made it clear to me that they are in reality Phœnicians, descendants of those who came with Cadmus into the country now called Bœotia. Here they received for their portion the district of Tanagra, in which they afterwards dwelt. On their expulsion from this country by the Bœotians (which happened some time after that of the Cadmeians from the same parts by the Argives[3]) they took

---

1 The fable of Memnon is one of those in which it is difficult to discover any germs of truth. The earliest author who is *known* to have connected Memnon with Susa is Æschylus, who made his mother a Cissian woman. It is clear, however, that by the time of Herodotus, the story that he built Susa, or its great palace, was generally accepted in Greece. Perhaps the adoption of this account may be regarded as indicating some knowledge of the *ethnic* connection which really existed between Ethiopia and Susiana.

2 From B.C. 514 to B.C. 510.

3 Herodotus alludes here to the legend of the Epigoni.

refuge at Athens. The Athenians received them among their citizens upon set terms, whereby they were excluded from a number of privileges which are not worth mentioning.

58. Now the Phœnicians who came with Cadmus, and to whom the Gephyræi belonged, introduced into Greece upon their arrival a great variety of arts, among the rest that of writing,[1] whereof the Greeks till then had, as I think, been ignorant. And originally they shaped their letters exactly like all the other Phœnicians, but afterwards, in course of time, they changed by degrees their language, and together with it the form likewise of their characters. Now the Greeks who dwelt about those parts at that time were chiefly the Ionians. The Phœnician letters were accordingly adopted by them, but with some variation in the shape of a few, and so they arrived at the present use, still calling the letters Phœnician, as justice required, after the name of those who were the first to introduce them into Greece. Paper rolls also were called from of old "parchments" by the Ionians, because formerly when paper was scarce they used, instead, the skins of sheep and goats – on which material many of the barbarians are even now wont to write.[2]

59. I myself saw Cadmeian characters[3] engraved upon some tripods in the temple of Apollo Ismenias[4] in Bœotian[5] Thebes, most of them shaped like the Ionian. One of the tripods has the inscription following:–

"Me did Amphitryon place, from the far Teleboans coming."

This would be about the age of Laïus, the son of Labdacus, the son of Polydorus, the son of Cadmus.

1 Homer (Il. vi. 168) shows that in his time the Greeks wrote on folding wooden tablets. [See *n.* on that passage, in my ed. of Homer, vol. i. – E. H. B.]

2 This is a remarkable statement. Among the "barbarians" alluded to, we may assume the Persians to be included. Stone and clay seem to have been the common material in Assyria and Babylonia; wood, leather, and paper in Egypt; the bark of trees and linen in Italy; stone, wood, and metal among the Jews. Parchment seems never to have been much used, even by the Greeks, till the time of Eumenes II (B.C. 197–159).

3 The old Greek letters, like the Phœnician, were written from right to left. They continued to be so written till a late time on vases; but this appears to have been then merely the imitation of an old fashion; for already, in the age of Psammetichus, the seventh century B.C., inscriptions were written from left to right.

4 Cf. i. 52.

5 *Bœotian* Thebes is here distinguished from *Egyptian*.

60. Another of the tripods has this legend in the hexameter measure:—

"I to far-shooting Phœbus was offered by Scæus the boxer,
    When he had won at the games – a wondrous beautiful offering."

This might be Scæus, the son of Hippocoön;[1] and the tripod, if dedicated by him, and not by another of the same name, would belong to the time of Œdipus, the son of Laïus.

61. The third tripod has also an inscription in hexameters, which runs thus:—

"King Laodamas gave this tripod to far-seeing Phœbus,
    When he was set on the throne – a wondrous beautiful offering."

It was in the reign of this Laodamas, the son of Eteocles, that the Cadmeians were driven by the Argives out of their country,[2] and found a shelter with the Encheleans.[3] The Gephyræans at that time remained in the country, but afterwards they retired before the Bœotians, and took refuge at Athens, where they have a number of temples for their separate use, which the other Athenians are not allowed to enter – among the rest, one of Achæan Demeter, in whose honour they likewise celebrate special orgies.

62. Having thus related the dream which Hipparchus saw, and traced the descent of the Gephyræans, the family whereto his murderers belonged, I must proceed with the matter whereof I was intending before to speak; to wit, the way in which the Athenians got quit of their tyrants. Upon the death of Hipparchus, Hippias, who was king, grew harsh towards the Athenians; and the Alcmæonidæ,[4] an Athenian family which had been banished by the Pisistratidæ,[5] joined the other exiles, and endeavoured to procure their own return, and to free Athens, by force. They seized and fortified Leipsydrium above Pæonia, and tried to gain their object by arms; but great disasters befell them, and

1 Hippocoön was the brother of Tyndareus and Icarion. Assisted by his twelve sons, he drove his two brothers from Lacedæmon. Afterwards Heracles slew him and his sons, and restored Tyndareus.

2 Laodamas succeeded his father Eteocles upon the throne of Thebes.

3 The Encheleans were an Illyrian tribe.

4 Vide infra, vi. 125–131, where the earlier history of the Alcmæonidæ is given.

5 That is by Pisistratus himself, who is included among the Pisistratidæ (vide supra, i. 64).

their purpose remained unaccomplished. They therefore resolved to shrink from no contrivance that might bring them success; and accordingly they contracted with the Amphictyons to build the temple which now stands at Delphi, but which in those days did not exist.[1] Having done this, they proceeded, being men of great wealth and members of an ancient and distinguished family, to build the temple much more magnificently than the plan obliged them. Besides other improvements, instead of the coarse stone whereof by the contract the temple was to have been constructed, they made the facings of Parian marble.

63. These same men, if we may believe the Athenians, during their stay at Delphi persuaded the Pythoness by a bribe[2] to tell the Spartans, whenever any of them came to consult the oracle, either on their own private affairs or on the business of the state, that they must free Athens. So the Lacedæmonians, when they found no answer ever returned to them but this, sent at last Anchimolius, the son of Aster – a man of note among their citizens – at the head of an army against Athens, with orders to drive out the Pisistratidæ, albeit they were bound to them by the closest ties of friendship. For they esteemed the things of heaven more highly than the things of men. The troops went by sea and were conveyed in transports. Anchimolius brought them to an anchorage at Phalerum;[3] and there the men disembarked. But the Pisistratidæ, who had previous knowledge of their intentions, had sent to Thessaly, between which country and Athens there was an alliance,[4] with a request for aid. The Thessalians, in reply to their entreaties, sent them by a public vote 1,000 horsemen,[5] under the command of their king, Cineas, who was a Coniæan. When this help came, the Pisistratidæ laid their plan accordingly: they cleared the whole plain about Phalerum so as to make it fit for the movements of cavalry, and then charged the enemy's

1 The old temple had been burnt (vide supra, ii. 180).

2 The Delphic oracle is again bribed by Cleomenes, infra, vi. 66.

3 Phalerum is the most ancient, as it is the most natural, harbour of Athens. It is nearer than Piræus to the city. The Piræus seems not to have been used as a port until the time of Pericles.

4 As Bœotia is found generally on the Spartan, so Thessaly appears on the Athenian side. Mutual jealousy of Bœotia would appear to be the chief ground of the alliance.

5 The country was favourable for pasturage; and Thessalian horses were of special excellency (vide infra, vii. 196).

camp with their horse, which fell with such fury upon the Lacedæmonians as to kill numbers, among the rest Anchimolius, the general, and to drive the remainder to their ships. Such was the fate of the first army sent from Lacedæmon, and the tomb of Anchimolius may be seen to this day in Attica; it is at Alopecæ (Foxtown), near the temple of Heracles in Cynosargos.[1]

64. Afterwards, the Lacedæmonians despatched a larger force against Athens, which they put under the command of Cleomenes, son of Anaxandridas, one of their kings. These troops were not sent by sea, but marched by the mainland. When they were come into Attica, their first encounter was with the Thessalian horse, which they shortly put to flight, killing above forty men; the remainder made good their escape, and fled straight to Thessaly. Cleomenes proceeded to the city, and, with the aid of such of the Athenians as wished for freedom, besieged the tyrants, who had shut themselves up in the Pelasgic fortress.[2]

65. And now there had been small chance of the Pisistratidæ falling into the hands of the Spartans, who did not even design to sit down before the place,[3] which had moreover been well provisioned beforehand with stores both of meat and drink, – nay, it is likely that after a few days' blockade the Lacedæmonians would have quitted Attica altogether, and gone back to Sparta, – had not an event occurred most unlucky for the besieged, and most advantageous for the besiegers. The children of the Pisistratidæ were made prisoners, as they were being removed out of the country. By this calamity all their plans were deranged, and – as the ransom of their children – they consented to the demands of the Athenians, and agreed within five days' time to quit Attica. Accordingly they soon afterwards left the country, and withdrew to Sigeum on the Scamander,[4] after reigning thirty-six years over the Athenians. By descent they were Pylians, of the family of the Neleids,[5] to which Codrus and Melanthus

---

1 Vide infra, vi. 116.

2 That is, the Acropolis.

3 Aware, apparently, of their inability to conduct sieges (vide infra, ix. 70). That the Acropolis was not at this time very strong appears from the account of its siege by Xerxes (viii. 52, 53). It was afterwards fortified by Cimon.

4 Vide infra, ch. 94, 95.

5 The tale went, that Melanthus (the fifth in descent from the Homeric Nestor, son of Neleus, and king of Pylos), was king of Messenia at the time of the return of the Heraclidæ. Being expelled, he sought a refuge in Attica, where

likewise belonged, men who in former times from foreign settlers became kings of Athens. And hence it was that Hippocrates[1] came to think of calling his son Pisistratus: he named him after the Pisistratus who was a son of Nestor. Such then was the mode in which the Athenians got quit of their tyrants. What they did and suffered worthy of note from the time when they gained their freedom until the revolt of Ionia from King Darius, and the coming of Aristagoras to Athens with a request that the Athenians would lend the Ionians aid, I shall now proceed to relate.

66. The power of Athens had been great before; but, now that the tyrants were gone, it became greater than ever. The chief authority was lodged with two persons, Clisthenes, of the family of the Alcmæonids, who is said to have been the persuader of the Pythoness,[2] and Isagoras, the son of Tisander, who belonged to a noble house, but whose pedigree I am not able to trace further. Howbeit his kinsmen offer sacrifice to the Carian Zeus. These two men strove together for the mastery; and Clisthenes, finding himself the weaker, called to his aid the common people. Hereupon, instead of the four tribes[3] among which the Athenians had been divided hitherto, Clisthenes made ten tribes, and parcelled out the Athenians among them. He likewise changed the names of the tribes; for whereas they had till now been called after Geleon, Ægicores, Argades, and Hoples, the four sons of Ion, Clisthenes set these names aside, and called his tribes after certain other heroes, all of whom were native, except Ajax. Ajax was associated because, although a foreigner, he was a neighbour and an ally of Athens.[4]

67. My belief is that in acting thus he did but imitate his maternal grandfather, Clisthenes, king of Sicyon.[5] This king, when he was at war with Argos, put an end to the contests of the rhapsodists at Sicyon, because in the Homeric poems Argos and the Argives were so constantly the theme of song. He

---

he was kindly received, and even placed upon the throne – Thymœtes, the existing monarch, being forced to abdicate in his favour. This will explain the terms "Pylians" and "Neleids."

1 Supra, i. 59.
2 Supra, ch. 62.
3 That is, the ancient *hereditary* tribes of Attica.
4 Ajax was the tutelary hero of Salamis (vide infra, viii. 64 and 121).
5 Concerning this king, see below, vi. 126.

likewise conceived the wish to drive Adrastus, the son of Talaüs, out of his country,[1] seeing that he was an Argive hero. For Adrastus had a shrine at Sicyon, which yet stands in the market-place of the town. Clisthenes therefore went to Delphi, and asked the oracle if he might expel Adrastus. To this the Pythoness is reported to have answered — "Adrastus is the Sicyonians' king, but thou art only a robber." So when the god would not grant his request, he went home and began to think how he might contrive to make Adrastus withdraw of his own accord. After a while he hit upon a plan which he thought would succeed. He sent envoys to Thebes in Bœotia, and informed the Thebans that he wished to bring Melanippus,[2] the son of Astacus, to Sicyon. The Thebans consenting, Clisthenes carried Melanippus back with him, assigned him a precinct within the government-house, and built him a shrine there in the safest and strongest part. The reason for his so doing (which I must not forbear to mention) was, because Melanippus was Adrastus' great enemy, having slain both his brother Mecistes and his son-in-law Tydeus.[3] Clisthenes, after assigning the precinct to Melanippus, took away from Adrastus the sacrifices and festivals wherewith he had till then been honoured, and transferred them to his adversary. Hitherto the Sicyonians had paid extraordinary honours to Adrastus, because the country had belonged to Polybus,[4] and Adrastus was Polybus' daughter's son; whence it came to pass that Polybus, dying childless, left Adrastus his kingdom. Besides other ceremonies, it had been their wont to honour Adrastus with tragic choruses, which they assigned to him rather than Dionysus, on account of his calamities. Clisthenes now gave the choruses to Dionysus, transferring to Melanippus the rest of the sacred rites.

68. Such were his doings in the matter of Adrastus. With respect to the Dorian tribes, not choosing the Sicyonians to have the same tribes as the Argives, he changed all the old names for new ones; and here he took special occasion to mock the

---

1 Adrastus, king of Argos, and leader of the first (mythic) attack upon Thebes, was worshipped as a hero in several places.

2 A *statue* of Melanippus is probably intended. See below, ch. 80.

3 Melanippus, the son of Astacus, is mentioned among the defenders of Thebes by Pherecydes (Fr. 51) and Apollodorus. He is said to have lost his own life at the siege, being slain by Amphiaraus.

4 Polybus was king of Corinth, and Sicyon was included in his dominions.

Sicyonians, for he drew his new names from the words "pig," and "ass," adding thereto the usual tribe-endings; only in the case of his own tribe he did nothing of the sort, but gave them a name drawn from his own kingly office. For he called his own tribe the Archelaï, or Rulers, while the others he named Hyatæ, or Pig-folk, Oneatæ, or Ass-folk, and Chœreatæ, or Swine-folk. The Sicyonians kept these names, not only during the reign of Clisthenes, but even after his death, by the space of sixty years: then, however, they took counsel together, and changed to the well-known names of Hyllæans, Pamphylians, and Dymanatæ, taking at the same time, as a fourth name, the title of Ægialeans, from Ægialeus the son of Adrastus.[1]

69. Thus had Clisthenes the Sicyonian done.[2] The Athenian Clisthenes, who was grandson by the mother's side of the other, and had been named after him, resolved, from contempt (as I believe) of the Ionians, that his tribes should not be the same as theirs; and so followed the pattern set him by his namesake of Sicyon. Having brought entirely over to his own side the common people of Athens, whom he had before disdained, he gave all the tribes new names, and made the number greater than formerly; instead of the four phylarchs he established ten; he likewise placed ten demes in each of the tribes; and he was, now that the common people took his part, very much more powerful than his adversaries.

70. Isagoras in his turn lost ground; and therefore, to counter-plot his enemy, he called in Cleomenes the Lacedæmonian, who had already, at the time when he was besieging the Pisistratidæ, made a contract of friendship with him. A charge is even brought against Cleomenes that he was on terms of too great familiarity with Isagoras's wife. At this time the first thing that he did, was to send a herald and require that Clisthenes, and

1 Ægialeans was the ancient name of the primitive Ionians of this tract.

2 Clisthenes was the youngest of three brothers, and had therefore, in the natural course of things, little hope of the succession. Myron, however, his eldest brother, having been guilty of adultery with the wife of Isodemus the second brother, Clisthenes persuaded the latter to revenge himself by slaying the adulterer. He then represented to him that he could not reign alone, as it was impossible for him to offer the sacrifices; and was admitted as joint king on this account. Finally, he had Isodemus persuaded to go into voluntary exile for a year, in order to purge his pollution; and during his absence made himself sole king.

a large number of Athenians besides, whom he called "The Accursed," should leave Athens. This message he sent at the suggestion of Isagoras: for in the affair referred to, the blood-guiltiness lay on the Alcmæonidæ and their partisans, while he and his friends were quite clear of it.

71. The way in which "The Accursed" at Athens got their name, was the following. There was a certain Athenian called Cylon, a victor at the Olympic games, who aspired to the sovereignty, and aided by a number of his companions, who were of the same age with himself, made an attempt to seize the citadel. But the attack failed; and Cylon became a suppliant at the image. Hereupon the Heads of the Naucraries, who at that time bore rule in Athens, induced the fugitives to remove by a promise to spare their lives. Nevertheless they were all slain; and the blame was laid on the Alcmæonidæ. All this happened before the time of Pisistratus.

72. When the message of Cleomenes arrived, requiring Clisthenes and "The Accursed" to quit the city, Clisthenes departed of his own accord. Cleomenes, however, notwithstanding his departure, came to Athens, with a small band of followers; and on his arrival sent into banishment seven hundred Athenian families, which were pointed out to him by Isagoras. Succeeding here, he next endeavoured to dissolve the council, and to put the government into the hands of three hundred of the partisans of that leader. But the council resisted, and refused to obey his orders; whereupon Cleomenes, Isagoras, and their followers took possession of the citadel. Here they were attacked by the rest of the Athenians, who took the side of the council, and were besieged for the space of two days: on the third day they accepted terms, being allowed — at least such of them as were Lacedæmonians — to quit the country. And so the word which came to Cleomenes received its fulfilment. For when he first went up into the citadel, meaning to seize it, just as he was entering the sanctuary of the goddess, in order to question her, the priestess arose from her throne, before he had passed the doors, and said — "Stranger from Lacedæmon, depart hence, and presume not to enter the holy place — it is not lawful for a Dorian to set foot there." But he answered, "Oh! woman, I am not a Dorian, but an Achæan."[1] Slighting this warning, Cleomenes made his

---

1 The Heraclidæ were, according to the unanimous tradition, the old royal family of the Peloponnese.

attempt, and so he was forced to retire, together with his Lacedæ-monians.[1] The rest were cast into prison by the Athenians, and condemned to die, – among them Timasitheüs the Delphian, of whose prowess and courage I have great things which I could tell.

73. So these men died in prison. The Athenians directly afterwards recalled Clisthenes, and the seven hundred families which Cleomenes had driven out; and, further, they sent envoys to Sardis, to make an alliance with the Persians, for they knew that war would follow with Cleomenes and the Lacedæmonians. When the ambassadors reached Sardis and delivered their message, Artaphernes, son of Hystaspes, who was at that time governor of the place, inquired of them "who they were, and in what part of the world they dwelt,[2] that they wanted to become allies of the Persians?" The messengers told him; upon which he answered them shortly – that "if the Athenians chose to give earth and water to King Darius, he would conclude an alliance with them; but if not, they might go home again." After consulting together, the envoys, anxious to form the alliance, accepted the terms; but on their return to Athens, they fell into deep disgrace on account of their compliance.

74. Meanwhile Cleomenes, who considered himself to have been insulted by the Athenians both in word and deed, was drawing a force together from all parts of the Peloponnese, without informing any one of his object; which was to revenge himself on the Athenians, and to establish Isagoras, who had escaped with him from the citadel,[3] as despot of Athens. Accordingly, with a large army, he invaded the district of Eleusis,[4] while the Bœotians, who had concerted measures with him, took Œnoë and Hysiæ,[5] two country towns upon the frontier; and at the same time the Chalcideans,[6] on another side, plundered divers places in Attica. The Athenians, notwithstanding that danger

1 The Athenians always cherished a lively recollection of this triumph over their great rivals. [Cf. Aristoph. *Lysist.* 271 sqq. – E. H. B.]

2 Vide supra, i. 153, and infra, ch. 105.

3 Disguised, probably as a Spartan.

4 Eleusis was the key to Attica on the south.

5 Hysiæ lay on the north side of Cithæron, in the plain of the Asopus.

6 Chalcis had been one of the most important cities in Greece. It was said to have been originally a colony from Athens. It is the modern *Egripo*, or *Negropont*.

threatened them from every quarter, put off all thought of the Bœotians and Chalcideans till a future time, and marched against the Peloponnesians, who were at Eleusis.

75. As the two hosts were about to engage, first of all the Corinthians, bethinking themselves that they were perpetrating a wrong, changed their minds, and drew off from the main army. Then Demaratus, son of Ariston, who was himself king of Sparta and joint-leader of the expedition, and who till now had had no sort of quarrel with Cleomenes, followed their example. On account of this rupture between the kings, a law was passed at Sparta, forbidding both monarchs to go out together with the army, as had been the custom hitherto. The law also provided, that, as one of the kings was to be left behind, one of the Tyndaridæ should also remain at home; whereas hitherto both had accompanied the expeditions, as auxiliaries. So when the rest of the allies saw that the Lacedæmonian kings were not of one mind, and that the Corinthian troops had quitted their post, they likewise drew off and departed.

76. This was the fourth time that the Dorians had invaded Attica: twice they came as enemies, and twice they came to do good service to the Athenian people. Their first invasion took place at the period when they founded Megara, and is rightly placed in the reign of Codrus at Athens; the second and third occasions were when they came from Sparta to drive out the Pisistratidæ; the fourth was the present attack, when Cleomenes, at the head of a Peloponnesian army, entered at Eleusis. Thus the Dorians had now four times invaded Attica.

77. So when the Spartan army had broken up from its quarters thus ingloriously, the Athenians, wishing to revenge themselves, marched first against the Chalcideans. The Bœotians, however, advancing to the aid of the latter as far as the Euripus, the Athenians thought it best to attack them first. A battle was fought accordingly; and the Athenians gained a very complete victory, killing a vast number of the enemy, and taking seven hundred of them alive. After this, on the very same day, they crossed into Eubœa, and engaged the Chalcideans with the like success; whereupon they left four thousand settlers[1] upon the

---

1 Literally, "allotment-holders" ($\kappa\lambda\eta\rho o\hat{v}\chi o\iota$). These allotment-holders are to be carefully distinguished from the ordinary colonists ($\check{\alpha}\pi o\iota\kappa o\iota$), who went out to find themselves a home wherever they might be able to settle, and who

lands of the Hippobotæ,[1] – which is the name the Chalcideans give to their rich men. All the Chalcidean prisoners whom they took were put in irons, and kept for a long time in close confinement, as likewise were the Bœotians, until the ransom asked for them was paid; and this the Athenians fixed at two minæ the man. The chains wherewith they were fettered the Athenians suspended in their citadel; where they were still to be seen in my day, hanging against the wall scorched by the Median flames,[2] opposite the chapel which faces the west. The Athenians made an offering of the tenth part of the ransom-money: and expended it on the brazen chariot drawn by four steeds, which stands on the left hand immediately that one enters the gateway[3] of the citadel. The inscription runs as follows:–

> "When Chalcis and Bœotia dared her might,
> Athens subdued their pride in valorous fight;
> Gave bonds for insults; and, the ransom paid,
> From the full tenths these steeds for Pallas made."

78. Thus did the Athenians increase in strength. And it is plain enough, not from this instance only, but from many everywhere, that freedom is an excellent thing; since even the Athenians, who, while they continued under the rule of tyrants, were not a whit more valiant than any of their neighbours, no sooner shook off the yoke than they became decidedly the first of all. These things show that, while undergoing oppression, they let themselves be beaten, since then they worked for a master; but so soon as they got their freedom, each man was eager to do the best he could for himself. So fared it now with the Athenians.

79. Meanwhile the Thebans, who longed to be revenged on the Athenians, had sent to the oracle, and been told by the

---

retained but a very slight connection with the mother-country. The cleruchs were a military garrison planted in a conquered territory, the best portions of which were given to them. They continued Athenian subjects, and retained their full rights as Athenian citizens, occupying a position closely analogous to that of the Roman *coloni* in the earlier times.

1 The Chalcidean Hippobotæ, or "horse-keepers," were a wealthy aristocracy and correspond to the knights (ἱππεῖς) of most Grecian states, and the "equites," or "celeres," of the Romans. In early times wealth is measured by the ability to maintain a horse, or horses.

2 Infra, viii. 53.

3 The great *Propylæa*, the most magnificent of the works of Pericles.

Pythoness that of their own strength they would be unable to accomplish their wish: "they must lay the matter," she said, "before the many-voiced, and ask the aid of those nearest them." The messengers, therefore, on their return, called a meeting, and laid the answer of the oracle before the people, who no sooner heard the advice to "ask the aid of those nearest them" than they exclaimed, – "What! are not they who dwell the nearest to us the men of Tanagra, of Coronæa, and Thespiæ? Yet these men always fight on our side, and have aided us with a good heart all through the war. Of what use is it to ask them? But maybe this is not the true meaning of the oracle."

80. As they were thus discoursing one with another, a certain man, informed of the debate, cried out, – "Methinks that I understand what course the oracle would recommend to us. Asôpus, they say, had two daughters, Thêbé and Egina. The god means that, as these two were sisters, we ought to ask the Eginetans to lend us aid." As no one was able to hit on any better explanation, the Thebans forthwith sent messengers to Egina, and, according to the advice of the oracle, asked their aid, as the people "nearest to them." In answer to this petition the Eginetans said, that they would give them the Æacidæ for helpers.

81. The Thebans now, relying on the assistance of the Æacidæ, ventured to renew the war; but they met with so rough a reception, that they resolved to send to the Eginetans again, returning the Æacidæ, and beseeching them to send some men instead. The Eginetans, who were at that time a most flourishing people, elated with their greatness, and at the same time calling to mind their ancient feud with Athens,[1] agreed to lend the Thebans aid, and forthwith went to war with the Athenians, without even giving them notice by a herald. The attention of these latter being engaged by the struggle with the Bœotians, the Eginetans in their ships of war made descents upon Attica, plundered Phalerum,[2] and ravaged a vast number of the townships upon the sea-board, whereby the Athenians suffered very grievous damage.

82. The ancient feud between the Eginetans and Athenians arose out of the following circumstances. Once upon a time the land of Epidaurus would bear no crops; and the Epidaurians sent to consult the oracle of Delphi concerning their affliction. The

---

1 Related in the next chapter.   2 The port of Athens at the time.

answer bade them set up the images of Damia and Auxesia, and promised them better fortune when that should be done. "Shall the images be made of bronze or stone?" the Epidaurians asked; but the Pythoness replied, "Of neither: but let them be made of the garden olive."[1] Then the Epidaurians sent to Athens and asked leave to cut olive wood in Attica, believing the Athenian olives to be the holiest; or, according to others, because there were no olives at that time anywhere else in all the world but at Athens.[2] The Athenians answered that they would give them leave, but on condition of their bringing offerings year by year to Athena Polias and to Erechtheus.[3] The Epidaurians agreed, and having obtained what they wanted, made the images of olive wood, and set them up in their own country. Henceforth their land bore its crops; and they duly paid the Athenians what had been agreed upon.

83. Anciently, and even down to the time when this took place, the Eginetans were in all things subject to the Epidaurians, and had to cross over to Epidaurus for the trial of all suits in which they were engaged one with another. After this, however, the Eginetans built themselves ships, and, growing proud, revolted from the Epidaurians. Having thus come to be at enmity with them, the Eginetans, who were masters of the sea, ravaged Epidaurus, and even carried off these very images of Damia and Auxesia, which they set up in their own country, in the interior, at a place called Œa, about twenty furlongs from their city. This done, they fixed a worship for the images, which consisted in part of sacrifices, in part of female satiric choruses; while at the same time they appointed certain men to furnish the choruses, ten for each goddess. These choruses did not abuse men, but only the women of the country. Holy orgies of a similar kind

1 Statues in wood preceded those in stone and bronze. The material suited a ruder state of the arts.

2 This is, of course, not true, for the olive had been cultivated in the east from a very remote antiquity. (Deuteronomy vi. 11; viii. 8, etc.) It is, however, very likely that the olive may have been introduced into Attica from Asia, before it was known to the rest of Greece.

3 By "Athena Polias" we are to understand the Athena who presided over the city ($\pi\delta\lambda\iota\varsigma$). Her temple in later times was a portion of the building known to the Athenians by the general name of Erechtheium, which stood on the north side of the Acropolis, nearly opposite the spot afterwards occupied by the Parthenon.

were in use also among the Epidaurians, and likewise another sort of holy orgies, whereof it is not lawful to speak.

84. After the robbery of the images the Epidaurians ceased to make the stipulated payments to the Athenians, wherefore the Athenians sent to Epidaurus to remonstrate. But the Epidaurians proved to them that they were not guilty of any wrong:— "While the images continued in their country," they said, "they had duly paid the offerings according to the agreement; now that the images had been taken from them, they were no longer under any obligation to pay: the Athenians should make their demand of the Eginetans, in whose possession the figures now were." Upon this the Athenians sent to Egina, and demanded the images back; but the Eginetans answered that the Athenians had nothing whatever to do with them.

85. After this the Athenians relate that they sent a trireme to Egina with certain citizens on board, and that these men, who bore commission from the state, landed in Egina, and sought to take the images away, considering them to be their own, inasmuch as they were made of their wood. And first they endeavoured to wrench them from their pedestals, and so carry them off; but failing herein, they in the next place tied ropes to them, and set to work to try if they could haul them down. In the midst of their hauling suddenly there was a thunderclap, and with the thunderclap an earthquake; and the crew of the trireme were forthwith seized with madness, and, like enemies, began to kill one another; until at last there was but one left, who returned alone to Phalerum.

86. Such is the account given by the Athenians. The Eginetans deny that there was only a single vessel:— "Had there been only one," they say, "or no more than a few, they would easily have repulsed the attack, even if they had had no fleet at all; but the Athenians came against them with a large number of ships, wherefore they gave way, and did not hazard a battle." They do not however explain clearly whether it was from a conviction of their own inferiority at sea that they yielded, or whether it was for the purpose of doing that which in fact they did. Their account is that the Athenians, disembarking from their ships, when they found that no resistance was offered, made for the statues, and failing to wrench them from their pedestals, tied ropes to them and began to haul. Then, they say, — and some people will perhaps believe them, though I for my part do not, — the two statues, as they were being

dragged and hauled, fell down both upon their knees; in which attitude they still remain. Such, according to them, was the conduct of the Athenians; they meanwhile, having learnt beforehand what was intended, had prevailed on the Argives to hold themselves in readiness; and the Athenians accordingly were but just landed on their coasts when the Argives came to their aid. Secretly and silently they crossed over from Epidaurus, and, before the Athenians were aware, cut off their retreat to their ships, and fell upon them; and the thunder came exactly at that moment, and the earthquake with it.

87. The Argives and the Eginetans both agree in giving this account; and the Athenians themselves acknowledge that but one of their men returned alive to Attica. According to the Argives, he escaped from the battle in which the rest of the Athenian troops were destroyed by them. According to the Athenians, it was the god who destroyed their troops; and even this one man did not escape, for he perished in the following manner. When he came back to Athens, bringing word of the calamity, the wives of those who had been sent out on the expedition took it sorely to heart, that he alone should have survived the slaughter of all the rest;– they therefore crowded round the man, and struck him with the brooches by which their dresses were fastened – each, as she struck, asking him, where he had left her husband. And the man died in this way. The Athenians thought the deed of the women more horrible even than the fate of the troops; as however they did not know how else to punish them, they changed their dress and compelled them to wear the costume of the Ionians. Till this time the Athenian women had worn a Dorian dress, shaped nearly like that which prevails at Corinth. Henceforth they were made to wear the linen tunic, which does not require brooches.[1]

88. In very truth, however, this dress is not originally Ionian, but Carian; for anciently the Greek women all wore the costume

---

1 The large horseshoe brooch with which ladies in our times occasionally fasten their shawls, closely resembles the ancient περόνη, which was not a buckle, but "a brooch, consisting of a pin, and a curved portion, furnished with a hook." The Dorian tunic was of woollen; it had no sleeves, and was fastened over both the shoulders by brooches. It was scanty and short, sometimes scarcely reaching the knee. The Ionic tunic was of linen: it had short loose sleeves, as we see in statues of the Muses, and so did not need brooches; it was a long and full dress hiding the form, and reaching down generally to the feet.

which is now called the Dorian. It is said further that the Argives
and Eginetans made it a custom, on this same account, for their
women to wear brooches half as large again as formerly, and to
offer brooches rather than anything else in the temple of these
goddesses. They also forbade the bringing of anything Attic into
the temple, were it even a jar of earthenware,[1] and made a law
that none but native drinking vessels should be used there in
time to come. From this early age to my own day the Argive and
Eginetan women have always continued to wear their brooches
larger than formerly, through hatred of the Athenians.

89. Such then was the origin of the feud which existed between the Eginetans and the Athenians. Hence, when the Thebans made their application for succour, the Eginetans, calling
to mind the matter of images, gladly lent their aid to the Bœotians. They ravaged all the sea-coast of Attica; and the Athenians
were about to attack them in return, when they were stopped by
the oracle of Delphi, which bade them wait till thirty years had
passed from the time that the Eginetans did the wrong, and in
the thirty-first year, having first set apart a precinct for Æacus,
then to begin the war. "So should they succeed to their wish,"
the oracle said; "but if they went to war at once, though they
would still conquer the island in the end, yet they must go
through much suffering and much exertion before taking it." On
receiving this warning the Athenians set apart a precinct for
Æacus – the same which still remains dedicated to him in their
market-place – but they could not hear with any patience of
waiting thirty years, after they had suffered such grievous wrong
at the hands of the Eginetans.

90. Accordingly they were making ready to take their revenge
when a fresh stir on the part of the Lacedæmonians hindered
their projects. These last had become aware of the truth – how
that the Alcmæonidæ had practised on the Pythoness, and the
Pythoness had schemed against themselves, and against the
Pisistratidæ; and the discovery was a double grief to them, for
while they had driven their own sworn friends into exile, they
found that they had not gained thereby a particle of good will
from Athens. They were also moved by certain prophecies,
which declared that many dire calamities should befall them at
the hands of the Athenians. Of these in times past they had been

1 The pottery of Athens was the most celebrated in ancient Greece.

ignorant; but now they had become acquainted with them by means of Cleomenes, who had brought them with him to Sparta, having found them in the Athenian citadel, where they had been left by the Pisistratidæ when they were driven from Athens: they were in the temple,[1] and Cleomenes having discovered them, carried them off.

91. So when the Lacedæmonians obtained possession of the prophecies, and saw that the Athenians were growing in strength, and had no mind to acknowledge any subjection to their control, it occurred to them that, if the people of Attica were free, they would be likely to be as powerful as themselves, but if they were oppressed by a tyranny, they would be weak and submissive. Under this feeling they sent and recalled Hippias, the son of Pisistratus, from Sigeum upon the Hellespont, where the Pisistratidæ had taken shelter.[2] Hippias came at their bidding, and the Spartans on his arrival summoned deputies from all their other allies, and thus addressed the assembly:—

"Friends and brothers in arms, we are free to confess that we did lately a thing which was not right. Misled by counterfeit oracles, we drove from their country those who were our sworn and true friends, and who had, moreover, engaged to keep Athens in dependence upon us; and we delivered the government into the hands of an unthankful people – a people who no sooner got their freedom by our means, and grew in power, than they turned us and our king, with every token of insult, out of their city. Since then they have gone on continually raising their thoughts higher, as their neighbours of Bœotia and Chalcis have already discovered to their cost, and as others too will presently discover if they shall offend them. Having thus erred, we will endeavour now, with your help, to remedy the evils we have caused, and to obtain vengeance on the Athenians. For this cause we have sent for Hippias to come here, and have summoned you likewise from your several states, that we may all now with heart and hand unite to restore him to Athens, and thereby give him back that which we took from him formerly."

92. (§ 1.) Such was the address of the Spartans. The greater number of the allies listened without being persuaded. None however broke silence, but Sosicles the Corinthian, who exclaimed –

1 The temple of Athena Polias (vide supra, chs. 72 and 82).
2 Vide supra, ch. 65 [and Bury's *Hist. of Greece*, ch. v. – E. H. B.].

"Surely the heaven will soon be below, and the earth above, and men will henceforth live in the sea, and fish take their place upon the dry land, since you, Lacedæmonians, propose to put down free governments in the cities of Greece, and to set up tyrannies in their room. There is nothing in the whole world so unjust, nothing so bloody, as a tyranny. If, however, it seems to you a desirable thing to have the cities under despotic rule, begin by putting a tyrant over yourselves, and then establish despots in the other states. While you continue yourselves, as you have always been, unacquainted with tyranny, and take such excellent care that Sparta may not suffer from it, to act as you are now doing is to treat your allies unworthily. If you knew what tyranny was as well as ourselves, you would be better advised than you now are in regard to it. (§ 2.) The government at Corinth was once an oligarchy – a single race, called Bacchiadæ, who intermarried only among themselves, held the management of affairs. Now it happened that Amphion, one of these, had a daughter, named Labda, who was lame, and whom therefore none of the Bacchiadæ would consent to marry; so she was taken to wife by Aëtion, son of Echecrates, a man of the township of Petra, who was, however, by descent of the race of the Lapithæ, and of the house of Cæneus. Aëtion, as he had no child, either by this wife or by any other, went to Delphi to consult the oracle concerning the matter. Scarcely had he entered the temple when the Pythoness saluted him in these words –

'No one honours thee now, Aëtion, worthy of honour;–
Labda shall soon be a mother – her offspring a rock, that will one day
Fall on the kingly race, and right the city of Corinth.'

By some chance this address of the oracle to Aëtion came to the ears of the Bacchiadæ, who till then had been unable to perceive the meaning of another earlier prophecy which likewise bore upon Corinth, and pointed to the same event as Aëtion's prediction. It was the following:–

'When mid the rocks an eagle shall bear a carnivorous lion,
Mighty and fierce, he shall loosen the limbs of many beneath them –
Brood ye well upon this, all ye Corinthian people,
Ye who dwell by fair Peirêné, and beetling Corinth.'

(§ 3.) The Bacchiadæ had possessed this oracle for some time; but they were quite at a loss to know what it meant until they heard the response given to Aëtion; then however they at once perceived its meaning, since the two agreed so well together. Nevertheless, though the bearing of the first prophecy was now clear to them, they remained quiet, being minded to put to death the child which Aëtion was expecting. As soon, therefore, as his wife was delivered, they sent ten of their number to the township where Aëtion lived, with orders to make away with the baby. So the men came to Petra, and went into Aëtion's house, and there asked if they might see the child; and Labda, who knew nothing of their purpose, but thought their inquiries arose from a kindly feeling towards her husband, brought the child, and laid him in the arms of one of them. Now they had agreed by the way that whoever first got hold of the child should dash it against the ground. It happened, however, by a providential chance, that the babe, just as Labda put him into the man's arms, smiled in his face. The man saw the smile, and was touched with pity, so that he could not kill it; he therefore passed it on to his next neighbour, who gave it to a third; and so it went through all the ten without any one choosing to be the murderer. The mother received her child back; and the men went out of the house, and stood near the door, and there blamed and reproached one another; chiefly however accusing the man who had first had the child in his arms, because he had not done as had been agreed upon. At last, after much time had been thus spent, they resolved to go into the house again and all take part in the murder. (§ 4.) But it was fated that evil should come upon Corinth from the progeny of Aëtion; and so it chanced that Labda, as she stood near the door, heard all that the men said to one another, and fearful of their changing their mind, and returning to destroy her baby, she carried him off and hid him in what seemed to her the most unlikely place to be suspected, viz., a 'cypsel' or corn-bin. She knew that if they came back to look for the child, they would search all her house; and so indeed they did, but not finding the child after looking everywhere, they thought it best to go away, and declare to those by whom they had been sent that they had done their bidding. And thus they reported on their return home. (§ 5.) Aëtion's son grew up, and, in remembrance of the danger from which he had escaped, was named Cypselus, after the corn-bin. When he reached to man's estate, he went to Delphi, and on consulting the oracle, received a response which was two-sided. It was the following:—

'See there comes to my dwelling a man much favour'd of fortune,
Cypselus, son of Aëtion, and king of the glorious Corinth, –
He and his children too, but not his children's children.'

Such was the oracle; and Cypselus put so much faith in it that
he forthwith made his attempt, and thereby became master of
Corinth. Having thus got the tyranny, he showed himself a harsh
ruler – many of the Corinthians he drove into banishment, many
he deprived of their fortunes, and a still greater number of their
lives. (§ 6.) His reign lasted thirty years, and was prosperous to
its close; insomuch that he left the government to Periander, his
son. This prince at the beginning of his reign was of a milder
temper than his father; but after he corresponded by means of
messengers with Thrasybulus, tyrant of Miletus, he became even
more sanguinary. On one occasion he sent a herald to ask Thrasybulus what mode of government it was safest to set up in order
to rule with honour. Thrasybulus led the messenger without the
city, and took him into a field of corn, through which he began
to walk, while he asked him again and again concerning his
coming from Corinth, ever as he went breaking off and throwing
away all such ears of corn as overtopped the rest. In this way he
went through the whole field, and destroyed all the best and
richest part of the crop; then, without a word, he sent the messenger back. On the return of the man to Corinth, Periander was
eager to know what Thrasybulus had counselled, but the messenger reported that he had said nothing; and he wondered that
Periander had sent him to so strange a man, who seemed to have
lost his senses, since he did nothing but destroy his own
property. And upon this he told how Thrasybulus had behaved
at the interview. (§ 7.) Periander, perceiving what the action
meant, and knowing that Thrasybulus advised the destruction of
all the leading citizens, treated his subjects from this time forward with the very greatest cruelty. Where Cypselus had spared
any, and had neither put them to death nor banished them,
Periander completed what his father had left unfinished.[1] One
day he stripped all the women of Corinth stark naked, for the
sake of his own wife Melissa. He had sent messengers into Thesprotia to consult the oracle of the dead upon the Acheron[2]

---

1 The cruel tyranny of Periander is agreed on by all writers.
2 [A river of Epirus; now known as the *Suliotiko* or *Phanariotiko:* see Frazer's
n. on *Pausanias*, I. xvii. 5. – E. H. B.]

concerning a pledge which had been given into his charge by a stranger, and Melissa appeared, but refused to speak or tell where the pledge was, – 'she was chill,' she said, 'having no clothes; the garments buried with her were of no manner of use, since they had not been burnt. And this should be her token to Periander, that what she said was true – the oven was cold when he baked his loaves in it.' When this message was brought him, Periander knew the token, for he had lain with Melissa's corpse; wherefore he straightway made proclamation, that all the wives of the Corinthians should go forth to the temple of Hera. So the women apparelled themselves in their bravest, and went forth, as if to a festival. Then, with the help of his guards, whom he had placed for the purpose, he stripped them one and all, making no difference between the free women and the slaves; and, taking their clothes to a pit, he called on the name of Melissa, and burnt the whole heap. This done, he sent a second time to the oracle; and Melissa's ghost told him where he would find the stranger's pledge. Such, O Lacedæmonians! is tyranny, and such are the deeds which spring from it. We Corinthians marvelled greatly when we first knew of your having sent for Hippias; and now it surprises us still more to hear you speak as you do. We adjure you, by the common gods of Greece, plant not despots in her cities. If however you are determined, if you persist, against all justice, in seeking to restore Hippias, – know, at least, that the Corinthians will not approve your conduct."

93. When Sosicles, the deputy from Corinth, had thus spoken, Hippias replied, and, invoking the same gods, he said, – "Of a surety the Corinthians will, beyond all others, regret the Pisistratidæ, when the fated days come for them to be distressed by the Athenians." Hippias spoke thus because he knew the prophecies better than any man living. But the rest of the allies, who till Sosicles spoke had remained quiet, when they heard him utter his thoughts thus boldly, all together broke silence, and declared themselves of the same mind; and withal, they conjured the Lacedæmonians "not to revolutionise a Grecian city." And in this way the enterprise came to nought.

94. Hippias hereupon withdrew; and Amyntas the Macedonian offered him the city of Anthemûs, while the Thessalians were willing to give him Iolcôs:[1] but he would accept neither

1 Iolcôs, the port from which the Argonauts were said to have sailed, lay at the bottom of the Pagasean gulf in the district called Magnesia.

the one nor the other, preferring to go back to Sigêum,[1] which city Pisistratus had taken by force of arms from the Mytilenæans. Pisistratus, when he became master of the place, established there as tyrant his own natural son, Hegesistratus, whose mother was an Argive woman. But this prince was not allowed to enjoy peaceably what his father had made over to him; for during very many years there had been war between the Athenians of Sigêum and the Mytilenæans of the city called Achillêum.[2] They of Mytilêné insisted on having the place restored to them: but the Athenians refused, since they argued that the Æolians had no better claim to the Trojan territory than themselves, or than any of the other Greeks who helped Menelaüs on occasion of the rape of Helen.

95. War accordingly continued, with many and various incidents, whereof the following was one. In a battle which was gained by the Athenians, the poet Alcæus took to flight, and saved himself, but lost his arms, which fell into the hands of the conquerors. They hung them up in the temple of Athena at Sigêum; and Alcæus made a poem, describing his misadventure to his friend Melanippus, and sent it to him at Mytilêné. The Mytilenæans and Athenians were reconciled by Periander, the son of Cypselus, who was chosen by both parties as arbiter — he decided that they should each retain that of which they were at the time possessed; and Sigêum passed in this way under the dominion of Athens.

96. On the return of Hippias to Asia from Lacedæmon, he moved heaven and earth to set Artaphernes against the Athenians, and did all that lay in his power to bring Athens into subjection to himself and Darius. So when the Athenians learnt what he was about, they sent envoys to Sardis, and exhorted the Persians not to lend an ear to the Athenian exiles. Artaphernes told them in reply, "that if they wished to remain safe, they must receive back Hippias." The Athenians, when this answer was reported to them, determined not to consent, and therefore made up their minds to be at open enmity with the Persians.

97. The Athenians had come to this decision, and were already in bad odour with the Persians, when Aristagoras the Milesian, dismissed from Sparta by Cleomenes the Lacedæmonian,

---

1 Supra, ch. 65.
2 So called because it was supposed to contain the tomb of Achilles.

arrived at Athens. He knew that, after Sparta, Athens was the most powerful of the Grecian states.[1] Accordingly he appeared before the people, and, as he had done at Sparta,[2] spoke to them of the good things which there were in Asia, and of the Persian mode of fight – how they used neither shield nor spear, and were very easy to conquer. All this he urged, and reminded them also, that Miletus was a colony from Athens,[3] and therefore ought to receive their succour, since they were so powerful – and in the earnestness of his entreaties, he cared little what he promised – till, at the last, he prevailed and won them over. It seems indeed to be easier to deceive a multitude than one man – for Aristagoras, though he failed to impose on Cleomenes the Lacedæmonian, succeeded with the Athenians, who were thirty thousand. Won by his persuasions, they voted that twenty ships should be sent to the aid of the Ionians, under the command of Melanthius, one of the citizens, a man of mark in every way. These ships were the beginning of mischief both to the Greeks and to the barbarians.

98. Aristagoras sailed away in advance, and when he reached Miletus, devised a plan, from which no manner of advantage could possibly accrue to the Ionians;– indeed, in forming it, he did not aim at their benefit, but his sole wish was to annoy King Darius. He sent a messenger into Phrygia to those Pæonians who had been led away captive by Megabazus from the river Strymon,[4] and who now dwelt by themselves in Phrygia, having a tract of land and a hamlet of their own. This man, when he reached the Pæonians, spoke thus to them:–

"Men of Pæonia, Aristagoras, king of Miletus, has sent me to you, to inform you that you may now escape, if you choose to follow the advice he proffers. All Ionia has revolted from the king; and the way is open to you to return to your own land. You have only to contrive to reach the sea-coast; the rest shall be our business."

When the Pæonians heard this, they were exceedingly rejoiced, and, taking with them their wives and children, they made all speed to the coast; a few only remaining in Phrygia through fear. The rest, having reached the sea, crossed over to Chios, where they had just landed, when a great troop of Persian horse

1 Compare, i. 56.   2 Supra, ch. 49
3 Supra, i. 147, and infra, ix. 97. 4 Vide supra, chs. 15–17.

came following upon their heels, and seeking to overtake them. Not succeeding, however, they sent a message across to Chios, and begged the Pæonians to come back again. These last refused, and were conveyed by the Chians from Chios to Lesbos, and by the Lesbians thence to Doriscus;[1] from which place they made their way on foot to Pæonia.

99. The Athenians now arrived with a fleet of twenty sail, and brought also in their company five triremes of the Eretrians;[2] which had joined the expedition, not so much out of goodwill towards Athens, as to pay a debt which they already owed to the people of Miletus. For in the old war between the Chalcideans and Eretrians, the Milesians fought on the Eretrian side throughout, while the Chalcideans had the help of the Samian people. Aristagoras, on their arrival, assembled the rest of his allies, and proceeded to attack Sardis, not however leading the army in person, but appointing to the command his own brother Charopinus, and Hermophantus, one of the citizens, while he himself remained behind in Miletus.

100. The Ionians sailed with this fleet to Ephesus, and, leaving their ships at Coressus in the Ephesian territory, took guides from the city, and went up the country, with a great host. They marched along the course of the river Caÿster,[3] and, crossing over the ridge of Tmôlus, came down upon Sardis and took it, no man opposing them;— the whole city fell into their hands, except only the citadel, which Artaphernes defended in person, having with him no contemptible force.

101. Though, however, they took the city, they did not succeed in plundering it; for, as the houses in Sardis were most of them built of reeds, and even the few which were of brick had a reed thatching for their roof, one of them was no sooner fired by a soldier than the flames ran speedily from house to house, and spread over the whole place.[4] As the fire raged, the Lydians, and such Persians as were in the city, inclosed on every side by

1 Herodotus gives the name of Doriscus to the great alluvial plain through which the river Hebrus (*Maritza*) empties itself into the sea.

2 Eretria lay upon the coast of Eubœa, 12 or 13 miles below Chalcis.

3 The Caÿster, now the Little Mendere, washed Ephesus on the north, and formed its harbour.

4 In Eastern capitals the houses are still rarely of brick or stone. Reeds and wood constitute the chief building materials. Hence the terrible conflagrations which from time to time devastate them.

the flames, which had seized all the skirts of the town, and finding themselves unable to get out, came in crowds into the market-place, and gathered themselves upon the banks of the Pactôlus. This stream, which comes down from Mount Tmôlus, and brings the Sardians a quantity of gold-dust, runs directly through the market-place of Sardis, and joins the Hermus, before that river reaches the sea. So the Lydians and Persians, brought together in this way in the market-place and about the Pactôlus, were forced to stand on their defence; and the Ionians, when they saw the enemy in part resisting, in part pouring towards them in dense crowds, took fright, and drawing off to the ridge which is called Tmôlus, when night came, went back to their ships.

102. Sardis however was burnt, and, among other buildings, a temple of the native goddess Cybelé was destroyed;[1] which was the reason afterwards alleged by the Persians for setting on fire the temples of the Greeks. As soon as what had happened was known, all the Persians who were stationed on this side the Halys drew together, and brought help to the Lydians. Finding however, when they arrived, that the Ionians had already withdrawn from Sardis, they set off, and, following close upon their track, came up with them at Ephesus. The Ionians drew out against them in battle array; and a fight ensued, wherein the Greeks had very greatly the worse. Vast numbers were slain by the Persians: among other men of note, they killed the captain of the Eretrians, a certain Eualcidas, a man who had gained crowns at the games, and received much praise from Simonides the Cean.[2] Such as made their escape from the battle, dispersed among the several cities.

103. So ended this encounter. Afterwards the Athenians quite forsook the Ionians, and, though Aristagoras besought them much by his ambassadors, refused to give him any further help. Still the Ionians, notwithstanding this desertion, continued unceasingly their preparations to carry on the war against the Persian king, which their late conduct towards him had rendered

1 Cybêbé, Cybelé, or Rhea, was the Magna Mater, or Mother of the Gods, a principal object of worship among all the Oriental nations. Her temple at Sardis was a magnificent structure, of the Ionic order, formed of blocks of white marble of an enormous size.

2 Simonides the Cean, like Pindar, wrote odes in praise of those who carried off prizes in the games.

unavoidable. Sailing into the Hellespont, they brought Byzantium, and all the other cities in that quarter, under their sway. Again, quitting the Hellespont, they went to Caria, and won the greater part of the Carians to their side; while Caunus, which had formerly refused to join with them, after the burning of Sardis, came over likewise.

104. All the Cyprians too, excepting those of Amathûs, of their own proper motion espoused the Ionian cause. The occasion of their revolting from the Medes was the following. There was a certain Onesilus, younger brother of Gorgus, king of Salamis, and son of Chersis, who was son of Siromus, and grandson of Evelthon. This man had often in former times entreated Gorgus to rebel against the king; but, when he heard of the revolt of the Ionians, he left him no peace with his importunity. As, however, Gorgus would not hearken to him, he watched his occasion, and when his brother had gone outside the town, he with his partisans closed the gates upon him. Gorgus, thus deprived of his city, fled to the Medes; and Onesilus, being now king of Salamis, sought to bring about a revolt of the whole of Cyprus. All were prevailed on except the Amathusians, who refused to listen to him; whereupon Onesilus sate down before Amathûs,[1] and laid siege to it.

105. While Onesilus was engaged in the siege of Amathûs, King Darius received tidings of the taking and burning of Sardis by the Athenians and Ionians; and at the same time he learnt that the author of the league, the man by whom the whole matter had been planned and contrived, was Aristagoras the Milesian. It is said that he no sooner understood what had happened, than, laying aside all thought concerning the Ionians, who would, he was sure, pay dear for their rebellion, he asked, "Who the Athenians were?"[2] and, being informed, called for his bow, and placing an arrow on the string, shot upward into the sky,[3] saying, as he let fly the shaft — "Grant me, Zeus,[4] to revenge myself on the Athenians!" After this speech, he bade one of his servants every

1 Amathus, one of the most ancient Phœnician settlements in Cyprus.

2 Compare i. 153, and supra, ch. 73.

3 Compare with this what is said of the Thracians (supra, iv. 94). The notion here seems to be, to send the message to heaven on the arrow.

4 That is, "Ormuzd." The Greeks identify the *supreme* God of each nation with their own Zeus (vide supra, i. 131; ii. 55, etc.).

day, when his dinner was spread, three times repeat these words to him – "Master, remember the Athenians."

106. Then he summoned into his presence Histiæus of Miletus, whom he had kept at his court for so long a time; and on his appearance addressed him thus – "I am told, O Histiæus, that thy lieutenant, to whom thou hast given Miletus in charge, has raised a rebellion against me. He has brought men from the other continent to contend with me, and, prevailing on the Ionians – whose conduct I shall know how to recompense – to join with this force, he has robbed me of Sardis! Is this as it should be, thinkest thou? Or can it have been done without thy knowledge and advice? Beware lest it be found hereafter that the blame of these acts is thine."

Histiæus answered – "What words are these, O king, to which thou hast given utterance? I advise aught from which unpleasantness of any kind, little or great, should come to thee! What could I gain by so doing? Or what is there that I lack now? Have I not all that thou hast, and am I not thought worthy to partake all thy counsels? If my lieutenant has indeed done as thou sayest, be sure he has done it all of his own head. For my part, I do not think it can really be that the Milesians and my lieutenant have raised a rebellion against thee. But if they have indeed committed aught to thy hurt, and the tidings are true which have come to thee, judge thou how ill-advised thou wert to remove me from the sea-coast. The Ionians, it seems, have waited till I was no longer in sight, and then sought to execute that which they long ago desired; whereas, if I had been there, not a single city would have stirred. Suffer me then to hasten at my best speed to Ionia, that I may place matters there upon their former footing, and deliver up to thee the deputy of Miletus, who has caused all the troubles. Having managed this business to thy heart's content, I swear by all the gods of thy royal house, I will not put off the clothes in which I reach Ionia till I have made Sardinia, the biggest island in the world, thy tributary."

107. Histiæus spoke thus, wishing to deceive the king; and Darius, persuaded by his words, let him go; only bidding him be sure to do as he had promised, and afterwards come back to Susa.

108. In the meantime – while the tidings of the burning of Sardis were reaching the king, and Darius was shooting the arrow and having the conference with Histiæus, and the latter, by permission of Darius, was hastening down to the sea – in

Cyprus the following events took place. Tidings came to One-silus, the Salaminian, who was still besieging Amathûs, that a certain Artybius, a Persian, was looked for to arrive in Cyprus with a great Persian armament. So Onesilus, when the news reached him, sent off heralds to all parts of Ionia, and besought the Ionians to give him aid. After brief deliberation, these last in full force passed over into the island; and the Persians about the same time crossed in their ships from Cilicia, and proceeded by land to attack Salamis; while the Phœnicians, with the fleet, sailed round the promontory which goes by the name of "the Keys of Cyprus."

109. In this posture of affairs the princes of Cyprus called together the captains of the Ionians, and thus addressed them:—

"Men of Ionia, we Cyprians leave it to you to choose whether you will fight with the Persians or with the Phœnicians. If it be your pleasure to try your strength on land against the Persians, come on shore at once, and array yourselves for the battle; we will then embark aboard your ships and engage the Phœnicians by sea. If, on the other hand, ye prefer to encounter the Phœni-cians, let that be your task: only be sure, whichever part you choose, to acquit yourselves so that Ionia and Cyprus, so far as depends on you, may preserve their freedom."

The Ionians made answer – "The commonwealth of Ionia sent us here to guard the sea, not to make over our ships to you, and engage with the Persians on shore. We will therefore keep the post which has been assigned to us, and seek therein to be of some service. Do you, remembering what you suffered when you were the slaves of the Medes, behave like brave warriors."

110. Such was the reply of the Ionians. Not long afterwards the Persians advanced into the plain before Salamis,[1] and the Cyprian kings[2] ranged their troops in order of battle against them, placing them so that while the rest of the Cyprians were drawn up against the auxiliaries of the enemy, the choicest troops of the Salaminians and the Solians[3] were set to oppose the Per-sians. At the same time Onesilus, of his own accord, took post opposite to Artybius, the Persian general.

1 Salamis was situated on the eastern coast of Cyprus.
2 Cyprus, like Phœnicia, seems to have been at all times governed by a number of petty kings.
3 Soli lay on the north coast of Cyprus.

111. Now Artybius rode a horse which had been trained to rear up against a foot-soldier. Onesilus, informed of this, called to him his shieldbearer, who was a Carian by nation, a man well skilled in war, and of daring courage; and thus addressed him:— "I hear," he said, "that the horse which Artybius rides, rears up and attacks with his fore legs and teeth the man against whom his rider urges him. Consider quickly therefore and tell me which wilt thou undertake to encounter, the steed or the rider?" Then the squire answered him, "Both, my liege, or either, am I ready to undertake, and there is nothing that I will shrink from at thy bidding. But I will tell thee what seems to me to make most for thy interests. As thou art a prince and a general, I think thou shouldest engage with one who is himself both a prince and also a general. For then, if thou slayest thine adversary, 'twill redound to thine honour, and if he slays thee (which may Heaven forefend!), yet to fall by the hand of a worthy foe makes death lose half its horror. To us, thy followers, leave his war-horse and his retinue. And have thou no fear of the horse's tricks. I warrant that this is the last time he will stand up against any one."

112. Thus spake the Carian; and shortly after, the two hosts joined battle both by sea and land. And here it chanced that by sea the Ionians, who that day fought as they have never done either before or since, defeated the Phœnicians, the Samians especially distinguishing themselves. Meanwhile the combat had begun on land, and the two armies were engaged in a sharp struggle, when thus it fell out in the matter of the generals. Artybius, astride upon his horse, charged down upon Onesilus, who, as he had agreed with his shieldbearer, aimed his blow at the rider; the horse reared and placed his fore feet upon the shield of Onesilus, when the Carian cut at him with a reaping-hook, and severed the two legs from the body. The horse fell upon the spot, and Artybius, the Persian general, with him.

113. In the thick of the fight, Stesanor, tyrant of Curium,[1] who commanded no inconsiderable body of troops, went over with them to the enemy. On this desertion of the Curians – Argive colonists, if report says true – forthwith the war-chariots of the Salaminians followed the example set them, and went over likewise; whereupon victory declared in favour of the Persians; and the army of the Cyprians being routed, vast numbers were

1 Curium lay upon the southern coast, between Paphos and Amathûs.

slain, and among them Onesilus, the son of Chersis, who was the author of the revolt, and Aristocyprus, king of the Solians. This Aristocyprus was son of Philocyprus, whom Solon the Athenian, when he visited Cyprus, praised in his poems[1] beyond all other sovereigns.

114. The Amathusians, because Onesilus had laid siege to their town, cut the head off his corpse, and took it with them to Amathûs, where it was set up over the gates. Here it hung till it became hollow; whereupon a swarm of bees took possession of it, and filled it with a honeycomb. On seeing this the Amathusians consulted the oracle, and were commanded "to take down the head and bury it, and thenceforth to regard Onesilus as a hero, and offer sacrifice to him year by year; so it would go the better with them." And to this day the Amathusians do as they were then bidden.

115. As for the Ionians who had gained the sea-fight, when they found that the affairs of Onesilus were utterly lost and ruined, and that siege was laid to all the cities of Cyprus excepting Salamis, which the inhabitants had surrendered to Gorgus,[2] the former king – forthwith they left Cyprus, and sailed away home. Of the cities which were besieged, Soli held out the longest: the Persians took it by undermining the wall in the fifth month from the beginning of the siege.

116. Thus, after enjoying a year of freedom, the Cyprians were enslaved for the second time. Meanwhile Daurises, who was married to one of the daughters of Darius, together with Hymeas, Otanes, and other Persian captains, who were likewise married to daughters of the king,[3] after pursuing the Ionians who had fought at Sardis, defeating them, and driving them to their ships, divided their efforts against the different cities, and proceeded in succession to take and sack each one of them.

117. Daurises attacked the towns upon the Hellespont, and took in as many days the five cities of Dardanus, Abydos, Percôté, Lampsacus, and Pæsus. From Pæsus he marched against

1 The poems of Solon were written chiefly in the elegiac metre, and were hortatory or gnomic.

2 Gorgus is still king at the time of the expedition of Xerxes (infra, vii. 98).

3 The practice of marrying the king's daughters to the most distinguished of the Persian nobles had in view the consolidation of the empire and the strengthening of the royal power, by attaching to the throne those who would have been most likely to stir up revolts.

Parium; but on his way receiving intelligence that the Carians had made common cause with the Ionians, and thrown off the Persian yoke, he turned round, and, leaving the Hellespont, marched away towards Caria.

118. The Carians by some chance got information of this movement before Daurises arrived, and drew together their strength to a place called "the White Columns," which is on the river Aresyas, a stream running from the Idrian country, and emptying itself into the Mæander. Here when they were met, many plans were put forth; but the best, in my judgment, was that of Pixodarus, the son of Mausôlus, a Cindyan, who was married to a daughter of Syennesis, the Cilician king. His advice was, that the Carians should cross the Mæander, and fight with the river at their back; that so, all chance of flight being cut off, they might be forced to stand their ground, and have their natural courage raised to a still higher pitch. His opinion, however, did not prevail; it was thought best to make the enemy have the Mæander behind them; that so, if they were defeated in the battle and put to flight, they might have no retreat open, but be driven headlong into the river.

119. The Persians soon afterwards approached, and, crossing the Mæander, engaged the Carians upon the banks of the Aresyas; where for a long time the battle was stoutly contested, but at last the Carians were defeated, being overpowered by numbers. On the side of the Persians there fell 2,000, while the Carians had not fewer than 10,000 slain. Such as escaped from the field of battle collected together at Labranda, in the vast precinct of Zeus Stratius – a deity worshipped only by the Carians – and in the sacred grove of plane-trees. Here they deliberated as to the best means of saving themselves, doubting whether they would fare better if they gave themselves up to the Persians, or if they abandoned Asia for ever.

120. As they were debating these matters a body of Milesians and allies came to their assistance; whereupon the Carians, dismissing their former thoughts, prepared themselves afresh for war, and on the approach of the Persians gave them battle a second time. They were defeated, however, with still greater loss than before; and while all the troops engaged suffered severely, the blow fell with most force on the Milesians.

121. The Carians, some while after, repaired their ill fortune in another action. Understanding that the Persians were about

to attack their cities, they laid an ambush for them on the road which leads to Pedasus; the Persians, who were making a night-march, fell into the trap, and the whole army was destroyed, together with the generals, Daurises, Amorges, and Sisimaces: Myrsus too, the son of Gyges, was killed at the same time. The leader of the ambush was Heraclides, the son of Ibanôlis, a man of Mylasa. Such was the way in which these Persians perished.

122. In the meantime Hymeas, who was likewise one of those by whom the Ionians were pursued after their attack on Sardis, directing his course towards the Propontis, took Cius,[1] a city of Mysia. Learning, however, that Daurises had left the Hellespont, and was gone into Caria, he in his turn quitted the Propontis, and marching with the army under his command to the Hellespont, reduced all the Æolians of the Troad, and likewise conquered the Gergithæ, a remnant of the ancient Teucrians. He did not, however, quit the Troad, but, after gaining these successes, was himself carried off by disease.

123. After his death, which happened as I have related, Artaphernes, the satrap of Sardis, and Otanes, the third general,[2] were directed to undertake the conduct of the war against Ionia and the neighbouring Æolis. By them Clazomenæ in the former,[3] and Cymé in the latter,[4] were recovered.

124. As the cities fell one after another, Aristagoras the Milesian (who was in truth, as he now plainly showed, a man of but little courage), notwithstanding that it was he who had caused the disturbances in Ionia and made so great a commotion, began, seeing his danger, to look about for means of escape. Being convinced that it was in vain to endeavour to overcome King Darius, he called his brothers-in-arms together, and laid before them the following project:— "'Twould be well," he said, "to have some place of refuge, in case they were driven out of Miletus. Should he go out at the head of a colony to Sardinia,[5] or should he sail to Myrcinus in Edonia, which Histiæus had received as a gift from King Darius, and had begun to fortify?"

1 Cius, like most other towns upon this coast, was a colony of the Milesians.
2 Supra, ch. 116.
3 Supra, i. 142.
4 Supra, i. 149.
5 Sardinia seems to have been viewed by the Greeks of this time as a sort of El Dorado.

125. To this question of Aristagoras, Hecatæus, the historian, son of Hegesander, made answer, that in his judgment neither place was suitable. "Aristagoras should build a fort," he said, "in the island of Leros,¹ and, if driven from Miletus, should go there and bide his time; from Leros attacks might readily be made, and he might re-establish himself in Miletus." Such was the advice given by Hecatæus.

126. Aristagoras, however, was bent on retiring to Myrcinus. Accordingly, he put the government of Miletus into the hands of one of the chief citizens, named Pythagoras, and, taking with him all who liked to go, sailed to Thrace, and there made himself master of the place in question. From thence he proceeded to attack the Thracians; but here he was cut off with his whole army, while besieging a city whose defenders were anxious to accept terms of surrender.

1 Leros, one of the Sporades, retains its ancient name almost unchanged.

ADDED NOTE BY THE EDITOR

"The theme of Herodotus – the struggle of Greece with the Orient – possessed for him a deeper meaning than the political result of the Persian War. It was the contact and collision of two different types of civilisation; of peoples of two different characters and different political institutions. In the last division of his work, where the final struggle of Persia and Greece is narrated, this contest between the slavery of the barbarian and the liberty of the Greek, between Oriental autocracy and Hellenic constitutionalism, is ever present and is forcibly brought out. But the contrast of Hellenic with Oriental culture pervades the whole work; it informs the unity of the external theme with the deeper unity of an inner meaning. It is the keynote of the History of Herodotus."

"Herodotus was the Homer of the Persian War; and that war originally inspired him. His work presents a picture of sixth century civilisation; and it is also a universal history in so far as it gathers the greater part of the known world into a narrative which is concentrated on a single issue. It is fortunate for literature that he was not too critical; if his criticism had been more penetrating and less naïve, he could not have been a second Homer." – From J. B. Bury's *Ancient Greek Historians* (1909), lecture ii.

THE SIXTH BOOK,
ENTITLED ERATO

1. ARISTAGORAS, the author of the Ionian revolt, perished in the way which I have described. Meanwhile Histiæus, tyrant of Miletus, who had been allowed by Darius to leave Susa, came down to Sardis. On his arrival, being asked by Artaphernes, the Sardian satrap, what he thought was the reason that the Ionians had rebelled, he made answer that he could not conceive, and it had astonished him greatly, pretending to be quite unconscious of the whole business. Artaphernes, however, who perceived that he was dealing dishonestly, and who had in fact full knowledge of the whole history of the outbreak, said to him, "I will tell thee how the case stands, Histiæus: this shoe is of thy stitching; Aristagoras has but put it on."

2. Such was the remark made by Artaphernes concerning the rebellion. Histiæus, alarmed at the knowledge which he displayed, so soon as night fell, fled away to the coast. Thus he forfeited his word to Darius; for though he had pledged himself to bring Sardinia, the biggest island in the whole world, under the Persian yoke,[1] he in reality sought to obtain the direction of the war against the king. Crossing over to Chios, he was there laid in bonds by the inhabitants, who accused him of intending some mischief against them in the interest of Darius. However, when the whole truth was laid before them, and they found that Histiæus was in reality a foe to the king, they forthwith set him at large again.

3. After this the Ionians inquired of him for what reason he had so strongly urged Aristagoras to revolt from the king, thereby doing their nation so ill a service. In reply, he took good care not to disclose to them the real cause, but told them that King Darius had intended to remove the Phœnicians from their own country, and place them in Ionia, while he planted the Ionians in Phœnicia, and that it was for this reason he sent Aristagoras

1 Vide supra, v. 106. "An expedition against Sardinia," as Grote observes, "seems to have been among the favourite fancies of the Ionic Greeks of that day."

the order. Now it was not true that the king had entertained any such intention, but Histiæus succeeded hereby in arousing the fears of the Ionians.[1]

4. After this, Histiæus, by means of a certain Hermippus, a native of Atarneus, sent letters to many of the Persians in Sardis, who had before held some discourse with him concerning a revolt. Hermippus, however, instead of conveying them to the persons to whom they were addressed, delivered them into the hands of Artaphernes, who, perceiving what was on foot, commanded Hermippus to deliver the letters according to their addresses, and then bring him back the answers which were sent to Histiæus. The traitors being in this way discovered, Artaphernes put a number of Persians to death, and caused a commotion in Sardis.

5. As for Histiæus, when his hopes in this matter were disappointed, he persuaded the Chians to carry him back to Miletus; but the Milesians were too well pleased at having got quit of Aristagoras to be anxious to receive another tyrant into their country; besides which they had now tasted liberty. They therefore opposed his return; and when he endeavoured to force an entrance during the night, one of the inhabitants even wounded him in the thigh. Having been thus rejected from his country, he went back to Chios; whence, after failing in an attempt to induce the Chians to give him ships, he crossed over to Mytilênê, where he succeeded in obtaining vessels from the Lesbians. They fitted out a squadron of eight triremes, and sailed with him to the Hellespont, where they took up their station, and proceeded to seize all the vessels which passed out from the Euxine, unless the crews declared themselves ready to obey his orders.

6. While Histiæus and the Mytilenæans were thus employed, Miletus was expecting an attack from a vast armament, which comprised both a fleet and also a land force. The Persian captains had drawn their several detachments together, and formed them into a single army; and had resolved to pass over all the other cities, which they regarded as of lesser account, and to march straight on Miletus. Of the naval states, Phœnicia showed

---

[1] The readiness with which this was believed proves, even better than historical instances, how frequent such transfers of population were in the great oriental empires.

the greatest zeal; but the fleet was composed likewise of the Cyprians (who had so lately been brought under),[1] the Cilicians, and also the Egyptians.

7. While the Persians were thus making preparations against Miletus and Ionia, the Ionians, informed of their intent, sent their deputies to the Panionium,[2] and held a council upon the posture of their affairs. Hereat it was determined that no land force should be collected to oppose the Persians, but that the Milesians should be left to defend their own walls as they could; at the same time they agreed that the whole naval force of the states, not excepting a single ship, should be equipped, and should muster at Ladé,[3] a small island lying off Miletus – to give battle on behalf of the place.

8. Presently the Ionians began to assemble in their ships, and with them came the Æolians of Lesbos; and in this way they marshalled their line:– The wing towards the east was formed of the Milesians themselves, who furnished eighty ships; next to them came the Prienians with twelve, and the Myusians with three ships; after the Myusians were stationed the Teians, whose ships were seventeen; then the Chians, who furnished a hundred. The Erythræans and Phocæans followed, the former with eight, the latter with three ships; beyond the Phocæans were the Lesbians, furnishing seventy; last of all came the Samians, forming the western wing, and furnishing sixty vessels. The fleet amounted in all to three hundred and fifty-three triremes. Such was the number on the Ionian side.

9. On the side of the barbarians the number of vessels was six hundred. These assembled off the coast of Milesia, while the land army collected upon the shore; but the leaders, learning the strength of the Ionian fleet, began to fear lest they might fail to defeat them, in which case, not having the mastery at sea, they would be unable to reduce Miletus, and might in consequence receive rough treatment at the hands of Darius. So when they thought of all these things, they resolved on the following course:– Calling together the Ionian tyrants, who had fled to the Medes for refuge when Aristagoras deposed them from their

1 Supra, v. 115, 116.
2 Supra, i. 141 and 148.
3 Ladé is now a hillock in the plain of the Mæander.

governments, and who were now in camp, having joined in the expedition against Miletus, the Persians addressed them thus: "Men of Ionia, now is the fit time to show your zeal for the house of the king. Use your best efforts, every one of you, to detach your fellow-countrymen from the general body. Hold forth to them the promise that, if they submit, no harm shall happen to them on account of their rebellion; their temples shall not be burnt, nor any of their private buildings; neither shall they be treated with greater harshness than before the outbreak. But if they refuse to yield, and determine to try the chance of a battle, threaten them with the fate which shall assuredly overtake them in that case. Tell them, when they are vanquished in fight, they shall be enslaved; their boys shall be made eunuchs, and their maidens transported to Bactra; while their country shall be delivered into the hands of foreigners.

10. Thus spake the Persians. The Ionian tyrants sent accordingly by night to their respective citizens, and reported the words of the Persians; but the people were all staunch, and refused to betray their countrymen, those of each state thinking that they alone had had overtures made to them. Now these events happened on the first appearance of the Persians before Miletus.

11. Afterwards, while the Ionian fleet was still assembled at Ladé, councils were held, and speeches made by divers persons – among the rest by Dionysius, the Phocæan captain, who thus expressed himself:– "Our affairs hang on the razor's edge, men of Ionia, either to be free or to be slaves; and slaves, too, who have shown themselves runaways. Now then you have to choose whether you will endure hardships, and so for the present lead a life of toil, but thereby gain ability to overcome your enemies and establish your own freedom; or whether you will persist in this slothfulness and disorder, in which case I see no hope of your escaping the king's vengeance for your rebellion. I beseech you, be persuaded by me, and trust yourselves to my guidance. Then, if the gods only hold the balance fairly between us, I undertake to say that our foes will either decline a battle, or, if they fight, suffer complete discomfiture."

12. These words prevailed with the Ionians, and forthwith they committed themselves to Dionysius; whereupon he proceeded every day to make the ships move in column, and the rowers ply their oars, and exercise themselves in breaking the

line;[1] while the marines were held under arms, and the vessels were kept, till evening fell, upon their anchors,[2] so that the men had nothing but toil from morning even to night. Seven days did the Ionians continue obedient, and do whatsoever he bade them; but on the eighth day, worn out by the hardness of the work and the heat of the sun, and quite unaccustomed to such fatigues, they began to confer together, and to say one to another, "What god have we offended to bring upon ourselves such a punishment as this? Fools and distracted that we were, to put ourselves into the hands of this Phocæan braggart, who does but furnish three ships to the fleet! He, now that he has got us, plagues us in the most desperate fashion; many of us, in consequence, have fallen sick already – many more expect to follow. We had better suffer anything rather than these hardships; even the slavery with which we are threatened, however harsh, can be no worse than our present thraldom. Come, let us refuse him obedience." So saying, they forthwith ceased to obey his orders, and pitched their tents, as if they had been soldiers, upon the island, where they reposed under the shade all day, and refused to go aboard the ships and train themselves.

13. Now when the Samian captains perceived what was taking place, they were more inclined than before to accept the terms which Æaces, the son of Syloson, had been authorised by the Persians to offer them, on condition of their deserting from the confederacy. For they saw that all was disorder among the Ionians, and they felt also that it was hopeless to contend with the power of the king; since if they defeated the fleet which had been sent against them, they knew that another would come five times as great. So they took advantage of the occasion which now offered, and as soon as ever they saw the Ionians refuse to work, hastened gladly to provide for the safety of their temples and their properties. This Æaces, who made the overtures to the Samians, was the son of Syloson, and grandson of the earlier Æaces. He had formerly been tyrant of Samos, but was ousted from his government by Aristagoras the Milesian, at the same time with the other tyrants of the Ionians.

1 This was the most important naval manœuvre with which the Greeks were acquainted. It is supposed to have had two objects; one, the breaking of the oars of the two vessels between which the ship using the manœuvre passed, and the other, the cutting off of a portion of the enemy's fleet from the rest.
2 Instead of being drawn up on shore, as was the usual practice.

14. The Phœnicians soon afterwards sailed to the attack; and the Ionians likewise put themselves in line, and went out to meet them. When they had now neared one another, and joined battle, which of the Ionians fought like brave men and which like cowards, I cannot declare with any certainty, for charges are brought on all sides; but the tale goes that the Samians, according to the agreement which they had made with Æaces, hoisted sail, and quitting their post bore away for Samos, except eleven ships, whose captains gave no heed to the orders of the commanders, but remained and took part in the battle. The state of Samos, in consideration of this action, granted to these men, as an acknowledgment of their bravery, the honour of having their names, and the names of their fathers, inscribed upon a pillar, which still stands in the market-place. The Lesbians also, when they saw the Samians, who were drawn up next them, begin to flee, themselves did the like; and the example, once set, was followed by the greater number of the Ionians.

15. Of those who remained and fought, none were so rudely handled as the Chians, who displayed prodigies of valour, and disdained to play the part of cowards. They furnished to the common fleet, as I mentioned above, one hundred ships, having each of them forty armed citizens, and those picked men, on board; and when they saw the greater portion of the allies betraying the common cause, they for their part, scorning to imitate the base conduct of these traitors, although they were left almost alone and unsupported, a very few friends continuing to stand by them, notwithstanding went on with the fight, and ofttimes cut the line of the enemy, until at last, after they had taken very many of their adversaries' ships, they ended by losing more than half of their own. Hereupon, with the remainder of their vessels, the Chians fled away to their own country.

16. As for such of their ships as were damaged and disabled, these, being pursued by the enemy, made straight for Mycalé,[1] where the crews ran them ashore, and abandoning them began their march along the continent. Happening in their way upon the territory of Ephesus, they essayed to cross it; but here a dire misfortune befell them. It was night, and the Ephesian women

1 For a description of Mycalé, vide supra, i. 148. It was the name given to the mountainous headland which runs out from the coast in the direction of Samos.

chanced to be engaged in celebrating the Thesmophoria – the previous calamity of the Chians had not been heard of[1] – so when the Ephesians saw their country invaded by an armed band, they made no question of the new-comers being robbers who purposed to carry off their women;[2] and accordingly they marched out against them in full force, and slew them all. Such were the misfortunes which befell them of Chios.

17. Dionysius, the Phocæan, when he perceived that all was lost, having first captured three ships from the enemy, himself took to flight. He would not, however, return to Phocæa, which he well knew must fall again, like the rest of Ionia, under the Persian yoke; but straightway, as he was, he set sail for Phœnicia, and there sunk a number of merchantmen, and gained a great booty; after which he directed his course to Sicily, where he established himself as a corsair, and plundered the Carthaginians and Tyrrhenians, but did no harm to the Greeks.

18. The Persians, when they had vanquished the Ionians in the sea-fight, besieged Miletus both by land and sea, driving mines under the walls, and making use of every known device, until at length they took both the citadel and the town, six years from the time when the revolt first broke out under Aristagoras. All the inhabitants of the city they reduced to slavery, and thus the event tallied with the announcement which had been made by the oracle.

19. For once upon a time, when the Argives had sent to Delphi to consult the god about the safety of their own city, a prophecy was given them, in which others besides themselves were interested; for while it bore in part upon the fortunes of Argos, it touched in a by-clause the fate of the men of Miletus. I shall set down the portion which concerned the Argives when I come to that part of my History,[3] mentioning at present only the passage in which the absent Milesians were spoken of. This passage was as follows:–

"Then shalt thou, Miletus, so oft the contriver of evil,
  Be, thyself, to many a feast and an excellent booty:
  Then shall thy matrons wash the feet of long-haired masters;–
  Others shall then possess our lov'd Didymian temple."

---

1 In this fact we seem to have another indication that Ephesus kept aloof from the revolt.
2 For the frequency of such outrages, vide infra, ch. 138.
3 Vide infra, ch. 77.

Such a fate now befell the Milesians; for the Persians, who wore their hair long, after killing most of the men, made the women and children slaves; and the sanctuary at Didyma,[1] the oracle no less than the temple was plundered and burnt; of the riches whereof I have made frequent mention in other parts of my History.

20. Those of the Milesians whose lives were spared, being carried prisoners to Susa, received no ill treatment at the hands of King Darius, but were established by him in Ampé, a city on the shores of the Erythræan sea, near the spot where the Tigris flows into it. Miletus itself, and the plain about the city, were kept by the Persians for themselves, while the hill-country was assigned to the Carians of Pedasus.[2]

21. And now the Sybarites, who after the loss of their city occupied Laüs and Scidrus, failed duly to return the former kindness of the Milesians. For these last, when Sybaris was taken by the Crotoniats,[3] made a great mourning, all of them, youths as well as men, shaving their heads; since Miletus and Sybaris were, of all the cities whereof we have any knowledge, the two most closely united to one another. The Athenians, on the other hand, showed themselves beyond measure afflicted at the fall of Miletus, in many ways expressing their sympathy, and especially by their treatment of Phrynichus.[4] For when this poet brought out upon the stage his drama of the Capture of Miletus, the whole theatre burst into tears; and the people sentenced him to pay a fine of a thousand drachms, for recalling to them their own misfortunes. They likewise made a law, that no one should ever again exhibit that piece.

22. Thus was Miletus bereft of its inhabitants. In Samos the people of the richer sort were much displeased with the doings of the captains, and the dealings they had had with the Medes; they therefore held a council, very shortly after the sea-fight, and resolved that they would not remain to become the slaves of Æaces and the Persians, but before the tyrant set foot in their country, would sail away and found a colony in another land.

1 Didyma was the name of the place called also Branchidæ, in the territory of Miletus, where the famous temple of Apollo stood.

2 Supra, i. 175.

3 Supra, v. 44.

4 Phrynichus, the disciple of Thespis, began to exhibit tragedies about the year B.C. 511.

Now it chanced that about this time the Zanclæans of Sicily had sent ambassadors to the Ionians, and invited them to Kalé-Acté, where they wished an Ionian city to be founded. This place, Kalé-Acté (or the Fair Strand) as it is called, is in the country of the Sicilians,[1] and is situated in the part of Sicily which looks towards Tyrrhenia.[2] The offer thus made to all the Ionians was embraced only by the Samians, and by such of the Milesians as had contrived to effect their escape.

23. Hereupon this is what ensued. The Samians on their voyage reached the country of the Epizephyrian Locrians,[3] at a time when the Zanclæans and their king Scythas were engaged in the siege of a Sicilian town which they hoped to take. Anaxilaüs, tyrant of Rhegium,[4] who was on ill terms with the Zanclæans, knowing how matters stood, made application to the Samians, and persuaded them to give up the thought of Kalé-Acté, the place to which they were bound, and to seize Zanclé itself, which was left without men. The Samians followed this counsel and possessed themselves of the town; which the Zanclæans no sooner heard than they hurried to the rescue, calling to their aid Hippocrates, tyrant of Gela,[5] who was one of their allies. Hippocrates came with his army to their assistance; but on his arrival he seized Scythas, the Zanclæan king, who had just lost his city, and sent him away in chains, together with his brother Pythogenes, to the town of Inycus; after which he came to an understanding with the Samians, exchanged oaths with them, and agreed to betray the people of Zanclé. The reward of his treachery was to be one-half of the goods and chattels, including slaves, which the town contained, and all that he could find in the open country. Upon this Hippocrates seized and bound the greater number of the Zanclæans as slaves; delivering, however, into the hands of the Samians three hundred of the principal citizens, to be slaughtered; but the Samians spared the lives of these persons.

1 [The Sicels (Σικελοὶ) (Σικελιῶται, Sicilian Greeks) were part of the pre-Hellenic population of Sicily. – E. H. B.]

2 That is, on the north coast.

3 The Epizephyrian or Western Locrians are the Locrians of Italy, who possessed a city, Locri, and a tract of country, near the extreme south of the modern Calabria.

4 Rhegium retains its name almost unchanged. It is the modern *Reggio*.

5 Infra, vii. 153, 154.

24. Scythas, the king of the Zanclæans, made his escape from Inycus, and fled to Himera;[1] whence he passed into Asia, and went up to the court of Darius. Darius thought him the most upright of all the Greeks to whom he afforded a refuge; for with the king's leave he paid a visit to Sicily, and thence returned back to Persia, where he lived in great comfort, and died by a natural death at an advanced age.

25. Thus did the Samians escape the yoke of the Medes, and possess themselves without any trouble of Zanclé,[2] a most beautiful city. At Samos itself the Phœnicians, after the fight which had Miletus for its prize was over, re-established Æaces, the son of Syloson, upon his throne. This they did by the command of the Persians, who looked upon Æaces as one who had rendered them a high service and therefore deserved well at their hands. They likewise spared the Samians, on account of the desertion of their vessels, and did not burn either their city or their temples, as they did those of the other rebels. Immediately after the fall of Miletus the Persians recovered Caria, bringing some of the cities over by force, while others submitted of their own accord.

26. Meanwhile tidings of what had befallen Miletus reached Histiæus the Milesian, who was still at Byzantium, employed in intercepting the Ionian merchantmen as they issued from the Euxine.[3] Histiæus had no sooner heard the news than he gave the Hellespont in charge to Bisaltes, son of Apollophanes, a native of Abydos, and himself, at the head of his Lesbians, set sail for Chios. One of the Chian garrisons which opposed him he engaged at a place called "The Hollows," situated in the Chian territory, and of these he slaughtered a vast number; afterwards, by the help of his Lesbians, he reduced all the rest of the Chians, who were weakened by their losses in the sea-fight, Polichné, a city of Chios, serving him as head-quarters.

27. It mostly happens that there is some warning when great misfortunes are about to befall a state or nation; and so it was in this instance, for the Chians had previously had some strange tokens sent to them. A choir of a hundred of their youths had

1 Himera was an important place, and the only Greek colony on the north coast of Sicily.
2 Zanclé, the modern *Messina*.
3 Supra, ch. 5.

been despatched to Delphi; and of these only two had returned; the remaining ninety-eight having been carried off by a pestilence. Likewise, about the same time, and very shortly before the sea-fight, the roof of a school-house had fallen in upon a number of their boys, who were at lessons; and out of a hundred and twenty children there was but one left alive. Such were the signs which God sent to warn them. It was very shortly afterwards that the sea-fight happened, which brought the city down upon its knees; and after the sea-fight came the attack of Histiæus and his Lesbians, to whom the Chians, weakened as they were, furnished an easy conquest.

28. Histiæus now led a numerous army, composed of Ionians and Æolians, against Thasos, and had laid siege to the place when news arrived that the Phœnicians were about to quit Miletus and attack the other cities of Ionia. On hearing this, Histiæus raised the siege of Thasos, and hastened to Lesbos with all his forces. There his army was in great straits for want of food; whereupon Histiæus left Lesbos and went across to the mainland, intending to cut the crops which were growing in the Atarnean territory, and likewise in the plain of the Caïcus, which belonged to Mysia. Now it chanced that a certain Persian named Harpagus was in these regions at the head of an army of no little strength. He, when Histiæus landed, marched out to meet him, and engaging with his forces destroyed the greater number of them, and took Histiæus himself prisoner.

29. Histiæus fell into the hands of the Persians in the following manner. The Greeks and Persians engaged at Malêna, in the region of Atarneus; and the battle was for a long time stoutly contested, till at length the cavalry came up, and, charging the Greeks, decided the conflict. The Greeks fled; and Histiæus, who thought that Darius would not punish his fault with death, showed how he loved his life by the following conduct. Overtaken in his flight by one of the Persians, who was about to run him through, he cried aloud in the Persian tongue that he was Histiæus the Milesian.

30. Now, had he been taken straightway before King Darius, I verily believe that he would have received no hurt, but the king would have freely forgiven him. Artaphernes, however, satrap of Sardis, and his captor Harpagus, on this very account, – because they were afraid that, if he escaped, he would be again received into high favour by the king, – put him to death as soon as he

arrived at Sardis. His body they impaled at that place,[1] while they embalmed his head and sent it up to Susa to the king. Darius, when he learnt what had taken place, found great fault with the men engaged in this business for not bringing Histiæus alive into his presence, and commanded his servants to wash and dress the head with all care, and then bury it, as the head of a man who had been a great benefactor to himself and the Persians.[2] Such was the sequel of the history of Histiæus.

31. The naval armament of the Persians wintered at Miletus, and in the following year proceeded to attack the islands off the coast, Chios, Lesbos, and Tenedos,[3] which were reduced without difficulty. Whenever they became masters of an island, the barbarians, in every single instance, netted the inhabitants. Now the mode in which they practise this netting is the following. Men join hands, so as to form a line across from the north coast to the south, and then march through the island from end to end and hunt out the inhabitants.[4] In like manner the Persians took also the Ionian towns upon the mainland, not however netting the inhabitants, as it was not possible.

32. And now their generals made good all the threats wherewith they had menaced the Ionians before the battle.[5] For no sooner did they get possession of the towns than they chose out all the best favoured boys and made them eunuchs, while the most beautiful of the girls they tore from their homes and sent as presents to the king, at the same time burning the cities themselves, with their temples. Thus were the Ionians for the third time reduced to slavery; once by the Lydians, and a second, and now a third time, by the Persians.

33. The sea force, after quitting Ionia, proceeded to the Hellespont, and took all the towns which lie on the left shore as one sails into the straits. For the cities on the right bank had already been reduced by the land force of the Persians. Now these are the places which border the Hellespont on the European side; the Chersonese, which contains a number of cities,

1 According to the Persian custom with rebels.
2 Compare Cæsar's conduct on receiving the head of Pompey.
3 Tenedos retains its name absolutely unchanged to the present day. It is a small but fertile island, producing an excellent wine.
4 Supra, iii. 149.
5 Supra, ch. 9.

Perinthus,[1] the forts in Thrace, Selybria,[2] and Byzantium.[3] The Byzantines at this time, and their opposite neighbours, the Chalcedonians, instead of awaiting the coming of the Phœnicians, quitted their country, and sailing into the Euxine, took up their abode at the city of Mesêmbria. The Phœnicians, after burning all the places above mentioned, proceeded to Proconnêsus[4] and Artaca, which they likewise delivered to the flames; this done, they returned to the Chersonese, being minded to reduce those cities which they had not ravaged in their former cruise. Upon Cyzicus they made no attack at all, as before their coming the inhabitants had made terms with Œbares, the son of Megabazus, and satrap of Dascyleium, and had submitted themselves to the king. In the Chersonese the Phœnicians subdued all the cities, excepting Cardia.[5]

34. Up to this time the cities of the Chersonese had been under the government of Miltiades, the son of Cimon, and grandson of Stesagoras, to whom they had descended from Miltiades, the son of Cypselus, who obtained possession of them in the following manner. The Dolonci, a Thracian tribe, to whom the Chersonese at that time belonged, being harassed by a war in which they were engaged with the Apsinthians,[6] sent their princes to Delphi to consult the oracle about the matter. The reply of the Pythoness bade them "take back with them as a colonist into their country the man who should first offer them hospitality after they quitted the temple." The Dolonci, following the Sacred Road,[7] passed through the regions of Phocis and Bœotia; after which, as still no one invited them in, they turned aside, and travelled to Athens.

35. Now Pisistratus was at this time sole lord of Athens; but Miltiades, the son of Cypselus, was likewise a person of much distinction. He belonged to a family which was wont to contend

1 Supra, v. 1.

2 A small town upon the Sea of Marmora, about 40 miles from Constantinople.

3 Supra, iv. 144.

4 Supra, iv. 13.

5 It was situated on the western side of the Thracian Chersonese.

6 A Thracian people who occupied the tract immediately north of the Chersonese.

7 By "the sacred road" is meant apparently the road which led from Delphi *eastward.*

in the four-horse chariot-races,[1] and traced its descent to Æacus and Egina, but which, from the time of Philæas, the son of Ajax, who was the first Athenian citizen of the house, had been naturalised at Athens. It happened that as the Dolonci passed his door Miltiades was sitting in his vestibule, which caused him to remark them, dressed as they were in outlandish garments, and armed moreover with lances.[2] He therefore called to them, and, on their approach, invited them in, offering them lodging and entertainment. The strangers accepted his hospitality, and, after the banquet was over, they laid before him in full the directions of the oracle, and besought him on their own part to yield obedience to the god. Miltiades was persuaded ere they had done speaking; for the government of Pisistratus was irksome to him, and he wanted to be beyond the tyrant's reach. He therefore went straightway to Delphi, and inquired of the oracle whether he should do as the Dolonci desired.

36. As the Pythoness backed their request, Miltiades, son of Cypselus, who had already won the four-horse chariot-race at Olympia, left Athens, taking with him as many of the Athenians as liked to join in the enterprise, and sailed away with the Dolonci. On his arrival at the Chersonese, he was made king by those who had invited him. After this his first act was to build a wall across the neck of the Chersonese from the city of Cardia to Pactya, to protect the country from the incursions and ravages of the Apsinthians. The breadth of the isthmus at this part is thirty-six furlongs, the whole length of the peninsula within the isthmus being four hundred and twenty furlongs.

37. When he had finished carrying the wall across the isthmus, and had thus secured the Chersonese against the Apsinthians, Miltiades proceeded to engage in other wars, and first of all attacked the Lampsacenians; but falling into an ambush which they had laid he had the misfortune to be taken prisoner. Now it happened that Miltiades stood high in the favour of Crœsus, king of Lydia. When Crœsus therefore heard of his calamity, he sent and commanded the men of Lampsacus to give Miltiades

---

[1] The maintenance of such a stud as could entitle a man to contend with any chance of success in the great games, marks the owner as a person of ample fortune.

[2] The wearing of arms had gone out of fashion in Greece some little time before.

his freedom; "if they refused," he said, "he would destroy them like a fir." Then the Lampsacenians were somewhile in doubt about this speech of Crœsus, and could not tell how to construe his threat "that he would destroy them like a fir;" but at last one of their elders divined the true sense, and told them that the fir is the only tree which, when cut down, makes no fresh shoots, but forthwith dies outright. So the Lampsacenians, being greatly afraid of Crœsus, released Miltiades, and let him go free.

38. Thus did Miltiades, by the help of Crœsus, escape this danger. Some time afterwards he died childless, leaving his kingdom and his riches to Stesagoras, who was the son of Cimon, his half-brother.[1] Ever since his death the people of the Chersonese have offered him the customary sacrifices of a founder; and they have further established in his honour a gymnic contest and a chariot-race, in neither of which is it lawful for any Lampsacenian to contend. Before the war with Lampsacus was ended Stesagoras too died childless: he was sitting in the hall of justice when he was struck upon the head with a hatchet by a man who pretended to be a deserter, but was in good sooth an enemy, and a bitter one.

39. Thus died Stesagoras; and upon his death the Pisistratidæ fitted out a trireme, and sent Miltiades, the son of Cimon, and brother of the deceased, to the Chersonese, that he might undertake the management of affairs in that quarter. They had already shown him much favour at Athens, as if, forsooth, they had been no parties to the death of his father Cimon − a matter whereof I will give an account in another place.[2] He upon his arrival remained shut up within the house, pretending to do honour to the memory of his dead brother; whereupon the chief people of the Chersonese gathered themselves together from all the cities of the land, and came in a procession to the place where Miltiades was, to condole with him upon his misfortune. Miltiades commanded them to be seized and thrown into prison; after which he made himself master of the Chersonese, maintained a body of five hundred mercenaries, and married Hegesipyla, daughter of the Thracian king Olorus.

40. This Miltiades, the son of Cimon, had not been long in the country when a calamity befell him yet more grievous than those in which he was now involved: for three years earlier he

---

1 Literally, "his brother on the mother's side."　　2 Infra, ch. 103.

had had to fly before an incursion of the Scyths. These nomads, angered by the attack of Darius, collected in a body and marched as far as the Chersonese.[1] Miltiades did not await their coming, but fled, and remained away until the Scyths retired, when the Dolonci sent and fetched him back. All this happened three years before the events which befell Miltiades at the present time.

41. He now no sooner heard that the Phœnicians were attacking Tenedos[2] than he loaded five triremes with his goods and chattels, and set sail for Athens. Cardia was the point from which he took his departure; and as he sailed down the gulf of Melas, along the shore of the Chersonese, he came suddenly upon the whole Phœnician fleet. However he himself escaped, with four of his vessels, and got into Imbrus, one trireme only falling into the hands of his pursuers. This vessel was under the command of his eldest son Metiochus, whose mother was not the daughter of the Thracian king Olorus, but a different woman. Metiochus and his ship were taken; and when the Phœnicians found out that he was a son of Miltiades they resolved to convey him to the king, expecting thereby to rise high in the royal favour. For they remembered that it was Miltiades who counselled the Ionians to hearken when the Scyths prayed them to break up the bridge and return home.[3] Darius, however, when the Phœnicians brought Metiochus into his presence, was so far from doing him any hurt, that he loaded him with benefits. He gave him a house and estate, and also a Persian wife, by whom there were children born to him who were accounted Persians. As for Miltiades himself, from Imbrus he made his way in safety to Athens.

42. At this time the Persians did no more hurt to the Ionians; but on the contrary, before the year was out, they carried into effect the following measures, which were greatly to their advantage. Artaphernes, satrap of Sardis, summoned deputies from all the Ionian cities, and forced them to enter into agreements with one another, not to harass each other by force of arms, but to settle their disputes by reference.[4] He likewise took the measurement of their whole country in parasangs – such is the name

1 This appears to have been a marauding expedition, to which the Scythians were encouraged by the success of the Ionian revolt up to that time.
2 Supra, ch. 31.
3 Supra, iv. 137.
4 These provisos were common in the Greek treaties.

which the Persians give to a distance of thirty furlongs[1] – and settled the tributes which the several cities were to pay, at a rate that has continued unaltered from the time when Artaphernes fixed it down to the present day. The rate was very nearly the same as that which had been paid before the revolt.[2] Such were the peaceful dealings of the Persians with the Ionians.

43. The next spring Darius superseded all the other generals, and sent down Mardonius, the son of Gobryas,[3] to the coast, and with him a vast body of men, some fit for sea, others for land service. Mardonius was a youth at this time, and had only lately married Artazôstra, the king's daughter. When Mardonius, accompanied by this numerous host, reached Cilicia, he took ship and proceeded along shore with his fleet, while the land army marched under other leaders towards the Hellespont. In the course of his voyage along the coast of Asia he came to Ionia; and here I have a marvel to relate which will greatly surprise those Greeks who cannot believe that Otanes advised the seven conspirators to make Persia a commonwealth. Mardonius put down all the despots throughout Ionia, and in lieu of them established democracies. Having so done, he hastened to the Hellespont, and when a vast multitude of ships had been brought together, and likewise a powerful land force, he conveyed his troops across the strait by means of his vessels, and proceeded through Europe against Eretria and Athens.[4]

44. At least these towns served as a pretext for the expedition, the real purpose of which was to subjugate as great a number as possible of the Grecian cities; and this became plain when the Thasians, who did not even lift a hand in their defence, were reduced by the sea force, while the land army added the Macedonians to the former slaves of the king. All the tribes on the hither side of Macedonia had been reduced previously.[5] From Thasos the fleet stood across to the mainland, and sailed along shore to Acanthus, whence an attempt was made to double Mount Athos. But here a violent north wind sprang up, against

1 Supra, ii. 6, and v. 53.

2 Supra, iii. 90. What necessitated the new rating and measurement was the alteration of territory which had taken place in consequence of the revolt.

3 This is another instance of the alternation of names among the Persians. (Compare iii. 160, etc.) Gobryas was the son of a Mardonius.

4 The aggressors in the late war (supra, v. 99).

5 Supra, v. 18.

which nothing could contend, and handled a large number of the ships with much rudeness, shattering them and driving them aground upon Athos. 'Tis said the number of the ships destroyed was little short of three hundred; and the men who perished were more than twenty thousand.[1] For the sea about Athos abounds in monsters beyond all others; and so a portion were seized and devoured by these animals, while others were dashed violently against the rocks; some, who did not know how to swim, were engulfed; and some died of the cold.

45. While thus it fared with the fleet, on land Mardonius and his army were attacked in their camp during the night by the Brygi, a tribe of Thracians; and here vast numbers of the Persians were slain, and even Mardonius himself received a wound. The Brygi, nevertheless, did not succeed in maintaining their own freedom: for Mardonius would not leave the country till he had subdued them and made them subjects of Persia. Still, though he brought them under the yoke, the blow which his land force had received at their hands, and the great damage done to his fleet off Athos, induced him to set out upon his retreat; and so this armament, having failed disgracefully, returned to Asia.

46. The year after these events, Darius received information from certain neighbours of the Thasians that those islanders were making preparations for revolt; he therefore sent a herald, and bade them dismantle their walls, and bring all their ships to Abdêra.[2] The Thasians, at the time when Histiæus the Milesian made his attack upon them,[3] had resolved that, as their income was very great, they would apply their wealth to building ships of war, and surrounding their city with another and a stronger wall. Their revenue was derived partly from their possessions upon the mainland, partly from the mines which they owned. They were masters of the gold-mines at Scapté-Hylé, the yearly produce of which amounted in all to eighty talents. Their mines in Thasos yielded less, but still were so far prolific that, besides being entirely free from land-tax, they had a surplus income, derived from the two sources of their territory on the main and their mines, in common years of two hundred, and in the best years of three hundred talents.

1 The navigation of this coast is still full of danger.
2 On its site, vide infra, vii. 109.
3 Supra, ch. 28.

47. I myself have seen the mines in question: by far the most curious of them are those which the Phœnicians discovered at the time when they went with Thasus and colonised the island, which afterwards took its name from him. These Phœnician workings are in Thasos itself, between Cœnyra and a place called Ænyra, over against Samothrace:[1] a huge mountain has been turned upside down in the search for ores. Such then was the source of their wealth. On this occasion no sooner did the Great King issue his commands than straightway the Thasians dismantled their wall, and took their whole fleet to Abdêra.

48. After this Darius resolved to prove the Greeks, and try the bent of their minds, whether they were inclined to resist him in arms or prepared to make their submission. He therefore sent out heralds in divers directions round about Greece, with orders to demand everywhere earth and water for the king. At the same time he sent other heralds to the various seaport towns which paid him tribute, and required them to provide a number of ships of war and horse-transports.

49. These towns accordingly began their preparations; and the heralds who had been sent into Greece obtained what the king had bid them ask from a large number of the states upon the mainland, and likewise from all the islanders whom they visited. Among these last were included the Eginetans, who, equally with the rest, consented to give earth and water to the Persian king.

When the Athenians heard what the Eginetans had done, believing that it was from enmity to themselves that they had given consent, and that the Eginetans intended to join the Persian in his attack upon Athens, they straightway took the matter in hand. In good truth it greatly rejoiced them to have so fair a pretext; and accordingly they sent frequent embassies to Sparta,[2] and made it a charge against the Eginetans that their conduct in this matter proved them to be traitors to Greece.

---

1 That is, on the south-east side of the island.

2 The great importance of this appeal is that it raised Sparta to the general protectorate of Greece. Hitherto she had been a leading power, frequently called in to aid the weaker against the stronger, but with no definite *hegemony*, excepting over the states of the Peloponnese (supra, v. 91). Now she was acknowledged to have a paramount authority over the whole of Greece, as the proper guardian of the Grecian liberties. It gave additional weight to the appeal that it was made by Athens, the second city of Greece.

50. Hereupon Cleomenes, the son of Anaxandridas, who was then king of the Spartans, went in person to Egina, intending to seize those whose guilt was the greatest. As soon however as he tried to arrest them, a number of the Eginetans made resistance, a certain Crius, son of Polycritus, being the foremost in violence. This person told him "he should not carry off a single Eginetan without it costing him dear – the Athenians had bribed him to make this attack, for which he had no warrant from his own government – otherwise *both* the kings would have come together to make the seizure." This he said in consequence of instructions which he had received from Demaratus.[1] Hereupon Cleomenes, finding that he must quit Egina, asked Crius his name; and when Crius told him, "Get thy horns tipped with brass with all speed, O Crius!"[2] he said, "for thou wilt have to struggle with a great danger."

51. Meanwhile Demaratus, son of Ariston, was bringing charges against Cleomenes at Sparta. He too, like Cleomenes, was king of the Spartans, but he belonged to the lower house – not indeed that his house was of any lower origin than the other, for both houses are of one blood – but the house of Eurysthenes is the more honoured of the two, inasmuch as it is the elder branch.

52. The Lacedæmonians declare, contradicting therein all the poets,[3] that it was king Aristodemus himself, son of Aristomachus, grandson of Cleodæus, and great-grandson of Hyllus, who conducted them to the land which they now possess, and not the sons of Aristodemus. The wife of Aristodemus, whose name (they say) was Argeia, and who was daughter of Autesion,[4] son of Tisamenus, grandson of Thersander, and great-grandson of Polynices, within a little while after their coming into the country, gave birth to twins. Aristodemus just lived to see his children, but died soon afterwards of a disease. The Lacedæmonians of that day determined, according to custom, to take for their king the elder of the two children; but they were so alike,

---

1 This was the *second* time that Demaratus had thwarted Cleomenes (vide supra, v. 75).

2 Cleomenes puns upon the name Crius, which signifies "a ram" in Greek.

3 These poets are not those of the Epic cycle, which concluded with the adventures of Telegonus, the son of Ulysses.

4 Sister therefore, according to the myth, of Theras, the coloniser of Thera (supra, iv. 147).

and so exactly of one size, that they could not possibly tell which of the two to choose: so when they found themselves unable to make a choice, or haply even earlier, they went to the mother and asked her to tell them which was the elder, whereupon she declared that "she herself did not know the children apart;" although in good truth she knew them very well, and only feigned ignorance in order that, if it were possible, both of them might be made kings of Sparta. The Lacedæmonians were now in a great strait; so they sent to Delphi and inquired of the oracle how they should deal with the matter. The Pythoness made answer, "Let both be taken to be kings; but let the elder have the greater honour." So the Lacedæmonians were in as great a strait as before, and could not conceive how they were to discover which was the first-born, till at length a certain Messenian, by name Panites, suggested to them to watch and see which of the two the mother washed and fed first; if they found she always gave one the preference, that fact would tell them all they wanted to know; if, on the contrary, she herself varied, and sometimes took the one first, sometimes the other, it would be plain that she knew as little as they; in which case they must try some other plan. The Lacedæmonians did according to the advice of the Messenian, and, without letting her know why, kept a watch upon the mother; by which means they discovered that, whenever she either washed or fed her children, she always gave the same child the preference. So they took the boy whom the mother honoured the most, and regarding him as the first-born, brought him up in the palace; and the name which they gave to the elder boy was Eurysthenes, while his brother they called Procles. When the brothers grew up, there was always, so long as they lived, enmity between them; and the houses sprung from their loins have continued the feud to this day.

53. Thus much is related by the Lacedæmonians, but not by any of the other Greeks; in what follows I give the tradition of the Greeks generally. The kings of the Dorians (they say) – counting up to Perseus, son of Danaë, and so omitting the god – are rightly given in the common Greek lists, and rightly considered to have been Greeks themselves; for even at this early time they ranked among that people. I say "up to Perseus," and not further, because Perseus has no mortal father by whose name he is called, as Heracles has in Amphitryon; whereby it appears that I have reason on my side, and am right in saying,

"up to Perseus." If we follow the line of Danaë, daughter of Acrisius, and trace her progenitors, we shall find that the chiefs of the Dorians are really genuine Egyptians.[1] In the genealogies here given I have followed the common Greek accounts.

54. According to the Persian story, Perseus was an Assyrian who became a Greek;[2] his ancestors, therefore, according to them, were not Greeks. They do not admit that the forefathers of Acrisius were in any way related to Perseus, but say they were Egyptians, as the Greeks likewise testify.

55. Enough however of this subject. How it came to pass that Egyptians obtained the kingdoms of the Dorians,[3] and what they did to raise themselves to such a position, these are questions concerning which, as they have been treated by others, I shall say nothing. I proceed to speak of points on which no other writer has touched.

56. The prerogatives which the Spartans have allowed their kings are the following. In the first place, two priesthoods, those (namely) of Lacedæmonian and of Celestial Zeus;[4] also the right of making war on what country soever they please, without hindrance from any of the other Spartans, under pain of outlawry; on service the privilege of marching first in the advance and last in the retreat, and of having a hundred[5] picked men for their body-guard while with the army; likewise the liberty of sacrificing as many cattle in their expeditions as it seems them good, and the right of having the skins and the chines of the slaughtered animals for their own use.

57. Such are their privileges in war; in peace their rights are as follows. When a citizen makes a public sacrifice the kings are given the first seats at the banquet; they are served before any

1 Supra. ii. 91. Herodotus believes in the tale which brings Danaüs from Egypt.

2 This is an entirely distinct story from that related below (vii. 150) – that Perseus, son of Danaë, had a son Perses, the progenitor of the Achæmenian kings – which latter the Greeks generally adopted. Both stories seem to me pure inventions.

3 That is to say, the kingdoms of the Peloponnese, afterwards conquered by the Dorians.

4 I.e. of king Zeus in the heavenly realm, and of the divine king from whom the royal line in Sparta was derived. – [E. H. B.] The necessary union of the priestly with the kingly office was an idea almost universal in early times.

5 The number of the knights who formed the king's body-guard is always elsewhere declared to be 300.

of the other guests, and have a double portion of everything; they take the lead in the libations; and the hides of the sacrificed beasts belong to them. Every month, on the first day, and again on the seventh of the first decade,[1] each king receives a beast without blemish at the public cost, which he offers up to Apollo; likewise a medimnus of meal,[2] and of wine a Laconian quart. In the contests of the games they have always the seat of honour; they appoint the citizens who have to entertain foreigners; they also nominate, each of them, two of the Pythians, officers whose business it is to consult the oracle at Delphi, who eat with the kings, and, like them, live at the public charge. If the kings do not come to the public supper, each of them must have two chœnixes of meal and a cotylè of wine sent home to him at his house; if they come, they are given a double quantity of each, and the same when any private man invites them to his table. They have the custody of all the oracles which are pronounced; but the Pythians must likewise have knowledge of them. They have the whole decision of certain causes, which are these, and these only:— When a maiden is left the heiress of her father's estate, and has not been betrothed by him to any one, they decide who is to marry her; in all matters concerning the public highways they judge; and if a person wants to adopt a child, he must do it before the kings. They likewise have the right of sitting in council with the eight-and-twenty senators; and if they are not present, then the senators nearest of kin to them have their privileges, and give two votes as the royal proxies, besides a third vote, which is their own.

58. Such are the honours which the Spartan people have allowed their kings during their lifetime; after they are dead other honours await them. Horsemen carry the news of their death through all Laconia, while in the city the women go hither and thither drumming upon a kettle. At this signal, in every house two free persons, a man and a woman, must put on mourning, or else be subject to a heavy fine. The Lacedæmonians have likewise a custom at the demise of their kings which is common

1 The division of the Greek month was into decades. The seventh day of each month was sacred to Apollo, who was believed to have been born on the seventh of Thargelion (May).

2 [The *medimnus* was about 12 gallons, the *chœnix* rather less than a quart, and a *cotylè* half a pint. – E. H. B.]

to them with the barbarians of Asia – indeed with the greater number of the barbarians everywhere – namely, that when one of their kings dies, not only the Spartans, but a certain number of the country people from every part of Laconia are forced, whether they will or no, to attend the funeral. So these persons and the Helots, and likewise the Spartans themselves,[1] flock together to the number of several thousands, men and women intermingled; and all of them smite their foreheads violently, and weep and wail without stint, saying always that their last king was the best. If a king dies in battle, then they make a statue of him, and placing it upon a couch right bravely decked, so carry it to the grave. After the burial, by the space of ten days there is no assembly, nor do they elect magistrates, but continue mourning the whole time.

59. They hold with the Persians also in another custom. When a king dies, and another comes to the throne, the newly-made monarch forgives all the Spartans the debts which they owe either to the king or to the public treasury. And in like manner among the Persians each king when he begins to reign remits the tribute due from the provinces.

60. In one respect the Lacedæmonians resemble the Egyptians. Their heralds and flute-players, and likewise their cooks, take their trades by succession from their fathers. A flute-player must be the son of a flute-player, a cook of a cook, a herald of a herald; and other people cannot take advantage of the loudness of their voice to come into the profession and shut out the heralds' sons; but each follows his father's business. Such are the customs of the Lacedæmonians.

61. At the time of which we are speaking, while Cleomenes in Egina was labouring for the general good of Greece, Demaratus at Sparta continued to bring charges against him, moved not so much by love of the Eginetans as by jealousy and hatred of his colleague. Cleomenes therefore was no sooner returned from Egina than he considered with himself how he might deprive Demaratus of his kingly office; and here the following

---

1 The three classes of which the Lacedæmonian population consisted are here very clearly distinguished from one another:– 1. The Periœci, or free inhabitants of the country districts; 2. The Helots, or serfs who tilled the soil; and 3. The Spartans, or Dorian conquerors, who were the only *citizens*, and who lived almost exclusively in the capital.

circumstance furnished a ground for him to proceed upon. Ariston, king of Sparta, had been married to two wives, but neither of them had borne him any children; as however he still thought it was possible he might have offspring, he resolved to wed a third; and this was how the wedding was brought about. He had a certain friend, a Spartan, with whom he was more intimate than with any other citizen. This friend was married to a wife whose beauty far surpassed that of all the other women in Sparta; and what was still more strange, she had once been as ugly as she now was beautiful. For her nurse, seeing how ill-favoured she was, and how sadly her parents, who were wealthy people, took her bad looks to heart, bethought herself of a plan, which was to carry the child every day to the temple of Helen at Therapna,[1] which stands above the Phœbeum,[2] and there to place her before the image, and beseech the goddess to take away the child's ugliness. One day, as she left the temple, a woman appeared to her, and begged to know what it was she held in her arms. The nurse told her it was a child, on which she asked to see it; but the nurse refused; the parents, she said, had forbidden her to show the child to any one. However the woman would not take a denial; and the nurse, seeing how highly she prized a look, at last let her see the child. Then the woman gently stroked its head, and said, "One day this child shall be the fairest dame in Sparta." And her looks began to change from that very day. When she was of marriageable age, Agêtus, son of Alcides, the same whom I have mentioned above as the friend of Ariston, made her his wife.

62. Now it chanced that Ariston fell in love with this person; and his love so preyed upon his mind that at last he devised as follows. He went to his friend, the lady's husband, and proposed to him, that they should exchange gifts, each taking that which pleased him best out of all the possessions of the other. His friend, who felt no alarm about his wife, since Ariston was also married, consented readily; and so the matter was confirmed between them by an oath. Then Ariston gave Agêtus the present, whatever it was, of which he had made choice, and when it came to his turn to name the present which he was to receive in

---

1 Therapna was a place of some importance on the left bank of the Eurotas, nearly opposite Sparta, from which it was distant probably about two miles.
2 A precinct sacred to Apollo, at a little distance from the town itself.

exchange, required to be allowed to carry home with him Agê-tus's wife. But the other demurred, and said, "except his wife, he might have anything else:" however, as he could not resist the oath which he had sworn, or the trickery which had been practised on him, at last he suffered Ariston to carry her away to his house.

63. Ariston hereupon put away his second wife and took for his third this woman; and she, in less than the due time – when she had not yet reached her full term of ten months, – gave birth to a child, the Demaratus of whom we have spoken. Then one of his servants came and told him the news, as he sat in council with the Ephors; whereat, remembering when it was that the woman became his wife, he counted the months upon his fingers, and having so done, cried out with an oath, "The boy cannot be mine." This was said in the hearing of the Ephors; but they made no account of it at the time. The boy grew up; and Ariston repented of what he had said; for he became altogether convinced that Demaratus was truly his son. The reason why he named him Demaratus was the following. Some time before these events the whole Spartan people, looking upon Ariston as a man of mark beyond all the kings that had reigned at Sparta before him, had offered up a prayer that he might have a son. On this account, therefore, the name Demaratus[1] was given.

64. In course of time Ariston died; and Demaratus received the kingdom: but it was fated, as it seems, that these words, when bruited abroad, should strip him of his sovereignty. This was brought about by means of Cleomenes, whom he had twice sorely vexed, once when he led the army home from Eleusis,[2] and a second time when Cleomenes was gone across to Egina against such as had espoused the side of the Medes.[3]

65. Cleomenes now, being resolved to have his revenge upon Demaratus, went to Leotychides, the son of Menares, and grandson of Agis, who was of the same family as Demaratus, and made agreement with him to this tenor following. Cleomenes was to lend his aid to make Leotychides king in the room of

---

1 Dem-aratus (ὃτῳ δήμῳ ἀρατός) is the "People-prayed-for" king. Compare the Louis *le Désiré* of French history.

2 Supra, v. 75.

3 Supra, chs. 50 and 51.

Demaratus; and then Leotychides was to take part with Cleomenes against the Eginetans. Now Leotychides hated Demaratus chiefly on account of Percalus, the daughter of Chilon, son of Demarmenus: this lady had been betrothed to Leotychides; but Demaratus laid a plot, and robbed him of his bride, forestalling him in carrying her off,[1] and marrying her. Such was the origin of the enmity. At the time of which we speak, Leotychides was prevailed upon by the earnest desire of Cleomenes to come forward against Demaratus and make oath "that Demaratus was not rightful king of Sparta, since he was not the true son of Ariston." After he had thus sworn, Leotychides sued Demaratus, and brought up against him the phrase which Ariston had let drop when, on the coming of his servant to announce to him the birth of his son, he counted the months, and cried out with an oath that the child was not his. It was on this speech of Ariston's that Leotychides relied to prove that Demaratus was not his son, and therefore not rightful king of Sparta; and he produced as witnesses the Ephors who were sitting with Ariston at the time and heard what he said.

66. At last, as there came to be much strife concerning this matter, the Spartans made a decree that the Delphic oracle should be asked to say whether Demaratus were Ariston's son or no. Cleomenes set them upon this plan; and no sooner was the decree passed than he made a friend of Cobon, the son of Aristophantus, a man of the greatest weight among the Delphians; and this Cobon prevailed upon Perialla, the prophetess, to give the answer which Cleomenes wished.[2] Accordingly, when the sacred messengers came and put their question, the Pythoness returned for answer, "that Demaratus was not Ariston's son." Some time afterwards all this became known; and Cobon was forced to fly from Delphi; while Perialla the prophetess was deprived of her office.

67. Such were the means whereby the deposition of Demaratus was brought about; but his flying from Sparta to the Medes was by reason of an affront which was put upon him. On losing his kingdom he had been made a magistrate; and in that office

---

1 The seizure of the bride was a necessary part of a Spartan marriage.

2 The venality of the Delphic oracle appears both by this instance, and by the former one of the Alcmæonidæ (v. 63). Such cases, however, appear to have been rare.

soon afterwards, when the feast of the Gymnopædiæ[1] came round, he took his station among the lookers-on; whereupon Leotychides, who was now king in his room, sent a servant to him and asked him, by way of insult and mockery, "how it felt to be a magistrate after one had been a king?"[2] Demaratus, who was hurt at the question, made answer – "Tell him I have tried them both, but he has not. Howbeit this speech will be the cause to Sparta of infinite blessings or else of infinite woes." Having thus spoken he wrapped his head in his robe, and, leaving the theatre, went home to his own house, where he prepared an ox for sacrifice, and offered it to Zeus, after which he called for his mother.

68. When she appeared, he took of the entrails, and placing them in her hand, besought her in these words following:–

"Dear mother, I beseech you, by all the gods, and chiefly by our own hearth-god Zeus, tell me the very truth, who was really my father. For Leotychides, in the suit which we had together, declared, that when thou becamest Ariston's wife thou didst already bear in thy womb a child by thy former husband; and others repeat a yet more disgraceful tale, that our groom found favour in thine eyes, and that I am his son. I entreat thee therefore by the gods to tell me the truth. For if thou hast gone astray, thou hast done no more than many a woman; and the Spartans remark it as strange, if I am Ariston's son, that he had no children by his other wives."

69. Thus spake Demaratus; and his mother replied as follows: "Dear son, since thou entreatest so earnestly for the truth, it shall indeed be fully told to thee. When Ariston brought me to his house, on the third night after my coming, there appeared to me one like to Ariston, who, after staying with me a while, rose, and taking the garlands from his own brows placed them upon my head, and so went away. Presently after Ariston entered, and when he saw the garlands which I still wore, asked me who gave them to me. I said, 'twas he; but this he stoutly denied; whereupon I solemnly swore that it was none other, and told him he did not do well to dissemble when he had so lately risen from my side and left the garlands with me. Then Ariston,

1 The feast of the Gymnopædiæ, or *naked youths*, was one of the most important at Sparta. [Warlike songs were sung by choruses. – E. H. B.]
2 Compare i. 129.

when he heard my oath, understood that there was something beyond nature in what had taken place. And indeed it appeared that the garlands had come from the hero-temple which stands by our court gates – the temple of him they call Astrabacus – and the soothsayers, moreover, declared that the apparition was that very person. And now, my son, I have told thee all thou wouldest fain know. Either thou art the son of that hero – either thou mayest call Astrabacus sire; or else Ariston was thy father. As for that matter which they who hate thee urge the most, the words of Ariston, who, when the messenger told him of thy birth, declared before many witnesses that 'thou wert not not his son, forasmuch as the ten months were not fully out,' it was a random speech, uttered from mere ignorance. The truth is, children are born not only at ten months, but at nine, and even at seven.[1] Thou wert thyself, my son, a seven months' child. Ariston acknowledged, no long time afterwards, that his speech sprang from thoughtlessness. Hearken not then to other tales concerning thy birth, my son: for be assured thou hast the whole truth. As for grooms, pray Heaven Leotychides and all who speak as he does may suffer wrong from them!" Such was the mother's answer.

70. Demaratus, having learnt all that he wished to know, took with him provision for the journey, and went into Elis, pretending that he purposed to proceed to Delphi, and there consult the oracle. The Lacedæmonians, however, suspecting that he meant to fly his country, sent men in pursuit of him; but Demaratus hastened, and leaving Elis before they arrived, sailed across to Zacynthus.[2] The Lacedæmonians followed, and sought to lay hands upon him, and to separate him from his retinue; but the Zacynthians would not give him up to them: so he escaping, made his way afterwards by sea to Asia,[3] and presented himself before King Darius, who received him generously, and gave him both lands and cities. Such was the chance which drove Demaratus to Asia, a man distinguished among the Lacedæmonians for many noble deeds and wise counsels, and who alone of all the Spartan kings[4] brought honour to his country by winning at Olympia the prize in the four-house chariot-race.

1 Supra, ch. 63.
2 Zacynthus is the modern *Zante*.
3 In B.C. 486 (infra, vii. 3).
4 Wealth was the chief requisite for success in this contest.

71. After Demaratus was deposed, Leotychides, the son of Menares, received the kingdom. He had a son, Zeuxidamus, called Cyniscus[1] by many of the Spartans. This Zeuxidamus did not reign at Sparta, but died before his father, leaving a son, Archidamus. Leotychides, when Zeuxidamus was taken from him, married a second wife, named Eurydamé, the sister of Menius and daughter of Diactorides. By her he had no male offspring, but only a daughter called Lampito, whom he gave in marriage to Archidamus, Zeuxidamus' son.

72. Even Leotychides, however, did not spend his old age in Sparta, but suffered a punishment whereby Demaratus was fully avenged. He commanded the Lacedæmonians when they made war against Thessaly, and might have conquered the whole of it, but was bribed by a large sum of money. It chanced that he was caught in the fact, being found sitting in his tent on a gauntlet, quite full of silver. Upon this he was brought to trial and banished from Sparta; his house was razed to the ground; and he himself fled to Tegea, where he ended his days. But these events took place long afterwards.

73. At the time of which we are speaking, Cleomenes, having carried his proceedings in the matter of Demaratus to a prosperous issue, forthwith took Leotychides with him, and crossed over to attack the Eginetans; for his anger was hot against them on account of the affront which they had formerly put upon him. Hereupon the Eginetans, seeing that both the kings were come against them, thought it best to make no further resistance. So the two kings picked out from all Egina the ten men who for wealth and birth stood the highest, among whom were Crius,[2] son of Polycritus, and Casambus, son of Aristocrates, who wielded the chief power; and these men they carried with them to Attica, and there deposited them in the hands of the Athenians, the great enemies of the Eginetans.

74. Afterwards, when it came to be known what evil arts had been used against Demaratus, Cleomenes was seized with fear of his own countrymen, and fled into Thessaly. From thence he passed into Arcadia, where he began to stir up troubles, and endeavoured to unite the Arcadians against Sparta. He bound them by various oaths to follow him whithersoever he should lead, and was even desirous of taking their chief leaders with him

1 Or "the Whelp."   2 Supra, ch. 50.

to the city of Nonacris, that he might swear them to his cause by the waters of the Styx. For the waters of Styx, as the Arcadians say, are in that city, and this is the appearance they present: you see a little water, dripping from a rock into a basin, which is fenced round by a low wall.[1] Nonacris, where this fountain is to be seen, is a city of Arcadia near Pheneus.

75. When the Lacedæmonians heard how Cleomenes was engaged, they were afraid, and agreed with him that he should come back to Sparta and be king as before. So Cleomenes came back; but had no sooner returned than he, who had never been altogether of sound mind,[2] was smitten with downright madness. This he showed by striking every Spartan he met upon the face with his sceptre. On his behaving thus, and showing that he was gone quite out of his mind, his kindred imprisoned him, and even put his feet in the stocks. While so bound, finding himself left alone with a single keeper, he asked the man for a knife. The keeper at first refused, whereupon Cleomenes began to threaten him, until at last he was afraid, being only a helot, and gave him what he required. Cleomenes had no sooner got the steel than, beginning at his legs, he horribly disfigured himself, cutting gashes in his flesh, along his legs, thighs, hips, and loins, until at last he reached his belly, which he likewise began to gash, whereupon in a little time he died. The Greeks generally think that this fate came upon him because he induced the Pythoness to pronounce against Demaratus; the Athenians differ from all others in saying that it was because he cut down the sacred grove of the goddesses[3] when he made his invasion by Eleusis; while the Argives ascribe it to his having taken from their refuge and cut to pieces certain Argives who had fled from battle into a precinct sacred to Argus, where Cleomenes slew them, burning likewise at the same time, through irreverence, the grove itself.

76. For once, when Cleomenes had sent to Delphi to consult the oracle, it was prophesied to him that he should take Argos; upon which he went out at the head of the Spartans, and led them to the river Erasinus. This stream is reported to flow from the Stymphalian[4] lake, the waters of which empty themselves

1 Superstitious feelings of dread still attach to the water, which is considered to be of a peculiarly noxious character.
2 Supra, v. 42.
3 The great goddesses, Demeter and Proserpine.
4 The lake Stymphalia, or Stymphâlis, was in Northern Arcadia.

into a pitch-dark chasm, and then (as they say) reappear in Argos, where the Argives call them the Erasinus. Cleomenes, having arrived upon the banks of this river, proceeded to offer sacrifice to it, but, in spite of all that he could do, the victims were not favourable to his crossing. So he said that he admired the god for refusing to betray his countrymen, but still the Argives should not escape him for all that. He then withdrew his troops, and led them down to Thyrea, where he sacrificed a bull to the sea, and conveyed his men on shipboard to Nauplia[1] in the Tirynthian territory.[2]

77. The Argives, when they heard of this, marched down to the sea, to defend their country; and arriving in the neighbourhood of Tiryns, at the place which bears the name of Sêpeia, they pitched their camp opposite to the Lacedæmonians, leaving no great space between the hosts. And now their fear was not so much lest they should be worsted in open fight as lest some trick should be practised on them; for such was the danger which the oracle given to them in common with the Milesians[3] seemed to intimate. The oracle ran as follows:—

"Time shall be when the female shall conquer the male,
    and shall chase him
Far away, – gaining so great praise and honour in Argos;
Then full many an Argive woman her cheeks shall mangle;–
Hence, in the times to come 'twill be said by the men
    who are unborn,
'Tamed by the spear expired the coilèd terrible serpent.' "[4]

At the coincidence of all these things the Argives were greatly cast down; and so they resolved that they would follow the signals of the enemy's herald. Having made this resolve, they proceeded to act as follows: whenever the herald of the Lacedæmonians gave any order to the soldiers of his own army, the Argives did the like on their side.

---

1 Nauplia, called in our maps by its Turkish name *Anapli*, is still known by its ancient appellation among the Greeks.

2 Tiryns was situated at a short distance from Argos. [For a description of the ruins of Tiryns, consult Frazer's *Pausanias*, vol. iii. pp. 217 sqq. – E. H. B.]

3 Vide supra, ch. 19.

4 It is hopeless to attempt a rational explanation of this oracle, the obscurity of which gives it a special claim to be regarded as a genuine Pythian response. [Query: is it prophetic of Sparta's victory over Argos? – E. H. B.]

78. Now when Cleomenes heard that the Argives were acting thus, he commanded his troops that, so soon as the herald gave the word for the soldiers to go to dinner, they should instantly seize their arms and charge the host of the enemy. Which the Lacedæmonians did accordingly, and fell upon the Argives just as, following the signal, they had begun their repast; whereby it came to pass that vast numbers of the Argives were slain, while the rest, who were more than they which died in the fight, were driven to take refuge in the grove of Argus hard by, where they were surrounded, and watch kept upon them.

79. When things were at this pass Cleomenes acted as follows: Having learnt the names of the Argives who were shut up in the sacred precinct from certain deserters who had come over to him, he sent a herald to summon them one by one, on pretence of having received their ransoms. Now the ransom of prisoners among the Peloponnesians is fixed at two minæ the man. So Cleomenes had these persons called forth severally, to the number of fifty, or thereabouts, and massacred them. All this while they who remained in the enclosure knew nothing of what was happening; for the grove was so thick that the people inside were unable to see what was taking place without. But at last one of their number climbed up into a tree and spied the treachery; after which none of those who were summoned would go forth.

80. Then Cleomenes ordered all the helots to bring brushwood, and heap it around the grove; which was done accordingly; and Cleomenes set the grove on fire. As the flames spread he asked a deserter "Who was the god of the grove?" whereto the other made answer, "Argus." So he, when he heard that, uttered a loud groan, and said –

"Greatly hast thou deceived me, Apollo, god of prophecy, in saying that I should take Argos. I fear me thy oracle has now got its accomplishment."

81. Cleomenes now sent home the greater part of his army, while with a thousand of his best troops he proceeded to the temple of Hera,[1] to offer sacrifice. When however he would have slain the victim on the altar himself, the priest forbade him, as it was not lawful (he said) for a foreigner to sacrifice in that temple. At this Cleomenes ordered his helots to drag the priest

1 This temple, one of the most famous in antiquity, was near Argos. [Discovered 1831. See Frazer's *Pausanias*, vol. iii. pp. 165–185. – E. H. B.]

from the altar and scourge him, while he performed the sacrifice himself, after which he went back to Sparta.

82. Thereupon his enemies brought him up before the Ephors, and made it a charge against him that he had allowed himself to be bribed, and on that account had not taken Argos when he might have captured it easily. To this he answered – whether truly or falsely I cannot say with certainty – but at any rate his answer to the charge was, that "so soon as he discovered the sacred precinct which he had taken to belong to Argus, he directly imagined that the oracle had received its accomplishment; he therefore thought it not good to attempt the town, at the least until he had inquired by sacrifice, and ascertained if the god meant to grant him the place, or was determined to oppose his taking it. So he offered in the temple of Hera, and when the omens were propitious, immediately there flashed forth a flame of fire from the breast of the image; whereby he knew of a surety that he was not to take Argos. For if the flash had come from the head, he would have gained the town, citadel and all; but as it shone from the breast, he had done so much as the god intended." And his words seemed to the Spartans so true and reasonable, that he came clear off from his adversaries.

83. Argos however was left so bare of men, that the slaves managed the state, filled the offices, and administered everything until the sons of those who were slain by Cleomenes grew up. Then these latter cast out the slaves, and got the city back under their own rule; while the slaves who had been driven out fought a battle and won Tiryns. After this for a time there was peace between the two; but a certain man, a soothsayer, named Cleander, who was by race a Phigalean[1] from Arcadia, joined himself to the slaves, and stirred them up to make a fresh attack upon their lords. Then were they at war with one another by the space of many years; but at length the Argives with much trouble gained the upper hand.

84. The Argives say that Cleomenes lost his senses, and died so miserably, on account of these doings. But his own countrymen declare that his madness proceeded not from any supernatural cause whatever, but only from the habit of drinking wine unmixed with water, which he learnt of the Scyths. These nomads, from the time that Darius made his inroad into their

---

1 Phigalea was an Arcadian town.

country, had always had a wish for revenge. They therefore sent ambassadors to Sparta to conclude a league, proposing to endeavour themselves to enter Media by the Phasis, while the Spartans should march inland from Ephesus, and then the two armies should join together in one. When the Scyths came to Sparta on this errand Cleomenes was with them continually; and growing somewhat too familiar, learnt of them to drink his wine without water, a practice which is thought by the Spartans to have caused his madness. From this distance of time the Spartans, according to their own account, have been accustomed, when they want to drink purer wine than common, to give the order to fill "Scythian fashion." The Spartans then speak thus concerning Cleomenes; but for my own part I think his death was a judgment on him for wronging Demaratus.

85. No sooner did the news of Cleomenes' death reach Egina than straightway the Eginetans sent ambassadors to Sparta to complain of the conduct of Leotychides in respect of their hostages, who were still kept at Athens. So they of Lacedæmon assembled a court of justice and gave sentence upon Leotychides, that whereas he had grossly affronted the people of Egina, he should be given up to the ambassadors, to be led away in place of the men whom the Athenians had in their keeping. Then the ambassadors were about to lead him away; but Theasides, the son of Leoprepes, who was a man greatly esteemed in Sparta, interfered, and said to them –

"What are ye minded to do, ye men of Egina? To lead away captive the king of the Spartans, whom his countrymen have given into your hands? Though now in their anger they have passed this sentence, yet belike the time will come when they will punish you, if you act thus, by bringing utter destruction upon your country."

The Eginetans, when they heard this, changed their plan, and, instead of leading Leotychides away captive, agreed with him that he should come with them to Athens, and give them back their men.

86. When however he reached that city, and demanded the restoration of his pledge, the Athenians, being unwilling to comply, proceeded to make excuses, saying, "that two kings had come and left the men with them, and they did not think it right to give them back to the one without the other." So when the Athenians refused plainly to restore the men, Leotychides said to them –

"Men of Athens, act which way you choose – give me up the hostages, and be righteous, or keep them, and be the contrary. I wish, however, to tell you what happened once in Sparta about a pledge. The story goes among us that three generations back there lived in Lacedæmon one Glaucus, the son of Epicydes, a man who in every other respect was on a par with the first in the kingdom, and whose character for justice was such as to place him above all the other Spartans. Now to this man at the appointed season the following events happened. A certain Milesian came to Sparta and having desired to speak with him, said, – 'I am of Miletus, and I have come hither, Glaucus, in the hope of profiting by thy honesty. For when I heard much talk thereof in Ionia and through all the rest of Greece, and when I observed that whereas Ionia is always insecure, the Peloponnese stands firm and unshaken, and noted likewise how wealth is continually changing hands in our country, I took counsel with myself and resolved to turn one-half of my substance into money, and place it in thy hands, since I am well assured that it will be safe in thy keeping. Here then is the silver – take it – and take likewise these tallies, and be careful of them; remember thou art to give back the money to the person who shall bring you their fellows.' Such were the words of the Milesian stranger; and Glaucus took the deposit on the terms expressed to him. Many years had gone by when the sons of the man by whom the money was left came to Sparta, and had an interview with Glaucus, whereat they produced the tallies, and asked to have the money returned to them. But Glaucus sought to refuse, and answered them: 'I have no recollection of the matter; nor can I bring to mind any of those particulars whereof ye speak. When I remember, I will certainly do what is just. If I had the money, you have a right to receive it back; but if it was never given to me, I shall put the Greek law in force against you. For the present I give you no answer; but four months hence I will settle the business.' So the Milesians went away sorrowful, considering that their money was utterly lost to them. As for Glaucus, he made a journey to Delphi, and there consulted the oracle. To his question if he should swear,[1] and so make prize of the money, the Pythoness returned for answer these lines following:—

1 The Greek law allowed an accused person, with the consent of the accuser, to clear himself of a crime imputed to him, by taking an oath that the charge was false.

'Best for the present it were, O Glaucus, to do as thou wishest,
Swearing an oath to prevail, and so to make prize of the money.
Swear then – death is the lot e'en of those who never swear
  falsely.
Yet hath the Oath-God a son who is nameless, footless, and
  handless;
Mighty in strength he approaches to vengeance, and whelms in
  destruction
All who belong to the race, or the house of the man who is
  perjured.
But oath-keeping men leave behind them a flourishing offspring.'

Glaucus when he heard these words earnestly besought the god
to pardon his question; but the Pythoness replied that it was as
bad to have tempted the god as it would have been to have done
the deed. Glaucus, however, sent for the Milesian strangers, and
gave them back their money. And now I will tell you, Athenians,
what my purpose has been in recounting to you this history.
Glaucus at the present time has not a single descendant; nor is
there any family known as his – root and branch has he been
removed from Sparta. It is a good thing, therefore, when a
pledge has been left with one, not even in thought to doubt
about restoring it."

Thus spake Leotychides; but, as he found that the Athenians
would not hearken to him, he left them and went his way.

87. The Eginetans had never been punished for the wrongs
which, to pleasure the Thebans, they had committed upon Athens.[1]
Now, however, conceiving that they were themselves wronged, and
had a fair ground of complaint against the Athenians, they instantly
prepared to revenge themselves. As it chanced that the Athenian
Theôris,[2] which was a vessel of five banks of oars, lay at Sunium,[3]
the Eginetans contrived an ambush, and made themselves masters of the holy vessel, on board of which were a number of
Athenians of the highest rank, whom they took and threw into
prison.

88. At this outrage the Athenians no longer delayed, but set
to work to scheme their worst against the Eginetans; and, as

1 Vide supra, v. 81, 89.

2 The Athenian *theôris* was the ship which conveyed the sacred messengers
(θεωροί) to Delos.

3 The situation of Sunium was on the extreme southern promontory of
Attica.

there was in Egina at that time a man of mark, Nicodromus by name, the son of Cnœthus, who was on ill terms with his countrymen because on a former occasion they had driven him into banishment, they listened to overtures from this man, who had heard how determined they were to do the Eginetans a mischief, and agreed with him that on a certain day he should be ready to betray the island into their hands, and they would come with a body of troops to his assistance. And Nicodromus, some time after, holding to the agreement, made himself master of what is called the old town.

89. The Athenians, however, did not come to the day; for their own fleet was not of force sufficient to engage the Eginetans, and while they were begging the Corinthians to lend them some ships, the failure of the enterprise took place. In those days the Corinthians were on the best of terms with the Athenians; and accordingly they now yielded to their request, and furnished them with twenty ships; but, as their law did not allow the ships to be given for nothing, they sold them to the Athenians for five drachms a-piece.[1] As soon then as the Athenians had obtained this aid, and, by manning also their own ships, had equipped a fleet of seventy sail,[2] they crossed over to Egina, but arrived a day later than the time agreed upon.

90. Meanwhile Nicodromus, when he found the Athenians did not come to the time appointed, took ship and made his escape from the island. The Eginetans who accompanied him were settled by the Athenians at Sunium, whence they were wont to issue forth and plunder the Eginetans of the island. But this took place at a later date.

91. When the wealthier Eginetans had thus obtained the victory over the common people who had revolted with Nicodromus,[3] they laid hands on a certain number of them, and led them out to death. But here they were guilty of a sacrilege, which, notwithstanding all their efforts, they were never able to atone,

---

1 In this way the letter of the law was satisfied, at an expense to the Athenians of 100 drachms (about £4 of our money).

2 Thus it appears that Athens at this time maintained a fleet of 50 ships.

3 In Egina, as in most Dorian states, the constitution was oligarchical. The Athenians, it appears, took advantage of this circumstance, and sought to bring about a revolution, which would have thrown the island, practically, into their hands. This is the first instance of *revolutionary* war in which Athens is known to have engaged.

being driven from the island before they had appeased the goddess whom they now provoked. Seven hundred of the common people had fallen alive into their hands; and they were all being led out to death, when one of them escaped from his chains, and flying to the gateway of the temple of Demeter the Lawgiver,[1] laid hold of the door-handles, and clung to them. The others sought to drag him from his refuge; but, finding themselves unable to tear him away, they cut off his hands, and so took him, leaving the hands still tightly grasping the handles.

92. Such were the doings of the Eginetans among themselves. When the Athenians arrived, they went out to meet them with seventy ships; and a battle took place, wherein the Eginetans suffered a defeat. Hereupon they had recourse again to their old allies,[2] the Argives; but these latter refused now to lend them any aid, being angry because some Eginetan ships, which Cleomenes had taken by force, accompanied him in his invasion of Argolis, and joined in the disembarkation. The same thing had happened at the same time with certain vessels of the Sicyonians; and the Argives had laid a fine of a thousand talents upon the misdoers, five hundred upon each: whereupon they of Sicyon acknowledged themselves to have sinned, and agreed with the Argives to pay them a hundred talents,[3] and so be quit of the debt; but the Eginetans would make no acknowledgment at all, and showed themselves proud and stiff-necked. For this reason, when they now prayed the Argives for aid, the state refused to send them a single soldier. Notwithstanding, volunteers joined them from Argos to the number of a thousand, under a captain, Eurybates, a man skilled in the pentathlic contests.[4] Of these men the greater part never returned, but were slain by the Athenians in Egina. Eurybates, their captain, fought a number of single combats, and, after killing three men in this way, was himself slain by the fourth, who was a Decelean,[5] named Sôphanes.

1 In whose honour the feast of the Thesmophoria was celebrated in almost all parts of Greece.

2 Supra, v. 86.

3 A sum exceeding £24,000 of our money.

4 The πένταθλον, or contest of five games, consisted of the five sports of leaping, running, throwing the quoit or discus, hurling the spear, and wrestling.

5 Decelêa was situated on the mountain-range north of Athens (Parnes), within sight of the city.

93. Afterwards the Eginetans fell upon the Athenian fleet when it was in some disorder and beat it, capturing four ships with their crews.

94. Thus did war rage between the Eginetans and Athenians. Meantime the Persian pursued his own design, from day to day exhorted by his servant to "remember the Athenians,"[1] and likewise urged continually by the Pisistratidæ, who were ever accusing their countrymen. Moreover it pleased him well to have a pretext for carrying war into Greece, that so he might reduce all those who had refused to give him earth and water. As for Mardonius, since his expedition had succeeded so ill, Darius took the command of the troops from him, and appointed other generals in his stead, who were to lead the host against Eretria and Athens; to wit, Datis, who was by descent a Mede, and Artaphernes, the son of Artaphernes, his own nephew. These men received orders to carry Athens and Eretria away captive, and to bring the prisoners into his presence.

95. So the new commanders took their departure from the court and went down to Cilicia, to the Aleïan plain, having with them a numerous and well-appointed land army. Encamping here, they were joined by the sea force which had been required of the several states, and at the same time by the horse-transports which Darius had, the year before, commanded his tributaries to make ready.[2] Aboard these the horses were embarked; and the troops were received by the ships of war; after which the whole fleet, amounting in all to six hundred triremes, made sail for Ionia. Thence, instead of proceeding with a straight course along the shore to the Hellespont and to Thrace, they loosed from Samos and voyaged across the Icarian sea[3] through the midst of the islands; mainly, as I believe, because they feared the danger of doubling Mount Athos, where the year before they had suffered so grievously on their passage; but a constraining cause also was their former failure to take Naxos.[4]

96. When the Persians, therefore, approaching from the Icarian sea, cast anchor at Naxos, which, recollecting what there

---

1 Supra, v. 105.

2 Supra, ch. 48.

3 The Icarian sea received its name from the island of Icaria (now *Nikaria*), which lay between Samos and Myconus.

4 Supra. v. 34.

befell them formerly, they had determined to attack before any other state, the Naxians, instead of encountering them, took to flight, and hurried off to the hills. The Persians however succeeded in laying hands on some, and them they carried away captive, while at the same time they burnt all the temples together with the town. This done, they left Naxos, and sailed away to the other islands.

97. While the Persians were thus employed, the Delians likewise quitted Delos, and took refuge in Tenos.[1] And now the expedition drew near, when Datis sailed forward in advance of the other ships; commanding them, instead of anchoring at Delos, to rendezvous at Rhênea, over against Delos, while he himself proceeded to discover whither the Delians had fled; after which he sent a herald to them with this message:–

"Why are ye fled, O holy men? Why have ye judged me so harshly and so wrongfully? I have surely sense enough, even had not the king so ordered, to spare the country which gave birth to the two gods, – to spare, I say, both the country and its inhabitants. Come back therefore to your dwellings; and once more inhabit your island."

Such was the message which Datis sent by his herald to the Delians. He likewise placed upon the altar three hundred talents' weight of frankincense, and offered it.

98. After this he sailed with his whole host against Eretria, taking with him both Ionians and Æolians. When he was departed, Delos (as the Delians told me) was shaken by an earthquake, the first and last shock that has been felt to this day.[2] And truly this was a prodigy whereby the god warned men of the evils that were coming upon them. For in the three following generations of Darius the son of Hystaspes, Xerxes the son of Darius, and Artaxerxes the son of Xerxes, more woes befell Greece than in the twenty generations preceding Darius;– woes caused in part by the Persians, but in part arising from the contentions among their own chief men respecting the supreme power. Wherefore it is not surprising that Delos,

1 Tenos (the modern *Tino*) was distant about 13 miles from Delos, in a direction almost due north.

2 The Delians, whose holy island was believed to be specially exempt from earthquakes, thought it to the credit of their god, that he should mark by such a prodigy the beginning of a great war.

though it had never before been shaken, should at that time have felt the shock of an earthquake. And indeed there was an oracle, which said of Delos –

"Delos' self will I shake, which never yet has been shaken."

Of the above names Darius may be rendered "Worker," Xerxes "Warrior," and Artaxerxes "Great Warrior." And so might we call these kings in our own language with propriety.

99. The barbarians, after loosing from Delos, proceeded to touch at the other islands, and took troops from each,[1] and likewise carried off a number of the children as hostages. Going thus from one to another, they came at last to Carystus;[2] but here the hostages were refused by the Carystians, who said they would neither give any, nor consent to bear arms against the cities of their neighbours, meaning Athens and Eretria. Hereupon the Persians laid siege to Carystus, and wasted the country round, until at length the inhabitants were brought over and agreed to do what was required of them.

100. Meanwhile the Eretrians, understanding that the Persian armament was coming against them, besought the Athenians for assistance. Nor did the Athenians refuse their aid, but assigned to them as auxiliaries the four thousand landholders to whom they had allotted the estates of the Chalcidean Hippobatæ.[3] At Eretria, however, things were in no healthy state; for though they had called in the aid of the Athenians, yet they were not agreed among themselves how they should act; some of them were minded to leave the city and to take refuge in the heights of Eubœa, while others, who looked to receiving a reward from the Persians, were making ready to betray their country. So when these things came to the ears of Æschines, the son of Nothon, one of the first men in Eretria, he made known the whole state of affairs to the Athenians who were already arrived, and besought them to return home to their own land, and not perish with his countrymen. And the Athenians hearkened to his counsel, and, crossing over to Orôpus, in this way escaped the danger.

---

1 Vide infra, ch. 133.
2 Carystus was one of the four principal cities of the ancient Eubœa (the *Egripo* of our maps).
3 Supra, v. 77.

101. The Persian fleet now drew near and anchored at Tamy-næ, Chœreæ, and Ægilia, three places in the territory of Eretria. Once masters of these posts, they proceeded forthwith to disembark their horses, and made ready to attack the enemy. But the Eretrians were not minded to sally forth and offer battle; their only care, after it had been resolved not to quit the city, was, if possible, to defend their walls. And now the fortress was assaulted in good earnest, and for six days there fell on both sides vast numbers, but on the seventh day Euphorbus, the son of Alcimachus, and Philagrus, the son of Cyneas, who were both citizens of good repute, betrayed the place to the Persians. These were no sooner entered within the walls than they plundered and burnt all the temples that there were in the town, in revenge for the burning of their own temples at Sardis; moreover, they did according to the orders of Darius, and carried away captive all the inhabitants.

102. The Persians, having thus brought Eretria into subjection after waiting a few days, made sail for Attica, greatly straitening the Athenians as they approached, and thinking to deal with them as they had dealt with the people of Eretria. And, because there was no place in all Attica so convenient for their horse as Marathon, and it lay moreover quite close to Eretria, therefore Hippias, the son of Pisistratus, conducted them thither.

103. When intelligence of this reached the Athenians, they likewise marched their troops to Marathon, and there stood on the defensive, having at their head ten generals,[1] of whom one was Miltiades.

Now this man's father, Cimon, the son of Stesagoras, was banished from Athens by Pisistratus, the son of Hippocrates. In his banishment it was his fortune to win the four-horse chariot-race at Olympia, whereby he gained the very same honour which had before been carried off by Miltiades,[2] his half-brother on the mother's side. At the next Olympiad he won the prize again with

1 The Ten Generals (Strategi) are a part of the constitution of Clisthenes, who modelled the Athenian army upon the political division of the tribes. Each tribe annually elected its Phylarch to command its contingent of cavalry, its Taxiarch to command its infantry, and its Strategus to direct both. Hence the *ten* Strategi, who seem immediately to have claimed equality with the Polemarch or War-Archon. [Note:– The Strategi were *elected*, unlike the Members of the Senate (Boulé), who were appointed by *lot*. – E. H. B.]

2 Miltiades, the son of Cypselus, the first king of the Chersonese.

the same mares; upon which he caused Pisistratus to be proclaimed the winner, having made an agreement with him that on
yielding him this honour he should be allowed to come back to
his country. Afterwards, still with the same mares, he won the
prize a third time; whereupon he was put to death by the sons
of Pisistratus, whose father was no longer living. They set men
to lie in wait for him secretly; and these men slew him near the
government-house in the night-time. He was buried outside the
city, beyond what is called the Valley Road; and right opposite
his tomb were buried the mares which had won the three prizes.
The same success had likewise been achieved once previously,
to wit, by the mares of Evagoras the Lacedæmonian, but never
except by them. At the time of Cimon's death Stesagoras, the
elder of his two sons, was in the Chersonese, where he lived with
Miltiades his uncle; the younger, who was called Miltiades after
the founder of the Chersonesite colony, was with his father in
Athens.

104. It was this Miltiades who now commanded the Athenians, after escaping from the Chersonese, and twice nearly
losing his life. First he was chased as far as Imbrus by the
Phœnicians,[1] who had a great desire to take him and carry him
up to the king; and when he had avoided this danger, and, having
reached his own country, thought himself to be altogether in
safety, he found his enemies waiting for him, and was cited by
them before a court and impeached for his tyranny in the Chersonese. But he came off victorious here likewise, and was thereupon made general of the Athenians by the free choice of the
people.

105. And first, before they left the city, the generals sent off
to Sparta a herald, one Pheidippides,[2] who was by birth an
Athenian, and by profession and practice a trained runner. This
man, according to the account which he gave to the Athenians
on his return, when he was near Mount Parthenium, above
Tegea, fell in with the god Pan, who called him by his name, and
bade him ask the Athenians "wherefore they neglected him so
entirely, when he was kindly disposed towards them, and had
often helped them in times past, and would do so again in time
to come?" The Athenians, entirely believing in the truth of this

1 Supra, ch. 41.
2 [See Browning's poem "Pheidippides" in his *Dramatic Idylls*. – E. H. B.]

report, as soon as their affairs were once more in good order, set up a temple to Pan under the Acropolis,[1] and, in return for the message which I have recorded, established in his honour yearly sacrifices and a torch-race.

106. On the occasion of which we speak, when Pheidippides was sent by the Athenian generals, and, according to his own account, saw Pan on his journey, he reached Sparta on the very next day after quitting the city of Athens.[2] Upon his arrival he went before the rulers, and said to them –

"Men of Lacedæmon, the Athenians beseech you to hasten to their aid, and not allow that state, which is the most ancient[3] in all Greece, to be enslaved by the barbarians. Eretria, look you, is already carried away captive; and Greece weakened by the loss of no mean city."

Thus did Pheidippides deliver the message committed to him. And the Spartans wished to help the Athenians, but were unable to give them any present succour, as they did not like to break their established law. It was then the ninth day of the first decade;[4] and they could not march out of Sparta on the ninth, when the moon had not reached the full. So they waited for the full of the moon.

107. The barbarians were conducted to Marathon by Hippias, the son of Pisistratus, who the night before had seen a strange vision in his sleep. He dreamt of lying in his mother's arms, and conjectured the dream to mean that he would be restored to Athens, recover the power which he had lost, and afterwards live to a good old age in his native country. Such was the sense in which he interpreted the vision. He now proceeded to act as guide to the Persians; and, in the first place, he landed the prisoners taken from Eretria upon the island that is called

1 The temple or rather chapel of Pan was contained in a hollow in the rock just below the Propylæa, or entrance to the citadel. The cavern still exists. [Bury, *Hist. of Greece*, chap. vi. – E. H. B.]

2 Moderns estimate the direct distance at 135 or 140 miles.

3 It was the favourite boast of Athens that her inhabitants were αὐτόχθονες – sprung from the soil. Hence the adoption of the symbol of the grasshopper.

4 The Greeks divided their month of 29 or 30 days into three periods:– 1, from the 1st day to the 10th inclusively; 2, from the 11th to the 20th; and 3, from the 21st to the end. The ninth day of the first decade is thus the ninth day of the month itself.

Ægileia,[1] a tract belonging to the Styreans,[2] after which he brought the fleet to anchor off Marathon, and marshalled the bands of the barbarians as they disembarked. As he was thus employed it chanced that he sneezed and at the same time coughed with more violence than was his wont. Now, as he was a man advanced in years, and the greater number of his teeth were loose, it so happened that one of them was driven out with the force of the cough, and fell down into the sand. Hippias took all the pains he could to find it; but the tooth was nowhere to be seen: whereupon he fetched a deep sigh, and said to the bystanders –

"After all, the land is not ours; and we shall never be able to bring it under. All my share in it is the portion of which my tooth has possession."

So Hippias believed that in this way his dream was out.

108. The Athenians were drawn up in order of battle in a sacred close belonging to Heracles,[3] when they were joined by the Platæans, who came in full force to their aid. Some time before, the Platæans had put themselves under the rule of the Athenians; and these last had already undertaken many labours on their behalf. The occasion of the surrender was the following. The Platæans suffered grievous things at the hands of the men of Thebes; so, as it chanced that Cleomenes, the son of Anaxandridas, and the Lacedæmonians were in their neighbourhood, they first of all offered to surrender themselves to them. But the Lacedæmonians refused to receive them, and said –

"We dwell too far off from you, and ours would be but chill succour. Ye might oftentimes be carried into slavery before one of us heard of it. We counsel you rather to give yourselves up to the Athenians, who are your next neighbours, and well able to shelter you."

This they said, not so much out of good will towards the Platæans as because they wished to involve the Athenians in trouble by engaging them in wars with the Bœotians. The Platæans, however, when the Lacedæmonians gave them this counsel, complied at once; and when the sacrifice to the Twelve Gods

---

1 Between Eubœa and Attica.
2 Styra was a town of southern Eubœa.
3 Heracles was among the gods specially worshipped at Marathon.

was being offered at Athens, they came and sat as suppliants about the altar,[1] and gave themselves up to the Athenians. The Thebans no sooner learnt what the Platæans had done than instantly they marched out against them, while the Athenians sent troops to their aid. As the two armies were about to join battle, the Corinthians, who chanced to be at hand, would not allow them to engage; both sides consented to take them for arbitrators, whereupon they made up the quarrel, and fixed the boundary-line between the two states upon this condition: to wit, that if any of the Bœotians wished no longer to belong to Bœotia, the Thebans should allow them to follow their own inclinations. The Corinthians, when they had thus decreed, forthwith departed to their homes: the Athenians likewise set off on their return; but the Bœotians fell upon them during the march, and a battle was fought wherein they were worsted by the Athenians. Hereupon these last would not be bound by the line which the Corinthians had fixed, but advanced beyond those limits, and made the Asôpus[2] the boundary-line between the country of the Thebans and that of the Platæans and Hysians. Under such circumstances did the Platæans give themselves up to Athens; and now they were come to Marathon to bear the Athenians aid.

109. The Athenian generals were divided in their opinions; and some advised not to risk a battle, because they were too few to engage such a host as that of the Medes, while others were for fighting at once; and among these last was Miltiades. He therefore, seeing that opinions were thus divided, and that the less worthy counsel appeared likely to prevail, resolved to go to the polemarch, and have a conference with him. For the man on whom the lot fell to be polemarch[3] at Athens was entitled to give his vote with the ten generals, since anciently[4] the Athenians allowed him an equal right of voting with them. The polemarch at this juncture was Callimachus of Aphidnæ; to him therefore Miltiades went, and said:—

"With thee it rests, Callimachus, either to bring Athens to slavery, or, by securing her freedom, to leave behind thee to all

---

1 The altar of the Twelve Gods at Athens has been mentioned before (ii. 7). It was in the Agora.
2 The Asôpus is the modern *Vuriéni*, the great river of southern Bœotia.
3 The Polemarch, or War-Archon, was the third archon in dignity.
4 When Herodotus wrote, the polemarch had no military functions at all.

future generations a memory beyond even Harmodius and Aristogeiton. For never since the time that the Athenians became a people were they in so great a danger as now. If they bow their necks beneath the yoke of the Medes, the woes which they will have to suffer when given into the power of Hippias are already determined on; if, on the other hand, they fight and overcome, Athens may rise to be the very first city in Greece. How it comes to pass that these things are likely to happen, and how the determining of them in some sort rests with thee, I will now proceed to make clear. We generals are ten in number, and our votes are divided; half of us wish to engage, half to avoid a combat. Now, if we do not fight, I look to see a great disturbance at Athens which will shake men's resolutions, and then I fear they will submit themselves; but if we fight the battle before any unsoundness show itself among our citizens, let the gods but give us fair play, and we are well able to overcome the enemy. On thee therefore we depend in this matter, which lies wholly in thine own power. Thou hast only to add thy vote to my side and thy country will be free, and not free only, but the first state in Greece. Or, if thou preferrest to give thy vote to them who would decline the combat, then the reverse will follow."

110. Miltiades by these words gained Callimachus; and the addition of the polemarch's vote caused the decision to be in favour of fighting. Hereupon all those generals who had been desirous of hazarding a battle, when their turn came to command the army, gave up their right to Miltiades. He however, though he accepted their offers, nevertheless waited, and would not fight, until his own day of command arrived in due course.

111. Then at length, when his own turn was come, the Athenian battle was set in array, and this was the order of it. Callimachus the polemarch led the right wing; for it was at that time a rule with the Athenians to give the right wing to the polemarch.[1] After this followed the tribes, according as they were numbered, in an unbroken line; while last of all came the Platæans, forming the left wing. And ever since that day it has

---

1 The *right* wing was the special post of honour (vide infra, ix. 27). The Polemarch took the post as representative of the king, whose position it had been in the ancient times.

been a custom with the Athenians, in the sacrifices and assemblies held each fifth year at Athens,[1] for the Athenian herald to implore the blessing of the gods on the Platæans conjointly with the Athenians. Now, as they marshalled the host upon the field of Marathon, in order that the Athenian front might be of equal length with the Median, the ranks of the centre were diminished, and it became the weakest part of the line, while the wings were both made strong with a depth of many ranks.

112. So when the battle was set in array, and the victims showed themselves favourable, instantly the Athenians, so soon as they were let go, charged the barbarians at a run. Now the distance between the two armies was little short of eight furlongs. The Persians, therefore, when they saw the Greeks coming on at speed, made ready to receive them, although it seemed to them that the Athenians were bereft of their senses, and bent upon their own destruction; for they saw a mere handful of men coming on at a run without either horsemen or archers. Such was the opinion of the barbarians; but the Athenians in close array fell upon them, and fought in a manner worthy of being recorded. They were the first of the Greeks, so far as I know, who introduced the custom of charging the enemy at a run, and they were likewise the first who dared to look upon the Median garb, and to face men clad in that fashion. Until this time the very name of the Medes had been a terror to the Greeks to hear.

113. The two armies fought together on the plain of Marathon for a length of time; and in the mid battle, where the Persians themselves and the Sacæ had their place, the barbarians were victorious, and broke and pursued the Greeks into the inner country; but on the two wings the Athenians and the Platæans defeated the enemy. Having so done, they suffered the routed barbarians to fly at their ease, and joining the two wings in one, fell upon those who had broken their own centre, and fought and conquered them. These likewise fled, and now the Athenians hung upon the runaways and cut them down, chasing them all the way to the shore, on reaching which they laid hold of the ships and called aloud for fire.

1 The Panathenaic festival is probably intended. It was held every fifth year (i.e. once in every four years, half-way between the Olympic festivals), and was the great religious assembly of the Athenians.

114. It was in the struggle here that Callimachus the pole-march, after greatly distinguishing himself, lost his life; Stesilaüs too, the son of Thrasilaüs, one of the generals, was slain; and Cynægirus, the son of Euphorion, having seized on a vessel of the enemy's by the ornament at the stern,[1] had his hand cut off by the blow of an axe, and so perished; as likewise did many other Athenians of note and name.

115. Nevertheless the Athenians secured in this way seven of the vessels; while with the remainder the barbarians pushed off, and taking aboard their Eretrian prisoners from the island where they had left them, doubled Cape Sunium, hoping to reach Athens before the return of the Athenians. The Alcmæonidæ were accused by their countrymen of suggesting this course to them; they had, it was said, an understanding with the Persians, and made a signal to them, by raising a shield, after they were embarked in their ships.

116. The Persians accordingly sailed round Sunium. But the Athenians with all possible speed marched away to the defence of their city, and succeeded in reaching Athens before the appearance of the barbarians:[2] and as their camp at Marathon had been pitched in a precinct of Heracles, so now they encamped in another precinct of the same god at Cynosarges.[3] The barbarian fleet arrived, and lay to off Phalerum, which was at that time the haven of Athens;[4] but after resting awhile upon their oars, they departed and sailed away to Asia.

117. There fell in this battle of Marathon, on the side of the barbarians, about six thousand and four hundred men; on that of the Athenians, one hundred and ninety-two. Such was the number of the slain on the one side and the other. A strange prodigy likewise happened at this fight. Epizêlus, the son of Cuphagoras, an Athenian, was in the thick of the fray, and behaving himself as a brave man should, when suddenly he was

1 The ornament at the stern consisted of wooden planks curved gracefully in continuance of the sweep by which the stern of the ancient ship rose from the sea. Vessels were ordinarily ranged along a beach with their sterns towards the shore, and thus were liable to be seized by the stern-ornament. [See Rich, *Dict. of Antiquities.* – E. H. B.]

2 Marathon is six-and-twenty miles from Athens by the common route.

3 Supra, v. 63. Cynosarges was situated very near the famous Lycæum, the school of Aristotle.

4 Supra, v. 63.

stricken with blindness, without blow of sword or dart; and this blindness continued thenceforth during the whole of his after life. The following is the account which he himself, as I have heard, gave of the matter: he said that a gigantic warrior, with a huge beard, which shaded all his shield, stood over against him; but the ghostly semblance passed him by, and slew the man at his side. Such, as I understand, was the tale which Epizê-lus told.[1]

118. Datis meanwhile was on his way back to Asia, and had reached Myconus,[2] when he saw in his sleep a vision. What it was is not known; but no sooner was day come than he caused strict search to be made throughout the whole fleet, and finding on board a Phœnician vessel an image of Apollo overlaid with gold, he inquired from whence it had been taken, and learning to what temple it belonged, he took it with him in his own ship to Delos, and placed it in the temple there, enjoining the Delians, who had now come back to their island, to restore the image to the Theban Delium,[3] which lies on the coast over against Chalcis. Having left these injunctions, he sailed away; but the Delians failed to restore the statue; and it was not till twenty years after-wards that the Thebans, warned by an oracle, themselves brought it back to Delium.

119. As for the Eretrians, whom Datis and Artaphernes had carried away captive, when the fleet reached Asia, they were taken up to Susa. Now King Darius, before they were made his prisoners, nourished a fierce anger against these men for having injured him without provocation; but now that he saw them brought into his presence, and become his subjects, he did them no other harm, but only settled them at one of his own stations in Cissia — a place called Ardericca — two hundred and ten furlongs distant from Susa, and forty from the well which yields produce of three different kinds. For from this well they get bitumen, salt, and oil, procuring it in the way that I will now

---

1 According to Plutarch, Theseus was seen by a great number of the Athenians fighting on their side against the Persians.

2 It lies between Tenos (*Tino*) and Icaria (*Nikaria*).

3 This temple acquired a special celebrity from the defeat which the Athenians suffered in its neighbourhood in the eighth year of the Peloponnesian war, B.C. 424. The name of Delium is said to have been given to it because it was built after the model of Apollo's temple at Delos.

describe: They draw with a swipe, and instead of a bucket make use of the half of a wine-skin; with this the man dips, and after drawing, pours the liquid into a reservoir, wherefrom it passes into another, and there takes three different shapes. The salt and the bitumen forthwith collect and harden, while the oil is drawn off into casks. It is called by the Persians "rhadinacé," is black, and has an unpleasant smell. Here then King Darius established the Eretrians; and here they continued to my time, and still spoke their old language. So thus it fared with the Eretrians.

120. After the full of the moon two thousand Lacedæmonians came to Athens. So eager had they been to arrive in time, that they took but three days to reach Attica from Sparta. They came, however, too late for the battle; yet, as they had a longing to behold the Medes, they continued their march to Marathon and there viewed the slain. Then, after giving the Athenians all praise for their achievement, they departed and returned home.

121. But it fills me with wonderment, and I can in no wise believe the report, that the Alcmæonidæ had an understanding with the Persians, and held them up a shield as a signal, wishing Athens to be brought under the yoke of the barbarians and of Hippias, – the Alcmæonidæ, who have shown themselves at least as bitter haters of tyrants as was Callias, the son of Phænippus, and father of Hipponicus.[1] This Callias was the only person at Athens who, when the Pisistratidæ were driven out, and their goods were exposed for sale by the vote of the people, had the courage to make purchases, and likewise in many other ways to display the strongest hostility.

[122. He was a man very worthy to be had in remembrance by all, on several accounts. For not only did he thus distinguish himself beyond others in the cause of his country's freedom; but likewise, by the honours which he gained at the Olympic games, where he carried off the prize in the horse-race, and was second in the four-horse chariot-race, and by his victory at an earlier period in the Pythian games, he showed himself in the eyes of all the Greeks a man most unsparing in his expenditure. He was remarkable too for his conduct in respect of his daughters, three in number; for when they came to be of marriageable age, he gave to each of them a most ample dowry, and placed it at their own disposal, allowing them to choose their husbands from

---

1 Vide infra, vii. 151.

among all the citizens of Athens,[1] and giving each in marriage
to the man of her own choice.[2]]

123. Now the Alcmæonidæ fell not a whit short of this person in their hatred of tyrants, so that I am astonished at the
charge made against them, and cannot bring myself to believe
that they held up a shield; for they were men who had remained
in exile during the whole time that the tyranny lasted, and they
even contrived the trick by which the Pisistratidæ were deprived
of their throne.[3] Indeed I look upon them as the persons who
in good truth gave Athens her freedom far more than Harmodius and Aristogeiton.[4] For these last did but exasperate the
other Pisistratidæ by slaying Hipparchus,[5] and were far from
doing anything towards putting down the tyranny; whereas the
Alcmæonidæ were manifestly the actual deliverers of Athens, if
at least it be true that the Pythoness was prevailed upon by them
to bid the Lacedæmonians set Athens free, as I have already
related.

124. But perhaps they were offended with the people of
Athens; and therefore betrayed their country. Nay, but on the
contrary there were none of the Athenians who were held in
such general esteem, or who were so laden with honours. So that
it is not even reasonable to suppose that a shield was held up
by them on this account. A shield was shown, no doubt; that
cannot be gainsaid; but who it was that showed it I cannot any
further determine.

125. Now the Alcmæonidæ were, even in days of yore, a
family of note at Athens; but from the time of Alcmæon, and
again of Megacles, they rose to special eminence. The former of
these two personages, to wit, Alcmæon, the son of Megacles,
when Crœsus the Lydian sent men from Sardis to consult the
Delphic oracle, gave aid gladly to his messengers, and assisted
them to accomplish their task. Crœsus, informed of Alcmæon's
kindnesses by the Lydians who from time to time conveyed his

1 In general the Athenian ladies – indeed, the *Greek* ladies without exception
– were not even asked to give their consent to the match prepared for them.

2 This chapter is generally regarded as an interpolation. It is wanting in
several of the best MSS.

3 Supra, v. 63.

4 It is plain that Herodotus was of the same opinion as Thucydides (vi. 54–59),
that far too much honour was paid to the memory of these persons.

5 Supra, v. 55, 62.

messages to the god,[1] sent for him to Sardis, and when he arrived, made him a present of as much gold as he should be able to carry at one time about his person. Finding that this was the gift assigned him, Alcmæon took his measures, and prepared himself to receive it in the following way. He clothed himself in a loose tunic, which he made to bag greatly at the waist, and placing upon his feet the widest buskins that he could anywhere find, followed his guides into the treasure-house. Here he fell to upon a heap of gold-dust, and in the first place packed as much as he could inside his buskins, between them and his legs; after which he filled the breast of his tunic quite full of gold, and then sprinkling some among his hair, and taking some likewise in his mouth, he came forth from the treasure-house, scarcely able to drag his legs along, like anything rather than a man, with his mouth crammed full, and his bulk increased every way. On seeing him, Crœsus burst into a laugh, and not only let him have all that he had taken, but gave him presents besides of fully equal worth. Thus this house became one of great wealth; and Alcmæon was able to keep horses for the chariot-race, and won the prize at Olympia.[2]

126. Afterwards, in the generation which followed, Clisthenes, king of Sicyon, raised the family to still greater eminence among the Greeks than even that to which it had attained before. For this Clisthenes, who was the son of Aristonymus, the grandson of Myron, and the great-grandson of Andreas, had a daughter, called Agarista, whom he wished to marry to the best husband that he could find in the whole of Greece. At the Olympic games, therefore, having gained the prize in the chariot-race, he caused public proclamation to be made to the following effect:– "Whoever among the Greeks deems himself worthy to become the son-in-law of Clisthenes, let him come, sixty days hence, or, if he will, sooner, to Sicyon; for within a year's time, counting from the end of the sixty days, Clisthenes will decide on the man to whom he shall contract his daughter." So all the Greeks who were proud of their own merit or of their country flocked to Sicyon as suitors; and Clisthenes had a foot-course and a wrestling-ground made ready, to try their powers.

1 Supra, i. 55.
2 There are strong reasons for suspecting the whole of this story.

127. From Italy there came Smindyrides, the son of Hippo-crates, a native of Sybaris – which city about that time was at the very height of its prosperity. He was a man who in luxur-iousness of living exceeded all other persons. Likewise there came Damasus, the son of Amyris, surnamed the Wise, a native of Siris. These two were the only suitors from Italy. From the Ionian Gulf appeared Amphimnestus, the son of Epistrophus, an Epidamnian; from Ætolia Males, the brother of that Titormus who excelled all the Greeks in strength, and who wishing to avoid his fellow-men, withdrew himself into the remotest parts of the Ætolian territory. From the Peloponnese came several – Leocêdes, son of that Pheidon, king of the Argives, who estab-lished weights and measures throughout the Peloponnese, and was the most insolent of all the Grecians – the same who drove out the Elean directors of the games, and himself presided over the contests at Olympia – Leocêdes, I say, appeared, this Phei-don's son; and likewise Amiantus, son of Lycurgus, an Arcadian of the city of Trapezus; Laphanes, an Azenian of Pæus, whose father, Euphorion, as the story goes in Arcadia, entertained the Dioscuri[1] at his residence, and thenceforth kept open house for all comers; and lastly, Onomastus, the son of Agæus, a native of Elis. These four came from the Peloponnese. From Athens there arrived Megacles, the son of that Alcmæon who visited Crœsus, and Tisander's son, Hippoclides, the wealthiest and handsomest of the Athenians. There was likewise one Eubœan, Lysanias, who came from Eretria, then a flourishing city. From Thessaly came Diactorides, a Cranonian, of the race of the Scopadæ; and Alcon arrived from the Molossians. This was the list of the suitors.

128. Now when they were all come, and the day appointed had arrived, Clisthenes first of all inquired of each concerning his country and his family; after which he kept them with him a year, and made trial of their manly bearing, their temper, their accomplishments, and their disposition, sometimes drawing them apart for converse, sometimes bringing them all together. Such as were still youths he took with him from time to time to the gymnasia; but the greatest trial of all was at the banquet-table. During the whole period of their stay he lived with them as I

1 [Castor and Pollux, "the great twin brethren, to whom the Dorians pray." – E. H. B.]

have said; and, further, from first to last he entertained them sumptuously. Somehow or other the suitors who came from Athens pleased him the best of all; and of these Hippoclides, Tisander's son, was specially in favour, partly on account of his manly bearing, and partly also because his ancestors were of kin to the Corinthian Cypselids.

129. When at length the day arrived which had been fixed for the espousals, and Clisthenes had to speak out and declare his choice, he first of all made a sacrifice of a hundred oxen, and held a banquet, whereat he entertained all the suitors and the whole people of Sicyon. After the feast was ended, the suitors vied with each other in music and in speaking on a given subject. Presently, as the drinking advanced, Hippoclides, who quite dumbfoundered the rest, called aloud to the flute-player, and bade him strike up a dance; which the man did, and Hippoclides danced to it. And he fancied that he was dancing excellently well; but Clisthenes, who was observing him, began to misdoubt the whole business. Then Hippoclides, after a pause, told an attendant to bring in a table; and when it was brought, he mounted upon it and danced first of all some Laconian figures, then some Attic ones; after which he stood on his head upon the table, and began to toss his legs about. Clisthenes, notwithstanding that he now loathed Hippoclides for a son-in-law, by reason of his dancing and his shamelessness, still, as he wished to avoid an outbreak, had restrained himself during the first and likewise during the second dance; when, however, he saw him tossing his legs in the air, he could no longer contain himself, but cried out, "Son of Tisander, thou hast danced thy wife away!" "What does Hippoclides care?" was the other's answer. And hence the proverb arose.

130. Then Clisthenes commanded silence, and spake thus before the assembled company:—

"Suitors of my daughter, well pleased am I with you all; and right willingly, if it were possible, would I content you all, and not by making choice of one appear to put a slight upon the rest. But as it is out of my power, seeing that I have but one daughter, to grant to all their wishes, I will present to each of you whom I must needs dismiss a talent of silver, for the honour that you have done me in seeking to ally yourselves with my house, and for your long absence from your homes. But my daughter, Agarista, I betroth to Megacles, the son of Alcmæon, to be his wife, according to the usage and wont of Athens."

Then Megacles expressed his readiness; and Clisthenes had the marriage solemnised.

131. Thus ended the affair of the suitors; and thus the Alcmæonidæ came to be famous throughout the whole of Greece. The issue of this marriage was the Clisthenes – so named after his grandfather the Sicyonian – who made the tribes at Athens, and set up the popular government.[1] Megacles had likewise another son, called Hippocrates, whose children were a Megacles and an Agarista, the latter named after Agarista the daughter of Clisthenes. She married Xanthippus, the son of Ariphron; and when she was with child by him had a dream, wherein she fancied that she was delivered of a lion; after which, within a few days, she bore Xanthippus a son, to wit, Pericles.

132. After the blow struck at Marathon, Miltiades, who was previously held in high esteem by his countrymen, increased yet more in influence. Hence, when he told them that he wanted a fleet of seventy ships,[2] with an armed force, and money, without informing them what country he was going to attack, but only promising to enrich them if they would accompany him, seeing that it was a right wealthy land, where they might easily get as much gold as they cared to have – when he told them this, they were quite carried away, and gave him the whole armament which he required.

133. So Miltiades, having got the armament, sailed against Paros, with the object, as he alleged, of punishing the Parians for having gone to war with Athens, inasmuch as a trireme of theirs had come with the Persian fleet to Marathon. This, however, was a mere pretence; the truth was, that Miltiades owed the Parians a grudge, because Lysagoras, the son of Tisias, who was a Parian by birth, had told tales against him to Hydarnes the Persian. Arrived before the place against which his expedition was designed, he drove the Parians within their walls, and forthwith laid siege to the city. At the same time he sent a herald to the inhabitants, and required of them a hundred talents, threatening that, if they refused, he would press the siege, and never give it over till the town was taken. But the Parians,

---

1 Supra, v. 69.

2 Seventy ships appear to have been the full complement of the Athenian navy, until the time when the number was raised by Themistocles to 200 (vide supra, ch. 89, and infra, vii. 144). Miltiades therefore took the whole Athenian navy on this expedition.

without giving his demand a thought, proceeded to use every means that they could devise for the defence of their city, and even invented new plans for the purpose, one of which was, by working at night to raise such parts of the wall as were likely to be carried by assault to double their former height.

134. Thus far all the Greeks agree in their accounts of this business; what follows is related upon the testimony of the Parians only. Miltiades had come to his wit's end, when one of the prisoners, a woman named Timo, who was by birth a Parian, and had held the office of under-priestess in the temple of the infernal goddesses, came and conferred with him. This woman, they say, being introduced into the presence of Miltiades, advised him, if he set great store by the capture of the place, to do something which she could suggest to him. When therefore she had told him what it was she meant, he betook himself to the hill which lies in front of the city, and there leapt the fence enclosing the precinct of Demeter Thesmophorus,[1] since he was not able to open the door. After leaping into the place he went straight to the sanctuary, intending to do something within it – either to remove some of the holy things which it was not lawful to stir, or to perform some act or other, I cannot say what – and had just reached the door, when suddenly a feeling of horror came upon him,[2] and he returned back the way he had come; but in jumping down from the outer wall, he strained his thigh, or, as some say, struck the ground with his knee.

135. So Miltiades returned home sick, without bringing the Athenians any money, and without conquering Paros, having done no more than to besiege the town for six-and-twenty days, and ravage the remainder of the island. The Parians, however, when it came to their knowledge that Timo, the under-priestess of the goddesses, had advised Miltiades what he should do, were minded to punish her for her crime; they therefore sent messengers to Delphi, as soon as the siege was at an end, and asked the god if they should put the under-priestess to death. "She had discovered," they said, "to the enemies of her country how they might bring it into subjection, and had exhibited to Miltiades mysteries which it was not lawful for a man to know." But the

---

1 Supra, ch. 16.

2 He would feel that he was doing an act of great impiety, since the sanctuaries of Demeter were not to be entered by men.

Pythoness forbade them, and said, "Timo was not in fault; 'twas decreed that Miltiades should come to an unhappy end; and she was sent to lure him to his destruction." Such was the answer given to the Parians by the Pythoness.

136. The Athenians, upon the return of Miltiades from Paros, had much debate concerning him; and Xanthippus, the son of Ariphron, who spoke more freely against him than all the rest, impleaded him before the people, and brought him to trial for his life, on the charge of having dealt deceitfully with the Athenians. Miltiades, though he was present in court, did not speak in his own defence; for his thigh had begun to mortify, and disabled him from pleading his cause. He was forced to lie on a couch while his defence was made by his friends, who dwelt at most length on the fight at Marathon, while they made mention also of the capture of Lemnos, telling how Miltiades took the island, and, after executing vengeance on the Pelasgians, gave up his conquest to Athens. The judgment of the people was in his favour so far as to spare his life; but for the wrong he had done them they fined him fifty talents.[1] Soon afterwards his thigh completely gangrened and mortified: and so Miltiades died; and the fifty talents were paid by his son Cimon.

137. Now the way in which Miltiades had made himself master of Lemnos was the following. There were certain Pelasgians whom the Athenians once drove out of Attica; whether they did it justly or unjustly I cannot say, since I only know what is reported concerning it, which is the following: Hecatæus, the son of Hegesander, says in his History that it was unjustly. "The Athenians," according to him, "had given to the Pelasgi a tract of land at the foot of Hymettus as payment for the wall with which the Pelasgians had surrounded their citadel. This land was barren, and little worth at the time; but the Pelasgians brought it into good condition; whereupon the Athenians begrudged them the tract, and desired to recover it. And so, without any better excuse, they took arms and drove out the Pelasgians." But the Athenians maintain that they were justified in what they did. "The Pelasgians," they say, "while they lived at the foot of Hymettus, were wont to sally forth from that region and commit outrages on their children. For the Athenians used at that time to send their sons and daughters to draw water at the fountain

---

1 Fifty talents (above £12,000) is certainly an enormous sum for the time.

called 'the Nine Springs,' inasmuch as neither they nor the other
Greeks had any household slaves in those days; and the maidens,
whenever they came, were used rudely and insolently by the
Pelasgians. Nor were they even content thus; but at the last they
laid a plot, and were caught by the Athenians in the act of
making an attempt upon their city. Then did the Athenians give
a proof how much better men they were than the Pelasgians; for
whereas they might justly have killed them all, having caught
them in the very act of rebelling, they spared their lives, and only
required that they should leave the country. Hereupon the
Pelasgians quitted Attica, and settled in Lemnos and other
places." Such are the accounts respectively of Hecatæus and the
Athenians.

138. These same Pelasgians, after they were settled in Lemnos, conceived the wish to be revenged on the Athenians. So,
as they were well acquainted with the Athenian festivals, they
manned some penteconters, and having laid an ambush to catch
the Athenian women as they kept the festival of Artemis at Brauron,[1] they succeeded in carrying off a large number, whom they
took to Lemnos and there kept as concubines. After a while the
women bore children, whom they taught to speak the language
of Attica and observe the manners of the Athenians. These boys
refused to have any commerce with the sons of the Pelasgian
women; and if a Pelasgian boy struck one of their number, they
all made common cause, and joined in avenging their comrade;
nay, the Greek boys even set up a claim to exercise lordship over
the others, and succeeded in gaining the upper hand. When these
things came to the ears of the Pelasgians, they took counsel
together, and, on considering the matter, they grew frightened,
and said one to another, "If these boys even now are resolved
to make common cause against the sons of our lawful wives, and
seek to exercise lordship over them, what may we expect when
they grow up to be men?" Then it seemed good to the Pelasgians
to kill all the sons of the Attic women; which they did accordingly,

---

1 Brauron, as is sufficiently evident from this place, was one of the
maritime demes of Attica. The Brauronia was a festival held once in four years,
wherein the Attic girls, between the ages of five and ten, went in procession,
dressed in crocus-coloured garments, to the sanctuary, and there performed a
rite wherein they imitated bears. No Attic woman was allowed to marry till she
had gone through this ceremony.

and at the same time slew likewise their mothers. From this deed, and that former crime of the Lemnian women, when they slew their husbands in the days of Thoas,[1] it has come to be usual throughout Greece to call wicked actions by the name of "Lemnian deeds."

139. When the Pelasgians had thus slain their children and their women, the earth refused to bring forth its fruits for them, and their wives bore fewer children, and their flocks and herds increased more slowly than before, till at last, sore pressed by famine and bereavement, they sent men to Delphi, and begged the god to tell them how they might obtain deliverance from their sufferings. The Pythoness answered, that "they must give the Athenians whatever satisfaction they might demand." Then the Pelasgians went to Athens and declared their wish to give the Athenians satisfaction for the wrong which they had done to them. So the Athenians had a couch prepared in their town-hall, and adorned it with the fairest coverlets, and set by its side a table laden with all manner of good things, and then told the Pelasgians they must deliver up their country to them in a similar condition. The Pelasgians answered and said, "When a ship comes with a north wind from your country to ours in a single day, then will we give it up to you." This they said because they knew that what they required was impossible, for Attica lies a long way to the south of Lemnos.[2]

140. No more passed at that time. But very many years afterwards, when the Hellespontian Chersonese had been brought under the power of Athens, Miltiades, the son of Cimon, sailed, during the prevalence of the Etesian winds, from Elæus in the Chersonese to Lemnos, and called on the Pelasgians to quit their island, reminding them of the prophecy which they had supposed it impossible to fulfil. The people of Hephæstia obeyed the call; but they of Myrina, not acknowledging the Chersonese to be any part of Attica, refused and were besieged and brought

1 The tale went that the Sintian Lemnians, the original inhabitants of the island, having become disgusted with their wives, on whom Aphrodite had sent a curse, married Thracian women from the continent. Hereupon their wives formed a conspiracy, and murdered their fathers and their husbands. Hypsipylé alone had compassion on her father Thoas, and concealed him. Her fraud was afterwards detected; Thoas was killed, and Hypsipylé sold into slavery.

2 Lemnos is nearly 140 miles north of Attica.

over by force. Thus was Lemnos gained by the Athenians and Miltiades.

ADDED NOTE ON THE BATTLE OF MARATHON:
BY THE EDITOR

The importance of the battle of Marathon can hardly be overestimated. The success of the Athenians inspired Greece to gird herself to withstand the later (and greater) invasion of Xerxes. It is one of those victories upon which the destinies of nations have hinged. But, apart from this aspect of the battle, we do well to remember that the great democracy of Athens was baptised, if it was not born, on that immortal field. Rightly did the Athenians regard Marathon as marking a decisive epoch in her history. "It was as if on that day the Gods had said to them: Go on and prosper."

For further information the student is referred to the histories of Thirlwall and of Grote. In Prof. Strachan's edition of the sixth book of Herodotus, a careful account of the battle is given (Appendix i.; see the map). Creasy, in his *Decisive Battles of the World*, supplies a popular description.

What Trafalgar and Waterloo have been to modern Europe, that – and more – Marathon and Salamis proved to the ancient world. Whereas in the former case, the sea-victory preceded the land-victory, in the latter the position is reversed. It is a curious coincidence that, in both these world struggles, a period of just ten years separated the naval and the land battles (B.C. 490 and 480; A.D. 1805, and 1815).

THE SEVENTH BOOK,
ENTITLED POLYMNIA

1. NOW when tidings of the battle that had been fought at Marathon reached the ears of King Darius, the son of Hystaspes, his anger against the Athenians, which had been already roused by their attack upon Sardis,[1] waxed still fiercer, and he became more than ever eager to lead an army against Greece. Instantly he sent off messengers to make proclamation through the several states, that fresh levies were to be raised, and these at an increased rate; while ships, horses, provisions, and transports were likewise to be furnished. So the men published his commands; and now all Asia was in commotion by the space of three years, while everywhere, as Greece was to be attacked, the best and bravest were enrolled for the service, and had to make their preparations accordingly.

After this, in the fourth year,[2] the Egyptians whom Cambyses had enslaved revolted from the Persians; whereupon Darius was more hot for war than ever,[3] and earnestly desired to march an army against both adversaries.

2. Now, as he was about to lead forth his levies against Egypt and Athens, a fierce contention for the sovereign power arose among his sons; since the law of the Persians was, that a king must not go out with his army, until he has appointed one to succeed him upon the throne.[4] Darius, before he obtained the kingdom, had had three sons born to him from his former wife, who was a daughter of Gobryas; while, since he began to reign, Atossa, the daughter of Cyrus, had borne him four. Artabazanes was the eldest of the first family, and Xerxes of the second. These two, therefore, being the sons of different mothers, were now at·variance. Artabazanes claimed the crown as the eldest of all the children, because it was an established custom all over the

1 Supra, v. 100–102.

2 B.C. 487. The reckoning is inclusive, as usual.

3 Probably the revolt of Egypt was attributed to the machinations of the Greeks.

4 An allusion to this custom is made in the first book (ch. 208), in connection with the expedition of Cyrus against the Massagetæ.

world for the eldest to have the pre-eminence; while Xerxes, on the other hand, urged that he was sprung from Atossa, the daughter of Cyrus, and that it was Cyrus who had won the Persians their freedom.[1]

3. Before Darius had pronounced on the matter, it happened that Demaratus, the son of Ariston, who had been deprived of his crown at Sparta, and had afterwards, of his own accord, gone into banishment, came up to Susa,[2] and there heard of the quarrel of the princes. Hereupon, as report says, he went to Xerxes, and advised him, in addition to all that he had urged before, to plead – that at the time when he was born Darius was already king, and bore rule over the Persians; but when Artabazanes came into the world, he was a mere private person. It would therefore be neither right nor seemly that the crown should go to another in preference to himself. "For at Sparta," said Demaratus, by way of suggestion, "the law is, that if a king has sons before he comes to the throne, and another son is born to him afterwards, the child so born is heir to his father's kingdom." Xerxes followed this counsel, and Darius, persuaded that he had justice on his side, appointed him his successor. For my own part I believe that, even without this, the crown would have gone to Xerxes; for Atossa was all-powerful.[3]

4. Darius, when he had thus appointed Xerxes his heir, was minded to lead forth his armies; but he was prevented by death while his preparations were still proceeding. He died in the year following[4] the revolt of Egypt and the matters here related, after having reigned in all six-and-thirty years, leaving the revolted Egyptians and the Athenians alike unpunished. At his death the kingdom passed to his son Xerxes.

5. Now Xerxes, on first mounting the throne, was coldly disposed towards the Grecian war, and made it his business to collect an army against Egypt. But Mardonius, the son of Gobryas, who was at the court, and had more influence with him than any of the other Persians, being his own cousin, the child

---

1 This was probably the real *right* on which the claim of Xerxes rested. Xerxes was of the blood of Cyrus; Artabazanes was not.

2 Supra, vi. 70.

3 Though Darius had several wives (supra, iii. 88), it is probable that he had but one queen, namely Atossa. This is the rule wherever there is a seraglio, and was clearly the custom of the Persian court.

4 B.C. 486.

of a sister of Darius, plied him with discourses like the following:—

"Master, it is not fitting that they of Athens escape scot-free, after doing the Persians such great injury. Complete the work which thou hast now in hand, and then, when the pride of Egypt is brought low, lead an army against Athens. So shalt thou thyself have good report among men, and others shall fear hereafter to attack thy country."

Thus far it was of vengeance that he spoke; but sometimes he would vary the theme, and observe by the way, "that Europe was a wondrous beautiful region, rich in all kinds of cultivated trees, and the soil excellent: no one, save the king, was worthy to own such a land."

6. All this he said, because he longed for adventures, and hoped to become satrap of Greece under the king; and after a while he had his way, and persuaded Xerxes to do according to his desires. Other things, however, occurring about the same time, helped his persuasions. For, in the first place, it chanced that messengers arrived from Thessaly, sent by the Aleuadæ, Thessalian kings, to invite Xerxes into Greece, and to promise him all the assistance which it was in their power to give. And further, the Pisistratidæ, who had come up to Susa, held the same language as the Aleuadæ, and worked upon him even more than they, by means of Onomacritus of Athens, an oracle-monger, and the same who set forth the prophecies of Musæus in their order.[1] The Pisistratidæ had previously been at enmity with this man, but made up the quarrel before they removed to Susa. He was banished from Athens by Hipparchus, the son of Pisistratus, because he foisted into the writings of Musæus a prophecy that the islands which lie off Lemnos would one day disappear in the sea. Lasus of Hermioné[2] caught him in the act of so doing. For this cause Hipparchus banished him, though till then they had been the closest of friends. Now, however, he went up to Susa with the sons of Pisistratus, and they talked very grandly of him to the king; while he, for his part, whenever he was in the king's

1 Of Musæus, as of Orpheus, with whom his name is commonly joined, scarcely anything is known. All perhaps that can be said with certainty is that poems believed to be ancient were current under his name as early as B.C. 520. [Campbell, *Religion in Greek Literature*, pp. 245–254.— E. H. B.]

2 Lasus of Hermione was a lyric and dithyrambic poet of the highest repute. He was said to have been the instructor of Pindar.

company, repeated to him certain of the oracles; and while he took care to pass over all that spoke of disaster to the barbarians, brought forward the passages which promised them the greatest success. " 'Twas fated," he told Xerxes, "that a Persian should bridge the Hellespont, and march an army from Asia into Greece." While Onomacritus thus plied Xerxes with his oracles, the Pisistratidæ and Aleuadæ did not cease to press on him their advice, till at last the king yielded, and agreed to lead forth an expedition.

7. First, however, in the year following the death of Darius,[1] he marched against those who had revolted from him; and having reduced them, and laid all Egypt under a far harder yoke than ever his father had put upon it, he gave the government to Achæmenes, who was his own brother, and son to Darius. This Achæmenes was afterwards slain in his government by Inarôs, the son of Psammetichus, a Libyan.

8. (§ 1.) After Egypt was subdued, Xerxes, being about to take in hand the expedition against Athens, called together an assembly of the noblest Persians, to learn their opinions, and to lay before them his own designs.[2] So, when the men were met, the king spake thus to them:—

"Persians, I shall not be the first to bring in among you a new custom — I shall but follow one which has come down to us from our forefathers. Never yet, as our old men assure me, has our race reposed itself, since the time when Cyrus overcame Astyages, and so we Persians wrested the sceptre from the Medes. Now in all this God guides us; and we, obeying his guidance, prosper greatly. What need have I to tell you of the deeds of Cyrus and Cambyses, and my own father Darius, how many nations they conquered, and added to our dominions? Ye know right well what great things they achieved. But for myself, I will say that, from the day on which I mounted the throne, I have not ceased to consider by what means I may rival those who have preceded me in this post of honour, and increase the power of Persia as much as any of them. And truly I have

1 B.C. 485.

2 These speeches have scarcely any higher historical character than those of the conspirators in the third book. They must be considered however as embodying *Persian* as well as Greek views of the circumstances out of which the war arose, and the feelings of those who engaged in it. Oriental respect for royalty strove to exonerate Xerxes from all blame.

pondered upon this, until at last I have found out a way whereby we may at once win glory, and likewise get possession of a land which is as large and as rich as our own – nay, which is even more varied in the fruits it bears – while at the same time we obtain satisfaction and revenge. For this cause I have now called you together, that I may make known to you what I design to do. (§ 2.) My intent is to throw a bridge over the Hellespont and march an army through Europe against Greece, that thereby I may obtain vengeance from the Athenians for the wrongs committed by them against the Persians and against my father. Your own eyes saw the preparations of Darius against these men; but death came upon him, and balked his hopes of revenge. In his behalf, therefore, and in behalf of all the Persians, I undertake the war, and pledge myself not to rest till I have taken and burnt Athens, which has dared, unprovoked, to injure me and my father. Long since they came to Asia with Aristagoras of Miletus, who was one of our slaves, and, entering Sardis, burnt its temples and its sacred groves;[1] again, more lately, when we made a landing upon their coast under Datis and Artaphernes, how roughly they handled us ye do not need to be told. (§ 3.) For these reasons, therefore, I am bent upon this war; and I see likewise therewith united no few advantages. Once let us subdue this people, and those neighbours of theirs who hold the land of Pelops the Phrygian, and we shall extend the Persian territory as far as God's heaven reaches. The sun will then shine on no land beyond our borders; for I will pass through Europe from one end to the other, and with your aid make of all the lands which it contains one country. For thus, if what I hear be true, affairs stand: The nations whereof I have spoken, once swept away, there is no city, no country left in all the world, which will venture so much as to withstand us in arms. By this course then we shall bring all mankind under our yoke, alike those who are guilty and those who are innocent of doing us wrong. (§ 4.) For yourselves, if you wish to please me, do as follows: When I announce the time for the army to meet together, hasten to the muster with a good will, every one of you; and know that to the man who brings with him the most gallant array I will give the gifts which our people consider the most honourable. This then is what ye have to do. But to show that I am not self-willed in

1 Supra, v. 100–102.

this matter, I lay the business before you, and give you full leave to speak your minds upon it openly."

Xerxes, having so spoken, held his peace.

9. (§ 1.) Whereupon Mardonius took the word, and said – "Of a truth, my lord, thou dost surpass, not only all living Persians, but likewise those yet unborn. Most true and right is each word that thou hast now uttered; but best of all thy resolve, not to let the Ionians[1] who live in Europe – a worthless crew – mock us any more. It were indeed a monstrous thing if, after conquering and enslaving the Sacæ,[2] the Indians, the Ethiopians, the Assyrians, and many other mighty nations, not for any wrong that they had done us, but only to increase our empire, we should then allow the Greeks, who have done us such wanton injury, to escape our vengeance. What is it that we fear in them? – not surely their numbers? – not the greatness of their wealth? We know the manner of their battle – we know how weak their power is; already have we subdued their children who dwell in our country, the Ionians, Æolians, and Dorians. I myself have had experience of these men when I marched against them by the orders of thy father; and though I went as far as Macedonia,[3] and came but a little short of reaching Athens itself, yet not a soul ventured to come out against me to battle. (§ 2.) And yet, I am told, these very Greeks are wont to wage wars against one another in the most foolish way, through sheer perversity and doltishness. For no sooner is war proclaimed than they search out the smoothest and fairest plain that is to be found in all the land, and there they assemble and fight; whence it comes to pass that even the conquerors depart with great loss: I say nothing of the conquered, for they are destroyed altogether. Now surely, as they are all of one speech, they ought to interchange heralds and messengers, and make up their differences by any means rather than battle; or, at the worst, if they must needs fight one against another, they ought to post themselves as strongly as possible, and so try their quarrels. But, notwithstanding that they have so

1 This use of the term "Ionian" for the European Greeks is not casual, but characteristic of the Oriental modes of speech, and marks Herodotus for a keen observer of little peculiarities. Here *two* Ionias are mentioned, one of which stands clearly for Asiatic, and the other for European Greece.

2 Apparently Mardonius means the Scythians of Europe, whom he represents as reduced to slavery by the expedition of Darius.

3 Supra, vi. 44, 45.

foolish a manner of warfare, yet these Greeks, when I led my army against them to the very borders of Macedonia, did not so much as think of offering me battle. (§ 3.) Who then will dare, O king! to meet thee in arms, when thou comest with all Asia's warriors at thy back, and with all her ships? For my part I do not believe the Greek people will be so foolhardy. Grant, however, that I am mistaken herein, and that they are foolish enough to meet us in open fight; in that case they will learn that there are no such soldiers in the whole world as we. Nevertheless let us spare no pains; for nothing comes without trouble; but all that men acquire is got by painstaking."

When Mardonius had in this way softened the harsh speech of Xerxes, he too held his peace.

10. The other Persians were silent; for all feared to raise their voice against the plan proposed to them. But Artabanus, the son of Hystaspes, and uncle of Xerxes, trusting to his relationship, was bold to speak:– "O king!" he said, "it is impossible, if no more than one opinion is uttered, to make choice of the best: a man is forced then to follow whatever advice may have been given him; but if opposite speeches are delivered, then choice can be exercised. In like manner pure gold is not recognised by itself; but when we test it along with baser ore, we perceive which is the better. I counselled thy father, Darius, who was my own brother, not to attack the Scyths,[1] a race of people who had no town in their whole land. He thought however to subdue those wandering tribes, and would not listen to me, but marched an army against them, and ere he returned home lost many of his bravest warriors. Thou art about, O king! to attack a people far superior to the Scyths, a people distinguished above others both by land and sea. 'Tis fit therefore that I should tell thee what danger thou incurrest hereby. (§ 2.) Thou sayest that thou wilt bridge the Hellespont, and lead thy troops through Europe against Greece. Now suppose some disaster befall thee by land or sea, or by both. It may be even so; for the men are reputed valiant. Indeed one may measure their prowess from what they have already done; for when Datis and Artaphernes led their huge army against Attica, the Athenians singly defeated them. But grant they are not successful on both elements. Still, if they man their ships, and, defeating us by sea, sail to the Hellespont,

1 Supra, iv. 83.

and there destroy our bridge, — that, sire, were a fearful hazard. (§ 3.) And here 'tis not by my own mother wit alone that I conjecture what will happen; but I remember how narrowly we escaped disaster once, when thy father, after throwing bridges over the Thracian Bosphorus and the Ister, marched against the Scythians, and they tried every sort of prayer to induce the Ionians, who had charge of the bridge over the Ister, to break the passage.[1] On that day, if Histiæus, the king of Miletus, had sided with the other princes, and not set himself to oppose their views, the empire of the Persians would have come to nought. Surely a dreadful thing is this even to hear said, that the king's fortunes depended wholly on one man.

(§ 4.) "Think then no more of incurring so great a danger when no need presses, but follow the advice I tender. Break up this meeting, and when thou hast well considered the matter with thyself, and settled what thou wilt do, declare to us thy resolve. I know not of aught in the world that so profits a man as taking good counsel with himself; for even if things fall out against one's hopes, still one has counselled well, though fortune has made the counsel of none effect: whereas if a man counsels ill and luck follows, he has gotten a windfall, but his counsel is none the less silly. (§ 5.) Seest thou how God with his lightning smites always the bigger animals, and will not suffer them to wax insolent, while those of a lesser bulk chafe him not? How likewise his bolts fall ever on the highest houses and the tallest trees? So plainly does He love to bring down everything that exalts itself. Thus ofttimes a mighty host is discomfited by a few men, when God in his jealousy sends fear or storm from heaven, and they perish in a way unworthy of them. For God allows no one to have high thoughts but Himself. (§ 6.) Again, hurry always brings about disasters, from which huge sufferings are wont to arise; but in delay lie many advantages, not apparent (it may be) at first sight, but such as in course of time are seen of all. Such then is my counsel to thee, O king!

(§ 7.) "And thou, Mardonius, son of Gobryas, forbear to speak foolishly concerning the Greeks, who are men that ought not to be lightly esteemed by us. For while thou revilest the Greeks, thou dost encourage the king to lead his own troops against them; and this, as it seems to me, is what thou art specially

1 Supra, iv. 133, 136–139.

striving to accomplish. Heaven send thou succeed not to thy wish! For slander is of all evils the most terrible. In it two men do wrong, and one man has wrong done to him. The slanderer does wrong, forasmuch as he abuses a man behind his back; and the hearer, forasmuch as he believes what he has not searched into thoroughly. The man slandered in his absence suffers wrong at the hands of both: for one brings against him a false charge; and the other thinks him an evildoer. (§ 8.) If, however, it must needs be that we go to war with this people, at least allow the king to abide at home in Persia. Then let thee and me both stake our children on the issue, and do thou choose out thy men, and, taking with thee whatever number of troops thou likest, lead forth our armies to battle. If things go well for the king, as thou sayest they will, let me and my children be put to death; but if they fall out as I prophesy, let thy children suffer, and thyself too, if thou shalt come back alive. But shouldest thou refuse this wager, and still resolve to march an army against Greece, sure I am that some of those whom thou leavest behind thee here will one day receive the sad tidings, that Mardonius has brought a great disaster upon the Persian people, and lies a prey to dogs and birds somewhere in the land of the Athenians, or else in that of the Lacedæmonians; unless indeed thou shalt have perished sooner by the way, experiencing in thy own person the might of those men on whom thou wouldest fain induce the king to make war."

11. Thus spake Artabanus. But Xerxes, full of wrath, replied to him –

"Artabanus, thou art my father's brother – that shall save thee from receiving the due meed of thy silly words. One shame however I will lay upon thee, coward and faint-hearted as thou art – thou shalt not come with me to fight these Greeks, but shalt tarry here with the women. Without thy aid I will accomplish all of which I spake. For let me not be thought the child of Darius, the son of Hystaspes, the son of Arsames, the son of Ariaramnes, the son of Teispes, the son of Cyrus,[1] the son of

---

1 The genealogy of himself which Darius caused to be engraved on the rocks of Behistun determines absolutely the number of generations between Xerxes and Achæmenes, *proving* what had been already surmised, that the names of Cyrus and Cambyses do not belong to the stem of Darius, but are thrown by Xerxes into the list of his ancestors in right of his mother Atossa, the daughter of Cyrus.

Cambyses, the son of Teispes, the son of Achæmenes, if I take not vengeance on the Athenians. Full well I know that, were we to remain at rest, yet would not they, but would most certainly invade our country, if at least it be right to judge from what they have already done; for, remember, it was they who fired Sardis and attacked Asia. So now retreat is on both sides impossible, and the choice lies between doing and suffering injury; either our empire must pass under the dominion of the Greeks, or their land become the prey of the Persians; for there is no middle course left in this quarrel. It is right then that we, who have in times past received wrong, should now avenge it, and that I should thereby discover what that great risk[1] is which I run in marching against these men – men whom Pelops the Phrygian, a vassal of my forefathers,[2] subdued so utterly, that to this day both the land, and the people who dwell therein, alike bear the name of the conqueror!"

12. Thus far did the speaking proceed. Afterwards evening fell; and Xerxes began to find the advice of Artabanus greatly disquiet him. So he thought upon it during the night, and concluded at last that it was not for his advantage to lead an army into Greece. When he had thus made up his mind anew, he fell asleep. And now he saw in the night, as the Persians declare, a vision of this nature – he thought a tall and beautiful man stood over him and said, "Hast thou then changed thy mind, Persian, and wilt thou not lead forth thy host against the Greeks, after commanding the Persians to gather together their levies? Be sure thou doest not well to change; nor is there a man here who will approve thy conduct. The course that thou didst determine on during the day, let that be followed." After thus speaking the man seemed to Xerxes to fly away.

13. Day dawned; and the king made no account of this dream, but called together the same Persians as before, and spake to them as follows:–

"Men of Persia, forgive me if I alter the resolve to which I came so lately. Consider that I have not yet reached to the full growth of my wisdom, and that they who urge me to engage in

---

1 Xerxes refers here to the earlier part of the speech of Artabanus, and the perils there put forward (supra, ch. 10, § 1–3).

2 Herodotus tells us at the beginning of his History that the Persians considered Asia and all its nations as their own always.

this war leave me not to myself for a moment. When I heard the advice of Artabanus, my young blood suddenly boiled; and I spake words against him little befitting his years: now however I confess my fault, and am resolved to follow his counsel. Understand then that I have changed my intent with respect to carrying war into Greece, and cease to trouble yourselves."

When they heard these words, the Persians were full of joy, and, falling down at the feet of Xerxes, made obeisance to him.

14. But when night came, again the same vision stood over Xerxes as he slept, and said, "Son of Darius, it seems thou hast openly before all the Persians renounced the expedition, making light of my words, as though thou hadst not heard them spoken. Know therefore and be well assured, that unless thou go forth to the war, this thing shall happen unto thee — as thou art grown mighty and puissant in a short space, so likewise shalt thou within a little time be brought low indeed."

15. Then Xerxes, greatly frightened at the vision which he had seen, sprang from his couch, and sent a messenger to call Artabanus, who came at the summons, when Xerxes spoke to him in these words:—

"Artabanus, at the moment I acted foolishly, when I gave thee ill words in return for thy good advice. However it was not long ere I repented, and was convinced that thy counsel was such as I ought to follow. But I may not now act in this way, greatly as I desire to do so. For ever since I repented and changed my mind a dream has haunted me, which disapproves my intentions, and has now just gone from me with threats. Now if this dream is sent to me from God, and if it is indeed his will that our troops should march against Greece, thou too wilt have the same dream come to thee and receive the same commands as myself. And this will be most sure to happen, I think, if thou puttest on the dress which I am wont to wear, and then, after taking thy seat upon my throne, liest down to sleep on my bed."

16. Such were the words of Xerxes. Artabanus would not at first yield to the command of the King; for he deemed himself unworthy to sit upon the royal throne. At the last however he was forced to give way, and did as Xerxes bade him; but first he spake thus to the king:—

"To me, sire, it seems to matter little whether a man is wise himself or willing to hearken to such as give good advice. In thee truly are found both tempers; but the counsels of evil men lead

thee astray: they are like the gales of wind which vex the sea —
else the most useful thing for man in the whole world — and
suffer it not to follow the bent of its own nature. For myself, it
irked me not so much to be reproached by thee, as to observe,
that when two courses were placed before the Persian people,
one of a nature to increase their pride, the other to humble it,
by showing them how hurtful it is to allow one's heart always
to covet more than one at present possesses, thou madest choice
of that which was the worse both for thyself and for the Persians. (§ 2.) Now thou sayest, that from the time when thou didst
approve the better course, and give up the thought of warring
against Greece, a dream has haunted thee, sent by some god or
other, which will not suffer thee to lay aside the expedition. But
such things, my son, have of a truth nothing divine in them. The
dreams, that wander to and fro among mankind, I will tell thee
of what nature they are, — I who have seen so many more years
than thou. Whatever a man has been thinking of during the day,
is wont to hover round him in the visions of his dreams at night.
Now we during these many days past have had our hands full
of this enterprise. (§ 3.) If however the matter be not as I suppose, but God has indeed some part therein, thou hast in brief
declared the whole that can be said concerning it — let it e'en
appear to me as it has to thee, and lay on me the same injunctions. But it ought not to appear to me any the more if I put on
thy clothes than if I wear my own, nor if I go to sleep in thy
bed than if I do so in mine — supposing, I mean, that it is about
to appear at all. For this thing, be it what it may, that visits thee
in thy sleep, surely is not so far gone in folly as to see me, and
because I am dressed in thy clothes, straightway to mistake me
for thee. Now however our business is to see if it will regard me
as of small account, and not vouchsafe to appear to me, whether
I wear mine own clothes or thine, while it keeps on haunting
thee continually. If it does so, and appears often, I should myself
say that it was from God. For the rest, if thy mind is fixed, and
it is not possible to turn thee from thy design, but I must needs
go and sleep in thy bed, well and good, let it be even so; and
when I have done as thou wishest, then let the dream appear to
me. Till such time, however, I shall keep to my former opinion."

17. Thus spake Artabanus; and when he had so said, thinking
to show Xerxes that his words were nought, he did according to
his orders. Having put on the garments which Xerxes was wont

to wear and taken his seat upon the royal throne, he lay down to sleep upon the king's own bed. As he slept, there appeared to him the very same dream which had been seen by Xerxes; it came and stood over Artabanus, and said –

"Thou art the man, then, who, feigning to be tender of Xerxes, seekest to dissuade him from leading his armies against the Greeks! But thou shalt not escape scathless, either now or in time to come, because thou hast sought to prevent that which is fated to happen. As for Xerxes, it has been plainly told to himself what will befall him, if he refuses to perform my bidding."

18. In such words, as Artabanus thought, the vision threatened him, and then endeavoured to burn out his eyes with red-hot irons.[1] At this he shrieked, and, leaping from his couch, hurried to Xerxes, and, sitting down at his side, gave him a full account of the vision; after which he went on to speak in the words which follow:–

"I, O King! am a man who has seen many mighty empires overthrown by weaker ones; and therefore it was that I sought to hinder thee from being quite carried away by thy youth; since I knew how evil a thing it is to covet more than one possesses. I could remember the expedition of Cyrus against the Massagetæ, and what was the issue of it; I could recollect the march of Cambyses against the Ethiops; I had taken part in the attack of Darius upon the Scyths;– bearing therefore all these things in mind, I thought with myself that if thou shouldst remain at peace, all men would deem thee fortunate. But as this impulse has plainly come from above, and a heaven-sent destruction seems about to overtake the Greeks, behold, I change to another mind, and alter my thoughts upon the matter. Do thou therefore

1 Putting out the eyes has been in all ages a common Oriental punishment. The earliest instance on record is that of Zedekiah, whose eyes were put out by Nebuchadnezzar (Jerem. xxxix. 7; lii. 11). [But see now a reference to this hideous form of penalty in the recently discovered "Code of Khammurâbi," circ. 2500 B.C. – E. H. B.] Grote sees in this whole narrative nothing but "religious imagination" – a *mythus* embodying the deep conviction, alike of Greeks and of Persians, that nothing short of a direct divine interposition could have brought about the transcendently great events which were connected with the expedition of Xerxes. I incline, with Bishop Thirlwall, to suspect a foundation in *fact* for the stories that were told. The weak mind of Xerxes may have been imposed upon by a pretended spectre; and the stronger one of Artabanus may have been subdued by threats.

make known to the Persians what the god has declared, and bid them follow the orders which were first given, and prepare their levies. Be careful to act so that the bounty of the god may not be hindered by slackness on thy part."

Thus spake these two together; and Xerxes, being in good heart on account of the vision, when day broke, laid all before the Persians; while Artabanus, who had formerly been the only person openly to oppose the expedition, now showed as openly that he favoured it.

19. After Xerxes had thus determined to go forth to the war, there appeared to him in his sleep yet a third vision. The Magi were consulted upon it,[1] and said that its meaning reached to the whole earth, and that all mankind would become his servants. Now the vision which the king saw was this: he dreamt that he was crowned with a branch of an olive-tree, and that boughs spread out from the olive-branch and covered the whole earth; then suddenly the garland, as it lay upon his brow, vanished. So when the Magi had thus interpreted the vision, straightway all the Persians who were come together departed to their several governments, where each displayed the greatest zeal, on the faith of the king's offers. For all hoped to obtain for themselves the gifts which had been promised. And so Xerxes gathered together his host, ransacking every corner of the continent.

20. Reckoning from the recovery of Egypt, Xerxes spent four full years[2] in collecting his host, and making ready all things that were needful for his soldiers. It was not till the close of the fifth year that he set forth on his march, accompanied by a mighty multitude. For of all the armaments whereof any mention has reached us, this was by far the greatest; insomuch that no other expedition compared to this seems of any account, neither that which Darius undertook against the Scythians, nor the expedition of the Scythians (which the attack of Darius was designed to avenge), when they, being in pursuit of the Cimmerians, fell upon the Median territory, and subdued and held for a time

1 Vide supra, i. 108. For the general practice among the Oriental nations to attend to dreams, and to require an interpretation of them from their priests, see Gen. xli. 8; and Dan. ii. 2; iv. 6.

2 Various modes have been adopted of explaining the chronology of the period between the battles of Marathon and Salamis. All accounts agree in stating the interval at ten years. The numbers in Herodotus are with difficulty brought within this interval.

almost the whole of Upper Asia;[1] nor, again, that of the Atridæ against Troy, of which we hear in story; nor that of the Mysians and Teucrians, which was still earlier, wherein these nations crossed the Bosphorus into Europe, and, after conquering all Thrace, pressed forward till they came to the Ionian sea,[2] while southward they reached as far as the river Peneus.

21. All these expeditions, and others, if such there were, are as nothing compared with this. For was there a nation in all Asia which Xerxes did not bring with him against Greece? Or was there a river, except those of unusual size, which sufficed for his troops to drink? One nation furnished ships; another was arrayed among the foot-soldiers; a third had to supply horses; a fourth, transports for the horse and men likewise for the transport service; a fifth, ships of war towards the bridges; a sixth, ships and provisions.

22. And in the first place, because the former fleet had met with so great a disaster about Athos,[3] preparations were made, by the space of about three years, in that quarter. A fleet of triremes lay at Elæus in the Chersonese; and from this station detachments were sent by the various nations whereof the army was composed, which relieved one another at intervals, and worked at a trench beneath the lash of taskmasters; while the people dwelling about Athos bore likewise a part in the labour. Two Persians, Bubares, the son of Megabazus, and Artachæes, the son of Artæus, superintended the undertaking.

Athos is a great and famous mountain, inhabited by men, and stretching far out into the sea. Where the mountain ends towards the mainland it forms a peninsula; and in this place there is a neck of land about twelve furlongs across, the whole extent whereof, from the sea of the Acanthians to that over against Torôné, is a level plain, broken only by a few low hills. Here, upon this isthmus where Athos ends, is Sané[4] a Greek city. Inside of Sané, and upon Athos itself, are a number of towns, which Xerxes · was now employed in disjoining from the continent:

1 Vide supra, i. 103–106; iv. 1, 12.
2 By the "Ionian Sea" Herodotus means the Adriatic (vide supra, vi. 127; and infra, ix. 92).
3 Supra, vi. 44.
4 Sané was situated on the southern coast of the isthmus, near the mouth of the canal of Xerxes.

these are, Dium, Olophyxus, Acrothôum, Thyssus, and Cleônæ. Among these cities Athos was divided.

23. Now the manner in which they dug was the following:[1] a line was drawn across by the city of Sané; and along this the various nations parcelled out among themselves the work to be done. When the trench grew deep, the workmen at the bottom continued to dig, while others handed the earth, as it was dug out, to labourers placed higher up upon ladders, and these taking it, passed it on further, till it came at last to those at the top, who carried it off and emptied it away. All the other nations, therefore, except the Phœnicians, had double labour; for the sides of the trench fell in continually, as could not but happen, since they made the width no greater at the top than it was required to be at the bottom. But the Phœnicians showed in this the skill which they are wont to exhibit in all their undertakings. For in the portion of the work which was allotted to them they began by making the trench at the top twice as wide as the prescribed measure, and then as they dug downwards approached the sides nearer and nearer together, so that when they reached the bottom their part of the work was of the same width as the rest. In a meadow near, there was a place of assembly and a market; and hither great quantities of corn, ready ground, were brought from Asia.

24. It seems to me, when I consider this work, that Xerxes, in making it, was actuated by a feeling of pride, wishing to display the extent of his power, and to leave a memorial behind him to posterity. For notwithstanding that it was open to him, with no trouble at all,[2] to have had his ships drawn across the isthmus, yet he issued orders that a canal should be made through which the sea might flow, and that it should be of such a width as would allow of two triremes passing through it abreast with the oars in action. He likewise gave to the same persons who were set over the digging of the trench, the task of making a bridge across the river Strymon.

---

1 Distinct appearances of the ancient cutting have been discovered almost across its whole extent, only failing where the canal approached the sea, and somewhat indistinctly marked in the alluvial plain north of the hills. The canal forms a line of ponds, from two to eight feet deep and from sixty to ninety broad, nearly from one sea to the other.

2 The light ships of the ancients were easily transported in this way across the land.

25. While these things were in progress, he was having cables prepared for his bridges, some of papyrus and some of white flax, a business which he entrusted to the Phœnicians and the Egyptians. He likewise laid up stores of provisions in divers places, to save the army and the beasts of burthen from suffering want upon their march into Greece. He inquired carefully about all the sites, and had the stores laid up in such as were most convenient, causing them to be brought across from various parts of Asia and in various ways, some in transports and others in merchantmen. The greater portion was carried to Leucé-Acté, upon the Thracian coast; some part, however, was conveyed to Tyrodiza,[1] in the country of the Perinthians, some to Doriscus,[2] some to Eïon[3] upon the Strymon, and some to Macedonia.

26. During the time that all these labours were in progress, the land army which had been collected was marching with Xerxes towards Sardis, having started from Critalla in Cappadocia. At this spot all the host which was about to accompany the king in his passage across the continent had been bidden to assemble. And here I have it not in my power to mention which of the satraps was adjudged to have brought his troops in the most gallant array, and on that account rewarded by the king according to his promise; for I do not know whether this matter ever came to a judgment. But it is certain that the host of Xerxes, after crossing the river Halys, marched through Phrygia till it reached the city of Celænæ.[4] Here are the sources of the river Mæander, and likewise of another stream of no less size, which bears the name of Catarrhactes (or the Cataract); the last-named river has its rise in the market-place of Celænæ, and empties itself into the Mæander. Here, too, in this market-place, is hung up to view the skin of the Silênus Marsyas, which Apollo, as the Phrygian story goes, stripped off and placed there.

27. Now there lived in this city a certain Pythius, the son of Atys, a Lydian. This man entertained Xerxes and his whole army in a most magnificent fashion, offering at the same time to give

1 The exact site cannot be fixed; but it was probably near the Serrhean promontory of Stephen.

2 Infra, ch. 59.

3 Infra, ch. 113.

4 It is the modern *Deenair* (lat. 38° 3', long. 30° 20'). This town, which abounds in remains of high antiquity, is situated near the source of the southern or main stream of the Mæander.

him a sum of money for the war. Xerxes, upon the mention of money, turned to the Persians who stood by, and asked of them, "Who is this Pythius, and what wealth has he, that he should venture on such an offer as this?" They answered him, "This is the man, O king! who gave thy father Darius the golden plane-tree, and likewise the golden vine;[1] and he is still the wealthiest man we know of in all the world, excepting thee."

28. Xerxes marvelled at these last words; and now, addressing Pythius with his own lips, he asked him what the amount of his wealth really was. Pythius answered as follows:—

"O king! I will not hide this matter from thee, nor make pretence that I do not know how rich I am; but as I know perfectly, I will declare all fully before thee. For when thy journey was noised abroad, and I heard thou wert coming down to the Grecian coast, straightway, as I wished to give thee a sum of money for the war, I made count of my stores, and found them to be two thousand talents of silver, and of gold four millions of Daric staters,[2] wanting seven thousand. All this I willingly make over to thee as a gift; and when it is gone, my slaves and my estates in land will be wealth enough for my wants."

29. This speech charmed Xerxes, and he replied, "Dear Lydian, since I left Persia there is no man but thou who has either desired to entertain my army, or come forward of his own free will to offer me a sum of money for the war. Thou hast done both the one and the other, feasting my troops magnificently, and now making offer of a right noble sum. In return, this is what I will bestow on thee. Thou shalt be my sworn friend from this day; and the seven thousand staters which are wanting to make up thy four millions I will supply, so that the full tale may be no longer lacking, and that thou mayest owe the completion of the round sum to me. Continue to enjoy all that thou hast acquired hitherto; and be sure to remain ever such as thou now art. If thou dost, thou wilt not repent of it so long as thy life endures."

---

1 The golden vine was even more famous than the plane-tree. The bunches of grapes were imitated by means of the most costly precious stones. It over-shadowed the couch on which the kings slept.

2 The stater was the only gold coin known to the Greeks generally. It was adopted by them from the Asiatics. The stater is equivalent to about £1 3s. The Persian Daric was a gold coin very like the stater and did not greatly differ in value from it.

30. When Xerxes had so spoken and had made good his promises to Pythius, he pressed forward upon his march; and passing Anaua, a Phrygian city, and a lake from which salt is gathered, he came to Colossæ,[1] a Phrygian city of great size, situated at a spot where the river Lycus plunges into a chasm and disappears. This river, after running under ground a distance of about five furlongs, reappears once more, and empties itself, like the stream above mentioned, into the Mæander. Leaving Colossæ, the army approached the borders of Phrygia where it abuts on Lydia; and here they came to a city called Cydrara,[2] where was a pillar set up by Crœsus, having an inscription on it, showing the boundaries of the two countries.

31. Where it quits Phrygia and enters Lydia the road separates; the way on the left leads into Caria, while that on the right conducts to Sardis. If you follow this route, you must cross the Mæander, and then pass by the city Callatêbus, where the men live who make honey out of wheat and the fruit of the tamarisk.[3] Xerxes, who chose this way, found here a plane-tree[4] so beautiful, that he presented it with golden ornaments, and put it under the care of one of his Immortals.[5] The day after, he entered the Lydian capital.

32. Here his first care was to send off heralds into Greece, who were to prefer a demand for earth and water, and to require that preparations should be made everywhere to feast the king. To Athens indeed and to Sparta he sent no such demand;[6] but these cities excepted, his messengers went everywhere. Now the reason why he sent for earth and water to states which had already refused, was this: he thought that although they had refused when Darius made the demand, they would now be too frightened to venture to say him nay. So he sent his heralds, wishing to know for certain how it would be.

33. Xerxes, after this, made preparations to advance to Abydos, where the bridge across the Hellespont from Asia to Europe

---

1 [A town on the Lycus (*Churuk Su*), a tributary of the Mæander, in that part of the Roman province of Asia called Phrygia by the Greeks. Ramsay, *Hist. Geogr. of Asia Minor*, pp. 36–7; *The Church in the Roman Empire*, p. 466. – E. H. B.]

2 The hot springs near *Sarai Kieui* seem to mark this site.

3 The tamarisk still grows here in abundance.

4 The plane-trees of this district are magnificent.

5 Infra, ch. 83.

6 The reason for this abstinence is given below (ch. 133).

was lately finished. Midway between Sestos and Madytus[1] in the Hellespontine Chersonese, and right over against Abydos, there is a rocky tongue of land which runs out for some distance into the sea. This is the place where no long time afterwards the Greeks under Xanthippus, the son of Ariphron, took Artaÿctes the Persian, who was at that time governor of Sestos, and nailed him living to a plank.[2] He was the Artaÿctes who brought women into the temple of Protesilaüs at Elæus, and there was guilty of most unholy deeds.

34. Towards this tongue of land then, the men to whom the business was assigned carried out a double bridge from Abydos; and while the Phœnicians constructed one line with cables of white flax, the Egyptians in the other used ropes made of papyrus. Now it is seven furlongs across from Abydos to the opposite coast. When, therefore, the channel had been bridged successfully, it happened that a great storm arising broke the whole work to pieces, and destroyed all that had been done.

35. So when Xerxes heard of it he was full of wrath, and straightway gave orders that the Hellespont should receive three hundred lashes, and that a pair of fetters should be cast into it. Nay, I have even heard it said, that he bade the branders take their irons and therewith brand the Hellespont. It is certain that he commanded those who scourged the waters to utter, as they lashed them, these barbarian and wicked words: "Thou bitter water, thy lord lays on thee this punishment because thou hast wronged him without a cause, having suffered no evil at his hands. Verily King Xerxes will cross thee, whether thou wilt or no. Well dost thou deserve that no man should honour thee with sacrifice; for thou art of a truth a treacherous and unsavoury river."[3] While the sea was thus punished by his orders, he likewise commanded that the overseers of the work should lose their heads.

36. Then they, whose business it was, executed the unpleasing task laid upon them; and other master-builders were set over the work, who accomplished it in the way which I will now describe.

---

1 Madytus was one of the less important cities of the Chersonese.

2 Vide infra, ix. 116–120.

3 The remark of Dean Blakesley is just, that "the Hellespont, perfectly land-locked, and with a stream running some three knots an hour, presents to a person who is sailing on it altogether the appearance of a river."

They joined together triremes and penteconters, 360 to support the bridge on the side of the Euxine Sea, and 314 to sustain the other; and these they placed at right angles to the sea, and in the direction of the current of the Hellespont, relieving by these means the tension of the shore cables. Having joined the vessels, they moored them with anchors of unusual size, that the vessels of the bridge towards the Euxine might resist the winds which blow from within the straits, and that those of the more western bridge facing the Ægean might withstand the winds which set in from the south and from the south-east. A gap was left in the penteconters in no fewer than three places, to afford a passage for such light craft as chose to enter or leave the Euxine. When all this was done, they made the cables taut from the shore by the help of wooden capstans. This time, moreover, instead of using the two materials separately, they assigned to each bridge six cables, two of which were of white flax, while four were of papyrus. Both cables were of the same size and quality; but the flaxen were the heavier, weighing not less than a talent the cubit. When the bridge across the channel was thus complete, trunks of trees were sawn into planks, which were cut to the width of the bridge, and these were laid side by side upon the tightened cables, and then fastened on the top. This done, brushwood was brought, and arranged upon the planks, after which earth was heaped upon the brushwood, and the whole trodden down into a solid mass. Lastly a bulwark was set up on either side of this causeway, of such a height as to prevent the sumpter-beasts and the horses from seeing over it and taking fright at the water.

37. And now when all was prepared – the bridges, and the works at Athos, the breakwaters about the mouths of the cutting, which were made to hinder the surf from blocking up the entrances,[1] and the cutting itself; and when the news came to Xerxes that this last was completely finished, – then at length the host, having first wintered at Sardis, began its march towards Abydos, fully equipped, on the first approach of spring. At the moment of departure, the sun suddenly quitted his seat in the heavens, and disappeared, though there were no clouds in sight, but the sky was clear and serene. Day was thus turned into night;

---

1 When these breakwaters were allowed to fall into decay, the two ends of the canal would soon be silted up and disappear.

whereupon Xerxes, who saw and remarked the prodigy, was seized with alarm, and sending at once for the Magians, inquired of them the meaning of the portent. They replied – "God is foreshowing to the Greeks the destruction of their cities; for the sun foretells for them, and the moon for us." So Xerxes, thus instructed,[1] proceeded on his way with great gladness of heart.

38. The army had begun its march, when Pythius the Lydian, affrighted at the heavenly portent, and emboldened by his gifts, came to Xerxes and said – "Grant me, O my lord! a favour which is to thee a light matter, but to me of vast account." Then Xerxes, who looked for nothing less than such a prayer as Pythius in fact preferred, engaged to grant him whatever he wished, and commanded him to tell his wish freely. So Pythius, full of boldness, went on to say –

"O my lord! thy servant has five sons; and it chances that all are called upon to join thee in this march against Greece. I beseech thee, have compassion upon my years; and let one of my sons, the eldest, remain behind, to be my prop and stay, and the guardian of my wealth. Take with thee the other four; and when thou hast done all that is in thy heart, mayest thou come back in safety."

39. But Xerxes was greatly angered, and replied to him: "Thou wretch! darest thou speak to me of thy son, when I am myself on the march against Greece, with sons, and brothers, and kinsfolk, and friends? Thou, who art my bond-slave, and art in duty bound to follow me with all thy household, not excepting thy wife! Know that man's spirit dwelleth in his ears, and when it hears good things, straightway it fills all his body with delight; but no sooner does it hear the contrary than it heaves and swells with passion. As when thou didst good deeds and madest good offers to me, thou wert not able to boast of having outdone the king in bountifulness, so now when thou art changed and grown impudent, thou shalt not receive all thy deserts, but less. For thyself and four of thy five sons, the entertainment which I had of thee shall gain protection; but as for him to whom thou clingest above the rest, the forfeit of his life shall be thy punishment." Having thus spoken, forthwith he commanded those to whom such tasks were assigned, to seek out the eldest of the sons of Pythius, and having cut his body asunder, to place the

1 The anecdote is probably apocryphal.

two halves, one on the right, the other on the left, of the great road, so that the army might march out between them.[1]

40. Then the king's orders were obeyed; and the army marched out between the two halves of the carcase. First of all went the baggage-bearers, and the sumpter-beasts, and then a vast crowd of many nations mingled together without any intervals,[2] amounting to more than one half of the army. After these troops an empty space was left, to separate between them and the king. In front of the king went first a thousand horsemen, picked men of the Persian nation – then spearmen a thousand, likewise chosen troops, with their spear-heads pointing towards the ground – next ten of the sacred horses called Nisæan, all daintily caparisoned. (Now these horses are called Nisæan, because they come from the Nisæan plain, a vast flat in Media, producing horses of unusual size.) After the ten sacred horses came the holy chariot of Zeus, drawn by eight milk-white steeds, with the charioteer on foot behind them holding the reins; for no mortal is ever allowed to mount into the car. Next to this came Xerxes himself, riding in a chariot drawn by Nisæan horses, with his charioteer, Patiramphes, the son of Otanes, a Persian, standing by his side.[3]

41. Thus rode forth Xerxes from Sardis – but he was accustomed every now and then, when the fancy took him, to alight from his chariot and travel in a litter. Immediately behind the king there followed a body of a thousand spearmen, the noblest and bravest of the Persians, holding their lances in the usual manner[4] – then came a thousand Persian horse, picked men – then ten thousand, picked also after the rest, and serving on foot.[5] Of these last one thousand carried spears with golden pomegranates at their lower end instead of spikes; and these encircled the other nine thousand, who bore on their spears

1 Compare with this the similar story of Œobazus (iv. 84). The tales are important, as indicating the rigour with which personal service was exacted among the Oriental nations, especially when the monarch was himself going to the field.

2 It is plain from the whole narrative (infra, ch. 60–86, 210; ix. 31), that in the Persian army, as in the Greek, the contingents of the several nations formed distinct and separate *corps*.

3 The Persian monarchs fought from chariots down to the era of the Macedonian conquest.

4 That is, with the point upward.

5 These were probably the Immortals, who are spoken of in ch. 83, and are there said to have served on foot.

pomegranates of silver. The spearmen too who pointed their lances towards the ground had golden pomegranates; and the thousand Persians who followed close after Xerxes had golden apples. Behind the ten thousand footmen came a body of Persian cavalry, likewise ten thousand; after which there was again a void space for as much as two furlongs; and then the rest of the army followed in a confused crowd.

42. The march of the army, after leaving Lydia, was directed upon the river Caïcus and the land of Mysia. Beyond the Caïcus the road, leaving Mount Cana upon the left, passed through the Atarnean plain, to the city of Carina. Quitting this, the troops advanced across the plain of Thebé,[1] passing Adramyttium, and Antandrus,[2] the Pelasgic city; then, holding Mount Ida upon the left hand,[3] it entered the Trojan territory. On this march the Persians suffered some loss; for as they bivouacked during the night at the foot of Ida, a storm of thunder and lightning burst upon them, and killed no small number.

43. On reaching the Scamander, which was the first stream, of all that they had crossed since they left Sardis, whose water failed them and did not suffice to satisfy the thirst of men and cattle,[4] Xerxes ascended into the Pergamus of Priam,[5] since he had a longing to behold the place. When he had seen everything, and inquired into all particulars, he made an offering of a thousand oxen to the Trojan Athena, while the Magians poured libations to the heroes who were slain at Troy. The night after, a panic fell upon the camp: but in the morning they set off with daylight, and skirting on the left hand the towns Rhœteum, Ophryneum, and Dardanus[6] (which borders on Abydos), on the right the Teucrians of Gergis,[7] so reached Abydos.[8]

1 The plain of Thebé was so called from an ancient town of that name in the northern part of the plain, at the foot of Mount Ida.

2 For the situation of Antandrus, vide supra, v. 26.

3 The true Ida must have been left considerably to the right.

4 Though the Scamander of Herodotus (the modern *Mendere*) has a bed from 200 to 300 feet broad, yet the stream in the dry season is reduced to a slender brook not more than three feet deep.

5 By the "Pergamus of Priam" is to be understood the acropolis of New Ilium.

6 These were all places of small importance on or near the coast.

7 Supra, v. 122.

8 The remains of Abydos lie a little north of the upper castle of the Dardanelles [famous in poetry for the loves of Hero and Leander. – E. H. B.]

44. Arrived here, Xerxes wished to look upon all his host; so as there was a throne of white marble upon a hill near the city, which they of Abydos had prepared beforehand, by the king's bidding, for his especial use, Xerxes took his seat on it, and, gazing thence upon the shore below, beheld at one view all his land forces and all his ships. While thus employed, he felt a desire to behold a sailing-match among his ships, which accordingly took place, and was won by the Phœnicians of Sidon, much to the joy of Xerxes, who was delighted alike with the race and with his army.

45. And now, as he looked and saw the whole Hellespont covered with the vessels of his fleet, and all the shore and every plain about Abydos as full as possible of men, Xerxes congratulated himself on his good fortune; but after a little while he wept.

46. Then Artabanus, the king's uncle (the same who at the first so freely spake his mind to the king, and advised him not to lead his army against Greece), when he heard that Xerxes was in tears, went to him, and said —

"How different, sire, is what thou art now doing, from what thou didst a little while ago! Then thou didst congratulate thyself; and now, behold! thou weepest."

"There came upon me," replied he, "a sudden pity, when I thought of the shortness of man's life, and considered that of all this host, so numerous as it is, not one will be alive when a hundred years are gone by."

"And yet there are sadder things in life than that," returned the other. "Short as our time is, there is no man, whether it be here among this multitude or elsewhere, who is so happy, as not to have felt the wish — I will not say once, but full many a time — that he were dead rather than alive. Calamities fall upon us; sicknesses vex and harass us, and make life, short though it be, to appear long. So death, through the wretchedness of our life, is a most sweet refuge to our race: and God, who gives us the tastes that we enjoy of pleasant times, is seen, in his very gift, to be envious."

47. "True," said Xerxes; "human life is even such as thou hast painted it, O Artabanus! But for this very reason let us turn our thoughts from it, and not dwell on what is so sad, when pleasant things are in hand. Tell me rather, if the vision which we saw had not appeared so plainly to thyself, wouldst thou have been still of the same mind as formerly, and have continued to

dissuade me from warring against Greece, or wouldst thou at this time think differently? Come now, tell me this honestly."

"O king!" replied the other, "may the dream which hath appeared to us have such issue as we both desire! For my own part, I am still full of fear, and have scarcely power to control myself, when I consider all our dangers, and especially when I see that the two things which are of most consequence are alike opposed to thee."

48. "Thou strange man!" said Xerxes in reply – "what, I pray thee, are the two things thou speakest of? Does my land army seem to thee too small in number, and will the Greeks, thinkest thou, bring into the field a more numerous host? Or is it our fleet which thou deemest weaker than theirs? Or art thou fearful on both accounts? If in thy judgment we fall short in either respect, it were easy to bring together with all speed another armament."

49. "O king!" said Artabanus, "it is not possible that a man of understanding should find fault with the size of thy army or the number of thy ships. The more thou addest to these, the more hostile will those two things, whereof I spake, become. Those two things are the land and the sea. In all the wide sea there is not, I imagine, anywhere a harbour large enough to receive thy vessels, in case a storm arise, and afford them a sure protection. And yet thou wilt want, not one such harbour only, but many in succession, along the entire coast by which thou art about to make thy advance. In default then of such harbours, it is well to bear in mind that chances rule men, and not men chances. Such is the first of the two dangers; and now I will speak to thee of the second. The land will also be thine enemy; for if no one resists thy advance, as thou proceedest further and further, insensibly allured onwards (for who is ever sated with success?), thou wilt find it more and more hostile. I mean this, that, should nothing else withstand thee, yet the mere distance, becoming greater as time goes on, will at last produce a famine. Methinks it is best for men, when they take counsel, to be timorous, and imagine all possible calamities, but when the time for action comes, then to deal boldy."

50. Whereto Xerxes answered – "There is reason, O Artabanus! in everything which thou hast said; but I pray thee, fear not all things alike, nor count up every risk. For if in each matter that comes before us thou wilt look to all possible chances, never

wilt thou achieve anything. Far better is it to have a stout heart always, and suffer one's share of evils, than to be ever fearing what may happen, and never incur a mischance. Moreover, if thou wilt oppose whatever is said by others, without thyself showing us the sure course which we ought to take, thou art as likely to lead us into failure as they who advise differently; for thou art but on a par with them. And as for that sure course, how canst thou show it us when thou art but a man? I do not believe thou canst. Success for the most part attends those who act boldly, not those who weigh everything, and are slack to venture. Thou seest to how great a height the power of Persia has now reached – never would it have grown to this point if they who sate upon the throne before me had been like-minded with thee, or even, though not like-minded, had listened to councillors of such a spirit. 'Twas by brave ventures that they extended their sway; for great empires can only be conquered by great risks. We follow then the example of our fathers in making this march; and we set forward at the best season of the year; so, when we have brought Europe under us, we shall return, without suffering from want or experiencing any other calamity. For while on the one hand we carry vast stores of provisions with us, on the other we shall have the grain of all the countries and nations that we attack; since our march is not directed against a pastoral people, but against men who are tillers of the ground."

51. Then said Artabanus – "If, sire, thou art determined that we shall not fear anything, at least hearken to a counsel which I wish to offer; for when the matters in hand are so many, one cannot but have much to say. Thou knowest that Cyrus the son of Cambyses reduced and made tributary to the Persians all the race of the Ionians, except only those of Attica.[1] Now my advice is, that thou on no account lead forth these men against their fathers;[2] since we are well able to overcome them without such aid. Their choice, if we take them with us to the war, lies between showing themselves the most wicked of men by helping to enslave their fatherland, or the most righteous by joining in the struggle to keep it free. If then they choose the side of injustice, they will do us but scant good; while if they determine to act

[1] This, of course, was not true; but the Persians might not unnaturally be supposed ignorant of all the Ionians of Europe except the Athenians.
[2] Vide infra, viii. 22, where Themistocles makes use of the same argument.

justly, they may greatly injure our host. Lay thou to heart the old proverb, which says truly, 'The beginning and end of a matter are not always seen at once.' "

52. "Artabanus," answered Xerxes, "there is nothing in all that thou hast said, wherein thou art so wholly wrong as in this, that thou suspectest the faith of the Ionians. Have they not given us the surest proof of their attachment, – a proof which thou didst thyself witness, and likewise all those who fought with Darius against the Scythians? When it lay wholly with them to save or to destroy the entire Persian army, they dealt by us honourably and with good faith, and did us no hurt at all. Besides, they will leave behind them in our country their wives, their children, and their properties – can it then be conceived that they will attempt rebellion? Have no fear, therefore, on this score; but keep a brave heart and uphold my house and empire. To thee, and thee only, do I intrust my sovereignty."

53. After Xerxes had thus spoken, and had sent Artabanus away to return to Susa, he summoned before him all the Persians of most repute, and when they appeared, addressed them in these words:–

"Persians, I have brought you together because I wished to exhort you to behave bravely, and not to sully with disgrace the former achievements of the Persian people, which are very great and famous. Rather let us one and all, singly and jointly, exert ourselves to the uttermost; for the matter wherein we are engaged concerns the common weal. Strain every nerve, then, I beseech you, in this war. Brave warriors are the men we march against, if report says true; and such that, if we conquer them, there is not a people in all the world which will venture thereafter to withstand our arms. And now let us offer prayers to the gods[1] who watch over the welfare of Persia, and then cross the channel."

54. All that day the preparations for the passage continued; and on the morrow they burnt all kinds of spices upon the bridges, and strewed the way with myrtle-boughs, while they waited anxiously for the sun, which they hoped to see as he rose. And now the sun appeared; and Xerxes took a golden goblet and poured from it a libation into the sea, praying the while with

---

1 Ormuzd is spoken of throughout the Inscriptions as "the chief of the gods." [See chap. on "Persian Religion," in Menzies' *Hist. of Religion.* – E. H. B.]

his face turned to the sun, "that no misfortune might befall him such as to hinder his conquest of Europe, until he had penetrated to its uttermost boundaries." After he had prayed, he cast the golden cup into the Hellespont, and with it a golden bowl, and a Persian sword of the kind which they call *acinaces*.[1] I cannot say for certain whether it was as an offering to the sun-god that he threw these things into the deep, or whether he had repented of having scourged the Hellespont, and thought by his gifts to make amends to the sea for what he had done.

55. When, however, his offerings were made, the army began to cross; and the foot-soldiers, with the horsemen, passed over by one of the bridges – that (namely) which lay towards the Euxine – while the sumpter-beasts and the camp-followers passed by the other, which looked on the Ægean. Foremost went the Ten Thousand Persians, all wearing garlands upon their heads; and after them a mixed multitude of many nations. These crossed upon the first day.

On the next day the horsemen began the passage; and with them went the soldiers who carried their spears with the point downwards, garlanded, like the Ten Thousand;– then came the sacred horses and the sacred chariot; next Xerxes with his lancers and the thousand horse; then the rest of the army. At the same time the ships sailed over to the opposite shore. According, however, to another account which I have heard, the king crossed the last.

56. As soon as Xerxes had reached the European side, he stood to contemplate his army as they crossed under the lash. And the crossing continued during seven days and seven nights, without rest or pause. 'Tis said that here, after Xerxes had made the passage, a Hellespontian exclaimed –

"Why, O Zeus, dost thou, in the likeness of a Persian man, and with the name of Xerxes instead of thine own, lead the whole race of mankind to the destruction of Greece? It would have been as easy for thee to destroy it without their aid!"

57. When the whole army had crossed, and the troops were now upon their march, a strange prodigy appeared to them, whereof the king made no account, though its meaning was not difficult to conjecture. Now the prodigy was this: – a mare brought forth a hare. Hereby it was shown plainly enough, that Xerxes would lead

---

1 The Persian *acinaces* was a short sword, not a scymitar. It was straight, not curved.

forth his host against Greece, with mighty pomp and splendour, but, in order to reach again the spot from which he set out, would have to run for his life. There had also been another portent, while Xerxes was still at Sardis – a mule dropped a foal, neither male nor female; but this likewise was disregarded.

58. So Xerxes, despising the omens, marched forwards; and his land army accompanied him. But the fleet held an opposite course, and, sailing to the mouth of the Hellespont, made its way along the shore. Thus the fleet proceeded westward, making for Cape Sarpêdon,[1] where the orders were that it should await the coming up of the troops; but the land army marched eastward along the Chersonese, leaving on the right the tomb of Hellé, the daughter of Athamas, and on the left the city of Cardia. Having passed through the town which is called Agora, they skirted the shores of the Gulf of Melas, and then crossed the river Melas, whence the gulf takes its name, the waters of which they found too scanty to supply the host. From this point their march was to the west; and after passing Ænos,[2] an Æolian settlement, and likewise Lake Stentoris,[3] they came to Doriscus.

59. The name Doriscus is given to a beach and a vast plain upon the coast of Thrace, through the middle of which flows the strong stream of the Hebrus. Here was the royal fort which is likewise called Doriscus, where Darius had maintained a Persian garrison ever since the time when he attacked the Scythians. This place seemed to Xerxes a convenient spot for reviewing and numbering his soldiers; which things accordingly he proceeded to do. The sea-captains, who had brought the fleet to Doriscus, were ordered to take the vessels to the beach adjoining, where Salé stands, a city of the Samothracians, and Zôné, another city. The beach extends to Serrhêum,[4] the well-known promontory; the whole district in former times was inhabited by the Ciconians.[5] Here then the captains were to bring their ships,

1 The modern Cape *Gremea*.

2 Ænos retains its name almost unchanged in the modern *Enos* (lat. 40° 45′, long. 26° 4′).

3 Herodotus appears to intend the vast lake or marsh on the left bank of the Hebrus (*Maritza*), near its mouth, which is one of the most remarkable features of this district.

4 Serrhêum is undoubtedly Cape *Makri*. It lay east of Mesambria.

5 The Ciconians were among the most celebrated of the early Thracian tribes. Homer represents them as inhabiting this same tract at the time of the Trojan war (Odyss. ix. 39–59).

and to haul them ashore for refitting, while Xerxes at Doriscus was employed in numbering the soldiers.

60. What the exact number of the troops of each nation was I cannot say with certainty – for it is not mentioned by any one – but the whole land army together was found to amount to one million seven hundred thousand men. The manner in which the numbering took place was the following. A body of ten thousand men was brought to a certain place, and the men were made to stand as close together as possible; after which a circle was drawn around them, and the men were let go: then where the circle had been, a fence was built about the height of a man's middle; and the enclosure was filled continually with fresh troops, till the whole army had in this way been numbered. When the numbering was over, the troops were drawn up according to their several nations.

61. Now these were the nations that took part in this expedition. The Persians, who wore on their heads the soft hat called the tiara, and about their bodies, tunics with sleeves, of divers colours, having iron scales upon them like the scales of a fish. Their legs were protected by trousers; and they bore wicker shields for bucklers; their quivers hanging at their backs, and their arms being a short spear, a bow of uncommon size, and arrows of reed. They had likewise daggers suspended from their girdles along their right thighs. Otanes, the father of Xerxes' wife, Amestris, was their leader. This people was known to the Greeks in ancient times by the name of Cephenians; but they called themselves and were called by their neighbours, Artæans. It was not till Perseus, the son of Jove and Danaë, visited Cepheus the son of Bel, and, marrying his daughter Andromeda, had by her a son called Perses (whom he left behind him in the country because Cepheus had no male offspring), that the nation took from this Perses the name of Persians.[1]

62. The Medes had exactly the same equipment as the Persians; and indeed the dress common to both is not so much Persian as Median.[2] They had for commander Tigranes, of the race of the Achæmenids. These Medes were called anciently by

[1] Vide infra, ch. 150.

[2] Compare Book i. ch. 135, where the adoption by the Persians of the ordinary Median costume is mentioned. It appears by this passage that they likewise adopted their military equipment.

all people Arians; but when Medêa, the Colchian, came to them from Athens, they changed their name. Such is the account which they themselves give.

The Cissians were equipped in the Persian fashion, except in one respect:— they wore on their heads, instead of hats, fillets.[1] Anaphes, the son of Otanes, commanded them.

The Hyrcanians were likewise armed in the same way as the Persians. Their leader was Megapanus, the same who was afterwards satrap of Babylon.

63. The Assyrians went to the war with helmets upon their heads made of brass, and plaited in a strange fashion which it is not easy to describe. They carried shields, lances, and daggers very like the Egyptian; but in addition, they had wooden clubs knotted with iron, and linen corselets.[2] This people, whom the Greeks call Syrians, are called Assyrians by the barbarians.[3] The Chaldæans[4] served in their ranks, and they had for commander Otaspes, the son of Artachæus.

64. The Bactrians went to the war wearing a head-dress very like the Median, but armed with bows of cane, after the custom of their country, and with short spears.

The Sacæ, or Scyths, were clad in trousers, and had on their heads tall stiff caps rising to a point. They bore the bow of their country and the dagger; besides which they carried the battle-axe, or *sagaris*. They were in truth Amyrgian[5] Scythians, but the Persians called them Sacæ, since that is the name which they give to all Scythians.[6] The Bactrians and the Sacæ had for leader Hystaspes, the son of Darius and of Atossa, the daughter of Cyrus.

1 The μίτρα, which was worn also by the Cyprian princes in the fleet of Xerxes (infra, ch. 90), and by the Babylonians as part of their ordinary costume (supra, i. 195), was regarded both by Greeks and Romans as a token of effeminacy. It is generally thought to have been a sort of turban.

2 This description agrees tolerably, but not quite exactly, with the costume seen in the sculptures. The difference is not surprising, as the latest sculptures are at the least two centuries earlier than the time of Xerxes.

3 "Syrian" and "Assyrian" are in reality two entirely different words. "Syrian" is nothing but a variant of "Tyrian."

4 Herodotus seems here to use the word "Chaldæan" in an ethnic sense, and to designate, not the priest-caste of his first Book (chs. 181–183), but the inhabitants of lower Babylonia.

5 According to Hellanicus, the word "Amyrgian" was strictly a geographical title, *Amyrgium* being the name of the plain in which these Scythians dwelt.

6 "*Saká*" is the word used throughout the Persian inscriptions.

65. The Indians wore cotton dresses, and carried bows of cane, and arrows also of cane with iron at the point. Such was the equipment of the Indians, and they marched under the command of Pharnazathres the son of Artabates.

66. The Arians carried Median bows, but in other respects were equipped like the Bactrians. Their commander was Sisamnes the son of Hydarnes.

The Parthians and Chorasmians, with the Sogdians, the Gandarians, and the Dadicæ, had the Bactrian equipment in all respects. The Parthians and Chorasmians were commanded by Artabazus the son of Pharnaces, the Sogdians by Azanes the son of Artæus, and the Gandarians and Dadicæ by Artyphius the son of Artabanus.

67. The Caspians were clad in cloaks of skin, and carried the cane bow of their country and the scymitar. So equipped they went to the war; and they had for commander Ariomardus the brother of Artyphius.

The Sarangians had dyed garments which showed brightly, and buskins which reached to the knee: they bore Median bows, and lances. Their leader was Pherendates, the son of Megabazus.

The Pactyans wore cloaks of skin, and carried the bow of their country and the dagger. Their commander was Artyntes, the son of Ithamatres.

68. The Utians, the Mycians, and the Paricanians were all equipped like the Pactyans. They had for leaders, Arsamenes, the son of Darius, who commanded the Utians and Mycians; and Siromitres, the son of Œobazus, who commanded the Paricanians.

69. The Arabians wore the *zeira*,[1] or long cloak, fastened about them with a girdle; and carried at their right side long bows, which when unstrung bent backwards.[2]

The Ethiopians were clothed in the skins of leopards and lions, and had long bows made of the stem of the palm-leaf, not less than four cubits in length. On these they laid short arrows made of reed, and armed at the tip, not with iron, but with a piece of stone,[3] sharpened to a point, of the kind used in

1 The flowing dress or petticoat called zeira (zira), supported by a girdle, is very similar to their present costume.

2 Bows of this kind were not usual among either the Greeks or the Oriental nations.

3 The stone used was an agate.

engraving seals. They carried likewise spears, the head of which was the sharpened horn of an antelope; and in addition they had knotted clubs. When they went into battle they painted their bodies, half with chalk, and half with vermilion. The Arabians,[1] and the Ethiopians who came from the region above Egypt, were commanded by Arsames, the son of Darius and of Artystônê daughter of Cyrus. This Artystônê was the best-beloved of all the wives of Darius; and it was she whose statue he caused to be made of gold wrought with the hammer. Her son Arsames commanded these two nations.

70. The eastern Ethiopians – for two nations of this name served in the army – were marshalled with the Indians. They differed in nothing from the other Ethiopians, save in their language, and the character of their hair. For the eastern Ethiopians have straight hair, while they of Libya are more woolly-haired than any other people in the world. Their equipment was in most points like that of the Indians; but they wore upon their heads the scalps of horses, with the ears and mane attached; the ears were made to stand upright, and the mane served as a crest. For shields this people made use of the skins of cranes.

71. The Libyans wore a dress of leather, and carried javelins made hard in the fire. They had for commander Massages, the son of Oarizus.

72. The Paphlagonians went to the war with plaited helmets upon their heads, and carrying small shields and spears of no great size. They had also javelins and daggers, and wore on their feet the buskin of their country, which reached half way up the shank. In the same fashion were equipped the Ligyans, the Matienians, the Mariandynians, and the Syrians (or Cappadocians, as they are called by the Persians). The Paphlagonians and Matienians were under the command of Dôtus the son of Megasidrus; while the Mariandynians, the Ligyans, and the Syrians had for leader Gobryas, the son of Darius and Artystônê.

73. The dress of the Phrygians closely resembled the Paphlagonian, only in a very few points differing from it. According to the Macedonian account, the Phrygians, during the time that they had their abode in Europe and dwelt with them in Macedonia,

---

1 The Arabians here spoken of, who served under the same commander as the Ethiopians, were probably those of Africa, who occupied the tract between the valley of the Nile and the Red Sea.

bore the name of Brigians; but on their removal to Asia they changed their designation at the same time with their dwelling-place.[1]

The Armenians, who are Phrygian colonists, were armed in the Phrygian fashion. Both nations were under the command of Artochmes, who was married to one of the daughters of Darius.

74. The Lydians were armed very nearly in the Grecian manner. These Lydians in ancient times were called Mæonians, but changed their name, and took their present title from Lydus the son of Atys.

The Mysians wore upon their heads a helmet made after the fashion of their country, and carried a small buckler; they used as javelins staves with one end hardened in the fire. The Mysians are Lydian colonists, and from the mountain-chain of Olympus, are called Olympiêni. Both the Lydians and the Mysians were under the command of Artaphernes, the son of that Artaphernes who, with Datis, made the landing at Marathon.

75. The Thracians went to the war wearing the skins of foxes upon their heads, and about their bodies tunics, over which was thrown a long cloak of many colours.[2] Their legs and feet were clad in buskins made from the skins of fawns; and they had for arms javelins, with light targes, and short dirks. This people, after crossing into Asia, took the name of Bithynians;[3] before, they had been called Strymonians, while they dwelt upon the Strymon; whence, according to their own account, they had been driven out by the Mysians and Teucrians.[4] The commander of these Asiatic Thracians was Bassaces the son of Artabanus.

76. [The Chalybians[5]] had small shields made of the hide of the ox, and carried each of them two spears such as are used in wolf-hunting. Brazen helmets protected their heads; and above these they wore the ears and horns of an ox fashioned in brass. They had also crests on their helms; and their legs were bound round with purple bands. There is an oracle of Areas in the country of this people.

77. The Cabalians, who are Mæonians, but are called Laso-nians, had the same equipment as the Cilicians — an equipment

---

1 The word "Bryges" in Macedonian would be identical with "Phryges."

2 The Thracians of Europe wore exactly the same costume.

3 Supra, i. 28.

4 Compare ch. 20 sub fin.

5 There is a defect here in the text of Herodotus; the name of the nation has been lost.

which I shall describe when I come in due course to the Cilician contingent.[1]

The Milyans bore short spears, and had their garments fastened with buckles. Some of their number carried Lycian bows.[2] They wore about their heads skull-caps made of leather. Badres the son of Hystanes led both nations to battle.

78. The Moschians wore helmets made of wood, and carried shields and spears of a small size: their spear-heads, however, were long. The Moschian equipment was that likewise of the Tibarenians, the Macronians, and the Mosynœcians.[3] The leaders of these nations were the following: the Moschians and Tibarenians were under the command of Ariomardus, who was the son of Darius and of Parmys, daughter of Smerdis son of Cyrus; while the Macronians and Mosynœcians had for leader Artaÿctes, the son of Cherasmis, the governor of Sestos upon the Hellespont.

79. The Mares wore on their heads the plaited helmet peculiar to their country, and used small leathern bucklers, and javelins.

The Colchians wore wooden helmets, and carried small shields of raw hide, and short spears; besides which they had swords. Both Mares and Colchians were under the command of Pharandates, the son of Teaspes.

The Alarodians and Saspirians were armed like the Colchians; their leader was Masistes, the son of Siromitras.

80. The Islanders who came from the Erythræan sea, where they inhabited the islands to which the king sends those whom he banishes, wore a dress and arms almost exactly like the Median. Their leader was Mardontes the son of Bagæus, who the year after perished in the battle of Mycalé, where he was one of the captains.

81. Such were the nations who fought upon the dry land, and made up the infantry of the Persians. And they were commanded by the captains whose names have been above recorded. The marshalling and numbering of the troops had been committed to them; and by them were appointed the captains over a thousand,

1 Infra, ch. 91.
2 That is, bows of *cornel-wood*. Vide infra, ch. 92.
3 These three nations had become independent of Persia by the time of Xenophon.

and the captains over ten thousand; but the leaders of ten men, or a hundred, were named by the captains over ten thousand. There were other officers also, who gave the orders to the various ranks and nations; but those whom I have mentioned above were the commanders.

82. Over these commanders themselves, and over the whole of the infantry, there were set six generals, – namely, Mardonius, son of Gobryas; Tritantæchmes, son of the Artabanus who gave his advice against the war with Greece; Smerdomenes, son of Otanes – these two were the sons of Darius' brothers, and thus were cousins of Xerxes – Masistes, son of Darius and Atossa; Gergis, son of Arizus; and Megabyzus, son of Zopyrus.

83. The whole of the infantry was under the command of these generals, excepting the Ten Thousand. The Ten Thousand, who were all Persians and all picked men, were led by Hydarnes, the son of Hydarnes. They were called "the Immortals," for the following reason. If one of their body failed either by the stroke of death or of disease, forthwith his place was filled up by another man, so that their number was at no time either greater or less than 10,000.

Of all the troops the Persians were adorned with the greatest magnificence, and they were likewise the most valiant. Besides their arms, which have been already described, they glittered all over with gold, vast quantities of which they wore about their persons.[1] They were followed by litters, wherein rode their concubines, and by a numerous train of attendants handsomely dressed. Camels and sumpter-beasts carried their provision, apart from that of the other soldiers.

84. All these various nations fight on horseback; they did not, however, at this time all furnish horsemen, but only the following:–

(i.) The Persians, who were armed in the same way as their own footmen, excepting that some of them wore upon their heads devices fashioned with the hammer in brass or steel.

85. (ii.) The wandering tribe known by the name of Sagartians – a people Persian in language, and in dress half Persian, half Pactyan, who furnished to the army as many as eight thousand horse. It is not the wont of this people to carry arms, either

---

1 All accounts agree in representing the use of ornaments in pure gold as common among the Persians.

of bronze or steel, except only a dirk; but they use lassoes made of thongs plaited together, and trust to these whenever they go to the wars. Now the manner in which they fight is the following: when they meet their enemy, straightway they discharge their lassoes, which end in a noose; then, whatever the noose encircles, be it man or be it horse, they drag towards them; and the foe, entangled in the toils, is forthwith slain.[1] Such is the manner in which this people fight; and now their horsemen were drawn up with the Persians.

86. (iii.) The Medes, and Cissians, who had the same equipment as their foot-soldiers.

(iv.) The Indians, equipped as their footmen, but some on horseback and some in chariots, – the chariots drawn either by horses, or by wild asses.

(v.) The Bactrians and Caspians, arrayed as their foot-soldiers.

(vi.) The Libyans, equipped as their foot-soldiers, like the rest; but all riding in chariots.[2]

(vii.) The Caspeirians and Paricanians, equipped as their foot-soldiers.

(viii.) The Arabians, in the same array as their footmen, but all riding on camels, not inferior in fleetness to horses.[3]

87. These nations, and these only, furnished horse to the army: and the number of the horse was eighty thousand, without counting camels or chariots. All were marshalled in squadrons, excepting the Arabians; who were placed last, to avoid frightening the horses, which cannot endure the sight of the camel.[4]

88. The horse was commanded by Armamithras and Tithæus, sons of Datis. The other commander, Pharnuches, who was to have been their colleague, had been left sick at Sardis; since at the moment that he was leaving the city, a sad mischance befell

1 The use of the lasso was common in ancient times to many of the nations of Western Asia. It is seen in the Assyrian sculptures from the palace of Asshur bani-pal.

2 Supra, iv. 170 and 189.

3 The speed of the dromedary being equal to that of a horse is an error; it scarcely exceeds nine miles an hour. The camel answers to the cart-horse, the dromedary to the saddle-horse. Each has one hump; the Bactrian camel has two. It is singular that the camel is not represented in the Egyptian sculptures. An instance occurs only of late time. But this does not prove its non-existence in Egypt, as it was there in the age of Abraham.

4 Supra, i. 80.

him:— a dog ran under the feet of the horse upon which he was mounted; and the horse, not seeing it coming, was startled, and, rearing bolt upright, threw his rider. After this fall Pharnuches spat blood, and fell into a consumption. As for the horse, he was treated at once as Pharnuches ordered: the attendants took him to the spot where he had thrown his master, and there cut off his four legs at the hough. Thus Pharnuches lost his command.

89. The triremes amounted in all to twelve hundred and seven; and were furnished by the following nations:—

(i.) The Phœnicians, with the Syrians of Palestine, furnished three hundred vessels, the crews of which were thus accoutred: upon their heads they wore helmets made nearly in the Grecian manner; about their bodies they had breastplates of linen;[1] they carried shields without rims;[2] and were armed with javelins. This nation, according to their own account, dwelt anciently upon the Erythræan sea, but, crossing thence, fixed themselves on the sea-coast of Syria, where they still inhabit. This part of Syria, and all the region extending from hence to Egypt, is known by the name of Palestine.[3]

(ii.) The Egyptians furnished two hundred ships. Their crews had plaited helmets upon their heads, and bore concave shields with rims of unusual size. They were armed with spears suited for a sea-fight, and with huge pole-axes. The greater part of them wore breastplates; and all had long cutlasses.

90. (iii.) The Cyprians furnished a hundred and fifty ships, and were equipped in the following fashion. Their kings had turbans bound about their heads, while the people wore tunics; in other respects they were clad like the Greeks. They are of various races; some are sprung from Athens and Salamis, some from Arcadia, some from Cythnus,[4] some from Phœnicia, and a portion, according to their own account, from Ethiopia.

91. (iv.) The Cilicians furnished a hundred ships. The crews wore upon their heads the helmet of their country, and carried instead·of shields light targes made of raw hide; they were clad

1 For a description of these corselets, see Book ii. ch. 182.

2 This was the characteristic of the *pelta*, or light targe. It consisted of a framework of wood or wickerwork, over which was stretched a covering of raw hide or leather.

3 The name Palestine is beyond a doubt the Greek form of the Hebrew *Philistia*.

4 Cythnus was one of the Cyclades.

in woollen tunics, and were each armed with two javelins, and a sword closely resembling the cutlass of the Egyptians. This people bore anciently the name of Hypachæans,[1] but took their present title from Cilix, the son of Agenor, a Phœnician.

(v.) The Pamphylians furnished thirty ships, the crews of which were armed exactly as the Greeks. This nation is descended from those who on the return from Troy were dispersed with Amphilochus and Calchas.

92. (vi.) The Lycians furnished fifty ships. Their crews wore greaves and breastplates, while for arms they had bows of cornel wood, reed arrows without feathers, and javelins. Their outer garment was the skin of a goat, which hung from their shoulders; their head-dress a hat encircled with plumes; and besides their other weapons they carried daggers and falchions. This people came from Crete, and were once called Termilæ; they got the name which they now bear from Lycus, the son of Pandion, an Athenian.[2]

93. (vii.) The Dorians of Asia furnished thirty ships. They were armed in the Grecian fashion, inasmuch as their forefathers came from the Peloponnese.

(viii.) The Carians furnished seventy ships, and were equipped like the Greeks, but carried, in addition, falchions and daggers. What name the Carians bore anciently was declared in the first part of this History.[3]

94. (ix.) The Ionians furnished a hundred ships, and were armed like the Greeks. Now these Ionians, during the time that they dwelt in the Peloponnese and inhabited the land now called Achæa (which was before the arrival of Danaüs and Xuthus in the Peloponnese), were called, according to the Greek account, Ægialean Pelasgi, or "Pelasgi of the Sea-shore;"[4] but afterwards, from Ion the son of Xuthus, they were called Ionians.

95. The Islanders furnished seventeen ships, and wore arms like the Greeks. They too were a Pelasgian race, who in later

1 The Cilicians were undoubtedly a kindred race to the Phœnicians.

2 Vide supra, i. 173.

3 Supra, i. 171. We may conclude from this passage that Herodotus regarded his work as divided into certain definite portions; though of course we are not entitled to identify these with the divisions which have come down to us.

4 See Book i. ch. 145, and Book v. ch. 68. The supposed date of the Ionic migration was about B.C. 1050. Danaüs, Xuthus, and Ion seem to be purely mythological personages.

times took the name of Ionians for the same reason as those who inhabited the twelve cities founded from Athens.[1]

The Æolians furnished sixty ships, and were equipped in the Grecian fashion. They too were anciently called Pelasgians, as the Greeks declare.

The Hellespontians from the Pontus,[2] who are colonists of the Ionians and Dorians, furnished a hundred ships, the crews of which wore the Grecian armour. This did not include the Abydenians, who stayed in their own country, because the king had assigned them the special duty of guarding the bridges.

96. On board of every ship was a band of soldiers, Persians, Medes, or Sacans. The Phœnician ships were the best sailers in the fleet, and the Sidonian the best among the Phœnicians. The contingent of each nation, whether to the fleet or to the land army, had at its head a native leader; but the names of these leaders I shall not mention, as it is not necessary for the course of my History. For the leaders of some nations were not worthy to have their names recorded; and besides, there were in each nation as many leaders as there were cities. And it was not really as commanders that they accompanied the army, but as mere slaves, like the rest of the host. For I have already mentioned the Persian generals who had the actual command, and were at the head of the several nations which composed the army.

97. The fleet was commanded by the following – Ariabignes, the son of Darius, Prêxaspes, the son of Aspathines, Megabazus, the son of Megabates, and Achæmenes, the son of Darius. Ariabignes, who was the child of Darius by a daughter of Gobryas, was leader of the Ionian and Carian ships; Achæmenes, who was own brother to Xerxes, of the Egyptian;[3] the rest of the fleet was commanded by the other two. Besides the triremes, there was an assemblage of thirty-oared and fifty-oared galleys, of cercuri,[4] and transports for conveying horses, amounting in all to three thousand.

98. Next to the commanders, the following were the most renowned of those who sailed aboard the fleet:– Tetramnêstus,

---

1 That is, they received colonies from Athens.

2 Herodotus includes in this expression the inhabitants of the Greek cities on both sides of the Hellespont, the Propontis, and the Bosphorus.

3 Achæmenes was satrap of Egypt (supra, ch. 7).

4 Cercuri were light boats of unusual length.

the son of Anysus, the Sidonian; Mapên, the son of Sirom,[1] the Tyrian; Merbal,[2] the son of Agbal, the Aradian; Syennesis, the son of Oromedon, the Cilician; Cyberniscus, the son of Sicas, the Lycian; Gorgus, the son of Chersis,[3] and Timônax, the son of Timagoras, the Cyprians; and Histiæus, the son of Timnes,[4] Pigres, the son of Seldômus, and Damasithymus, the son of Candaules, the Carians.

99. Of the other lower officers I shall make no mention, since no necessity is laid on me; but I must speak of a certain leader named Artemisia,[5] whose participation in the attack upon Greece, notwithstanding that she was a woman, moves my special wonder. She had obtained the sovereign power after the death of her husband; and, though she had now a son grown up, yet her brave spirit and manly daring sent her forth to the war, when no need required her to adventure. Her name, as I said, was Artemisia, and she was the daughter of Lygdamis; by race she was on his side a Halicarnassian, though by her mother a Cretan. She ruled over the Halicarnassians, the men of Cos, of Nisyrus, and of Calydna; and the five triremes which she furnished to the Persians were, next to the Sidonian, the most famous ships in the fleet. She likewise gave to Xerxes sounder counsel than any of his other allies. Now the cities over which I have mentioned that she bore sway, were one and all Dorian; for the Halicarnassians were colonists from Trœzen,[6] while the remainder were from Epidaurus.[7] Thus much concerning the sea-force.

100. Now when the numbering and marshalling of the host was ended, Xerxes conceived a wish to go himself throughout the forces, and with his own eyes behold everything. Accordingly he traversed the ranks seated in his chariot, and, going from nation to nation, made manifold inquiries, while his scribes wrote down the answers; till at last he had passed from end to

---

1 Sirom is probably the same name with Hiram.

2 Merbal seems to be the Carthaginian Maharbal.

3 Supra, v. 104.

4 Histiæus was king of Termera (supra, v. 37).

5 The special notice taken of Artemisia is undoubtedly due in part to her having been queen of Halicarnassus, the native place of the historian.

6 Trœzen was situated on the eastern coast of the Peloponnese.

7 Epidaurus was situated on the same coast with Trœzen, but higher up, and close upon the sea-shore.

end of the whole land army, both the horsemen and likewise the foot. This done, he exchanged his chariot for a Sidonian galley, and, seated beneath a golden awning, sailed along the prows of all his vessels (the vessels having now been hauled down and launched into the sea), while he made inquiries again, as he had done when he reviewed the land-force, and caused the answers to be recorded by his scribes. The captains took their ships to the distance of about four hundred feet from the shore, and there lay to, with their vessels in a single row, the prows facing the land, and with the fighting-men upon the decks accoutred as if for war, while the king sailed along in the open space between the ships and the shore, and so reviewed the fleet.

101. Now after Xerxes had sailed down the whole line and was gone ashore, he sent for Demaratus the son of Ariston, who had accompanied him in his march upon Greece, and bespake him thus:—

"Demaratus, it is my pleasure at this time to ask thee certain things which I wish to know. Thou art a Greek, and, as I hear from the other Greeks with whom I converse, no less than from thine own lips, thou art a native of a city which is not the meanest or the weakest in their land. Tell me, therefore, what thinkest thou? Will the Greeks lift a hand against us? Mine own judgment is, that even if all the Greeks and all the barbarians of the West were gathered together in one place, they would not be able to abide my onset, not being really of one mind. But I would fain know what thou thinkest hereon."

Thus Xerxes questioned; and the other replied in his turn, — "O king! is it thy will that I give thee a true answer, or dost thou wish for a pleasant one?"

Then the king bade him speak the plain truth, and promised that he would not on that account hold him in less favour than heretofore.

102. So Demaratus, when he heard the promise, spake as follows:—

"O king! since thou biddest me at all risks speak the truth, and not say what will one day prove me to have lied to thee, thus I answer. Want has at all times been a fellow-dweller with us in our land, while Valour is an ally whom we have gained by dint of wisdom and strict laws. Her aid enables us to drive out want and escape thraldom. Brave are all the Greeks who dwell in any Dorian land; but what I am about to say does not concern all, but only the Lacedæmonians. First then, come what may, they will never accept thy terms, which would reduce Greece to slavery; and further, they are sure to join battle with thee, though all the rest of the Greeks should submit to thy will. As for their numbers, do not ask how many they are, that their resistance should be a possible thing; for if a thousand of them should take the field, they will meet thee in battle, and so will any number, be it less than this, or be it more."

103. When Xerxes heard this answer of Demaratus, he laughed and answered, –

"What wild words, Demaratus! A thousand men join battle with such an army as this! Come then, wilt thou – who wert once, as thou sayest, their king – engage to fight this very day with ten men? I trow not. And yet, if all thy fellow-citizens be indeed such as thou sayest they are, thou oughtest, as their king, by thine own country's usages,[1] to be ready to fight with twice the number. If then each one of them be a match for ten of my soldiers, I may well call upon thee to be a match for twenty. So wouldest thou assure the truth of what thou hast now said. If, however, you Greeks, who vaunt yourselves so much, are of a truth men like those whom I have seen about my court, as thyself, Demaratus, and the others with whom I am wont to converse, – if, I say, you are really men of this sort and size, how is the speech that thou hast uttered more than a mere empty boast? For, to go to the very verge of likelihood, – how could a thousand men, or ten thousand, or even fifty thousand, particularly if they were all alike free, and not under one lord, – how could such a force, I say, stand against an army like mine? Let them be five thousand, and we shall have more than a thousand men to each one of theirs.[2] If, indeed, like our troops, they had a single master, their fear of him might make them courageous beyond their natural bent; or they might be urged by lashes against an enemy which far outnumbered them.[3] But left to their own free choice, assuredly they will act differently. For mine own part, I believe, that if the Greeks had to contend with the Persians

---

1 The allusion is apparently to the "double portion" whereto the kings were entitled at banquets.

2 See below, ch. 186, where the entire Persian host is reckoned to exceed five millions of men!

3 Supra, vi. 70.

only, and the numbers were equal on both sides, the Greeks would find it hard to stand their ground. We too have among us such men as those of whom thou spakest – not many indeed, but still we possess a few. For instance, some of my body-guard would be willing to engage singly with three Greeks. But this thou didst not know; and therefore it was thou talkedst so foolishly."

104. Demaratus answered him, – "I knew, O king! at the outset, that if I told thee the truth, my speech would displease thine ears. But as thou didst require me to answer thee with all possible truthfulness, I informed thee what the Spartans will do. And in this I spake not from any love that I bear them – for none knows better than thou what my love towards them is likely to be at the present time, when they have robbed me of my rank and my ancestral honours, and made me a homeless exile, whom thy father did receive, bestowing on me both shelter and sustenance. What likelihood is there that a man of understanding should be unthankful for kindness shown him, and not cherish it in his heart? For mine own self, I pretend not to cope with ten men, nor with two, – nay, had I the choice, I would rather not fight even with one. But, if need appeared, or if there were any great cause urging me on, I would contend with right good will against one of those persons who boast themselves a match for any three Greeks. So likewise the Lacedæmonians, when they fight singly, are as good men as any in the world, and when they fight in a body, are the bravest of all. For though they be freemen, they are not in all respects free; Law is the master whom they own; and this master they fear more than thy subjects fear thee. Whatever he commands they do; and his commandment is always the same: it forbids them to flee in battle, whatever the number of their foes, and requires them to stand firm, and either to conquer or die. If in these words, O king! I seem to thee to speak foolishly, I am content from this time forward evermore to hold my peace. I had not now spoken unless compelled by thee. Certes, I pray that all may turn out according to thy wishes."

105. Such was the answer of Demaratus; and Xérxes was not angry with him at all, but only laughed, and sent him away with words of kindness.

After this interview, and after he had made Mascames the son of Megadostes governor of Doriscus, setting aside the governor appointed by Darius, Xerxes started with his army, and marched upon Greece through Thrace.

106. This man, Mascames, whom he left behind him, was a person of such merit that gifts were sent him yearly by the king as a special favour, because he excelled all the other governors that had been appointed either by Xerxes or by Darius. In like manner, Artaxerxes, the son of Xerxes, sent gifts yearly to the descendants of Mascames. Persian governors had been established in Thrace and about the Hellespont before the march of Xerxes began; but these persons, after the expedition was over, were all driven from their towns by the Greeks, except the governor of Doriscus: no one succeeded in driving out Mascames, though many made the attempt. For this reason the gifts are sent him every year by the king who reigns over the Persians.

107. Of the other governors whom the Greeks drove out, there was not one who, in the judgment of Xerxes, showed himself a brave man, excepting Boges, the governor of Eïon. Him Xerxes never could praise enough; and such of his sons as were left in Persia, and survived their father, he very specially honoured. And of a truth this Boges was worthy of great commendation; for when he was besieged by the Athenians under Cimon, the son of Miltiades, and it was open to him to retire from the city upon terms, and return to Asia, he refused, because he feared the king might think he had played the coward to save his own life, wherefore, instead of surrendering, he held out to the last extremity. When all the food in the fortress was gone, he raised a vast funeral pile, slew his children, his wife, his concubines, and his household slaves, and cast them all into the flames. Then, collecting whatever gold and silver there was in the place, he flung it from the walls into the Strymon; and, when that was done, to crown all, he himself leaped into the fire. For this action Boges is with reason praised by the Persians even at the present day.

108. Xerxes, as I have said, pursued his march from Doriscus against Greece; and on his way he forced all the nations through which he passed to take part in the expedition. For the whole country as far as the frontiers of Thessaly had been (as I have already shown) enslaved and made tributary to the king by the conquests of Megabazus, and, more lately, of Mardonius.[1] And

1 Supra, v. 2–18; vi. 44, 45.

first, after leaving Doriscus, Xerxes passed the Samothracian fortresses, whereof Mesambria is the furthermost as one goes toward the west. The next city is Strymé, which belongs to Thasos. Midway between it and Mesambria flows the river Lissus, which did not suffice to furnish water for the army, but was drunk up and failed. This region was formerly called Gallaïca; now it bears the name of Briantica; but in strict truth it likewise is really Ciconian.[1]

109. After crossing the dry channel of the Lissus, Xerxes passed the Grecian cities of Marôneia, Dicæa, and Abdêra, and likewise the famous lakes which are in their neighbourhood, Lake Ismaris between Marôneia and Strymé, and Lake Bistonis near Dicæa, which receives the waters of two rivers, the Travus and the Compsatus. Near Abdêra there was no famous lake for him to pass; but he crossed the river Nestus, which there reaches the sea. Proceeding further upon his way, he passed by several continental cities, one of them possessing a lake nearly thirty furlongs in circuit, full of fish, and very salt, of which the sumpter-beasts only drank, and which they drained dry. The name of this city was Pistyrus. All these towns, which were Grecian, and lay upon the coast, Xerxes kept upon his left hand as he passed along.

110. The following are the Thracian tribes through whose country he marched: the Pæti, the Ciconians, the Bistonians, the Sapæans, the Dersæans, the Edonians, and the Satræ. Some of these dwelt by the sea, and furnished ships to the king's fleet; while others lived in the more inland parts, and of these all the tribes which I have mentioned, except the Satræ, were forced to serve on foot.

111. The Satræ, so far as our knowledge goes, have never yet been brought under by any one, but continue to this day a free and unconquered people, unlike the other Thracians. They dwell amid lofty mountains clothed with forests of different trees and capped with snow, and are very valiant in fight. They are the Thracians who have an oracle of Dionysus in their country, which is situated upon their highest mountain-range. The Bessi, a Satrian race, deliver the oracles; but the prophet, as at Delphi, is a woman; and her answers are not harder to read.

1 See above, ch. 59.

112. When Xerxes had passed through the region mentioned above, he came next to the Pierian fortresses, one of which is called Phagres, and another Pergamus.[1] Here his line of march lay close by the walls, with the long high range of Pangæum[2] upon his right, a tract in which there are mines both of gold and silver, some worked by the Pierians and Odomantians, but the greater part by the Satræ.

113. Xerxes then marched through the country of the Pæonian tribes – the Doberians and the Pæoplæ – which lay to the north of Pangæum, and, advancing westward, reached the river Strymon and the city Eïon, whereof Boges, of whom I spoke a short time ago,[3] and who was then still alive, was governor. The tract of land lying about Mount Pangæum, is called Phyllis; on the west it reaches to the river Angites, which flows into the Strymon, and on the south to the Strymon itself, where at this time the Magi were sacrificing white horses to make the stream favourable.[4]

114. After propitiating the stream by these and many other magical ceremonies, the Persians crossed the Strymon, by bridges made before their arrival, at a place called "The Nine Ways,"[5] which was in the territory of the Edonians. And when they learnt that the name of the place was "The Nine Ways," they took nine of the youths of the land and as many of their maidens, and buried them alive on the spot. Burying alive is a Persian custom. I have heard that Amestris, the wife of Xerxes, in her old age buried alive seven pairs of Persian youths, sons of illustrious men, as a thank-offering to the god who is supposed to dwell underneath the earth.

115. From the Strymon the army, proceeding westward, came to a strip of shore, on which there stands the Grecian town of Argilus. This shore, and the whole tract above it, is called Bisaltia.[6] Passing this, and keeping on the left hand the Gulf of Posideium, Xerxes crossed the Sylean plain,[7] as it is called, and

---

1 The original Pieria was the district between the Haliacmon and the Peneus.
2 Vide supra, v. 16.
3 Supra, ch. 107.
4 *White* horses seem to have been regarded as especially sacred (supra, ch. 40).
5 Afterwards Amphipolis.
6 The Bisaltæ were a brave and powerful Thracian people.
7 By the Sylean plain, which no other writer mentions, is to be understood the flat tract, about a mile in width, near the mouth of the river which drains the lake of Bolbé (*Besikia*).

passing by Stagirus,[1] a Greek city, came to Acanthus. The inhabitants of these parts, as well as those who dwelt about Mount Pangæum, were forced to join the armament, like those others of whom I spoke before; the dwellers along the coast being made to serve in the fleet, while those who lived more inland had to follow with the land forces. The road which the army of Xerxes took remains to this day untouched: the Thracians neither plough nor sow it, but hold it in great honour.

116. On reaching Acanthus, the Persian king, seeing the great zeal of the Acanthians for his service, and hearing what had been done about the cutting, took them into the number of his sworn friends, sent them as a present a Median dress,[2] and besides commended them highly.

117. It was while he remained here that Artachæes, who presided over the canal,[3] a man in high repute with Xerxes, and by birth an Achæmenid, who was moreover the tallest of all the Persians, being only four fingers short of five cubits, royal measure,[4] and who had a stronger voice than any other man in the world, fell sick and died. Xerxes therefore, who was greatly afflicted at the mischance, carried him to the tomb and buried him with all magnificence; while the whole army helped to raise a mound over his grave. The Acanthians, in obedience to an oracle, offer sacrifice to this Artachæes as a hero, invoking him in their prayers by name. But King Xerxes sorrowed greatly over his death.

118. Now the Greeks who had to feed the army, and to entertain Xerxes, were brought thereby to the very extremity of distress, insomuch that some of them were forced even to forsake house and home. When the Thasians received and feasted the host, on account of their possessions upon the mainland, Antipater, the son of Orges, one of the citizens of best repute, and the man to whom the business was assigned, proved that the cost of the meal was four hundred talents of silver.[5]

119. And estimates almost to the same amount were made by the superintendents in other cities. For the entertainment, which had been ordered long beforehand and was reckoned to be of much consequence, was, in the manner of it, such as I will now describe. No sooner did the heralds who brought the

---

1 Now *Stavros*.   2 Compare iii. 84.   3 Supra, ch. 21.
4 That is, about 8 feet 2 inches.   5 Nearly £100,000 of our money.

orders[1] give their message, than in every city the inhabitants made a division of their stores of corn, and proceeded to grind flour of wheat and of barley for many months together. Besides this, they purchased the best cattle that they could find, and fattened them; and fed poultry and water-fowl in ponds and buildings, to be in readiness for the army; while they likewise prepared gold and silver vases and drinking-cups, and whatsoever else is needed for the service of the table. These last preparations were made for the king only, and those who sat at meat with him; for the rest of the army nothing was made ready beyond the food for which orders had been given. On the arrival of the Persians, a tent ready pitched for the purpose received Xerxes, who took his rest therein, while the soldiers remained under the open heaven. When the dinner hour came, great was the toil of those who entertained the army; while the guests ate their fill, and then, after passing the night at the place, tore down the royal tent next morning, and seizing its contents, carried them all off, leaving nothing behind.

120. On one of these occasions Megacreon of Abdêra wittily recommended his countrymen "to go to the temples in a body, men and women alike, and there take their station as suppliants, and beseech the gods that they would in future always spare them one-half of the woes which might threaten their peace – thanking them at the same time very warmly for their past goodness in that they had caused Xerxes to be content with one meal in the day." For had the order been to provide breakfast for the king as well as dinner, the Abderites must either have fled before Xerxes came, or, if they awaited his coming, have been brought to absolute ruin. As it was, the nations, though suffering heavy pressure, complied nevertheless with the directions that had been given.

121. At Acanthus Xerxes separated from his fleet, bidding the captains sail on ahead and await his coming at Therma, on the Thermaic Gulf, the place from which the bay takes its name. Through this town lay, he understood, his shortest road. Previously, his order of march had been the following:– from Doriscus to Acanthus his land force had proceeded in three bodies, one of which took the way along the sea-shore in company with the fleet, and was commanded by Mardonius and Masistes, while

another pursued an inland track under Tritantæchmes and Gergis; the third, with which was Xerxes himself, marching midway between the other two, and having for its leaders Smerdomenes and Megabyzus.[1]

122. The fleet, therefore, after leaving the king, sailed through the channel which had been cut for it by Mount Athos, and came into the bay whereon lie the cities of Assa, Pilôrus, Singus, and Sarta; from all which it received contingents. Thence it stood on for the Thermaic Gulf, and rounding Cape Ampelus, the promontory of the Torônæans, passed the Grecian cities Torônê, Galepsus, Sermyla, Mecyberna, and Olynthus, receiving from each a number of ships and men. This region is called Sithonia.[2]

123. From Cape Ampelus the fleet stretched across by a short course to Cape Canastræum,[3] which is the point of the peninsula of Pallênê that runs out furthest into the sea,[4] and gathered fresh supplies of ships and men from Potidæa, Aphytis, Neapolis, Æga, Therambus, Sciônê, Mendé, and Sané.[5] These are the cities of the tract called anciently Phlegra, but now Pallênê.[6] Hence they again followed the coast, still advancing towards the place appointed by the king, and had accessions from all the cities that lie near Pallênê, and border on the Thermaic Gulf, whereof the names are Lipaxus, Cômbreia, Lisæ, Gigônus, Campsa, Smila, and Ænêa. The tract where these towns lie still retains its old name of Crossæa.[7] After passing Ænêa, the city which I last named, the fleet found itself arrived in the Thermaic Gulf, off the land of Mygdonia. And so at length they reached Therma, the appointed place, and came likewise to Sindus and Chalestra upon the river Axius, which separates Bottiæa from

---

1 See above, ch. 82.

2 The Sithonians were probably an ancient Thracian people.

3 It is plain from this that only a portion of the ships made the circuit of the bay in order to collect ships and men. The main body of the fleet sailed across the mouth of the bay.

4 This description sufficiently identifies the Canastræan promontory with the modern Cape *Paliúri*.

5 The situation and origin of Potidæa are well known from Thucydides (i. 56–65).

6 Pallênê was the name of the peninsula extending from Potidæa to Cape Canastræum.

7 Now called *Kalamariá*.

Mygdonia. Bottiæa has a scanty sea-board, which is occupied by the two cities Ichnæ and Pella.[1]

124. So the fleet anchored off the Axius, and off Therma, and the towns that lay between, waiting the king's coming. Xerxes meanwhile with his land force[2] left Acanthus, and started for Therma, taking his way across the land. This road led him through Pæonia and Crestonia to the river Echeidôrus,[3] which rising in the country of the Crestonians, flows through Mygdonia, and reaches the sea near the marsh upon the Axius.

125. Upon this march the camels that carried the provisions of the army were set upon by lions, which left their lairs and came down by night, but spared the men and the sumpter-beasts, while they made the camels their prey. I marvel what may have been the cause which compelled the lions to leave the other animals untouched and attack the camels, when they had never seen that beast before, nor had any experience of it.

126. That whole region is full of lions, and wild bulls,[4] with gigantic horns which are brought into Greece. The lions are confined within the tract lying between the river Nestus (which flows through Abdêra) on the one side, and the Acheloüs (which waters Acarnania) on the other.[5] No one ever sees a lion in the fore part of Europe east of the Nestus, nor through the entire continent west of the Acheloüs; but in the space between these bounds lions are found.[6]

127. On reaching Therma Xerxes halted his army, which encamped along the coast, beginning at the city of Therma in

1 Pella (which became under Philip the capital of Macedonia) was not upon the coast, as we should gather from this passage, but above twenty miles from the sea, on the borders of a lake.

2 The bulk of the land force would undoubtedly have kept the direct road through Apollonia which St. Paul followed (Acts xvii. 1); while Xerxes with his immediate attendants visited Acanthus, to see the canal, and then rejoined the main army by a mountain-path which fell into the main road beyond Apollonia.

3 The Echeidôrus is undoubtedly the *Galliko*, which flows from the range of *Karadagh* (Cerciné), and running nearly due south, empties itself into the Gulf of *Saloniki*.

4 The bonasus has been thought to be the modern *auroch;* but Sir G. C. Lewis regards it as "a species of wild ox, cognate, but not identical, with the auroch."

5 Vide supra, ii. 10.

6 Aristotle, a native of this district, makes the same statement as Herodotus; and the elder Pliny follows him.

Mygdonia, and stretching out as far as the rivers Lydias and Haliacmon, two streams which, mingling their waters in one, form the boundary between Bottiæa and Macedonia. Such was the extent of country through which the barbarians encamped. The rivers here mentioned were all of them sufficient to supply the troops, except the Echeidôrus, which was drunk dry.

128. From Therma Xerxes beheld the Thessalian mountains, Olympus and Ossa,[1] which are of a wonderful height. Here, learning that there lay between these mountains a narrow gorge[2] through which the river Peneus ran, and where there was a road that gave an entrance into Thessaly, he formed the wish to go by sea himself, and examine the mouth of the river. His design was to lead his army by the upper road through the country of the inland Macedonians, and so to enter Perrhæbia, and come down by the city of Gonnus;[3] for he was told that that way was the most secure. No sooner therefore had he formed this wish than he acted accordingly. Embarking, as was his wont on all such occasions, aboard a Sidonian vessel,[4] he gave the signal to the rest of the fleet to get under weigh, and quitting his land army, set sail and proceeded to the Peneus. Here the view of the mouth caused him to wonder greatly; and sending for his guides, he asked them whether it were possible to turn the course of the stream, and make it reach the sea at any other point.

129. Now there is a tradition that Thessaly was in ancient times a lake, shut in on every side by huge hills. Ossa and Pelion – ranges which join at the foot[5] – do in fact inclose it upon the east, while Olympus forms a barrier upon the north,[6] Pindus

---

1 In clear weather Olympus and Ossa are in full view from Therma (*Saloniki*), though the latter is more than 70 miles distant.

2 This description of the pass of Tempé (vide infra, ch. 173), though brief, is remarkably accurate.

3 Gonnus was at the western extremity of the pass of Tempé, near the modern *Dereli*.

4 Supra, ch. 100.

5 Mount Pelium (the modern *Plessídhi*) lies south-east of Ossa at a distance of about 40 miles. The bases of the two mountains nevertheless join, as Herodotus states. The height of Pelium is estimated at 5,300 feet. It is richly clothed with wood, nearly to the summit.

6 The name Olympus is here applied to the entire range.

upon the west,[1] and Othrys towards the south.[2] The tract contained within these mountains, which is a deep basin, is called Thessaly. Many rivers pour their waters into it; but five of them are of more note than the rest, namely, the Peneus, the Apidanus, the Onochônus, the Enipeus, and the Pamisus. These streams flow down from the mountains which surround Thessaly, and, meeting in the plain, mingle their waters together, and discharge themselves into the sea by a single outlet, which is a gorge of extreme narrowness. After the junction all the other names disappear, and the river is known as the Peneus. It is said that of old the gorge which allows the waters an outlet did not exist; accordingly the rivers, which were then, as well as the Lake Bœbêïs,[3] without names, but flowed with as much water as at present, made Thessaly a sea. The Thessalians tell us that the gorge through which the water escapes was caused by Poseidon; and this is likely enough; at least any man who believes that Poseidon causes earthquakes, and that chasms so produced are his handiwork, would say, upon seeing this rent, that Poseidon did it. For it plainly appeared to me that the hills had been torn asunder by an earthquake.[4]

130. When Xerxes therefore asked the guides if there were any other outlet by which the waters could reach the sea, they, being men well acquainted with the nature of their country, made answer —

"O king! there is no other passage by which this stream can empty itself into the sea save that which thine eye beholds. For Thessaly is girt about with a circlet of hills."

Xerxes is said to have observed upon this —

"Wise men truly are they of Thessaly, and good reason had they to change their minds in time and consult for their own safety. For, to pass by other matters, they must have felt that they lived in a country which may easily be brought under and

---

1 Mount Pindus, the back-bone of Greece, runs in a direction nearly due north and south.

2 Othrys, now Mount *Iérako*, is situated due south of Ossa, and south-west of Pelion. Its height is estimated at 5,670 feet.

3 Lake Bœbêïs, so called from a small town Bœbé, at its eastern extremity, is the modern lake of *Karla*, a piece of water which has no outlet to the sea.

4 Modern science will scarcely quarrel with this description of Thessaly, which shows Herodotus to have had the eye of a physical geographer and the imagination of a geologist.

subdued. Nothing more is needed than to turn the river upon their lands by an embankment which should fill up the gorge and force the stream from its present channel, and lo! all Thessaly, except the mountains, would at once be laid under water."

The king aimed in this speech at the sons of Aleuas, who were Thessalians, and had been the first of all the Greeks to make submission to him. He thought that they had made their friendly offers in the name of the whole people.[1] So Xerxes, when he had viewed the place, and made the above speech, went back to Therma.

131. The stay of Xerxes in Pieria lasted for several days, during which a third part of his army was employed in cutting down the woods on the Macedonian mountain-range to give his forces free passage into Perrhæbia. At this time the heralds who had been sent into Greece to require earth for the king returned to the camp, some of them empty-handed, others with earth and water.

132. Among the number of those from whom earth and water were brought, were the Thessalians, Dolopians,[2] Enianians,[3] Perrhæbians, Locrians, Magnetians, Malians, Achæans of Phthiôtis,[4] Thebans, and Bœotians generally, except those of Platæa and Thespiæ. These are the nations against whom the Greeks that had taken up arms to resist the barbarians swore the oath, which ran thus – "From all those of Greek blood who delivered themselves up to the Persians without necessity, when their affairs were in good condition, we will take a tithe of their goods, and give it to the god at Delphi." So ran the words of the Greek oath.

133. King Xerxes had sent no heralds either to Athens or Sparta to ask earth and water, for a reason which I will now relate. When Darius some time before sent messengers for the same purpose,[5] they were thrown, at Athens, into the pit of punishment,[6] at Sparta into a well, and bidden to take therefrom

1 This was not the case.
2 The Dolopes inhabited the mountain tract at the base of Pindus.
3 The Enianes occupied the upper valley of the Spercheius.
4 The Magnetians, Achæans, and Malians, were the inhabitants of the coast tract between Thessaly and Locris.
5 Supra, vi. 48.
6 The barathrum, or "pit of punishment" at Athens, was a deep hole like a well into which criminals were precipitated.

earth and water for themselves, and carry it to their king. On this account Xerxes did not send to ask them. What calamity came upon the Athenians to punish them for their treatment of the heralds I cannot say, unless it were the laying waste of their city and territory; but that I believe was not on account of this crime.

134. On the Lacedæmonians, however, the wrath of Talthybius, Agamemnon's herald, fell with violence. Talthybius has a temple at Sparta; and his descendants, who are called Talthybiadæ, still live there, and have the privilege of being the only persons who discharge the office of herald. When therefore the Spartans had done the deed of which we speak, the victims at their sacrifices failed to give good tokens; and this failure lasted for a very long time. Then the Spartans were troubled; and, regarding what had befallen them as a grievous calamity, they held frequent assemblies of the people, and made proclamation through the town, "Was any Lacedæmonian willing to give his life for Sparta?" Upon this two Spartans, Sperthias, the son of Anêristus, and Bulis, the son of Nicolaüs, both men of noble birth, and among the wealthiest in the place, came forward and freely offered themselves as an atonement to Xerxes for the heralds of Darius slain at Sparta. So the Spartans sent them away to the Medes to undergo death.

135. Nor is the courage which these men hereby displayed alone worthy of wonder; but so likewise are the following speeches which were made by them. On their road to Susa they presented themselves before Hydarnes.[1] This Hydarnes was a Persian by birth, and had the command of all the nations that dwelt along the sea-coast of Asia. He accordingly showed them hospitality, and invited them to a banquet, where, as they feasted, he said to them:—

"Men of Lacedæmon, why will ye not consent to be friends with the king? Ye have but to look at me and my fortune to see that the king knows well how to honour merit. In like manner ye yourselves, were ye to make your submission to him, would receive at his hands, seeing that he deems you men of merit, some government in Greece."

"Hydarnes," they answered, "thou art a one-sided counsellor. Thou hast experience of half the matter; but the other half is

1 This Hydarnes seems to be the person alluded to in Book vi. ch. 133.

beyond thy knowledge. A slave's life thou understandest; but, never having tasted liberty, thou canst not tell whether it be sweet or no. Ah! hadst thou known what freedom is, thou wouldst have bidden us fight for it, not with the spear only, but with the battle-axe."

So they answered Hydarnes.

136. And afterwards, when they were come to Susa into the king's presence, and the guards ordered them to fall down and do obeisance, and went so far as to use force to compel them, they refused, and said they would never do any such thing, even were their heads thrust down to the ground; for it was not their custom to worship men, and they had not come to Persia for that purpose. So they fought off the ceremony; and having done so, addressed the king in words much like the following:—

"O king of the Medes! the Lacedæmonians have sent us hither, in the place of those heralds of thine who were slain in Sparta, to make atonement to thee on their account."

Then Xerxes answered with true greatness of soul "that he would not act like the Lacedæmonians, who, by killing the heralds, had broken the laws which all men hold in common. As he had blamed such conduct in them, he would never be guilty of it himself. And besides, he did not wish, by putting the two men to death, to free the Lacedæmonians from the stain of their former outrage."

137. This conduct on the part of the Spartans caused the anger of Talthybius to cease for a while, notwithstanding that Sperthias and Bulis returned home alive. But many years afterwards it awoke once more, as the Lacedæmonians themselves declare, during the war between the Peloponnesians and the Athenians.

In my judgment this was a case wherein the hand of Heaven was most plainly manifest. That the wrath of Talthybius should have fallen upon ambassadors, and not slacked till it had full vent, so much justice required; but that it should have come upon the sons of the very men who were sent up to the Persian king on its account – upon Nicolaüs, the son of Bulis, and Anêristus, the son of Sperthias (the same who carried off fishermen from Tiryns, when cruising in a well-manned merchantship), – this does seem to me to be plainly a supernatural circumstance. Yet certain it is that these two men, having been sent to Asia as ambassadors by the Lacedæmonians, were betrayed by Sitalces, the son of Teres, king of Thrace, and Nym-phodôrus, the son of Pythes, a native of Abdêra, and being made prisoners at Bisanthé, upon the Hellespont, were conveyed to Attica, and there put to death by the Athenians, at the same time as Aristeas, the son of Adeimantus,[1] the Corinthian. All this happened, however, very many years after the expedition of Xerxes.[2]

138. To return, however, to my main subject, — the expedi-tion of the Persian king, though it was in name directed against Athens, threatened really the whole of Greece. And of this the Greeks were aware some time before; but they did not all view the matter in the same light. Some of them had given the Persian earth and water, and were bold on this account, deeming them-selves thereby secured against suffering hurt from the barbarian army; while others, who had refused compliance, were thrown into extreme alarm. For whereas they considered all the ships in Greece too few to engage the enemy, it was plain that the greater number of states would take no part in the war, but warmly favoured the Medes.

139. And here I feel constrained to deliver an opinion, which most men, I know, will mislike, but which, as it seems to me to be true, I am determined not to withhold. Had the Athenians, from fear of the approaching danger, quitted their country, or had they without quitting it submitted to the power of Xerxes, there would certainly have been no attempt to resist the Persians by sea; in which case the course of events by land would have been the following. Though the Peloponnesians might have car-ried ever so many breastworks across the Isthmus, yet their allies would have fallen off from the Lacedæmonians, not by voluntary desertion, but because town after town must have been taken by the fleet of the barbarians; and so the Lacedæmonians would at last have stood alone, and, standing alone, would have displayed prodigies of valour, and died nobly. Either they would have done thus, or else, before it came to that extremity, seeing one Greek state after another embrace the cause of the Medes, they would have come to terms with King Xerxes;— and thus, either way Greece would have been brought under Persia. For I cannot

---

1 Concerning Adeimantus, see below, viii. 59, 61, 94.
2 The event took place in the year B.C. 430, nearly sixty years after the murder of the Persian envoys.

understand of what possible use the walls across the Isthmus could have been, if the king had had the mastery of the sea. If then a man should now say that the Athenians were the saviours of Greece, he would not exceed the truth. For they truly held the scales; and whichever side they espoused must have carried the day. They too it was who, when they had determined to maintain the freedom of Greece, roused up that portion of the Greek nation which had not gone over to the Medes; and so, next to the gods, *they* repulsed the invader. Even the terrible oracles which reached them from Delphi, and struck fear into their hearts, failed to persuade them to fly from Greece. They had the courage to remain faithful to their land, and await the coming of the foe.

140. When the Athenians, anxious to consult the oracle, sent their messengers to Delphi, hardly had the envoys completed the customary rites about the sacred precinct, and taken their seats inside the sanctuary of the god, when the Pythoness, Aristonicé by name, thus prophesied —

"Wretches, why sit ye here? Fly, fly to the ends of creation,
  Quitting your homes, and the crags which your city crowns with
    her circlet.
Neither the head, nor the body is firm in its place, nor at bottom
Firm the feet, nor the hands; nor resteth the middle uninjur'd.
All — all ruined and lost. Since fire, and impetuous Ares,
Speeding along in a Syrian chariot,[1] hastes to destroy her.
Not alone shalt thou suffer; full many the towers he will level,
Many the shrines of the gods he will give to a fiery destruction.
Even now they stand with dark sweat horribly dripping,
Trembling and quaking for fear; and lo! from the high roofs
  trickleth
Black blood, sign prophetic of hard distresses impending.
Get ye away from the temple; and brood on the ills that await ye!"

141. When the Athenian messengers heard this reply, they were filled with the deepest affliction: whereupon Timon, the son of Androbûlus, one of the men of most mark among the Delphians, seeing how utterly cast down they were at the gloomy prophecy, advised them to take an olive-branch, and entering the sanctuary again, consult the oracle as suppliants. The Athenians followed this advice, and going in once more, said — "O king!

---

1 That is, Assyrian.

we pray thee reverence these boughs of supplication which we bear in our hands, and deliver to us something more comforting concerning our country. Else we will not leave thy sanctuary, but will stay here till we die." Upon this the priestess gave them a second answer, which was the following:–

"Pallas has not been able to soften the lord of Olympus,
Though she has often prayed him, and urged him with excellent
    counsel.
Yet once more I address thee in words than adamant firmer.
When the foe shall have taken whatever the limit of Cecrops[1]
Holds within it, and all which divine Cithæron shelters,
Then far-seeing Zeus grants this to the prayers of Athena;
Safe shall the wooden wall continue for thee and thy children.
Wait not the tramp of the horse, nor the footmen mightily moving
Over the land, but turn your back to the foe, and retire ye.
Yet shall a day arrive when ye shall meet him in battle.
Holy Salamis, thou shalt destroy the offspring of women,
When men scatter the seed, or when they gather the harvest."

142. This answer seemed, as indeed it was, gentler than the former one; so the envoys wrote it down, and went back with it to Athens. When, however, upon their arrival, they produced it before the people, and inquiry began to be made into its true meaning, many and various were the interpretations which men put on it; two, more especially, seemed to be directly opposed to one another. Certain of the old men were of opinion that the god meant to tell them the citadel would escape; for this was anciently defended by a palisade; and they supposed that barrier to be the "wooden wall" of the oracle. Others maintained that the fleet was what the god pointed at; and their advice was that nothing should be thought of except the ships, which had best be at once got ready. Still such as said the "wooden wall" meant the fleet, were perplexed by the last two lines of the oracle –

"Holy Salamis, thou shalt destroy the offspring of women,
When men scatter the seed, or when they gather the harvest."

These words caused great disturbance among those who took the wooden wall to be the ships; since the interpreters understood them to mean, that, if they made preparations for a sea-fight, they would suffer a defeat off Salamis.

1 By the "limit of Cecrops" the boundaries of Attica are intended.

143. Now there was at Athens a man who had lately made his way into the first rank of citizens: his true name was Themistocles; but he was known more generally as the son of Neocles.[1] This man came forward and said, that the interpreters had not explained the oracle altogether aright – "for if," he argued, "the clause in question had really respected the Athenians, it would not have been expressed so mildly; the phrase used would have been 'Luckless Salamis,' rather than 'Holy Salamis,' had those to whom the island belonged been about to perish in its neighbourhood. Rightly taken, the response of the god threatened the enemy, much more than the Athenians." He therefore counselled his countrymen to make ready to fight on board their ships, since *they* were the wooden wall in which the god told them to trust. When Themistocles had thus cleared the matter, the Athenians embraced his view, preferring it to that of the interpreters. The advice of these last had been against engaging in a sea-fight; "all the Athenians could do," they said, "was, without lifting a hand in their defence, to quit Attica, and make a settlement in some other country."[2]

144. Themistocles had before this given a counsel which prevailed very seasonably. The Athenians, having a large sum of money in their treasury, the produce of the mines at Laureium,[3] were about to share it among the full-grown citizens, who would have received ten drachmas apiece,[4] when Themistocles persuaded them to forbear the distribution, and build with the money two hundred ships, to help them in their war against the Eginetans. It was the breaking out of the Eginetan war which was at this time the saving of Greece; for hereby were the Athenians forced to become a maritime power. The new ships were not used for the purpose for which they had been built, but became a help to Greece in her hour of need. And the Athenians had not only

1 The practice of addressing persons by their fathers' names was common in Greece.

2 This plan appears to have been seriously entertained.

3 Laureium or Laurion was the name of the mountainous country immediately above Cape *Colonna* (Sunium). The silver-mines, with which the whole tract abounded, had been worked from time immemorial.

4 If the number of citizens at this time was, according to the estimate already made, 30,000 (supra, v. 97), the entire sum which they were about to have shared among them must have been fifty talents, or rather more than £12,000.

these vessels ready before the war, but they likewise set to work to build more; while they determined, in a council which was held after the debate upon the oracle, that, according to the advice of the god, they would embark their whole force aboard their ships, and, with such Greeks as chose to join them, give battle to the barbarian invader. Such, then, were the oracles which had been received by the Athenians.

145. The Greeks who were well affected to the Grecian cause, having assembled in one place, and there consulted together, and interchanged pledges with each other, agreed that, before any other step was taken, the feuds and enmities which existed between the different nations should first of all be appeased. Many such there were; but one was of more importance than the rest, namely, the war which was still going on between the Athenians and the Eginetans.[1] When this business was concluded, understanding that Xerxes had reached Sardis with his army, they resolved to despatch spies into Asia to take note of the king's affairs. At the same time they determined to send ambassadors to the Argives, and conclude a league with them against the Persians; while they likewise despatched messengers to Gelo, the son of Deinomenes, in Sicily, to the people of Corcyra, and to those of Crete, exhorting them to send help to Greece. Their wish was to unite, if possible, the entire Greek name in one, and so to bring all to join in the same plan of defence, inasmuch as the approaching dangers threatened all alike. Now the power of Gelo was said to be very great, far greater than that of any single Grecian people.

146. So when these resolutions had been agreed upon, and the quarrels between the states made up, first of all they sent into Asia three men as spies. These men reached Sardis, and took note of the king's forces, but, being discovered, were examined by order of the generals who commanded the land army, and, having been condemned to suffer death, were led out to execution. Xerxes, however, when the news reached him, disapproving the sentence of the generals, sent some of his body-guard with instructions, if they found the spies still alive, to bring them into his presence. The messengers found the spies alive, and brought them before the king, who, when he heard the purpose for which

1 Supra, v. 81, 89; vi. 87-93. The council appears to have assembled at the Isthmus (infra, ch. 172).

they had come, gave orders to his guards to take them round the camp, and show them all the footmen and all the horse, letting them gaze at everything to their hearts' content; then, when they were satisfied, to send them away unharmed to whatever country they desired.

147. For these orders Xerxes gave afterwards the following reasons. "Had the spies been put to death," he said, "the Greeks would have continued ignorant of the vastness of his army, which surpassed the common report of it; while he would have done them a very small injury by killing three of their men. On the other hand, by the return of the spies to Greece, his power would become known; and the Greeks," he expected, "would make surrender of their freedom before he began his march, by which means his troops would be saved all the trouble of an expedition." This reasoning was like to that which he used upon another occasion. While he was staying at Abydos, he saw some corn-ships, which were passing through the Hellespont from the Euxine,[1] on their way to Egina and the Peloponnese. His attendants, hearing that they were the enemy's, were ready to capture them, and looked to see when Xerxes would give the signal. He, however, merely asked, "Whither the ships were bound?" and when they answered, "For thy foes, master, with corn on board," — "We too are bound thither," he rejoined, "laden, among other things, with corn. What harm is it, if they carry our provisions for us?"

So the spies, when they had seen everything, were dismissed, and came back to Europe.

148. The Greeks who had banded themselves together against the Persian king, after despatching the spies into Asia, sent next ambassadors to Argos. The account which the Argives give of their own proceedings is the following. They say that they had information from the very first of the preparations which the barbarians were making against Greece. So, as they expected that the Greeks would come upon them for aid against the assailant, they sent envoys to Delphi to inquire of the god what it would be best for them to do in the matter. They had lost, not long before, six thousand citizens, who had been slain by the Lacedæmonians under Cleomenes the son of

---

1 The corn-growing countries upon the Black Sea, in ancient as in modern times, supplied the commercial nations with their chief article of food.

Anaxandridas;[1] which was the reason why they now sent to
Delphi. When the Pythoness heard their question, she replied –

> "Hated of all thy neighbours, beloved of the blessed Immortals,
>   Sit thou still, with thy lance drawn inward, patiently watching;
>   Warily guard thine head, and the head will take care of the body."

This prophecy had been given them some time before the
envoys came; but still, when they afterwards arrived, it was permitted them to enter the council-house, and there deliver their
message. And this answer was returned to their demands –
"Argos is ready to do as ye require, if the Lacedæmonians will
first make a truce for thirty years, and will further divide with
Argos the leadership of the allied army. Although in strict right
the whole command should be hers,[2] she will be content to have
the leadership divided equally."

149. Such, they say, was the reply made by the council, in
spite of the oracle which forbade them to enter into a league
with the Greeks. For, while not without fear of disobeying the
oracle, they were greatly desirous of obtaining a thirty years'
truce, to give time for their sons to grow to man's estate. They
reflected, that if no such truce were concluded, and it should be
their lot to suffer a second calamity at the hands of the Persians,
it was likely they would fall hopelessly under the power of Sparta.
But to the demands of the Argive council the Lacedæmonian
envoys made answer – "They would bring before the people the
question of concluding a truce. With regard to the leadership,
they had received orders what to say, and the reply was, that
Sparta had two kings, Argos but one – it was not possible that
either of the two Spartans should be stripped of his dignity –
but they did not oppose the Argive king having one vote like
each of them." The Argives say, that they could not brook this
arrogance on the part of Sparta, and rather than yield one jot to
it, they preferred to be under the rule of the barbarians. So they

---

1 We have here an estimate of the Argive loss in the battle and massacre
of which an account was given above (see vi. 78–80). If, as is probable, the
number of citizens was not greater than at Sparta (about 10,000), the blow was
certainly tremendous.

2 Argos never forgot her claim or relinquished her hopes of the hegemony.
It induced her to stand aloof from great struggles – from the Peloponnesian as
well as from this – in order to nurse her strength.

told the envoys to be gone, before sunset, from their territory, or they should be treated as enemies.

150. Such is the account which is given of these matters by the Argives themselves. There is another story, which is told generally through Greece, of a different tenor. Xerxes, it is said, before he set forth on his expedition against Greece, sent a herald to Argos, who on his arrival spoke as follows:—

"Men of Argos, King Xerxes speaks thus to you. We Persians deem that the Perses from whom we descend was the child of Perseus the son of Danaë, and of Andromeda the daughter of Cepheus. Hereby it would seem that we come of your stock and lineage. So then it neither befits us to make war upon those from whom we spring; nor can it be right for you to fight, on behalf of others, against us. Your place is to keep quiet and hold yourselves aloof. Only let matters proceed as I wish, and there is no people whom I shall have in higher esteem than you."

This address, says the story, was highly valued by the Argives, who therefore at the first neither gave a promise to the Greeks nor yet put forward a demand. Afterwards, however, when the Greeks called upon them to give their aid, they made the claim which has been mentioned, because they knew well that the Lacedæmonians would never yield it, and so they would have a pretext for taking no part in the war.

151. Some of the Greeks say that this account agrees remarkably with what happened many years afterwards. Callias, the son of Hipponicus, and certain others with him, had gone up to Susa, the city of Memnon,[1] as ambassadors of the Athenians, upon a business quite distinct from this. While they were there, it happened that the Argives likewise sent ambassadors to Susa, to ask Artaxerxes, the son of Xerxes, "if the friendship which they had formed with his father still continued, or if he looked upon them as his enemies?" – to which King Artaxerxes replied, "Most certainly it continues; and there is no city which I reckon more my friend than Argos."

152. For my own part I cannot positively say whether Xerxes did send the herald to Argos or not; nor whether Argive ambassadors at Susa did really put this question to Artaxerxes about the friendship between them and him; neither do I deliver any opinion hereupon other than that of the Argives themselves.

---

1 Supra, ii. 106, and v. 53, 54.

This, however, I know – that if every nation were to bring all its evil deeds to a given place, in order to make an exchange with some other nation, when they had all looked carefully at their neighbours' faults, they would be truly glad to carry their own back again. So, after all, the conduct of the Argives was not perhaps more disgraceful than that of others. For myself, my duty is to report all that is said; but I am not obliged to believe it all alike – a remark which may be understood to apply to my whole History. Some even go so far as to say that the Argives first invited the Persians to invade Greece, because of their ill success in the war with Lacedæmon, since they preferred anything to the smart of their actual sufferings. Thus much concerning the Argives.

153. Other ambassadors, among whom was Syagrus from Lacedæmon, were sent by the allies into Sicily, with instructions to confer with Gelo.

The ancestor of this Gelo, who first settled at Gela, was a native of the isle of Telos, which lies off Triopium.[1] When Gela was colonised by Antiphêmus and the Lindians of Rhodes,[2] he likewise took part in the expedition. In course of time his descendants became the high-priests of the gods who dwell below – an office which they held continually, from the time that Têlines, one of Gelo's ancestors, obtained it in the way which I will now mention. Certain citizens of Gela, worsted in a sedition, had found a refuge at Mactôrium, a town situated on the heights above Gela. Têlines reinstated these men, without any human help, solely by means of the sacred rites of these deities. From whom he received them, or how he himself acquired them, I cannot say; but certain it is, that relying on their power he brought the exiles back. For this his reward was to be, the office of high-priest of those gods for himself and his seed for ever. It surprises me especially that such a feat should have been performed by Têlines; for I have always looked upon acts of this nature as beyond the abilities of common men, and only to be achieved by such as are of a bold and manly spirit; whereas

1 Telos, still known by its old name, but more commonly called *Piscopi*, lies due south of the Triopian promontory (near Cape *Crio*, supra, i. 174), at the distance of about twenty miles.

2 Gela, like most of the Sicilian towns, derived its name from the stream on whose banks it was built.

Têlines is said by those who dwell about Sicily to have been a soft-hearted and womanish person. He however obtained this office in the manner above described.

154. Afterwards, on the death of Cleander the son of Pantares,[1] who was slain by Sabyllus, a citizen of Gela, after he had held the tyranny for seven years, Hippocrates, Cleander's brother, mounted the throne. During his reign, Gelo, a descendant of the high-priest Têlines, served with many others – of whom Ænesidêmus, son of Pataïcus,[2] was one – in the king's body-guard. Within a little time his merit caused him to be raised to the command of all the horse. For when Hippocrates laid siege to Callipolis,[3] and afterwards to Naxos,[4] to Zanclé,[5] to Leontini,[6] and moreover to Syracuse, and many cities of the barbarians, Gelo in every war distinguished himself above all the combatants. Of the various cities above named, there was none but Syracuse which was not reduced to slavery. The Syracusans were saved from this fate, after they had suffered defeat on the river Elôrus, by the Corinthians and Corcyræans, who made peace between them and Hippocrates, on condition of their ceding Camarina[7] to him; for that city anciently belonged to Syracuse.

155. When, however, Hippocrates, after a reign of the same length as that of Cleander his brother, perished near the city Hybla, as he was warring with the native Sicilians, then Gelo, pretending to espouse the cause of the two sons of Hippocrates, Eucleides and Cleander, defeated the citizens who were seeking to recover their freedom, and having so done, set aside the children, and himself took the kingly power. After this piece of good fortune, Gelo likewise became master of Syracuse, in the following manner. The Syracusan landholders, as they were called, had been driven from their city by the common people

1 Cleander was the first tyrant.

2 Ænesidêmus was the father of Theron, tyrant of Agrigentum not long afterwards.

3 Callipolis was a Naxian settlement, and lay at no great distance from Naxos.

4 Naxos, according to Thucydides (vi. 3), the first of the Greek settlements in Sicily, was founded about the year B.C. 735.

5 Supra, vi. 23.

6 Leontini was founded from Naxos, six years after the arrival of the Chalcideans in Sicily.

7 Camarina was founded from Syracuse about the year B.C. 599.

assisted by their own slaves, the Cyllyrians, and had fled to Cas-menæ. Gelo brought them back to Syracuse, and so got posses-sion of the town; for the people surrendered themselves, and gave up their city on his approach.

156. Being now master of Syracuse, Gelo cared less to govern Gela, which he therefore entrusted to his brother Hiero, while he strengthened the defences of his new city, which indeed was now all in all to him. And Syracuse sprang up rapidly to power and became a flourishing place. For Gelo razed Camarina to the ground, and brought all the inhabitants to Syracuse, and made them citizens; he also brought thither more than half the citizens of Gela, and gave them the same rights as the Camarinæans. So likewise with the Megarians of Sicily – after besieging their town and forcing them to surrender, he took the rich men, who, hav-ing made the war, looked now for nothing less than death at his hands, and carrying them to Syracuse, established them there as citizens; while the common people, who, as they had not taken any share in the struggle, felt secure that no harm would be done to them, he carried likewise to Syracuse, where he sold them all as slaves to be conveyed abroad. He did the like also by the Eubœans of Sicily,[1] making the same difference. His conduct towards both nations arose from his belief, that a "people" was a most unpleasant companion. In this way Gelo became a great king.

157. When the Greek envoys reached Syracuse, and were admitted to an audience, they spoke as follows –

"We have been sent hither by the Lacedæmonians and Athen-ians, with their respective allies, to ask thee to join us against the barbarian. Doubtless thou hast heard of his invasion, and art aware that a Persian is about to throw a bridge over the Helles-pont, and, bringing with him out of Asia all the forces of the East, to carry war into Greece, – professing indeed that he only seeks to attack Athens, but really bent on bringing all the Greeks into subjection. Do thou therefore, we beseech thee, aid those who would maintain the freedom of Greece, and thyself assist to free her; since the power which thou wieldest is great, and thy portion in Greece, as lord of Sicily, is no small one. For if all Greece join together in one, there will be a mighty host collected, and we shall be a match for our assailants; but if some

---

1 Eubœa seems never to have recovered from this blow.

turn traitors, and others refuse their aid, and only a small part of the whole body remains sound, then there is reason to fear that all Greece may perish. For do not thou cherish a hope that the Persian, when he has conquered our country, will be content and not advance against thee. Rather take thy measures beforehand, and consider that thou defendest thyself when thou givest aid to us. Wise counsels, be sure, for the most part have prosperous issues."

158. Thus spake the envoys; and Gelo replied with vehemence –

"Greeks, ye have had the face to come here with selfish words, and exhort me to join in league with you against the barbarian. Yet when I erewhile asked you to join with me in fighting barbarians, what time the quarrel broke out between me and Carthage;[1] and when I earnestly besought you to revenge on the men of Egesta their murder of Dorieus, the son of Anaxandridas, promising to assist you in setting free the trading-places, from which you receive great profits and advantages, you neither came hither to give me succour, nor yet to revenge Dorieus; but, for any efforts on your part to hinder it, these countries might at this time have been entirely under the barbarians. Now, however, that matters have prospered and gone well with me, while the danger has shifted its ground and at present threatens yourselves, lo! you call Gelo to mind. But though ye slighted me then, I will not imitate you now: I am ready to give you aid, and to furnish as my contribution two hundred triremes, twenty thousand men-at-arms, two thousand cavalry, and an equal number of archers, slingers, and light horsemen, together with corn for the whole Grecian army so long as the war shall last. These services, however, I promise on one condition – that ye appoint me chief captain and commander of the Grecian forces during the war with the barbarian. Unless ye agree to this, I will neither send succours, nor come myself."

159. Syagrus, when he heard these words, was unable to contain himself, and exclaimed –

"Surely a groan would burst from Pelops' son, Agamemnon, did he hear that her leadership was snatched from Sparta by Gelo and the men of Syracuse. Speak then no more of any such condition, as that we should yield thee the chief command; but

1 No particulars are known of this war.

if thou art minded to come to the aid of Greece, prepare to serve under Lacedæmonian generals. Wilt thou not serve under a leader? – then, prithee, withhold thy succours."

160. Hereupon Gelo, seeing the indignation which showed itself in the words of Syagrus, delivered to the envoys his final offer:– "Spartan stranger," he said, "reproaches cast forth against a man are wont to provoke him to anger; but the insults which thou hast uttered in thy speech shall not persuade me to outstep good breeding in my answer. Surely if you maintain so stoutly your right to the command, it is reasonable that I should be still more stiff in maintaining mine, forasmuch as I am at the head of a far larger fleet and army. Since, however, the claim which I have put forward is so displeasing to you, I will yield, and be content with less. Take, if it please you, the command of the land-force, and I will be admiral of the fleet; or assume, if you prefer it, the command by sea, and I will be leader upon the land. Unless you are satisfied with these terms, you must return home by yourselves, and lose this great alliance." Such was the offer which Gelo made.

161. Hereat broke in the Athenian envoy, before the Spartan could answer, and thus addressed Gelo –

"King of the Syracusans! Greece sent us here to thee to ask for an army, and not to ask for a general. Thou, however, dost not promise to send us any army at all, if thou art not made leader of the Greeks; and this command is what alone thou sticklest for. Now when thy request was to have the whole command, we were content to keep silence; for well we knew that we might trust the Spartan envoy to make answer for us both. But since, after failing in thy claim to lead the whole armament, thou hast now put forward a request to have the command of the fleet, know that, even should the Spartan envoy consent to this, we will not consent. The command by sea, if the Lacedæmonians do not wish for it, belongs to us. While they like to keep this command, we shall raise no dispute; but we will not yield our right to it in favour of any one else. Where would be the advantage of our having raised up a naval force greater than that of any other Greek people, if nevertheless we should suffer Syracusans to take the command away from us? – from us, I say, who are Athenians, the most ancient nation in Greece, the only Greeks who have never changed their abode – the people who are said by the poet Homer to have sent to Troy the man best able of all the Greeks to array and marshal an army – so that we may be allowed to boast somewhat."

162. Gelo replied – "Athenian stranger, ye have, it seems, no lack of commanders; but ye are likely to lack men to receive their orders. As ye are resolved to yield nothing and claim everything, ye had best make haste back to Greece, and say that the spring of her year is lost to her." The meaning of this expression was the following: as the spring is manifestly the finest season of the year, so (he meant to say) were his troops the finest of the Greek army – Greece, therefore, deprived of his alliance, would be like a year with the spring taken from it.

163. Then the Greek envoys, without having any further dealings with Gelo, sailed away home. And Gelo, who feared that the Greeks would be too weak to withstand the barbarians, and yet could not any how bring himself to go to the Peloponnese, and there, though king of Sicily, serve under the Lacedæmonians, left off altogether to contemplate that course of action, and betook himself to quite a different plan. As soon as ever tidings reached him of the passage of the Hellespont by the Persians, he sent off three penteconters, under the command of Cadmus, the son of Scythas, a native of Cos, who was to go to Delphi, taking with him a large sum of money and a stock of friendly words: there he was to watch the war, and see what turn it would take: if the barbarians prevailed, he was to give Xerxes the treasure, and with it earth and water for the lands which Gelo ruled – if the Greeks won the day, he was to convey the treasure back.

164. This Cadmus had at an earlier time received from his father the kingly power at Cos in a right good condition, and had of his own free will and without the approach of any danger, from pure love of justice, given up his power into the hands of the people at large, and departed to Sicily; where he assisted in the Samian seizure and settlement of Zanclé,[1] or Messana, as it was afterwards called. Upon this occasion Gelo chose him to send into Greece, because he was acquainted with the proofs of honesty which he had given. And now he added to his former honourable deeds an action which is not the least of his merits. With a vast sum entrusted to him and completely in his power, so that he might have kept it for his own use if he had liked, he

---

1 See above, vi. 23.

did not touch it; but when the Greeks gained the sea-fight and Xerxes fled away with his army, he brought the whole treasure back with him to Sicily.

165. They, however, who dwell in Sicily, say that Gelo, though he knew that he must serve under the Lacedæmonians, would nevertheless have come to the aid of the Greeks, had not it been for Têrillus, the son of Crinippus, king of Himera; who, driven from his city by Thero, the son of Ænesidêmus, king of Agrigentum,[1] brought into Sicily at this very time an army of three hundred thousand men, Phœnicians, Libyans, Iberians, Ligurians, Helisycians, Sardinians, and Corsicans,[2] under the command of Hamilcar the son of Hanno, king[3] of the Carthaginians. Têrillus prevailed upon Hamilcar, partly as his sworn friend, but more through the zealous aid of Anaxilaüs the son of Cretines, king of Rhegium;[4] who, by giving his own sons to Hamilcar as hostages, induced him to make the expedition. Anaxilaüs herein served his own father-in-law; for he was married to a daughter of Têrillus, by name Cydippé. So, as Gelo could not give the Greeks any aid, he sent (they say) the sum of money to Delphi.

166. They say too, that the victory of Gelo and Thero in Sicily over Hamilcar the Carthaginian, fell out upon the very day that the Greeks defeated the Persians at Salamis. Hamilcar, who was a Carthaginian on his father's side only, but on his mother's a Syracusan, and who had been raised by his merit to the throne of Carthage, after the battle and the defeat, as I am informed, disappeared from sight: Gelo made the strictest search for him, but he could not be found anywhere, either dead or alive.

167. The Carthaginians, who take probability for their guide, give the following account of this matter:— Hamilcar, they say, during all the time that the battle raged between the Greeks and the barbarians, which was from early dawn till evening, remained in the camp, sacrificing and seeking favourable omens, while he burned on a huge pyre the entire bodies of the victims which he offered. Here, as he poured libations upon the sacrifices, he saw the rout of his army; whereupon he cast himself headlong into

1 Agrigentum was founded from Gela, about B.C. 582.

2 This is the first instance of the mixed mercenary armies of Carthage, by which her conquests were ordinarily effected.

3 That is, Suffes. The Greek writers always speak of the Suffetes as "kings" (βασιλεῖς).

4 Supra, vi. 23.

the flames, and so was consumed and disappeared. But whether Hamilcar's disappearance happened, as the Phœnicians tell us, in this way, or, as the Syracusans maintain, in some other, certain it is that the Carthaginians offer him sacrifice, and in all their colonies have monuments erected to his honour, as well as one, which is the grandest of all, at Carthage. Thus much concerning the affairs of Sicily.

168. As for the Corcyræans, whom the envoys that visited Sicily took in their way, and to whom they delivered the same message as to Gelo, – their answers and actions were the following. With great readiness they promised to come and give their help to the Greeks; declaring that "the ruin of Greece was a thing which they could not tamely stand by to see; for should she fall, they must the very next day submit to slavery; so that they were bound to assist her to the very uttermost of their power." But notwithstanding that they answered so smoothly, yet when the time came for the succours to be sent, they were of quite a different mind; and though they manned sixty ships, it was long ere they put to sea with them; and when they had so done, they went no further than the Peloponnese, where they lay to with their fleet, off the Lacedæmonian coast, about Pylos[1] and Tænarum,[2] – like Gelo, watching to see what turn the war would take. For they despaired altogether of the Greeks gaining the day, and expected that the Persians would win a great battle, and then be masters of the whole of Greece. They therefore acted as I have said, in order that they might be able to address Xerxes in words like these: "O king! though the Greeks sought to obtain our aid in their war with thee, and though we had a force of no small size, and could have furnished a greater number of ships than any Greek state except Athens, yet we refused, since we would not fight against thee, nor do aught to cause thee annoyance." The Corcyræans hoped that a speech like this would gain them better treatment from the Persians than the rest of the Greeks; and it would have done so, in my judgment. At the same time, they had an excuse ready to give their countrymen,

1 Pylos, celebrated in poetry as the abode of Nestor (Il. ii. 591–602), and in history as the scene of the first important defeat suffered by the Spartans (Thucyd. iv. 32–40), was situated on the west coast of the Peloponnese, near the site of the modern *Navarino*.

2 Tænarum was the ancient name of the promontory now called Cape *Matapan*.

which they used when the time came. Reproached by them for sending no succours, they replied, "that they had fitted out a fleet of sixty triremes, but that the Etesian winds did not allow them to double Cape Malea, and this hindered them from reaching Salamis – it was not from any bad motive that they had missed the sea-fight." In this way the Corcyræans eluded the reproaches of the Greeks.

169. The Cretans, when the envoys sent to ask aid from them came and made their request, acted as follows. They despatched messengers in the name of their state of Delphi, and asked the god, whether it would make for their welfare if they should lend succour to Greece. "Fools!" replied the Pythoness, "do ye not still complain of the woes which the assisting of Menelaüs cost you at the hands of angry Minos? How wroth was he, when, in spite of their having lent you no aid towards avenging his death at Camicus, you helped them to avenge the carrying off by a barbarian of a woman from Sparta!" When this answer was brought from Delphi to the Cretans, they thought no more of assisting the Greeks.

170. Minos, according to tradition, went to Sicania, or Sicily, as it is now called, in search of Dædalus, and there perished by a violent death. After a while the Cretans, warned by some god or other, made a great expedition into Sicania, all except the Polichnites and the Præsians, and besieged Camicus (which in my time belonged to Agrigentum) by the space of five years. At last, however, failing in their efforts to take the place, and unable to carry on the siege any longer from the pressure of hunger, they departed and went their way. Voyaging homewards they had reached Iapygia,[1] when a furious storm arose and threw them upon the coast. All their vessels were broken in pieces; and so, as they saw no means of returning to Crete, they founded the town of Hyria, where they took up their abode, changing their name from Cretans to Messapian Iapygians, and at the same time becoming inhabitants of the mainland instead of islanders. From Hyria they afterwards founded those other towns which the Tarentines at a much later period endeavoured to take, but could not, being defeated signally. Indeed so dreadful a slaughter of Greeks never happened at any other time, so far as my knowledge

---

1 Iapygia coincides generally with the *Terra di Otranto* of our maps, extending, however, somewhat further round the Gulf of *Taranto*.

extends: nor was it only the Tarentines who suffered; but the men of Rhegium too, who had been forced to go to the aid of the Tarentines by Micythus the son of Chœrus, lost here three thousand of their citizens; while the number of the Tarentines who fell was beyond all count. This Micythus had been a household slave of Anaxilaüs, and was by him left in charge of Rhegium: he is the same man who was afterwards forced to leave Rhegium, when he settled at Tegea in Arcadia, from which place he made his many offerings of statues to the shrine at Olympia.

171. This account of the Rhegians and the Tarentines is a digression from the story which I was relating. To return – the Præsians say that men of various nations now flocked to Crete, which was stript of its inhabitants; but none came in such numbers as the Grecians. Three generations after the death of Minos the Trojan war took place; and the Cretans were not the least distinguished among the helpers of Menelaüs. But on this account, when they came back from Troy, famine and pestilence fell upon them, and destroyed both the men and the cattle. Crete was a second time stript of its inhabitants, a remnant only being left; who form, together with fresh settlers, the third "Cretan" people by whom the island has been inhabited. These were the events of which the Pythoness now reminded the men of Crete; and thereby she prevented them from giving the Greeks aid, though they wished to have gone to their assistance.

172. The Thessalians did not embrace the cause of the Medes until they were forced to do so; for they gave plain proof that the intrigues of the Aleuadæ[1] were not at all to their liking. No sooner did they hear that the Persian was about to cross over into Europe than they despatched envoys to the Greeks who were met to consult together at the Isthmus, whither all the states which were well inclined to the Grecian cause had sent their delegates. These envoys on their arrival thus addressed their countrymen:–

"Men of Greece, it behoves you to guard the pass of Olympus; for thus will Thessaly be placed in safety, as well as the rest of Greece. We for our parts are quite ready to take our share in this work; but you must likewise send us a strong force: otherwise we give you fair warning that we shall make terms with the Persians. For we ought not to be left, exposed as we are in front

1 Supra, ch. 6. Compare ch. 140, ad fin.

of all the rest of Greece, to die in your defence alone and un-
assisted. If however you do not choose to send us aid, you cannot
force us to resist the enemy; for there is no force so strong as
inability. We shall therefore do our best to secure our own safety."

Such was the declaration of the Thessalians.

173. Hereupon the Greeks determined to send a body of foot
to Thessaly by sea, which should defend the pass of Olympus.
Accordingly a force was collected, which passed up the Euripus,
and disembarking at Alus, on the coast of Achæa, left the ships
there, and marched by land into Thessaly. Here they occupied
the defile of Tempé; which leads from Lower Macedonia into
Thessaly along the course of the Peneus, having the range of
Olympus on the one hand and Ossa upon the other. In this place
the Greek force that had been collected, amounting to about
10,000 heavy-armed men, pitched their camp; and here they were
joined by the Thessalian cavalry. The commanders were, on the
part of the Lacedæmonians, Evænetus, the son of Carênus, who
had been chosen out of the Polemarchs, but did not belong to
the blood royal; and on the part of the Athenians, Themistocles,
the son of Neocles. They did not however maintain their station
for more than a few days; since envoys came from Alexander,
the son of Amyntas, the Macedonian, and counselled them to
decamp from Tempé, telling them that if they remained in the
pass they would be trodden under foot by the invading army,
whose numbers they recounted, and likewise the multitude of
their ships. So when the envoys thus counselled them, and the
counsel seemed to be good, and the Macedonian who sent it
friendly, they did even as he advised. In my opinion what chiefly
wrought on them was the fear that the Persians might enter by
another pass,[1] whereof they now heard, which led from Upper
Macedonia[2] into Thessaly through the territory of the Perrhæbi,
and by the town of Gonnus, – the pass by which soon afterwards
the army of Xerxes actually made its entrance. The Greeks therefore went back to their ships and sailed away to the Isthmus.

174. Such were the circumstances of the expedition into
Thessaly; they took place when the king was at Abydos, preparing

1 Vide supra, ch. 128. The pass intended is probably that which crossed
the Olympic range by the town of Petra.

2 By "Upper Macedonia" Herodotus appears to mean the upper portion
of Pieria.

to pass from Asia into Europe. The Thessalians, when their allies forsook them, no longer wavered, but warmly espoused the side of the Medes; and afterwards, in the course of the war, they were of the very greatest service to Xerxes.

175. The Greeks, on their return to the Isthmus, took counsel together concerning the words of Alexander, and considered where they should fix the war, and what places they should occupy. The opinion which prevailed was, that they should guard the pass of Thermopylæ; since it was narrower than the Thessalian defile, and at the same time nearer to them. Of the pathway, by which the Greeks who fell at Thermopylæ were intercepted, they had no knowledge, until, on their arrival at Thermopylæ, it was discovered to them by the Trachinians. This pass then it was determined that they should guard, in order to prevent the barbarians from penetrating into Greece through it; and at the same time it was resolved that the fleet should proceed to Artemisium, in the region of Histiæôtis;[1] for, as those places are near to one another, it would be easy for the fleet and army to hold communication. The two places may be thus described.

176. Artemisium is where the sea of Thrace[2] contracts into a narrow channel, running between the isle of Sciathus and the mainland of Magnesia. When this narrow strait is passed you come to the line of coast called Artemisium; which is a portion of Eubœa, and contains a temple of Artemis (Artemis). As for the entrance into Greece by Trachis,[3] it is, at its narrowest point, about fifty feet wide. This however is not the place where the passage is most contracted; for it is still narrower a little above and a little below Thermopylæ. At Alpêni,[4] which is lower down than that place, it is only wide enough for a single carriage; and up above, at the river Phœnix, near the town called Anthêla, it is the same. West of Thermopylæ rises a lofty and precipitous hill, impossible to climb, which runs up into the chain of Œta; while to the east the road is shut in by the sea and by marshes. In this place are the warm springs, which the natives call "The

1 The northern tract of Eubœa was called Histiæôtis.

2 The northern portion of the Ægean, extending from Magnesia to the Thracian Chersonese.

3 Trachis was one of the chief cities of the Malians (infra, chs. 198, 199). It afterwards became Heraclea, on being colonised by the Lacedæmonians.

4 Infra, ch. 216.

Cauldrons;" and above them stands an altar sacred to Heracles.[1] A wall had once been carried across the opening;[2] and in this there had of old times been a gateway. These works were made by the Phocians, through fear of the Thessalians, at the time when the latter came from Thesprôtia to establish themselves in the land of Æolis, which they still occupy. As the Thessalians strove to reduce Phocis, the Phocians raised the wall to protect themselves, and likewise turned the hot springs upon the pass, that so the ground might be broken up by watercourses, using thus all possible means to hinder the Thessalians from invading their country. The old wall had been built in very remote times; and the greater part of it had gone to decay through age. Now however the Greeks resolved to repair its breaches, and here make their stand against the barbarian. At this point there is a village very nigh the road, Alpêni by name, from which the Greeks reckoned on getting corn for their troops.

177. These places, therefore, seemed to the Greeks fit for their purpose. Weighing well all that was likely to happen, and considering that in this region the barbarians could make no use of their vast numbers, nor of their cavalry, they resolved to await here the invader of Greece. And when news reached them of the Persians being in Pieria, straightway they broke up from the Isthmus, and proceeded, some on foot to Thermopylæ, others by sea to Artemisium.

178. The Greeks now made all speed to reach the two stations;[3] and about the same time the Delphians, alarmed both for themselves and for their country, consulted the god, and received for answer a command to "pray to the winds, for the winds would do Greece good service." So when this answer was given them, forthwith the Delphians sent word of the prophecy to those Greeks who were zealous for freedom, and, cheering them thereby amid the fears which they entertained with respect to the barbarian, earned their everlasting gratitude. This done, they raised an altar to the winds at Thyia (where Thyia, the daughter of Cephissus, from whom the region takes its name, has a precinct), and worshipped them with sacrifices. And even

---

1 The whole district was regarded as ennobled by the sufferings of Heracles, and as sacred to him.

2 Vide infra, chs. 208, 223, 225.

3 Thermopylæ and Artemisium.

to the present day the Delphians sacrifice to the winds, because of this oracle.

179. The fleet of Xerxes now departed from Therma; and ten of the swiftest sailing ships ventured to stretch across direct for Sciathus, at which place there were upon the look-out three vessels belonging to the Greeks, one a ship of Trœzen,[1] another of Egina, and the third from Athens. These vessels no sooner saw from a distance the barbarians approaching than they all hurriedly took to flight.

180. The barbarians at once pursued, and the Trœzenian ship, which was commanded by Prexînus, fell into their hands. Hereupon the Persians took the handsomest of the men-at-arms, and drew him to the prow of the vessel, where they sacrificed him; for they thought the man a good omen to their cause, seeing that he was at once so beautiful, and likewise the first captive they had made. The man who was slain in this way was called Leo; and it may be that the name he bore helped him to his fate in some measure.

181. The Eginetan trireme, under its captain, Asônides, gave the Persians no little trouble, one of the men-at-arms, Pythes, the son of Ischenoüs, distinguishing himself beyond all the others who fought on that day. After the ship was taken this man continued to resist, and did not cease fighting till he fell quite covered with wounds. The Persians who served as men-at-arms in the squadron, finding that he was not dead, but still breathed, and being very anxious to save his life, since he had behaved so valiantly, dressed his wounds with myrrh, and bound them up with bandages of cotton. Then, when they were returned to their own station, they displayed their prisoner admiringly to the whole host, and behaved towards him with much kindness; but all the rest of the ship's crew were treated merely as slaves.

182. Thus did the Persians succeed in taking two of the vessels. The third, a trireme commanded by Phormus of Athens, took to flight and ran aground at the mouth of the river Peneus. The barbarians got possession of the bark, but not of the men. For the Athenians had no sooner run their vessel aground than they leapt out, and made their way through Thessaly back to Athens.

1 Supra, ch. 99.

When the Greeks stationed at Artemisium learnt what had happened by fire-signals¹ from Sciathus, so terrified were they, that, quitting their anchorage-ground at Artemisium, and leaving scouts to watch the foe on the highlands of Eubœa, they removed to Chalcis, intending to guard the Euripus.

183. Meantime three of the ten vessels sent forward by the barbarians advanced as far as the sunken rock between Sciathus and Magnesia, which is called "The Ant," and there set up a stone pillar which they had brought with them for that purpose. After this, their course being now clear, the barbarians set sail with all their ships from Therma, eleven days from the time that the king quitted the town. The rock, which lay directly in their course, had been made known to them by Pammon of Scyros.² A day's voyage without a stop brought them to Sepias in Magnesia,³ and to the strip of coast which lies between the town of Casthanæa and the promontory of Sepias.

184. As far as this point then, and on land, as far as Thermopylæ, the armament of Xerxes had been free from mischance; and the numbers were still, according to my reckoning, of the following amount. First there was the ancient complement of the twelve hundred and seven vessels which came with the king from Asia – the contingents of the nations severally – amounting, if we allow to each ship a crew of two hundred men,⁴ to 241,400. Each of these vessels had on board, besides native soldiers, thirty fighting men, who were either Persians, Medes, or Sacans;⁵ which gives an addition of 36,210. To these two numbers I shall further add the crews of the penteconters; which may be reckoned, one with another, at fourscore men each. Of such vessels there were (as I said before⁶) three thousand; and the men on board them accordingly would be 240,000. This was the sea force brought by the king from Asia; and it amounted

1 The employment of fire-signals among the Greeks was very common. Æschylus represents it as known to them at the time of the Trojan war. [Compare the opening of the *Agamemnon* of Æschylus. – E. H. B.]

2 Scyros, still called *Skyro*, lay off the east coast of Eubœa, at the distance of about 23 miles.

3 The distance is calculated to be about 900 stades or 103˙ miles.

4 The crew of a *Greek* trireme seems always to have been 200 (vide infra, viii. 17).

5 Vide supra, ch. 96.

6 Supra, ch. 97. It appears from that passage that in these 3,000 vessels are included, besides penteconters, various other craft of a much smaller size.

in all to 517,610 men. The number of the foot soldiers was 1,700,000;[1] that of the horsemen 80,000;[2] to which must be added the Arabs who rode on camels, and the Libyans who fought in chariots, whom I reckon at 20,000. The whole number, therefore, of the land and sea forces added together amounts to 2,317,610 men. Such was the force brought from Asia, without including the camp followers, or taking any account of the provision-ships and the men whom they had on board.

185. To the amount thus reached we have still to add the forces gathered in Europe, concerning which I can only speak from conjecture. The Greeks dwelling in Thrace, and in the islands off the coast of Thrace, furnished to the fleet one hundred and twenty ships; the crews of which would amount to 24,000 men. Besides these, footmen were furnished by the Thracians, the Pæonians, the Eordians, the Bottiæans, by the Chalcidean tribes, by the Brygians, the Pierians, the Macedonians, the Perrhæbians, the Enianians, the Dolopians, the Magnesians, the Achæans, and by all the dwellers upon the Thracian sea-board; and the forces of these nations amounted, I believe, to three hundred thousand men. These numbers, added to those of the force which came out of Asia, make the sum of the fighting men 2,641,610.

186. Such then being the number of the fighting men, it is my belief that the attendants who followed the camp, together with the crews of the corn-barks, and of the other craft accompanying the army, made up an amount rather above than below that of the fighting men. However I will not reckon them as either fewer or more, but take them at an equal number. We have therefore to add to the sum already reached an exactly equal amount. This will give 5,283,220 as the whole number of men brought by Xerxes, the son of Darius, as far as Sepias and Thermopylæ.[3]

187. Such then was the amount of the entire host of Xerxes. As for the number of the women who ground the corn, of the concubines, and the eunuchs, no one can give any sure account

1 Supra, ch. 60.
2 See ch. 87.
3 [These numbers are probably wholly fabulous. Modern historians (e.g. Bury) estimate the land forces at 300,000, and the number of the fleet at about 800 triremes. – E. H. B.]

of it; nor can the baggage-horses and other sumpter-beasts, nor the Indian hounds which followed the army, be calculated, by reason of their multitude. Hence I am not at all surprised that the water of the rivers was found too scant for the army in some instances; rather it is a marvel to me how the provisions did not fail, when the numbers were so great. For I find on calculation that if each man consumed no more than a chœnix of corn a-day, there must have been used daily by the army 110,340 medimni,[1] and this without counting what was eaten by the women, the eunuchs, the sumpter-beasts, and the hounds. Among all this multitude of men there was not one who, for beauty and stature, deserved more than Xerxes himself to wield so vast a power.

188. The fleet then, as I said, on leaving Therma, sailed to the Magnesian territory, and there occupied the strip of coast between the city of Casthanæa and Cape Sepias. The ships of the first row were moored to the land, while the remainder swung at anchor further off. The beach extended but a very little way, so that they had to anchor off the shore, row upon row, eight deep. In this manner they passed the night. But at dawn of day calm and stillness gave place to a raging sea, and a violent storm, which fell upon them with a strong gale from the east — a wind which the people in those parts call Hellespontias. Such of them as perceived the wind rising, and were so moored as to allow of it, forestalled the tempest by dragging their ships up on the beach, and in this way saved both themselves and their vessels. But the ships which the storm caught out at sea were driven ashore, some of them near the place called Ipni, or "The Ovens," at the foot of Pelion; others on the strand itself; others again about Cape Sepias; while a portion were dashed to pieces near the cities of Melibœa and Casthanæa. There was no resisting the tempest.

189. It is said that the Athenians had called upon Boreas[2] to aid the Greeks, on account of a fresh oracle which had reached them, commanding them to "seek help from their son-in-law." For Boreas, according to the tradition of the Greeks, took to wife a woman of Attica, viz., Orithyia, the daughter of Erechtheus. So the Athenians, as the tale goes, considering that this marriage made Boreas their son-in-law, and perceiving, while

1 The medimnus contained about 12 gallons English.
2 The name Bora is still retained in the Adriatic for the N.E. wind.

they lay with their ships at Chalcis of Eubœa,[1] that the wind was rising, or, it may be, even before it freshened, offered sacrifice both to Boreas and likewise to Orithyia, entreating them to come to their aid and to destroy the ships of the barbarians, as they did once before off Mount Athos. Whether it was owing to this that Boreas fell with violence on the barbarians at their anchorage I cannot say; but the Athenians declare that they had received aid from Boreas before, and that it was he who now caused all these disasters. They therefore, on their return home, built a temple to this god on the banks of the Ilissus.

190. Such as put the loss of the Persian fleet in this storm at the lowest, say that four hundred of their ships were destroyed, that a countless multitude of men were slain, and a vast treasure engulfed. Ameinocles, the son of Crêtines, a Magnesian, who farmed land near Cape Sepias, found the wreck of these vessels a source of great gain to him; many were the gold and silver drinking-cups, cast up long afterwards by the surf, which he gathered; while treasure-boxes too which had belonged to the Persians, and golden articles of all kinds and beyond count, came into his possession. Ameinocles grew to be a man of great wealth in this way; but in other respects things did not go over well with him: he too, like other men, had his own grief — the calamity of losing his offspring.

191. As for the number of the provision craft and other merchant ships which perished, it was beyond count. Indeed, such was the loss, that the commanders of the sea force, fearing lest in their shattered condition the Thessalians should venture on an attack, raised a lofty barricade around their station out of the wreck of the vessels cast ashore. The storm lasted three days. At length the Magians, by offering victims to the Winds, and charming them with the help of conjurers, while at the same time they sacrificed to Thetis and the Nereids, succeeded in laying the storm four days after it first began; or perhaps it ceased of itself. The reason of their offering sacrifice to Thetis was this: they were told by the Ionians that here was the place whence Peleus carried her off, and that the whole promontory was sacred to her and to her sister Nereids. So the storm lulled upon the fourth day.

192. The scouts left by the Greeks about the highlands of Eubœa hastened down from their stations on the day following

that whereon the storm began, and acquainted their countrymen with all that had befallen the Persian fleet. These no sooner heard what had happened than straightway they returned thanks to Poseidon the Saviour, and poured libations in his honour; after which they hastened back with all speed to Artemisium, expecting to find a very few ships left to oppose them, and arriving there for the second time, took up their station on that strip of coast: nor from that day to the present have they ceased to address Poseidon by the name then given him, of "Saviour."

193. The barbarians, when the wind lulled and the sea grew smooth, drew their ships down to the water, and proceeded to coast along the mainland. Having then rounded the extreme point of Magnesia, they sailed straight into the bay that runs up to Pagasæ.[1] There is a place in this bay, belonging to Magnesia, where Hercules is said to have been put ashore to fetch water by Jason and his companions; who then deserted him and went on their way to Æa in Colchis, on board the ship Argo, in quest of the golden fleece. From the circumstance that they intended, after watering their vessel at this place, to quit the shore and launch forth into the deep, it received the name of Aphetæ. Here then it was that the fleet of Xerxes came to an anchor.

194. Fifteen ships, which had lagged greatly behind the rest, happening to catch sight of the Greek fleet at Artemisium, mistook it for their own, and sailing down into the midst of it, fell into the hands of the enemy. The commander of this squadron was Sandôces, the son of Thamasius, governor of Cymé,[2] in Æolis. He was of the number of the royal judges,[3] and had been crucified by Darius some time before, on the charge of taking a bribe to determine a cause wrongly; but while he yet hung on the cross, Darius bethought him that the good deeds of Sandôces towards the king's house were more numerous than his evil deeds; and so, confessing that he had acted with more haste than wisdom, he ordered him to be taken down and set at large. Thus Sandôces escaped destruction at the hands of Darius, and was alive at this time; but he was not fated to come off so cheaply from his second peril; for as soon as the Greeks saw the ships making towards them, they guessed their mistake, and putting to sea, took them without difficulty.

1 The modern Gulf of *Volo*.   2 Supra, i. 149.   3 Supra, iii. 31.

195. Aridôlis, tyrant of Alabanda in Caria, was on board one of the ships, and was made prisoner; as also was the Paphian general, Penthylus, the son of Demonoüs, who was on board another. This person had brought with him twelve ships from Paphos,[1] and, after losing eleven in the storm off Sepias, was taken in the remaining one as he sailed towards Artemisium. The Greeks, after questioning their prisoners as much as they wished concerning the forces of Xerxes, sent them away in chains to the Isthmus of Corinth.

196. The sea force of the barbarians, with the exception of the fifteen ships commanded (as I said) by Sandôces, came safe to Aphetæ. Xerxes meanwhile, with the land army, had proceeded through Thessaly and Achæa, and three days earlier, had entered the territory of the Malians. In Thessaly, he matched his own horses against the Thessalian, which he heard were the best in Greece;[2] but the Greek coursers were left far behind in the race. All the rivers in this region had water enough to supply his army, except only the Onochônus;[3] but in Achæa, the largest of the streams, the Apidanus, barely held out.

197. On his arrival at Alus[4] in Achæa, his guides, wishing to inform him of everything, told him the tale known to the dwellers in those parts concerning the temple of the Laphystian Zeus[5] – how that Athamas the son of Æolus took counsel with Ino and plotted the death of Phrixus;[6] and how that afterwards the Achæans, warned by an oracle, laid a forfeit upon his posterity, forbidding the eldest of the race ever to enter into the courthouse (which they call the people's house), and keeping watch

---

1 Paphos seems to have been one of the earliest Phœnician settlements in Cyprus.

2 The excellency of the Thessalian horses was proverbial.

3 Supra, ch. 129.

4 Supra, ch. 173.

5 The most famous temple of Zeus Laphystius was in Bœotia.

6 The tale went, that Ino, wishing to destroy the children of Athamas by his first wife Nephelé, produced a dearth by having the seed-corn secretly parched before it was sown, and when Athamas consulted the oracle on the subject, persuaded the messengers to bring back word, that Phrixus must be sacrificed to Zeus. Athamas was imposed upon, and prepared to offer his son; but Nephelé snatched Phrixus from the altar, and placed him upon a ram with a golden fleece which she had obtained from Hermes, and the ram carried him through the air to Colchis, where it was offered by Phrixus to Zeus. The fleece he gave to Æetes the Colchian king.

themselves to see the law obeyed. If one comes within the doors, he can never go out again except to be sacrificed. Further, they told him, how that many persons, when on the point of being slain, are seized with such fear that they flee away and take refuge in some other country; and that these, if they come back long afterwards, and are found to be the persons who entered the court-house, are led forth covered with chaplets, and in a grand procession, and are sacrificed. This forfeit is paid by the descendants of Cytissorus the son of Phrixus, because, when the Achæans, in obedience to an oracle, made Athamas the son of Æolus their sin-offering, and were about to slay him, Cytissorus came from Æa in Colchis and rescued Athamus; by which deed he brought the anger of the god upon his own posterity. Xerxes, therefore, having heard this story, when he reached the grove of the god, avoided it, and commanded his army to do the like. He also paid the same respect to the house and precinct of the descendants of Athamas.

198. Such were the doings of Xerxes in Thessaly and in Achæa. From hence he passed on into Malis, along the shores of a bay, in which there is an ebb and flow of the tide daily.[1] By the side of this bay lies a piece of flat land, in one part broad, but in another very narrow indeed, around which runs a range of lofty hills, impossible to climb, enclosing all Malis within them, and called the Trachinian cliffs. The first city upon the bay, as you come from Achæa, is Anticyra, near which the river Spercheius, flowing down from the country of the Enianians, empties itself into the sea. About twenty furlongs from this stream there is a second river, called the Dyras,[2] which is said to have appeared first to help Heracles when he was burning. Again, at the distance of twenty furlongs, there is a stream called the Melas, near which, within about five furlongs, stands the city of Trachis.

199. At the point where this city is built, the plain between the hills and the sea is broader than at any other, for it there measures 22,000 plethra.[3] South of Trachis there is a cleft in the

1 The tides in the Mediterranean seldom rise more than a few feet, in some places not above 12 or 13 inches. The flatness of the coast róund the Maliac Gulf would render the rise and fall more perceptible there than elsewhere.

2 Colonel Leake has satisfactorily identified this stream as well as the Melas.

3 This is certainly an incorrect reading. Twenty-two thousand plethra are above 420 miles, whereas the plain is even now, at the utmost, seven miles across.

mountain-range which shuts in the territory of Trachinia; and the river Asôpus[1] issuing from this cleft flows for a while along the foot of the hills.

200. Further to the south, another river, called the Phœnix, which has no great body of water, flows from the same hills, and falls into the Asôpus. Here is the narrowest place of all; for in this part there is only a causeway wide enough for a single carriage. From the river Phœnix to Thermopylæ is a distance of fifteen furlongs; and in this space is situate the village called Anthêla, which the river Asôpus passes ere it reaches the sea. The space about Anthêla is of some width; and contains a temple of Amphictyonian Demeter, as well as the seats of the Amphictyonic deputies,[2] and a temple of Amphictyon himself.[3]

201. King Xerxes pitched his camp in the region of Malis called Trachinia, while on their side the Greeks occupied the straits. These straits the Greeks in general call Thermopylæ (the Hot Gates); but the natives, and those who dwell in the neighbourhood, call them Pylæ (the Gates). Here then the two armies took their stand; the one master of all the region lying north of Trachis, the other of the country extending southward of that place to the verge of the continent.

202. The Greeks who at this spot awaited the coming of Xerxes were the following:— From Sparta, three hundred men-at-arms: from Arcadia, a thousand Tegeans and Mantineans, five hundred of each people; a hundred and twenty Orchomenians, from the Arcadian Orchomenus;[4] and a thousand from other cities: from Corinth, four hundred men: from Phlius, two hundred: and from Mycenæ eighty. Such was the number from the Peloponnese. There were also present, from Bœotia, seven hundred Thespians and four hundred Thebans.

203. Besides these troops, the Locrians of Opus and the Phocians had obeyed the call of their countrymen, and sent, the former all the force they had, the latter a thousand men. For

---

1 The Asôpus is clearly the *Karvunaria*.

2 Amphictyonies were religious leagues of states possessing a common sanctuary.

3 Amphictyon would seem to be most clearly an invented name, formed, according to the Greek custom of referring all appellatives to a *heros eponymus*, from the word Amphictyony.

4 The Arcadian is here distinguished from the Bœotian city of the same name (infra, viii. 34).

envoys had gone from the Greeks at Thermopylæ among the Locrians and Phocians, to call on them for assistance, and to say – "They were themselves but the vanguard of the host, sent to precede the main body, which might every day be expected to follow them. The sea was in good keeping, watched by the Athenians, the Eginetans, and the rest of the fleet. There was no cause why they should fear; for after all the invader was not a god but a man; and there never had been, and never would be, a man who was not liable to misfortunes from the very day of his birth, and those misfortunes greater in proportion to his own greatness. The assailant therefore, being only a mortal, must needs fall from his glory." Thus urged, the Locrians and the Phocians had come with their troops to Trachis.

204. The various nations had each captains of their own under whom they served; but the one to whom all especially looked up, and who had the command of the entire force, was the Lacedæmonian, Leonidas. Now Leonidas was the son of Anaxandridas, who was the son of Leo, who was the son of Eurycratidas, who was the son of Anaxander, who was the son of Eurycrates, who was the son of Polydôrus, who was the son of Alcamenes, who was the son of Têlecles, who was the son of Archelaüs, who was the son of Agesilaüs, who was the son of Doryssus, who was the son of Labôtas, who was the son of Echestratus, who was the son of Agis, who was the son of Eurysthenes, who was the son of Aristodêmus, who was the son of Aristomachus, who was the son of Cleodæus, who was the son of Hyllus, who was the son of Hercules.

Leonidas had come to be king of Sparta quite unexpectedly.

205. Having two elder brothers, Cleomenes and Dorieus, he had no thought of ever mounting the throne. However, when Cleomenes died without male offspring, as Dorieus was likewise deceased, having perished in Sicily,[1] the crown fell to Leonidas, who was older than Cleombrotus, the youngest of the sons of Anaxandridas, and, moreover, was married to the daughter of Cleomenes. He had now come to Thermopylæ, accompanied by the three hundred[2] men which the law assigned him, whom he

---

1 Supra, v. 46.
2 Leonidas seems to have been fully aware of the desperate nature of the service which he now undertook. He therefore, instead of taking with him his ordinary body-guard of *youths*, selected a body-guard from among the men of

had himself chosen from among the citizens, and who were all of them fathers with sons living. On his way he had taken the troops from Thebes, whose number I have already mentioned, and who were under the command of Leontiades the son of Eurymachus. The reason why he made a point of taking troops from Thebes, and Thebes only, was, that the Thebans were strongly suspected of being well inclined to the Medes. Leonidas therefore called on them to come with him to the war, wishing to see whether they would comply with his demand, or openly refuse, and disclaim the Greek alliance. They, however, though their wishes leant the other way, nevertheless sent the men.

206. The force with Leonidas was sent forward by the Spartans in advance of their main body, that the sight of them might encourage the allies to fight, and hinder them from going over to the Medes, as it was likely they might have done had they seen that Sparta was backward. They intended presently, when they had celebrated the Carneian festival,[1] which was what now kept them at home, to leave a garrison in Sparta, and hasten in full force to join the army. The rest of the allies also intended to act similarly; for it happened that the Olympic festival fell exactly at this same period.[2] None of them looked to see the contest at Thermopylæ decided so speedily; wherefore they were content to send forward a mere advanced guard. Such accordingly were the intentions of the allies.

207. The Greek forces at Thermopylæ, when the Persian army drew near to the entrance of the pass, were seized with fear; and a council was held to consider about a retreat. It was the wish of the Peloponnesians generally that the army should fall back upon the Peloponnese, and there guard the Isthmus. But Leonidas, who saw with what indignation the Phocians and Locrians heard of this plan, gave his voice for remaining where they were, while they sent envoys to the several cities to ask for

---

advanced age, taking none but such as had male offspring living, in order that no family might altogether perish.

1 The Carneian festival fell in the Spartan month Carneius, the Athenian Metageitnion, corresponding nearly to our August. It was held in honour of Apollo Carneius.

2 Vide infra, viii. 26. The Olympic festival was celebrated at the time of the first full moon after the summer solstice. It therefore ordinarily preceded the Spartan Carneia, falling in the latter end of June or in July.

help, since they were too few to make a stand against an army like that of the Medes.

208. While this debate was going on, Xerxes sent a mounted spy to observe the Greeks, and note how many they were, and see what they were doing. He had heard, before he came out of Thessaly, that a few men were assembled at this place, and that at their head were certain Lacedæmonians, under Leonidas, a descendant of Heracles. The horseman rode up to the camp, and looked about him, but did not see the whole army; for such as were on the further side of the wall (which had been rebuilt and was now carefully guarded) it was not possible for him to behold; but he observed those on the outside, who were encamped in front of the rampart. It chanced that at this time the Lacedæmonians held the outer guard, and were seen by the spy, some of them engaged in gymnastic exercises, others combing their long hair. At this the spy greatly marvelled, but he counted their number, and when he had taken accurate note of everything, he rode back quietly; for no one pursued after him, nor paid any heed to his visit. So he returned, and told Xerxes all that he had seen.

209. Upon this, Xerxes, who had no means of surmising the truth — namely, that the Spartans were preparing to do or die manfully — but thought it laughable that they should be engaged in such employments, sent and called to his presence Demaratus the son of Ariston, who still remained with the army. When he appeared, Xerxes told him all that he had heard, and questioned him concerning the news, since he was anxious to understand the meaning of such behaviour on the part of the Spartans. Then Demaratus said —

"I spake to thee, O king! concerning these men long since,[1] when we had but just begun our march upon Greece; thou, however, didst only laugh at my words, when I told thee of all this, which I saw would come to pass. Earnestly do I struggle at all times to speak truth to thee, sire; and now listen to it once more. These men have come to dispute the pass with us; and it is for this that they are now making ready. 'Tis their custom, when they are about to hazard their lives, to adorn their heads with care.[2] Be assured, however, that if thou canst subdue the

1 Supra, chs. 101–104.

2 The Spartan custom of wearing the hair long has been already noticed (supra, i. 82).

men who are here and the Lacedæmonians who remain in Sparta, there is no other nation in all the world which will venture to lift a hand in their defence. Thou hast now to deal with the first kingdom and town in Greece, and with the bravest men."

Then Xerxes, to whom what Demaratus said seemed altogether to surpass belief, asked further, "how it was possible for so small an army to contend with his?"

"O king!" Demaratus answered, "let me be treated as a liar, if matters fall not out as I say."

210. But Xerxes was not persuaded any the more. Four whole days he suffered to go by, expecting that the Greeks would run away. When, however, he found on the fifth that they were not gone, thinking that their firm stand was mere impudence and recklessness, he grew wroth, and sent against them the Medes and Cissians, with orders to take them alive and bring them into his presence. Then the Medes rushed forward and charged the Greeks, but fell in vast numbers: others however took the places of the slain, and would not be beaten off, though they suffered terrible losses. In this way it became clear to all, and especially to the king, that though he had plenty of combatants, he had but very few warriors. The struggle, however, continued during the whole day.

211. Then the Medes, having met so rough a reception, withdrew from the fight; and their place was taken by the band of Persians under Hydarnes, whom the king called his "Immortals:"[1] they, it was thought, would soon finish the business. But when they joined battle with the Greeks, 'twas with no better success than the Median detachment − things went much as before − the two armies fighting in a narrow space, and the barbarians using shorter spears than the Greeks, and having no advantage from their numbers. The Lacedæmonians fought in a way worthy of note, and showed themselves far more skilful in fight than their adversaries, often turning their backs, and making as though they were all flying away, on which the barbarians would rush after them with much noise and shouting, when the Spartans at their approach would wheel round and face their pursuers, in this way destroying vast numbers of the enemy. Some Spartans likewise fell in these encounters, but only a very few. At last the Persians, finding that all their efforts to gain the

1 Supra, ch. 83.

pass availed nothing, and that, whether they attacked by divisions or in any other way, it was to no purpose, withdrew to their own quarters.

212. During these assaults, it is said that Xerxes, who was watching the battle, thrice leaped from the throne on which he sate, in terror for his army.

Next day the combat was renewed, but with no better success on the part of the barbarians. The Greeks were so few that the barbarians hoped to find them disabled, by reason of their wounds, from offering any further resistance; and so they once more attacked them. But the Greeks were drawn up in detachments according to their cities, and bore the brunt of the battle in turns, — all except the Phocians, who had been stationed on the mountain to guard the pathway. So, when the Persians found no difference between that day and the preceding, they again retired to their quarters.

213. Now, as the king was in a great strait, and knew not how he should deal with the emergency, Ephialtes, the son of Eurydêmus, a man of Malis, came to him and was admitted to a conference. Stirred by the hope of receiving a rich reward at the king's hands, he had come to tell him of the pathway which led across the mountain to Thermopylæ; by which disclosure he brought destruction on the band of Greeks who had there withstood the barbarians. This Ephialtes afterwards, from fear of the Lacedæmonians, fled into Thessaly; and during his exile, in an assembly of the Amphictyons held at Pylæ, a price was set upon his head by the Pylagoræ. When some time had gone by, he returned from exile, and went to Anticyra, where he was slain by Athênades, a native of Trachis. Athênades did not slay him for his treachery, but for another reason, which I shall mention in a later part of my history: yet still the Lacedæmonians honoured him none the less. Thus then did Ephialtes perish a long time afterwards.

214. Besides this there is another story told, which I do not at all believe — to wit, that Onêtas the son of Phanagoras, a native of Carystus, and Corydallus, a man of Anticyra, were the persons who spoke on this matter to the king, and took the Persians across the mountain. One may guess which story is true, from the fact that the deputies of the Greeks, the Pylagoræ, who must have had the best means of ascertaining the truth, did not offer the reward for the heads of Onêtas and Corydallus, but for

that of Ephialtes of Trachis; and again from the flight of Ephialtes, which we know to have been on this account. Onêtas, I allow, although he was not a Malian, might have been acquainted with the path, if he had lived much in that part of the country; but as Ephialtes was the person who actually led the Persians round the mountain by the pathway, I leave his name on record as that of the man who did the deed.

215. Great was the joy of Xerxes on this occasion; and as he approved highly of the enterprise which Ephialtes undertook to accomplish, he forthwith sent upon the errand Hydarnes, and the Persians under him.[1] The troops left the camp about the time of the lighting of the lamps. The pathway along which they went was first discovered by the Malians of these parts, who soon afterwards led the Thessalians by it to attack the Phocians, at the time when the Phocians fortified the pass with a wall,[2] and so put themselves under covert from danger. And ever since, the path has always been put to an ill use by the Malians.

216. The course which it takes is the following:– Beginning at the Asôpus, where that stream flows through the cleft in the hills,[3] it runs along the ridge of the mountain (which is called, like the pathway over it, Anopæa), and ends at the city of Alpênus – the first Locrian town as you come from Malis – by the stone called Melampygus and the seats of the Cercopians. Here it is as narrow as at any other point.

217. The Persians took this path, and, crossing the Asôpus, continued their march through the whole of the night, having the mountains of Œta on their right hand, and on their left those of Trachis. At dawn of day they found themselves close to the summit. Now the hill was guarded, as I have already said,[4] by a thousand Phocian men-at-arms, who were placed there to defend the pathway, and at the same time to secure their own country. They had been given the guard of the mountain path, while the other Greeks defended the pass below, because they had volunteered for the service, and had pledged themselves to Leonidas to maintain the post.

218. The ascent of the Persians became known to the Phocians in the following manner:– During all the time that they were making their way up, the Greeks remained unconscious of

1 The 10,000 Immortals.   2 Supra, ch. 176.
3 Supra, ch. 199.   4 Supra, ch. 212.

it, inasmuch as the whole mountain was covered with groves of oak; but it happened that the air was very still, and the leaves which the Persians stirred with their feet made, as it was likely they would, a loud rustling, whereupon the Phocians jumped up and flew to seize their arms. In a moment the barbarians came in sight, and, perceiving men arming themselves, were greatly amazed; for they had fallen in with an enemy when they expected no opposition. Hydarnes, alarmed at the sight, and fearing lest the Phocians might be Lacedæmonians, inquired of Ephialtes to what nation these troops belonged. Ephialtes told him the exact truth, whereupon he arrayed his Persians for battle. The Phocians, galled by the showers of arrows to which they were exposed, and imagining themselves the special object of the Persian attack, fled hastily to the crest of the mountain, and there made ready to meet death; but while their mistake continued, the Persians, with Ephialtes and Hydarnes, not thinking it worth their while to delay on account of Phocians, passed on and descended the mountain with all possible speed.

219. The Greeks at Thermopylæ received the first warning of the destruction which the dawn would bring on them from the seer Megistias,[1] who read their fate in the victims as he was sacrificing. After this deserters came in, and brought the news that the Persians were marching round by the hills: it was still night when these men arrived. Last of all, the scouts came running down from the heights, and brought in the same accounts, when the day was just beginning to break. Then the Greeks held a council to consider what they should do, and here opinions were divided: some were strong against quitting their post, while others contended to the contrary. So when the council had broken up, part of the troops departed and went their ways homeward to their several states; part however resolved to remain, and to stand by Leonidas to the last.

220. It is said that Leonidas himself sent away the troops who departed, because he tendered their safety, but thought it unseemly that either he or his Spartans should quit the post which they had been especially sent to guard. For my own part, I incline to think that Leonidas gave the order, because he perceived the allies to be out of heart and unwilling to encounter the danger to which his own mind was made up. He therefore

1 Infra, chs. 221 and 228.

commanded them to retreat, but said that he himself could not draw back with honour; knowing that, if he stayed, glory awaited him, and that Sparta in that case would not lose her prosperity. For when the Spartans, at the very beginning of the war, sent to consult the oracle concerning it, the answer which they received from the Pythoness was, "that either Sparta must be overthrown by the barbarians, or one of her kings must perish." The prophecy was delivered in hexameter verse, and ran thus:—

"O ye men who dwell in the streets of broad Lacedæmon!
  Either your glorious town shall be sacked by the children of
      Perseus,
  Or, in exchange, must all through the whole Laconian country
  Mourn for the loss of a king, descendant of great Hêrácles.
  He cannot be withstood by the courage of bulls nor of lions,
  Strive as they may; he is mighty as Jove; there is nought that shall
      stay him,
  Till he have got for his prey your king, or your glorious city."

The remembrance of this answer, I think, and the wish to secure the whole glory for the Spartans, caused Leonidas to send the allies away. This is more likely than that they quarrelled with him, and took their departure in such unruly fashion.

221. To me it seems no small argument in favour of this view, that the seer also who accompanied the army, Megistias, the Acarnanian,[1] – said to have been of the blood of Melampus,[2] and the same who was led by the appearance of the victims to warn the Greeks of the danger which threatened them, – received orders to retire (as it is certain he did) from Leonidas, that he might escape the coming destruction. Megistias, however, though bidden to depart, refused, and stayed with the army; but he had an only son present with the expedition, whom he now sent away.

222. So the allies, when Leonidas ordered them to retire, obeyed him and forthwith departed. Only the Thespians and the Thebans remained with the Spartans; and of these the Thebans were kept back by Leonidas as hostages, very much against their will. The Thespians, on the contrary, stayed entirely of their own accord, refusing to retreat, and declaring that they would not

---

1 The celebrity of the Acarnanian seers has been already mentioned (supra, i. 62).

2 Melampus was placed in the generation before the Trojan war.

forsake Leonidas and his followers. So they abode with the Spartans, and died with them. Their leader was Demophilus, the son of Diadromes.

223. At sunrise Xerxes made libations, after which he waited until the time when the forum is wont to fill, and then began his advance. Ephialtes had instructed him thus, as the descent of the mountain is much quicker, and the distance much shorter, than the way round the hills, and the ascent. So the barbarians under Xerxes began to draw nigh; and the Greeks under Leonidas, as they now went forth determined to die, advanced much further than on previous days, until they reached the more open portion of the pass. Hitherto they had held their station within the wall, and from this had gone forth to fight at the point where the pass was the narrowest. Now they joined battle beyond the defile, and carried slaughter among the barbarians, who fell in heaps. Behind them the captains of the squadrons, armed with whips, urged their men forward with continual blows. Many were thrust into the sea, and there perished; a still greater number were trampled to death by their own soldiers; no one heeded the dying. For the Greeks, reckless of their own safety and desperate, since they knew that, as the mountain had been crossed, their destruction was nigh at hand, exerted themselves with the most furious valour against the barbarians.

224. By this time the spears of the greater number were all shivered, and with their swords they hewed down the ranks of the Persians; and here, as they strove, Leonidas fell fighting bravely, together with many other famous Spartans, whose names I have taken care to learn on account of their great worthiness, as indeed I have those of all the three hundred. There fell too at the same time very many famous Persians: among them, two sons of Darius, Abrocomes and Hyperanthes, his children by Phrataguné, the daughter of Artanes. Artanes was brother of King Darius, being a son of Hystaspes, the son of Arsames; and when he gave his daughter to the king, he made him heir likewise of all his substance; for she was his only child.

225. Thus two brothers of Xerxes here fought and fell. And now there arose a fierce struggle between the Persians and the Lacedæmonians over the body of Leonidas, in which the Greeks four times drove back the enemy, and at last by their great bravery succeeded in bearing off the body. This combat was scarcely ended when the Persians with Ephialtes approached;

and the Greeks, informed that they drew nigh, made a change in the manner of their fighting. Drawing back into the narrowest part of the pass, and retreating even behind the cross wall, they posted themselves upon a hillock, where they stood all drawn up together in one close body, except only the Thebans. The hillock whereof I speak is at the entrance of the straits, where the stone lion stands which was set up in honour of Leonidas.[1] Here they defended themselves to the last, such as still had swords using them, and the others resisting with their hands and teeth; till the barbarians, who in part had pulled down the wall and attacked them in front, in part had gone round and now encircled them upon every side, overwhelmed and buried the remnant which was left beneath showers of missile weapons.

226. Thus nobly did the whole body of Lacedæmonians and Thespians behave; but nevertheless one man is said to have distinguished himself above all the rest, to wit, Diêneces the Spartan. A speech which he made before the Greeks engaged the Medes, remains on record. One of the Trachinians told him, "Such was the number of the barbarians, that when they shot forth their arrows the sun would be darkened by their multitude." Diêneces, not at all frightened at these words, but making light of the Median numbers, answered, "Our Trachinian friend brings us excellent tidings. If the Medes darken the sun, we shall have our fight in the shade." Other sayings too of a like nature are reported to have been left on record by this same person.

227. Next to him two brothers, Lacedæmonians, are reputed to have made themselves conspicuous: they were named Alpheus and Maro, and were the sons of Orsiphantus. There was also a Thespian who gained greater glory than any of his countrymen: he was a man called Dithyrambus, the son of Harmatidas.

228. The slain were buried where they fell; and in their honour, nor less in honour of those who died before Leonidas sent the allies away, an inscription was set up, which said:—

> "Here did four thousand men from Pelops' land[2]
> Against three hundred myriads bravely stand."

1 The monument seems to have been standing at least as late as the time of Tiberius.

2 Herodotus seems to have misconceived this inscription. He regarded it as an epitaph upon the Greeks slain at Thermopylæ. Hence he sets the number of the slain at 4000 (infra, viii. 25). But it plainly appears from the wording to

This was in honour of all. Another was for the Spartans alone:–

> "Go, stranger, and to Lacedæmon tell
> That here, obeying her behests, we fell."[1]

This was for the Lacedæmonians. The seer had the following:–

> "The great Megistias' tomb you here may view,
> Whom slew the Medes, fresh from Spercheius' fords.
> Well the wise seer the coming death foreknew,
> Yet scorned he to forsake his Spartan lords."

These inscriptions, and the pillars likewise, were all set up by the Amphictyons, except that in honour of Megistias, which was inscribed to him (on account of their sworn friendship) by Simônides, the son of Leôprepes.[2]

229. Two of the three hundred, it is said, Aristodêmus and Eurytus, having been attacked by a disease of the eyes, had received orders from Leonidas to quit the camp; and both lay at Alpêni in the worst stage of the malady. These two men might, had they been so minded, have agreed together to return alive to Sparta; or if they did not like to return, they might have gone both to the field and fallen with their countrymen. But at this time, when either way was open to them, unhappily they could not agree, but took contrary courses. Eurytus no sooner heard that the Persians had come round the mountain than straightway he called for his armour, and having buckled it on, bade his Helot[3] lead him to the place where his friends were fighting. The Helot did so, and then turned and fled; but Eurytus plunged into the thick of the battle, and so perished. Aristodêmus, on the other hand, was faint of heart, and remained at Alpêni. It is my belief that if Aristodêmus only had been sick and returned, or if both had come back together, the Spartans would have been content and felt no anger; but when there were two men with

---

have been an inscription set up in honour of the *Peloponnesians* only, and to have referred to *all who fought*, not merely to those who fell.

1 This famous inscription Cicero has translated in the Tusculans (i. 42):–
> "Dic, hospes, Spartæ nos te hic vidisse jacentes;
> Dum sanctis patriæ *legibus* obsequimur."

2 Simonides was the poet laureate of the time.

3 By the expression "*his* Helot," we are to understand the special servant (θεράπων), whose business it was to attend constantly upon the Spartan warrior.

the very same excuse, and one of them was chary of his life, while the other freely gave it, they could not but be very wroth with the former.

230. This is the account which some give of the escape of Aristodêmus. Others say that he, with another, had been sent on a message from the army, and, having it in his power to return in time for the battle, purposely loitered on the road, and so survived his comrades; while his fellow-messenger came back in time, and fell in the battle.

231. When Aristodêmus returned to Lacedæmon, reproach and disgrace awaited him; disgrace, inasmuch as no Spartan would give him a light to kindle his fire, or so much as address a word to him; and reproach, since all spoke of him as "the craven." However he wiped away all his shame afterwards at the battle of Platæa.[1]

232. Another of the three hundred is likewise said to have survived the battle, a man named Pantites, whom Leonidas had sent on an embassy into Thessaly. He, they say, on his return to Sparta, found himself in such disesteem that he hanged himself.

233. The Thebans under the command of Leontiades remained with the Greeks, and fought against the barbarians, only so long as necessity compelled them. No sooner did they see victory inclining to the Persians, and the Greeks under Leonidas hurrying with all speed towards the hillock, than they moved away from their companions, and with hands upraised advanced towards the barbarians, exclaiming, as was indeed most true, – "that they for their part wished well to the Medes, and had been among the first to give earth and water to the king; force alone had brought them to Thermopylæ; and so they must not be blamed for the slaughter which had befallen the king's army." These words, the truth of which was attested by the Thessalians, sufficed to obtain the Thebans the grant of their lives. However, their good fortune was not without some drawback; for several of them were slain by the barbarians on their first approach; and the rest, who were the greater number, had the royal mark branded upon their bodies by the command of Xerxes, – Leontiades, their captain, being the first to suffer. (This man's son, Eurymachus, was afterwards slain by the Platæans, when he came with a band of 400 Thebans, and seized their city.)

1 Vide infra, ix. 71.

234. Thus fought the Greeks at Thermopylæ. And Xerxes, after the fight was over, called for Demaratus to question him; and began as follows:—

"Demaratus, thou art a worthy man; thy true-speaking proves it. All has happened as thou didst forewarn. Now then, tell me, how many Lacedæmonians are there left, and of those left how many are such brave warriors as these? Or are they all alike?"

"O king!" replied the other, "the whole number of the Lacedæmonians is very great; and many are the cities which they inhabit. But I will tell thee what thou really wishest to learn. There is a town of Lacedæmon called Sparta, which contains within it about eight thousand full-grown men. *They* are, one and all, equal to those who have fought here. The other Lacedæmonians are brave men, but not such warriors as these."

"Tell me now, Demaratus," rejoined Xerxes, "how we may with least trouble subdue these men. Thou must know all the paths of their counsels, as thou wert once their king."

235. Then Demaratus answered – "O king! since thou askest my advice so earnestly, it is fitting that I should inform thee what I consider to be the best course. Detach three hundred vessels from the body of thy fleet, and send them to attack the shores of Laconia. There is an island called Cythera in those parts, not far from the coast, concerning which Chilon, one of our wisest men,[1] made the remark, that Sparta would gain if it were sunk to the bottom of the sea – so constantly did he expect that it would give occasion to some project like that which I now recommend to thee. I mean not to say that he had a foreknowledge of thy attack upon Greece; but in truth he feared all armaments. Send thy ships then to this island, and thence affright the Spartans. If once they have a war of their own close to their doors, fear not their giving any help to the rest of the Greeks while thy land force is engaged in conquering them. In this way may all Greece· be subdued; and then Sparta, left to herself, will be powerless. But if thou wilt not take this advice, I will tell thee what thou mayest look to see. When thou comest to the Peloponnese, thou wilt find a narrow neck of land, where all the Peloponnesians who are leagued against thee will be gathered

1 Chilon was included among the seven wise men. The maxims "γνῶθι σεαυτόν" (*know thyself*) and "μηδὲν ἄγαν" (*nothing in excess*) were ascribed to him.

together; and there thou wilt have to fight bloodier battles than any which thou hast yet witnessed. If, however, thou wilt follow my plan, the Isthmus and the cities of the Peloponnese will yield to thee without a battle."

236. Achæmenes, who was present, now took the word, and spoke – he was brother to Xerxes, and, having the command of the fleet, feared lest Xerxes might be prevailed upon to do as Demaratus advised –

"I perceive, O king" (he said), "that thou art listening to the words of a man who is envious of thy good fortune, and seeks to betray thy cause. This is indeed the common temper of the Grecian people – they envy good fortune, and hate power greater than their own. If in this posture of our affairs, after we have lost four hundred vessels by shipwreck,[1] three hundred more be sent away to make a voyage round the Peloponnese, our enemies will become a match for us. But let us keep our whole fleet in one body, and it will be dangerous for them to venture on an attack, as they will certainly be no match for us then. Besides, while our sea and land forces advance together, the fleet and army can each help the other; but if they be parted, no aid will come either from thee to the fleet, or from the fleet to thee. Only order thy own matters well, and trouble not thyself to inquire concerning the enemy, – where they will fight, or what they will do, or how many they are. Surely they can manage their own concerns without us, as we can ours without them. If the Lacedæmonians come out against the Persians to battle, they will scarce repair the disaster which has befallen them now."

237. Xerxes replied – "Achæmenes, thy counsel pleases me well, and I will do as thou sayest. But Demaratus advised what he thought best – only his judgment was not so good as thine. Never will I believe that he does not wish well to my cause; for that is disproved both by his former counsels, and also by the circumstances of the case. A citizen does indeed envy any fellow-citizen who is more lucky than himself, and often hates him secretly; if such a man be called on for counsel, he will not give his best thoughts, unless indeed he be a man of very exalted virtue; and such are but rarely found. But a friend of another country delights in the good fortune of his foreign bond-friend, and will give him, when asked, the best advice in his power.

1 Supra, ch. 190.

Therefore I warn all men to abstain henceforth from speaking ill of Demaratus, who is my bond-friend."

238. When Xerxes had thus spoken, he proceeded to pass through the slain; and finding the body of Leonidas, whom he knew to have been the Lacedæmonian king and captain, he ordered that the head should be struck off, and the trunk fastened to a cross. This proves to me most clearly, what is plain also in many other ways, — namely, that King Xerxes was more angry with Leonidas, while he was still in life, than with any other mortal. Certes, he would not else have used his body so shamefully. For the Persians are wont to honour those who show themselves valiant in fight more highly than any nation that I know. They, however, to whom the orders were given, did according to the commands of the king.

239. I return now to a point in my History, which at the time I left incomplete. The Lacedæmonians were the first of the Greeks to hear of the king's design against their country; and it was at this time that they sent to consult the Delphic oracle, and received the answer of which I spoke a while ago.[1] The discovery was made to them in a very strange way. Demaratus, the son of Ariston, after he took refuge with the Medes, was not, in my judgment, which is supported by probability, a well-wisher to the Lacedæmonians. It may be questioned, therefore, whether he did what I am about to mention from good-will or from insolent triumph. It happened that he was at Susa at the time when Xerxes determined to lead his army into Greece; and in this way becoming acquainted with his design, he resolved to send tidings of it to Sparta. So as there was no other way of effecting his purpose, since the danger of being discovered was great, Demaratus framed the following contrivance. He took a pair of tablets, and, clearing the wax away from them, wrote what the king was purposing to do upon the wood whereof the tablets were made; having done this, he spread the wax once more over the writing, and so sent it. By these means, the guards placed to watch the roads, observing nothing but a blank tablet, were sure to give no trouble to the bearer. When the tablet reached Lacedæmon, there was no one, I understand, who could find out the secret, till Gorgo, the daughter of Cleomenes and wife of Leonidas, discovered it, and told the others. "If they would scrape the wax

1 Supra, ch. 220.

off the tablet," she said, "they would be sure to find the writing upon the wood." The Lacedæmonians took her advice, found the writing, and read it;[1] after which they sent it round to the other Greeks. Such then is the account which is given of this matter.

1 Here we have one out of many instances of the common practice of writing among the Spartans, so strangely called in question by Grote.

ADDED NOTES BY THE EDITOR

(1.) *The Character of Xerxes.* – Unlike Cyrus, who was a great soldier, or Darius, who was a clear-headed statesman, Xerxes was typical of the Persian character on its weakest side. He trusted to mere numbers to win the day at Salamis and elsewhere, forgetting that battles (as Herodotus implies) are fought with the head as well as with the hands. As a ruler, he was arbitrary and unscrupulous; as a man, effeminate, extravagant, and cruel.

(2.) *The Battle of Salamis* (book viii.). The story of this decisive battle is clear enough in the pages of Herodotus; but we have the good luck to possess the statement of an eye-witness, in the poetical description given us in the *Persæ* of Æschylus (ll. 355–434). This fine battle-picture should be carefully studied – see the verse rendering in Prof. Lewis Campbell's translation of the plays of Æschylus (Oxford University Press). Readers will, perhaps, recall Byron's lines (*Don Juan*, canto iii.):–

> "A king sate on the rocky brow
>   That looks o'er sea-born Salamis;
> And ships, by thousands, lay below,
>   And men in nations, – all were his!
> He counted them at break of day –
>   And, when the sun set, where were they?"

Compare book viii. chap. 90.

THE EIGHTH BOOK,
ENTITLED URANIA

1. THE Greeks engaged in the sea-service were the following. The Athenians furnished a hundred and twenty-seven vessels to the fleet, which were manned in part by the Platæans, who, though unskilled in such matters, were led by their active and daring spirit to undertake this duty; the Corinthians furnished a contingent of forty vessels; the Megarians sent twenty; the Chalcideans also manned twenty, which had been furnished to them by the Athenians;[1] the Eginetans came with eighteen; the Sicyonians with twelve; the Lacedæmonians with ten; the Epidaurians with eight; the Eretrians with seven; the Trœzenians with five; the Styreans with two; and the Cêans[2] with two triremes and two penteconters. Last of all, the Locrians of Opus came in aid with a squadron of seven penteconters.

2. Such were the nations which furnished vessels to the fleet now at Artemisium; and in mentioning them I have given the number of ships furnished by each. The total number of the ships thus brought together, without counting the penteconters, was two hundred and seventy-one; and the captain, who had the chief command over the whole fleet, was Eurybiades the son of Eurycleides. He was furnished by Sparta, since the allies had said that, "if a Lacedæmonian did not take the command, they would break up the fleet, for never would they serve under the Athenians."

3. From the first, even earlier than the time when the embassy went to Sicily[3] to solicit alliance, there had been a talk of intrusting the Athenians with the command at sea; but the allies were averse to the plan, wherefore the Athenians did not press it; for there was nothing they had so much at heart as the salvation of Greece, and they knew that, if they quarrelled among themselves about the command, Greece would be brought to

---

1 These Chalcideans are beyond a doubt Athenian cleruchs or colonists.
2 Ceos, one of the Cyclades, now *Tzia* or *Zea*, lies off the promontory of Sunium, at the distance of about 12 miles.
3 Supra, vii. 153, et sqq.

ruin.¹ Herein they judged rightly; for internal strife is a thing as much worse than war carried on by a united people, as war itself is worse than peace. The Athenians therefore, being so persuaded, did not push their claims, but waived them, so long as they were in such great need of aid from the other Greeks. And they afterwards showed their motive; for at the time when the Persians had been driven from Greece, and were now threatened by the Greeks in their own country, they took occasion of the insolence of Pausanias to deprive the Lacedæmonians of their leadership. This, however, happened afterwards.

4. At the present time the Greeks, on their arrival at Artemisium, when they saw the number of the ships which lay at anchor near Aphetæ, and the abundance of troops everywhere, feeling disappointed that matters had gone with the barbarians so far otherwise than they had expected, and full of alarm at what they saw, began to speak of drawing back from Artemisium towards the inner parts of their country. So when the Eubœans heard what was in debate, they went to Eurybiades, and besought him to wait a few days, while they removed their children and their slaves to a place of safety. But, as they found that they prevailed nothing, they left him and went to Themistocles, the Athenian commander, to whom they gave a bribe of thirty talents,² on his promise that the fleet should remain and risk a battle in defence of Eubœa.

5. And Themistocles succeeded in detaining the fleet in the way which I will now relate. He made over to Eurybiades five talents out of the thirty paid him, which he gave as if they came from himself; and having in this way gained over the admiral, he addressed himself to Adeimantus, the son of Ocytus, the Corinthian leader, who was the only remonstrant now, and who still threatened to sail away from Artemisium and not wait for the other captains. Addressing himself to this man, Themistocles said with an oath, – "Thou forsake us? By no means! I will pay thee better for remaining than the Mede would for leaving thy friends" – and straightway he sent on board the ship of Adeimantus a present of three talents of silver. So these two captains were won by gifts, and came over to the views of Themistocles, who was thereby enabled to gratify the wishes of the Eubœans.

---

1 Athens prudently waived her claim.
2 Thirty talents would be above £7,000 of our money.

He likewise made his own gain on the occasion; for he kept the rest of the money, and no one knew of it. The commanders who took the gifts thought that the sums were furnished by Athens, and had been sent to be used in this way.

6. Thus it came to pass that the Greeks stayed at Eubœa and there gave battle to the enemy.

Now the battle was on this wise. The barbarians reached Aphetæ early in the afternoon, and then saw (as they had previously heard reported) that a fleet of Greek ships, weak in number, lay at Artemisium. At once they were eager to engage, fearing that the Greeks would fly, and hoping to capture them before they should get away. They did not however think it wise to make straight for the Greek station, lest the enemy should see them as they bore down, and betake themselves to flight immediately; in which case night might close in before they came up with the fugitives, and so they might get clean off and make their escape from them; whereas the Persians were minded not to let a single soul slip through their hands.

7. They therefore contrived a plan, which was the following:— They detached two hundred of their ships from the rest, and — to prevent the enemy from seeing them start — sent them round outside the island of Sciathos, to make the circuit of Eubœa by Caphareus[1] and Geræstus,[2] and so to reach the Euripus. By this plan they thought to enclose the Greeks on every side; for the ships detached would block up the only way by which they could retreat, while the others would press upon them in front. With these designs therefore they dispatched the two hundred ships, while they themselves waited, – since they did not mean to attack the Greeks upon that day, or until they knew, by signal, of the arrival of the detachment which had been ordered to sail round Eubœa. Meanwhile they made a muster of the other ships at Aphetæ.

8. Now the Persians had with them a man named Scyllias, a native of Sciôné, who was the most expert diver of his day. At the time of the shipwreck off Mount Pelion he had recovered for the Persians a great part of what they lost; and at the same

---

1 Caphereus (or Caphareus) was the name of the south-eastern promontory of Eubœa, now called *Capo Doro*.

2 Geræstus was a town and promontory at the extreme southern point of Eubœa.

time he had taken care to obtain for himself a good share of the treasure. He had for some time been wishing to go over to the Greeks; but no good opportunity had offered till now, when the Persians were making the muster of their ships. In what way he contrived to reach the Greeks I am not able to say for certain: I marvel much if the tale that is commonly told be true. 'Tis said he dived into the sea at Aphetæ, and did not once come to the surface till he reached Artemisium, a distance of nearly eighty furlongs.[1] Now many things are related of this man which are plainly false; but some of the stories seem to be true. My own opinion is that on this occasion he made the passage to Artemisium in a boat.

However this might be, Scyllias no sooner reached Artemisium than he gave the Greek captains a full account of the damage done by the storm, and likewise told them of the ships sent to make the circuit of Eubœa.

9. So the Greeks on receiving these tidings held a council, whereat, after much debate, it was resolved that they should stay quiet for the present where they were, and remain at their moorings, but that after midnight they should put out to sea, and encounter the ships which were on their way round the island. Later in the day, when they found that no one meddled with them, they formed a new plan, which was, to wait till near evening, and then sail out against the main body of the barbarians, for the purpose of trying their mode of fight and skill in manœuvring.

10. When the Persian commanders and crews saw the Greeks thus boldly sailing towards them with their few ships, they thought them possessed with madness,[2] and went out to meet them, expecting (as indeed seemed likely enough) that they would take all their vessels with the greatest ease. The Greek ships were so few, and their own so far outnumbered them, and sailed so much better, that they resolved, seeing their advantage, to encompass their foe on every side. And now such of the Ionians as wished well to the Grecian cause and served in the Persian fleet unwillingly, seeing their countrymen surrounded, were sorely distressed; for they felt sure that not one of them would ever make his escape, so poor an opinion had they of the strength of

1 The distance across the strait is about 7 miles.
2 Vide supra, vi. 112.

the Greeks. On the other hand, such as saw with pleasure the attack on Greece, now vied eagerly with each other which should be the first to make prize of an Athenian ship, and thereby to secure himself a rich reward from the king. For through both the hosts none were so much accounted of as the Athenians.

11. The Greeks, at a signal, brought the sterns of their ships together into a small compass, and turned their prows on every side towards the barbarians; after which, at a second signal, although inclosed within a narrow space, and closely pressed upon by the foe, yet they fell bravely to work, and captured thirty ships of the barbarians, at the same time taking prisoner Philaon, the son of Chersis, and brother of Gorgus king of Salamis,[1] a man of much repute in the fleet. The first who made prize of a ship of the enemy was Lycomêdes the son of Æschreas, an Athenian, who was afterwards adjudged the meed of valour. Victory however was still doubtful when night came on, and put a stop to the combat. The Greeks sailed back to Artemisium; and the barbarians returned to Aphetæ, much surprised at the result, which was far other than they had looked for. In this battle only one of the Greeks who fought on the side of the king deserted and joined his countrymen. This was Antidôrus of Lemnos, whom the Athenians rewarded for his desertion by the present of a piece of land in Salamis.

12. Evening had barely closed in when a heavy rain – it was about midsummer[2] – began to fall, which continued the whole night, with terrible thunderings and lightnings from Mount Pelion: the bodies of the slain and the broken pieces of the damaged ships were drifted in the direction of Aphetæ, and floated about the prows of the vessels there, disturbing the action of the oars. The barbarians, hearing the storm, were greatly dismayed, expecting certainly to perish, as they had fallen into such a multitude of misfortunes. For before they were well recovered from the tempest and the wreck of their vessels off Mount Pelion, they had been surprised by a sea-fight which had taxed all their strength, and now the sea-fight was scarcely over

---

1 Supra, v. 104.

2 From this passage, and from the fact mentioned above (vii. 206), that the engagements at Thermopylæ and Artemisium coincided with the time of the Olympic games, we may be justified in fixing the battles to the latter part of June or the beginning of July.

when they were exposed to floods of rain, and the rush of swollen streams into the sea, and violent thunderings.

13. If, however, they who lay at Aphetæ passed a comfortless night, far worse were the sufferings of those who had been sent to make the circuit of Eubœa; inasmuch as the storm fell on them out at sea, whereby the issue was indeed calamitous. They were sailing along near the Hollows of Eubœa,[1] when the wind began to rise and the rain to pour: overpowered by the force of the gale, and driven they knew not whither, at the last they fell upon rocks, – Heaven so contriving, in order that the Persian fleet might not greatly exceed the Greek, but be brought nearly to its level. This squadron, therefore, was entirely lost about the Hollows of Eubœa.

14. The barbarians at Aphetæ were glad when day dawned, and remained in quiet at their station, content if they might enjoy a little peace after so many sufferings. Meanwhile there came to the aid of the Greeks a reinforcement of fifty-three ships from Attica.[2] Their arrival, and the news (which reached Artemisium about the same time) of the complete destruction by the storm of the ships sent to sail round Eubœa, greatly cheered the spirits of the Greek sailors. So they waited again till the same hour as the day before, and, once more putting out to sea, attacked the enemy. This time they fell in with some Cilician vessels, which they sank; when night came on, they withdrew to Artemisium.

15. The third day was now come, and the captains of the barbarians, ashamed that so small a number of ships should harass their fleet, and afraid of the anger of Xerxes, instead of waiting for the others to begin the battle, weighed anchor themselves, and advanced against the Greeks about the hour of noon, with shouts encouraging one another. Now it happened that these sea-fights took place on the very same days with the combats at Thermopylæ; and as the aim of the struggle was in the one case to maintain the pass, so in the other it was to defend the Euripus. While the Greeks, therefore, exhorted one another not to let the barbarians burst in upon Greece, these latter shouted to their fellows to destroy the Grecian fleet, and get possession of the channel.

---

1 "The Hollows" seem to have had at all times a bad name among sailors.
2 This seems to have been the whole of the Athenian reserve fleet. The policy of Themistocles had raised their navy of 200 vessels.

16. And now the fleet of Xerxes advanced in good order to the attack, while the Greeks on their side remained quite motionless at Artemisium. The Persians therefore spread themselves, and came forward in a half-moon, seeking to encircle the Greeks on all sides, and thereby prevent them from escaping. The Greeks, when they saw this, sailed out to meet their assailants; and the battle forthwith began. In this engagement the two fleets contended with no clear advantage to either, – for the armament of Xerxes injured itself by its own greatness, the vessels falling into disorder, and oft-times running foul of one another; yet still they did not give way, but made a stout fight, since the crews felt it would indeed be a disgrace to turn and fly from a fleet so inferior in number. The Greeks therefore suffered much, both in ships and men; but the barbarians experienced a far larger loss of each. So the fleets separated after such a combat as I have described.

17. On the side of Xerxes the Egyptians distinguished themselves above all the combatants; for besides performing many other noble deeds, they took five vessels from the Greeks with their crews on board. On the side of the Greeks the Athenians bore off the meed of valour; and among them the most distinguished was Clinias, the son of Alcibiades, who served at his own charge with two hundred men,[1] on board a vessel which he had himself furnished.[2]

18. The two fleets, on separating, hastened very gladly to their anchorage-grounds. The Greeks, indeed, when the battle was over, became masters of the bodies of the slain and the wrecks of the vessels; but they had been so roughly handled, especially the Athenians, one-half of whose vessels had suffered damage, that they determined to break up from their station, and withdraw to the inner parts of their country.

19. Then Themistocles, who thought that if the Ionian and Carian ships could be detached from the barbarian fleet, the Greeks might be well able to defeat the rest, called the captains together. They met upon the sea-shore, where the Eubœans were now assembling their flocks and herds; and here Themistocles

1 This was the ordinary crew of a trireme.
2 The state usually furnished the vessel and its equipment, the trierarch being bound to keep the whole in repair. Trierarchs often went to the expense of equipping their vessels at their own cost.

told them he thought that he knew of a plan whereby he could detach from the king those who were of most worth among his allies. This was all that he disclosed to them of his plan at that time. Meanwhile, looking to the circumstances in which they were, he advised them to slaughter as many of the Eubœan cattle as they liked – for it was better (he said) that their own troops should enjoy them than the enemy – and to give orders to their men to kindle the fires as usual. With regard to the retreat, he said that he would take upon himself to watch the proper moment, and would manage matters so that they should return to Greece without loss. These words pleased the captains; so they had the fires lighted, and began the slaughter of the cattle.

20. The Eubœans, until now, had made light of the oracle of Bacis, as though it had been void of all significancy, and had neither removed their goods from the island, nor yet taken them into their strong places; as they would most certainly have done if they had believed that war was approaching. By this neglect they had brought their affairs into the very greatest danger. Now the oracle of which I speak ran as follows:–

"When o'er the main shall be thrown a byblus yoke[1] by a stranger,
  Be thou ware, and drive from Eubœa the goats' loud-bleating."

So, as the Eubœans had paid no regard to this oracle when the evils approached and impended, now that they had arrived, the worst was likely to befall them.

21. While the Greeks were employed in the way described above,[2] the scout who had been on the watch at Trachis arrived at Artemisium. For the Greeks had employed two watchers:– Polyas, a native of Anticyra, had been stationed off Artemisium, with a row-boat at his command ready to sail at any moment, his orders being that, if an engagement took place by sea, he should convey the news at once to the Greeks at Thermopylæ; and in like manner Abrônychus, the son of Lysicles, an Athenian, had been stationed with a triaconter near Leonidas, to be ready, in case of disaster befalling the land force, to carry tidings of it to Artemisium. It was this Abrônychus who now arrived with news of what had befallen Leonidas and those who were with him. When the Greeks heard the tidings they no longer delayed

---

1 [That is, a yoke (or *bridge*) fastened with cords of papyrus. – E. H. B.]
2 Supra, ch. 19, end.

to retreat, but withdrew in the order wherein they had been stationed, the Corinthians leading, and the Athenians sailing last of all.

22. And now Themistocles chose out the swiftest sailers from among the Athenian vessels, and, proceeding to the various watering-places along the coast, cut inscriptions on the rocks, which were read by the Ionians the day following, on their arrival at Artemisium. The inscriptions ran thus:— "Men of Ionia, ye do wrong to fight against your own fathers, and to give your help to enslave Greece. We beseech you therefore to come over, if possible, to our side: if you cannot do this, then, we pray you, stand aloof from the contest yourselves, and persuade the Carians to do the like. If neither of these things be possible, and you are hindered, by a force too strong to resist, from venturing upon desertion, at least when we come to blows fight backwardly, remembering that you are sprung from us, and that it was through you we first provoked the hatred of the barbarian."[1] Themistocles, in putting up these inscriptions, looked, I believe, to two chances — either Xerxes would not discover them, in which case they might bring over the Ionians to the side of the Greeks; or they would be reported to him and made a ground of accusation against the Ionians, who would thereupon be distrusted, and would not be allowed to take part in the sea-fights.

23. Shortly after the cutting of the inscriptions, a man of Histiæa went in a merchant-ship to Aphetæ, and told the Persians that the Greeks had fled from Artemisium. Disbelieving his report, the Persians kept the man a prisoner, while they sent some of their fastest vessels to see what had happened. These brought back word how matters stood; whereupon at sunrise the whole fleet advanced together in a body, and sailed to Artemisium, where they remained till mid-day; after which they went on to Histiæa.[2] That city fell into their hands immediately; and they shortly overran the various villages upon the coast in the district of Hellopia,[3] which was part of the Histiæan territory.

24. It was while they were at this station that a herald reached them from Xerxes, whom he had sent after making the following

1 Alluding to the assistance given by Athens to the Ionians in the great revolt.

2 The most important town of northern Eubœa.

3 The Hellopians, one of the early Pelasgic tribes, seem to have been the original inhabitants of Eubœa, which anciently bore the name of Hellopia.

dispositions with respect to the bodies of those who fell at Thermopylæ. Of the twenty thousand who had been slain on the Persian side, he left one thousand upon the field while he buried the rest in trenches; and these he carefully filled up with earth, and hid with foliage, that the sailors might not see any signs of them. The herald, on reaching Histiæa, caused the whole force to be collected together, and spake thus to them:

"Comrades, King Xerxes gives permission to all who please, to quit their posts, and see how he fights with the senseless men who think to overthrow his armies."

25. No sooner had these words been uttered, than it became difficult to get a boat, so great was the number of those who desired to see the sight. Such as went crossed the strait, and passing among the heaps of dead, in this way viewed the spectacle. Many Helots were included in the slain,[1] but every one imagined that the bodies were all either Lacedæmonians or Thespians. However, no one was deceived by what Xerxes had done with his own dead. It was indeed most truly a laughable device – on the one side a thousand men were seen lying about the field, on the other four thousand crowded together into one spot. This day then was given up to sight-seeing; on the next the seamen embarked on board their ships and sailed back to Histiæa, while Xerxes and his army proceeded upon their march.

26. There came now a few deserters from Arcadia to join the Persians – poor men who had nothing to live on, and were in want of employment. The Persians brought them into the king's presence, and there inquired of them, by a man who acted as their spokesman, "what the Greeks were doing?" The Arcadians answered – "They are holding the Olympic games, seeing the athletic sports and the chariot-races." "And what," said the man, "is the prize for which they contend?" "An olive-wreath," returned the others, "which is given to the man who wins." On hearing this, Tritantæchmes, the son of Artabanus,[2] uttered a speech which was in truth most noble, but which caused him to be taxed with cowardice by King Xerxes. Hearing the men say that the prize was not money but a wreath of olive, he could not

1 Herodotus had not directly mentioned these Helots before. If they bore the proportion, found elsewhere (infra, ix. 10, 28), of seven to each Spartan, they must have amounted to 2100 men.

2 Supra, vii. 82.

forbear from exclaiming before them all: "Good heavens! Mardonius, what manner of men are these against whom thou hast brought us to fight? – men who contend with one another, not for money, but for honour!"

27. A little before this, and just after the blow had been struck at Thermopylæ, a herald was sent into Phôcis by the Thessalians, who had always been on bad terms with the Phocians, and especially since their last overthrow. For it was not many years previous to this invasion of Greece by the king, that the Thessalians, with their allies, entered Phôcis in full force, but were defeated by the Phocians in an engagement wherein they were very roughly handled. The Phocians, who had with them as soothsayer Tellias of Elis, were blocked up in the mountain of Parnassus, when the following stratagem was contrived for them by their Elean ally. He took six hundred of their bravest men, and whitened their bodies and their arms with chalk; then instructing them to slay every one whom they should meet that was not whitened like themselves, he made a night attack upon the Thessalians. No sooner did the Thessalian sentries, who were the first to see them, behold this strange sight, than, imagining it to be a prodigy, they were all filled with affright. From the sentries the alarm spread to the army, which was seized with such a panic that the Phocians killed four thousand of them, and became masters of their dead bodies and shields. Of the shields one half were sent as an offering to the temple at Abæ,[1] the other half were deposited at Delphi; while from the tenth part of the booty gained in the battle, were made the gigantic figures which stand round the tripod in front of the Delphic shrine, and likewise the figures of the same size and character at Abæ.

28. Besides this slaughter of the Thessalian foot when it was blockading them, the Phocians had dealt a blow to their horse upon its invading their territory, from which they had never recovered. There is a pass near the city of Hyampolis,[2] where the Phocians, having dug a broad trench, filled up the void with empty wine-jars, after which they covered the place with mould, so that the ground all looked alike, and then awaited the coming of the Thessalians. These, thinking to destroy the Phocians at

---

1 For the great celebrity of this temple, see above, i. 46.
2 Hyampolis lay very near to Abæ.

one sweep, rushed rapidly forward, and became entangled in the wine-jars, which broke the legs of their horses.

29. The Thessalians had therefore a double cause of quarrel with the Phocians, when they dispatched the herald above mentioned, who thus delivered his message:—

"At length acknowledge, ye men of Phôcis, that ye may not think to match with us. In times past, when it pleased us to hold with the Greeks, we had always the vantage over you; and now our influence is such with the barbarian, that, if we choose it, you will lose your country, and (what is even worse) you will be sold as slaves. However, though we can now do with you exactly as we like, we are willing to forget our wrongs. Quit them with a payment of fifty talents of silver,[1] and we undertake to ward off the evils which threaten your country."

30. Such was the message which the Thessalians sent. The Phocians were the only people in these parts who had not espoused the cause of the Medes; and it is my deliberate opinion that the motive which swayed them was none other – neither more nor less – than their hatred of the Thessalians: for had the Thessalians declared in favour of the Greeks, I believe that the men of Phôcis would have joined the Median side. As it was, when the message arrived, the Phocians made answer, that "they would not pay anything – it was open to them, equally with the Thessalians, to make common cause with the Medes, if they only chose so to do – but they would never of their own free will become traitors to Greece."

31. On the return of this answer, the Thessalians, full of wrath against the Phocians, offered themselves as guides to the barbarian army, and led them forth from Trachinia into Dôris. In this place there is a narrow tongue of Dorian territory, not more than thirty furlongs across, interposed between Malis and Phôcis; it is the tract in ancient times called Dryopis; and the land, of which it is a part, is the mother-country of the Dorians in the · Peloponnese.[2] This territory the barbarians did not plunder, for the inhabitants had espoused their side; and besides, the Thessalians wished that they should be spared.

32. From Dôris they marched forward into Phôcis; but here the inhabitants did not fall into their power: for some of them

---

1 Rather more than £12,000 of our money.
2 Supra, i. 56.

had taken refuge in the high grounds of Parnassus — one summit of which, called Tithorea, standing quite by itself, not far from the city of Neon, is well fitted to give shelter to a large body of men, and had now received a number of the Phocians with their movables; while the greater portion had fled to the country of the Ozolian Locrians,[1] and placed their goods in the city called Amphissa, which lies above the Crissæan plain. The land of Phôcis, however, was entirely overrun, for the Thessalians led the Persian army through the whole of it; and wherever they went, the country was wasted with fire and sword, the cities and even the temples being wilfully set alight by the troops.

33. The march of the army lay along the valley of the Cephissus;[2] and here they ravaged far and wide, burning the towns of Drymus, Charadra, Erôchus, Tethrônium, Amphicæa, Neon, Pedieis, Triteis, Elateia, Hyampolis, Parapotamii, and Abæ. At the last-named place there was a temple of Apollo, very rich, and adorned with a vast number of treasures and offerings. There was likewise an oracle there in those days, as indeed there is at the present time. This temple the Persians plundered and burnt; and here they captured a number of the Phocians before they could reach the hills,[3] and caused the death of some of their women by ill-usage.

34. After passing Parapotamii, the barbarians marched to Panopeis; and now the army separated into two bodies, whereof one, which was the more numerous and the stronger of the two, marched, under Xerxes himself, towards Athens, entering Bœotia by the country of the Orchomenians.[4] The Bœotians had one and all embraced the cause of the Medes; and their towns were in the possession of Macedonian garrisons, whom Alexander had sent there, to make it manifest to Xerxes that the Bœotians were on the Median side. Such then was the road followed by one division of the barbarians.

35. The other division took guides, and proceeded towards the temple of Delphi, keeping Mount Parnassus on their right hand. They too laid waste such parts of Phôcis as they passed

1 The Ozolian Locrians dwelt on the shores of the Corinthian Gulf.
2 The Cephissus rises from the base of Parnassus.
3 The Persians were determined, however, in true iconoclastic spirit, to destroy, if possible, all the principal Greek fanes.
4 Orchomenus, the most famous of the Bœotian cities next to Thebes.

through, burning the city of the Panopeans, together with those of the Daulians and of the Æolidæ. This body had been detached from the rest of the army, and made to march in this direction, for the purpose of plundering the Delphian temple and conveying to King Xerxes the riches which were there laid up. For Xerxes, as I am informed, was better acquainted with what there was worthy of note at Delphi, than even with what he had left in his own house; so many of those about him were continually describing the treasures — more especially the offerings made by Crœsus the son of Alyattes.[1]

36. Now when the Delphians heard what danger they were in, great fear fell on them. In their terror they consulted the oracle concerning the holy treasures, and inquired if they should bury them in the ground, or carry them away to some other country. The god, in reply, bade them leave the treasures untouched — "He was able," he said, "without help to protect his own." So the Delphians, when they received this answer, began to think about saving themselves. And first of all they sent their women and children across the gulf into Achæa; after which the greater number of them climbed up into the tops of Parnassus,[2] and placed their goods for safety in the Corycian cave;[3] while some effected their escape to Amphissa in Locris.[4] In this way all the Delphians quitted the city, except sixty men, and the Prophet.

37. When the barbarian assailants drew near and were in sight of the place,[5] the Prophet, who was named Acêratus, beheld, in front of the temple, a portion of the sacred armour, which it was not lawful for any mortal hand to touch, lying upon the ground, removed from the inner shrine where it was wont to hang. Then went he and told the prodigy to the Delphians who had remained behind. Meanwhile the enemy pressed forward briskly, and had reached the shrine of Athena Pronaia, when they were overtaken by other prodigies still more wonder-

1 Supra, i. 50, 51.

2 The two peaks rising immediately above Delphi (*Kastri*), are probably intended.

3 The Corycian cave, sacred to Pan and the Nymphs.

4 Whither the other Phocians had already fled (supra, ch. 32).

5 Delphi stood on the side of a rocky hill, in the form of a theatre, to which a succession of terraces gave it a still greater resemblance. The Temple of Apollo was about the centre of the curve.

ful than the first. Truly it was marvel enough, when warlike harness was seen lying outside the temple, removed there by no power but its own; what followed, however, exceeded in strangeness all prodigies that had ever before been seen. The barbarians had just reached in their advance the chapel of Athena Pronaia, when a storm of thunder burst suddenly over their heads – at the same time two crags split off from Mount Parnassus, and rolled down upon them with a loud noise, crushing vast numbers beneath their weight – while from the temple of Athena there went up the war-cry and the shout of victory.

38. All these things together struck terror into the barbarians, who forthwith turned and fled. The Delphians, seeing this, came down from their hiding-places, and smote them with a great slaughter, from which such as escaped fled straight into Bœotia. These men, on their return, declared (as I am told) that besides the marvels mentioned above, they witnessed also other supernatural sights. Two armed warriors, they said, of a stature more than human, pursued after their flying ranks, pressing them close and slaying them.

39. These men, the Delphians maintain, were two Heroes belonging to the place – by name Phylacus and Autonoüs – each of whom has a sacred precinct near the temple; one, that of Phylacus, hard by the road which runs above the temple of Pronaia; the other, that of Autonoüs, near the Castalian spring,[1] at the foot of the peak called Hyampeia. The blocks of stone which fell from Parnassus might still be seen in my day; they lay in the precinct of Pronaia, where they stopped, after rolling through the host of the barbarians. Thus was this body of men forced to retire from the temple.

40. Meanwhile, the Grecian fleet, which had left Artemisium, proceeded to Salamis, at the request of the Athenians, and there cast anchor. The Athenians had begged them to take up this position, in order that they might convey their women and children out of Attica, and further might deliberate upon the course which it now behoved them to follow. Disappointed in the

---

1 The Castalian spring may be distinctly recognised in the modern fountain of *Aio Jánni*. It lies at the base of the precipices of Parnassus. [For a description of Delphi and its surroundings – so famous in antiquity – see the exhaustive note in Frazer's monumental edition of *Pausanias*, vol. v. pp. 248, sqq. – E. H. B.]

hopes which they had previously entertained, they were about to hold a council concerning the present posture of their affairs. For they had looked to see the Peloponnesians drawn up in full force to resist the enemy in Bœotia, but found nothing of what they had expected; nay, they learnt that the Greeks of those parts, only concerning themselves about their own safety, were building a wall across the Isthmus, and intended to guard the Peloponnese, and let the rest of Greece take its chance. These tidings caused them to make the request whereof I spoke, that the combined fleet should anchor at Salamis.

41. So while the rest of the fleet lay to off this island, the Athenians cast anchor along their own coast. Immediately upon their arrival, proclamation was made, that every Athenian should save his children and household as he best could;[1] whereupon some sent their families to Egina, some to Salamis, but the greater number to Trœzen.[2] This removal was made with all possible haste, partly from a desire to obey the advice of the oracle,[3] but still more for another reason. The Athenians say that they have in their Acropolis a huge serpent, which lives in the temple, and is the guardian of the whole place. Nor do they only say this, but, as if the serpent really dwelt there, every month they lay out its food, which consists of a honey-cake. Up to this time the honey-cake had always been consumed; but now it remained untouched. So the priestess told the people what had happened; whereupon they left Athens the more readily, since they believed that the goddess had already abandoned the citadel. As soon as all was removed, the Athenians sailed back to their station.

42. And now, the remainder of the Grecian sea-force, hearing that the fleet which had been at Artemisium, was come to Salamis, joined it at that island from Trœzen — orders having been issued previously that the ships should muster at Pôgon, the port of the Trœzenians. The vessels collected were many more in number than those which had fought at Artemisium, and were furnished by more cities. The admiral was the same

1 The Athenian who, without such proclamation, left his country at a time of danger, was considered guilty of a capital offence.

2 The Trœzenians received them with much kindness, and voted them sustenance-money at the rate of two obols ($3\frac{1}{4}$ d.) per diem for each person.

3 Supra, vii. 141.

who had commanded before, to wit, Eurybiades, the son of Eurycleides, who was a Spartan, but not of the family of the kings: the city, however, which sent by far the greatest number of ships, and the best sailers, was Athens.

43. Now these were the nations who composed the Grecian fleet. From the Peloponnese, the following – the Lacedæmonians with sixteen ships; the Corinthians with the same number as at Artemisium; the Sicyonians with fifteen; the Epidaurians with ten; the Trœzenians with five; and the Hermionians with three. These were Dorians and Macednians[1] all of them (except those from Hermioné), and had emigrated last from Erineus, Pindus, and Dryopis. The Hermionians were Dryopians, of the race which Heracles and the Malians drove out of the land now called Dôris. Such were the Peloponnesian nations.

44. From the mainland of Greece beyond the Peloponnese, came the Athenians with a hundred and eighty ships, a greater number than that furnished by any other people; and these were now manned wholly by themselves; for the Platæans did not serve aboard the Athenian ships at Salamis, owing to the following reason. When the Greeks, on their withdrawal from Artemisium, arrived off Chalcis, the Platæans disembarked upon the opposite shore of Bœotia, and set to work to remove their households, whereby it happened that they were left behind. (The Athenians, when the region which is now called Greece was held by the Pelasgi, were Pelasgians, and bore the name of Cranaans; but under their king Cecrops, they were called Cecropidæ; when Erechtheus got the sovereignty, they changed their name to Athenians; and when Ion, the son of Xuthus, became their general, they were named after him Ionians.)

45. The Megarians served with the same number of ships as at Artemisium; the Ambraciots came with seven; the Leucadians (who were Dorians from Corinth) with three.

46. Of the islanders, the Eginetans furnished thirty ships – they had a larger number equipped; but some were kept back to guard their own coasts, and only thirty, which however were their best sailers, took part in the fight at Salamis. (The Eginetans are Dorians from Epidaurus;[2] their island was called formerly Œnône). The Chalcideans came next in order; they furnished the twenty ships with which they had served at Artemisium. The

---

1 Supra, i. 56.   2 Supra, v. 83.

Eretrians likewise furnished their seven. These races are Ionian.
Cêos gave its old number[1] – the Ceans are Ionians from Attica.
Naxos furnished four: this detachment, like those from the other
islands, had been sent by the citizens at home to join the Medes;
but they made light of the orders given them, and joined the
Greeks, at the instigation of Democritus, a citizen of good report, who was at that time captain of a trireme. The Naxians are
Ionians, of the Athenian stock. The Styreans served with the
same ships as before; the Cythnians contributed one, and likewise a penteconter – these two nations are Dryopians: the Seriphians, Siphnians, and Melians, also served;[2] they were the only
islanders who had not given earth and water to the barbarian.

47. All these nations dwelt inside the river Acheron and the
country inhabited by the Thesprotians; for that people borders
on the Ambraciots and Leucadians, who are the most remote of
all those by whom the fleet was furnished. From the countries
beyond, there was only one people which gave help to the
Greeks in their danger. This was the people of Crotôna,[3] who
contributed a single ship, under the command of Phaÿllus, a man
who had thrice carried off the prize at the Pythian games. The
Crotoniats are, by descent, Achæans.

48. Most of the allies came with triremes; but the Melians,
Siphnians, and Seriphians, brought penteconters. The Melians,
who draw their race from Lacedæmon, furnished two; the
Siphnians and Seriphians, who are Ionians of the Athenian stock,
one each. The whole number of the ships, without counting the
penteconters, was three hundred and seventy-eight.[4]

49. When the captains from these various nations were come
together at Salamis, a council of war was summoned; and Eurybiades proposed that any one who liked to advise, should say
which place seemed to him the fittest, among those still in the

---

1 Two triremes and two penteconters (supra, ch. 1).
2 Seriphus, Siphnus, and Melos – the *Serpho*, *Siphanto*, and *Milo* of the present day – form, together with Ceos and Cythnus, the western Cyclades, which
were now especially threatened by the advance of the Persian fleet. Their
remoteness from Asia had emboldened them to refuse submission; their danger
now induced them to appear in arms.
3 Supra, iii. 126.
4 The actual number of the Greek ships *engaged* is variously stated. Æschylus, who was one of the combatants, makes them 300, or 310; Thucydides, 400,
or according to some MSS., 300.

possession of the Greeks, to be the scene of a naval combat. Attica, he said, was not to be thought of now; but he desired their counsel as to the remainder. The speakers mostly advised that the fleet should sail away to the Isthmus, and there give battle in defence of the Peloponnese; and they urged as a reason for this, that if they were worsted in a sea-fight at Salamis, they would be shut up in an island where they could get no help; but if they were beaten near the Isthmus, they could escape to their homes.

50. As the captains from the Peloponnese were thus advising, there came an Athenian to the camp, who brought word that the barbarians had entered Attica, and were ravaging and burning everything. For the division of the army under Xerxes was just arrived at Athens from its march through Bœotia, where it had burnt Thespiæ and Platæa – both which cities were forsaken by their inhabitants, who had fled to the Peloponnese – and now it was laying waste all the possessions of the Athenians. Thespiæ and Platæa had been burnt by the Persians, because they knew from the Thebans that neither of those cities had espoused their side.

51. Since the passage of the Hellespont and the commencement of the march upon Greece, a space of four months had gone by; one, while the army made the crossing, and delayed about the region of the Hellespont; and three while they proceeded thence to Attica, which they entered in the archonship of Calliades. They found the city forsaken; a few people only remained in the temple,[1] either keepers of the treasures,[2] or men of the poorer sort. These persons having fortified the citadel[3] with planks and boards, held out against the enemy. It was in some measure their poverty which had prevented them from seeking shelter in Salamis; but there was likewise another reason which in part induced them to remain. They imagined themselves to have discovered the true meaning of the oracle uttered by the Pythoness, which promised that "the wooden wall" should never be taken[4] – the wooden wall, they thought, did not mean the ships, but the place where they had taken refuge.

1 The temple of Athena Polias in the Acropolis.
2 The keepers of the sacred treasures of Athena were ten in number.
3 The Athenian citadel, or Acropolis.
4 Supra, vii. 141.

52. The Persians encamped upon the hill over against the citadel, which is called Ares' hill by the Athenians,[1] and began the siege of the place, attacking the Greeks with arrows whereto pieces of lighted tow were attached, which they shot at the barricade. And now those who were within the citadel found themselves in a most woeful case; for their wooden rampart betrayed them; still, however, they continued to resist. It was in vain that the Pisistratidæ came to them and offered terms of surrender – they stoutly refused all parley, and among their other modes of defence, rolled down huge masses of stone upon the barbarians as they were mounting up to the gates: so that Xerxes was for a long time very greatly perplexed, and could not contrive any way to take them.

53. At last, however, in the midst of these many difficulties, the barbarians made discovery of an access. For verily the oracle had spoken truth; and it was fated that the whole mainland of Attica should fall beneath the sway of the Persians. Right in front of the citadel, but behind the gates and the common ascent – where no watch was kept, and no one would have thought it possible that any foot of man could climb – a few soldiers mounted from the sanctuary of Aglaurus, Cecrops' daughter,[2] notwithstanding the steepness of the precipice. As soon as the Athenians saw them upon the summit, some threw themselves headlong from the wall, and so perished; while others fled for refuge to the inner part of the temple. The Persians rushed to the gates and opened them, after which they massacred the suppliants. When all were slain, they plundered the temple, and fired every part of the citadel.[3]

54. Xerxes, thus completely master of Athens, despatched a horseman to Susa, with a message to Artabanus, informing him of his success hitherto. The day after, he collected together all the Athenian exiles who had come into Greece in his train, and bade them go up into the citadel, and there offer sacrifice after their own fashion. I know not whether he had had a dream

1 Ares' Hill, the seat of the celebrated court of the Areopagus, made still more famous by the preaching of St. Paul (Acts xvii. 22), is one of the features of Athenian topography which cannot be mistaken.

2 Aglaurus, the daughter of Cecrops, was said to have thrown herself over the precipices of the Acropolis.

3 The traces of this destruction may still be seen, though the structures have been rebuilt. [Cf. Gardner, *New Chapters in Greek History*, chap. viii. – E. H. B.]

which made him give this order, or whether he felt some re-morse on account of having set the temple on fire. However this may have been, the exiles were not slow to obey the command given them.

55. I will now explain why I have made mention of this circumstance: there is a temple of Erechtheus the Earth-born, as he is called, in this citadel, containing within it an olive-tree and a sea.[1] The tale goes among the Athenians, that they were placed there as witnesses by Poseidon and Athena, when they had their contention about the country.[2] Now this olive-tree had been burnt with the rest of the temple when the barbarians took the place. But when the Athenians, whom the king had commanded to offer sacrifice, went up into the temple for the purpose, they found a fresh shoot, as much as a cubit in length, thrown out from the old trunk. Such at least was the account which these persons gave.

56. Meanwhile, at Salamis, the Greeks no sooner heard what had befallen the Athenian citadel, than they fell into such alarm that some of the captains did not even wait for the council to come to a vote, but embarked hastily on board their vessels, and hoisted sail as though they would take to flight immediately. The rest, who stayed at the council board, came to a vote that the fleet should give battle at the Isthmus. Night now drew on; and the captains, dispersing from the meeting, proceeded on board their respective ships.

57. Themistocles, as he entered his own vessel, was met by Mnesiphilus, an Athenian, who asked him what the council had resolved to do. On learning that the resolve was to stand away

1 Pausanias tells us that this "sea" was a well of salt water.
2 The myth is given more fully by Apollodorus than by any other writer. "The gods," he says, "were minded to choose themselves cities where they should be specially worshipped. Poseidon was the first to reach Attica, where he smote with his trident, and made a sea spring up in the midst of the Acropolis, where it remains to this day, and is called the Sea of Erechtheus. Athena followed, and calling Cecrops to be witness that she took the land in possession, planted the olive which still grows in the temple of Pandrosus. Then a strife arose concerning the country: so Zeus, to reconcile the rivals, appointed judges, who were not Cecrops and Cranaus, as some say, nor yet Erechtheus, but the twelve deities. Their decision adjudged the land to Athena, upon the witness of Cecrops; and so Athens gained its name, being called after the goddess."

for the Isthmus, and there give battle on behalf of the Peloponnese, Mnesiphilus exclaimed —

"If these men sail away from Salamis, thou wilt have no fight at all for the one fatherland; for they will all scatter themselves to their own homes; and neither Eurybiades nor any one else will be able to hinder them, nor to stop the breaking up of the armament. Thus will Greece be brought to ruin through evil counsels. But haste thee now; and, if there be any possible way, seek to unsettle these resolves — mayhap thou mightest persuade Eurybiades to change his mind, and continue here."

58. The suggestion greatly pleased Themistocles; and without answering a word, he went straight to the vessel of Eurybiades. Arrived there, he let him know that he wanted to speak with him on a matter touching the public service. So Eurybiades bade him come on board, and say whatever he wished. Then Themistocles, seating himself at his side, went over all the arguments which he had heard from Mnesiphilus, pretending as if they were his own, and added to them many new ones besides; until at last he persuaded Eurybiades, by his importunity, to quit his ship and again collect the captains to council.

59. As soon as they were come, and before Eurybiades had opened to them his purpose in assembling them together, Themistocles, as men are wont to do when they are very anxious, spoke much to divers of them; whereupon the Corinthian captain, Adeimantus, the son of Ocytus, observed — "Themistocles, at the games they who start too soon are scourged." "True," rejoined the other in his excuse, "but they who wait too late are not crowned."

60. Thus he gave the Corinthian at this time a mild answer; and towards Eurybiades himself he did not now use any of those arguments which he had urged before, or say aught of the allies betaking themselves to flight if once they broke up from Salamis; it would have been ungraceful for him, when the confederates were present, to make accusation against any: but he had recourse to quite a new sort of reasoning, and addressed him as follows:—

"With thee it rests, O Eurybiades! to save Greece, if thou wilt only hearken unto me, and give the enemy battle here, rather than yield to the advice of those among us, who would have the fleet withdrawn to the Isthmus. Hear now, I beseech thee, and judge between the two courses. At the Isthmus thou wilt fight in an open sea, which is greatly to our disadvantage, since our ships are heavier and fewer in number than the enemy's; and further, thou wilt in any case lose Salamis, Megara, and Egina, even if all the rest goes well with us. The land and sea force of the Persians will advance together; and thy retreat will but draw them towards the Peloponnese, and so bring all Greece into peril. If, on the other hand, thou doest as I advise, these are the advantages which thou wilt so secure: in the first place, as we shall fight in a narrow sea with few ships against many, if the war follows the common course, we shall gain a great victory; for to fight in a narrow space is favourable to us – in an open sea, to them. Again, Salamis will in this case be preserved, where we have placed our wives and children. Nay, that very point by which ye set most store, is secured as much by this course as by the other; for whether we fight here or at the Isthmus, we shall equally give battle in defence of the Peloponnese. Assuredly ye will not do wisely to draw the Persians upon that region. For if things turn out as I anticipate, and we beat them by sea, then we shall have kept your Isthmus free from the barbarians, and they will have advanced no further than Attica, but from thence have fled back in disorder; and we shall, moreover, have saved Megara, Egina, and Salamis itself, where an oracle has said that we are to overcome our enemies.[1] When men counsel reasonably, reasonable success ensues; but when in their counsels they reject reason, God does not choose to follow the wanderings of human fancies."

61. When Themistocles had thus spoken, Adeimantus the Corinthian again attacked him, and bade him be silent, since he was a man without a city; at the same time he called on Eurybiades not to put the question at the instance of one who had no country, and urged that Themistocles should show of what state he was envoy, before he gave his voice with the rest. This reproach he made, because the city of Athens had been taken, and was in the hands of the barbarians. Hereupon Themistocles spake many bitter things against Adeimantus and the Corinthians generally; and for proof that he had a country, reminded the captains, that with two hundred ships at his command, all fully manned for battle, he had both city and territory as good as

1 Supra, vii. 141, ad fin.

theirs; since there was no Grecian state which could resist his men if they were to make a descent.[1]

62. After this declaration, he turned to Eurybiades, and addressing him with still greater warmth and earnestness — "If thou wilt stay here," he said, "and behave like a brave man, all will be well — if not, thou wilt bring Greece to ruin. For the whole fortune of the war depends on our ships. Be thou persuaded by my words. If not, we will take our families on board, and go, just as we are, to Siris, in Italy, which is ours from of old, and which the prophecies declare we are to colonise some day or other. You then, when you have lost allies like us, will hereafter call to mind what I have now said."

63. At these words of Themistocles, Eurybiades changed his determination; principally, as I believe, because he feared that if he withdrew the fleet to the Isthmus, the Athenians would sail away, and knew that without the Athenians, the rest of their ships could be no match for the fleet of the enemy. He therefore decided to remain, and give battle at Salamis.

64. And now, the different chiefs, notwithstanding their skirmish of words, on learning the decision of Eurybiades, at once made ready for the fight. Morning broke; and, just as the sun rose, the shock of an earthquake was felt both on shore and at sea: whereupon the Greeks resolved to approach the gods with prayer, and likewise to send and invite the Æacids to their aid. And this they did, with as much speed as they had resolved on it. Prayers were offered to all the gods; and Telamon and Ajax were invoked at once from Salamis, while a ship was sent to Egina to fetch Æacus himself, and the other Æacids.

65. The following is a tale which was told by Dicæus, the son of Theocŷdes, an Athenian, who was at this time an exile, and had gained a good report among the Medes. He declared that after the army of Xerxes had, in the absence of the Athenians, wasted Attica, he chanced to be with Demaratus the Lacedæmonian in the Thriasian plain, and that while there, he saw a cloud of dust advancing from Eleusis, such as a host of thirty thousand men might raise. As he and his companion were wondering who the men, from whom the dust arose, could possibly

---

[1] Two hundred ships would imply at least 40,000 men, a force greater (probably) than that which any Greek state, except Sparta, could have brought into the field.

be, a sound of voices reached his ear, and he thought that he recognised the mystic hymn to Dionysus.[1] Now Demaratus was unacquainted with the rites of Eleusis, and so he inquired of Dicæus what the voices were saying. Dicæus made answer – "O Demaratus! beyond a doubt some mighty calamity is about to befall the king's army! For it is manifest, inasmuch as Attica is deserted by its inhabitants, that the sound which we have heard is an unearthly one, and is now upon its way from Eleusis to aid the Athenians and their confederates. If it descends upon the Peloponnese, danger will threaten the king himself and his land army – if it moves towards the ships at Salamis, 'twill go hard but the king's fleet there suffers destruction. Every year the Athenians celebrate this feast to the Mother and the Daughter;[2] and all who wish, whether they be Athenians or any other Greeks, are initiated. The sound thou hearest is the Dionysiac song, which is wont to be sung at that festival." "Hush now," rejoined the other; "and see thou tell no man of this matter. For if thy words be brought to the king's ear, thou wilt assuredly lose thy head because of them; neither I nor any man living can then save thee. Hold thy peace therefore. The gods will see to the king's army." Thus Demaratus counselled him; and they looked, and saw the dust, from which the sound arose, become a cloud, and the cloud rise up into the air and sail away to Salamis, making for the station of the Grecian fleet. Then they knew that it was the fleet of Xerxes which would suffer destruction. Such was the tale told by Dicæus the son of Theocýdes; and he appealed for its truth to Demaratus and other eye-witnesses.

66. The men belonging to the fleet of Xerxes, after they had seen the Spartan dead at Thermopylæ,[3] and crossed the channel from Trachis to Histiæa, waited there by the space of three days, and then sailing down through the Euripus,[4] in three more came to Phalêrum. In my judgment, the Persian forces both by land and sea when they invaded Attica were not less numerous than

1 The chief details concerning the greater Eleusinia, of which the mystic hymn to Dionysus was a part, are carefully collected in Smith's *Dictionary of Antiquities* (ad voc. ELEUSINIA) [and in chap. ix. of Jevons and Gardiner's *Manual of Greek Antiquities*. – E. H. B.].

2 Demeter [Kore] and Proserpine.

3 Supra, ch. 25.

4 The name Euripus applies, strictly speaking, only to the very narrowest part of the channel between Eubœa and the mainland.

they had been on their arrival at Sêpias and Thermopylæ. For against the Persian loss in the storm and at Thermopylæ, and again in the sea-fights off Artemisium, I set the various nations which had since joined the king – as the Malians, the Dorians, the Locrians, and the Bœotians – each serving in full force in his army except the last, who did not number in their ranks either the Thespians or the Platæans; and together with these, the Carystians, the Andrians, the Tenians, and the other people of the islands, who all fought on this side except the five states already mentioned.¹ For as the Persians penetrated further into Greece, they were joined continually by fresh nations.

67. Reinforced by the contingents of all these various states, except Paros, the barbarians reached Athens. As for the Parians, they tarried at Cythnus, waiting to see how the war would go. The rest of the sea forces came safe to Phalêrum; where they were visited by Xerxes, who had conceived a desire to go aboard and learn the wishes of the fleet. So he came and sate in a seat of honour; and the sovereigns of the nations, and the captains of the ships, were sent for, to appear before him, and as they arrived took their seats according to the rank assigned them by the king. In the first seat sate the king of Sidon; after him, the king of Tyre;² then the rest in their order. When the whole had taken their places, one after another, and were set down in orderly array, Xerxes, to try them, sent Mardonius and questioned each, whether a sea-fight should be risked or no.

68. Mardonius accordingly went round the entire assemblage, beginning with the Sidonian monarch, and asked this question; to which all gave the same answer, advising to engage the Greeks, except only Artemisia, who spake as follows:–

"Say to the king, Mardonius, that these are my words to him: I was not the least brave of those who fought at Eubœa, nor were my achievements there among the meanest; it is my right, therefore, O my lord, to tell thee plainly what I think to be most for thy advantage now. This then is my advice. Spare thy ships, and do not risk a battle; for these people are as much superior to thy people in seamanship, as men to women. What so great need is there for thee to incur hazard at sea? Art thóu not master of Athens, for which thou didst undertake thy expedition?³ Is

---

1 Naxos, Cythnus, Seriphus, Siphnus, and Melos (vide supra, ch. 46).
2 Compare vii. 98.   3 Supra, vii. 8, § 2.

not Greece subject to thee? Not a soul now resists thy advance. They who once resisted, were handled even as they deserved. (§ 2.) Now learn how I expect that affairs will go with thy adversaries. If thou art not over-hasty to engage with them by sea, but wilt keep thy fleet near the land, then whether thou abidest as thou art, or marchest forward towards the Peloponnese, thou wilt easily accomplish all for which thou art come hither. The Greeks cannot hold out against thee very long; thou wilt soon part them asunder, and scatter them to their several homes. In the island where they lie, I hear they have no food in store; nor is it likely, if thy land force begins its march towards the Peloponnese, that they will remain quietly where they are – at least such as come from that region. Of a surety *they* will not greatly trouble themselves to give battle on behalf of the Athenians. (§ 3.) On the other hand, if thou art hasty to fight, I tremble lest the defeat of thy sea force bring harm likewise to thy land army. This, too, thou shouldst remember, O king; good masters are apt to have bad servants, and bad masters good ones. Now, as thou art the best of men, thy servants must needs be a sorry set. These Egyptians, Cyprians, Cilicians, and Pamphylians, who are counted in the number of thy subject-allies, of how little service are they to thee!"

69. As Artemisia spake, they who wished her well were greatly troubled concerning her words, thinking that she would suffer some hurt at the king's hands, because she exhorted him not to risk a battle; they, on the other hand, who disliked and envied her, favoured as she was by the king above all the rest of the allies, rejoiced at her declaration, expecting that her life would be the forfeit. But Xerxes, when the words of the several speakers were reported to him, was pleased beyond all others with the reply of Artemisia; and whereas, even before this, he had always esteemed her much, he now praised her more than ever. Nevertheless, he gave orders that the advice of the greater number should be followed; for he thought that at Euboea the fleet had not done its best, because he himself was not there to see – whereas this time he resolved that he would be an eye-witness of the combat.

70. Orders were now given to stand out to sea; and the ships proceeded towards Salamis, and took up the stations to which they were directed, without let or hindrance from the enemy. The day, however, was too far spent for them to begin the battle, since night already approached: so they prepared to engage upon

the morrow. The Greeks, meanwhile, were in great distress and alarm, more especially those of the Peloponnese, who were troubled that they had been kept at Salamis to fight on behalf of the Athenian territory, and feared that, if they should suffer defeat, they would be pent up and besieged in an island, while their own country was left unprotected.

71. The same night the land army of the barbarians began its march towards the Peloponnese, where, however, all that was possible had been done to prevent the enemy from forcing an entrance by land. As soon as ever news reached the Peloponnese of the death of Leonidas and his companions at Thermopylæ, the inhabitants flocked together from the various cities, and encamped at the Isthmus, under the command of Cleombrotus, son of Anaxandridas, and brother of Leonidas. Here their first care was to block up the Scironian Way;[1] after which it was determined in council to build a wall across the Isthmus.[2] As the number assembled amounted to many tens of thousands, and there was not one who did not give himself to the work, it was soon finished. Stones, bricks, timber, baskets filled full of sand, were used in the building; and not a moment was lost by those who gave their aid; for they laboured without ceasing either by night or day.

72. Now the nations who gave their aid, and who had flocked in full force to the Isthmus, were the following: the Lacedæmonians, all the tribes of the Arcadians, the Eleans, the Corinthians, the Sicyonians, the Epidaurians, the Phliasians, the Trœzenians, and the Hermionians. These all gave their aid, being greatly alarmed at the danger which threatened Greece. But the other inhabitants of the Peloponnese took no part in the matter; though the Olympic and Carneian festivals were now over.[3]

73. Seven nations inhabit the Peloponnese. Two of them are aboriginal, and still continue in the regions where they dwelt at the first — to wit, the Arcadians[4] and the Cynurians.[5] A third,

1 The Scironian Way led from Megara to Corinth, along the eastern shore of the Isthmus.

2 The Isthmus is about four miles across at its narrowest point, and nearly five where the wall was built.

3 Supra, vii. 206.

4 That the Arcadians were aboriginal inhabitants of the Peloponnese was the unanimous tradition of antiquity.

5 Cynuria, or Cynosuria, was the border territory between Sparta and Argos upon the coast.

that of the Achæans, has never left the Peloponnese, but has been dislodged from its own proper country, and inhabits a district which once belonged to others.[1] The remaining nations, four out of the seven, are all immigrants – namely, the Dorians, the Ætolians, the Dryopians, and the Lemnians. To the Dorians belong several very famous cities;[2] to the Ætolians one only, that is, Elis; to the Dryopians, Hermioné and that Asiné which lies over against Cardamylé in Laconia;[3] to the Lemnians, all the towns of the Paroreats.[4] The aboriginal Cynurians alone seem to be Ionians; even they, however, have, in course of time, grown to be Dorians, under the government of the Argives, whose Orneats and vassals they were. All the cities of these seven nations, except those mentioned above, stood aloof from the war; and by so doing, if I may speak freely, they in fact took part with the Medes.

74. So the Greeks at the Isthmus toiled unceasingly, as though in the greatest peril; since they never imagined that any great success would be gained by the fleet. The Greeks at Salamis, on the other hand, when they heard what the rest were about, felt greatly alarmed; but their fear was not so much for themselves as for the Peloponnese. At first they conversed together in low tones, each man with his fellow, secretly, and marvelled at the folly shown by Eurybiades; but presently the smothered feeling broke out, and another assembly was held; whereat the old subjects provoked much talk from the speakers, one side maintaining that it was best to sail to the Peloponnese and risk battle for that, instead of abiding at Salamis and fighting for a land already taken by the enemy; while the other, which consisted of the Athenians, Eginetans, and Megarians, was urgent to remain and have the battle fought where they were.

75. Then Themistocles, when he saw that the Peloponnesians would carry the vote against him, went out secretly from the council, and, instructing a certain man what he should say, sent him on board a merchant ship to the fleet of the Medes. The man's name was Sicinnus; he was one of Themistocles'

---

1 Supra, vii. 94; compare i. 145.

2 Sparta, Argos, Mycenæ, Trœzen, Epidaurus, Corinth, and Sicyon.

3 Cardamylé was on the opposite side of the Coronæan Gulf to Asiné. It was an old Achæan settlement, and important enough to be mentioned by Homer (Il. ix. 150).

4 Supra, iv. 148.

household slaves, and acted as tutor to his sons;[1] in after times, when the Thespians were admitting persons to citizenship, Themistocles made him a Thespian, and a rich man to boot. The ship brought Sicinnus to the Persian fleet, and there he delivered his message to the leaders in these words:—

"The Athenian commander has sent me to you privily, without the knowledge of the other Greeks. He is a well-wisher to the king's cause, and would rather success should attend on you than on his countrymen; wherefore he bids me tell you that fear has seized the Greeks and they are meditating a hasty flight. Now then it is open to you to achieve the best work that ever ye wrought, if only ye will hinder their escaping. They no longer agree among themselves, so that they will not now make any resistance – nay, 'tis likely ye may see a fight already begun between such as favour and such as oppose your cause." The messenger, when he had thus expressed himself, departed and was seen no more.

76. Then the captains, believing all that the messenger had said, proceeded to land a large body of Persian troops on the islet of Psyttaleia,[2] which lies between Salamis and the mainland; after which, about the hour of midnight, they advanced their western wing towards Salamis, so as to inclose the Greeks. At the same time the force stationed about Ceos and Cynosura moved forward, and filled the whole strait as far as Munychia with their ships. This advance was made to prevent the Greeks from escaping by flight, and to block them up in Salamis, where it was thought that vengeance might be taken upon them for the battles fought near Artemisium. The Persian troops were landed on the islet of Psyttaleia, because, as soon as the battle began, the men and wrecks were likely to be drifted thither, as the isle lay in the very path of the coming fight, – and they would thus be able to save their own men and destroy those of the enemy. All these movements were made in silence, that the Greeks might have no knowledge of them; and they occupied the whole night, so that the men had no time to get their sleep.

77. I cannot say that there is no truth in prophecies, or feel inclined to call in question those which speak with clearness, when I think of the following:—

---

1 Themistocles is said to have had five sons.
2 Psyttaleia is the small island now called *Lipsokutáli*, which lies between the Piræus and the eastern extremity of Salamis.

"When they shall bridge with their ships to the sacred strand of
    Artemis
Girt with the golden falchion, and eke to marine Cynosura,[1]
Mad hope swelling their hearts at the downfall of beautiful
    Athens[2] –
Then shall godlike Right extinguish haughty Presumption,
Insult's furious offspring, who thinketh to overthrow all things.
Brass with brass shall mingle, and Ares with blood shall empurple
Ocean's waves. Then – then shall the day of Grecia's freedom
Come from Victory fair, and Cronos' son all-seeing."

When I look to this, and perceive how clearly Bacis[3] spoke, I
neither venture myself to say anything against prophecies, nor
do I approve of others impugning them.

78. Meanwhile, among the captains at Salamis, the strife of
words grew fierce. As yet they did not know that they were
encompassed, but imagined that the barbarians remained in the
same places where they had seen them the day before.

79. In the midst of their contention, Aristides, the son of
Lysimachus, who had crossed from Egina, arrived in Salamis. He
was an Athenian, and had been ostracised by the commonalty;[4]
yet I believe, from what I have heard concerning his character,
that there was not in all Athens a man so worthy or so just as
he. He now came to the council, and, standing outside, called
for Themistocles. Now Themistocles was not his friend, but his
most determined enemy. However, under the pressure of the
great dangers impending, Aristides forgot their feud, and called
Themistocles out of the council, since he wished to confer with
him. He had heard before his arrival of the impatience of the
Peloponnesians to withdraw the fleet to the Isthmus. As soon
therefore as Themistocles came forth, Aristides addressed him
in these words:–

"Our rivalry at all times, and especially at the present season,
ought to be a struggle, which of us shall most advantage our

---

1 The Marathonian promontory of the name.

2 "Brilliant" or "fruitful Athens" would be a closer translation. The epithet
λιπαραὶ is a favourite one in this connection.

3 Supra, ch. 20.

4 After a long struggle, Aristides had been ostracised through the influence
of Themistocles, three years earlier, B.C. 483. The stories told in connection with
his ostracism are well known, and will be found in Plutarch.

country. Let me then say to thee, that so far as regards the departure of the Peloponnesians from this place, much talk and little will be found precisely alike. I have seen with my own eyes that which I now report: that, however much the Corinthians or Eurybiades himself may wish it, they cannot now retreat; for we are inclosed on every side by the enemy. Go in to them, and make this known."

80. "Thy advice is excellent," answered the other; "and thy tidings are also good. That which I earnestly desired to happen, thine eyes have beheld accomplished. Know that what the Medes have now done was at my instance; for it was necessary, as our men would not fight here of their own free will, to make them fight whether they would or no. But come now, as thou hast brought the good news, go in and tell it. For if I speak to them, they will think it a feigned tale, and will not believe that the barbarians have inclosed us around. Therefore do thou go to them, and inform them how matters stand. If they believe thee, 'twill be for the best; but if otherwise, it will not harm. For it is impossible that they should now flee away, if we are indeed shut in on all sides, as thou sayest."

81. Then Aristides entered the assembly, and spoke to the captains: he had come, he told them, from Egina, and had but barely escaped the blockading vessels – the Greek fleet was entirely inclosed by the ships of Xerxes – and he advised them to get themselves in readiness to resist the foe. Having said so much, he withdrew. And now another contest arose; for the greater part of the captains would not believe the tidings.

82. But while they still doubted, a Tenian trireme, commanded by Panætius the son of Sôsimenes, deserted from the Persians and joined the Greeks, bringing full intelligence. For this reason the Tenians were inscribed upon the tripod at Delphi among those who overthrew the barbarians. With this ship, which deserted to their side at Salamis, and the Lemnian vessel which came over before at Artemisium,[1] the Greek fleet was brought to the full number of 380 ships; otherwise it fell short by two of that amount.

83. The Greeks now, not doubting what the Tenians told them, made ready for the coming fight. At the dawn of day, all

1 Supra, ch. 11. The calculation here made confirms the *total* in ch. 48, ad fin.

the men-at-arms[1] were assembled together, and speeches were made to them, of which the best was that of Themistocles; who throughout contrasted what was noble with what was base, and bade them, in all that came within the range of man's nature and constitution, *always* to make choice of the nobler part. Having thus wound up his discourse, he told them to go at once on board their ships, which they accordingly did; and about this time the trireme, that had been sent to Egina for the Æacidæ,[2] returned; whereupon the Greeks put to sea with all their fleet.

84. The fleet had scarce left the land when they were attacked by the barbarians. At once most of the Greeks began to back water, and were about touching the shore, when Ameinias of Pallênê,[3] one of the Athenian captains, darted forth in front of the line, and charged a ship of the enemy. The two vessels became entangled, and could not separate, whereupon the rest of the fleet came up to help Ameinias, and engaged with the Persians. Such is the account which the Athenians give of the way in which the battle began; but the Eginetans maintain that the vessel which had been to Egina for the Æacidæ, was the one that brought on the fight. It is also reported, that a phantom in the form of a woman appeared to the Greeks, and, in a voice that was heard from end to end of the fleet, cheered them on to the fight; first, however, rebuking them, and saying – "Strange men, how long are ye going to back water?"

85. Against the Athenians, who held the western extremity of the line towards Eleusis, were placed the Phœnicians; against the Lacedæmonians, whose station was eastward towards the Piræus, the Ionians. Of these last a few only followed the advice of Themistocles, to fight backwardly; the greater number did far otherwise. I could mention here the names of many trierarchs who took vessels from the Greeks, but I shall pass over all excepting Theomêstor, the son of Androdamas, and Phylacus, the son of Histiæus, both Samians. I show this preference to them, inasmuch as for this service Theomêstor was made tyrant of Samos by the Persians, while Phylacus was enrolled among

---

1 The Epibatæ, or armed portion of the crew of a trireme, corresponding to our marines, varied in amount at different periods of Greek history. The greatest number ever found is forty.

2 Supra, ch. 64.

3 Pallênê was one of the most famous of the Athenian provincial towns.

the king's benefactors, and presented with a large estate in land. In the Persian tongue the king's benefactors are called *Orosangs*.

86. Far the greater number of the Persian ships engaged in this battle were disabled, either by the Athenians or by the Eginetans. For as the Greeks fought in order and kept their line, while the barbarians were in confusion and had no plan in anything that they did, the issue of the battle could scarce be other than it was. Yet the Persians fought far more bravely here than at Eubœa, and indeed surpassed themselves; each did his utmost through fear of Xerxes, for each thought that the king's eye was upon himself.[1]

87. What part the several nations, whether Greek or barbarian, took in the combat, I am not able to say for certain; Artemisia, however, I know, distinguished herself in such a way as raised her even higher than she stood before in the esteem of the king. For after confusion had spread throughout the whole of the king's fleet, and her ship was closely pursued by an Athenian trireme, she, having no way to fly, since in front of her were a number of friendly vessels, and she was nearest of all the Persians to the enemy, resolved on a measure which in fact proved her safety. Pressed by the Athenian pursuer, she bore straight against one of the ships of her own party, a Calyndian, which had Damasithymus, the Calyndian king, himself on board. I cannot say whether she had had any quarrel with the man while the fleet was at the Hellespont, or no – neither can I decide whether she of set purpose attacked his vessel, or whether it merely chanced that the Calyndian ship came in her way – but certain it is that she bore down upon his vessel and sank it, and that thereby she had the good fortune to procure herself a double advantage. For the commander of the Athenian trireme, when he saw her bear down on one of the enemy's fleet, thought immediately that her vessel was a Greek, or else had deserted from the Persians, and was now fighting on the Greek side; he therefore gave up the chase, and turned away to attack others.

88. Thus in the first place she saved her life by the action, and was enabled to get clear off from the battle; while further, it fell out that in the very act of doing the king an injury she raised herself to a greater height than ever in his esteem. For as

[1] Supra, ch. 69, and infra, ch. 90. The anger of Xerxes, as we see in the latter passage, led to very serious consequences.

Xerxes beheld the fight, he remarked (it is said) the destruction of the vessel, whereupon the bystanders observed to him – "Seest thou, master, how well Artemisia fights, and how she has just sunk a ship of the enemy?" Then Xerxes asked if it were really Artemisia's doing; and they answered, "Certainly; for they knew her ensign:" while all made sure that the sunken vessel belonged to the opposite side. Everything, it is said, conspired to prosper the queen – it was especially fortunate for her that not one of those on board the Calyndian ship survived to become her accuser. Xerxes, they say, in reply to the remarks made to him, observed – "My men have behaved like women, my women like men!"

89. There fell in this combat Ariabignes, one of the chief commanders of the fleet, who was son of Darius and brother of Xerxes; and with him perished a vast number of men of high repute, Persians, Medes, and allies. Of the Greeks there died only a few; for, as they were able to swim, all those that were not slain outright by the enemy escaped from the sinking vessels and swam across to Salamis. But on the side of the barbarians more perished by drowning than in any other way, since they did not know how to swim. The great destruction took place when the ships which had been first engaged began to fly; for they who were stationed in the rear, anxious to display their valour before the eyes of the king, made every effort to force their way to the front, and thus became entangled with such of their own vessels as were retreating.

90. In this confusion the following event occurred: Certain Phœnicians belonging to the ships which had thus perished made their appearance before the king, and laid the blame of their loss on the Ionians, declaring that they were traitors, and had wilfully destroyed the vessels. But the upshot of this complaint was, that the Ionian captains escaped the death which threatened them, while their Phœnician accusers received death as their reward. For it happened that, exactly as they spoke, a Samothracian vessel bore down on an Athenian and sank it, but was attacked and crippled immediately by one of the Eginetan squadron. Now the Samothracians were expert with the javelin, and aimed their weapons so well, that they cleared the deck of the vessel which had disabled their own, after which they sprang on board, and took it. This saved the Ionians. Xerxes, when he saw the exploit, turned fiercely on the Phœnicians – (he was ready, in his extreme

vexation, to find fault with any one) – and ordered their heads to be cut off, to prevent them, he said, from casting the blame of their own misconduct upon braver men. During the whole time of the battle Xerxes sate at the base of the hill called Ægaleôs, over against Salamis; and whenever he saw any of his own captains perform any worthy exploit he inquired concerning him; and the man's name was taken down by his scribes,[1] together with the names of his father and his city. Ariaramnes too, a Persian,[2] who was a friend of the Ionians, and present at the time whereof I speak, had a share in bringing about the punishment of the Phœnicians.

91. When the rout of the barbarians began, and they sought to make their escape to Phalêrum, the Eginetans, awaiting them in the channel, performed exploits worthy to be recorded. Through the whole of the confused struggle the Athenians employed themselves in destroying such ships as either made resistance or fled to shore, while the Eginetans dealt with those which endeavoured to escape down the strait; so that the Persian vessels were no sooner clear of the Athenians than forthwith they fell into the hands of the Eginetan squadron.

92. It chanced here that there was a meeting between the ship of Themistocles, which was hasting in pursuit of the enemy, and that of Polycritus, son of Crius the Eginetan,[3] which had just charged a Sidonian trireme. The Sidonian vessel was the same that captured the Eginetan guard-ship off Sciathus,[4] which had Pytheas, the son of Ischenoüs, on board – that Pytheas, I mean, who fell covered with wounds, and whom the Sidonians kept on board their ship, from admiration of his gallantry. This man afterwards returned in safety to Egina; for when the Sidonian vessel with its Persian crew fell into the hands of the Greeks, he was still found on board. Polycritus no sooner saw the Athenian trireme than, knowing at once whose vessel it was, as he observed that it bore the ensign of the admiral, he shouted to Themistocles jeeringly, and asked him, in a tone of reproach, if the Eginetans did not show themselves rare friends to the Medes. At the same time, while he thus reproached

---

1 Supra, vii. 100.
2 He was probably one of the royal house.
3 Crius has been mentioned as one of the chief men in Egina (supra, vi. 73).
4 Supra, vii. 181.

Themistocles, Polycritus bore straight down on the Sidonian. Such of the barbarian vessels as escaped from the battle fled to Phalêrum, and there sheltered themselves under the protection of the land army.

93. The Greeks who gained the greatest glory of all in the sea-fight off Salamis were the Eginetans, and after them the Athenians. The individuals of most distinction were Polycritus the Eginetan, and two Athenians, Eumenes of Anagyrus,[1] and Ameinias of Pallênê; the latter of whom had pressed Artemisia so hard. And assuredly, if he had known that the vessel carried Artemisia on board, he would never have given over the chase till he had either succeeded in taking her, or else been taken himself. For the Athenian captains had received special orders touching the queen; and moreover a reward of ten thousand drachmas[2] had been proclaimed for any one who should make her prisoner; since there was great indignation felt that a woman should appear in arms against Athens. However, as I said before, she escaped; and so did some others whose ships survived the engagement; and these were all now assembled at the port of Phalêrum.

94. The Athenians say that Adeimantus, the Corinthian commander, at the moment when the two fleets joined battle, was seized with fear, and being beyond measure alarmed, spread his sails, and hasted to fly away; on which the other Corinthians, seeing their leader's ship in full flight, sailed off likewise. They had reached in their flight that part of the coast of Salamis where stands the temple of Athena Sciras, when they met a light bark, a very strange apparition: it was never discovered that any one had sent it to them; and till it appeared they were altogether ignorant how the battle was going. That there was something beyond nature in the matter they judged from this – that when the men, in the bark drew near to their ships they addressed them, saying – "Adeimantus, while thou playest the traitor's part, by withdrawing all these ships, and flying away from the fight, the Greeks whom thou hast deserted are defeating their foes as completely as they ever wished in their prayers." Adeimantus, however, would not believe what the men said; whereupon they

1 Anagyrus was one of the maritime demes [or *parishes*] between the Piræus and Sunium.

2 Ten thousand drachmas would be equal to £400 of our money.

told him, "he might take them with him as hostages, and put them to death if he did not find the Greeks winning." Then Adeimantus put about, both he and those who were with him; and they re-joined the fleet when the victory was already gained. Such is the tale which the Athenians tell concerning them of Corinth; these latter however do not allow its truth.[1] On the contrary, they declare that they were among those who distinguished themselves most in the fight. And the rest of Greece bears witness in their favour.

95. In the midst of the confusion Aristides, the son of Lysimachus, the Athenian, of whom I lately spoke as a man of the greatest excellence, performed the following service. He took a number of the Athenian heavy-armed troops, who had previously been stationed along the shore of Salamis, and, landing with them on the islet of Psyttaleia, slew all the Persians by whom it was occupied.

96. As soon as the sea-fight was ended,[2] the Greeks drew together to Salamis all the wrecks that were to be found in that quarter, and prepared themselves for another engagement, supposing that the king would renew the fight with the vessels which still remained to him. Many of the wrecks had been carried away by a westerly wind to the coast of Attica, where they were thrown upon the strip of shore called Côlias. Thus not only were the prophecies of Bacis and Musæus[3] concerning this battle fulfilled completely, but likewise, by the place to which the wrecks were drifted, the prediction of Lysistratus, an Athenian soothsayer, uttered many years before these events, and quite forgotten at the time by all the Greeks, was fully accomplished. The words were –

"Then shall the sight of the oars fill Colian dames with amazement."

Now this must have happened as soon as the king was departed.

97. Xerxes, when he saw the extent of his loss, began to be afraid lest the Greeks might be counselled by the Ionians, or

---

1 There can be no doubt that the tale was altogether false.

2 The description of the battle of Salamis in Æschylus (Pers. 359–438), as the account of an eye-witness and combatant, must always hold a primary place among the records of the time. It does not appear to have been known to Herodotus, yet it confirms his account in all the principal features.

3 Concerning these poets, see above, vii. 6, and viii. 20.

without their advice might determine to sail straight to the Hellespont and break down the bridges there; in which case he would be blocked up in Europe, and run great risk of perishing. He therefore made up his mind to fly; but, as he wished to hide his purpose alike from the Greeks and from his own people, he set to work to carry a mound across the channel to Salamis, and at the same time began fastening a number of Phœnician merchant ships together, to serve at once for a bridge and a wall. He likewise made many warlike preparations, as if he were about to engage the Greeks once more at sea. Now, when these things were seen, all grew fully persuaded that the king was bent on remaining, and intended to push the war in good earnest. Mardonius, however, was in no respect deceived; for long acquaintance enabled him to read all the king's thoughts. Meanwhile, Xerxes, though engaged in this way, sent off a messenger to carry intelligence of his misfortune to Persia.

98. Nothing mortal travels so fast as these Persian messengers. The entire plan is a Persian invention; and this is the method of it. Along the whole line of road there are men (they say) stationed with horses, in number equal to the number of days which the journey takes, allowing a man and horse to each day; and these men will not be hindered from accomplishing at their best speed the distance which they have to go, either by snow, or rain, or heat, or by the darkness of night. The first rider delivers his despatch to the second, and the second passes it to the third; and so it is borne from hand to hand along the whole line, like the light in the torch-race, which the Greeks celebrate to Hephaistos. The Persians give the riding post in this manner, the name of "Angarum."[1]

99. At Susa, on the arrival of the first message, which said that Xerxes was master of Athens, such was the delight of the Persians who had remained behind, that they forthwith strewed all the streets with myrtle boughs, and burnt incense, and fell to feasting and merriment. In like manner, when the second message reached them, so sore was their dismay, that they all with one accord rent their garments, and cried aloud, and wept and wailed without stint. They laid the blame of the disaster on

1 Probably in the time of Herodotus swift camels were employed in the postal service of the Persian Empire. [For the verb (ἀγγαρεύειν) see Matt. v. 41, and Esther, viii. 10. – E. H. B.].

Mardonius; and their grief on the occasion was less on account of the damage done to their ships, than owing to the alarm which they felt about the safety of the king. Hence their trouble did not cease till Xerxes himself, by his arrival, put an end to their fears.

100. And now Mardonius, perceiving that Xerxes took the defeat of his fleet greatly to heart, and suspecting that he had made up his mind to leave Athens and fly away, began to think of the likelihood of his being visited with punishment for having persuaded the king to undertake the war. He therefore considered that it would be the best thing for him to adventure further, and either become the conqueror of Greece – which was the result he rather expected – or else die gloriously after aspiring to a noble achievement. So with these thoughts in his mind, he said one day to the king –

"Do not grieve, master, or take so greatly to heart thy late loss. Our hopes hang not altogether on the fate of a few planks, but on our brave steeds and horsemen. These fellows, whom thou imaginest to have quite conquered us, will not venture – no, not one of them – to come ashore and contend with our land army; nor will the Greeks who are upon the mainland fight our troops; such as did so have received their punishment. If thou so pleasest, we may at once attack the Peloponnese; if thou wouldst rather wait a while, that too is in our power. Only be not disheartened. For it is not possible that the Greeks can avoid being brought to account, alike for this and for their former injuries; nor can they anyhow escape being thy slaves. Thou shouldst therefore do as I have said. If, however, thy mind is made up, and thou art resolved to retreat and lead away thy army, listen to the counsel which, in that case, I have to offer. Make not the Persians, O king! a laughing-stock to the Greeks. If thy affairs have succeeded ill, it has not been by their fault; thou canst not say that thy Persians have ever shown themselves cowards. What matters it if Phœnicians and Egyptians, Cyprians and Cilicians, have misbehaved? – their misconduct touches not us. Since then thy Persians are without fault, be advised by me. Depart home, if thou art so minded, and take with thee the bulk of thy army; but first let me choose out 300,000 troops, and let it be my task to bring Greece beneath thy sway."

101. Xerxes, when he heard these words, felt a sense of joy and delight, like a man who is relieved from care. Answering

Mardonius, therefore, "that he would consider his counsel, and let him know which course he might prefer," Xerxes proceeded to consult with the chief men among the Persians; and because Artemisia on the former occasion had shown herself the only person who knew what was best to be done, he was pleased to summon her to advise him now. As soon as she arrived, he put forth all the rest, both councillors and body-guards, and said to her:—

"Mardonius wishes me to stay and attack the Peloponnese. My Persians, he says, and my other land forces, are not to blame for the disasters which have befallen our arms; and of this he declares they would very gladly give me the proof. He therefore exhorts me, either to stay and act as I have said, or to let him choose out 300,000 of my troops – wherewith he undertakes to reduce Greece beneath my sway – while I myself retire with the rest of my forces, and withdraw into my own country. Do thou, therefore, as thou didst counsel me so wisely to decline the sea-fight, now also advise me in this matter, and say, which course of the twain I ought to take for my own good."

102. Thus did the king ask Artemisia's counsel; and the following are the words wherewith she answered him:—

" 'Tis a hard thing, O king! to give the best possible advice to one who asks our counsel. Nevertheless, as thy affairs now stand, it seemeth to me that thou wilt do right to return home. As for Mardonius, if he prefers to remain, and undertakes to do as he has said, leave him behind by all means, with the troops which he desires. If his design succeeds, and he subdues the Greeks, as he promises, thine is the conquest, master; for thy slaves will have accomplished it. If, on the other hand, affairs run counter to his wishes, we can suffer no great loss, so long as thou art safe, and thy house is in no danger. The Greeks, too, while thou livest, and thy house flourishes, must be prepared to fight full many a battle for their freedom; whereas if Mardonius fall, it matters nothing – they will have gained but a poor triumph – a victory over one of thy slaves! Remember also, thou goest home having gained the purpose of thy expedition;[1] for thou hast burnt Athens!"

103. The advice of Artemisia pleased Xerxes well; for she had exactly uttered his own thoughts. I, for my part, do not

---

1 Vide supra, ch. 68, § 1.

believe that he would have remained had all his counsellors, both men and women, united to urge his stay, so great was the alarm that he felt. As it was, he gave praise to Artemisia, and entrusted certain of his children to her care, ordering her to convey them to Ephesus; for he had been accompanied on the expedition by some of his natural sons.

104. He likewise sent away at this time one of the principal of his eunuchs,[1] a man named Hermotimus, a Pedasian, who was bidden to take charge of these sons. Now the Pedasians inhabit the region above Halicarnassus; and it is related of them, that in their country the following circumstance happens: When a mischance is about to befall any of their neighbours within a certain time, the priestess of Athena in their city grows a long beard. This has already taken place on two occasions.

105. The Hermotimus of whom I spoke above was, as I said, a Pedasian; and he, of all men whom we know, took the most cruel vengeance on the person who had done him an injury. He had been made a prisoner of war, and when his captors sold him, he was bought by a certain Panionius, a native of Chios, who made his living by a most nefarious traffic. Whenever he could get any boys of unusual beauty, he made them eunuchs, and, carrying them to Sardis or Ephesus, sold them for large sums of money. For the barbarians value eunuchs more than others, since they regard them as more trustworthy. Many were the slaves that Panionius, who made his living by the practice, had thus treated; and among them was this Hermotimus of whom I have here made mention. However, he was not without his share of good fortune; for after a while he was sent from Sardis, together with other gifts, as a present to the king. Nor was it long before he came to be esteemed by Xerxes more highly than all his eunuchs.

106. When the king was on his way to Athens with the Persian army, and abode for a time at Sardis, Hermotimus happened to make a journey upon business into Mysia; and there, in a district which is called Atarneus, but belongs to Chios,[2] he chanced to fall in with Panionius. Recognising him at once, he entered into a long and friendly talk with him, wherein he counted

---

1 We have here the first instance in authentic Persian history of the influence of the eunuchs, which afterwards became so great an evil.

2 Vide supra, i. 160; vi. 28, 29.

up the numerous blessings he enjoyed through his means, and promised him all manner of favours in return, if he would bring his household to Sardis and live there. Panionius was overjoyed, and, accepting the offer made him, came presently, and brought with him his wife and children. Then Hermotimus, when he had got Panionius and all his family into his power, addressed him in these words:—

"Thou man, who gettest a living by viler deeds than any one else in the whole world, what wrong to thee or thine had I or any of mine done, that thou shouldst have made me the *nothing* that I now am? Ah! surely thou thoughtest that the gods took no note of thy crimes. But they in their justice have delivered thee, the doer of unrighteousness, into my hands; and now thou canst not complain of the vengeance which I am resolved to take on thee."

After these reproaches, Hermotimus commanded the four sons of Panionius to be brought, and forced the father to make them eunuchs with his own hand. Unable to resist, he did as Hermotimus required; and then his sons were made to treat him in the self-same way. So in this way there came to Panionius requital at the hands of Hermotimus.

107. Xerxes, after charging Artemisia to convey his sons safe to Ephesus,[1] sent for Mardonius, and bade him choose from all his army such men as he wished, and see that he made his achievements answer to his promises. During this day he did no more; but no sooner was night come, than he issued his orders, and at once the captains of the ships left Phalêrum, and bore away for the Hellespont, each making all the speed he could, and hasting to guard the bridges against the king's return. On their way, as they sailed by Zôster, where certain narrow points of land project into the sea,[2] they took the cliffs for vessels, and fled far away in alarm. Discovering their mistake, however, after a time, they joined company once more, and proceeded upon their voyage.

108. Next day the Greeks, seeing the land force of the barbarians encamped in the same place, thought that their ships must still be lying at Phalêrum; and, expecting another attack from that quarter, made preparations to defend themselves.

---

1 Supra, ch. 103.
2 Cape Zôster is undoubtedly the modern Cape *Lumbardha*.

Soon however news came that the ships were all departed and gone away; whereupon it was instantly resolved to make sail in pursuit. They went as far as Andros; but, seeing nothing of the Persian fleet, they stopped at that place, and held a council of war. At this council Themistocles advised that the Greeks should follow on through the islands, still pressing the pursuit, and making all haste to the Hellespont, there to break down the bridges. Eurybiades, however, delivered a contrary opinion. "If," he said, "the Greeks should break down the bridges, it would be the worst thing that could possibly happen for Greece. The Persian, supposing that his retreat were cut off, and he compelled to remain in Europe, would be sure never to give them any peace. Inaction on his part would ruin all his affairs, and leave him no chance of ever getting back to Asia – nay, would even cause his army to perish by famine: whereas, if he bestirred himself, and acted vigorously, it was likely that the whole of Europe would in course of time become subject to him; since, by degrees, the various towns and tribes would either fall before his arms, or else agree to terms of submission; and in this way, his troops would find food sufficient for them, since each year the Greek harvest would be theirs. As it was, the Persian, because he had lost the sea-fight, intended evidently to remain no longer in Europe. The Greeks ought to let him depart; and when he was gone from among them, and had returned into his own country, then would be the time for them to contend with him for the possession of *that*."

The other captains of the Peloponnesians declared themselves of the same mind.

109. Whereupon Themistocles, finding that the majority was against him, and that he could not persuade them to push on to the Hellespont, changed round, and addressing himself to the Athenians, who of all the allies were the most nettled at the enemy's escape, and who eagerly desired, if the other Greeks would not stir, to sail on by themselves to the Hellespont and break the bridges, spake as follows:—

"I have often myself witnessed occasions, and I have heard of many more from others, where men who had been conquered by an enemy, having been driven quite to desperation, have renewed the fight, and retrieved their former disasters. We have now had the great good luck to save both ourselves and all Greece by the repulse of this vast cloud of men; let us then be content and not press them too hard, now that they have begun to fly. Be sure we have not done this by our own might. It is the work of gods and heroes, who were jealous[1] that one man should be king at once of Europe and of Asia – more especially a man like this, unholy and presumptuous – a man who esteems alike things sacred and things profane; who has cast down and burnt the very images of the gods themselves; who even caused the sea to be scourged with rods and commanded fetters to be thrown into it.[2] At present all is well with us – let us then abide in Greece, and look to ourselves and to our families. The barbarian is clean gone – we have driven him off – let each now repair his own house, and sow his land diligently. In the spring we will take ship and sail to the Hellespont and to Ionia!"

All this Themistocles said in the hope of establishing a claim upon the king; for he wanted to have a safe retreat in case any mischance should befall him at Athens – which indeed came to pass afterwards.

110. At present, however, he dissembled; and the Athenians were persuaded by his words. For they were ready now to do whatever he advised; since they had always esteemed him a wise man, and he had lately proved himself most truly wise and well-judging. Accordingly, they came in to his views; whereupon he lost no time in sending messengers, on board a light bark, to the king, choosing for this purpose men whom he could trust to keep his instructions secret, even although they should be put to every kind of torture. Among them was the house-slave Sicinnus, the same whom he had made use of previously.[3] When the men reached Attica, all the others stayed with the boat; but Sicinnus went up to the king, and spake to him as follows:–

"I am sent to thee by Themistocles, the son of Neocles, who is the leader of the Athenians, and the wisest and bravest man of all the allies, to bear thee this message: 'Themistocles the Athenian, anxious to render thee a service, has restrained the Greeks, who were impatient to pursue thy ships, and to break up the bridges at the Hellespont. Now, therefore, return home at thy leisure.'"

The messengers, when they had performed their errand, sailed back to the fleet.

1 Supra, vii. 10, § 5. 2 Supra, vii. 35. 3 Supra, ch. 75.

111. And the Greeks, having resolved that they would neither proceed further in pursuit of the barbarians, nor push forward to the Hellespont and destroy the passage, laid siege to Andros, intending to take the town by storm. For Themistocles had required the Andrians to pay down a sum of money; and they had refused, being the first of all the islanders who did so. To his declaration, "that the money must needs be paid, as the Athenians had brought with him two mighty gods – Persuasion and Necessity," they made reply, that "Athens might well be a great and glorious city, since she was blest with such excellent gods; but *they* were wretchedly poor, stinted for land, and cursed with two unprofitable gods, who always dwelt with them and would never quit their island – to wit, Poverty and Helplessness. These were the gods of the Andrians, and therefore they would not pay the money. For the power of Athens could not possibly be stronger than their inability." This reply, coupled with the refusal to pay the sum required, caused their city to be besieged by the Greeks.

112. Meanwhile Themistocles, who never ceased his pursuit of gain,[1] sent threatening messages to the other islanders with demands for different sums, employing the same messengers and the same words as he had used towards the Andrians. "If," he said, "they did not send him the amount required, he would bring the Greek fleet upon them, and besiege them till he took their cities." By these means he collected large sums from the Carystians[2] and the Parians, who, when they heard that Andros was already besieged, and that Themistocles was the best esteemed of all the captains, sent the money through fear. Whether any of the other islanders did the like, I cannot say for certain; but I think some did besides those I have mentioned. However, the Carystians, though they complied, were not spared any the more; but Themistocles was softened by the Parians' gift, and therefore they received no visit from the army. In this way it was that Themistocles, during his stay at Andros, obtained money from the islanders, unbeknown to the other captains.

113. King Xerxes and his army waited but a few days after the sea-fight, and then withdrew into Bœotia by the road which they had followed on their advance. It was the wish of Mardonius to escort the king a part of the way; and as the time of year

1 Cf. supra, ch. 4.　　2 Supra, vi. 99.

was no longer suitable for carrying on war, he thought it best to winter in Thessaly, and wait for the spring before he attempted the Peloponnese. After the army was come into Thessaly, Mardonius made choice of the troops that were to stay with him; and, first of all, he took the whole body called the "Immortals,"[1] except only their leader, Hydarnes, who refused to quit the person of the king. Next, he chose the Persians who wore breastplates, and the thousand picked horse;[2] likewise the Medes, the Sacans, the Bactrians, and the Indians, foot and horse equally. These nations he took entire: from the rest of the allies he culled a few men, taking either such as were remarkable for their appearance, or else such as had performed, to his knowledge, some valiant deed. The Persians furnished him with the greatest number of troops, men who were adorned with chains and armlets. Next to them were the Medes, who in number equalled the Persians, but in valour fell short of them. The whole army, reckoning the horsemen with the rest, amounted to 300,000 men.

114. At the time when Mardonius was making choice of his troops, and Xerxes still continued in Thessaly, the Lacedæmonians received a message from the Delphic oracle, bidding them seek satisfaction at the hands of Xerxes for the death of Leonidas, and take whatever he chose to give them. So the Spartans sent a herald with all speed into Thessaly, who arrived while the entire Persian army was still there. This man, being brought before the king, spake as follows:—

"King of the Medes, the Lacedæmonians and the Heracleids of Sparta require of thee the satisfaction due for bloodshed, because thou slewest their king, who fell fighting for Greece."

Xerxes laughed, and for a long time spake not a word. At last, however, he pointed to Mardonius, who was standing by him, and said:— "Mardonius here shall give them the satisfaction they deserve to get." And the herald accepted the answer, and forthwith went his way.

115. Xerxes, after this, left Mardonius in Thessaly, and marched away himself, at his best speed, toward the Hellespont. In five-and-forty days he reached the place of passage, where he arrived with scarce a fraction, so to speak, of his former army. All along their line of march, in every country where they

---

1 Supra, vii. 83, 211, 215.
2 Troops specially attached to the king's person (supra, vii. 40).

chanced to be, his soldiers seized and devoured whatever corn they could find belonging to the inhabitants; while, if no corn was to be found, they gathered the grass that grew in the fields, and stripped the trees, whether cultivated or wild, alike of their bark and of their leaves, and so fed themselves. They left nothing anywhere, so hard were they pressed by hunger. Plague too and dysentery attacked the troops while still upon their march, and greatly thinned their ranks. Many died; others fell sick and were left behind in the different cities that lay upon the route, the inhabitants being strictly charged by Xerxes to tend and feed them. Of these some remained in Thessaly, others in Siris of Pæonia, others again in Macedon. Here[1] Xerxes, on his march into Greece, had left the sacred car and steeds of Jove; which upon his return he was unable to recover; for the Pæonians had disposed of them to the Thracians, and, when Xerxes demanded them back, they said that the Thracian tribes who dwelt about the sources of the Strymon had stolen the mares as they pastured.

116. Here too a Thracian chieftain, king of the Bisaltians and of Crestonia, did a deed which went beyond nature. He had refused to become the willing slave of Xerxes, and had fled before him into the heights of Rhodopé,[2] at the same time forbidding his sons to take part in the expedition against Greece. But they, either because they cared little for his orders, or because they wished greatly to see the war, joined the army of Xerxes. At this time they had all returned home to him – the number of the men was six – quite safe and sound. But their father took them, and punished their offence by plucking out their eyes from the sockets. Such was the treatment which these men received.

117. The Persians, having journeyed through Thrace and reached the passage, entered their ships hastily and crossed the Hellespont to Abydos. The bridges were not found stretched across the strait; since a storm had broken and dispersed them. At Abydos the troops halted, and, obtaining more abundant provision than they had yet got upon their march, they fed without stint; from which cause, added to the change in their water, great numbers of those who had hitherto escaped

1 At Siris, not in Macedonia.
2 Rhodopé proper appears to have been the chain now called *Despoto Dagh*.

perished. The remainder, together with Xerxes himself, came safe to Sardis.[1]

118. There is likewise another account given of the return of the king. It is said that when Xerxes on his way from Athens arrived at Eïon upon the Strymon, he gave up travelling by land, and, intrusting Hydarnes with the conduct of his forces to the Hellespont, embarked himself on board a Phœnician ship, and so crossed into Asia. On his voyage the ship was assailed by a strong wind blowing from the mouth of the Strymon, which caused the sea to run high. As the storm increased, and the ship laboured heavily, because of the number of the Persians who had come in the king's train, and who now crowded the deck, Xerxes was seized with fear, and called out to the helmsman in a loud voice, asking him, if there were any means whereby they might escape the danger. "No means, master," the helmsman answered, "unless we could be quit of these too numerous passengers." Xerxes, they say, on hearing this, addressed the Persians as follows: "Men of Persia," he said, "now is the time for you to show what love ye bear your king. My safety, as it seems, depends wholly upon you." So spake the king; and the Persians instantly made obeisance, and then leapt over into the sea. Thus was the ship lightened, and Xerxes got safe to Asia. As soon as he had reached the shore, he sent for the helmsman, and gave him a golden crown because he had preserved the life of the king, – but because he had caused the death of a number of Persians, he ordered his head to be struck from his shoulders.

119. Such is the other account which is given of the return of Xerxes; but to me it seems quite unworthy of belief, alike in other respects, and in what relates to the Persians. For had the helmsman made any such speech to Xerxes, I suppose there is not one man in ten thousand who will doubt that this is the course which the king would have followed:– he would have made the men upon the ship's deck,[2] who were not only Persians, but Persians of the very highest rank, quit their place and go down below; and would have cast into the sea an equal number of the rowers, who were Phœnicians. But the truth is,

1 Xerxes remained at Sardis the whole of the winter, and during a considerable portion of the next year (infra, ix. 107, ad fin.).
2 The Epibatæ, or "marines," of which each trireme in the Persian fleet carried thirty (supra, 184).

that the king, as I have already said, returned into Asia by the same road as the rest of the army.

120. I will add a strong proof of this. It is certain that Xerxes on his way back from Greece passed through Abdêra, where he made a contract of friendship with the inhabitants, and presented them with a golden scymitar, and a tiara broidered with gold. The Abderites declare – but I put no faith in this part of their story – that from the time of the king's leaving Athens, he never once loosed his girdle till he came to their city, since it was not till then that he felt himself in safety. Now Abdêra is nearer to the Hellespont than Eïon and the Strymon, where Xerxes, according to the other tale, took ship.

121. Meanwhile the Greeks, finding that they could not capture Andros, sailed away to Carystus, and wasted the lands of the Carystians, after which they returned to Salamis. Arrived here, they proceeded, before entering on any other matter, to make choice of the first-fruits which should be set apart as offerings to the gods. These consisted of divers gifts; among them were three Phœnician triremes, one of which was dedicated at the Isthmus, where it continued to my day; another at Sunium; and the third, at Salamis itself, which was devoted to Ajax. This done, they made a division of the booty, and sent away the first-fruits to Delphi. Thereof was made the statue, holding in its hand the beak of a ship, which is twelve cubits high, and which stands in the same place with the golden one of Alexander the Macedonian.

122. After the first-fruits had been sent to Delphi, the Greeks made inquiry of the god, in the name of their whole body, if he had received his full share of the spoils and was satisfied therewith. The god made answer, that all the other Greeks had paid him his full due, except only the Eginetans; on them he had still a claim for the prize of valour which they had gained at Salamis.[1] So the Eginetans, when they heard this, dedicated the three golden stars which stand on the top of a bronze mast in the corner near the bowl offered by Crœsus.[2]

123. When the spoils had been divided, the Greeks sailed to the Isthmus, where a prize of valour was to be awarded to the

---

1 Supra, ch. 93.

2 Supra, i. 51. The *silver* bowl of Crœsus is intended, which stood "in the corner of the ante-chapel."

man who, of all the Greeks, had shown the most merit during the war. When the chiefs were all come, they met at the altar of Poseidon, and took the ballots wherewith they were to give their votes for the first and for the second in merit. Then each man gave himself the first vote, since each considered that he was himself the worthiest; but the second votes were given chiefly to Themistocles. In this way, while the others received but one vote apiece, Themistocles had for the second prize a large majority of the suffrages.

124. Envy, however, hindered the chiefs from coming to a decision, and they all sailed away to their homes without making any award. Nevertheless Themistocles was regarded everywhere as by far the wisest man of all the Greeks; and the whole country rang with his fame. As the chiefs who fought at Salamis, notwithstanding that he was really entitled to the prize, had withheld his honour from him, he went without delay to Lacedæmon, in the hope that he would be honoured there. And the Lacedæmonians received him handsomely, and paid him great respect. The prize of valour indeed, which was a crown of olive, they gave to Eurybiades; but Themistocles was given a crown of olive too, as the prize of wisdom and dexterity. He was likewise presented with the most beautiful chariot that could be found in Sparta; and after receiving abundant praises, was, upon his departure, escorted as far as the borders of Tegea, by the three hundred picked Spartans, who are called the Knights. Never was it known, either before or since, that the Spartans escorted a man out of their city.

125. On the return of Themistocles to Athens, Timodêmus of Aphidnæ,[1] who was one of his enemies, but otherwise a man of no repute, became so maddened with envy that he openly railed against him, and, reproaching him with his journey to Sparta, said – " 'Twas not his own merit that had won him honour from the men of Lacedæmon, but the fame of Athens, his country." Then Themistocles, seeing that Timodêmus repeated this phrase unceasingly, replied –

"Thus stands the case, friend. I had never got this honour from the Spartans, had I been a Belbinite[2] – nor thou, hadst thou been an Athenian!"

---

1 Aphidnæ, or Aphidna, was one of the most ancient of the Attic demi.
2 An island at the mouth of the Saronic Gulf.

126. Artabazus, the son of Pharnaces,[1] a man whom the Persians had always held in much esteem, but who, after the affair of Platæa, rose still higher in their opinion, escorted King Xerxes as far as the strait, with sixty thousand of the chosen troops of Mardonius. When the king was safe in Asia, Artabazus set out upon his return; and on arriving near Pallêné, and finding that Mardonius had gone into winter-quarters in Thessaly and Macedonia, and was in no hurry for him to join the camp, he thought it his bounden duty, as the Potidæans had just revolted, to occupy himself in reducing them to slavery. For as soon as the king had passed beyond their territory, and the Persian fleet had made its hasty flight from Salamis, the Potidæans revolted from the barbarians openly; as likewise did all the other inhabitants of that peninsula.

127. Artabazus, therefore, laid siege to Potidæa; and having a suspicion that the Olynthians were likely to revolt shortly, he besieged their city also. Now Olynthus was at that time held by the Bottiæans, who had been driven from the parts about the Thermaic Gulf by the Macedonians. Artabazus took the city, and, having so done, led out all the inhabitants to a marsh in the neighbourhood, and there slew them. After this he delivered the place into the hands of the people called Chalcideans, having first appointed Critobûlus of Torôné to be governor. Such was the way in which the Chalcideans got Olynthus.

128. When this town had fallen, Artabazus pressed the siege of Potidæa all the more unremittingly; and was pushing his operations with vigour, when Timoxenus, captain of the Scionæans, entered into a plot to betray the town to him. How the matter was managed at first, I cannot pretend to say, for no account has come down to us: but at the last this is what happened. Whenever Timoxenus wished to send a letter to Artabazus, or Artabazus to send one to Timoxenus, the letter was written on a strip of paper, and rolled round the notched end of an arrow-shaft; the feathers were then put on over the paper, and the arrow thus prepared was shot to some place agreed upon. But after a while the plot of Timoxenus to betray Potidæa was discovered in this way. Artabazus, on one occasion, shot off his arrow, intending to send it to the accustomed place, but, missing

1 Artabazus had previously commanded the Parthians and Chorasmians (supra, vii. 66). His prudent conduct at Platæa is noticed (infra, ix. 66).

his mark, hit one of the Potidæans in the shoulder. A crowd gathered about the wounded man, as commonly happens in war; and when the arrow was pulled out, they noticed the paper, and straightway carried it to the captains who were present from the various cities of the peninsula. The captains read the letter, and, finding who the traitor was, nevertheless resolved, out of regard for the city of Sciônê, that as they did not wish the Scionæans to be thenceforth branded with the name of traitors, they would not bring against him any charge of treachery. Such accordingly was the mode in which this plot was discovered.

129. After Artabazus had continued the siege by the space of three months, it happened that there was an unusual ebb of the tide, which lasted a long while. So when the barbarians saw that what had been sea was now no more than a swamp, they determined to push across it into Pallênê. And now the troops had already made good two-fifths of their passage, and three-fifths still remained before they could reach Pallênê, when the tide came in with a very high flood, higher than had ever been seen before, as the inhabitants of those parts declare, though high floods are by no means uncommon. All who were not able to swim perished immediately; the rest were slain by the Potidæans, who bore down upon them in their sailing vessels. The Potidæans say that what caused this swell and flood, and so brought about the disaster of the Persians which ensued therefrom, was the profanation, by the very men now destroyed in the sea, of the temple and image of Poseidon, situated in their suburb. And in this they seem to me to say well. Artabazus afterwards led away the remainder of his army, and joined Mardonius in Thessaly. Thus fared it with the Persians who escorted the king to the strait.

130. As for that part of the fleet of Xerxes which had survived the battle, when it had made good its escape from Salamis to the coast of Asia, and conveyed the king with his army across the strait from the Chersonese to Abydos, it passed the winter at Cymé.[1] On the first approach of spring, there was an early muster of the ships at Samos, where some of them indeed had remained throughout the winter. Most of the men-at-arms who served on board were Persians, or else Medes; and the command of the fleet had been taken by Mardontes, the son of Bagæus,

---

1 Supra, i. 149.

and Artaÿntes, the son of Artachæus; while there was likewise a third commander, Ithamitres, the nephew of Artaÿntes,[1] whom his uncle had advanced to the post. Further west than Samos, however, they did not venture to proceed; for they remembered what a defeat they had suffered, and there was no one to compel them to approach any nearer to Greece. They therefore remained at Samos, and kept watch over Ionia, to hinder it from breaking into revolt. The whole number of their ships, including those furnished by the Ionians, was three hundred. It did not enter into their thoughts that the Greeks would proceed against Ionia; on the contrary, they supposed that the defence of their own country would content them, more especially as they had not pursued the Persian fleet when it fled from Salamis, but had so readily given up the chase. They despaired, however, altogether of gaining any success by sea themselves, though by land they thought that Mardonius was quite sure of victory. So they remained at Samos, and took counsel together, if by any means they might harass the enemy, at the same time that they waited eagerly to hear how matters would proceed with Mardonius.

131. The approach of spring, and the knowledge that Mardonius was in Thessaly, roused the Greeks from inaction. Their land force indeed was not yet come together; but the fleet, consisting of one hundred and ten ships, proceeded to Egina, under the command of Leotychides.[2] This Leotychides, who was both general and admiral, was the son of Menares, the son of Agesilaüs, the son of Hippocratides, the son of Leotychides, the son of Anaxilaüs, the son of Archidamus, the son of Anaxandrides, the son of Theopompus, the son of Nicander, the son of Charillus, the son of Eunomus, the son of Polydectes, the son of Prytanis, the son of Euryphon, the son of Procles, the son of Aristodêmus, the son of Aristomachus, the son of Cleodæus, the son of Hyllus, the son of Heracles. He belonged to the younger branch of the royal house.[3] All his ancestors, except the two next in the above list to himself, had been kings of Sparta. The Athenian vessels were commanded by Xanthippus, the son of Ariphron.[4]

132. When the whole fleet was collected together at Egina, ambassadors from Ionia arrived at the Greek station; they had

---

1 Infra, ix. 102.   2 Supra, vi. 71.   3 Supra, vi. 52.
4 Supra, vi. 131. That Xanthippus had succeeded Themistocles in the command of the fleet, does not imply that the latter had ceased to be a Strategus.

but just come from paying a visit to Sparta, where they had been intreating the Lacedæmonians to undertake the deliverance of their native land. One of these ambassadors was Herodotus, the son of Basileides. Originally they were seven in number; and the whole seven had conspired to slay Strattis the tyrant of Chios; one, however, of those engaged in the plot betrayed the enterprise; and the conspiracy being in this way discovered, Herodotus, and the remaining five, quitted Chios, and went straight to Sparta, whence they had now proceeded to Egina, their object being to beseech the Greeks that they would pass over to Ionia. It was not, however, without difficulty that they were induced to advance even so far as Delos. All beyond that seemed to the Greeks full of danger; the places were quite unknown to them, and to their fancy swarmed with Persian troops; as for Samos, it appeared to them as far off as the Pillars of Heracles.[1] Thus it came to pass, that at the very same time the barbarians were hindered by their fears from venturing any further west than Samos, and the prayers of the Chians failed to induce the Greeks to advance any further east than Delos. Terror guarded the mid region.

133. The Greek fleet was now on its way to Delos; but Mardonius still abode in his winter-quarters in Thessaly. When he was about to leave them, he despatched a man named Mys, a Europian by birth, to go and consult the different oracles, giving him orders to put questions everywhere to all the oracles whereof he found it possible to make trial. What it was that he wanted to know, when he gave Mys these orders, I am not able to say, for no account has reached me of the matter; but for my own part, I suppose that he sent to inquire concerning the business which he had in hand, and not for any other purpose.

134. Mys, it is certain, went to Lebadeia,[2] and, by the payment of a sum of money, induced one of the inhabitants to go down to Trophônius;[3] he likewise visited Abæ of the Phocians, and there consulted the god; while at Thebes, to which place he went first of all, he not only got access to Apollo Ismenius (of

1 Rhetorical exaggeration. The passage from Europe to Asia, through the islands, must have been thoroughly familiar to the Greeks of this period. Even the Spartans were accustomed to make it.

2 One of the most flourishing towns of Northern Greece.

3 The cave of Trophonius was situated at a little distance from the city.

whom inquiry is made by means of victims, according to the custom practised also at Olympia), but likewise prevailed on a man, who was not a Theban but a foreigner, to pass the night in the temple of Amphiaraüs.[1] No Theban can lawfully consult this oracle, for the following reason: Amphiaraüs by an oracle gave the Thebans their choice, to have him for their prophet or for their helper in war; he bade them elect between the two, and forego either one or the other; so they chose rather to have him for their helper. On this account it is unlawful for a Theban to sleep in his temple.

135. One thing which the Thebans declare to have happened at this time is to me very surprising. Mys, the Europian, they say, after he had gone about to all the oracles, came at last to the sacred precinct of Apollo Ptôüs. The place itself bears the name of Ptôüm; it is in the country of the Thebans, and is situate on the mountain side overlooking Lake Copaïs, only a very little way from the town called Acræphia. Here Mys arrived, and entered the temple, followed by three Theban citizens – picked men whom the state had appointed to take down whatever answer the god might give. No sooner was he entered than the prophet delivered him an oracle, but in a foreign tongue; so that his Theban attendants were astonished, hearing a strange language when they expected Greek, and did not know what to do. Mys, however, the Europian, snatched from their hands the tablet which they had brought with them, and wrote down what the prophet uttered. The reply, he told them, was in the Carian dialect. After this, Mys departed and returned to Thessaly.

136. Mardonius, when he had read the answers given by the oracles, sent next an envoy to Athens. This was Alexander, the son of Amyntas, a Macedonian, of whom he made choice for two reasons. Alexander was connected with the Persians by family ties; for Gygæa, who was the daughter of Amyntas, and sister to Alexander himself, was married to Bubares, a Persian, and by him had a son, to wit, Amyntas of Asia; who was named after his mother's father, and enjoyed the revenues of Alabanda, a large city of Phrygia,[2] which had been assigned him by the king. Alexander was likewise (and of this too Mardonius was well

---

1 Prophetic dreams were supposed to visit those who slept in this temple on the fleece of a ram which they had first offered to the god.

2 Alabanda is said above (vii. 195) to have belonged to Caria.

aware), both by services which he had rendered, and by formal compact of friendship, connected with Athens. Mardonius therefore thought that, by sending him, he would be most likely to gain over the Athenians to the Persian side. He had heard that they were a numerous and a warlike people, and he knew that the disasters which had befallen the Persians by sea were mainly their work; he therefore expected that, if he could form alliance with them, he would easily get the mastery of the sea (as indeed he would have done, beyond a doubt), while by land he believed that he was already greatly superior; and so he thought by this alliance to make sure of overcoming the Greeks. Perhaps, too, the oracles leant this way, and counselled him to make Athens his friend: so that it may have been in obedience to them that he sent the embassy.

137. This Alexander was descended in the seventh degree from Perdiccas, who obtained the sovereignty over the Macedonians in the way which I will now relate. Three brothers, descendants of Têmenus, fled from Argos to the Illyrians; their names were Gauanes, Aëropus, and Perdiccas. From Illyria they went across to Upper Macedonia, where they came to a certain town called Lebæa. There they hired themselves out to serve the king in different employs; one tended the horses; another looked after the cows; while Perdiccas, who was the youngest, took charge of the smaller cattle. In those early times poverty was not confined to the people: kings themselves were poor, and so here it was the king's wife who cooked the victuals. Now, whenever she baked the bread, she always observed that the loaf of the labouring boy Perdiccas swelled to double its natural size. So the queen, finding this never fail, spoke of it to her husband. Directly that it came to his ears, the thought struck him that it was a miracle, and boded something of no small moment. He therefore sent for the three labourers, and told them to begone out of his dominions. They answered, "they had a right to their wages; if he would pay them what was due, they were quite willing to go." Now it happened that the sun was shining down the chimney into the room where they were; and the king, hearing them talk of wages, lost his wits, and said, "There are the wages which you deserve; take that – I give it you!" and pointed, as he spoke, to the sunshine. The two elder brothers, Gauanes and Aëropus, stood aghast at the reply, and did nothing; but the boy, who had a knife in his hand, made a mark with it round the sunshine on

the floor of the room, and said, "O king! we accept your payment." Then he received the light of the sun three times into his bosom, and so went away; and his brothers went with him.

138. When they were gone, one of those who sat by told the king what the youngest of the three had done, and hinted that he must have had some meaning in accepting the wages given. Then the king, when he heard what had happened, was angry, and sent horsemen after the youths to slay them. Now there is a river in Macedonia to which the descendants of these Argives offer sacrifice as their saviour. This stream swelled so much, as soon as the sons of Têmenus were safe across, that the horsemen found it impossible to follow. So the brothers escaped into another part of Macedonia, and took up their abode near the place called "the Gardens of Midas, son of Gordias." In these gardens there are roses which grow of themselves, so sweet that no others can come near them, and with blossoms that have as many as sixty petals apiece. It was here, according to the Macedonians, that Silenus was made a prisoner.[1] Above the gardens stands a mountain called Bermius, which is so cold that none can reach the top. Here the brothers made their abode;[2] and from this place by degrees they conquered all Macedonia.

139. From the Perdiccas of whom we have here spoken, Alexander was descended in the following way:– Alexander was the son of Amyntas, Amyntas of Alcetas; the father of Alcetas was Aëropus; of Aëropus, Philip; of Philip, Argæus; of Argæus, Perdiccas, the first sovereign. Such was the descent of Alexander.

140. (§ 1.) When Alexander reached Athens as the ambassador of Mardonius, he spoke as follows:–

"O men of Athens, these be the words of Mardonius. 'The king has sent a message to me, saying, "All the trespasses which the Athenians have committed against me I freely forgive. Now then, Mardonius, thus shalt thou act towards them. Restore to them their territory; and let them choose for themselves whatever land they like besides, and let them dwell therein as a free people. Build up likewise all their temples which I burned, if on these terms they will consent to enter into a league with me."

1 The tale went that Midas, one day when he was hunting, caught Silenus, and forced him to answer a number of questions.
2 Mount Bermius is undoubtedly the range which shuts in the Macedonian maritime plain upon the west.

Such are the orders which I have received, and which I must needs obey, unless there be a hindrance on your part. And now I say unto you, – why are ye so mad as to levy war against the king, whom ye cannot possibly overcome, or even resist for ever? Ye have seen the multitude and the bravery of the host of Xerxes; ye know also how large a power remains with me in your land; suppose then ye should get the better of us, and defeat this army – a thing whereof ye will not, if ye be wise, entertain the least hope – what follows even then but a contest with a still greater force? Do not, because you would fain match yourselves with the king, consent to lose your country and live in constant danger of your lives. Rather agree to make peace; which ye can now do without any tarnish to your honour, since the king invites you to it. Continue free, and make an alliance with us, without fraud or deceit.'

(§ 2.) "These are the words, O Athenians! which Mardonius had bid me speak to you. For my own part, I will say nothing of the good will I bear your nation, since ye have not now for the first time to become acquainted with it.[1] But I will add my intreaties also, and beseech you to give ear to Mardonius; for I see clearly that it is impossible for you to go on for ever contending against Xerxes. If that had appeared to me possible, I would not now have come hither the bearer of such a message. But the king's power surpasses that of man, and his arm reaches far. If then ye do not hasten to conclude a peace, when such fair terms are offered you, I tremble to think of what you will have to endure – you, who of all the allies lie most directly in the path of danger, whose land will always be the chief battleground of the contending powers, and who will therefore constantly have to suffer alone. Hearken then, I pray you, to Mardonius! Surely it is no small matter that the Great King chooses you out from all the rest of the Greeks, to offer you forgiveness of the wrongs you have done him, and to propose himself as your friend and ally!"

141. Such were the words of Alexander. Now the Lacedæmonians, when tidings reached them that Alexander was gone to Athens to bring about a league between the Athenians and the barbarians, and when at the same time they called to mind the prophecies which declared that the Dorian race should one

---

1 Supra, vii. 173.

day be driven from the Peloponnese by the Medes and the Athenians, were exceedingly afraid lest the Athenians might consent to the alliance with Persia. They therefore lost no time in sending envoys to Athens; and it so happened that these envoys were given their audience at the same time with Alexander: for the Athenians had waited and made delays, because they felt sure that the Lacedæmonians would hear that an ambassador was come to them from the Persians, and as soon as they heard it would with all speed send an embassy. They contrived matters therefore of set purpose, so that the Lacedæmonians might hear them deliver their sentiments on the occasion.

142. As soon as Alexander had finished speaking, the ambassadors from Sparta took the word and said, –

"We are sent here by the Lacedæmonians to entreat of you that ye will not do a new thing in Greece, nor agree to the terms which are offered you by the barbarian. Such conduct on the part of any of the Greeks were alike unjust and dishonourable; but in you 'twould be worse than in others, for divers reasons. 'Twas by you that this war was kindled at the first among us – our wishes were in no way considered; the contest began by your seeking to extend your empire – now the fate of Greece is involved in it. Besides it were surely an intolerable thing that the Athenians, who have always hitherto been known as a nation to which many men owed their freedom, should now become the means of bringing all other Greeks into slavery. We feel, however, for the heavy calamities which press on you – the loss of your harvest these two years, and the ruin in which your homes have lain for so long a time. We offer you, therefore, on the part of the Lacedæmonians and the allies, sustenance for your women and for the unwarlike portion of your households, so long as the war endures. Be ye not seduced by Alexander the Macedonian, who softens down the rough words of Mardonius. He does as is natural for him to do – a tyrant himself, he helps forward a tyrant's cause.[1] But ye, Athenians, should do differently, at least if ye be truly wise; for ye should know that with barbarians there is neither faith nor truth."

143. Thus spake the envoys. After which the Athenians returned this answer to Alexander:–

---

1 Alexander was not a tyrant ($\tau \acute{v} \rho a \nu \nu o \varsigma$) in any proper acceptation of the word. He was a king ($\beta a \sigma \iota \lambda \epsilon \acute{v} \varsigma$) as truly as Xerxes or Leonidas.

"We know, as well as thou dost, that the power of the Mede is many times greater than our own: we did not need to have *that* cast in our teeth. Nevertheless we cling so to freedom that we shall offer what resistance we may. Seek not to persuade us into making terms with the barbarian – say what thou wilt, thou wilt never gain our assent. Return rather at once, and tell Mardonius that our answer to him is this:– 'So long as the sun keeps his present course, we will never join alliance with Xerxes. Nay, we shall oppose him unceasingly, trusting in the aid of those gods and heroes whom he has lightly esteemed, whose houses and whose images he has burnt with fire.' And come not thou again to us with words like these; nor, thinking to do us a service, persuade us to unholy actions. Thou art the guest and friend of our nation – we would not that thou shouldst receive hurt at our hands."

144. Such was the answer which the Athenians gave to Alexander. To the Spartan envoys they said, –

" 'Twas natural no doubt that the Lacedæmonians should be afraid we might make terms with the barbarian; but nevertheless 'twas a base fear in men who knew so well of what temper and spirit we are. Not all the gold that the whole earth contains – not the fairest and most fertile of all lands – would bribe us to take part with the Medes and help them to enslave our countrymen. Even could we anyhow have brought ourselves to such a thing, there are many very powerful motives which would now make it impossible. The first and chief of these is the burning and destruction of our temples and the images of our gods, which forces us to make no terms with their destroyer, but rather to pursue him with our resentment to the uttermost. Again, there is our common brotherhood with the Greeks: our common language, the altars and the sacrifices of which we all partake, the common character which we bear – did the Athenians betray all these, of a truth it would not be well. Know then now, if ye have not known it before, that while one Athenian remains alive, we will never join alliance with Xerxes. We thank you, however, for your forethought on our behalf, and for your wish to give our families sustenance, now that ruin has fallen on us – the kindness is complete on your part; but for ourselves, we will endure as we may, and not be burdensome to you. Such then is our resolve. Be it your care with all speed to lead out your troops; for if we surmise aright, the barbarian will not wait long ere he invade our territory, but will set out so soon as he learns our answer to be, that we will do none of those things which he requires of us. Now then is the time for us, before he enters Attica, to go forth ourselves into Bœotia, and give him battle."

When the Athenians had thus spoken, the ambassadors from Sparta departed, and returned back to their own country.

ADDED NOTE BY THE EDITOR

The great historical drama is now drawing to its close. The opposing forces of East and West, of Barbarism and Hellenism, have met at Salamis, in one of the most decisive sea-battles ever fought; Platæa is yet to decide their fortunes by land; at Mykale the Greeks are no longer in the position of those who act merely on the defensive; they are to begin a system of retaliation on the foe. This system is to reach its climax 150 years later in the great victories of Alexander.

THE NINTH BOOK,
ENTITLED CALLIOPÉ

1. MARDONIUS, when Alexander upon his return made known to him the answer of the Athenians, forthwith broke up from Thessaly,[1] and led his army with all speed against Athens; forcing the several nations through whose land he passed to furnish him with additional troops. The chief men of Thessaly, far from repenting of the part which they had taken in the war hitherto, urged on the Persians to the attack more earnestly than ever. Thorax of Larissa in particular, who had helped to escort Xerxes on his flight to Asia, now openly encouraged Mardonius in his march upon Greece.

2. When the army reached Bœotia, the Thebans sought to induce Mardonius to make a halt: "He would not," they told him, "find anywhere a more convenient place in which to pitch his camp; and their advice to him was, that he should go no further, but fix himself there, and thence take measures to subdue all Greece without striking a blow. If the Greeks, who had held together hitherto, still continued united among themselves, it would be difficult for the whole world to overcome them by force of arms. But if thou wilt do as we advise," they went on to say, "thou mayest easily obtain the direction of all their counsels. Send presents to the men of most weight in the several states, and by so doing thou wilt sow division among them. After that, it will be a light task, with the help of such as side with thee, to bring under all thy adversaries."

3. Such was the advice of the Thebans: but Mardonius did not follow it. A strong desire of taking Athens a second time possessed him, in part arising from his inborn stubbornness, in part from a wish to inform the king at Sardis, by fire-signals along the islands, that he was master of the place. However, he

---

1 Mardonius wintered his army in Thessaly *and Macedonia* (supra, viii. 126). The difficulty of procuring supplies, after the exhaustion caused by the presence of the immense host of Xerxes, made it necessary to fall back upon those rich and fertile countries, the chief granaries of Greece. The same cause compelled the wide dispersion of his troops, indicated by their occupation of both regions.

did not on his arrival in Attica find the Athenians in their country – they had again withdrawn, some to their ships, but the greater part to Salamis – and he only gained possession of a deserted town. It was ten months after the taking of the city by the king that Mardonius came against it for the second time.

4. Mardonius, being now in Athens, sent an envoy to Salamis, one Murychides, a Hellespontine Greek, to offer the Athenians once more the same terms which had been conveyed to them by Alexander. The reason for his sending a second time, though he knew beforehand their unfriendly feelings towards him, was, – that he hoped, when they saw the whole land of Attica conquered and in his power, their stubbornness would begin to give way. On this account, therefore, he dispatched Murychides to Salamis.

5. Now, when Murychides came before the council, and delivered his message, one of the councillors, named Lycidas, gave it as his opinion – "that the best course would be, to admit the proposals brought by Murychides, and lay them before the assembly of the people." This he stated to be his opinion, perhaps because he had been bribed by Mardonius, or it may be because that course really appeared to him the most expedient. However, the Athenians – both those in the council, and those who stood without, when they heard of the advice – were full of wrath, and forthwith surrounded Lycidas, and stoned him to death. As for Murychides, the Hellespontine Greek, him they sent away unharmed. Now there was a stir in the island about Lycidas, and the Athenian women learnt what had happened. Then each exhorted her fellow, and one brought another to take part in the deed; and they all flocked of their own accord to the house of Lycidas, and stoned to death his wife and his children.

6. The circumstances under which the Athenians had sought refuge in Salamis were the following. So long as any hope remained that a Peloponnesian army would come to give them aid, they abode still in Attica; but when it appeared that the allies were slack and slow to move, while the invader was reported to be pressing forward and to have already entered Bœotia, then they proceeded to remove their goods and chattels from the mainland, and themselves again crossed the strait to Salamis. At the same time they sent ambassadors to Lacedæmon, who were to reproach the Lacedæmonians for having allowed the barbarian to advance into Attica, instead of joining them and going out to

meet him in Bœotia. They were likewise to remind the Lacedæmonians of the offers by which the Persian had sought to win
Athens over to his side,[1] and to warn them, that if no aid came
from Sparta, the Athenians must consult for their own safety.

7. The truth was, the Lacedæmonians were keeping holiday
at that time; for it was the feast of the Hyacinthia,[2] and they
thought nothing of so much moment as to perform the service
of the god. They were also engaged in building their wall across
the Isthmus, which was now so far advanced that the battlements had begun to be placed upon it.

When the envoys of the Athenians, accompanied by ambassadors from Megara and Platæa, reached Lacedæmon, they came
before the Ephors, and spoke as follows:—

"The Athenians have sent us to you to say, — the king of the
Medes offers to give us back our country, and wishes to conclude
an alliance with us on fair and equal terms, without fraud or
deceit. He is willing likewise to bestow on us another country
besides our own, and bids us choose any land that we like. But
we, because we reverenced Hellenic Zeus, and thought it a
shameful act to betray Greece, instead of consenting to these
terms, refused them; notwithstanding that we have been
wronged and deserted by the other Greeks, and are fully aware
that it is far more for our advantage to make peace with the
Persian than to prolong the war with him. Still we shall not, of
our own free will, consent to any terms of peace. Thus do we,
in all our dealings with the Greeks, avoid what is base and
counterfeit: while contrariwise, ye, who were but now so full of
fear lest we should make terms with the enemy,[3] having learnt
of what temper we are, and assured yourselves that we shall not
prove traitors to our country — having brought moreover your
wall across the Isthmus to an advanced state — cease altogether
to have any care for us. Ye covenanted with us to go out and
meet the Persian in Bœotia; but when the time came, ye were

---

1 Supra, viii. 140, § 1.

2 Held annually at midsummer. Hyacinthus, the beautiful youth slain accidentally by Apollo, was the chief object of the worship. He took his name
from the flower, which was an emblem of death; and the original feast seems
to have been altogether a mournful ceremony, — a lamentation over the destruction of the flowers of spring by the summer heat, passing on to a more
general lament over death itself.

3 Supra, viii. 142.

false to your word, and looked on while the barbarian host advanced into Attica. At this time, therefore, the Athenians are angered with you; and justly, – for ye have not done what was right. They bid you, however, make haste to send forth your army, that we may even yet meet Mardonius in Attica. Now that Bœotia is lost to us, the best place for the fight within our country, will be the plain of Thria."

8. The Ephors, when they had heard this speech, delayed their answer till the morrow; and when the morrow came, till the day following. And thus they acted for ten days, continually putting off the ambassadors from one day to the next. Meanwhile the Peloponnesians generally were labouring with great zeal at the wall, and the work nearly approached completion. I can give no other reason for the conduct of the Lacedæmonians in showing themselves so anxious, at the time when Alexander came, that the Athenians should not join the Medes, and now being quite careless about it, except that at the former time the wall across the Isthmus was not complete, and they worked at it in great fear of the Persians, whereas now the bulwark had been raised, and so they imagined that they had no further need of the Athenians.

9. At last the ambassadors got an answer, and the troops marched forth from Sparta, under the following circumstances. The last audience had been fixed for the ambassadors, when, the very day before it was to be given, a certain Tegean, named Chileüs, a man who had more influence at Sparta than any other foreigner, learning from the Ephors exactly what the Athenians had said, addressed these words to them – "The case stands thus, O ye Ephors! If the Athenians are not our friends, but league themselves with the barbarians, however strong our wall across the Isthmus may be, there will be doors enough, and wide enough open too, by which the Persian may gain entrance to the Peloponnese.[1] Grant their request then, before they make any fresh resolve, which may bring Greece to ruin."

10. Such was the counsel which Chileüs gave: and the Ephors, taking the advice into consideration, determined forthwith, without speaking a word to the ambassadors from the three cities, to despatch to the Isthmus a body of five thousand

---

1 That is, the naval power of Athens would lay the whole coast of the Peloponnese open to the Persians.

Spartans; and accordingly they sent them forth the same night, appointing to each Spartan a retinue of seven Helots, and giving the command of the expedition to Pausanias the son of Cleombrotus. The chief power belonged of right at this time to Pleistarchus, the son of Leonidas; but as he was still a child, Pausanias, his cousin, was regent in his room. For the father of Pausanias, Cleombrotus, the son of Anaxandridas, no longer lived; he had died a short time after bringing back from the Isthmus the troops who had been employed in building the wall. A prodigy had caused him to bring his army home; for while he was offering sacrifice to know if he should march out against the Persian, the sun was suddenly darkened in mid sky. Pausanias took with him, as joint-leader of the army, Euryanax, the son of Dorieus, a member of his own family.

11. The army accordingly had marched out from Sparta with Pausanias: while the ambassadors, when day came, appeared before the Ephors, knowing nothing of the march of the troops, and purposing themselves to leave Sparta forthwith, and return each man to his own country. They therefore addressed the Ephors in these words:– "Lacedæmonians, as you do not stir from home, but keep the Hyacinthian festival, and amuse yourselves, deserting the cause of your confederates, the Athenians, whom your behaviour wrongs, and who have no other allies, will make such terms with the Persians as they shall find possible. Now when terms are once made, it is plain that, having become the king's allies, we shall march with the barbarians whithersoever they choose to lead. Then at length you will perceive what the consequences will be to yourselves." When the envoys had spoken, the Ephors declared to them with an oath:– "Our troops must be at Orestêum[1] by this time, on their march against the strangers." (The Spartans say "strangers" for "barbarians.") At this the ambassadors, quite ignorant of what had happened, questioned them concerning their meaning; and when, by much questioning, they had discovered the truth, they were greatly astonished thereat, and forthwith set off, at their best speed, to overtake the Spartan army. At the same time a body of five thousand Lacedæmonian Periœci, all picked men and fully armed, set forth from Sparta, in the company of the ambassadors.

---

1 Orestêum, or Orestasium, was a small town in the district of Arcadia called Mænalia.

12. So these troops marched in haste towards the Isthmus. Meanwhile the Argives, who had promised Mardonius that they would stop the Spartans from crossing their borders, as soon as they learnt that Pausanias with his army had started from Sparta, took the swiftest courier they could find, and sent him off to Attica. The message which he delivered, on his arrival at Athens, was the following: "Mardonius," he said, "the Argives have sent me to tell thee that the Lacedæmonian youth are gone forth from their city, and that the Argives are too weak to hinder them. Take good heed therefore to thyself at this time." After thus speaking, without a word more, he returned home.

13. When Mardonius learnt that the Spartans were on their march, he no longer cared to remain in Attica. Hitherto he had kept quiet, wishing to see what the Athenians would do, and had neither ravaged their territory, nor done it any the least harm; for till now he had cherished the hope that the Athenians would come to terms with him. As, however, he found that his persuasions were of no avail, and as their whole policy was now clear to him, he determined to withdraw from Attica before Pausanias with his army reached the Isthmus; first, however, he resolved to burn Athens, and to cast down and level with the ground whatever remained standing of the walls, temples, and other buildings. His reason for retreating was, that Attica was not a country where horse could act with advantage; and further, that if he suffered defeat in a battle, no way of escape was open to him, except through defiles,[1] where a handful of troops might stop all his army. So he determined to withdraw to Thebes, and give the Greeks battle in the neighbourhood of a friendly city, and on ground well suited for cavalry.

14. After he had quitted Attica and was already upon his march, news reached him that a body of a thousand Lacedæmonians, distinct from the army of Pausanias, and sent on in advance, had arrived in the Megarid. When he heard it, wishing, if possible, to destroy this detachment first, Mardonius considered with himself how he might compass their ruin. With a sudden change of march he made for Megara, while the horse, pushing on in advance, entered and ravaged the Megarid. (Here

---

1 Three roads only connected Attica with Bœotia. The one, which Mardonius now followed, led from Athens into the Tanagræa by the fortress of Deceleia. This is comparatively an easy route.

was the furthest point in Europe towards the setting sun to which this Persian army ever penetrated.)

15. After this, Mardonius received another message, whereby he learnt that the forces of the Greeks were collected together at the Isthmus; which tidings caused him to draw back, and leave Attica by the way of Deceleia. The Bœotarchs[1] had sent for some of the neighbours of the Asopians;[2] and these persons served as guides to the army, and led them first to Sphendalé, and from thence to Tanagra,[3] where Mardonius rested a night; after which, upon the morrow, he bent his course to Scôlus, which brought him into the territory of the Thebans. And now, although the Thebans had espoused the cause of the Medes, yet Mardonius cut down all the trees in these parts; not however from any enmity towards the Thebans, but on account of his own urgent needs; for he wanted a rampart to protect his army from attack, and he likewise desired to have a place of refuge, whither his troops might flee, in case the battle should go contrary to his wishes. His army at this time lay on the Asôpus, and stretched from Erythræ, along by Hysiæ, to the territory of the Platæans. The wall, however, was not made to extend so far, but formed a square of about ten furlongs each way.

While the barbarians were employed in this work, a certain citizen of Thebes, Attagînus by name, the son of Phrynon, having made great preparations, gave a banquet, and invited Mardonius thereto, together with fifty of the noblest Persians. Now the banquet was held at Thebes; and all the guests who were invited came to it.

16. What follows was recounted to me by Thersander, a native of Orchomenus,[4] a man of the first rank in that city. Thersander told me that he was himself among those invited to the feast, and that besides the Persians fifty Thebans were asked;[5] and the two nations were not arranged separately, but a Persian and a Theban were set side by side upon each couch. After the feast was ended, and the drinking had begun, the Persian who shared Thersander's couch addressed him in the Greek tongue,

1 The Bœotarchs, or chief magistrates of the Bœotians.
2 The Asopians are the inhabitants of the rich valley of the Asôpus, which lay immediately beyond the Attic frontier.
3 Tanagra was situated on the left or northern bank of the Asôpus.
4 Vide supra, viii. 34.
5 By Thebans we must understand here Bœotians.

and inquired of him from what city he came. He answered, that he was of Orchomenus; whereupon the other said –

"Since thou hast eaten with me at one table, and poured libation from one cup, I would fain leave with thee a memorial of the belief I hold – the rather that thou mayest have timely warning thyself, and so be able to provide for thy own safety. Seest thou these Persians here feasting, and the army which we left encamped yonder by the river-side? Yet a little while, and of all this number thou wilt behold but a few surviving!"

As he spake, the Persian let fall a flood of tears: whereon Thersander, who was astonished at his words, replied – "Surely thou shouldest say all this to Mardonius, and the Persians who are next him in honour" – but the other rejoined – "Dear friend, it is not possible for man to avert that which God has decreed shall happen. No one believes warnings, however true. Many of us Persians know our danger, but we are constrained by necessity to do as our leader bids us. Verily 'tis the sorest of all human ills, to abound in knowledge and yet have no power over action." All this I heard myself from Thersander the Orchomenian; who told me further, that he mentioned what had happened to divers persons, before the battle was fought at Platæa.

17. When Mardonius formerly held his camp in Bœotia, all the Greeks of those parts who were friendly to the Medes sent troops to join his army, and these troops accompanied him in his attack upon Athens. The Phocians alone abstained, and took no part in the invasion; for, though they had espoused the Median cause warmly, it was very much against their will, and only because they were compelled so to do.[1] However, a few days after the arrival of the Persian army at Thebes, a thousand of their heavy-armed soldiers came up, under the command of Harmocŷdes, one of their most distinguished citizens. No sooner had these troops reached Thebes, than some horsemen came to them from Mardonius, with orders that they should take up a position upon the plain, away from the rest of the army. The Phocians did so, and forthwith the entire Persian cavalry drew nigh to them: whereupon there went a rumour through the whole of the Greek force encamped with the Medes, that Mardonius was about to destroy the Phocians with missiles. The same conviction ran through the Phocian troops themselves; and

1 Supra, viii. 30–33.

Harmocŷdes, their leader, addressed them thus with words of encouragement – "Phocians," said he, " 'tis plain that these men have resolved beforehand to take our lives, because of the accusations of the Thessalians, as I imagine. Now, then, is the time for you all to show yourselves brave men. 'Tis better to die fighting and defending our lives, than tamely to allow them to slay us in this shameful fashion. Let them learn that they are barbarians, and that the men whose death they have plotted are Greeks!"

18. Thus spake Harmocŷdes; and the Persian horse, having encircled the Phocians, charged towards them, as if about to deal out death, with bows bent, and arrows ready to be let fly; nay, here and there some did even discharge their weapons. But the Phocians stood firm, keeping close one to another, and serrying their ranks as much as possible: whereupon the horse suddenly wheeled round and rode off. I cannot say with certainty whether they came, at the prayer of the Thessalians, to destroy the Phocians, but seeing them prepared to stand on their defence, and fearing to suffer damage at their hands, on that account beat a retreat, having orders from Mardonius so to act; or whether his sole intent was to try the temper of the Phocians and see whether they had any courage or no. However this may have been, when the horsemen retired, Mardonius sent a herald to the Phocians, saying – "Fear not, Phocians – ye have shown yourselves valiant men – much unlike the report I had heard of you. Now therefore be forward in the coming war. Ye will not readily outdo either the king or myself in services." Thus ended the affair of the Phocians.

19. The Lacedæmonians, when they reached the Isthmus, pitched their camp there; and the other Peloponnesians who had embraced the good side, hearing or else seeing that they were upon the march, thought it not right to remain behind when the Spartans were going forth to the war. So the Peloponnesians went out in one body from the Isthmus, the victims being favourable for setting forth; and marched as far as Eleusis, where again they offered sacrifices, and, finding the omens still encouraging, advanced further. At Eleusis they were joined by the Athenians, who had come across from Salamis, and now accompanied the main army. On reaching Erythræ[1] in Bœotia, they

---

1 Supra, ch. 15.

learnt that the barbarians were encamped upon the Asôpus; wherefore they themselves, after considering how they should act, disposed their forces opposite to the enemy upon the slopes of Mount Cithæron.

20. Mardonius, when he saw that the Greeks would not come down into the plain, sent all his cavalry, under Masistius (or Macistius, as the Greeks call him), to attack them where they were. Now Masistius was a man of much repute among the Persians, and rode a Nisæan charger with a golden bit, and otherwise magnificently caparisoned. So the horse advanced against the Greeks, and made attacks upon them in divisions, doing them great damage at each charge, and insulting them by calling them women.

21. It chanced that the Megarians were drawn up in the position most open to attack, and where the ground offered the best approach to the cavalry. Finding themselves therefore hard pressed by the assaults upon their ranks, they sent a herald to the Greek leaders, who came and said to them, "This is the message of the Megarians — We cannot, brothers-in-arms, continue to resist the Persian horse in that post which we have occupied from the first, if we are left without succours. Hitherto, although hard pressed, we have held out against them firmly and courageously. Now, however, if you do not send others to take our place, we warn you that we shall quit our post." Such were the words of the herald. Pausanias, when he heard them, inquired among his troops if there were any who would volunteer to take the post, and so relieve the Megarians. Of the rest none were willing to go, whereupon the Athenians offered themselves; and a body of picked men, three hundred in number, commanded by Olympiodôrus, the son of Lampo, undertook the service.

22. Selecting, to accompany them, the whole body of archers, these men relieved the Megarians, and occupied a post which all the other Greeks collected at Erythræ had shrunk from holding. After the struggle had continued for a while, it came to an end on this wise. As the barbarians continued charging in divisions, the horse of Masistius, which was in front of the others, received an arrow in his flank, the pain of which caused him to rear and throw his rider. Immediately the Athenians rushed upon Masistius as he lay, caught his horse, and when he himself made resistance, slew him. At first, however, they were not able to take

his life; for his armour hindered them. He had on a breastplate formed of golden scales,[1] with a scarlet tunic covering it. Thus the blows, all falling upon his breastplate, took no effect, till one of the soldiers, perceiving the reason, drove his weapon into his eye and so slew him. All this took place without any of the other horsemen seeing it: they had neither observed their leader fall from his horse, nor beheld him slain; for he fell as they wheeled round and prepared for another charge, so that they were quite ignorant of what had happened. When, however, they halted, and found that there was no one to marshal their line, Masistius was missed; and instantly his soldiers, understanding what must have befallen him, with loud cheers charged the enemy in one mass, hoping to recover the dead body.

23. So when the Athenians saw that, instead of coming up in squadrons, the whole mass of the horse was about to charge them at once, they called out to the other troops to make haste to their aid. While the rest of the infantry, however, was moving to their assistance, the contest waxed fierce about the dead body of Masistius. The three hundred, so long as they fought by themselves, had greatly the worse of the encounter, and were forced to retire and yield up the body to the enemy; but when the other troops approached, the Persian horse could no longer hold their ground, but fled without carrying off the body, having incurred in the attempt a further loss of several of their number. They therefore retired about two furlongs, and consulted with each other what was best to be done. Being without a leader, it seemed to them the fittest course to return to Mardonius.

24. When the horse reached the camp, Mardonius and all the Persian army made great lamentation for Masistius. They shaved off all the hair from their own heads, and cut the manes from their war-horses and their sumpter-beasts, while they vented their grief in such loud cries that all Bœotia resounded with the clamour,[2] because they had lost the man who, next to Mardonius, was held in the greatest esteem, both by the king and by the Persians generally. So the barbarians, after their own fashion, paid honours to the dead Masistius.

25. The Greeks, on the other hand, were greatly emboldened by what had happened, seeing that they had not only stood their

1 Vide supra, vii. 6, and viii. 113.
2 Such free indulgence of grief is characteristic of the Oriental temper.

ground against the attacks of the horse, but had even compelled them to beat a retreat. They therefore placed the dead body of Masistius upon a cart, and paraded it along the ranks of the army. Now the body was a sight which well deserved to be gazed upon, being remarkable both for stature and for beauty; and it was to stop the soldiers from leaving their ranks to look at it, that they resolved to carry it round. After this the Greeks determined to quit the high ground and go nearer Platæa, as the land there seemed far more suitable for an encampment than the country about Erythræ, particularly because it was better supplied with water. To this place therefore, and more especially to a spring-head which was called Gargaphia, they considered that it would be best for them to remove, after which they might once more encamp in their order. So they took their arms, and proceeded along the slopes of Cithæron, past Hysiæ, to the territory of the Platæans; and here they drew themselves up, nation by nation, close by the fountain Gargaphia, and the sacred precinct of the Hero Androcrates, partly along some hillocks of no great height, and partly upon the level of the plain.

26. Here, in the marshalling of the nations, a fierce battle of words arose between the Athenians and the Tegeans, both of whom claimed to have one of the wings assigned to them. On each side were brought forward the deeds which they had done, whether in earlier or in later times; and first the Tegeans urged their claim as follows:–

"This post has been always considered our right, and not the right of any of the other allies, in all the expeditions which have been entered into conjointly by the Peloponnesians, both anciently and in later times. Ever since the Heraclidæ made their attempt, after the death of Eurystheus, to return by force of arms into the Peloponnese, this custom has been observed. It was then that the right became ours, and this was the way in which we gained it:- When, in company with the Achæans and Ionians who then dwelt in the Peloponnese,[1] we marched out to the Isthmus, and pitched our camp over against the invaders, then,

1 Before the Dorian immigration the entire Peloponnese was occupied, with trifling exceptions, by three races:– the Arcadians, the Achæans, and the Ionians. The Ionians occupied the country along the Corinthian Gulf, which in later times became Achæa (supra, i. 145); the Arcadians held the strong central position in which they always maintained themselves; the Achæans were masters of the remainder.

as the tale goes, that Hyllus made proclamation, saying – 'It needs not to imperil two armies in a general battle; rather let one be chosen from the Peloponnesian ranks, whomseover they deem the bravest, and let him engage with me in single combat, on such terms as shall be agreed upon.' The saying pleased the Peloponnesians, and oaths were sworn to the effect following:– 'If Hyllus conquer the Peloponnesian champion, the Heraclidæ shall return to their inheritance; if, on the other hand, he be conquered, the Heraclidæ shall withdraw, lead back their army, and engage for the next hundred years to make no further endeavours to force their return.' Hereupon Echemus, the son of Aëropus and grandson of Phêgeus, who was our leader and king, offered himself, and was preferred before all his brothers-in-arms as champion, engaged in single combat with Hyllus, and slew him upon the spot. For this exploit we were rewarded by the Peloponnesians of that day with many goodly privileges, which we have ever since enjoyed; and, among the rest, we obtained the right of holding the leading post in one wing, whenever a joint expedition goes forth beyond our borders. With you then, O Lacedæmonians, we do not claim to compete; choose you which wing ye please; we yield and grant you the preference: but we maintain that the command of the other wing belongs of right to us, now no less than formerly. Moreover, set aside this exploit which we have related, and still our title to the chief post is better than that of the Athenians: witness the many glorious fights in which we have been engaged against yourselves, O Spartans! as well as those which we have maintained with others. We have therefore more right to this place than they; for they have performed no exploits to be compared to ours, whether we look to earlier or to later times."

27. Thus spake the Tegeans; and the Athenians made reply as follows:– "We are not ignorant that our forces were gathered here, not for the purpose of speech-making, but for battle against the barbarian. Yet as the Tegeans have been pleased to bring into debate the exploits performed by our two nations, alike in earlier and in later times, we have no choice but to set before you the grounds on which we claim it as our heritage, deserved by our unchanging bravery, to be preferred above Arcadians. In the first place, then, those very Heraclidæ, whose leader they boast to have slain at the Isthmus, and whom the other Greeks would not receive when they asked a refuge from

the bondage wherewith they were threatened by the people of Mycênæ, were given a shelter by us; and we brought down the insolence of Eurystheus, and helped to gain the victory over those who were at that time lords of the Peloponnese. Again, when the Argives led their troops with Polynices against Thebes, and were slain and refused burial, it is our boast that we went out against the Cadmeians, recovered the bodies, and buried them at Eleusis in our own territory. Another noble deed of ours was that against the Amazons, when they came from their seats upon the Thermôdon, and poured their hosts into Attica; and in the Trojan war too we were not a whit behind any of the Greeks. But what boots it to speak of these ancient matters? A nation which was brave in those days might have grown cowardly since, and a nation of cowards then might now be valiant. Enough therefore of our ancient achievements. Had we performed no other exploit than that at Marathon – though in truth we have performed exploits as many and as noble as any of the Greeks – yet had we performed no other, we should deserve this privilege, and many a one beside. There we stood alone, and singly fought with the Persians; nay, and venturing on so dangerous a cast, we overcame the enemy, and conquered on that day forty and six nations! Does not this one achievement suffice to make good our title to the post we claim? Nevertheless, Lacedæmonians, as to strive concerning place at such a time as this is not right, we are ready to do as ye command, and to take our station at whatever part of the line, and face whatever nation ye think most expedient. Wheresoever ye place us, 'twill be our endeavour to behave as brave men. Only declare your will, and we shall at once obey you."[1]

28. Such was the reply of the Athenians; and forthwith all the Lacedæmonian troops cried out with one voice, that the Athenians were worthier to have the left wing than the Arcadians. In this way were the Tegeans overcome; and the post was assigned to the Athenians.

When this matter had been arranged, the Greek army, which was in part composed of those who came at the first, in part of such as had flocked in from day to day, drew up in the following order:– Ten thousand Lacedæmonian troops held the right wing, five thousand of whom were Spartans; and these five thousand

1 [See n. on p. 727, infra. E. H. B]

were attended by a body of thirty-five thousand Helots, who were only lightly armed – seven Helots to each Spartan.[1] The place next to themselves the Spartans gave to the Tegeans, on account of their courage and of the esteem in which they held them. They were all fully armed, and numbered fifteen hundred men. Next in order came the Corinthians, five thousand strong; and with them Pausanias had placed, at their request,[2] the band of three hundred which had come from Potidæa in Pallênê. The Arcadians of Orchomenus, in number six hundred, came next; then the Sicyonians, three thousand; then the Epidaurians, eight hundred; then the Trœzenians, one thousand; then the Lepreats, two hundred; the Mycenæans and Tirynthians,[3] four hundred; the Phliasians, one thousand; the Hermionians, three hundred; the Eretrians and Styreans, six hundred; the Chalcideans,[4] four hundred; and the Ambraciots, five hundred. After these came the Leucadians and Anactorians,[5] who numbered eight hundred; the Paleans of Cephallênia, two hundred; the Eginetans, five hundred; the Megarians, three thousand; and the Platæans, six hundred. Last of all, but first at their extremity of the line, were the Athenians, who, to the number of eight thousand, occupied the left wing, under the command of Aristides, the son of Lysimachus.

29. All these, except the Helots – seven of whom, as I said, attended each Spartan – were heavy-armed troops; and they amounted to thirty-eight thousand seven hundred men. This was the number of Hoplites, or heavy-armed soldiers, which was brought together against the barbarian. The light-armed troops consisted of the thirty-five thousand ranged with the Spartans, seven in attendance upon each, who were all well equipped for war; and of thirty-four thousand five hundred others, belonging to the Lacedæmonians and the rest of the Greeks, at the rate (nearly) of one light to one heavy armed. Thus the entire number of the light-armed was sixty-nine thousand five hundred.

30. The Greek army, therefore, which mustered at Platæa, counting light-armed as well as heavy-armed, was but eighteen

1 Vide supra, ch. 10.
2 The Corinthians naturally desired to have *their colonists* under their immediate protection.
3 For the site of Tiryns, vide supra, vi. 76.
4 Not the Chalcideans of Thrace, but those of Eubœa.
5 Anactorium was a Corinthian, or perhaps a joint Corinthian and Corcyræan colony situated at the mouth of the Ambracian gulf.

hundred men short of one hundred and ten thousand; and this amount was exactly made up by the Thespians who were present in the camp; for eighteen hundred Thespians, being the whole number left,[1] were likewise with the army; but these men were without arms. Such was the array of the Greek troops when they took post on the Asôpus.

31. The barbarians under Mardonius, when the mourning for Masistius was at an end, and they learnt that the Greeks were in the Platæan territory, moved likewise towards the river Asôpus, which flows in those parts. On their arrival Mardonius marshalled them against the Greeks in the following order:— Against the Lacedæmonians he posted his Persians; and as the Persians were far more numerous, he drew them up with their ranks deeper than common, and also extended their front so that part faced the Tegeans; and here he took care to choose out the best troops to face the Lacedæmonians, whilst against the Tegeans he arrayed those on whom he could not so much depend. This was done at the suggestion and by the advice of the Thebans. Next to the Persians he placed the Medes, facing the Corinthians, Potidæans, Orchomenians, and Sicyonians; then the Bactrians, facing the Epidaurians, Trœzenians, Lepreats, Tirynthians, Mycenæans, and Phliasians; after them the Indians, facing the Hermionians, Eretrians, Styreans, and Chalcidians; then the Sacans, facing the Ambraciots, Anactorians, Leucadians, Paleans, and Eginetans; last of all, facing the Athenians, the Platæans, and the Megarians, he placed the troops of the Bœotians, Locrians, Malians, and Thessalians, and also the thousand Phocians.[2] The whole nation of the Phocians had not joined the Medes; on the contrary, there were some who had gathered themselves into bands about Parnassus, and made expeditions from thence, whereby they distressed Mardonius and the Greeks who sided with him, and so did good service to the Grecian cause. Besides those mentioned above, Mardonius likewise arrayed against the Athenians the Macedonians and the tribes dwelling about Thessaly.

32. I have named here the greatest of the nations which were marshalled by Mardonius on this occasion, to wit, all those of

1 That is, the whole number left after the destruction of the 700 at Thermopylæ (supra, vii. 222–225).

2 That is, the thousand Phocians who had been previously mentioned (supra, chs. 17, 18).

most renown and account. Mixed with these, however, were men of divers other peoples,[1] as Phrygians, Thracians, Mysians, Pæonians, and the like; Ethiopians again, and Egyptians, both of the Hermotybian and Calasirian races,[2] whose weapon is the sword, and who are the only fighting men in that country. These persons had formerly served on board the fleet of Xerxes, but Mardonius disembarked them before he left Phalêrum; in the land force which Xerxes brought to Athens there were no Egyptians. The number of the barbarians, as I have already mentioned,[3] was three hundred thousand; that of the Greeks who had made alliance with Mardonius is known to none, for they were never counted: I should guess that they mustered near fifty thousand strong. The troops thus marshalled were all foot soldiers. As for the horse, it was drawn up by itself.

33. When the marshalling of Mardonius' troops by nations and by maniples was ended, the two armies proceeded on the next day to offer sacrifice. The Grecian sacrifice was offered by Tisamenus, the son of Antiochus, who accompanied the army as soothsayer: he was an Elean, and belonged to the Clytiad branch of the Iamidæ, but had been admitted among their own citizens by the Lacedæmonians. Now his admission among them was on this wise:— Tisamenus had gone to Delphi to consult the god concerning his lack of offspring, when it was declared to him by the Pythoness that he would win five very glorious combats.[4] Misunderstanding the oracle, and imagining that he was to win combats in the games, Tisamenus at once applied himself to the practice of gymnastics. He trained himself for the Pentathlum,[5] and, on contending at Olympia, came within a little of winning it; for he was successful in everything, except the wrestling-match, which was carried off by Hieronymus the Andrian. Hereon the Lacedæmonians perceived that the combats of which the oracle spoke were not combats in the games, but battles: they therefore sought to induce Tisamenus to hire out his services to them, in order that they might join him with their Heracleid

1 See above, viii. 113, ad fin.
2 The whole of the former amounted to 160,000 men, the Calisiries to 250,000. (Bk. ii. chs. 164, 165, 166.)
3 Supra, viii. 113, end.
4 On the habit of the Pythoness to disregard the question asked, and to answer on an entirely different subject, see above, iv. 151 and 155; v. 63.
5 For the nature of the Pentathlum, vide supra, vi. 92.

kings in the conduct of their wars. He however, when he saw that they set great store by his friendship, forthwith raised his price, and told them, "If they would receive him among their citizens, and give him equal rights with the rest, he was willing to do as they desired, but on no other terms would they ever gain his consent." The Spartans, when they heard this, at first thought it monstrous, and ceased to implore his aid. Afterwards, however, when the fearful danger of the Persian war hung over their heads, they sent for him and agreed to his terms; but Tisamenus now, perceiving them so changed, declared, "He could no longer be content with what he had asked before: they must likewise make his brother Hagias[1] a Spartan, with the same rights as himself."

34. In acting thus he did but follow the example once set by Melampus, at least if kingship may be compared with citizenship. For when the women of Argos were seized with madness, and the Argives would have hired Melampus to come from Pylos and heal them of their disease, he demanded as his reward one-half of the kingdom; but as the Argives disdained to stoop to this, they left him and went their way. Afterwards, however, when many more of their women were seized, they brought themselves to agree to his terms; and accordingly they went again to him, and said they were content to give what he required. Hereon Melampus, seeing them so changed, raised his demand, and told them, "Except they would give his brother Bias one-third of the kingdom likewise, he would not do as they wished." So, as the Argives were in a strait, they consented even to this.

35. In like manner the Spartans, as they were in great need of Tisamenus, yielded everything: and Tisamenus the Elean, having in this way become a Spartan citizen, afterwards, in the capacity of soothsayer, helped the Spartans to gain five very glorious combats. He and his brother were the only men whom the Spartans ever admitted to citizenship.[2] The five combats were these following:— The first was the combat at Platæa; the second, that near Tegea, against the Tegeans and the Argives; the third, that at Dipæeis, against all the Arcadians excepting those of Mantinea;

1 Hagias the *brother* must be distinguished from Hagias the *grandson* of Tisamenus.

2 Herodotus must be supposed to mean the only *foreigners*; otherwise his statement will be very incorrect.

the fourth, that at the Isthmus, against the Messenians; and the fifth, that at Tanagra, against the Athenians and the Argives. The battle here fought was the last of all the five.

36. The Spartans had now brought Tisamenus with them to the Platæan territory, where he acted as soothsayer for the Greeks. He found the victims favourable, if the Greeks stood on the defensive, but not if they began the battle or crossed the river Asôpus.

37. With Mardonius also, who was very eager to begin the battle, the victims were not favourable for so doing; but he likewise found they bode him well, if he was content to stand on his defence. He too had made use of the Grecian rites; for Hêgêsistratus, an Elean, and the most renowned of the Telliads, was his soothsayer. This man had once been taken captive by the Spartans, who, considering that he had done them many grievous injuries, laid him in bonds, with the intent to put him to death. Thereupon Hêgêsistratus, finding himself in so sore a case, since not only was his life in danger, but he knew that he would have to suffer torments of many kinds before his death, – Hêgêsistratus, I say, did a deed for which no words suffice. He had been set with one foot in the stocks, which were of wood but bound with iron bands; and in this condition received from without an iron implement, wherewith he contrived to accomplish the most courageous deed upon record. Calculating how much of his foot he would be able to draw through the hole, he cut off the front portion with his own hand; and then, as he was guarded by watchmen, forced a way through the wall of his prison, and made his escape to Tegea, travelling during the night, but in the daytime stealing into the woods, and staying there. In this way, though the Lacedæmonians went out in full force to search for him, he nevertheless escaped, and arrived the third evening at Tegea. So the Spartans were amazed at the man's endurance, when they saw on the ground the piece which he had cut off his foot, and yet for all their seeking could not find him anywhere. Hêgêsistratus, having thus escaped the Lacedæmonians, took refuge in Tegea; for the Tegeans at that time were ill friends with the Lacedæmonians. When his wound was healed, he procured himself a wooden foot, and became an open enemy to Sparta. At the last, however, this enmity brought him to trouble; for the Spartans took him captive as he was exercising his office in Zacynthus, and forthwith put him to death. But

these things happened some while after the fight at Platæa. At present he was serving Mardonius on the Asôpus, having been hired at no inconsiderable price; and here he offered sacrifice with a right good will, in part from his hatred of the Lacedæmonians, in part for lucre's sake.

38. So when the victims did not allow either the Persians or their Greek allies to begin the battle – these Greeks had their own soothsayer in the person of Hippomachus, a Leucadian – and when soldiers continued to pour into the opposite camp and the numbers on the Greek side to increase continually, Timagenidas, the son of Herpys, a Theban, advised Mardonius to keep a watch on the passes of Cithæron, telling him how supplies of men kept flocking in day after day, and assuring him that he might cut off large numbers.

39. It was eight days after the two armies first encamped opposite to one another when this advice was given by Timagenidas. Mardonius, seeing it to be good, as soon as evening came, sent his cavalry to that pass of Mount Cithæron which opens out upon Platæa, a pass called by the Bœotians the "Three Heads," but called the "Oak-Heads" by the Athenians.¹ The horse sent on this errand did not make the movement in vain. They came upon a body of five hundred sumpter-beasts which were just entering the plain, bringing provisions to the Greek camp from the Peloponnese, with a number of men driving them. Seeing this prey in their power, the Persians set upon them and slaughtered them, sparing none, neither man nor beast; till at last, when they had had enough of slaying, they secured such as were left, and bore them off to the camp to Mardonius.

40. After this they waited again for two days more, neither army wishing to begin the fight. The barbarians indeed advanced as far as the Asôpus, and endeavoured to tempt the Greeks to cross; but neither side actually passed the stream. Still the cavalry of Mardonius harassed and annoyed the Greeks incessantly; for the Thebans, who were zealous in the cause of the Medes, pressed the war forward with all eagerness, and often led the charge till the lines met, when the Medes and Persians took their place, and displayed, many of them, uncommon válour.

---

1 The name "Oak-Heads" (Dryos-Cephalæ) seems to have belonged to the entire dip in the mountain range through which passed both the roads above mentioned.

41. For ten days nothing was done more than this; but on the eleventh day from the time when the two hosts first took station, one over against the other, near Platæa – the number of the Greeks being now much greater than it was at the first, and Mardonius being impatient of the delay – there was a conference held between Mardonius, son of Gobryas, and Artabazus, son of Pharnaces,[1] a man who was esteemed by Xerxes more than almost any of the Persians. At this consultation the following were the opinions delivered:– Artabazus thought it would be best for them to break up from their quarters as soon as possible, and withdraw the whole army to the fortified town of Thebes, where they had abundant stores of corn for themselves, and of fodder for the sumpter-beasts. There, he said, they had only to sit quiet, and the war might be brought to an end on this wise:– Coined gold was plentiful in the camp, and uncoined gold too; they had silver moreover in great abundance, and drinking-cups. Let them not spare to take of these, and distribute them among the Greeks, especially among the leaders in the several cities; 'twould not be long before the Greeks gave up their liberty, without risking another battle for it. Thus the opinion of Artabazus agreed with that of the Thebans;[2] for he too had more foresight than some. Mardonius, on the other hand, expressed himself with more fierceness and obstinacy, and was utterly disinclined to yield. "Their army," he said, "was vastly superior to that of the Greeks; and they had best engage at once, and not wait till greater numbers were gathered against them. As for Hêgêsistratus and his victims, they should let them pass unheeded, not seeking to force them to be favourable, but, according to the old Persian custom, hasting to join battle."

42. When Mardonius had thus declared his sentiments, no one ventured to say him nay; and accordingly his opinion prevailed, for it was to him, and not to Artabazus, that the king had given the command of the army.

Mardonius now sent for the captains of the squadrons, and the leaders of the Greeks in his service, and questioned them:– "Did they know of any prophecy which said that the Persians were to be destroyed in Greece?" All were silent; some because they did not know the prophecies, but others, who knew them full well, because they did not think it safe to speak out. So

---

1 Supra, viii. 126–129.   2 Supra, ch. 2.

Mardonius, when none answered, said, "Since ye know of no such oracle, or do not dare to speak of it, I, who know it well, will myself declare it to you. There is an oracle which says that the Persians shall come into Greece, sack the temple at Delphi, and when they have so done, perish one and all. Now we, as we are aware of the prediction, will neither go against the temple nor make any attempt to sack it: we therefore shall not perish for this trespass. Rejoice then thus far, all ye who are well-wishers to the Persians, and doubt not we shall get the better of the Greeks." When he had so spoken, he further ordered them to prepare themselves, and to put all in readiness for a battle upon the morrow.

43. As for the oracle of which Mardonius spoke, and which he referred to the Persians, it did not, I am well assured, mean them, but the Illyrians and the Enchelean host. There are, however, some verses of Bacis which did speak of this battle:—

"By Thermôdon's stream, and the grass-clad banks of Asôpus,
See where gather the Grecians, and hark to the foreigners'
    war-shout —
There in death shall lie, ere fate or Lachesis doomed him,
Many a bow-bearing Mede, when the day of calamity cometh."

These verses, and some others like them which Musæus wrote, referred, I well know, to the Persians. The river Thermôdon flows between Tanagra and Glisas.[1]

44. After Mardonius had put his question about the prophecies, and spoken the above words of encouragement, night drew on apace, and on both sides the watches were set. As soon then as there was silence throughout the camp, — the night being now well advanced, and the men seeming to be in their deepest sleep, — Alexander, the son of Amyntas, king and leader of the Macedonians, rode up on horseback to the Athenian outposts, and desired to speak with the generals. Hereupon, while the greater part continued on guard, some of the watch ran to the chiefs, and told them, "There had come a horseman from the Median camp who would not say a word, except that he wished to speak with the generals, of whom he mentioned the names."

45. They at once, hearing this, made haste to the outpost, where they found Alexander, who addressed them as follows:—

1 Glisas was one of the most ancient of the Bœotian towns. It is mentioned by Homer.

"Men of Athens, that which I am about to say I trust to your honour; and I charge you to keep it secret from all excepting Pausanias, if you would not bring me to destruction. Had I not greatly at heart the common welfare of Greece, I should not have come to tell you; but I am myself a Greek by descent,[1] and I would not willingly see Greece exchange freedom for slavery. Know then that Mardonius and his army cannot obtain favourable omens; had it not been for this, they would have fought with you long ago. Now, however, they have determined to let the victims pass unheeded, and, as soon as day dawns, to engage in battle. Mardonius, I imagine, is afraid that, if he delays, you will increase in number. Make ready then to receive him. Should he however still defer the combat, do you abide where you are; for his provisions will not hold out many more days.[2] If ye prosper in this war, forget not to do something for my freedom; consider the risk I have run, out of zeal for the Greek cause, to acquaint you with what Mardonius intends, and to save you from being surprised by the barbarians. I am Alexander of Macedon."

As soon as he had said this, Alexander rode back to the camp, and returned to the station assigned him.

46. Meanwhile the Athenian generals hastened to the right wing, and told Pausanias all that they had learnt from Alexander. Hereupon Pausanias, who no sooner heard the intention of the Persians than he was struck with fear, addressed the generals, and said, –

"Since the battle is to come with to-morrow's dawn, it were well that you Athenians should stand opposed to the Persians, and we Spartans to the Bœotians and the other Greeks; for ye know the Medes and their manner of fight, since ye have already fought with them once at Marathon, but we are quite ignorant and without any experience of their warfare. While, however, there is not a Spartan here present who has ever fought against a Mede, of the Bœotians and Thessalians we have had experience. Take then your arms, and march over to our post upon the right, while we supply your place in the left wing."

Hereto the Athenians replied – "We, too, long ago, when we saw that the Persians were drawn up to face you, were minded to suggest to you the very course which you have now been the

---

1 Supra, v. 22; viii. 137, 138.
2 It seems very unlikely that this could be true.

first to bring forward. We feared, however, that perhaps our words might not be pleasing to you. But, as you have now spoken of these things yourselves, we gladly give our consent, and are ready to do as ye have said."

47. Both sides agreeing hereto, at the dawn of day the Spartans and Athenians changed places. But the movement was perceived by the Bœotians, and they gave notice of it to Mardonius; who at once, on hearing what had been done, made a change in the disposition of his own forces, and brought the Persians to face the Lacedæmonians. Then Pausanias, finding that his design was discovered, led back his Spartans to the right wing; and Mardonius, seeing this, replaced his Persians upon the left of his army.

48. When the troops again occupied their former posts, Mardonius sent a herald to the Spartans, who spoke as follows:–

"Lacedæmonians, in these parts the men say that you are the bravest of mankind, and admire you because you never turn your backs in flight nor quit your ranks, but always stand firm, and either die at your posts or else destroy your adversaries.[1] But in all this which they say concerning you there is not one word of truth; for now have we seen you, before battle was joined or our two hosts had come to blows, flying and leaving your posts, wishing the Athenians to make the first trial of our arms, and taking your own station against our slaves. Surely these are not the deeds of brave men. Much do we find ourselves deceived in you; for we believed the reports of you that reached our ears, and expected that you would send a herald with a challenge to us, proposing to fight by yourselves against our division of native Persians. We for our part were ready to have agreed to this; but ye have made us no such offer – nay! ye seem rather to shrink from meeting us. However, as no challenge of this kind comes from you to us, lo! we send a challenge to you. Why should not you on the part of the Greeks, as you are thought to be the bravest of all, and we on the part of the barbarians, fight a battle with equal numbers on both sides? Then, if it seems good to the others to fight likewise, let them engage afterwards – but if not, – if they are content that we should fight on behalf of all, let us so do – and whichever side wins the battle, let them win it for their whole army."

---

1 Vide supra, vii. 209.

49. When the herald had thus spoken, he waited a while, but, as no one made him any answer, he went back, and told Mardonius what had happened. Mardonius was full of joy thereat, and so puffed up by the empty victory, that he at once gave orders to his horse to charge the Greek line. Then the horsemen drew near, and with their javelins and their arrows – for though horsemen they used the bow[1] – sorely distressed the Greek troops, which could not bring them to close combat. The fountain of Gargaphia,[2] whence the whole Greek army drew its water, they at this time choked up and spoiled. The Lacedæmonians were the only troops who had their station near this fountain; the other Greeks were more or less distant from it, according to their place in the line; they however were not far from the Asôpus. Still, as the Persian horse with their missile weapons did not allow them to approach, and so they could not get their water from the river, these Greeks, no less than the Lacedæmonians, resorted at this time to the fountain.

50. When the fountain was choked, the Grecian captains, seeing that the army had no longer a watering-place, and observing moreover that the cavalry greatly harassed them, held a meeting on these and other matters at the head-quarters of Pausanias upon the right. For besides the above-named difficulties, which were great enough, other circumstances added to their distress. All the provisions that they had brought with them were gone; and the attendants who had been sent to fetch supplies from the Peloponnese, were prevented from returning to camp by the Persian horse, which had now closed the passage.

51. The captains therefore held a council, whereat it was agreed, that if the Persians did not give battle that day, the Greeks should move to the Island – a tract of ground which lies in front of Platæa, at the distance of ten furlongs from the Asôpus and fount Gargaphia, where the army was encamped at that time. This tract was a sort of island in the continent: for there is a river which, dividing near its source, runs down from Mount Cithæron into the plain below in two streams, flowing in channels about three furlongs apart, which after a while unite and become one. The name of this river is Oëroë, and the dwellers in those parts call it, the daughter of the Asôpus. This

---

1 Supra, vii. 84 (compare vii. 61). The custom is noticed by several writers.
2 Supra, ch. 25.

was the place to which the Greeks resolved to remove; and they chose it, first because they would there have no lack of water, and secondly, because the horse could not harass them as when it was drawn up right in their front. They thought it best to begin their march at the second watch of the night, lest the Persians should see them as they left their station, and should follow and harass them with their cavalry. It was agreed likewise, that after they had reached the place, which the Asôpus-born Oëroë surrounds, as it flows down from Cithæron, they should despatch, the very same night, one half of their army towards that mountain-range, to relieve those whom they had sent to procure provisions, and who were now blocked up in that region.

52. Having made these resolves, they continued during that whole day to suffer beyond measure from the attacks of the enemy's horse. At length when towards dusk the attacks of the horse ceased, and, night having closed in, the hour arrived at which the army was to commence its retreat, the greater number struck their tents and began the march towards the rear. They were not minded, however, to make for the place agreed upon; but in their anxiety to escape from the Persian horse, no sooner had they begun to move than they fled straight to Platæa; where they took post at the temple of Hera, which lies outside the city, at the distance of about twenty furlongs from Gargaphia; and here they pitched their camp in front of the sacred building.

53. As soon as Pausanias saw a portion of the troops in motion, he issued orders to the Lacedæmonians to strike their tents and follow those who had been the first to depart, supposing that they were on their march to the place agreed upon. All the captains but one were ready to obey his orders: Amompharetus, however, the son of Poliadas, who was leader of the Pitanate cohort, refused to move, saying, "He for one would not fly from the strangers,[1] or of his own will bring disgrace upon Sparta." It had happened that he was absent from the former conference of the captains;[2] and so what was now taking place astonished him. Pausanias and Euryanax[3] thought it a monstrous thing that Amompharetus would not hearken to them; but considered that

1 Vide supra, ch. 11, and infra, ch. 55.
2 Vide supra, ch. 51.
3 Euryanax has been mentioned as having some share in the command, supra, ch. 10.

it would be yet more monstrous, if, when he was so minded, they were to leave the Pitanates to their fate; seeing that, if they forsook them to keep their agreement with the other Greeks, Amompharetus and those with him might perish. On this account, therefore, they kept the Lacedæmonian force in its place, and made every endeavour to persuade Amompharetus that he was wrong to act as he was doing.

54. While the Spartans were engaged in these efforts to turn Amompharetus – the only man unwilling to retreat either in their own army or in that of the Tegeans – the Athenians on their side did as follows. Knowing that it was the Spartan temper to say one thing and do another,[1] they remained quiet in their station until the army began to retreat, when they despatched a horseman to see whether the Spartans really meant to set forth, or whether after all they had do intention of moving. The horseman was also to ask Pausanias what he wished the Athenians to do.

55. The herald on his arrival found the Lacedæmonians drawn up in their old position, and their leaders quarrelling with one another. Pausanias and Euryanax had gone on urging Amompharetus not to endanger the lives of his men by staying behind while the others drew off, but without succeeding in persuading him; until at last the dispute had waxed hot between them just at the moment when the Athenian herald arrived. At this point Amompharetus, who was still disputing, took up with both his hands a vast rock, and placed it at the feet of Pausanias, saying – "With this pebble I give my vote not to run away from the strangers." (By "strangers" he meant barbarians.[2]) Pausanias, in reply, called him a fool and a madman, and, turning to the Athenian herald, who had made the inquiries with which he was charged, bade him tell his countrymen how he was occupied, and ask them to approach nearer, and retreat or not according to the movements of the Spartans.

56. So the herald went back to the Athenians; and the Spartans continued to dispute till morning began to dawn upon them. Then Pausanias, who as yet had not moved, gave the signal for retreat – expecting (and rightly, as the event proved) that Amompharetus, when he saw the rest of the Lacedæmonians in motion, would be unwilling to be left behind. No sooner was the signal given, than all the army except the Pitanates began their march,

1 Vide supra, chs. 6 and 8.   2 Vide supra, ch. 11.

and retreated along the line of the hills; the Tegeans accompanying them. The Athenians likewise set off in good order, but proceeded by a different way from the Lacedæmonians. For while the latter clung to the hilly ground and the skirts of Mount Cithæron, on account of the fear which they entertained of the enemy's horse, the former betook themselves to the low country and marched through the plain.

57. As for Amompharetus, at first he did not believe that Pausanias would really dare to leave him behind; he therefore remained firm in his resolve to keep his men at their post; when, however, Pausanias and his troops were now some way off, Amompharetus, thinking himself forsaken in good earnest, ordered his band to take their arms, and led them at a walk towards the main army. Now the army was waiting for them at a distance of about ten furlongs, having halted upon the river Moloeis at a place called Argiopius, where stands a temple dedicated to Eleusinian Demeter. They had stopped here, that, in case Amompharetus and his band should refuse to quit the spot where they were drawn up, and should really not stir from it, they might have it in their power to move back and lend them assistance. Amompharetus, however, and his companions rejoined the main body; and at the same time the whole mass of the barbarian cavalry arrived and began to press hard upon them. The horsemen had followed their usual practice and ridden up to the Greek camp, when they discovered that the place where the Greeks had been posted hitherto was deserted. Hereupon they pushed forward without stopping, and, as soon as they overtook the enemy, pressed heavily on them.

58. Mardonius, when he heard that the Greeks had retired under cover of the night, and beheld the place, where they had been stationed, empty, called to him Thorax of Larissa,[1] and his brethren, Eurypylus and Thrasideius, and said —

"O sons of Aleuas! what will ye say now, when ye see yonder place empty? Why, you, who dwell in their neighbourhood, told me the Lacedæmonians never fled from battle, but were brave beyond all the rest of mankind. Lately, however, you yourselves beheld them change their place in the line;[2] and here, as all may see, they have run away during the night. Verily, when their turn came to fight with those who are of a truth the bravest warriors

1 Supra, ch. 1.   2 Supra, ch. 47.

in all the world, they showed plainly enough that they are men of no worth, who have distinguished themselves among *Greeks* – men likewise of no worth at all. However, I can readily excuse you, who, knowing nothing of the Persians, praised these men from your acquaintance with certain exploits of theirs; but I marvel all the more at Artabazus, that *he* should have been afraid of the Lacedæmonians, and have therefore given us so dastardly a counsel, – bidding us, as he did, break up our camp, and remove to Thebes, and there allow ourselves to be besieged by the Greeks[1] – advice whereof I shall take care to inform the king. But of this hereafter. Now we must not allow them to escape us, but must pursue after them till we overtake them; and then we must exact vengeance for all the wrongs which have been suffered at their hands by the Persians."

59. When he had so spoken, he crossed the Asôpus, and led the Persians forward at a run directly upon the track of the Greeks, whom he believed to be in actual flight. He could not see the Athenians; for, as they had taken the way of the plain, they were hidden from his sight by the hills; he therefore led on his troops against the Lacedæmonians and the Tegeans only. When the commanders of the other divisions of the barbarians saw the Persians pursuing the Greeks so hastily, they all forthwith seized their standards, and hurried after at their best speed in great disorder and disarray. On they went with loud shouts and in a wild rout, thinking to swallow up the runaways.

60. Meanwhile Pausanias had sent a horseman to the Athenians, at the time when the cavalry first fell upon him, with this message:–

"Men of Athens! now that the great struggle has come, which is to decide the freedom or the slavery of Greece, we twain, Lacedæmonians and Athenians, are deserted by all the other allies, who have fled away from us during the past night. Nevertheless, we are resolved what to do – we must endeavour, as best we may, to defend ourselves and to succour one another. Now, had the horse fallen upon you first, we ourselves with the Tegeans (who remain faithful to the Greek cause) would have been bound to render you assistance against them. As, however, the entire body has advanced upon us, 'tis your place to come to our aid, sore pressed as we are by the enemy. Should you yourselves

1 Supra, ch. 41.

be so straitened that you cannot come, at least send us your archers, and be sure you will earn our gratitude. We acknowledge that throughout this whole war there has been no zeal to be compared to yours – we therefore doubt not that you will do us this service."

61. The Athenians, as soon as they received this message, were anxious to go to the aid of the Spartans, and to help them to the uttermost of their power; but, as they were upon the march, the Greeks on the king's side, whose place in the line had been opposite theirs, fell upon them, and so harassed them by their attacks that it was not possible for them to give the succour they desired. Accordingly the Lacedæmonians, and the Tegeans – whom nothing could induce to quit their side – were left alone to resist the Persians. Including the light-armed, the number of the former was 50,000; while that of the Tegeans was 3,000. Now, therefore, as they were about to engage with Mardonius and the troops under him, they made ready to offer sacrifice. The victims, however, for some time were not favourable; and, during the delay, many fell on the Spartan side, and a still greater number were wounded. For the Persians had made a rampart of their wicker shields,[1] and shot from behind them such clouds of arrows, that the Spartans were sorely distressed. The victims continued unpropitious; till at last Pausanias raised his eyes to the Heræum of the Platæans, and calling the goddess to his aid, besought her not to disappoint the hopes of the Greeks.

62. As he offered his prayer, the Tegeans, advancing before the rest, rushed forward against the enemy; and the Lacedæmonians, who had obtained favourable omens the moment that Pausanias prayed, at length, after their long delay, advanced to the attack; while the Persians, on their side, left shooting, and prepared to meet them. And first the combat was at the wicker shields. Afterwards, when these were swept down, a fierce contest took place by the side of the temple of Demeter, which lasted long, and ended in a hand-to-hand struggle. The barbarians many times seized hold of the Greek spears and brake them; for in boldness and warlike spirit the Persians were not a whit inferior to the Greeks; but they were without bucklers,[2] untrained, and

1 The wicker shield used by the Persians seems to have been adopted from the Assyrians.
2 The wicker shields of the Persians were useless for close combat.

far below the enemy in respect of skill in arms. Sometimes singly, sometimes in bodies of ten, now fewer and now more in number, they dashed forward upon the Spartan ranks, and so perished.

63. The fight went most against the Greeks, where Mardonius, mounted upon a white horse, and surrounded by the bravest of all the Persians, the thousand picked men,[1] fought in person. So long as Mardonius was alive, this body resisted all attacks, and, while they defended their own lives, struck down no small number of Spartans; but after Mardonius fell, and the troops with him, which were the main strength of the army, perished, the remainder yielded to the Lacedæmonians, and took to flight. Their light clothing, and want of bucklers, were of the greatest hurt to them: for they had to contend against men heavily armed, while they themselves were without any such defence.

64. Then was the warning of the oracle fulfilled; and the vengeance which was due to the Spartans for the slaughter of Leonidas was paid them by Mardonius – then too did Pausanias, the son of Cleombrotus, and grandson of Anaxandridas (I omit to recount his other ancestors, since they are the same with those of Leonidas), win a victory exceeding in glory all those to which our knowledge extends. Mardonius was slain by Aeimnêstus, a man famous in Sparta – the same who in the Messenian war, which came after the struggle against the Medes, fought a battle near Stenyclêrus with but three hundred men against the whole force of the Messenians, and himself perished, and the three hundred with him.

65. The Persians, as soon as they were put to flight by the Lacedæmonians, ran hastily away, without preserving any order, and took refuge in their own camp, within the wooden defence which they had raised in the Theban territory.[2] It is a marvel to me how it came to pass, that although the battle was fought quite close to the grove of Demeter, yet not a single Persian appears to have died on the sacred soil, nor even to have set foot upon it, while round about the precinct, in the unconsecrated ground, great numbers perished. I imagine – if it is lawful, in matters which concern the gods, to imagine anything – that the goddess herself kept them out, because they had burnt her dwelling at Eleusis. Such, then, was the issue of this battle.

---

1 Supra, vii. 40 and viii. 113.   2 Supra, ch. 15.

66. Artabazus, the son of Pharnaces, who had disapproved from the first of the king's leaving Mardonius behind him, and had made great endeavours, but all in vain, to dissuade Mardonius from risking a battle,[1] when he found that the latter was bent on acting otherwise than he wished, did as follows. He had a force under his orders which was far from inconsiderable, amounting, as it did, to near forty thousand men. Being well aware, therefore, how the battle was likely to go, as soon as the two armies began to fight, he led his soldiers forward in an orderly array, bidding them one and all proceed at the same pace, and follow him with such celerity as they should observe him to use. Having issued these commands, he pretended to lead them to the battle. But when, advancing before his army, he saw that the Persians were already in flight, instead of keeping the same order, he wheeled his troops suddenly round, and beat a retreat; nor did he even seek shelter within the palisade or behind the walls of Thebes, but hurried on into Phocis, wishing to make his way to the Hellespont with all possible speed. Such accordingly was the course which these Persians took.

67. As for the Greeks upon the king's side, while most of them played the coward purposely, the Bœotians, on the contrary, had a long struggle with the Athenians. Those of the Thebans who were attached to the Medes, displayed especially no little zeal; far from playing the coward, they fought with such fury that three hundred of the best and bravest among them were slain by the Athenians in this passage of arms. But at last they too were routed, and fled away – not, however, in the same direction as the Persians and the crowd of allies, who, having taken no part in the battle, ran off without striking a blow – but to the city of Thebes.

68. To me it shows very clearly how completely the rest of the barbarians were dependent upon the Persian troops, that here they all fled at once, without ever coming to blows with the enemy, merely because they saw the Persians running away. And so it came to pass that the whole army took to flight, except only the horse, both Persian and Bœotian. These did good service to the flying foot-men, by advancing close to the enemy, and separating between the Greeks and their own fugitives.

---

1 Supra, ch. 41.

69. The victors however pressed on, pursuing and slaying the remnant of the king's army.

Meantime, while the flight continued, tidings reached the Greeks who were drawn up round the Heræum,[1] and so were absent from the battle, that the fight was begun, and that Pausanias was gaining the victory. Hearing this, they rushed forward without any order, the Corinthians taking the upper road across the skirts of Cithæron and the hills, which led straight to the temple of Demeter; while the Megarians and Phliasians followed the level route through the plain. These last had almost reached the enemy, when the Theban horse espied them, and, observing their disarray, despatched against them the squadron of which Asôpodôrus, the son of Timander, was captain. Asôpodôrus charged them with such effect that he left six hundred of their number dead upon the plain, and, pursuing the rest, compelled them to seek shelter in Cithæron. So these men perished without honour.

70. The Persians, and the multitude with them, who fled to the wooden fortress, were able to ascend into the towers before the Lacedæmonians came up. Thus placed, they proceeded to strengthen the defences as well as they could; and when the Lacedæmonians arrived, a sharp fight took place at the rampart. So long as the Athenians were away, the barbarians kept off their assailants, and had much the best of the combat, since the Lacedæmonians were unskilled in the attack of walled places:[2] but on the arrival of the Athenians, a more violent assault was made, and the wall was for a long time attacked with fury. In the end the valour of the Athenians and their perseverance prevailed – they gained the top of the wall, and, breaking a breach through it, enabled the Greeks to pour in. The first to enter here were the Tegeans, and they it was who plundered the tent of Mardonius; where among other booty they found the manger from which his horses ate, all made of solid brass, and well worth looking at. This manger was given by the Tegeans to the temple of Athena Alea, while the remainder of their booty was brought into the common stock of the Greeks. As soon as the wall was broken down, the barbarians no longer kept together in any

1 Supra, ch. 52.
2 The inability to conduct sieges is one of the most striking features of the Spartan military character. The Athenian skill contrasted remarkably with the Spartan inefficiency.

array, nor was there one among them who thought of making further resistance – in good truth, they were all half dead with fright, huddled as so many thousands were into so narrow and confined a space. With such tameness did they submit to be slaughtered by the Greeks, that of the 300,000 men who composed the army – omitting the 40,000 by whom Artabazus was accompanied in his flight – no more than 3,000 outlived the battle. Of the Lacedæmonians from Sparta there perished in this combat ninety-one; of the Tegeans, sixteen; of the Athenians, fifty-two.

71. On the side of the barbarians, the greatest courage was manifested, among the foot-soldiers, by the Persians; among the horse, by the Sacæ; while Mardonius himself, as a man, bore off the palm from the rest. Among the Greeks, the Athenians and the Tegeans fought well; but the prowess shown by the Lacedæmonians was beyond either. Of this I have but one proof to offer – since all the three nations overthrew the force opposed to them – and that is, that the Lacedæmonians fought and conquered the best troops. The bravest man by far on that day was, in my judgment, Aristodêmus – the same who alone escaped from the slaughter of the three hundred at Thermopylæ, and who on that account had endured disgrace and reproach:[1] next to him were Posidônius, Philocyon, and Amompharetus the Spartan. The Spartans, however, who took part in the fight, when the question of "who had distinguished himself most," came to be talked over among them, decided – "that Aristodêmus, who, on account of the blame which attached to him, had manifestly courted death, and had therefore left his place in the line and behaved like a madman, had done of a truth very notable deeds; but that Posidônius, who, with no such desire to lose his life, had quitted himself no less gallantly, was by so much a braver man than he." Perchance, however, it was envy that made them speak after this sort. Of those whom I have named above as slain in this battle, all, save and except Aristodêmus, received public honours: Aristodêmus alone had no honours, because he courted death for the reason which I have mentioned.

72. These then were the most distinguished of those who fought at Platæa. As for Callicrates, – the most beautiful man, not among the Spartans only, but in the whole Greek camp, –

---

1 Supra, vii. 229–231.

he was not killed in the battle; for it was while Pausanias was still consulting the victims, that as he sat in his proper place in the line, an arrow struck him on the side. While his comrades advanced to the fight, he was borne out of the ranks, very loath to die, as he showed by the words which he addressed to Arimnestus, one of the Platæans;— "I grieve," said he, "not because I have to die for my country, but because I have not lifted my arm against the enemy, nor done any deed worthy of me, much as I have desired to achieve something."

73. The Athenian who is said to have distinguished himself the most was Sôphanes, the son of Eutychides, of the Deceleian canton. The men of this canton, once upon a time, did a deed, which (as the Athenians themselves confess) has ever since been serviceable to them. When the Tyndaridæ, in days of yore, invaded Attica with a mighty army to recover Helen,[1] and, not being able to find out whither she had been carried, desolated the cantons, – at this time, they say, the Deceleians (or Decelus himself, according to some), displeased at the rudeness of Theseus, and fearing that the whole territory would suffer, discovered everything to the enemy, and even showed them the way to Aphidnæ, which Titacus, a native of the place, betrayed into their hands. As a reward for this action, Sparta has always, from that time to the present, allowed the Deceleians to be free from all dues, and to have seats of honour at their festivals; and hence too, in the war which took place many years after these events between the Peloponnesians and the Athenians, the Lacedæmonians, while they laid waste all the rest of Attica, spared the lands of the Deceleians.

74. Of this canton was Sôphanes, the Athenian, who most distinguished himself in the battle. Two stories are told concerning

---

1 Pirithoüs and Theseus resolved to wed daughters of Zeus, and to help one another. They had heard of the beauty of Helen, though she was no more than seven years old, and went to Sparta to carry her off. There they found her dancing in the temple of Artemis Orthia. Having seized her and borne her away, they cast lots whose she should be, and Theseus was the winner. So he brought Helen to Attica, and secreted her at Aphidnæ, giving her in charge to his friend Aphidnus, and his mother Æthra. Theseus then accompanied Pirithoüs into Thesprotia, to obtain Persephoné for him. Meanwhile the Dioscûri had collected a vast host, and invaded Attica, where they sought everywhere for their sister. At length her hiding-place was pointed out to them; and they laid siege to Aphidnæ, and having taken it, recovered Helen, and made Æthra prisoner.

him: according to the one, he wore an iron anchor fastened to the belt which secured his breastplate by a brazen chain; and this, when he came near the enemy, he threw out; to the intent that, when they made their charge, it might be impossible for him to be driven from his post: as soon, however, as the enemy fled, his wont was to take up his anchor and join the pursuit. Such, then, is one of the said stories. The other, which is contradictory to the first, relates that Sôphanes, instead of having an iron anchor fastened to his breastplate, bore the device of an anchor upon his shield,[1] which he never allowed to rest, but made to run round continually.

75. Another glorious deed was likewise performed by this same Sôphanes. At the time when the Athenians were laying siege to Egina, he took up the challenge of Eurybates the Argive, a winner of the Pentathlum, and slew him.[2] The fate of Sôphanes in after times was the following: he was leader of an Athenian army in conjunction with Leagrus, the son of Glaucon, and in a battle with the Edonians near Datum,[3] about the gold-mines there, he was slain, after displaying uncommon bravery.

76. As soon as the Greeks at Platæa had overthrown the barbarians, a woman came over to them from the enemy. She was one of the concubines of Pharandates, the son of Teäspes, a Persian; and when she heard that the Persians were all slain and that the Greeks had carried the day, forthwith she adorned herself and her maids with many golden ornaments, and with the bravest of the apparel that she had brought with her, and, alighting from her litter, came forward to the Lacedæmonians, ere the work of slaughter was well over. When she saw that all the orders were given by Pausanias, with whose name and country she was well acquainted, as she had oftentimes heard tell of them, she knew who he must be; wherefore she embraced his knees, and said –

"O king of Sparta! save thy suppliant from the slavery that awaits the captive. Already I am beholden to thee for one service – the slaughter of these men, wretches who had no regard either for gods or angels. I am by birth a Coan, the daughter of

---

1 Devices upon shields were in use among the Greeks from very early times.
2 Supra, vi. 92.
3 The battle here mentioned was fought about the year B.C. 465, on occasion of the first attempt which the Athenians made to colonise Amphipolis.

Hêgêtoridas, son of Antagoras. The Persian seized me by force in Cos, and kept me against my will."

"Lady," answered Pausanias, "fear nothing: as a suppliant thou art safe – and still more, if thou hast spoken truth, and Hêgêtoridas of Cos is thy father – for he is bound to me by closer ties of friendship than any other man in those regions."

When he had thus spoken, Pausanias placed the woman in the charge of some of the Ephors who were present, and afterwards sent her to Egina, whither she had a desire to go.

77. About the time of this woman's coming, the Mantineans arrived upon the field, and found that all was over, and that it was too late to take any part in the battle. Greatly distressed hereat, they declared themselves to deserve a fine, as laggarts; after which, learning that a portion of the Medes had fled away under Artabazus, they were anxious to go after them as far as Thessaly. The Lacedæmonians however would not suffer the pursuit; so they returned again to their own land, and sent the leaders of their army into banishment. Soon after the Mantineans, the Eleans likewise arrived, and showed the same sorrow; after which they too returned home, and banished their leaders. But enough concerning these nations.

78. There was a man at Platæa among the troops of the Eginetans, whose name was Lampon; he was the son of Pytheas, and a person of the first rank among his countrymen. Now this Lampon went about this same time to Pausanias, and counselled him to do a deed of exceeding wickedness. "Son of Cleombrotus," he said very earnestly, "what thou hast already done is passing great and glorious. By the favour of Heaven thou hast saved Greece, and gained a renown beyond all the Greeks of whom we have any knowledge. Now then so finish thy work, that thine own fame may be increased thereby, and that henceforth barbarians may fear to commit outrages on the Grecians. When Leonidas was slain at Thermopylæ, Xerxes and Mardonius commanded that he should be beheaded and crucified.[1] Do thou the like at this time by Mardonius, and thou wilt have glory in Sparta, and likewise through the whole of Greece. For, by hanging him upon a cross, thou wilt avenge Leonidas, who was thy father's brother."

1 Supra, vii. 238.

79. Thus spake Lampon, thinking to please Pausanias; but Pausanias answered him – "My Eginetan friend, for thy foresight and thy friendliness I am much beholden to thee: but the counsel which thou hast offered is not good. First hast thou lifted me up to the skies, by thy praise of my country and my achievement; and then thou hast cast me down to the ground, by bidding me maltreat the dead, and saying that thus I shall raise myself in men's esteem. Such doings befit barbarians rather than Greeks; and even in barbarians we detest them. On such terms then I could not wish to please the Eginetans, nor those who think as they think – enough for me to gain the approval of my own countrymen, by righteous deeds as well as by righteous words. Leonidas, whom thou wouldst have me avenge, is, I maintain, abundantly avenged already. Surely the countless lives here taken are enough to avenge not him only, but all those who fell at Thermopylæ. Come not thou before me again with such a speech, nor with such counsel; and thank my forbearance that thou art not now punished." Then Lampon, having received this answer, departed, and went his way.

80. After this Pausanias caused proclamation to be made, that no one should lay hands on the booty, but that the Helots should collect it and bring it all to one place. So the Helots went and spread themselves through the camp, wherein were found many tents richly adorned with furniture of gold and silver, many couches covered with plates of the same, and many golden bowls, goblets, and other drinking-vessels. On the carriages were bags containing silver and golden kettles; and the bodies of the slain furnished bracelets and chains, and scymitars with golden ornaments – not to mention embroidered apparel, of which no one made any account. The Helots at this time stole many things of much value, which they sold in after times to the Eginetans; however, they brought in likewise no small quantity, chiefly such things as it was not possible for them to hide. And this was the beginning of the great wealth of the Eginetans, who bought the gold of the Helots as if it had been mere brass.[1]

---

1 This ignorance of the helots has been well compared to that of the Swiss after the battle of Granson, when, according to Philippe de Comines they "ne connurent les biens qu'ils eurent en leurs mains . . . il y en eut qui vendirent grande quantité de plats et d'escuelles d'argent, pour deux grands blancs la pièce, *cuidans que ce fust estaing*" (Mémoires, v. 2).

81. When all the booty had been brought together, a tenth of the whole was set apart for the Delphian god; and hence was made the golden tripod which stands on the bronze serpent with the three heads, quite close to the altar.[1] Portions were also set apart for the gods of Olympia, and of the Isthmus; from which were made, in the one case, a bronze Zeus ten cubits high; and in the other, a bronze Poseidon of seven cubits. After this, the rest of the spoil was divided among the soldiers, each of whom received less or more according to his deserts; and in this way was a distribution made of the Persian concubines, of the gold, the silver, the beasts of burthen, and all the other valuables. What special gifts were presented to those who had most distinguished themselves in the battle, I do not find mentioned by any one;[2] but I should suppose that they must have had some gifts beyond the others. As for Pausanias, the portion which was set apart for him consisted of ten specimens of each kind of thing – women, horses, talents, camels, or whatever else there was in the spoil.

82. It is said that the following circumstance happened likewise at this time. Xerxes, when he fled away out of Greece, left his war-tent with Mardonius:[3] when Pausanias, therefore, saw the tent with its adornments of gold and silver, and its hangings of divers colours, he gave commandment to the bakers and the cooks to make him ready a banquet in such fashion as was their wont for Mardonius. Then they made ready as they were bidden; and Pausanias, beholding the couches of gold and silver daintily decked out with their rich covertures, and the tables of gold and silver laid, and the feast itself prepared with all magnificence, was astonished at the good things which were set before him, and, being in a pleasant mood, gave commandment to his own followers to make ready a Spartan supper. When the suppers were both served, and it was apparent how vast a difference lay

1 Upon this tripod Pausanias placed the inscription which was one of the first indications of his ambitious aims:–
  "Pausanias, Grecia's chief, the Mede o'erthrew,
   And gave Apollo that which here ye view."
2 This is one of the very few passages of his History in which Herodotus seems to imply that he consulted *authors* in compiling it. For the most part he derives his materials from personal observation and inquiry.
3 The capture of this tent was commemorated at Athens by the erection of a building in imitation of it. This was the Odeum.

between the two, Pausanias laughed, and sent his servants to call to him the Greek generals. On their coming, he pointed to the two boards, and said:—

"I sent for you, O Greeks, to show you the folly of this Median captain, who, when he enjoyed such fare as this, must needs come here to rob us of our penury."

Such, it is said, were the words of Pausanias to the Grecian generals.

83. During many years afterwards, the Platæans used often to find upon the field of battle concealed treasures of gold, and silver, and other valuables. More recently they likewise made discovery of the following: the flesh having all fallen away from the bodies of the dead, and their bones having been gathered together into one place, the Platæans found a skull without any seam, made entirely of a single bone; likewise a jaw, both the upper bone and the under, wherein all the teeth, front and back, were joined together and made of one bone; also, the skeleton of a man not less than five cubits in height.

84. The body of Mardonius disappeared the day after the battle; but who it was that stole it away I cannot say with certainty. I have heard tell of a number of persons, and those too of many different nations, who are said to have given him burial; and I know that many have received large sums on this score from Artontes the son of Mardonius: but I cannot discover with any certainty which of them it was who really took the body away, and buried it. Among others, Dionysophanes, an Ephesian, is rumoured to have been the actual person.

85. The Greeks, after sharing the booty upon the field of Platæa, proceeded to bury their own dead, each nation apart from the rest. The Lacedæmonians made three graves; in one they buried their youths, among whom were Posidônius, Amompharetus, Philocyon, and Callicrates;— in another, the rest of the Spartans; and in the third, the Helots. Such was their mode of burial. The Tegeans buried all their dead in a single grave; as likewise did the Athenians theirs, and the Megarians and Phliasians those who were slain by the horse. These graves, then, had bodies buried in them: as for the other tombs which are to be seen at Platæa, they were raised, as I understand, by the Greeks whose troops took no part in the battle; and who, being ashamed of themselves, erected empty barrows upon the field, to obtain credit with those who should come after them. Among others,

the Eginetans have a grave there, which goes by their name; but which, as I learn, was made ten years later by Cleades, the son of Autodicus, a Platæan, at the request of the Eginetans, whose agent he was.

86. After the Greeks had buried their dead at Platæa, they presently held a council, whereat it was resolved to make war upon Thebes, and to require that those who had joined the Medes should be delivered into their hands. Two men, who had been the chief leaders on the occasion, were especially named – to wit, Timagenidas and Attagînus.[1] If the Thebans should refuse to give these men up, it was determined to lay siege to their city, and never stir from before it till it should surrender. After this resolve, the army marched upon Thebes; and having demanded the men, and been refused, began the siege, laying waste the country all around, and making assaults upon the wall in divers places.

87. When twenty days were gone by, and the violence of the Greeks did not slacken, Timagenidas thus bespake his countrymen –

"Ye men of Thebes, since the Greeks have so decreed, that they will never desist from the siege till either they take Thebes or we are delivered to them, we would not that the land of Bœotia should suffer any longer on our behalf. If it be money that they in truth desire, and their demand of us be no more than a pretext, let money from the treasury of the state be given them; for the state, and not we alone, embraced the cause of the Medes. If, however, they really want our persons, and on that account press this siege, we are ready to be delivered to them and to stand our trial."

The Thebans thought this offer very right and seasonable; wherefore they despatched a herald without any delay to Pausanias, and told him they were willing to deliver up the men.

88. As soon as an agreement had been concluded upon these terms, Attagînus made his escape from the city; his sons, however, were surrendered in his place; but Pausanias refused to hold them guilty, since children (he said) could have had no part in such an offence. The rest of those whom the Thebans gave up had expected to obtain a trial, and in that case their trust was to escape by means of bribery; but Pausanias, afraid of this,

1 Supra, chs. 15 and 38.

dismissed at once the whole army of allies, and took the men with him to Corinth, where he slew them all. Such were the events which happened at Platæa and at Thebes.

89. Artabazus, the son of Pharnaces, who fled away from Platæa, was soon far sped on his journey. When he reached Thessaly, the inhabitants received him hospitably, and made inquiries of him concerning the rest of the army, since they were still altogether ignorant of what had taken place at Platæa: whereupon the Persian, knowing well that, if he told them the truth, he would run great risk of perishing himself, together with his whole army – for if the facts were once blazoned abroad, all who learnt them would be sure to fall upon him – the Persian, I say, considering this, as he had before kept all secret from the Phocians, so now answered the Thessalians after the following fashion:–

"I myself, Thessalians, am hastening, as ye see, into Thrace; and I am fain to use all possible despatch, as I am sent with this force on special business from the main army. Mardonius and his host are close behind me, and may be looked for shortly. When he comes, receive him as ye have received me, and show him every kindness. Be sure ye will never hereafter regret it, if ye so do."

With these words he took his departure, and marched his troops at their best speed through Thessaly and Macedon straight upon Thrace, following the inland route, which was the shortest, and, in good truth, using all possible despatch. He himself succeeded in reaching Byzantium; but a great part of his army perished upon the road – many being cut to pieces by the Thracians, and others dying from hunger and excess of toil. From Byzantium Artabazus set sail, and crossed the strait; returning into Asia in the manner which has been here described.

90. On the same day that the blow was struck at Platæa, another defeat befell the Persians at Mycalé in Ionia. While the Greek fleet under Leotychides the Lacedæmonian was still lying inactive at Delos, there arrived at that place an embassy from Samos, consisting of three men, Lampon the son of Thrasycles, Athenagoras the son of Archestratidas, and Hêgêsistratus the son of Aristagoras. The Samians had sent them secretly, concealing their departure both from the Persians and from their own tyrant Theomestor, the son of Androdamas, whom the Persians had made ruler of Samos.[1] When the ambassadors came before

---

1 The reason of this was given, viii. 85.

the Greek captains Hêgêsistratus took the word, and urged them with many and various arguments, saying, "that the Ionians only needed to see them arrive in order to revolt from the Persians; and that the Persians would never abide their coming; or if they did, 'twould be to offer them the finest booty that they could anywhere expect to gain;" while at the same time he made appeal to the gods of their common worship, and besought them to deliver from bondage a Grecian race, and withal to drive back the barbarians. "This," he said, "might very easily be done, for the Persian ships were bad sailers, and far from a match for theirs;" adding, moreover, "that if there was any suspicion lest the Samians intended to deal treacherously, they were themselves ready to become hostages, and to return on board the ships of their allies to Asia."

91. When the Samian stranger continued importunately beseeching him, Leotychides, either because he wanted an omen, or by a mere chance, as God guided him, asked the man – "Samian stranger! prithee, tell me thy name?" "Hêgêsistratus (army-leader)," answered the other, and might have said more, but Leotychides stopped him by exclaiming – "I accept, O Samian! the omen which thy name affords. Only, before thou goest back, swear to us, thyself and thy brother-envoys, that the Samians will indeed be our warm friends and allies."

92. No sooner had he thus spoken than he proceeded to hurry forward the business. The Samians pledged their faith upon the spot; and oaths of alliance were exchanged between them and the Greeks. This done, two of the ambassadors forthwith sailed away; as for Hêgêsistratus, Leotychides kept him to accompany his own fleet, for he considered his name to be a good omen. The Greeks abode where they were that day, and on the morrow sacrificed, and found the victims favourable. Their soothsayer was Deïphonus, the son of Evênius, a man of Apollonia – I mean the Apollonia which lies upon the Ionian Gulf.

93. A strange thing happened to this man's father, Evênius. The Apolloniats have a flock of sheep sacred to the sun. During the day-time these sheep graze along the banks of the river which flows from Mount Lacmon through their territory and empties itself into the sea by the port of Oricus;[1] while at night they are guarded by the richest and noblest of the citizens, who

---

[1] The geography of Herodotus is here somewhat at fault.

are chosen to serve the office, and who keep the watch each for one year. Now the Apolloniats set great store by these sheep, on account of an oracle which they received concerning them. The place where they are folded at night is a cavern, a long way from the town. Here it happened that Evênius, when he was chosen to keep the watch, by some accident fell asleep upon his guard; and while he slept, the cave was entered by wolves, which destroyed some sixty of the flock under his care. Evênius, when he woke and found what had occurred, kept silence about it and told no one; for he thought to buy other sheep and put them in the place of the slain. But the matter came to the ears of the Apolloniats, who forthwith brought Evênius to trial, and condemned him to lose his eyes, because he had gone to sleep upon his post. Now when Evênius was blinded, straightway the sheep had no young, and the land ceased to bear its wonted harvests. Then the Apolloniats sent to Dodôna, and to Delphi, and asked the prophets, what had caused the woes which so afflicted them. The answer which they received was this − "The woes were come for Evênius, the guardian of the sacred sheep, whom the Apolloniats had wrongfully deprived of sight. They (the gods) had themselves sent the wolves; nor would they ever cease to exact vengeance for Evênius, till the Apolloniats made him whatever atonement he liked to ask. When this was paid, *they* would likewise give him a gift, which would make many men call him blessed."

94. Such was the tenor of the prophecies. The Apolloniats kept them close, but charged some of their citizens to go and make terms with Evênius; and these men managed the business for them in the way which I will now describe. They found Evênius sitting upon a bench, and, approaching him, they sat down by his side, and began to talk: at first they spoke of quite other matters, but in the end they mentioned his misfortune, and offered him their condolence. Having thus beguiled him, at last they put the question − "What atonement would he desire, if the Apolloniats were willing to make him satisfaction for the wrong which they had done to him?" Hereupon Evênius, who had not heard of the oracle, made answer − "If I were given the lands of this man and that −" (here he named the two men whom he knew to have the finest farms in Apollonia), "and likewise the house of this other" − (and here he mentioned the house which he knew to be the handsomest in the town), "I would, when

master of these, be quite content, and my wrath would cease altogether." As soon as Evênius had thus spoken, the men who sat by him rejoined – "Evênius, the Apolloniats give thee the atonement which thou hast desired, according to the bidding of the oracles." Then Evênius understood the whole matter, and was enraged that they had deceived him so; but the Apolloniats bought the farms from their owners, and gave Evênius what he had chosen. After this was done, straightway Evênius had the gift of prophecy, insomuch that he became a famous man in Greece.

95. Deïphonus, the son of this Evênius, had accompanied the Corinthians, and was soothsayer, as I said before, to the Greek armament. One account, however, which I have heard, declares that he was not really the son of this man, but only took the name, and then went about Greece and let out his services for hire.

96. The Greeks, as soon as the victims were favourable, put to sea, and sailed across from Delos to Samos. Arriving off Calami, a place upon the Samian coast, they brought the fleet to an anchor near the temple of Hera which stands there,[1] and prepared to engage the Persians by sea. These latter, however, no sooner heard of the approach of the Greeks, than, dismissing the Phœnician ships, they sailed away with the remainder to the mainland. For it had been resolved in council not to risk a battle, since the Persian fleet was thought to be no match for that of the enemy. They fled, therefore, to the main, to be under the protection of their land army, which now lay at Mycalé,[2] and consisted of the troops left behind by Xerxes to keep guard over Ionia. This was an army of sixty thousand men, under the command of Tigranes, a Persian of more than common beauty and stature. The captains resolved therefore to betake themselves to these troops for defence, to drag their ships ashore, and to build a rampart around them, which might at once protect the fleet, and serve likewise as a place of refuge for themselves.

97. Having so resolved, the commanders put out to sea; and passing the temple of the Eumenides, arrived at Gæson and

1 Supra, iii. 60. I understand by this the *great* temple of Hera near the town of Samos.

2 Supra, i. 148. Mycalé is the modern *Cape St. Mary*, the promontory which runs out towards Samos.

Scolopoeis, which are in the territory of Mycalé. Here is a temple of Eleusinian Demeter, built by Philistus the son of Pasicles, who came to Asia with Neileus the son of Codrus,[1] what time he founded Miletus. At this place they drew the ships up on the beach, and surrounded them with a rampart made of stones and trunks of trees, cutting down for this purpose all the fruit-trees which grew near, and defending the barrier by means of stakes firmly planted in the ground. Here they were prepared either to win a battle, or undergo a siege – their thoughts embracing both chances.

98. The Greeks, when they understood that the barbarians had fled to the mainland, were sorely vexed at their escape: nor could they determine at first what they should do, whether they should return home, or proceed to the Hellespont. In the end, however, they resolved to do neither, but to make sail for the continent. So they made themselves ready for a sea-fight by the preparation of boarding-bridges, and what else was necessary; provided with which they sailed to Mycalé. Now when they came to the place where the camp was, they found no one venture out to meet them, but observed the ships all dragged ashore within the barrier, and a strong land-force drawn up in battle array upon the beach; Leotychides therefore sailed along the shore in his ship, keeping as close hauled to the land as possible, and by the voice of a herald thus addressed the Ionians:–

"Men of Ionia – ye who can hear me speak – do *ye* take heed to what I say; for the Persians will not understand a word that I utter. When we join battle with them, before aught else, re-member Freedom – and next, recollect our watchword, which is Hêbé. If there be any who hear me not, let those who hear report my words to the others."

In all this Leotychides had the very same design which Them-istocles entertained at Artemisium.[2] Either the barbarians would not know what he had said, and the Ionians would be persuaded to revolt from them; or if his words were reported to the former, they would mistrust their Greek soldiers.

99. After Leotychides had made this address, the Greeks brought their ships to the land, and, having disembarked, arrayed themselves for the battle. When the Persians saw them marshall-ing their array, and bethought themselves of the advice which had been offered to the Ionians, their first act was to disarm the

---

1 Supra, i. 147.   2 Supra, viii. 22, end.

Samians, whom they suspected of complicity with the enemy. For it had happened lately that a number of the Athenians who lingered in Attica, having been made prisoners by the troops of Xerxes, were brought to Asia on board the barbarian fleet; and these men had been ransomed, one and all, by the Samians, who sent them back to Athens, well furnished with provisions for the way. On this account, as much as on any other, the Samians were suspected, as men who had paid the ransom of five hundred of the king's enemies. After disarming them, the Persians next despatched the Milesians to guard the paths which lead up into the heights of Mycalé, because (they said) the Milesians were well acquainted with that region: their true object, however, was to remove them to a distance from the camp. In this way the Persians sought to secure themselves against such of the Ionians as they thought likely, if occasion offered, to make rebellion. They then joined shield to shield, and so made themselves a breastwork against the enemy.[1]

100. The Greeks now, having finished their preparations, began to move towards the barbarians; when, lo! as they advanced, a rumour flew through the host from one end to the other – that the Greeks had fought and conquered the army of Mardonius in Bœotia. At the same time a herald's wand was observed lying upon the beach. Many things prove to me that the gods take part in the affairs of man. How else, when the battles of Mycalé and Platæa were about to happen on the self same day, should such a rumour have reached the Greeks in that region, greatly cheering the whole army, and making them more eager than before to risk their lives.

101. A strange coincidence too it was, that both the battles should have been fought near a precinct of Eleusinian Demeter. The fight at Platæa took place, as I said before, quite close to one of Demeter's temples; and now the battle at Mycalé was to be fought hard by another. Rightly, too, did the rumour run, that the Greeks with Pausanias *had gained* their victory; for the fight at Platæa fell early in the day, whereas that at Mycalé was towards evening. That the two battles were really fought on the same day of the same month became apparent when inquiries were made a short time afterwards. Before the rumour reached them, the Greeks were full of fear, not so much on their own account, as

1 See above, chapters 61 and 62.

for their countrymen, and for Greece herself, lest she should be worsted in her struggle with Mardonius. But when the voice fell on them, their fear vanished, and they charged more vigorously and at a quicker pace. So the Greeks and the barbarians rushed with like eagerness to the fray; for the Hellespont and the Islands formed the prize for which they were about to fight.

102. The Athenians, and the force drawn up with them, who formed one half of the army, marched along the shore, where the country was low and level; but the way for the Lacedæmonians, and the troops with them, lay across hills and a torrent-course. Hence, while the Lacedæmonians were effecting their passage round, the Athenians on the other wing had already closed with the enemy. So long as the wicker bucklers of the Persians continued standing, they made a stout defence, and had not even the worst of the battle; but when the Athenians, and the allies with them, wishing to make the victory their own, and not share it with the Lacedæmonians, cheered each other on with shouts, and attacked them with the utmost fierceness, then at last the face of things became changed. For, bursting through the line of shields, and rushing forwards in a body, the Greeks fell upon the Persians; who, though they bore the charge and for a long time maintained their ground, yet at length took refuge in their intrenchment. Here the Athenians themselves, together with those who followed them in the line of battle, the Corinthians, the Sicyonians, and the Trœzenians, pressed so closely on the steps of their flying foes, that they entered along with them into the fortress. And now, when even their fortress was taken, the barbarians no longer offered resistance, but fled hastily away, all save only the Persians. *They* still continued to fight in knots of a few men against the Greeks, who kept pouring into the intrenchment. And here, while two of the Persian commanders fled, two fell upon the field: Artaÿntes and Ithamitres, who were leaders of the fleet,[1] escaped; Mardontes, and the commander of the land force, Tigranes, died fighting.

103. The Persians still held out, when the Lacedæmonians, and their part of the army, reached the camp, and joined in the remainder of the battle. The number of Greeks who fell in the struggle here was not small; the Sicyonians especially lost many, and, among the rest, Perilaüs their general.

---

1 Supra, viii. 130.

The Samians, who served with the Medes, and who, although disarmed, still remained in the camp, seeing from the very beginning of the fight that the victory was doubtful, did all that lay in their power to render help to the Greeks. And the other Ionians likewise, beholding their example, revolted and attacked the Persians.

104. As for the Milesians, who had been ordered, for the better security of the Persians, to guard the mountain-paths, – that, in case any accident befell them such as had now happened, they might not lack guides to conduct them into the high tracts of Mycalé, – and who had also been removed to hinder them from making an outbreak in the Persian camp; they, instead of obeying their orders, broke them in every respect. For they guided the flying Persians by wrong roads, which brought them into the presence of the enemy; and at last they set upon them with their own hands, and showed themselves the hottest of their adversaries. Ionia, therefore, on this day revolted a second time from the Persians.

105. In this battle the Greeks who behaved with the greatest bravery were the Athenians; and among them the palm was borne off by Hermolycus, the son of Euthynus, a man accomplished in the Pancratium.[1] This Hermolycus was afterwards slain in the war between the Athenians and Carystians. He fell in the fight near Cyrnus in the Carystian territory, and was buried in the neighbourhood of Geræstus. After the Athenians, the most distinguished on the Greek side were the Corinthians, the Trœzenians, and the Sicyonians.

106. The Greeks, when they had slaughtered the greater portion of the barbarians, either in the battle or in the rout, set fire to their ships and burnt them, together with the bulwark which had been raised for their defence, first however removing therefrom all the booty, and carrying it down to the beach. Besides other plunder, they found here many caskets of money. When they had burnt the rampart and the vessels, the Greeks sailed away to Samos, and there took counsel together concerning the Ionians, whom they thought of removing out of Asia. Ionia they proposed to abandon to the barbarians; and their doubt was, in what part of their own possessions in Greece they should settle its inhabitants. For it seemed to them a thing impossible that they should be ever on the watch to guard and protect Ionia;

---

1 The Pancratium was a contest in which wrestling and boxing were united.

and yet otherwise there could be no hope that the Ionians would escape the vengeance of the Persians. Hereupon the Peloponnesian leaders proposed, that the seaport towns of such Greeks as had sided with the Medes should be taken away from them, and made over to the Ionians. The Athenians, on the other hand, were very unwilling that any removal at all should take place, and misliked the Peloponnesians holding councils concerning their colonists. So, as they set themselves against the change, the Peloponnesians yielded with a good will. Hereupon the Samians, Chians, Lesbians, and other islanders, who had helped the Greeks at this time, were received into the league of the allies; and took the oaths, binding themselves to be faithful, and not desert the common cause. Then the Greeks sailed away to the Hellespont, where they meant to break down the bridges, which they supposed to be still extended across the strait.

107. The barbarians who escaped from the battle − a scanty remnant − took refuge in the heights of Mycalé, whence they made good their retreat to Sardis. During the march, Masistes, the son of Darius, who had been present at the disaster, had words with Artaÿntes, the general, on whom he showered many reproaches. He called him, among other things, "worse than a woman," for the way in which he had exercised his command, and said there was no punishment which he did not deserve to suffer for doing the king's house such grievous hurt. Now with the Persians there is no greater insult than to call a man "worse than a woman."[1] So when Artaÿntes had borne the reproaches for some while, at last he fell in a rage, and drew his scymitar upon Masistes, being fain to kill him. But a certain Halicarnassian, Xenagoras by name, the son of Praxilaüs, who stood behind Artaÿntes at the time, seeing him in the act of rushing forward, seized him suddenly round the waist, and, lifting him from his feet, dashed him down upon the ground; which gave time for the spearmen who guarded Masistes to come to his aid. By his conduct here Xenagoras gained the favour, not of Masistes only, but likewise of Xerxes himself, whose brother he had preserved from death; and the king rewarded his action by setting him over the whole land of Cilicia.[2] Except this, nothing happened upon

1 Supra, viii. 88, and ix. 20.
2 Probably this is an overstatement, natural in one jealous for the honour of a countryman.

the road; and the men continued their march and came all safe to Sardis. At Sardis they found the king, who had been there ever since he lost the sea-fight and fled from Athens to Asia.

108. During the time that Xerxes abode at this place, he fell in love with the wife of Masistes, who was likewise staying in the city. He therefore sent her messages, but failed to win her consent; and he could not dare to use violence, out of regard to Masistes, his brother. This the woman knew well enough, and hence it was that she had the boldness to resist him. So Xerxes, finding no other way open, devised a marriage between his own son Darius and a daughter of this woman and Masistes – thinking that he might better obtain his ends if he effected this union. Accordingly he betrothed these two persons to one another, and, after the usual ceremonies were completed, took his departure for Susa. When he was come there, and had received the woman into his palace as his son's bride, a change came over him, and, losing all love for the wife of Masistes, he conceived a passion for his son's bride, Masistes' daughter. And Artaÿnta – for so was she called – very soon returned his love.

109. After a while the thing was discovered in the way which I will now relate. Amestris, the wife of Xerxes, had woven with her own hands a long robe, of many colours, and very curious, which she presented to her husband as a gift. Xerxes, who was greatly pleased with it, forthwith put it on; and went in it to visit Artaÿnta, who happened likewise on this day to please him greatly. He therefore bade her ask him whatever boon she liked, and promised that, whatever it was, he would assuredly grant her request. Then Artaÿnta, who was doomed to suffer calamity together with her whole house, said to him – "Wilt thou indeed give me whatever I like to ask?" So the king, suspecting nothing less than that her choice would fall where it did, pledged his word, and swore to her. She then, as soon as she heard his oath, asked boldly for the robe. Hereupon Xerxes tried all possible means to avoid the gift; not that he grudged to give it, but because he dreaded Amestris, who already suspected, and would now, he feared, detect his love. So he offered her cities instead, and heaps of gold, and an army which should obey no other leader. (The last of these is a thoroughly Persian gift.) But, as nothing could prevail on Artaÿnta to change her mind, at the last he gave her the robe. Then Artaÿnta was very greatly rejoiced, and she often wore the garment and was proud of it. And

so it came to the ears of Amestris that the robe had been given to her.

110. Now when Amestris learnt the whole matter, she felt no anger against Artaÿnta; but, looking upon her mother, the wife of Masistes, as the cause of all the mischief, she determined to compass her death. She waited, therefore, till her husband gave the great royal banquet, a feast which takes place once every year, in celebration of the king's birthday[1] – "Tykta" the feast is called in the Persian tongue, which in our language may be rendered "perfect" – and this is the only day in all the year on which the king soaps his head, and distributes gifts to the Persians. Amestris waited, accordingly, for this day, and then made request of Xerxes, that he would please to give her, as her present, the wife of Masistes. But he refused; for it seemed to him shocking and monstrous to give into the power of another a woman who was not only his brother's wife, but was likewise wholly guiltless of what had happened – the more especially as he knew well enough with what intent Amestris had preferred her request.

111. At length, however, wearied by her importunity, and constrained moreover by the law of the feast, which required that no one who asked a boon that day at the king's board should be denied his request, he yielded, but with a very ill will, and gave the woman into her power.[2] Having so done, and told Amestris she might deal with her as she chose, the king called his brother into his presence, and said –

"Masistes, thou art my brother, the son of my father Darius; and, what is more, thou art a good man. I pray thee, live no longer with the wife whom thou now hast. Behold, I will give thee instead my own daughter in marriage; take her to live with thee. But part first with the wife thou now hast – I like not that thou keep to her."

To this Masistes, greatly astonished, answered –

"My lord and master, how strange a speech hast thou uttered! Thou biddest me put away my wife, who has borne me three goodly youths, and daughters besides, whereof thou hast taken

1 The custom of celebrating birthdays by a feast was universal in Persia. Even the poorest are said to have conformed to it.

2 Few readers can fail to be struck by the resemblance between this scene and that described by St. Matthew, ch. xiv. 6–9, and St. Mark, vi. 21–26. In the East kings celebrated their birthdays by holding feasts and granting graces from very early times (see Gen. ch. xl. 20, 21).

one and espoused her to a son of thine own – thou biddest me put away this wife, notwithstanding that she pleases me greatly, and marry a daughter of thine! In truth, O king! that I am accounted worthy to wed thy daughter, is an honour which I mightily esteem; but yet to do as thou sayest am I in no wise willing. I pray thee, use not force to compel me to yield to thy prayer. Be sure thy daughter will find a husband to the full as worthy as myself. Suffer me then to live on with my own wife."

Thus did Masistes answer; and Xerxes, in wrath, replied – "I will tell thee, Masistes, what thou hast gained by these words. I will not give thee my daughter; nor shalt thou live any longer with thy own wife. So mayest thou learn, in time to come, to take what is offered thee." Masistes, when he heard this, withdrew, only saying – "Master, thou hast not yet taken my life."

112. While these things were passing between Xerxes and his brother Masistes, Amestris sent for the spearmen of the royal body-guard, and caused the wife of Masistes to be mutilated in a horrible fashion. Her two breasts, her nose, ears, and lips were cut off and thrown to the dogs; her tongue was torn out by the roots, and thus disfigured she was sent back to her home.

113. Masistes, who knew nothing of what had happened, but was fearful that some calamity had befallen him, ran hastily to his house. There, finding his wife so savagely used, he forthwith took counsel with his sons, and, accompanied by them and certain others also, set forth on his way to Bactria, intending to stir up revolt in that province, and hoping to do great hurt to Xerxes: all which, I believe, he would have accomplished, if he had once reached the Bactrian and Sacan people; for he was greatly beloved by them both, and was moreover satrap of Bactria. But Xerxes, hearing of his designs, sent an armed force upon his track, and slew him while he was still upon the road, with his sons and his whole army. Such is the tale of King Xerxes' love and of the death of his brother Masistes.

114. Meanwhile the Greeks, who had left Mycalé, and sailed for the Hellespont, were forced by contrary winds to anchor near Lectum;[1] from which place they afterwards sailed on to Abydos. On arriving here, they discovered that the bridges, which they had thought to find standing, and which had been the chief cause

---

1 Lectum is the modern *Cape Baba*, the extreme point of the Troas towards the south-west. It is mentioned by Homer.

of their proceeding to the Hellespont, were already broken up and destroyed. Upon this discovery, Leotychides, and the Peloponnesians under him, were anxious to sail back to Greece; but the Athenians, with Xanthippus their captain, thought good to remain, and resolved to make an attempt upon the Chersonese. So, while the Peloponnesians sailed away to their homes, the Athenians crossed over from Abydos to the Chersonese, and there laid siege to Sestos.

115. Now, as Sestos was the strongest fortress in all that region, the rumour had no sooner gone forth that the Greeks were arrived at the Hellespont, than great numbers flocked thither from all the towns in the neighbourhood. Among the rest there came a certain Œobazus, a Persian, from the city of Cardia, where he had laid up the shore-cables which had been used in the construction of the bridges. The town was guarded by its own Æolian inhabitants, but contained also some Persians, and a great multitude of their allies.

116. The whole district was under the rule of Artaÿctes, one of the king's satraps; who was a Persian, but a wicked and cruel man. At the time when Xerxes was marching against Athens, he had craftily possessed himself of the treasures belonging to Protesilaüs the son of Iphiclus,[1] which were at Elæûs in the Chersonese. For at this place is the tomb of Protesilaüs, surrounded by a sacred precinct; and here there was great store of wealth, vases of gold and silver, works in brass, garments, and other offerings, all which Artaÿctes made his prey, having got the king's consent by thus cunningly addressing him –

"Master, there is in this region the house of a Greek, who, when he attacked thy territory, met his due reward, and perished. Give me his house, I pray thee, that hereafter men may fear to carry arms against *thy* land."

By these words he easily persuaded Xerxes to give him the man's house; for there was no suspicion of his design in the king's mind. And he could say in a certain sense that Protesilaüs had borne arms against the land of the king; because the Persians consider all Asia to belong to them, and to their king for the time being. So when Xerxes allowed his request, he brought all

---

1 Protesilaüs, the son of Iphiclus, was one of the Trojan heroes. He led the Thessalians of Phthlôtis, and was the first Greek who fell on the disembarkation of the army (Hom. Il. ii. 695–702).

the treasures from Elæûs to Sestos, and made the sacred land into
cornfields and pasture grounds; nay, more, whenever he paid a
visit to Elæûs, he polluted the shrine itself by having intercourse
with women within the inner sanctuary. It was this Artaÿctes who
was now besieged by the Athenians – and he was but ill prepared
for defence; since the Greeks had fallen upon him quite una-
wares, nor had he in the least expected their coming.

117. When it was now late in the autumn, and the siege still
continued, the Athenians began to murmur that they were kept
abroad so long; and, seeing that they were not able to take the
place, besought their captains to lead them back to their own
country. But the captains refused to move, till either the city had
fallen, or the Athenian people ordered them to return home. So
the soldiers patiently bore up against their sufferings.

118. Meanwhile those within the walls were reduced to the
last straits, and forced even to boil the very thongs of their beds
for food. At last, when these too failed them, Artaÿctes and
Œobazus, with the native Persians, fled away from the place by
night, having let themselves down from the wall at the back of
the town, where the blockading force was scantiest. As soon as
day dawned, they of the Chersonese made signals to the Greeks
from the walls, and let them know what had happened, at the
same time throwing open the gates of their city. Hereupon, while
some of the Greeks entered the town, others, and those the
more numerous body, set out in pursuit of the enemy.

119. Œobazus fled into Thrace; but there the Apsinthian Thracians seized him, and offered him, after their wonted fashion, to
Pleistôrus, one of the gods of their country. His companions
they likewise put to death, but in a different manner. As for
Artaÿctes and the troops with him, who had been the last to
leave the town, they were overtaken by the Greeks, not far from
Ægos-potami,[1] and defended themselves stoutly for a time, but
were at last either killed or taken prisoners. Those whom they
made prisoners the Greeks bound with chains, and brought with
them to Sestos. Artaÿctes and his son were among the number.

120. Now the Chersonesites relate that the following prodigy
befell one of the Greeks who guarded the captives. He was
broiling upon a fire some salted fish, when of a sudden they

1 Celebrated for the final defeat of the Athenians in the Peloponnesian war.
[See Thirlwall, *History of Greece*, vol. iv. chap. xxx. – E. H. B.]

began to leap and quiver, as if they had been only just caught. Hereat, the rest of the guards hurried round to look, and were greatly amazed at the sight. Artaÿctes, however, beholding the prodigy, called the man to him, and said –

"Fear not, Athenian stranger, because of this marvel. It has not appeared on thy account, but on mine. Protesilaüs of Elæûs has sent it to show me, that albeit he is dead and embalmed with salt, he has power from the gods to chastise his injurer. Now then I would fain acquit my debt to him thus. For the riches which I took from his temple, I will fix my fine at one hundred talents – while for myself and this boy of mine, I will give the Athenians two hundred talents,[1] on condition that they will spare our lives."

Such were the promises of Artaÿctes; but they failed to persuade Xanthippus. For the men of Elæûs, who wished to avenge Protesilaüs, entreated that he might be put to death; and Xanthippus himself was of the same mind. So they led Artaÿctes to the tongue of land where the bridges of Xerxes had been fixed[2] – or, according to others, to the knoll above the town of Madytus; and, having nailed him to a board, they left him hanging thereupon. As for the son of Artaÿctes, him they stoned to death before his eyes.

121. This done, they sailed back to Greece, carrying with them, besides other treasures, the shore cables from the bridges of Xerxes, which they wished to dedicate in their temples. And this was all that took place that year.

122. It was the grandfather of this Artaÿctes, one Artembares by name, who suggested to the Persians a proposal which they readily embraced, and thus urged upon Cyrus:– "Since Zeus," they said, "has overthrown Astyages, and given the rule to the Persians, and to thee chiefly, O Cyrus! come now, let us quit this land wherein we dwell – for it is a scant land and a rugged – and let us choose ourselves some other better country. Many such lie around us, some nearer, some further off: if we take one of these, men will admire us far more than they do now. Who that had the power would not so act? And when shall we have a fairer time than now, when we are lords of so many nations, and rule all Asia?" Then Cyrus, who did not greatly esteem the

---

1 Two hundred talents would be nearly £50,000 of our money.
2 Supra, vii. 33.

counsel, told them, – "they might do so, if they liked – but he warned them not to expect in that case to continue rulers, but to prepare for being ruled by others – soft countries gave birth to soft men – there was no region which produced very delightful fruits, and at the same time men of a warlike spirit." So the Persians departed with altered minds, confessing that Cyrus was wiser than they; and chose rather to dwell in a churlish land, and exercise lordship, than to cultivate plains, and be the slaves of others.[1]

1 The work of Herodotus, though not finished throughout, is *concluded*. This is, I think, the case both historically and artistically. Historically, the action ends with the victorious return of the Athenian fleet from the cruise in which they had destroyed the last remnant of the invading host, and recovered the key of their continent, which was still held, after all his defeats, by the invader. Artistically, – by this last chapter – the end is brought back into a connection with the beginning – the tail of the snake is curved round into his mouth; while at the same time the key-note of the whole narrative is struck, its moral suggested – that victory is to the hardy dwellers in rough and mountainous countries, defeat to the soft inhabitants of fertile plains, who lay aside old warlike habits and sink into sloth and luxury.

[Note the phil-Athenian feelings of Herodotus, and his anti-Ionian prejudices all through the latter books of his history. For the former cf. vii. 161, ix. 27. The claim of Athens to a hegemony of the Greeks at the time of the Persian war is an anachronism. At that time Sparta was the leader. Cf. Bury, *Ancient Greek Historians*, p. 63. – E. H. B.]

INDEX